Contents

Hiking colour section
following p.152

The Vikings colour
section following p.344

◄◄ Puffin, Hornøya Island ◄ Sognefjord

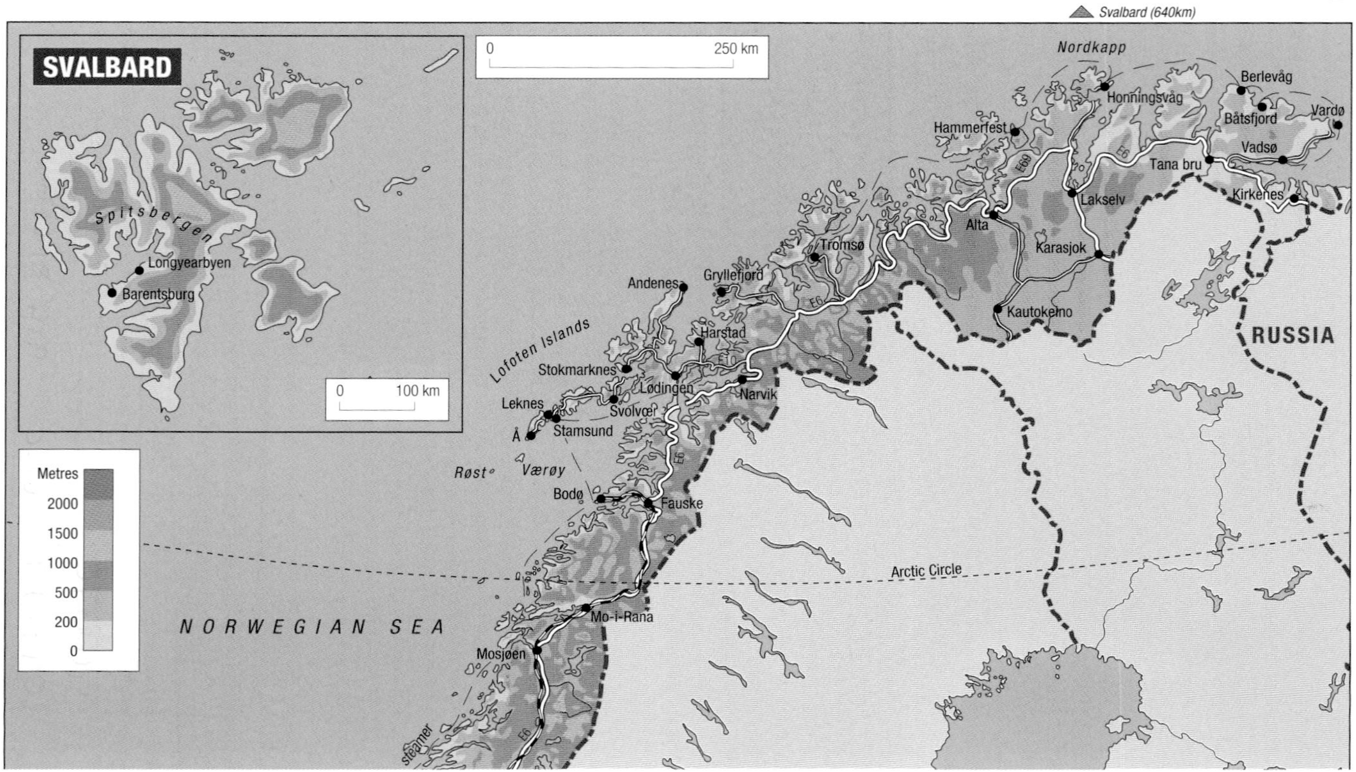

▲ Svalbard (640km)

SVALBARD

Spitsbergen

Longyearbyen

Barentsburg

0   100 km

Nordkapp

Honningsvåg

Hammerfest

Alta

Karasjok

Kautokeino

Lakselv

Tana bru

Vardø

Berlevåg

Båtsfjord

Vadsø

Kirkenes

RUSSIA

Tromsø

Gryllefjord

Harstad

Narvik

Andenes

Stokmarknes

Leknes

Svolvær

Lødingen

Å

Stamsund

Værøy

Røst

Bodø

Fauske

Mo-i-Rana

Mosjøen

Steigen

Lofoten Islands

Arctic Circle

NORWEGIAN SEA

0   250 km

Metres	
2000	
1500	
1000	
500	
200	
0	

written and researched by

Phil Lee

with additional contributions by
Suzanne Morton Taylor

ROUGH
GUIDES

www.roughguides.com

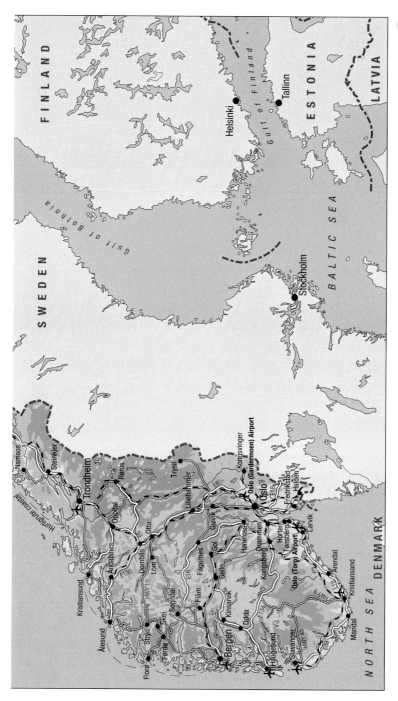

Introduction to

Norway

With its rearing mountains and deep, blue-black fjords, Norway remains a wilderness outpost in a tamed and crowded continent. Everything here is on a grand scale with the country boasting some of Europe's harshest and most beautiful land- and seascapes, whose vastness is merely pinpricked by a clutch of likeable cities, most memorably Trondheim, Bergen and Oslo. From the Skagerrak – the choppy channel that separates the country from Denmark – Norway stretches north in a long, slender band, its coastline buffeted by the Atlantic as it reaches up across the Arctic Circle to the Barents Sea and the Russian border. Behind this rough and rocky coast are great mountain ranges, harsh upland plateaux, plunging river valleys, rippling glaciers, deep forests and, most famously, the mighty fjords that gash deep inland.

The **fjords** are the apple of the tourist industry's eye, and they are indeed magnificent, but with the exception of Oslo, the capital city, and Bergen, its nearest rival, the rest of the country might as well be blank for all that many visitors know. Few seem aware of the sheer variety of the landscape or the lovely little towns that are sprinkled over it. Neither are the Norwegians given enough credit for their careful construction of one of the most civilized, educated and **tolerant societies** in the world – one whose even-handed internationalism has set standards that few other

▲ Sunset in a pine forest near Oslo

European nations can approach. With every justification, the bulk of the population have a deep loyalty for – and pride in – their country, partly at least because independence was so long in coming: after the heady days of the Vikings, Norway was governed by the Danes for four centuries and was then passed to the Swedes, who only left in 1905.

It is the **Vikings** who continue to grab the historical headlines, prompting book after book and film upon (foreign) film. These formidable warriors burst upon an unsuspecting Europe from the remoteness of Scandinavia in the ninth century. The Norwegian Vikings sailed west, raiding every seaboard from the Shetlands to Sicily, even venturing as far as Greenland and Newfoundland. Wherever they settled, the speed of their assimilation

Fact file

• Norway is one of the five **Nordic nations**, along with Denmark, Sweden, Finland and Iceland. It is bordered to the east by Sweden, Finland and Russia, but otherwise is flanked by the sea – the Atlantic to the west, the Barents Sea to the north and the Skagerrak, which leads off the North Sea, to the south. Extremely long and thin, Norway has a surface area of 386,000 square kilometres, of which half is mountain and a further third forest, lake and river.

• The **population** numbers about 4.6 million Norwegians, of whom about ten percent (half a million) live in the capital, Oslo. Norway's second city, Bergen, clocks up about 250,000 residents, while around 40,000 indigenous Sámi (Lapps) live mostly in the north of the country.

• Norway is a **constitutional monarchy** and the present king, Harald V, came to the throne in 1991. The parliament – the Storting – sits in Oslo, but many functions are devolved to a complex network of local authorities. The Lutheran **Church of Norway** is the official state church and over eighty percent of the population belong to it, however nominally. Norway is not a member of the EU, but has signed up to the EEA (European Economic Agreement) free-trade deal.

• The **economy** is buoyed up by the oil and gas industries, which account for eighty percent of the country's total exports. Machinery, metals and fish products come a distant second, third and fourth respectively.

into the indigenous population was extraordinary – William the Conqueror, the archetypal Norman baron, was only a few generations removed from his Viking ancestors – but in the unpopulated Faroes and Iceland, the settlers could begin from scratch, creating societies which then developed in a similar fashion to that of their original homeland.

Norway's so-called "period of greatness" came to an abrupt end: in 1349, an English ship unwittingly brought the **Black Death** to the country, and in the next two years somewhere between half and two-thirds of the population was wiped out. The enfeebled country was easy meat for the **Danes**, who took control at the end of the fourteenth century and remained in command until 1814. As colonial powers go, the Danes were comparatively benign, but everything specifically "Norwegian" – from language to dress – became associated with the primitive and uncouth. To redress this state of affairs, Norway's bourgeois nationalists of the mid- to late nineteenth century sought to redis-cover – and sometimes to reinvent – a national identity. This ambitious enterprise, enthusiastically under-taken, fuelled a cultural renaissance which formed the backdrop to the work of acclaimed painters, writers and musicians, most notably Munch, Ibsen and Grieg, and the endeav-ours of explorers like Amundsen and Nansen. Its reverberations can be felt to this day, for example in Norway's **"No" vote on EU membership**.

Where to go

◂ Sardine tin labels, Canning Museum, Stavanger

Norway is one of Europe's most sparsely inhabited countries, and for the most part its people live in small towns and villages, but the country's five largest cities are the obvious – and the most popular – initial targets for a visit. The five begin with urbane, vivacious **Oslo**, one of the world's most prettily sited capitals, with a flourishing café scene and a clutch of outstanding museums. Beyond Oslo, in roughly descending order of interest, are **Trondheim**, with its superb cathedral

Roald Amundsen

One of Norway's most celebrated sons, Roald Amundsen (1872–1928) was intent on becoming a polar explorer from his early teens. He read everything there was to read on the subject, even training as a sea captain in preparation, and, in 1897, embarked upon his first trip to Antarctica, with a Belgian expedition. Undeterred by a winter on the ice after the ship broke up, he was soon planning his own expedition, the first ever crossing of the Northwest Passage, from the Atlantic to the Pacific round the north of the American continent. He left in the *Gjøa* in June 1903 and finally reached Alaskan waters three years later.

His next target was the North Pole, but during his preparations, in 1909, the American Robert Peary got there first. Amundsen immediately switched his attention to the South Pole, which he reached on December 14, 1911, famously beating the British expedition of Captain Scott. Neither did Amundsen's ambitions end there: in 1926, he became one of the first men to fly over the North Pole in the airship of the Italian Umberto Nobile. It was, however, the Italian who was to do for Amundsen: in 1928, the Norwegian flew north out of Tromsø in a bid to rescue a stranded Nobile and was never seen again.

◄ Seven Sisters Waterfall, Geirangerfjord

and charming, antique centre; the beguiling port of **Bergen**, gateway to the western fjords; gritty, bustling **Stavanger** in the southwest; and northern **Tromsø**. All are likeable, walkable cities worthy of time in themselves, as well as being within comfortable reach of some startlingly handsome scenery. Indeed, each can serve as either a base or a starting point for further explorations: the trains, buses and ferries of Norway's finely tuned public transport system will take you almost anywhere you want to go, although services are curtailed in winter.

Outside of the cities, the perennial draw remains the **western fjords** – a must, and every bit as scenically stunning as the publicity suggests.

The Puffin (*Fratercula arctica*)

Some 30cm tall, with a triangular, red, blue and yellow striped bill, the puffin is the most distinctive of the many sea birds that congregate along the Norwegian coast. It feeds on small fish, and breeds in holes it excavates in turf on cliffs or grassy flatlands, sometimes even adapting former rabbit burrows. When hunting, puffins use their wings to propel themselves underwater and, indeed, are much better at swimming than flying, finding it difficult both to get airborne and to land – collisions of one sort or another are commonplace. Their nesting habits and repetitive flight paths make them easy to catch, and puffin has long been a west-coast delicacy, though hunting them is now severely restricted. In the summer, puffins nest along the whole of the Atlantic coast from Stavanger to Nordkapp, with Værøy (see p.346) and Runde (see p.273) being two of the most likely places for a sighting. In the autumn the puffins move south, though residual winter populations remain on the southerly part of the west coast between Stavanger and Ålesund.

Norway: Distance Chart (distance in kilometres)

	Ålesund	Bergen	Bodø	Hamar	Hammerfest	Kirkenes	Kristiansand	Lillehammer	Narvik	Nordkapp	Oslo	Røros	Stavanger	Tromsø	Trondheim
Ålesund	0	378	1010	441	1844	2218	811	382	1191	1913	533	430	621	1519	287
Bergen	378	0	1380	471	2214	2588	492	439	1561	2283	478	637	170	1844	657
Bodø	1010	1380	0	1108	962	1392	1534	1065	304	1059	1217	936	1560	562	723
Hamar	441	471	1108	0	1942	2316	443	59	1279	2011	123	289	575	1606	385
Hammerfest	1844	2214	962	1942	0	494	2368	1899	652	181	2051	1810	2394	549	1567
Kirkenes	2218	2588	1392	2316	494	0	2742	2273	1027	517	2425	2185	2768	944	1931
Kristiansand	811	492	1534	443	2368	2742	0	471	1715	2437	320	753	245	2054	811
Lillehammer	382	439	1065	59	1899	2273	471	0	1246	1968	167	282	587	1562	342
Narvik	1191	1561	304	1279	652	1027	1715	1246	0	721	1398	1123	1741	251	904
Nordkapp	1913	2283	1059	2011	181	517	2437	1968	721	0	2120	1869	2463	609	1626
Oslo	533	478	1217	123	2051	2425	320	167	1398	2120	0	423	452	1733	494
Røros	430	637	936	289	1810	2185	753	282	1123	1869	423	0	740	1352	166
Stavanger	621	170	1560	575	2394	2768	245	587	1741	2463	452	740	0	1852	837
Tromsø	1519	1844	562	1606	549	944	2054	1562	251	609	1733	1352	1852	0	1205
Trondheim	287	657	723	385	1567	1931	811	342	904	1626	494	166	837	1205	0

Ferry crossings not included in distances quoted.

Dip into the region from Bergen or **Åndalsnes**, both accessible by direct train from Oslo, or take more time to appreciate the subtle charms of the tiny, fjordside villages, among which **Balestrand** and **Mundal** are especially appealing. This is great hiking country too, with a network of cairned trails and lodges (maintained by the nationwide hiking association DNT) threading along the valleys and over the hills. However, many of the country's finest hikes are to be had further inland, within the confines of a trio of marvellous **national parks**: the **Hardangervidda**, a vast mountain plateau of lunar-like appearance; the **Rondane**, with its bulging mountains;

Stokfisk, klippfisk and lutefisk

The Vikings were able to sail long distances without starving to death because they had learnt how to dry white fish, mostly cod, in the open air. This dried fish, **stokfisk**, remained edible for years and was eaten either raw or after soaking in water – chewy and smelly no doubt, but very nutritious. In time, *stokfisk* became the staple diet of western Norway and remained so until the early twentieth century, with every fishing port festooned with wooden A-frames carrying hundreds of drying white fish, headless and paired for size.

Only in the 1690s did the Dutch introduce the idea of salting and drying white fish, again usually cod, to the Norwegians. The fish was decapitated, cleaned and split before being heavily salted and left for several weeks. Then it was dried for a further four to six weeks, by being left outside on rocky drying grounds, *klipper* in Norwegian, hence **klippfisk** – or **bacalao** in Spanish. The Norwegians never really took

 to eating *klippfisk*, but they (or rather their merchants) made fortunes by exporting it to Spain, Portugal, Africa and the Caribbean, where salted cod remains extremely popular to this day. The Norwegians did, however, take to eating **lutefisk**, in which either *stokfisk* or *klippfisk* is soaked in cold water and, at certain stages lye, to create a jelly-like substance that many Norwegians regard as a real delicacy. It is, however, very much an acquired taste and one that never convinced the American storyteller and humourist Garrison Keillor, who suggested in *Pontoon: A Lake Wobegon Novel* that "Most lutefisk is not edible by normal people."

and the **Jotunheimen**, famous for its jagged peaks. Of these three, the first is most easily approached from Finse, Rjukan or Kinsarvik, the Rondane from small-town Otta, the Jotunheimen from Sogndal or Lom. Nudging the Skagerrak, the **south coast** is different again. The climate is more hospitable, the landscape gentler and the coast is confetti-ed with hundreds of little islands. Every summer, holidaying Norwegians sail down here to explore every nautical nook and cranny, popping into a string of pretty, little ports, the most inviting being **Arendal** and **Mandal**, the latter the proud possessor of the country's finest sandy beach.

Away to the **north**, beyond Trondheim, Norway grows increasingly wild and inhospitable as it humps and bumps across the Arctic Circle on the way to the modern, workaday port of **Bodø**. From here, ferries shuttle over to the rugged **Lofoten** islands, which hold some of the most ravishing scenery in the whole of Europe – tiny fishing villages of ochre- and red-painted houses tucked in between the swell of the deep blue sea and the severest of grey-green mountains. Back on the mainland, it's a long haul north from Bodø to the iron-ore town of **Narvik**, and on to **Tromsø**. These towns are, however, merely the froth of a vast wilderness that extends up to **Nordkapp** (North Cape), one of the northernmost accessible points of mainland Europe, and the spot where the tourist trail peters out. Yet Norway continues east for several hundred kilometres, round to remote **Kirkenes** near the Russian border, while inland stretches an immense and hostile upland plateau, the **Finnmarksvidda**, one of the last haunts of the Sámi (formerly Lapp) reindeer-herders.

When to go

Norway is widely regarded as remote and cold – spectacular enough but climatically inhospitable. There is some truth in this, of course, but **when to go** is not, perhaps, as clear-cut a choice as you might imagine. There are advantages to travelling during the long, dark **winters** with their reduced everything: daylight, opening times and transport services. If you are equipped and hardy enough to reach the north, seeing the phenomenal **northern lights** (aurora borealis) is a distinct possibility and later, once the days begin to lighten, the **skiing** – and for that matter the dog-sledging and ice fishing – is excellent. There are skiing packages to Norway from abroad, but perhaps more appealing – and certainly less expensive – is the ease with which you can arrange a few days' skiing wherever you happen to be. As the year advances, **Easter** is the time of the colourful Sámi festivals, and **mid–May** can be absolutely delightful if your visit coincides with the brief Norwegian **spring**, though this is difficult to gauge. Springtime is particularly beguiling in the fjords, with myriad cascading waterfalls fed by the melting snow, and wildflowers in abundance. **Autumn** can be exquisite too, with **September** often bathed in the soft sunshine of an Indian summer, but – especially in the far north – it is frequently cold, often bitterly so, from late September to mid- to late May and this guide has been deliberately weighted towards the **summer** season, when most people travel and when bus, ferry and train connections are at their most frequent. This is the time of the **midnight sun**: the further north you go, the longer the day becomes, until at Nordkapp the sun is continually visible from mid-May to the end of July. Something worth noting, however, is that the **summer season** in Norway is relatively short, stretching roughly

▼ Waterside café, Stavanger

The midnight sun

The **midnight sun** is visible at the following places on the following dates, though climbing the nearest hill can – trees and clouds permitting – extend this by a day or two either way:

Bodø: June 2–July 10
Hammerfest: May 14–July 28
Longyearbyen April 19–Aug 23
Nordkapp: May 12–July 29
Tromsø: May 20–July 21

from the beginning of June to the end of August. Come in September and you'll find that many tourist offices, museums and other sights cut back their hours and buses, ferries and trains often switch to reduced schedules.

As regards **climate**, the Gulf Stream keeps all of coastal Norway temperate throughout the year. Inland, the climate is more extreme – bitterly cold in winter and hot in summer, when temperatures can soar to surprising heights. January and February are normally the coldest months in all regions, July and August the warmest. Rain is a regular occurrence throughout the year, particularly on the west coast, though there are significant local variations in precipitation.

Average daytime temperatures (°C) and rainfall (mm)

	Jan	Feb	Mar	Apr	May	June	July	Aug	Sept	Oct	Nov	Dec
Oslo												
°C	-3.7	-2.8	1.3	6.3	12.6	17.0	18.2	17.2	12.8	7.5	1.5	-2.6
mm	49	36	47	41	53	65	81	89	90	84	73	55
Bergen												
°C	1.5	1.6	3.3	5.9	10.5	13.5	14.5	14.4	11.5	8.7	4.6	1.6
mm	190	152	170	114	106	132	148	190	283	271	259	235
Trondheim												
°C	-3.3	-1.8	1.9	5.4	10.9	13.8	15.1	14.8	11.2	7.0	1.1	-1.8
mm	63	52	54	49	53	68	84	87	113	104	71	84
Tromsø												
°C	-4.7	-4.1	-1.9	1.1	5.6	10.1	12.7	11.8	7.7	2.9	-1.5	-3.7
mm	95	87	72	64	48	59	77	82	102	131	108	106

things not to miss

It's not possible to see everything Norway has to offer in one trip — and we don't suggest you try. What follows is a selective taste of the country's highlights: outstanding scenery, picturesque villages and dramatic wildlife safaris. They're arranged in five colour-coded categories, which you should browse through to find the very best things to see and experience. All highlights have a page reference to take you straight into the Guide, where you can find out more.

01 **Walking in the Jotunheimen mountains** Pages **177 & 251** • Norway's most celebrated hiking area, the Jotunheimen National Park, is crisscrossed with trails and includes northern Europe's two highest peaks.

02 The Norsk Fiskevaersmuseum in Å Page **344** • Hanging on for dear life between the mountains and the sea, the tiny village of Å has preserved its nineteenth-century buildings as the Norwegian Fishing Village Museum.

03 The Flåmsbana Page **235** • A trip on the Flåm railway from the mountains to the fjords down below is one of the most dramatic train rides in the world.

04 Vigelandsparken Page **103** • Before his death in 1943, Gustav Vigeland populated Oslo's favourite park with his fantastical, phantasmagorical sculptures.

05 Sea-bird colonies on Værøy
Page **346** • This remote Lofoten island is renowned for its birdlife, including puffins, cormorants, kittiwakes, guillemots and rare sea eagles.

06 Alta rock carvings
Page **363** • Simple in design but complex in their symbolism, the prehistoric rock carvings of Alta provide an intriguing insight into the lives and beliefs of the region's earliest inhabitants.

07 Troldhaugen
Page **216** • The one-time home of Norway's most famous composer, the modest and extraordinarily likeable Edvard Grieg, has been preserved pretty much as he left it.

08 Whale-watching
Page **327** • Take a whale-watching safari from Andenes between late May and mid-September, and you're virtually assured of a sighting.

09 **The Jostedalsbreen glacier** Page **255** • Take a guided walk out on to this mighty ice plateau that grinds and groans, slips and slithers its way across the mountains of the fjordland.

10 **Kjerringøy** Page **312** • The scenic journey to this extraordinarily well-preserved Arctic trading post makes the excursion doubly enjoyable.

11 **The Oslofjord** Page **108** • The islands of the Oslofjord are great for swimming, sunbathing and walking – and they lie just a short ferry-ride from the city centre.

12 **Trondheim cathedral**
Page **288** • Scandinavia's largest medieval building is a stirring – and sterling – edifice built of blue and green-grey soapstone.

13 **Geirangerfjord** Page **259** •
Shadowed by rearing mountains, the S-shaped Geirangerfjord is one of Norway's most beautiful fjords.

14 Urnes stave church
Page **249** • Perhaps the finest of Norway's stave churches, Urnes is distinguished by the frenzied intricacy of its woodcarving.

15 Edvard Munch Page **89** •
Munch's unsettling, highly charged paintings appear in several of the country's museums, most memorably at the National Gallery in Oslo.

16 Bergen Page **200** • Bergen, Norway's second city, is an eminently appealing place with a clutch of fine old buildings and a lovely coastal setting.

18 Union Hotel, Øye Page 262
• Bend your budget to stay in one of fjordland's most original hotels, whose antique charms are to be found in Øye, a remote hamlet at the end of the brutally beautiful Norangsdal.

17 Ålesund Page 269
• The trim, west-coast fishing port of Ålesund holds a delightful mix of Art Nouveau buildings, whose towers and turrets, floral patterns and even the odd Pharaoh date from 1904.

19 Hjørundfjord Page 262
• A wild and remote fjord, whose deep, dark waters and icy peaks make it one of Norway's most elegiac.

20 **Henningsvær** Page **338** • The Lofoten islands are strewn with picture-postcard fishing villages, but Henningsvær is perhaps the most beguiling of all.

21 **Wildlife safaris** Page **385** • From whale-watching to polar-bear spotting, Norway offers an extravagant range of wildlife safaris, nowhere more so than among the icy wastes of Svalbard.

22 The northern lights Page 354 • Strange, eerily disconcerting and stunningly beautiful, the northern lights roll across the winter skies of northern Norway at regular, if unpredictable intervals.

23 The Oseberg ship Page 99 • This superbly preserved Viking longboat can be seen at Oslo's Viking Ships Museum.

24 Mandal Page 144 • This pretty and laid-back south-coast town boasts the country's finest sandy beach.

25 Svalbard archipelago Page 385 • Glaciers cover two-thirds of the surface of Norway's wild and chilly Svalbard archipelago, which enjoys continuous daylight from April to August.

Basics

Basics

Getting there

From the UK, there's a good selection of inexpensive flights to Norway from London and a reasonable selection from the UK's regional airports. Oslo Gardermoen airport is the main point of arrival, but from London other Norwegian airports are fairly easy to reach too – notably Haugesund, Stavanger, Bergen, Trondheim and Tromsø. Flights are almost invariably much less expensive than the long and arduous journey from the UK to Norway by train or coach. There are currently no ferry services direct from the UK to Norway, but this situation may change and it's worth checking out if you're considering taking your car. From Ireland, there is much less choice, but there are regular flights to Oslo Gardermoen airport.

For travellers arriving from North America, the main decision is whether to fly direct to Oslo – though the options are limited – or via another European city, probably London. Australians, New Zealanders and South Africans have to fly via another country – there are no non-stop, direct flights. Finally, getting to Norway from the rest of Scandinavia (Denmark, Sweden and Finland) is quick, easy and relatively inexpensive, whether you travel by plane, bus or train.

Flights from the UK and Ireland

From the UK, there's a good choice of **direct flights** from London to Oslo's Gardermoen airport plus a scattering of flights there from the UK's **regional airports**. Other Norwegian cities and towns are less well served, though there are a handful of direct flights from the UK to Haugesund, Stavanger, Bergen, Trondheim, Tromsø and the deceptively named Oslo (Torp) airport, which is actually just outside Sandefjord, 110km from Oslo. You may well end up flying to Oslo and catching a connecting flight from there, not necessarily for much more money than a direct flight. Scandinavian Airlines (SAS) is the largest local carrier, but it is now under intense pressure from several budget airlines, including Ryanair and more especially Norwegian Air Shuttle. Current routings from the UK are as follows: **Scandinavian Airlines (SAS)** flies from Aberdeen to Stavanger; Manchester to Oslo; Bristol to Oslo; and London to Ålesund, Bergen, Stavanger and Oslo. **Widerøe**, a subsidiary

of SAS, has flights from Aberdeen to Bergen and Stavanger; Edinburgh to Bergen; and Newcastle to Stavanger. **Ryanair** offers flights from Birmingham, Glasgow, Liverpool and London Stansted to Oslo (Torp); and London Stansted to Haugesund. **British Airways** has flights from London to Oslo and, in the summertime, the Shetland Islands to Bergen. **bmi** has direct flights from London Heathrow to Oslo and Stavanger. **Norwegian Air Shuttle** has direct flights from Edinburgh to Oslo Gardermoen; London Stansted to Tromsø, Trondheim and Oslo Gardermoen; and London Gatwick to Bergen and Stavanger.

Flying from Ireland, there's much less choice, but Ryanair has flights from Dublin to Oslo (Torp) and SAS flies between Dublin and Oslo Gardermoen.

Whichever route and carrier you choose, what you'll **pay** at any given time depends on when you book and when you fly, what offers are available, and how lucky you get. However, if you are flying non-stop to Oslo or any other Norwegian airport between April and September you'll probably pay around £100 return (including taxes), £150 at the weekend, though sometimes the price can drop to £40 return or rise to £250. If you want flexibility with your ticket you'll pay more, as you will if you book at the last minute. All carriers offer their lowest prices online.

Flying times are insignificant: Aberdeen to Stavanger takes just one hour, London to Oslo a little over two, and its three and a half hours to Tromsø.

Fly less – stay longer! Travel and climate change

Climate change is perhaps the single biggest issue facing our planet. It is caused by a build-up in the atmosphere of carbon dioxide and other greenhouse gases, which are emitted by many sources – including planes. Already, **flights** account for three to four percent of human-induced global warming: that figure may sound small, but it is rising year on year and threatens to counteract the progress made by reducing greenhouse emissions in other areas.

Rough Guides regard travel as a **global benefit**, and feel strongly that the advantages to developing economies are important, as are the opportunities for greater contact and awareness among peoples. But we also believe in travelling responsibly, which includes giving thought to how often we fly and what we can do to redress any harm that our trips may create.

We can travel less or simply reduce the amount we travel by air (taking fewer trips and staying longer, or taking the train if there is one); we can avoid night flights (which are more damaging); and we can make the trips we do take "climate neutral" via a carbon offset scheme. **Offset schemes** run by **climatecare.org**, **carbonneutral.com** and others allow you to "neutralize" the greenhouse gases that you are responsible for releasing. Their websites have simple calculators that let you work out the impact of any flight – as does our own. Once that's done, you can pay to fund projects that will reduce future emissions by an equivalent amount. Please take the time to visit our website and make your trip climate neutral, or get a copy of the *Rough Guide to Climate Change* for more detail on the subject.

www.roughguides.com/climatechange

From the US and Canada

From the **US**, you can fly direct to Oslo from New York City by Continental Airlines, but you'll usually find cheaper deals if you're prepared to stop once, either in the US or mainland Europe. Return fares to Oslo can be found for as little as $800 if you're prepared to change, but otherwise reckon on spending around $1000–1500 return for a non-stop New York–Oslo return flight with Continental. There are no direct flights to Norway from the West Coast, but plenty of carriers will get you to Oslo with one stop, for as little as $1200 return.

From **Canada**, the best deals are offered by Air Canada, which flies non-stop to London Heathrow, with onward connections to Norway. From Toronto to Oslo, expect to pay around CDN$1800 in high season and CDN$1300 in low season, while typical fares from Vancouver are around CDN$2050 in high season and CDN$1350 in low season.

The **flying time** on a direct, non-stop flight from the east coast of North America to Norway is just over seven hours.

From Australia and New Zealand

There are no direct flights from **Australia** or **New Zealand** to Norway. Most itineraries will involve two changes, one in the Far East – Singapore, Bangkok or Kuala Lumpur – and then another in the gateway city of the airline you're flying with: most commonly Copenhagen, Amsterdam or London. You can get tickets to Oslo from Sydney or Melbourne for AUS$1500–2000 if you shop around, and from Auckland for slightly more.

From South Africa

There are no direct flights from South Africa to Norway, but KLM does offer direct flights to Amsterdam, a short flight away from Oslo, from both Cape Town and Johannesburg. Alternatively, South African Airways fly direct to London and Frankfurt, from either of which hub city it's a short hop on to Norway; Lufthansa also links South Africa with Frankfurt. Flights with KLM from Cape Town to Amsterdam **cost** around R7400, R8200 from Johannesburg. Indirect flights via London or Frankfurt cost around R8000.

The **flying time** on a direct, non-stop flight from South Africa to London is just over eleven hours.

By train from the UK

Eurostar services running through the Channel Tunnel to Brussels put Norway within reasonable striking distance of the UK by **train**, but the whole journey from London to Oslo, which is usually routed via Brussels and Copenhagen, still takes about 22 hours and costs about £300 one-way, £340 return, though special deals and concessionary rates can reduce these fares considerably. If you're visiting Norway as part of a longer European trip, it may be worth considering a **pan-European rail pass**. There are lots to choose from and **Rail Europe** (⊛www .raileurope.com and ⊛www.raileurope .co.uk), the umbrella company for all national and international passes, operates a comprehensive website detailing all the options with prices. Note in particular that some passes have to be bought before leaving home, others can only be bought in specific countries. Note also that **Inter-Rail Pass** and **Eurail Pass** holders get discounts on some internal ferry and bus journeys within Norway. For information on the **Norway Pass**, which can only be purchased by non-European residents, see "Getting around", p.33.

Driving from the UK

To reach Norway by **car or motorbike** from the UK, you'll have to use Eurotunnel's shuttle train through the Channel Tunnel. Note that Eurotunnel only carries cars (including occupants) and motorbikes, not cyclists and foot passengers. From the Eurotunnel exit in Calais, it's a somewhat epic journey of around 1400km or so to Oslo.

Eurotunnel

There are up to four **Eurotunnel shuttle trains** per hour (only 1 per hour midnight–6am), taking 35 minutes (45min for some night departures); you must check-in at Folkestone at least 30minutes before departure. It's possible to turn up and buy your ticket at the toll booths (exit the M20 at junction 11a), though at busy times booking is advisable. **Fares** depend on the time of year, time of day

and length of stay, and are charged per vehicle rather than per passenger, starting at around £50 for a single fare and £100 return. It's cheaper to travel between 10pm and 6am, while the highest fares are reserved for weekend departures and returns in July and August.

By ferry from the UK

There are currently no **car ferries** from the UK to Norway; the nearest you'll get is Esbjerg in Denmark with DFDS Seaways from Harwich. **Tariffs** vary enormously, depending on when you leave, how long you stay, what size your vehicle is and how many passengers are in it; on overnight sailings, there is also the cost of a cabin to consider. As a sample fare, a seven-day, peak season return fare for two adults in an ordinary car costs around £160. Reservations are strongly recommended. There are three or four Harwich-to-Esbjerg sailings every week and the journey time is about eighteen hours.

By bus from the UK

Given the low cost of budget-airline airfares, travelling by long-distance **bus** from the UK

to Norway may not seem an attractive proposition, but it may still be the cheapest way of getting there. **Eurolines**, part of National Express, has a once-daily service to **Copenhagen**, either via Brussels or Amsterdam, with connections on to **Oslo** (five weekly). The whole journey takes around 32 hours. **Fares** to Oslo start at £170 single (£180 return), less for passengers over 60 and under 26.

By train, bus and ferry from the rest of Scandinavia

By train you can reach **Oslo** from both Stockholm (2–3 daily; 6hr) and Copenhagen (3–4 daily; 8–16hr). There are also regular services from Stockholm to **Trondheim** (2 daily; 12–16hr) and **Narvik** (2 daily; 19hr).

Three main **bus** companies provide services into Norway from other parts of Scandinavia. Eurolines buses from London to Oslo pass through several Danish and Swedish towns, including Copenhagen, Malmö and Gothenburg; Safflebussen has a fast and frequent service from **Stockholm** to Oslo and also operates buses to Oslo from

Copenhagen, Malmö and Gothenburg; and Swebuss runs the same routes as Safflebussen. Note that there are no direct long-distance express buses to Norway from **Finland**, not even in the far north where the two countries share a common border.

A number of **car ferries** shuttle across the Skagerrak **from Denmark** to Norway. There are sailings to Oslo from Copenhagen with DFDS Seaways (16hr), and from Frederikshavn with Stena Line (8hr 30min–12hr). Color Line links Hirtshals with both Kristiansand (3hr 15min) and Larvik (4hr), and Fjordline sails from Hirtshals to Stavanger and Bergen (12/20hr). There's also a Color Line ferry service to Norway **from Sweden**, linking Strömstad, north of Gothenburg, with Sandefjord, 120km or so from Oslo (2hr 30min).

Airlines, agents and operators

Online booking agents

Ⓦ www.expedia.co.uk (in UK), Ⓦ www.expedia.com (in US), Ⓦ www.expedia.ca (in Canada) Ⓦ www.lastminute.com (in UK)

ⓦwww.opodo.co.uk (in UK)
ⓦwww.orbitz.com (in US)
ⓦwww.travelocity.ca (in Canada) ⓦwww
.travelocity.co.uk (in UK), ⓦwww.travelocity
.com (in US), ⓦwww.travelocity.co.nz
(in New Zealand)
ⓦwww.travelonline.co.za (in South Africa)
ⓦwww.zuji.com.au (in Australia)

Airlines

Air Canada ☏1-888/247-2262, UK ☏0871/220
1111, Republic of Ireland ☏01/679 3958, Australia
☏1300/655 767, New Zealand ☏0508/747 767;
ⓦwww.aircanada.com.
Air France US ☏1-800/237-2747, Canada
☏1-800/667-2747, UK ☏0870/142 4343,
Australia ☏1300/390 190, South Africa
☏0861/340 340; ⓦwww.airfrance.com.
Air New Zealand ☏0800/737000, Australia
☏0800/132 476, UK ☏0800/028 4149, Republic
of Ireland ☏1800/551 447, US ☏1800-262/1234,
Canada ☏1800-663/5494; ⓦwww.airnz.co.nz.
American Airlines ☏1-800/433-7300, UK
☏020/7365 0777, Republic of Ireland ☏01/602
0550, Australia ☏1800/673 486, New Zealand
☏0800/445 442; ⓦwww.aa.com.
bmi US ☏1-800/788-0555, UK ☏0870/607
0555 or 607 0222, Republic of Ireland ☏01/283
0700, Australia ☏02/8644 1881, New Zealand
☏09/623 4293, South Africa ☏11/289 8111;
ⓦwww.flybmi.com.
bmibaby UK ☏0871/224 0224, Republic of Ireland
☏1890/340 122; ⓦwww.bmibaby.com.
British Airways US & Canada ☏1-800/AIRWAYS,
UK ☏0844/493 0787, Republic of Ireland
☏1890/626 747, Australia ☏1300/767 177, New
Zealand ☏09/966 9777, South Africa ☏114/418
600; ⓦwww.ba.com.
Continental Airlines US & Canada
☏1-800/523-3273, UK ☏0845/607 6760, Republic
of Ireland ☏1890/925 252, Australia ☏1300/737
640, New Zealand ☏09/308 3350, International
☏1800/231 0856; ⓦwww.continental.com.
Delta US & Canada ☏1-800/221-1212, UK
☏0845/600 0950, Republic of Ireland ☏1850/882
031 or 01/407 3165, Australia ☏1300/302 849,
New Zealand ☏09/9772232; ⓦwww.delta.com.
easyJet UK ☏0905/821 0905, ⓦwww.easyjet
.com.
Finnair US ☏1-800/950-5000, UK ☏0870/241
4411, Republic of Ireland ☏01/844 6565, Australia
☏1300/798 188, South Africa ☏11/339 4865/9;
ⓦwww.finnair.com.
JAL (Japan Air Lines) US & Canada
☏1-800/525-3663, UK ☏0845/774 7700,

Republic of Ireland ☏01/408 3757, Australia
☏1-300/525 287 or 02/9272 1111, New Zealand
☏0800/525 747 or 09/379 9906,
South Africa ☏11/214 2560; ⓦwww.jal.com or
www.japanair.com.
KLM (Royal Dutch Airlines) See Northwest/KLM.
US & Canada ☏1-800/225-2525, UK ☏0870/507
4074, Republic of Ireland ☏1850/747 400,
Australia ☏1300/392 192, New Zealand
☏09/921 6040, South Africa ☏0860/247 747;
ⓦwww.klm.com.
Lufthansa US ☏1-800/3995-838, Canada
☏1-800/563-5954, UK ☏0871/945 9747, Republic
of Ireland ☏01/844 5544, Australia ☏1300/655
727, New Zealand ☏0800/945 220, South Africa
☏0861/842 538; ⓦwww.lufthansa.com.
Northwest/KLM US ☏1-800/225-2525, UK
☏0870/507 4074, Australia ☏1-300/767-310;
ⓦwww.nwa.com.
Norwegian Air Shuttle ☏0047/21 49 00 15
(from outside Norway), ☏815 21 815 (within
Norway); ⓦwww.norwegian.no.
Qantas Airways US & Canada ☏1-800/227-
4500, UK ☏0845/774 7767, Republic of Ireland
☏01/407 3278, Australia ☏13 13 13, New Zealand
☏0800/808 767 or 09/357 8900, South Africa
☏11/441 8550; ⓦwww.qantas.com.
Ryanair UK ☏0871/246 0000, Republic of Ireland
☏0818/30 30 30; ⓦwww.ryanair.com.
SAS (Scandinavian Airlines) US & Canada
☏1-800/221-2350, UK ☏0871/521 2772,
Republic of Ireland ☏01/844 5440, Australia
☏1300/727 707; ⓦwww.scandinavian.net.
Singapore Airlines US ☏1-800/742-3333,
Canada ☏1-800/663-3046, UK ☏0844/800 2380,
Republic of Ireland ☏01/671 0722, Australia
☏13 10 11, New Zealand ☏0800/808 909, South
Africa ☏11/880 8560 or 880 8566; ⓦwww
.singaporeair.com.
South African Airways ☏11/978 1111, US &
Canada ☏1-800/722-9675, UK ☏0870/747 1111,
Australia ☏1300/435 972, New Zealand ☏09/977
2237; ⓦwww.flysaa.com.
Thai Airways US ☏1-212/949-8424, UK
☏0870/606 0911, Australia ☏1300/651 960, New
Zealand ☏09/377 3886, South Africa ☏11/268
2580; ⓦwww.thaiair.com.
United Airlines US ☏1-800/864-8331, UK
☏0845/844 4777, Australia ☏13 17 77; ⓦwww
.united.com.
Virgin Atlantic US ☏1-800/821-5438, UK
☏0870/574 7747, Australia ☏1300/727 340,
South Africa ☏11/340 3400; ⓦwww
.virgin-atlantic.com.
Widerøe Norway ☏0047/75 11 11 11, ⓦwww
.wideroe.no.

B

Agents and operators

ebookers UK ☎0871/223 5000, Republic of Ireland ☎01/431 1311; ⓦwww.ebookers.com and www.ebookers.ie. Low fares on an extensive selection of scheduled flights and package deals.
North South Travel UK ☎01245/608 291, ⓦwww.northsouthtravel.co.uk. Friendly, competitive travel agency, offering discounted fares worldwide. Profits are used to support projects in the developing world, especially the promotion of sustainable tourism.
STA Travel US ☎1-800/781-4040, UK ☎0871/2300 040, Australia ☎134 782, New Zealand ☎0800/474 400, South Africa ☎0861/781 781; ⓦwww.statravel.com. Worldwide specialists in independent travel; also student IDs, travel insurance, car rental, rail passes, and more. Good discounts for students and under-26s.
Trailfinders UK ☎0845/058 5858, Republic of Ireland ☎01/677 7888; ⓦwww.trailfinders.com. One of the best-informed and most efficient agents for independent travellers.

Rail contacts

European Rail UK ☎020/7619 1083, ⓦwww.europeanrail.com.
Eurostar UK ☎0870/518 6186, outside UK ☎0044/12336 17575; ⓦwww.eurostar.com.
Norwegian Railways Norway ☎0047/815 00 888, ⓦwww.nsb.no.
Rail Europe US ☎1-888/382-7245, Canada ☎1-800/361-7245, UK ☎0844/848 4064, Australia ☎03/9642 8644, South Africa ☎11/628 2319; ⓦwww.raileurope.com and www.raileurope.co.uk.
SJ Sweden ☎0046/771 75 75 75 ⓦwww.sj.se. Swedish company operating the Narvik-to-Stockholm line.

Bus contacts

Eurolines UK ☎0871/781 8181, ⓦwww.eurolines.co.uk.
Lavprisekspressen Norway ☎0047/67 98 04 80, ⓦwww.lavprisekspressen.no.
Nor-Way Bussekspress Norway ☎0047/81 54 44 44, ⓦwww.nor-way.no.
Säfflebussen Norway ☎815 66 010, ⓦwww.safflebussen.se.
Swebuss Norway ☎800 58 444, ⓦwww.swebusexpress.no.

Ferry contacts

Color Line Norway ☎810 00 811, ⓦwww.colorline.no).
DFDS Seaways Norway ☎21 62 13 40, ⓦwww.dfds.no.
Fjordline Norway ☎815 33 500, ⓦwww.fjordline.no.
Stena Line Norway ☎02 010, ⓦwww.stenaline.no.

Eurotunnel contact

Eurotunnel UK ☎0870/53 53 535, ⓦwww.eurotunnel.com.

Packages and organized tours – a small selection

Anglers' World Holidays ☎01246/221 717, ⓦwww.anglers-world.co.uk. Sea- and river-fishing holidays in Norway.
Arctic Experience/Discover the World ☎01737/218 800, ⓦwww.discover-the-world.co.uk. Specialist adventure tours including

Fjord Tours AS

Tourism in Norway is a multi-million dollar industry that has spawned a small army of tour operators, but easily the best non-specialist is Bergen's **Fjord Tours** (☎815 68 222, ⓦwww.fjordtours.com). The company manages the first-rate **Fjord Pass** scheme (see p.43) and organizes a creative menu of Norwegian tours. It is the main organizer of the much-vaunted **Norway in a Nutshell** excursion (see p.224), and they also offer **Sognefjord in a Nutshell** (1115kr round-trip from Bergen); **Hardanger in a Nutshell** (770kr round-trip from Bergen); and a wonderful four-day tour from Bergen to Oslo and Trondheim followed by a Hurtigrute cruise back to Bergen (2845kr). There are no tour guides on any of these excursions, which suits most independent travellers just fine, and all use public transport – bus, train and ferry. Fjord Tours also offer **adventure packages** – cycling on the Rallarvegen (see p.236) or winter skiing for example – and, if you're travelling by car, they will book accommodation on your behalf with Fjord Pass hotels and advise on itineraries – see their 'Recommended travel routes'.

whale-watching in Norway, wildlife in Spitsbergen and dog-sledging in Lapland.

Brekke Tours – Spirit of Scandinavia
☏ 1-800/437-5302, ⓦ www.brekketours.com. A well-established company offering a host of sightseeing and cultural tours in Scandinavia.

Exodus ☏ 0845/863 9600, ⓦ www.exodus.co.uk. Large activity-holiday specialist offering cross-country skiing and all sorts of other winter sports plus whale-watching, hiking and Spitsbergen excursions.

Headwater Holidays ☏ 01606/720 199, ⓦ www .headwater.com. Guided walking holidays in the Rondane national park and the Gudbrandsdal valley in the summer, cross-country skiing on the Hardangervidda in winter. Canoeing and cycling holidays too.

Hurtigruten ☏ 0845/225 6640, ⓦ www .hurtigruten.com. UK contact for the Hurtigrute coastal boat (see p.36), Norway's most famous cruise. Extremely helpful and efficient.

Inntravel ☏ 01653/617 949, ⓦ www.inntravel .co.uk. Outdoor holidays in Norway including skiing, walking, dog-sledging, fjord cruises, and whale- and reindeer-watching.

Passage Tours ☏ 1-800/548-5960, ⓦ www .passagetours.com. Scandinavian specialist offering an extensive range of Norwegian tours, for example the "Fjord Crescendo" and the "Oslo and Bergen Rhapsody", which mix time in the city with time in the sticks. Also coastal cruises, dog-sledging, whale-watching and ski packages.

Saddle Skedaddle ☏ 0191/265 1110, ⓦ www .skedaddle.co.uk. Highly recommended company organizing a couple of cycling tours of Norway each year, usually one to the Lofoten islands and another round the western fjords.

Scanam World Tours ☏ 1-800/545-2204, ⓦ www.scanamtours.com. Scandinavian specialist offering an extensive programme of group and individual tours and cruises within Norway.

Scand-America Tours ☏ 1-727/415-5088, ⓦ www.scandamerica.com. A wide variety of packages – everything from dog-sledging to garden tours – throughout Scandinavia. Florida based.

Scantours ☏ 020/7554 3530, ⓦ www .scantoursuk.com. Huge range of packages and tailor-made holidays to every Scandinavian nook and cranny.

Getting around

Norway's public transport system – a huge mesh of trains, buses, car ferries and passenger express ferries – is comprehensive and reliable. In the winter (especially in the north) services can be cut back severely, but no part of the country is unreachable for long. Bear in mind, however, that Norwegian villages and towns usually spread over a large distance, so don't be surprised if you end up walking a kilometre or two from the bus stop, ferry terminal or train station to get where you want to go. It's this sprawling nature of the country's towns and, more especially, the remoteness of many of the sights, that encourages visitors to rent a car. This is an expensive business, but costs can be reduced if you hire locally for a day or two rather than for the whole trip, though in high season spare vehicles can get very thin on the ground.

Timetables for most of the principal train, bus and ferry services are detailed in the *NRI Guide to Transport and Accommodation*, a free and easy-to-use booklet available in your home country from the Norwegian Tourist Board. In Norway itself, almost every tourist office carries a comprehensive range of free local and regional public-transport timetables. In addition, all major train stations carry the *NSB Regiontog i Norge*, a brochure detailing Norway's principal train timetables, while long-distance bus routes operated by the national carrier, Nor-Way Bussekspress, are listed in the free *Rutehefte* (timetable), available at principal bus stations. Norwegian public-transport timetables are also widely

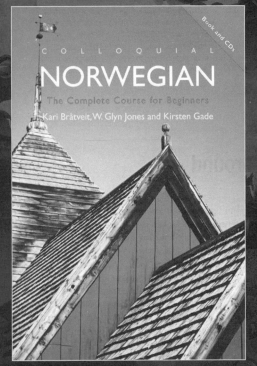

available on the internet, but although the major carriers are easy enough to track down, other companies are more elusive in English, less so if you can read Norwegian; we have provided public-transport websites throughout the Guide.

Trains

With the exception of the Narvik line into Sweden, operated by SJ (Sweden ☎0046/771 75 75 75, ⓦwww.sj.se), all Norwegian **train** services are run by Norges Statsbaner (NSB; ☎815 00 888, ⓦwww .nsb.no). Apart from a sprinkling of branch lines, NSB services operate on three main domestic routes, linking Oslo to Stavanger in the southwest, to Bergen in the west and to Trondheim and on to Bodø in the north. In places, the rail system is extended by a **TogBuss** (literally train-bus) service, with connecting coaches continuing on from train terminals. The nature of the country has made several of the routes engineering feats of some magnitude, worth the trip in their own right – the tiny **Flåm line** and the sweeping **Rauma line** from Dombås to Åndalsnes are exciting examples.

Fully flexible, standard-fare prices are bearable with the popular Oslo–Bergen run, for example, costing around 740kr one-way, Oslo–Trondheim 820kr – twice that for a return. Both journeys take around six and a half to seven hours; costs can be reduced by purchasing a **rail pass** in advance (see p.29). Inside Norway, NSB offers a variety of **discount fares**. The main discount ticket scheme is the **Minipris** (mini-price), under which you can cut up to fifty percent off the price of long-distance journeys. In general, the further you travel, the more economic they become. The drawback is that Minipris tickets must be purchased at least one day in advance, are not available at peak periods and on certain trains, and stopovers are not permitted. In addition, NSB offers a variety of special deals and discounts – inquire locally (and ahead of time) for details on any specific route.

In terms of **concessionary fares**, there are group and family reductions; children under 4 travel free; 4–15-year-olds pay half-fare, and so do senior citizens (67+) and the disabled. It's worth noting that on many intercity trains and on all overnight and international services, an advance **seat reservation** is **compulsory** whether you have a rail pass or not. In high season it's wise to reserve a seat on main routes anyway, as trains can be packed. **Sleepers** (*sove*) are reasonably priced from 750kr if you consider you'll save a night's hotel accommodation.

NSB have two main sorts of train – local (Lokaltog) and regional (Regiontog). There is one standard class on both, but certain regional trains have a "Komfort" (read more luxurious, spacious) carriage, for which you pay a supplement of 75kr. General **NSB timetables** are available free at every train station and there are individual route time tables too. In the case of the more scenic routes, there are also leaflets describing the sights as you go.

Rail passes

Both **Inter-Rail** and **Eurail** passes (see p.29) are valid on the Norwegian railway system. The other alternative for non-European residents only is the **Norway Rail Pass**, which allows unlimited travel on all NSB services (except the Oslo Airport Express) on a specified number of days within a specific period. Three days in one month costs 1830kr, four days 1980kr, six days 2490kr and eight days 2770kr. The Norway Rail Pass should be purchased before you arrive in Europe – most readily from Rail Europe (see p.32). Children under 4 travel free and there are substantial discounts for the under-26s and the over-60s.

All rail-pass holders have to shell out a small additional surcharge on certain trains on certain routes, and also have to pay the compulsory seat reservation fee on many intercity trains and all overnight and international services. On the plus side, rail passes are good for travel on connecting Togbuss services and two of them (Eurail, and Inter-Rail) give a fifty-percent discount on specified intercity bus and boat routes.

Buses

Both supplementing – and on occasion duplicating – the train network, **buses** reach almost every corner of the country. Costs are passable – especially as all tolls and ferry costs are included in the price of a ticket – and bus travel is almost invariably less expensive than the train, but prices are still fairly high. For instance, the ten-hour bus ride between Ålesund and Bergen costs 600kr, the seven-hour trip from Oslo to Haugesund 560kr.

Most long-distance buses are operated by the leading national carrier, **Nor-Way Bussekspress** (T815 44 444, Wwww.nor -way.no). Supplementing these services is a dense network of local buses, whose time tables are available at most tourist offices and bus stations as well as on the internet. In the more mountainous regions, many local buses only run in June, July and August. **Tickets** are usually bought on board, but bus stations do sell advance tickets on some of the more popular long-distance routes.

In terms of **concessionary fares**, there are group and family reductions; children under 4 travel free, and youngsters (under 16) plus seniors (over 67) pay half fare. Nor-Way Bussekspress also offers Inter-Rail pass-holders a fifty-percent reduction on certain services and some local bus companies have comparable deals. Indeed, rail-pass and student-card holders should always ask about discounts when purchasing a ticket.

Ferries

Using a **ferry** is one of the highlights of any visit to Norway – indeed, among the western fjords and around the Lofotens they are all but impossible to avoid. The majority are roll-on, roll-off **car ferries**. These represent an economical means of transport, with **prices** fixed on a nationwide sliding scale: short journeys (10–20min) cost foot passengers 20–30kr, whereas car and driver will pay 50–100kr. Ferry procedures are straightfor-ward: foot passengers walk on and pay the conductor, car drivers usually wait in line with their vehicles on the jetty till the conductor comes to the car window to collect the money – although some busier routes have a drive-by ticket office. One or two of the longer car ferries – in particular Bodø–Moskenes – take advance reservations, but the rest operate on a first-come, first-served basis. In the off season, there's no real need to arrive more than twenty minutes before

departure – with the possible exception of the Lofoten Island ferries – but in the summer allow two hours, or two and a half hours to be really safe.

Hurtigbåt passenger express boats

Norway's **Hurtigbåt passenger express boats** are catamarans that make up in speed what they lack for in enjoyment: unlike in ordinary ferries, you're cooped up and have to view the passing landscape through a window, and in choppy seas the ride can be disconcertingly bumpy. Nonetheless, they're a convenient time-saving option: it takes just four hours on the Hurtigbåt service from Bergen to Balestrand, for instance, the same from Narvik to Svolvær, and a mere two and a half hours from Harstad to Tromsø. Hurtigbåt services are concentrated on the west coast around Bergen and the neighbouring fjords; the majority operate all year. There's no fixed tariff table, so **rates** vary considerably, though Hurtigbåt boats are significantly more expensive per kilometre than car ferries – Bergen–Flåm, for instance, costs 625kr for the five-and-a-half-hour journey, 720kr for the four-hour trip from Bergen to Stavanger. There are **conces-sionary fares** on all routes, with infants up to the age of 3 travelling free, and children (4–15) and senior citizens (over 67) getting a fifty-percent discount. In addition, rail-pass holders and students are often eligible for a fifty-percent reduction on the full adult rate and on some routes you get a similar discount for reservations on the internet.

The Hurtigrute

Norway's most celebrated ferry journey is the long and beautiful haul up the coast from Bergen to Kirkenes on the **Hurtigrute** (literally "rapid route"; Wwww.hurtigruten .com) **coastal boat** – or "coastal steamer", in honour of its past rather than present means of locomotion. To many, the Hurti-grute remains the quintessential Norwegian experience, and it's certainly the best way to observe the drama of the country's extraor-dinary coastline. Twelve ships combine to provide one daily service in each direction, and the boats stop off at over thirty ports on the way.

Hurtigrute sailing schedule

Northbound departure times from principal ports
Summer schedule (mid-April to mid-Sept):

Bergen 8pm	Stamsund 7.30pm
Florø 2.15am	Svolvær 10pm
Ålesund 9.30am	Harstad 8am
Geiranger 1.30pm	Tromsø 6.30pm
Ålesund 6.45pm	Hammerfest 6.45am
Trondheim noon	Honningsvåg 3.15pm
Bodø 3pm	Arrive Kirkenes 10am

Winter schedule (mid-Sept to mid-April):

Bergen 10.30pm	Svolvær 10pm
Florø 4.45am	Harstad 8am
Ålesund 3pm	Tromsø 6.30pm
(No service to Geiranger)	Hammerfest 6.45am
Trondheim noon	Honningsvåg 3.15pm
Bodø 3pm	Arrive Kirkenes 10am
Stamsund 7.30pm	

Southbound: year-round departure times from principal ports:

Kirkenes 12.45pm	Bodø 4am
Honningsvåg 6.15am	Trondheim 10am
Hammerfest 12.45pm	Ålesund 00.45am
Tromsø 1.30am	Doesn't stop at Geiranger
Harstad 8.30am	southbound
Svolvær 7.30pm	Florø 8.15am
Stamsund 9.45pm	Arrives Bergen 2.30pm

The whole round-trip lasts thirteen days (and 12 nights), and in peak season (June & July) the one-way **fare** from Bergen to end-of-the-line Kirkenes is 13,000kr per person in a twin-bed cabin, forty percent less in the depths of winter, including all meals. There are, however, all sorts of special deals for early reservations and so forth – see the website for details. Making a Hurtigrute booking within Norway is easy too, either on the website, by phone (☎810 30 000), or via most west-coast tourist offices.

A **short or medium-sized hop** along the coast on a portion of the Hurtigrute route is also well worth considering. **Port-to-port fares** are not particularly cheap, especially in comparison with the bus, but they are affordable providing you are not sleeping on board, in which case you are required to have a cabin. The standard, mid-season (spring or autumn), one-way passenger fare from Harstad to Trondheim (6hr 30min), for example, costs 453kr without a cabin or meals, 849kr in high season; breakfast costs an extra 105kr, lunch 225kr and dinner 320kr. This compares very favourably with the cost of the 24-hour yomp from Trondheim to Bodø, which costs 2526kr per person in high season, including a berth in a cabin and breakfast – but not dinner or lunch. Last-minute bargains, however, can bring the rates down to amazingly low levels and there are often substantial one-off discounts in winter too. All the tourist offices in the Hurtigrute ports have the latest details and should be willing to telephone the captain of the nearest ship to make a reservation on your behalf.

As for specifics, sleeping in the lounges is no longer allowed; bikes travel free. There are luggage racks and laundry as well as a restaurant and a 24-hour cafeteria supplying coffee and snacks on all Hurtigrute boats; the restaurant is very popular, so reserve a table as soon as you board.

Domestic flights

Internal flights can prove a surprisingly inexpensive way of hopping about Norway, and are especially useful if you're short on time and want to reach, say, the far north: Tromsø to Kirkenes takes the best part of two days by bus, but it's just an hour by plane. Domestic air routes are serviced by several companies, but the major carrier is **SAS** (⊛www.sas.no), a conglomerate with many (airline) subsidiaries. A standard one-way fare with SAS from Oslo to Trondheim costs in the region of 620kr, 770kr from Oslo to Tromsø. SAS also offer all sorts of deals and discounts, especially on return fares, which often cost just ten percent more than single tickets, but these bargains usually come with restrictions, regarding, for example, advance booking. In terms of **concessionary fares**, SAS permits infants under 2 to travel free, while children under the age of 16 receive a 25 percent discount on most flights, providing they are travelling in a group that includes at least one full-fare-paying adult. The details of these various discounts vary from year to year, so it's always worth checking them out.

You might also want to check out the special deals offered by Widerøe (⊛www.wideroe.no), a subsidiary of SAS, which specializes in internal flights. They fly to 35 Norwegian airports, mostly in the north, and, among their several offerings, they do an "ODD" one-way ticket on all of their domestic flights for just 350kr. Another good bet is the budget airline **Norwegian Airlines** (⊛www.norwegian.no), which operates flights between twelve domestic airports at what can be staggeringly low prices – Bergen to Oslo, for example, for just 400kr.

Driving

Norway's **main roads** are excellent, especially when you consider the rigours of the climate, and nowadays, with most of the more hazardous sections either ironed out or tunnelled through, driving is comparatively straightforward. Nonetheless, you still have to be careful on some of the higher sections and in the longer, fume-filled tunnels. Once you leave the main roads for the narrow mountain byroads, however, you'll be in for some nail-biting experiences – and that's in

the summertime. In winter the Norwegians close many roads and concentrate their efforts on keeping the main highways open, but obviously blizzards and ice can make driving difficult- to-dangerous anywhere, even with winter tyres, studs and chains. At any time of the year, the more adventurous the drive, the better equipped you need to be: on remote drives you should pack provisions, have proper hiking gear, check the car thoroughly before departure, carry a spare can of petrol and take a mobile phone.

Norway's main highways have an **E prefix** – E6, E18, etc; all the country's other significant roads (**riksvei**, or **rv**) are assigned a number and, as a general rule, the lower the number, the busier the road. In our guide, we've used the E prefix, but designated other roads as Highways, or "Hwy" (followed by the number). The E roads are the nearest thing Norway has to motorways, but only rarely are they dual carriageways and they are often interrupted by roundabouts and even traffic lights. **Tolls** are imposed on certain roads to pay for construction projects such as bridges, tunnels and motorway improvements. Once the costs are covered the toll is normally removed. The older projects levy a fee of around 15–30kr, but the toll for some of the newer works runs to well over 100kr per vehicle. There's also a modest toll on entering the country's larger cities (15–20kr), but whether this is an environmental measure or a means of boosting city coffers is a moot point.

Paying on a toll road

On most **toll-roads**, you simply pay at the toll booth, but at others drivers are presented with three lanes and choices: the *abonnement* lanes (with blue signs) are for pass-holders only and are always on the left; the *mynt/coin* lanes (with yellow signs) are for exact cash payments only and usually have a bucket-shaped receptacle where you throw your money; and the *manuell* lanes (grey) are also used for cash payments, but provide change. The busiest toll roads, like those into Oslo and Bergen, are now automatic – and are signed *automatisk bomstasjon*. At these, all number plates are read electronically and an invoice is sent to

Opening dates of major mountain passes

Obviously enough, there's no preordained date for the opening of **mountain roads** in the springtime – it depends on the weather, and the threat of avalanche is often much more a limitation than actual snowfalls. The dates below should therefore be treated with caution; if in doubt, seek advice from a local tourist office. If you do head along a mountain road that's closed, sooner or later you'll come to a barrier and have to turn round.

E6: Dovrefjell (Oslo–Trondheim). Usually open all year.

E69: Skarsvåg–Nordkapp. Closed late October to April.

E134: Haukelifjell (Oslo–Bergen/Stavanger). Usually open all year.

Hwy 7: Hardangervidda (Oslo–Bergen). Usually open all year.

Hwy 51: Valdresflya. Closed December to early May.

Hwy 55: Sognefjellet. Closed November to early May.

Hwy 63: Grotli–Geiranger–Åndalsnes (Trollstigen). Closed mid-October to May.

either the car hire company concerned or the registered owner of the vehicle wherever he or she may be.

To avoid getting flustered at toll booths, Norwegians tend to carry a supply of coins ready to hand. Finally, there's often a modest toll of 10–20kr on privately maintained country roads; drivers are expected to deposit their money in a roadside **honesty box**, and these are easy to spot.

Fuel

Fuel is readily available, even in the north of Norway, though here the settlements are so widely separated that you'll need to keep your tank pretty full; if you're using the byroads extensively, remember to carry an extra can. Current fuel prices are 12–15kr a litre, and there are four main grades, all unleaded (*blyfri*): 95 octane, 98 octane, super 98 octane, and diesel. It's worth remembering that some petrol stations don't accept credit cards, so be sure to double-check before filling up.

Documentation

All EU/EEA **driving licences** are honoured in Norway, but other nationals will need – or are recommended to have – an **International Driver's Licence** (available at minimal cost from your home motoring organization). No form of provisional licence is accepted. If you're bringing your own car, you must have vehicle registration papers, adequate insurance, a first-aid kit, a warning

triangle and a green card (available from your insurers or motoring organization). Extra insurance coverage for unforeseen legal costs is also well worth having, as is an appropriate **breakdown policy** from a motoring organization. In Britain, for example, the AA charges members and non-members about £100 for a month's Europe-wide breakdown cover, with all the appropriate documentation, including green card, provided.

Rules of the road

Norway has strict **rules of the road**: you drive on the right, with dipped headlights required at all times; seat belts are compulsory for drivers and front-seat passengers, and for back-seat passengers too, if fitted. There's a speed limit of 30kph in residential areas, 50kph in built-up areas, 80kph on open roads and 80kph, 90kph or sometimes 100kph on motorways. Speed cameras monitor hundreds of kilometres of road – watch out for the **Automatisk Trafikkontroll** warning signs – and they are far from popular with the locals: there are all sorts of folkloric (and largely apocryphal) tales of men in masks appearing at night with chain saws to chop them down. **Speeding fines** are so heavy that local drivers stick religiously within the speed limit. If you're filmed breaking the limit in a hire car, expect your credit card to be stung by the car hire company to the tune of at least 600kr and a maximum of 7,800kr (yes, that's right). If you're stopped for speeding, large spot fines are payable within the same price range and, if you are way over the limit (say 60kph in a 30kph zone) you could well end up in jail; rarely is any leniency shown to unwitting foreigners. **Drunken driving** is also severely frowned upon. You can be asked to take a breath test on a routine traffic-check; if you're over the limit, you will have your licence confiscated and may face a stretch in prison. It is also an offence to drive while using a hand-held mobile/cell phone. On-street parking restrictions are rigorously enforced and clearly signed with a white 'P' on a blue background; below the 'P' are the hours where parking restrictions apply – Monday to Friday first and Saturday in brackets afterwards; below this are any particular limits – most commonly denoting the maximum (*maks*) number of hours (*timer*) – and then there's *mot avgift*, which means there's a fee to pay at the meter.

If you **break down** in a hire car, you'll get roadside assistance from the particular repair company the car hire firm has contracted. This is a free service, though some car hire companies charge you if you need help changing a tyre in the expectation that you should be able to do it yourself. The same principles work with your own vehicle's breakdown policy (see p.39). Two major **breakdown companies** in Norway are Norges Automobil-Forbund and Viking Redningstjeneste, who combine to operate a 24-hour emergency assistance line on ☏810 00 505. There are emergency telephones along some motorways, and NAF trucks patrol all mountain passes between mid-June and mid-August.

Car rental

All the major international **car rental** companies are represented in Norway – see below and the "Listings" sections of larger cities for contact details. To rent a car, you'll need to be 21 or over (and have been driving for at least a year), and you'll need a credit card. Rental **charges** are fairly high, beginning at around 3500kr per week for unlimited mileage in the smallest vehicle, but include collision damage waiver and vehicle (but not personal) insurance. To cut costs, watch for special local deals – a

Friday-to-Monday weekend rental might, for example, cost you as little as 800kr. If you hire from a local company rather than one of the big names, you should proceed with care. In particular, check the policy for the excess applied to claims and ensure that it includes collision damage waiver (applicable if an accident is your fault). There are lots of these local car-hire companies in Norway and they are listed in the *Yellow Pages* under *Bilutleie*. Bear in mind, too, that one-way car rental **drop-off charges** are almost always wallet-searing: if you pick up a car in Oslo and drop it in Bodø, it will cost you 6000kr – nearer 8000kr in Tromsø.

Car rental agencies

Alamo US ☏1-800/462-5266, ⓦwww.alamo.com.
Avis US ☏1-800/331-1212, Canada ☏1-800/879-2847, UK ☏0844/581 8181, Republic of Ireland ☏021/428 1111, Australia ☏13 63 33 or 02/9353 9000, New Zealand ☏09/526 2847 or 0800/655 111, South Africa ☏11/923 3660; ⓦwww.avis.com.
Budget US ☏1-800/527-0700, Canada ☏1-800/268-8900, UK ☏0870/156 5656, Australia ☏1300/362 848, New Zealand ☏0800/283 438; ⓦwww.budget.com.
Europcar US & Canada ☏1-877/940 6900, UK ☏0845/758 5375, Republic of Ireland ☏01/614 2800, Australia ☏1300/131 390; ⓦwww.europcar.com.
Hertz US & Canada ☏1-800/654-3131, UK ☏0870/040 9000, Republic of Ireland ☏01/870 5777, Australia ☏13 30 39, New Zealand ☏0800/654 321, South Africa ☏21/935 4800; ⓦwww.hertz.com.
Holiday Autos US & Canada ☏0866/392 9288, UK ☏0870/400 4482, Republic of Ireland ☏01/872 9366, Australia ☏1300/554 432, New Zealand ☏0800/144 040, South Africa ☏11/234 0597; ⓦwww.holidayautos.co.uk. Part of the LastMinute.com group.
National US ☏1-800/227-7368, UK ☏0870/400 4588, Australia ☏0870/600 6666, New Zealand ☏03/366 5574; ⓦwww.nationalcar.com.
SIXT US & Canada ☏1-888/749-8227, UK ☏0870/156 7567, Republic of Ireland ☏06/120 6088, Australia ☏1300/660 660, South Africa ☏0860/031 666; ⓦwww.sixt.com.
Thrifty US & Canada ☏1-800/847-4389, UK ☏01494/751 540, Republic of Ireland ☏1800/515 800, Australia ☏1300/367 227, New Zealand ☏0800/737 070; ⓦwww.thrifty.com.

Cycling

Cycling is a great way to enjoy Norway's scenery – just be sure to wrap up warm and dry, and don't be overambitious in the distances you expect to cover. Cycle tracks as such are few and far between, and are mainly confined to the larger towns, but there's precious little traffic on most of the minor roads and cycling along them is a popular pastime. Furthermore, whenever a road is improved or rerouted, the old highway is usually redesigned as a cycle route. At almost every place you're likely to stay in, you can anticipate that someone will **rent bikes** – either the tourist office, a sports shop, youth hostel or campsite. Costs are pretty uniform: reckon on paying between 120kr and 200kr a day for a seven-speed bike, plus a refundable deposit of up to 1000kr; mountain bikes are about thirty percent more.

A few tourist offices have maps of recommended **cycling routes**, but this is a rarity. It is, however, important to check your itinerary thoroughly, especially in the more mountainous areas. Cyclists aren't allowed through the longer tunnels for their own protection (the fumes can be life-threatening), so discuss your plans with whoever you hire the bike from. With regard to bike carriage, bikes mostly go free on car ferries and attract a nominal charge on passenger express boats, but buses vary. National carrier Nor-Way Bussekspress (🌐 www.nor-way.no) accepts bikes only when there is space and charges a child fare, while local rural buses sometimes take them free, sometimes charge and sometimes do not take them at all. Taking a bike on an NSB train (🌐 www.nsb.no) costs ten percent of the price of your ticket with a minimum price of 57kr; on some services, you have to make an advance reservation.

If you're planning a **cycling holiday**, your first port of call should be the Norwegian Tourist Board (see p.61), where you can get general cycling advice, a map showing roads and tunnels inaccessible to cyclists and a list of companies offering all-inclusive cycling tours. Obviously enough, tour costs vary enormously, but as a baseline reckon on about 6000kr per week all-inclusive.

The Norwegian Cyclist Association, Syklistenes Landsforening, Storgata 23D, Oslo (☎22 47 30 42, 🌐 www.slf.no), has an excellent range of specific cycling **books** and **maps**, some of which are in English. Finally, the website Sykkelturisme i Norge (🌐 www.bike-norway.com) has ideas for a dozen routes around the country from 100km to 400km, plus useful practical information about road conditions, repair facilities and places of interest en route.

Accommodation

Inevitably, accommodation is one of the major expenses you will incur on a trip to Norway – indeed, if you're after a degree of comfort, it's going to be the costliest item by far. There are, however, budget alternatives, principally guest-houses (pensjonater), rooms in private houses (broadly this is bed and breakfast arranged via the local tourist office), campsites and cabins, and last but certainly not least, an abundance of HI-registered hostels. Also bear in mind that many hotels offer special deals as well as substantial weekend discounts of 25–40 percent.

Almost everywhere, you can reserve ahead easily enough by calling or emailing the establishment direct; English is almost always spoken. Most tourist offices also operate an on-the-spot service for same-night accommodation for free or at minimal charge.

Hotels

Almost universally, Norwegian **hotels** are of a high standard: neat, clean and efficient. Special bargains and impromptu weekend deals also make many of them, by European standards at least, comparatively economical. Another plus is that the price of a hotel room always includes a buffet breakfast – in mid- to top-range hotels especially, these can be sumptuous banquets. The only negatives are the sizes of rooms, which tend to be small – singles especially – and their sameness: Norway abounds in mundanely modern, concrete-and-glass, sky-rise chain hotels. In addition to the places we've detailed in this Guide, many Norwegian hotels, along with their room rates, summer discounts and facilities, are listed in the free booklet *Transport and Accommodation*, available from Norwegian tourist offices abroad (see p.61).

Prices are very sensitive to demand – a double room that costs 1000kr when a hotel is slack, soon hits the 2000kr mark if there's a rush on. Generally speaking, however, 1200kr should cover the cost of two people in a double room at most hotels most of the time, nearer to 1000kr at the weekend, slightly more in Oslo. Typically, the stated price includes breakfast.

Hotel and guesthouse passes

One way to cut costs is to join one of Norway's **hotel discount and pass**

Scandic Hotels and the environment

A Swedish-owned company, Scandic Hotels (@www.scandichotels.com) has around 130 properties in ten countries, though in Norway it has just ten hotels, which makes it one of that country's smaller chains. Scandic hotels are extremely pleasant to stay in – and several are detailed in our Guide – and, most commendably, the company's environmental policies are exemplary. The company is committed to the elimination of all carbon emissions by 2025. This will be achieved partly by concentrating on the minutiae of hotel life – all of their hotel rooms have recycling bins and there's no bottled water – and Scandic has committed itself to focus on concerns such as water efficiencies and the use of renewable energy. Having spent time and money training its staff on environmental issues and the need for sustainability, it is hoped the company will prove to be a trendsetter. In a similar vein, Scandic has a full-time disability coordinator responsible for ensuring all their properties have proper disabled access.

schemes, though this will put paid to any idea you might have of a flexible itinerary as advance booking is a prerequisite. Most Norwegian hotels are members of one discount/pass scheme or another, and you can usually join the scheme at any one of them or in advance on the internet. There are half a dozen major schemes to choose from, most are limited to the summertime, and the majority are tied to a particular hotel chain, which obviously affects the variety of your accommodation. Among the hotel chains, Rica has a particularly varied portfolio of around ninety hotels, making their **Rica Holiday Pass** (*Rica Feriepass*; @www.rica .no) more appealing than most. Valid from late June to mid-August, this pass is basically a free loyalty card that promises the bearer the best rate available and every fifth night free; you can join at any Rica hotel. With only ten properties in Norway, **Scandic Hotels** (@www.scandichotels.com) cannot offer the range of accommodation provided by some of their rivals, but they do have a "Frequent Guest Programme" in which points received for staying with them are exchanged for discounts; for more on Scandic Hotels, see box, p.42.

Much more enticing, however, is the **Fjord Pass** (@815 68 222, @www.fjord-pass .com), which offers discounts of around 30 percent at 170 hotels, guesthouses, cottages and apartments all over Norway with a particular concentration in the western fjords. The Fjord Pass card costs just 120kr and is valid for two adults and children under the age of fifteen for the whole year in which it is purchased. Under the scheme, you can either book online with the place you want to stay at or leave it to the booking service of the company who run the scheme, the exemplary **Fjord Tours** (see p.32 for more details). The discount card itself can be bought direct from Fjord Tours or at the sales outlets detailed on the website.

Pensions, guesthouses and inns

For something a little less anonymous than the average hotel, **pensions** (*pensjonater*) are your best bet – small, sometimes intimate guesthouses, which can usually be found in the larger cities and more touristy towns.

Rooms go for 650–750kr single, 700–800kr double, and breakfast is generally extra. Broadly comparable in price and character is a *gjestgiveri* or *gjestehus*, a **guesthouse** or **inn**, though some of these offer superb lodgings in historic premises with prices to match. Facilities in all of these establish-ments are usually adequate and homely without being overwhelmingly comfortable; at the least-expensive places you'll share a bathroom with others. Some pensions and guesthouses also have kitchens available for the use of guests, which means you're very likely to meet other residents – a real boon (perhaps) if you're travelling alone.

Hostels

For many budget travellers, as well as hikers, climbers and skiers, the country's **HI hostels** (*vandrerhjem*; @www.vandrerhjem.no) are the accommodation mainstay. There are around seventy in total, with handy concentrations in the western fjords, the central hiking and skiing regions and in Oslo. The Norwegian hostelling association, **Norske Vandrerhjem**, has its headquarters in Oslo (@23 12 45 10). It maintains an excellent website – where you can make bookings at any hostel – and publishes a free booklet, *Norske Vandrerhjem*, which details locations, opening dates, prices and telephone numbers; the booklet is available at most hostels. The hostels themselves are almost invariably excellent – the only quibble, at the risk of being churlish, is that those occupying schools tend to be rather drab and institutional.

Prices for a single bed per night range from 170kr to 220kr with the more expensive hostels nearly always including a grand breakfast. Where breakfast isn't included, it will cost you around 90kr extra; many hostels also offer a hot evening meal at around 110–140kr. Bear in mind also that almost all hostels have at least a few regular double and family rooms: at 450–700kr a double, these are among the least expensive rooms you'll find in Norway. If you're not a member of Hostelling International (HI) you can still use the hostels, though there's a surcharge of 15 percent – considering the low cost of annual membership, it's better to join up at the first hostel you stay at or through your

Accommodation price codes

All the accommodation detailed in this guide has been graded according to the following price categories, based on the cost of the **least expensive double room during the high season** (usually June to mid-Aug). However, almost every hotel offers seasonal and/or weekend discounts, which can reduce the rate by one or even two grades. Wherever hotels have an **official off-peak or weekend rate** we've given two grades, covering both the regular and the special rate – the latter signified by **sp/r**. Single rooms, where available, usually cost between 60 and 80 percent of a double. At hostels, we have also given the price of a dormitory bed.

❶ 600kr and under	❹ 1001–1200kr	❼ 1601–1800kr
❷ 601–800kr	❺ 1201–1400kr	❽ 1801–2000kr
❸ 801–1000kr	❻ 1401–1600kr	❾ 2001kr and over

national organization before you leave home (see below). If you don't have your own sheet sleeping bag, you'll mostly have to rent bedsheets for around 40–50kr a time.

It cannot be stressed too strongly that **reserving** a hostel bed will save you lots of unnecessary legwork. Many hostels are only open from mid-June to mid-August and many close between 11am and 4pm. There's sometimes an 11pm or midnight curfew, though this isn't a huge drawback in a country where carousing is so expensive. Where breakfast is included – as it usually is – ask for a breakfast packet if you have to leave early to catch transport; otherwise note that hostel **meals** are nearly always excellent value, though of variable quality, ranging from the bland and filling to the delicious. Most, though not all, hostels have small **kitchens**, but often no pots, pans, cutlery or crockery, so self-caterers should take their own.

Youth hostel associations

US and Canada

Hostelling International–American Youth Hostels US ☎1-301/495-1240, ⓦwww.hiayh.org. **Hostelling International Canada** ☎1-800/663-5777, ⓦwww.hihostels.ca.

UK and Ireland

Youth Hostel Association (YHA) ☎01629/592 700, ⓦwww.yha.org.uk. **Scottish Youth Hostel Association** ☎0870/155 3255, ⓦwww.syha.org.uk. **Irish Youth Hostel Association** Republic of Ireland ☎01/830 4555, ⓦwww.anoige.ie.

Hostelling International Northern Ireland ☎028/9032 4733, ⓦwww.hini.org.uk.

Australia, New Zealand and South Africa

Australia Youth Hostels Association ☎02/9281 9444, ⓦwww.yha.com.au. **Youth Hostelling Association New Zealand** ☎0800/278 299 or 03/379 9970, ⓦwww.yha .co.nz. **South African Youth Hostel Association** ☎+27 21 788 2301, ⓦwww.hisa.org.za.

Rooms in private houses

Tourist offices in the larger towns and the more touristy settlements can often fix you up with a **private room** in someone's house, possibly including kitchen facilities. Prices are competitive – from 300 to 350kr per single, 400 to 500kr per double – though there's usually a reservation fee (30–35kr) on top, and the rooms themselves are frequently some way out of the centre. Nonetheless, they're often the best bargain available and, in certain instances, an improvement on the local hostel. Where this is the case, we've said so in the Guide. If you don't have a sleeping bag, check the room comes with bedding – not all of them do; and if you're cooking for yourself, a few basic utensils may not go amiss.

Camping

Camping is a popular pastime in Norway, and there are literally hundreds of sites to choose from – anything from a field with a few tent pitches to extensive complexes with all mod cons. The Norwegian tourist authorities detail several hundred campsites in their free *Norway Camping* brochure (also online at ⓦ www.camping.no), classifying them on a one- to five-star grading depending on the facilities offered (and not on the aesthetics and/or the location). Most sites are situated with the motorist (rather than the cyclist or walker) in mind, and a good few occupy key locations beside the main roads, though in summer these prime sites can be inundated by seasonal workers. The vast majority of campsites have at least a few cabins or chalets, called *hytter* – see below.

The majority of campsites are two- and three-star establishments, where prices are usually per tent, plus a small charge per person and then for vehicles; on average expect to pay around 200–250kr for two people using a tent and with a car, though four- and five-star sites average around twenty percent more. During peak season it can be a good idea to **reserve ahead** if you have a car and a large tent or trailer; contact details are listed online, in the free camping booklet and, in some cases, in this guide. The Scandinavia **Camping Card** brings faster registration at many campsites across **Scandinavia** and occasionally entitles the bearer to special camping rates. It is valid for one year, costs 120kr and can be purchased from participating campsites or online at ⓦ www.camping.no.

Camping rough in Norway is a tradition enshrined in law. You can camp anywhere in open areas as long as you are at least 150m away from any houses or cabins. As a courtesy, ask farmers for permission to use their land – it is rarely refused. Fires are not permitted in woodland areas or in fields between April 15 and September 15, and camper vans are not allowed (ever) to overnight in lay-bys. A good sleeping bag is essential, since even in summer it can get very cold, and, in the north at least, mosquito repellent is absolutely vital.

Cabins

The Norwegian countryside is dotted with thousands of timber **cabins/chalets** (called *hytter*), ranging from simple wooden huts through to comfortable lodges. They are usually two- or four-bedded affairs, with full kitchen facilities and sometimes a bathroom, even TV, but not necessarily **bed linen**. Some hostels have them on their grounds, there are nearly always at least a handful at every campsite, and in the Lofoten Islands they are the most popular form of accommodation, many occupying refurbished fishermen's huts called *rorbuer*. **Costs** vary enormously, depending on location, size and amenities, and there are significant seasonal variations, too. However, a four-bed *hytter* will rarely cost more than 800kr per night – a more usual average would be about 600kr. If you're travelling in a group, they are easily the cheapest way to see the countryside – and in some comfort. Hundreds of *hytter* are also rented out as holiday cottages by the week.

Mountain huts

One further option for hikers is the **mountain huts** (again called *hytter*), which are strategically positioned on every major hiking route. Some are privately run, but the majority are operated by **Den Norske Turistforening** (DNT; see *Hiking* colour section), and although you don't have to be a member of DNT to use their huts, you'll soon recoup your outlay through reduced hut charges for members. For members staying in staffed huts, a bunk in a dormitory costs 120kr, a family or double room 220kr per person; meals start at 90kr for breakfast, 210kr for a three-course dinner. At unstaffed huts, where you leave the money for your stay in a box provided, an overnight stay costs 170kr.

Lighthouses

The **Norsk Fyrhistorisk Forening** (Norwegian Lighthouse Association; ⓦ www.lighthouses.no) is an umbrella organization that has taken the lead in preserving and conserving the country's **lighthouses**. Norway's coastal waters are notoriously treacherous and in the second half of the nineteenth century scores of lighthouses were built from one end of the country to the other. Initially, they were manned, but from the 1950s onwards they were mechanized and the old lighthouse-men's quarters risked falling into decay. The Norsk Fyrhistorisk Forening is keen for new uses to be found for these quarters and already around forty are open to the public for overnight stays or day-trips – and more will follow. Some of these forty lighthouses can be reached by road, but others can only be reached by boat and, with one or two lavish exceptions, the **accommodation** on offer – where it is on offer – is fairly frugal and inexpensive with doubles averaging around 600kr. The reward is the scenery – almost by definition these lighthouses occupy some of the wildest locations imaginable. A few of the forty are mentioned in our guide, including Kråkenes (see p.274), Ryvarden (see p.157), Ulvesund (see p.274) and Ryvingen (see p.145).

Farm holidays

In Norway, rural tourism is coordinated by Norsk Bygdeturisme og Gardsmat (@www .nbg-nett.no), whose assorted members, spread one end of the country to the other, offer accommodation, local food, hunting and fishing. NBG's compendious website details everything that's on offer and costs do vary enormously, but for a night's bed and breakfast on a farm you can expect to pay around 400kr per person.

Food and drink

At its best, Norwegian food can be excellent: fish is plentiful, and carnivores can have a field day trying meats like reindeer and elk or even, conscience permitting, seal and whale. Admittedly it's not inexpensive, and those on a tight budget may have problems varying their diet, but by exercising a little prudence in the face of the average menu (which is almost always in Norwegian and English), you can keep costs down to reasonable levels. Vegetarians, however, will have slim pickings (except in Oslo), and drinkers will have to dig very deep into their pockets to maintain much of an intake. Indeed, most drinkers end up visiting the supermarkets and state off-licences (Vinmonopolet) so that they can sup away at home (in true Norwegian style) before setting out for the evening.

Food

Many travellers to Norway exist almost entirely on a mixture of picnic food and by cooking their own meals, with the odd café meal thrown in to boost morale. Frankly, this isn't really necessary (except on the tightest of budgets), as there are a number of ways to eat out inexpensively. To begin with, a good self-service buffet breakfast, served in almost every hostel and hotel, goes some way to solving the problem, while special lunch deals will get you a tasty hot meal for 100–150kr. Finally, alongside the regular restaurants – which are expensive – there's the usual array of budget pizzerias, cafeterias and café-bars in most towns.

Breakfast, picnics and snacks

More often than not, **breakfast** (*frokost*) in Norway is a substantial self-service affair of bread, crackers, cheese, eggs, preserves, cold meat and fresh and pickled fish, washed down with tea and ground coffee. It's usually first-rate at youth hostels, and often memorable in hotels, filling you up for the day for 100–130kr when and wherever it's not thrown in with the price of your room, as it mostly is.

If you're buying your own **picnic food**, bread, cheese, yoghurt and local fruit are all relatively good value, but other staple foodstuffs – rice, pasta, meat, cereals and vegetables – can be way above the European average. Anything tinned is particularly dear (with the exception of fish), but coffee and tea are quite reasonably priced. **Supermarkets** are ten-a-penny.

As ever, **fast food** offers the best chance of a hot, bargain-basement takeaway snack. The indigenous Norwegian stuff, served up from street kiosks or stalls – **gatekjøkken** – in every town, consists mainly of rubbery hot dogs (*varm pølse*), while pizza slices and chicken pieces and chips are much in evidence too. American burger bars are also creeping in – both at motorway service stations and in the towns and cities. A better choice, if rather more expensive, is simply to get a sandwich, normally a huge open affair called a **smørbrød** (pronounced "smurrbrur"), heaped with a variety of garnishes. You'll see them groaning with meat or shrimps, salad and mayonnaise in the windows of bakeries and cafés, or in the newer, trendier sandwich bars in the cities.

Good **coffee** is available everywhere, rich and strong, and served black or with cream. **Tea**, too, is ubiquitous, but the local preference is for lemon tea or a variety of flavoured infusions; if you want milk, ask for it. All the familiar **soft drinks** are also available.

Lunch and dinner

For the best deals, you're going to have to eat your main meal of the day at lunch or possibly tea time, when **kafeterias** (often self-service restaurants) lay on daily specials, the *dagens rett*. This is a fish or meat dish served with potatoes and a vegetable or salad, often including a drink, sometimes bread, and occasionally coffee, too; it should go for 100–150kr. Dipping into the menu is more expensive, but not cripplingly so if you stick to omelettes and suchlike. You'll find *kafeterias* hidden above shops and offices and adjoining hotels in larger towns, where they might be called *kaffistovas*. Most close at around 6pm, and many don't open at all on Sunday. As a general rule, the food these places serve is plain-verging-on-the-ordinary (though there are exceptions), but the same cannot be said of the continental-style **café-bars** which abound in Oslo and, increasingly, in all of Norway's larger towns and cities.

These eminently affordable establishments offer much tastier and much more adventurous meals like pasta dishes, salads and vegetarian options with main courses in the region of 160–200kr. Slightly different again are the coffee houses which have sprung up in all of Norway's cities and towns; the big deal here is the coffee and although many also offer light bites, few do it especially well.

In all of the cities, there are first-class **restaurants**, serving dinner (*middag*) in quite formal – and/or smart and chic – surroundings. Apart from exotica such as reindeer and elk, the one real speciality is the seafood, simply prepared and wonderfully fresh – whatever you do, don't go home without treating yourself at least once. In the smaller towns and villages, gourmets will be harder pressed – many of the restaurants are pretty mundane, though the general standard is improving rapidly. Main courses begin at around 220kr, starters and desserts at around 110kr. If in doubt, smoked salmon comes highly recommended, as does catfish and monkfish. Again, the best deals are at lunchtime, though some restaurants don't open till the evening. In the western fjords, look out also for the help-yourself, all-you-can-eat **buffets** available in many of the larger hotels from around 6pm; go early to get the best choice and expect to pay around 300–350kr to be confronted by mounds of pickled herring, salmon (*laks*), cold cuts of meat, a feast of breads and crackers, and usually a few hot dishes too – meatballs, soup and scrambled eggs.

In the towns, and especially in Oslo, there is also a sprinkling of **non-Scandinavian restaurants**, mostly Italian with a good helping of Chinese and Indian places. Other cuisines pop up here and there, too – Japanese, Moroccan and Persian to name but three.

Most restaurants have bilingual menus (in Norwegian and English), but we have provided a **menu reader**, on pp.463–466.

Vegetarians

Vegetarians are in for a hard time. Apart from a handful of specialist restaurants in the big cities, there's little option other than to make do with salads, look out for egg dishes in *kafeterias* and supplement your diet from supermarkets. If you are a **vegan** the problem is greater: when the Norwegians are not eating meat and fish, they are attacking a fantastic selection of milks, cheeses and yoghurts. At least you'll know what's in every dish you eat, since everyone speaks English. If you're self-catering, look for **health food shops** (*helsekost*), found in some of the larger towns and cities.

Drink

One of the less savoury sights in Norway – and especially common in the north – is the fall-over drunk: you can spot one at any time of the day or night zigzagging along the street, a strangely disconcerting counter to the usual stereotype of the Norwegian as a healthy, hearty figure in a wholesome woolly jumper. For reasons that remain obscure – or at least culturally complex – many Norwegians can't just have a drink or two, but have to get absolutely wasted. The majority of their compatriots deplore such behaviour and have consequently imposed what amounts to alcoholic rationing: thus, although booze is readily available in the bars and restaurants, it's taxed up to the eyeballs and the distribution of wines and spirits is strictly controlled by a state-run monopoly, **Vinmonopolet**. Whether this paternalistic type of control makes matters better or worse is a moot point, but the majority of Norwegians support it.

What to drink

If you decide to splash out on a few drinks, you'll find Norwegian **beer** is lager-like and characteristically uninspiring; major brands include Hansa and Ringsnes. There's no domestically produced **wine** to speak of and most **spirits** are imported, too, but one local brew worth experimenting with at least once is **aquavit** (*akevitt*), a bitter concoction served ice-cold in little glasses and, at forty percent proof or more, real headache material – though it's more palatable with beer chasers: Linie aquavit, made in Norway from potatoes, is one of the more popular brands.

Where to buy alcohol

Beer is sold in supermarkets and shops all over Norway, though some local communities, particularly in the west, have their own rules and restrictions; at around 25kr per third of a litre, the supermarket price is about seventy percent of the price you'd pay in a bar. The strongest beers, along with **wines and spirits**, can only be purchased from the state-run **Vinmonopolet** (@ www.vinmonopolet.no) shops. There's generally one branch in each medium-sized town and many more in each of Norway's cities. Specific opening hours are given in the Guide, but characteristically they are Monday to Friday 10am–4/6pm and Saturday 10am–1/3pm; they all close on public holidays. At Vinmonopolet stores, wine is quite a bargain, from 70kr a bottle, and there's generally a wide choice.

Where t o drink

Wherever you **go for a drink**, a third of a litre of beer should cost between 35 and 45kr, and a glass of wine from 30kr. You can get a drink at most outdoor cafés, in restaurants and at bars, pubs and cocktail bars, but only in the towns and cities is there any kind of "European" bar life: in Oslo, Bergen, Stavanger, Trondheim and Tromsø you will be able to keep drinking in bars until at least 1am, 3.30am in some places.

The media

You can buy British and some American daily newspapers, plus the occasional periodical, in any major Norwegian city, but elsewhere things are very patchy. The most likely outlets are the Narvesen kiosks at train stations and airports. Most hotels have cable or satellite TV access.

The press

British newspapers – from tabloid through to broadsheet – as well as the more popular **English-language magazines** are widely available either on the day of publication or the day after in all major Norwegian cities, along with internationally distributed **American newspapers** – principally the *Wall Street Journal*, *USA Today* and the *nternational Herald Tribune*.

As for the **Norwegian press**, state advertising, loans and subsidized production costs sustain a wealth of smaller papers that would bite the dust elsewhere. Most are closely linked with political parties, although the bigger city-based titles tend to be independent. The most popular newspapers in Oslo are the independent *Verdens Gang* and the independent-conservative *Aftenposten*; in Bergen it's the liberal *Bergens Tidende*. *Aftenposten* runs a very competent English-language summary of Norwegian news on the web (Ⓦ www .aftenposten.no/english).

TV and radio

Norway's **television** network has expanded over the last few years in line with the rest of Europe. Alongside the state channels, NRK1, NRK2 and TV2, there are satellite channels like TV Norge, while TV3 is a channel common to Norway, Denmark and Sweden; you can also pick up Swedish TV in many parts of the country. Many of the programmes are English-language imports with Norwegian subtitles, so there's invariably something on that you'll understand, though much of it is pretty unadventurous stuff. The big global cable and satellite channels like MTV and CNN are commonly accessible in hotel rooms.

Local tourist **radio**, giving details of events and festivals, is broadcast during the summer months; watch for signposts by the roadside and tune in. Shortwave frequencies and schedules for the BBC World Service (Ⓦ www.bbc.co.uk/worldservice), Radio Canada (Ⓦ www.rcinet.ca) and Voice of America (Ⓦ www.voanews.com) are listed on their respective websites.

Festivals and events

Almost every town in Norway has some sort of summer shindig and there are winter celebrations too. For the most part, these are worth attending if you are already in the area – rather than meriting a special journey. There are two main sorts of festival, one being celebrations of historical or folkloric events, the other more contemporary-based jazz, pop and classical music. As you might expect, most tourist-oriented events take place in summer and, as always, national and local tourist offices can supply details of exact dates, which tend to vary from year to year. Below we have listed the more important festivals, some of which are mentioned in the Guide.

Selected festivals and events

January

Nordlysfestivalen Tromsø, (Northern Lights Festival). Mid-Jan. ☎77 68 90 70, ⓦwww .nordlysfestivalen.no. This week-long festival of classical and contemporary music takes place in Tromsø. It coincides with the return of the sun, hence its name.

March

Birkebeinerrennet Lillehammer, late March. ☎41 77 29 00, ⓦwww.birkebeiner.no. Famous 58km cross-country ski race from Rena to Lillehammer, which celebrates the dramatic events of 1206, when the young prince Håkon Håkonsson was rushed over the mountains to safety. The race follows what is thought to have been the original route.

May

Constitution or **National Day** Nationwide, May 17. Many processions and flag-waving, cheering crowds celebrate the signing of the Norwegian constitution on May 17, 1814.

Festspillene i Bergen Bergen, (Bergen International Festival). Late May until early June. ⓦwww.fib.no. Much-praised festival of contemporary music that puts a real spring in Bergen's summer step. Venues across the city.

June

Ekstremsportveko Voss, (Extreme Sport Week). Late June. ⓦwww.ekstremsportveko.com. Every reckless sport imaginable and then some – from paragliding and base jumping through to rafting and bungee jumping.

Norwegian Wood Oslo, mid-June. ⓦwww .norwegianwood.no. Three-day, open-air rock festival, arguably Norway's best, that takes place in Frogner Park; showcases big-name international artists as well as up-and-coming local bands.

July

Jazz Festival Molde, mid-July. ☎71 20 31 50, ⓦwww.moldejazz.no. Held over a six-day period in the middle of the month, this is one of the best festivals of its type, attracting big international names.

Olavsfestdagene Stiklestad, late July. ☎73 84 14 50, ⓦwww.olavsfestdagene.no. St Olav, Norway's first Christian king, was killed at the battle of Stiklestad in 1030 (see p.300). Historical pageants and plays honouring him are staged on the King's feast day (July 29) and on the days before. There are also jazz and contemporary music acts.

Rauma Rock Åndalsnes, late July to early Aug. ⓦwww.raumarock.com. Three-day knees-up showcasing the talents of a wide range of local and international acts from the likes of the Bare Egil Band to the Raga Rockers and the Toy Dolls.

August

Jazz Festival Oslo, mid-Aug. ☎22 42 91 20, ⓦ www.oslojazz.no. A five-day event attracting a veritable raft of big international names.

October

Ultimafestivalen Oslo, three weeks in Oct. ☎22 40 18 90, ⓦ www.ultima.no. Much-vaunted festival showcasing the talents of contemporary (classical)

musicians from Scandinavia and beyond. Various venues.

UKA Trondheim, three weeks in Oct. ⓦ www .uka.no. Prestigious music festival, one of Norway's largest, featuring a battery of international stars in everything from Goth Rock to hip-hop.

Bergen Internasjonale Filmfestival (BIFF) Bergen, mid- to late Oct. ☎55 30 08 40, ⓦ www .biff.no. Week-long international film festival, one of the best of its type in the country. Various venues across the city centre.

Outdoor activities

Most Norwegians have a deep and abiding love of the great outdoors. They enjoy many kinds of sports – from dog-sledging and downhill skiing in winter, through to mountaineering, angling and whitewater rafting in the summer – but the two most popular activities are hiking and cross-country skiing.

Hiking

Norway boasts some of the most beautiful mountain landscapes in the world and substantial portions of these mountain ranges have been protected by the creation of a string of **national parks**. These parks attract thousands of hikers, who take full advantage of the excellent network of hiking trails and several hundred mountain cabins, which provide the most congenial of accommodation.

For more on hiking areas, national parks, mountain lodges and DNT (the Norwegian Mountain Touring Association), see *Hiking* colour section.

Glaciers

These slow-moving masses of ice are in constant, if generally imperceptible, motion, and are therefore potentially dangerous. People, often tourists, die on them nearly every year. Never climb a glacier without a guide, never walk beneath one and always heed the instructions at the site. Guided crossings can be terrific – see the relevant accounts in the Guide.

Skiing

Norway has as good a claim as anywhere to be regarded as the home of **skiing**: a 4000-year-old rock carving found in northern Norway is the oldest-known illustration of a person on skis; the first recorded ski competition was held in Norway in 1767; and Norwegians were the first to introduce skis to North America. Furthermore, one of the oldest cross-country ski races in the world, the 55km **Birkebeinerrennet**, is held annually in late March, attracting five thousand skiers to participate in the dash between Rena and Lillehammer. The race follows the route taken by Norwegian mountain-men in 1206 when they rescued the two-year-old Prince Håkon. The rescuers wore birch-bark leggings known as Birkebeiners, hence the name of the race.

Downhill skiing and **snowboarding** conditions in Norway are usually excellent from mid-November through to late April, though daylight hours are at a premium around the winter solstice. Otherwise, Norway scores well in comparison with the better-known skiing regions of southern

Europe: temperatures tend to be a good bit colder and the country has, in general terms at least, a more consistent snowfall; Norway's resorts tend to be less crowded, have smaller class sizes, shorter lift queues, and are at a lower altitude. Three main centres for downhill skiing are Voss (see p.233), Oppdal (see p.182) and Geilo (see p.188).

Cross-country skiing

Cross-country skiing is a major facet of winter life in Norway. Approximately half the population are active in the sport, and many Norwegians still use skis to get to work or school. In the classic style of cross-country skiing, the whole body is angled forwards and the skis remain parallel except when braking or turning. For forward propulsion the skier transfers all weight to one ski, then straightens that leg while kicking downwards and backwards. At the same time, the arm on the opposite side of the body pushes down and back on the ski pole close to the line of the un-weighted ski, which glides forward. At the finish of the kick, weight is transferred to what was the gliding ski, ready for the next kick. An un-weighted cross-country ski is arc shaped, with the central section not touching the ground until the skier's down-kick flattens it on to the snow; the ends of the skis glide while the middle grips. Near major ski resorts, sets of parallel ski tracks called *loipe* are cut in the snow by machine. They provide good gliding conditions and help keep the skis parallel; some *loipe* are floodlit.

Skis can be **waxed** or **waxless**. Waxless skis have a rough tread in the middle called "fishscales", which grips adequately at temperatures around zero. Waxed skis work better at low temperatures and on new snow. Grip wax is rubbed onto the middle third of the ski's length, but a sticky substance called *klister* is used instead in icy conditions. All skis benefit from hard glide wax applied to the front and back thirds of the base.

Telemarking

In the Telemark region of southern Norway a technique has been developed to enable skiers to descend steep slopes on free-heel touring skis. This technique, known as "**Telemarking**", provides a stable and effective turning platform in powder snow. Essentially the skier traverses a slope in an upright position, but goes down on a right knee to execute a right turn and vice versa.

Ski holidays and skiing independently

For companies specializing in downhill **ski packages** to Norway, see p.32; nearly all of them will also deal with cross-country skiing and other, more obscure winter activities such as frozen waterfall climbing and ice fishing. Several specialist operators organize **cross-country skiing tours** (see p.32), and DNT (see *Hiking* colour section) arranges a limited range of guided excursions too. Touring skiers should adopt the precautions taken by winter hill-walkers: if going out for more than a couple of hours the skier should have emergency clothing, food and a vacuum flask with a hot drink. Detailed advice about coping with winter conditions is available from DNT (again, see *Hiking* colour section).

Although you may be tempted to go on a ski package, remember that in most places you should find it easy (and comparatively inexpensive) to go skiing independently. Even in Oslo, there are downhill ski runs within the city boundaries, and plenty of places from which to **rent equipment**; cross-country skiers will also have few difficulties in renting skiing tackle by the day (or week) in Oslo and elsewhere. In terms of **preparation**, lessons on a dry slope are useful in so far as they develop confidence and balance, but cross-country skiing needs stamina and upper body as well as leg strength.

Finally, **summer skiing** on Norway's mountains and glaciers – both alpine and cross-country – is now very popular. Lots of places offer this, but one of the largest and most convenient spots is the **Folgefonn Sommar Skisenter** (late May to late Sept daily 10am–4pm; ☏53 66 80 28, ⓦwww.folgefonn.no), not far from Bergen, which has ski rental, a ski school, a café and a ski lift to the slopes; see p.227 for more details.

Fishing

Norway's myriad rivers and lakes offer some of Europe's finest **freshwater fishing** with common species including trout, char, pike and perch, not to mention the salmon that once brought English aristocrats here by the buggy load. In the south of the country, the fishing is at its best from June to September, July and August in the north. **Seawater fishing** is more the preserve of professionals, but (amateur) sea angling off the Lofoten Islands is a popular pastime. Fresh- and seawater fishing are both tightly controlled. To do the first, you need a local licence, which costs anything from 50kr to 400kr per day, and a national licence if you're after salmon, sea trout and char, while, that is, these fish are in freshwater. **Seawater fishing** does not require a national licence, but is subject to local restrictions. National licences are available at any post office and online (◉www.inatur.no) for 210kr and local licences (*fiskekort*) are sold at sports shops, a few tourist offices, some hotels and many campsites; the cost varies enormously from 50kr to 350kr per day. If you take your own fishing tackle, you must have it disinfected before use.

A number of tour companies specialize in Norwegian fishing trips and holidays, but if you're just after a day or two's fishing, it's easy enough to get fixed up locally – start off by asking down at the nearest tourist office.

River-rafting

Norway has literally dozens of top-notch **whitewater river-rafting** runs. Two of the best places are Voss (see p.233) and Sjoa (see p.174). For a full list of **tour operators** offering rafting trips, consult the Norges Padleforbund (the Norwegian Canoe Association) website, ◉www.padling.no.

Fjord kayaking

Fjord kayaking is something of a minority interest in Norway, but Moreld (☎40 46 71 00, ◉www.moreld.net) offers a good programme of guided excursions in and around the Sognefjord from its base in Skjolden.

Shopping

Norway has a flourishing retail sector and all the large towns and cities are jammed with department stores and international chains. There are a handful of obvious Norwegian goods – cheese, knitted pullovers and dried fish (klippfisk) are three that spring to mind – but it's the Norwegian flair for design that is the country's most striking feature, especially as reflected in its fine art and interior design. You will, however, have to dig deep to bring any of it home – Norway is not a land of bargains. If you're visiting the far north, resist the temptation to bring back reindeer antlers – they really are naff.

Regular shopping hours are Monday through Friday 10am to 5pm, with late opening on Thursdays till 6pm, 7pm or 8pm, plus Saturdays 10am to 1pm, 2pm or 3pm. Most supermarkets stay open much longer – from 9am until 8pm in the week and from 9am to 6pm on Saturdays, but close on Sundays. See also "Tax-free shopping", p.61.

Clothing and shoe sizes

Women's clothing
American	4	6	8	10	12	14	16	18	
British	6	8	10	12	14	16	18	20	
Continental	34	36	38	40	42	44	46	48	

Women's shoes
American	5	6	7	8	9	10	11		
British	3	4	5	6	7	8	9		
Continental	36	37	38	39	40	41	42		

Men's shirts
American	14	15	15.5	16	16.5	17	17.5	18	
British	14	15	15.5	16	16.5	17	17.5	18	
Continental	36	38	39	41	42	43	44	45	

Men's shoes
American	7	7.5	8	8.5	9.5	10	10.5	11	11.5
British	6	7	7.5	8	9	9.5	10	11	12
Continental	39	40	41	42	43	44	44	45	46

Men's suits
American	34	36	38	40	42	44	46	48	
British	34	36	38	40	42	44	46	48	
Continental	44	46	48	50	52	54	56	58	

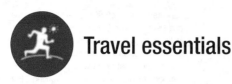 **Travel essentials**

Addresses

Norwegian addresses are always written with the number after the street name. In multi-floored buildings, the ground floor is always counted as the first floor, the first the second and so on.

Alphabet

The letters Æ, Ø and Å come at the end of the alphabet, after Z (and in that order).

Borders

There is (usually) little formality at either the Norway–Sweden or Norway–Finland borders, but the northern border with Russia is a different story. Despite the break-up of the Soviet Union, border patrols (on either side) won't be overjoyed at the prospect of you nosing around. If you have a genuine wish to visit Russia from Norway, it's best to sort out the paperwork – visas and so forth – before you leave home. Kirkenes (see p.384) is the main starting-point for tours into Russia from Norway.

Children

In general terms at least, Norwegian society is sympathetic to its **children** and the tourist industry follows suit. Extra beds in hotel rooms are usually easy to arrange, baby-changing stations are commonplace and concessionary rates are the rule, from public transport through to museums. Pharmacists carry all the kiddie stuff you would expect – nappies, baby food and so forth – but this being Norway they cost a lot, so try to bring the gubbins with you.

Costs

Norway has a reputation as one of the most expensive of European holiday destinations, and in some ways (but only some) this is entirely justified. Most of what you're likely to need – from a cup of coffee to a bottle of beer – is very costly, but on the other hand certain major items are reasonably priced, most notably accommodation which, compared with other North European countries, can be remarkably inexpensive: Norway's (usually) first-rate youth hostels, almost all of which have family, double and dormitory rooms, are particularly good value. Getting around is reasonably good news too, as the relatively high cost of normal bus, boat and train tickets can be offset by a number of passes and there are myriad discounts and deals. Furthermore, concessions are almost universally available at attractions and on public transport, with infants (under 4) going everywhere free, plus children and seniors (over 67, sometimes 60) paying – on average at least – half the standard rate. Food is, however, a different matter. With few exceptions – such as tinned fish – it's expensive, while the cost of alcohol is enough to make even a heavy drinker contemplate abstinence.

Travelling by bicycle, eating picnics bought from supermarkets and cooking your own food at campsites, it's possible to keep **average costs** down to 350kr a day per person. Moving up a notch, if you picnic at lunch, stick to less expensive cafés and restaurants, and stay in cheap hotels or hostels, you could get by on around 850kr a day. Staying in three-star hotels and eating out in medium-range restaurants, you should reckon on about 1300kr a day, the main variable being the cost of your room. On 1800kr a day and upwards, you'll be limited only by time, though if you're planning to stay in a five-star hotel and have a big night out, this still won't be enough. As always, if you're travelling alone you'll spend much more on accommodation than you would in a group of two or more: most hotels do have single rooms, but they're usually around sixty to eighty percent of the price of a double. For further information on accommodation costs, see pp.42–46. See also "Tax-free shopping", p.61.

Crime and personal safety

This is one of the least troublesome corners of Europe, so there's little reason why you should ever come into contact with the Norwegian police. You will find that most public places are well lit and secure, most people genuinely friendly and helpful, and street crime and hassle relatively rare even late at night. It would be foolish, however, to assume that problems don't exist. Oslo in particular has its share of **petty crime**, fuelled – as elsewhere – by drug addicts and alcoholics after easy money. But keep tabs on your possessions, use the same common sense you would use at home and you should have little reason to visit the police. If you do, you'll find them courteous, concerned, and usually able to speak English. If you have something stolen, make sure you get a copy of the police report or its number – essential if you are to make a claim against your insurance.

As for offences *you* might commit, drinking alcohol in public places is not permitted, and being drunk on the streets can get you arrested. Drinking and driving is treated especially rigorously. Drugs offences, too, are met with the same attitudes that prevail throughout most of Europe.

Electricity

The current is 220 volts AC, with standard European-style two-pin plugs. British equipment needs only a plug adaptor; American apparatus requires a transformer and an adaptor.

Entry requirements

Citizens of the EU/EEA, US, Canada, Australia and New Zealand need only a valid passport to enter Norway for up to three months. All other nationals should consult the relevant embassy or consulate about visa requirements. For **longer stays**, EU/EEA nationals (excluding citizens of some of the newer EU countries) can apply for a residence permit while in the country, which, if it's granted, may be valid for up to five years. In most cases, the permit is renewable, and also grants the holder the right to work (though most EU/EEA nationals

can start work before the residence permit has been obtained) and to reside anywhere in Norway. Non-EU/EEA nationals can only apply for residence permits before leaving home, and must be able to prove they can support themselves without working. For further information, contact the relevant embassy in your country of origin.

Norwegian embassies and consulates abroad

Australia Embassy: 17 Hunter St, Yarralumia, Canberra ACT 2600 ☏02/6273 3444, ⓦwww .norway.org.au. Also consulates in Adelaide, Brisbane, Darwin, Fremantle, Hobart, Melbourne and Sydney.
Canada Embassy: 150 Metcalfe St, Suite 1300, Ottawa, Ontario K2P 1P1 ☏613/238 6571, ⓦwww .emb-norway.ca. Also consulates in Calgary, Edmonton, Halifax, Montréal, Québec, Regina, Saint John, St John's, Toronto, Vancouver, Victoria, Ville de la Baie and Winnipeg.
Ireland Embassy: 34 Molesworth St, Dublin 2 ☏01/662 1800, ⓦ www.norway.ie.
New Zealand Consulate General: Deloitte House, Levels 11–16, 10 Brandon St, Wellington ☏04/471 2503, ⓦ www.norway.org.au. Also consulates in Auckland and Christchurch.
South Africa Embassy: iParioli Building A2, 1166 Park St, Hatfield 0083, Pretoria ☏ 12 342 6100, ⓦ www.norway.org.za. Also consulates in Cape Town and Durban, plus a second embassy in Cape Town.
UK Embassy: 25 Belgrave Square, London SW1X 8QD ☏020/7591 5500, ⓦ www.norway.org.uk Consulate: 86 George St, Edinburgh EH2 3BU ☏0131/226 5701, ⓦ www.norway.org .uk/edinburgh
USA Embassy: 2720 34th St NW, Washington, DC 20008 ☏ 202/333-6000, ⓦ www.norway.org /embassy. Also consulates in New York, Minneapolis, Houston and San Francisco.

Gay and lesbian travellers

In 1981, Norway was one of the first countries in the world to pass a law making discrimination against homosexuals and lesbians illegal. Twelve years later, it followed this up by becoming only the second country to pass legislation giving lesbian and gay couples the same rights as married couples, while retaining a bar on church weddings and the right to adopt children. Further legislation in 2002 and 2003 relaxed the restrictions on gay adoption and same-sex marriages became legal in 2009. All this progressiveness, however, has more to do with respect for the rights and freedoms of the individual than a positive attitude to homosexuality – Norway remains, in essence at least, very much a (heterosexual) family-oriented society. Nevertheless, the general attitude to gays is so tolerant that few feel the need to disguise their sexuality. The age of consent for both gays and straights is sixteen.

It's commonplace for bars and pubs to have a mixture of straights and gays in their clientele. There is something of a separate scene in Bergen, Trondheim and especially Oslo (see p.120), but it's pretty low-key stuff and barely worth seeking out – and the same applies to the weekly gay and lesbian nights held in some small-town nightclubs. The best source of information on the **Oslo scene** is **Ungdomsinformasjonen** or Use-it, a youth information shop near Oslo S train station at Møllergata 3 (July & Aug Mon & Wed–Fri 9am–6pm, Tues 11am–6pm; Sept–June Mon–Fri 11am–5pm; ☏24 14 98 20, ⊛www.use-it.no). They produce a free annual booklet, *Streetwise*, which is also online, and this includes a "gay guide" to the city. The main gay event in the Oslo calendar, the **Skeive Dager** (Queer Days; ⊛www.skeivedager.no), takes place over ten days each June and includes the city's Gay Pride celebrations.

Landsforeningen for Lesbisk og Homofil frigjøing (LLH; ⊛www.llh.no), Norway's strong and effective gay and lesbian organization, has an office in Oslo at Kongensgate 12.

Health

Under reciprocal health arrangements, all citizens of the EU and EEA (European Economic Area) are entitled to discounted medical treatment within Norway's public health-care system. Non-EU/EEA nationals are not entitled to discounted treatment and should, therefore, take out their own medical insurance to cover them while travelling in Norway. EU/EEA citizens may want to consider private health insurance too, in order to cover the cost of the discounted treatment as well as items not

within the EU/EEA's scheme, such as dental treatment and repatriation on medical grounds. Note also that the more worthwhile policies promise to sort matters out before you pay (rather than after) in the case of major expense; if you do have to pay upfront, get and keep the receipts. For more on insurance policies and what they cover, see below.

Health care in Norway is of a very high standard and widely available: even the remotest communities are within relatively easy – or well-organized – reach of medical attention. Rarely will **English speakers** encounter language problems – if the doctor or nurse can't speak English themselves (which is unlikely) there will almost certainly be someone at hand who can. Your local pharmacy, tourist office or hotel should be able to provide the address of an English-speaking doctor or dentist. For **medical emergencies**, call ☏113.

If you're seeking treatment under EU/EEA **reciprocal public health agreements**, double-check that the doctor/dentist is working within (and seeing you as) a patient of the relevant public health-care system. This being the case, you'll receive reduced-cost/government-subsidized treatment just as the locals do; any fees must be paid upfront, or at least at the end of your treatment, and are non-refundable. Sometimes you will be asked to produce documentation to prove you are eligible for EU/EEA health care, sometimes no-one bothers, but technically at least you should have your passport and your **European Health Insurance Card** (**EHIC**) to hand. If, on the other hand, you have a travel insurance policy covering medical expenses, you can seek treatment in either the public or private health sectors, the main issue being whether – at least in major cases – you have to pay the costs upfront and then wait for reimbursement or not.

Insurance

Prior to travelling, you'd do well to take out an insurance policy to cover against theft, loss and illness or injury. Before paying for a new policy, however, it's worth checking whether you already have some degree of cover: for instance, EU/EEA health-care

Rough Guides travel insurance

Rough Guides has teamed up with Columbus Direct to offer you tailor-made **travel insurance**. Products include a low-cost **backpacker** option for long stays; a **short break** option for city getaways; a typical **holiday package** option; and others. There are also annual **multi-trip** policies for those who travel regularly. Different sports and activities (trekking, skiing, etc) can usually be included.

See our website (ⓦwww.roughguides.com /shop) or call UK ☎0870/033 9988, Australia ☎1300/669 999, New Zealand ☎0800/559 911, or worldwide ☎+44 870/890 2843.

privileges apply in Norway (see p.57), some all-risks home insurance policies may cover your possessions when overseas, and many private medical schemes include cover when abroad.

After exhausting the possibilities above, you might want to contact a specialist travel insurance company. A typical travel insurance policy usually provides cover for loss of baggage, tickets and – up to a certain limit – cash or cheques, as well as cancellation or curtailment of your journey and medical costs. Most of them exclude so-called dangerous sports – climbing, horseriding, rafting, windsurfing and so forth – unless an extra premium is paid. Many policies can be chopped and changed to exclude coverage you don't need – for example, sickness and accident benefits can often be excluded or included at will. If you do take medical coverage, ascertain whether benefits will be paid as treatment proceeds or only after your return home, and whether there is a 24-hour medical emergency number. When securing baggage cover, make sure that the per-article limit will cover your most valuable possessions. If you need to make a claim, keep receipts for medicines and medical treatment. In the event you have anything stolen, you must obtain a crime report statement or number.

Internet

Norway is well geared up for **internet** access. There are internet cafés in all the big cities, and most hotels and hostels provide internet access for their guests either free or at minimal charge. Nearly all libraries provide free, albeit time-limited, internet access too.

The useful website ⓦwww.kropla.com gives details of how to plug your laptop in when abroad, phone country-codes around the world, and information about electrical systems in different countries.

Left luggage

There are coin-operated lockers in most railway and bus stations and at all major ferry terminals.

Mail

Norway has a very efficient postal system. Post offices are plentiful and mostly open 8am/9am–4/5pm and Saturday 9am–1/3pm. **Postage** costs are currently 7kr for either a postcard or a letter under 20g sent within Norway, 9kr to the EU, and 11kr to everywhere else. Mail to the USA takes a week, two to three days within Europe.

Maps

The **maps** in this book should be adequate for most general purposes, especially as they can be readily supplemented by the free local maps given out by almost every tourist office. Drivers, cyclists and hikers will, however, require something more detailed and buying one before you go helps in planning.

For **Scandinavia** as a whole, Cappelen (ⓦwww.cappelenkart.no) produces a good-quality road map on a scale of 1:800,000, though this can be hard to get hold of outside the region, in which case plump for the more readily available AA map (ⓦwww .theaa.com) at the same scale. For an excellent road map of Norway, complete with index, choose Hallwag's *Norge* (ⓦwww.swisstravelcenter.com), which has two scales – one for the south (1:800,000) and one for the north (1:900,000) – plus a handy distance calculator on the back. Michelin (Ⓦwww.viamichelin.com) also publish a widely available *Norway* map (1:1,250,000); although this is useful for route planning, the index is very scanty.

Currently, the best **book of Norwegian road maps** is the *Stort bilatlas Norge* (1:325,000) produced by Cappelen (Ⓦwww .cappelenkart.no); it has a comprehensive index and includes 75 good-quality city and town maps. Unfortunately, it's hard to get hold of outside of Norway, so you might opt instead for the more widely available **book of Norwegian road maps** (1:400,000) published by Freytag & Berndt (Ⓦwww .freytagberndt.com). The main disadvantages of these maps – as distinct from the Cappelen – are that the pages are much smaller, which makes it much harder to plan a route, and they're not nearly as accurate. The best **Norwegian road-map books** are the *Veiatlas Norge* produced by the state-run Statens Kartverk (Ⓦwww.statkart.no), an arm of the highways department. They consist of a number of two-page road maps (1:300,000) and a bevy of city and town maps (1:20,000); the last one was printed in 2004, but a new edition is, apparently, in the making.

Statens Kartverk also publishes authoritative **hiking maps** at a scale of 1:50,000. This series covers every part of the country and is extremely accurate. In addition, the same people publish maps to all the more popular hiking areas at a scale of 1:100,000, which gives the hiking trails greater prominence. Statens Kartverk maps are available abroad at any good map shop, though there's usually a significant mark-up on the domestic price of 70–80kr. For more on hiking, see *Hiking* colour section. Cappelen produce excellent city maps covering Bergen, Oslo, Trondheim and so on; they are at a variety of scales (1:4000 to 1:10,000) and are on sale locally at any good book shop.

Cycling maps, with route suggestions, are usually on sale at tourist offices in the more popular cycling areas; for more on cycling see p.41.

Money and exchange

Norway has its own currency, the **kroner**, one of which, a krone (literally "crown";

abbreviated **kr** or **NOK**), is divided into 100 øre. Coins in circulation are 50 øre, 1kr, 5kr and 10kr; notes are for 50kr, 100kr, 200kr, 500kr and 1000kr. At time of writing the rate of exchange for 1kr is £0.09, €0.12, US$0.17, CDN$0.18, AUS$0.21, NZ$0.26, SAR1.40. For the most up-to-date rates, check the currency converter website Ⓦwww.oanda.com.

ATMs are liberally dotted around every city, town and large village in Norway – and they accept a host of debit cards without charging a transaction fee. Credit cards can be used in ATMs too, but in this case transactions are treated as loans, with interest accruing daily from the date of withdrawal. All major credit cards, including American Express, Visa and MasterCard, are widely accepted. Typically, ATMs give instructions in a variety of languages.

All well-known brands of traveller's cheque in all major currencies are widely accepted in Norway, and you can change them as well as foreign currency into kroner at most banks, which are ubiquitous; banking hours are usually Monday to Friday 9am–3.30pm, sometimes till 5/6pm on Thursdays. All major **post offices** change foreign currency and traveller's cheques too, and they generally have longer opening hours, characteristically Monday to Friday 8/9am–4/5pm and Saturday 9am–2/3pm. Outside banking and post office hours, most major hotels, many travel agents and some hostels and campsites will change money at less generous rates and with variable commissions.

Mosquitoes

These pesky blighters thrive in the myriad lakes and lochs of northern Norway, though they can be a handful (or mouthful) in the south too. They are especially bothersome if you are camping. An antihistamine cream such as Phenergan is the best antidote, although this can be difficult to find – in which case preventative sticks like Autan or Citronella are the best bet.

Opening hours and public holidays

Business hours (ie office hours) normally run from Monday to Friday 9.30/10am to

B

BASICS | Travel essentials

Norway's public holidays

New Year's Day
Palm Sunday week before Easter
Maundy Thursday Thursday before Easter
Good Friday
Easter Sunday
Easter Monday
Labour Day May 1
Ascension Day early to mid-May
National (or Constitution) Day May 17
Whit Sunday seventh Sunday after Easter
Whit Monday
Christmas Day
Boxing Day day after Christmas Day

Note that when a public holiday falls on a Sunday, then the next day becomes a holiday as well.

4.30/5pm. Normal **shopping hours** are Monday through Friday 10am to 5pm, with late opening on Thursdays till 6pm, 7pm or 8pm, plus Saturdays 10am to 1pm, 2pm or 3pm. Most supermarkets stay open much longer – from 9am until 8pm in the week and from 9am to 6pm on Saturdays, but close on Sundays. In addition, the majority of kiosks-cum-newsstands stay open till 9pm or 10pm every night of the week (including Sun), but much more so in the cities and towns than in the villages. Many fuel stations sell a basic range of groceries and stay open till 11pm daily. Vinmonopolet, the state-run liquor chain, has outlets in almost every town and large village, but they operate limited opening hours; each store fixes its own schedule, but generally they're open Monday to Friday 10am–4/6pm and Saturday 10am–1/3pm. Norway has literally hundreds of **museums**. The more important open all year, but many

close for winter from October or November to April, May or even mid-June. Opening hours are usually 9.30/10am–5pm every day, including Saturday and Sunday, but some limit their hours on the weekend and many more close on Mondays.

There are thirteen national **public holidays** per year, most of which are keenly observed and, although much of the tourist industry carries on regardless, almost every museum and gallery in the land is closed. The result is that Easter, when four of these public holidays fall, is not a good time for museum-lovers to visit. Otherwise most businesses and shops close, and the public transport system operates a skeleton or Sunday service. Some of these public holidays are also **official flag-flying days**, but there are additional flag days as well – for example on Queen Sonja's birthday (July 4).

Phones

Given the sheer size of the country, it's no wonder that **mobile phone** (**cell phone**) coverage is partial, but the Norwegians are spreading the network at a rate of knots. Norway is on the mobile phone (cell phone) network at GSM900/1800, the band common to the rest of Europe, Australia and New Zealand. Mobile/cell phones bought in North America need to be of the triband variety to access this GSM band. If you intend to use your mobile/cell phone in Norway, note that call charges can be excruciating – particularly irritating is the supplementary charge you often have to pay on incoming calls – so check with your supplier before you depart. You might also consider buying a Norwegian SIM card. The basic card costs 200kr, including 100kr worth of calls, and they are on sale at some 7-Eleven and Narvesen kiosks; note, however, that not all mobiles/cell phones take foreign SIM cards – check with your supplier. Text messages, on the other hand,

Emergency numbers

Ambulance ☎113
Fire ☎110
Police ☎112

Useful telephone numbers

Domestic directory enquiries ☎1881
International directory enquiries & operator assistance ☎1882

International calls

Phoning home from Norway

To make an international phone call from within Norway, dial the appropriate international access code as below, then the number you require, omitting the initial zero where there is one.

Australia ☎0061
Canada ☎001
New Zealand ☎0064
Republic of Ireland ☎00353
South Africa ☎0027
UK ☎0044
USA ☎001

Phoning Norway from abroad

To call a number in Norway, dial the local international access code, then ☎47, followed by the number you require.

---

are usually charged at ordinary rates – and with your existing SIM card in place.

Domestic and international **phone cards** for use in public phones can be bought at many outlets, including post offices, some supermarkets and most Narvesen kiosks. The most common card is Telenor's Telekort, which comes in several specified denominations, beginning at 40kr. To make a reverse-charge or collect call, phone the international operator (almost all speak English). Remember also that although virtually all hotel rooms have phones, there is almost always an exorbitant surcharge for their use.

There are **no area codes** in Norway and the vast majority of Norwegian telephone numbers have eight digits; where this isn't the case, it's probably a premium-rated line, except those numbers beginning ☎800, which are toll-free.

Smoking

Smoking has long been prohibited in all public buildings, including train stations, as well as on flights and bus services. In June 2004, these restrictions were widened and smoking is now banned inside restaurants, bars and cafés. Nonetheless, one in four Norwegians still puffs away.

Tax-free shopping

Taking advantage of their decision not to join the EU, the Norwegians run a **tax-free shopping scheme** for tourists. If you spend more than 315kr at any of the three thousand outlets in the tax-free shopping scheme, you'll get a voucher for the amount of VAT you paid. On departure at an airport, ferry terminal or frontier crossing, present the goods, the voucher and your passport and – provided you haven't used the item – you'll get 12–19 percent refund, depending on the price of the item. There isn't a reclaim point at every exit from the country, however – pick up a leaflet at any participating shop to find out where they are – and note that many of the smaller reclaim points keep normal shop hours, closing for the weekend at 2/3pm on Saturday. The downside is the shops themselves: the bulk are dedicated to selling souvenir goods you can well manage without.

Time zones

Norway is on **Central European Time (CET)** – one hour ahead of Greenwich Mean Time, six hours ahead of US Eastern Standard Time, nine hours ahead of US Pacific Standard Time, nine hours behind Australian Eastern Standard Time and eleven hours behind New Zealand except for periods during the changeovers made in the respective countries to and from daylight saving. Norway operates daylight saving time, moving clocks forward one hour in the spring and one hour back in the autumn.

Tipping

Cafés and restaurants often add a service charge to their bills and this is – or at least should be – clearly indicated. Otherwise, few people **tip** at cafés or bars, but restaurant waiters and taxi drivers will be disappointed not to get a tip of between 10 and 15 percent. Rounding your bill up by a few kroner to make a round number is considered polite.

Tourist information

The Norwegian Tourist Board operates an all-encompassing website, covering everything from hotels and campsites to

Some useful websites

Ⓦ **www.goscandinavia.com** The official website of the Scandinavian Tourist Board in North America, offering a general introduction to Scandinavia, latest travel deals and links to the Norwegian Tourist Board website.

Ⓦ **www.kulturnett.no** Comprehensive information on the country's museums and current exhibitions.

Ⓦ **www.regjeringen.no** Government site of ODIN (Official Documentation and Information from Norway); despite the plain presentation, this has everything you ever wanted to know about contemporary Norway and then some. Especially good on political issues.

Ⓦ **www.visitnorway.com** The official site of the Norwegian Tourist Board, with links to all things Norwegian and good sections on outdoor activities and events.

forthcoming events. It also publishes a wide range of glossy, free booklets of both a general and specific nature and, for the most part at least, these are available at all the larger tourist offices throughout the country. Inside Norway, every town and most of the larger villages have their own **tourist office**; we've given their addresses, opening hours, websites and telephone numbers throughout the Guide. Staff almost invariably speak good-to-fluent English and dispense, among much else, free local maps, local brochures and public transport timetables; many will also help arrange accommodation (see "Accommodation", pp.42–46). In addition, Norway is spectacularly well represented on the internet in terms of everything from activity holidays through to bus timetables; we've listed a few general websites below – many more are in the Guide.

Travellers with disabilities

As you might expect, the Norwegians have adopted a progressive and thoughtful approach to the issues surrounding disability and, as a result, there are decent facilities for travellers with disabilities across the whole country. An increasing number of hotels, hostels and campsites are equipped for disabled visitors, and are credited as such in the tourist literature by means of the standard wheelchair-in-a-box icon. Furthermore, on most main routes the trains have special carriages with wheelchair space, hydraulic lifts and disabled toilets; domestic flights either cater for or provide assistance to disabled customers; and the latest ships on all ferry routes have lifts and cabins designed for disabled people.

In the cities and larger towns, many **restaurants** and most **museums** and public places are wheelchair-accessible, and although facilities are not so advanced in the countryside, things are improving rapidly. Drivers will find that most motorway **service stations** are wheelchair-accessible and that, if you have a UK-registered vehicle, the disabled **car parking badge** is honoured. Note also that several of the larger car-rental companies have modified vehicles available. On a less positive note, city pavements can be uneven and difficult to negotiate and, inevitably, winter snow and ice can make things much, much worse.

Getting to Norway should be relatively straightforward too. Most airlines and shipping companies provide assistance to disabled travellers, while some also have specific facilities, such as DFDS Scandinavian Seaways ferries' specially adapted cabins.

Guide

Guide

1

Oslo and the Oslofjord

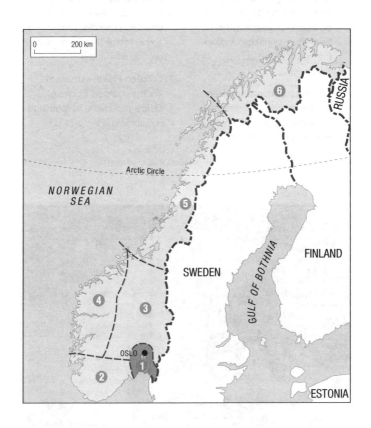

0   200 km

NORWEGIAN SEA

Arctic Circle

RUSSIA

SWEDEN

GULF OF BOTHNIA

FINLAND

OSLO

ESTONIA

CHAPTER 1 # Highlights

✱ **The Nasjonalgalleriet (National Gallery)** Norway's most ambitious collection of fine art, with a bit of everything from Munch to Manet, Dahl to Degas. **See p.88**

✱ **The Vikingskipshuset (Viking Ships Museum)** This fine museum contains a trio of Viking longships retrieved from ritual burial grounds in the south of the country. **See p.99**

✱ **The Vigelandsparken** Take a stroll round the fantastical creations of Gustav Vigeland in this open-air sculpture park. **See p.103**

✱ **The Munch-museet (Munch Museum)** Extraordinary collection of paintings, woodcuts and lithographs by Norway's most extraordinary artist. **See p.105**

✱ **Hovedøya** You can swim, walk through woods or laze on the beach on this charming Oslofjord island, just a short ferry-ride from the city centre. **See p.108**

✱ **Lofoten Fiskerestaurant** Try the seafood at one of Oslo's top-class, harbourside restaurants. **See p.113**

▲ Vigelandsparken in winter

![1]

Oslo and the Oslofjord

O**SLO** is a vibrant, self-confident city whose urbane, easy-going air makes it one of Europe's most amenable capitals, though this was not always the case: the city was something of a poor relation to Stockholm until Norway's break for independence from Sweden at the beginning of the twentieth century and it remained dourly provincial until well into the 1950s. Since then, however, Oslo has transformed itself, forging ahead to become an enterprising and cosmopolitan commercial hub with a population of about half a million. Oslo is also the only major metropolis in a country brimming with small towns and villages – its nearest rival, Bergen, being less than half its size. This gives Oslo a powerful – some say overweening – voice in the political, cultural and economic life of the nation and has pulled in all of Norway's big companies, as a rash of concrete and glass tower blocks testifies. Fortunately, these monoliths rarely interrupt the stately Neoclassical lines of the late nineteenth-century **city centre**, Oslo's most beguiling district, which boasts a lively restaurant and bar scene as well as a clutch of excellent museums. Indeed, Oslo's biggest single draw is its **museums**, which cover a hugely varied and stimulating range of topics: the fabulous Viking Ships Museum, the Munch Museum showcasing a good chunk of the painter's work, the sculpture park devoted to the stirring bronze and granite works of Gustav Vigeland, and the moving historical documents of the Resistance Museum, are, to name just four, enough to keep even the most museum-averse visitor busy for days. There's also a first-rate **outdoor life** with Oslo rustling up a good range of parks, pavement cafés, street entertainers and festivals, especially in summer when virtually the whole population seems to live outdoors – and visiting is a real delight. Winter is also a good time to be here, when Oslo's location amid hills and forests makes it a thriving, convenient and affordable ski centre.

Although Oslo's centre is itself compact, the **outer districts** spread over a vast 453 square kilometres, encompassing huge chunks of forest, beach and water. Almost universally, the city's inhabitants have a deep and abiding affinity for these wide-open spaces and, as a result, the waters of the Oslofjord to the south and the forested hills of the Nordmarka to the north are tremendously popular for everything from boating and swimming to hiking and skiing. On all but the shortest of stays, there's ample opportunity to join in – the open forest and

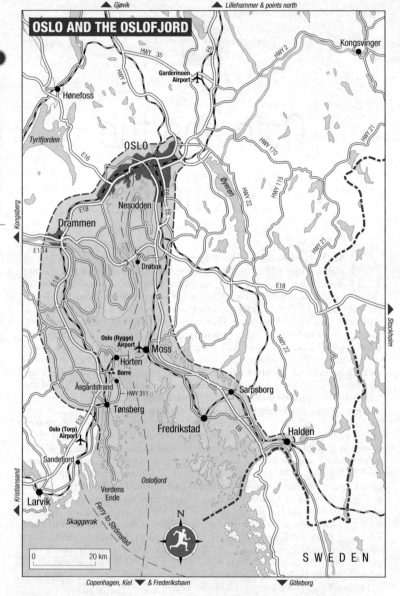

OSLO AND THE OSLOFJORD

Gjøvik · Lillehammer & points north

Kongsvinger

HWY 35
HWY 2
E6
HWY 4
Gardermoen Airport
Hønefoss
Tyrifjorden
E16
OSLO
HWY 170
HWY 115
Øyeren
HWY 22
HWY 21
Nesodden
E18
Drammen
E134
Drøbak
E18
HWY 21
Kongsberg
E18
Oslo (Rygge) Airport
Moss
Horten
Borre
Sarpsborg
HWY 22
Åsgårdstrand
HWY 311
Stockholm
E18
Tønsberg
Fredrikstad
E6
Halden
Oslo (Torp) Airport
Sandefjord
Oslofjord
Kristiansand
Larvik
Verdens Ende
Skagerrak
Ferry to Strömstad
N
SWEDEN

0   20 km

Copenhagen, Kiel ▼ & Frederikshavn · Göteborg ▼

cross-country ski routes of the Nordmarka and the **island beaches** just offshore in the Oslofjord are both easily reached by metro or ferry.

Oslo curves round the innermost shore of the **Oslofjord**, whose tapered waters extend for some 100km from the Skagerrak, the choppy channel separating Norway and Sweden from Denmark. As Norwegian fjords go, the Oslofjord is not particularly beautiful – the rocky shores are generally low and unprepossessing – but scores of pretty little islets diversify the seascape. Many of these forested bumps accommodate summer chalets, but several have been protected from development and one of them – Hovedøya – makes a lovely excursion. By comparison, the towns that trail along the shores of the Oslofjord are of little immediate appeal, being for the most part workaday industrial settlements. The few exceptions include, on the eastern shore, **Fredrikstad**, Norway's only surviving fortified town, and on the western shore, the Viking burial mounds of **Borre** and the popular holiday resort of **Tønsberg**.

Oslo

If Oslo is your first taste of Norway, you'll be struck by the wide-open spaces and by the light – soft and brilliantly clear in the summer and broodingly gloomy in winter. The grand, late nineteenth- and early twentieth-century buildings of central Oslo, doughty structures that once gave a sense of security to the emergent nation, suit the climate well and still look reassuringly sturdy today. Largely as a result, most of **downtown Oslo** remains easy and pleasant to walk around, a humming, good-natured place whose breezy streets and squares combine these appealing remnants of the city's early days with a clutch of good museums – in particular the Nasjonalgalleriet (National Gallery) and the Hjemmefrontmuseum (Resistance Museum) – plus dozens of lively bars, cafés and restaurants.

The city's showpiece museums – most memorably the remarkable Viking-skipshuset (Viking Ships Museum) – are on the **Bygdøy peninsula**, which is easily reached by ferry from the jetty behind the **Rådhus** (City Hall); other ferries head south from the Vippetangen quay behind the Akershus to the string of rusticated **islands** that necklace the inner waters of the Oslofjord with wooded Hovedøya being the cream of the scenic crop. Back on the mainland, **east Oslo** is the least prepossessing part of town, a gritty sprawl housing the poorest of the city's inhabitants, though the recently revived district of **Grünerløkka** is now home to a slew of fashionable bars and clubs. The main sight on the east side of town is the **Munch-museet** (Munch Museum), which boasts a superb collection of the artist's work. Afterwards, it's mildly tempting to pop along the eastern shore of Oslo's principal harbour for the views over the city and to look at the skimpy remains of the medieval town. **Northwest Oslo** is far more prosperous, with big old houses lining the avenues immediately to the west of the Slottsparken. Beyond is the **Frognerparken**, a chunk of parkland where the wondrous open-air sculptures of Gustav Vigeland are displayed in the **Vigelandsparken**. Further west still, beyond the city limits in suburban Høvikodden, the **Henie–Onstad Kunstsenter** displays more prestigious modern art, enhanced by the museum's splendid setting on a headland overlooking the Oslofjord.

The city's enormous reach becomes apparent only to the north of the centre in the **Nordmarka**. This massive forested wilderness, stretching far inland, is patterned by hiking trails and cross-country ski routes. Two T-bane (Tunnel-banen) lines provide ready access, weaving their way up into the rocky hills that herald the region. The more westerly T-bane rolls past **Holmenkollen**, a ski resort where the ski-jump makes a crooked finger on Oslo's skyline, before terminating at **Frognerseteren**. Here the station is still within the municipal boundaries, but the surrounding forested hills and lakes feel anything but urban. The more easterly T-bane is perhaps even more appealing, ending up near **Sognsvannet**, a pretty little lake set amidst the woods and an ideal place for an easy stroll and/or a picnic.

Compared to most other European capitals, Oslo is extremely safe, though the usual cautions apply to walking around on your own late at night, when you should be particularly careful in the vicinity of Oslo S – the main train station, where the junkies gather.

Some history

Oslo is the oldest of the Scandinavian capital cities. Its name is derived from *Às*, a Norse word for God, and *Lo*, meaning field. Harald Hardrada founded the city in around 1048, but it wasn't until Harald's son, Olav Kyrre, established a bishopric and built a cathedral here, that the city really began to take off. Despite this, the kings of Norway continued to live in Bergen – an oddly inefficient division of state and church considering the difficulty of communication. At the start of the fourteenth century, **Håkon V** rectified matters by moving to Oslo, where he built himself the Akershus fortress, and the town boomed until 1349, when bubonic plague wiped out almost half the population. The slow decline that followed this catastrophe accelerated when Norway came under Danish control in 1397. No longer the seat of power, Oslo became a neglected backwater until its fortunes were revived by the Danish king **Christian IV**. He moved Oslo lock, stock and barrel, shifting it west to its present site and modestly renaming it **Christiania** in 1624. The new city prospered, and continued to do so after 1814, when Norway broke away from Denmark and united with Sweden. In the event, this political realignment was a short-lived affair, and by the 1880s, Christiania – and the country as a whole – was clamouring for independence. This was eventually achieved in 1905, though the city didn't revert to its original name for another twenty years – and has hardly looked back since, except during the dark days of the German occupation of World War II.

Arrival

Downtown Oslo is at the heart of a superb public-transport system, which makes arriving and departing convenient and straightforward. The principal arrival hub is **Oslo Sentralstasjon** (usually shortened to **Oslo S**), a large complex that includes the main train and bus stations, city tram, metro and bus stops, a tourist office and exchange facilities; it is at the eastern end of the main thoroughfare, **Karl Johans gate**. The other transport hub is **Nationaltheatret**, at the west end of Karl Johans gate, which is handier for most city-centre sights and Oslo's main harbour. There's a **tourist information** office at Oslo S and another close to Nationaltheatret, on Fridtjof Nansens plass.

Arriving by air: Gardermoen airport

Opened in 1998, **Oslo Gardermoen airport** is a lavish affair designed in true pan-Scandinavian style, with cool stone floors, high ceilings and acres of lightly varnished pine. Departures is on the upper level, Arrivals on the lower, where there are also currency exchange facilities, car rental offices (see p.119 for details) and a visitor information desk.

Gardermoen is 45km north of the city centre, just off the E6 motorway. There are three ways to get from the airport to the centre of Oslo by **public transport** – express train, local train, and airport bus. The fastest and most expensive option is the **FlyToget** (Express train; daily 5.30am–12.30pm every 10–20 min; 170kr one-way, 340kr return; ⓦwww.flytoget.no), which takes twenty minutes to reach Oslo S, a couple more to Nationaltheatret. Alternatively, several NSB (Norwegian Railway) regional trains – including the hourly Lillehammer-to-Skien service – stop at the airport before proceeding on to Oslo S and usually Nationaltheatret. These trains take between thirty and forty minutes to make the journey and the one-way fare costs 86kr, 172kr return. Note also that there are express trains north from Gardermoen to a number of destinations, including Røros and Trondheim; long-distance services often require a reservation – details and reservations at the train ticket office in Arrivals.

By bus, **SAS Flybussen** (daily 5.20am–1am, every 20–30min; 140kr one-way, 240kr return; ⓦwww.flybussen.no/oslo) depart from outside the Arrivals concourse for the main downtown bus station, Oslo Bussterminalen, part of the Oslo S complex; the journey takes about 45 minutes, traffic depending. These buses then continue on to St Olavs plass and the Radisson *SAS Scandinavia Hotel* on Holbergs gate. **For Gardermoen departures**, the Flybussen follows the same route in the opposite direction. In addition, **Flybussekspressen** (ⓣ177 from within Oslo, ⓣ815 00 176 from without; ⓦwww.flybussekspressen.no) operates a variety of bus services from the airport direct to the small towns surrounding Oslo at regular intervals and at reasonable rates.

The **taxi fare** from Gardermoen to the city centre is 650kr. Finally, note that if you're heading into Oslo from Gardermoen by **car**, there is a 20kr toll on all approach roads into the city; it's an automatic toll, so you don't actually do anything: your number plate is read electronically and the bill is either sent to your car rental company or to the address of the owner of your vehicle.

Arriving by air: Oslo (Torp) and Oslo (Rygge) airports

Oslo has two other airports. The larger one, **Oslo (Torp)**, is just outside the town of Sandefjord, about 110km southwest of Oslo. The **Torp-Ekspressen bus** (ⓣ177 from within Oslo, ⓣ815 00 176 from without; ⓦwww.torpekspressen.no) links this airport with the main downtown bus station, Oslo Bussterminalen, part of the Oslo S complex, about six times daily; the bus schedule, both to and from Torp, links with flight arrivals and departures. The bus journey takes a little under two hours and costs 180kr one-way, 300kr return; you buy tickets from the driver. There is also a train service. (see p.134) The third airport, Oslo (Rygge), is 8km west of Moss, a small town about 60km south of Oslo. From here, the **Rygge-Ekspressen bus** (ⓣ177 from within Oslo, ⓣ815 00 176 from without; ⓦwww.rygge-ekspressen.no) runs to the main bus terminal at Oslo S. Again, the bus schedule links with flight arrivals and departures and you buy tickets from the driver. A one-way fare is 120kr, return 210kr, and the journey time is about 45 minutes.

Arriving by train

International and domestic **trains** use **Oslo Sentralstasjon**, known as Oslo S (train information and reservations ⓣ815 00 888, ⓦwww.nsb.no), which is beside Jernbanetorget, the square at the eastern end of the main drag, Karl Johans gate. There are money exchange facilities and a post office here, and just outside is a tourist office. Many domestic trains also pass through the

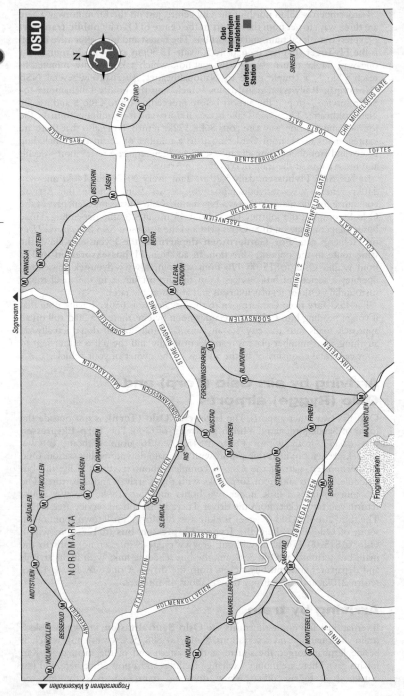

▲ Sognsvann

▲ Frognerseteren & Voksenkollen

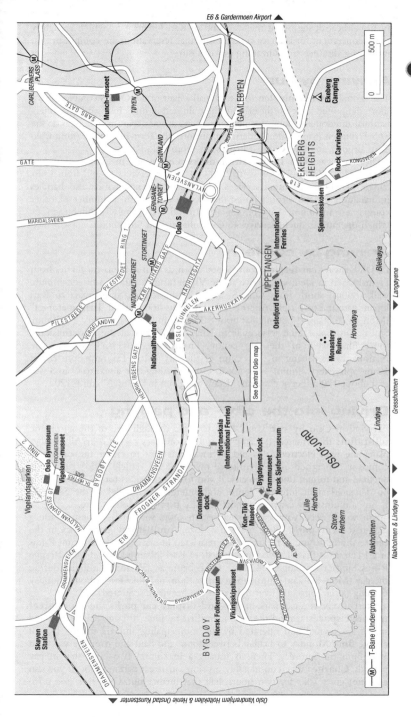

▲ E6 & Gardermoen Airport

CARL BERNERS PLASS Ⓜ

Munch-museet

Ⓜ TØYEN

SARS GATE

GATE

MARIDALSVEIEN

RING 1

PILESTREDET

PILESTREDET

VERGELANDVN

HENRIK IBSENS GATE

NATIONALTHEATRET

Ⓜ STORTINGET

KARL JOHANS GATE

RÅDHUSGATA

Nationaltheatret

Ⓜ JERNBANE TORGET

Ⓜ GRØNLAND

NYLANDSVEIEN

Oslo S

GAMLEBYEN

SCHWEIGAARDS

EKEBERG HEIGHTS

Rock Carvings

△ Ekeberg Camping

KONGSVEIEN

E18

Sjømannsskolen

KONGSVEIEN

International Ferries

VIPPETANGEN

Oslofjord Ferries

AKERSHUSKAIA

OSLO TUNNELEN

See Central Oslo map

Bleikøya

Langøyene ▶

Hovedøya

Monastery Ruins

Gressholmen ▶

Lindøya

Nakholmen & Lindøya ▶

OSLO-FJORD

HALDVAN SVARTES GT

Vigelandsparken

Oslo Bymuseum

Vigeland-museet

FROGNERVEIEN

RING 2

TH HEFTYES GATE

BYGDØY ALLE

DRAMMENSVEIEN

FROGNER STRANDA

E18

Hjortneskaia (International Ferries)

Dronningen dock

Bygdøynes dock

Frammuseet

Norsk Sjøfartsmuseum

Kon-Tiki Museet

Lille Herbern

Store Herbern

Nakholmen

DRAMMENSVEIEN

Skøyen Station

DRONNING BLANCAS

BYGDØYVEIEN

DRONNING MAUDS VEI

MYNTEVIKVEIEN

LANGVIKVEIEN

BYGDØY

Norsk Folkemuseum

Vikingskipshuset

500 m

0

Ⓜ — T-Bane (Underground)

▲ Oslo Vandrerhjem Holtekilen & Henie Onstad Kunstenter

Nationaltheatret station, at the west end of Karl Johans gate, which is slightly more convenient for the city centre. Note that reservations are compulsory on most long-distance trains heading out of Oslo.

Arriving by bus

The central **Bussterminalen** (bus terminal) is part of the Oslo S complex; it is a short, signposted walk northeast from the train station on Schweigårdsgate. International and domestic long-distance buses arrive at and depart from here, as do the SAS Flybussen (from Oslo Gardermoen airport), the Torp-Ekspressen (from Oslo Torp airport), and the **Rygge-Ekspressen** (from Oslo Rygge airport).

There are two **bus information desks**. One is for the largest domestic carrier, Nor-Way Bussekspress (℡23 00 24 00 for services to and from Oslo, ℡815 44 444 for all other services; ⓦwww.nor-way.no), which also handles information on the airport buses; the second deals with a number of other companies, including Säfflebussen (℡815 66 010, ⓦwww.safflebussen.se), which operates frequent services to Copenhagen and Stockholm.

Arriving by car ferry

DFDS Seaways **car ferries** from Copenhagen, as well as Stena car ferries from Fredrikshavn in Denmark, arrive at the **Vippetangen quays**, a fifteen-minute walk (800m) south from Oslo S: take Akershusstranda/Skippergata to Karl Johans gate and turn right. Alternatively, catch bus #60 marked "Jernbanetorget" (Mon–Fri 6.30am–11.30pm, Sat from 8.30am, Sun from 9am, every 20–30min; 5min). On Color Line services from Kiel, you'll arrive at the **Hjortneskaia**, some 3km west of the city centre. From here, bus #33 runs to the Nationaltheatret, bang in the centre of the city (Mon–Fri 7am–8pm & Sat 10am–5pm every 30min) – but not to Oslo S. Failing that, a taxi to Oslo S will cost about 170kr. Ferry company details are given in "Listings", on p.120.

Driving into the city – and parking

Arriving in Oslo **by car**, you'll have to drive through one of the automatic **toll-points** that encircle the city; the toll for ordinary cars is 20kr. All number plates are read electronically and an invoice is sent to either the car rental company concerned or the registered owner of the vehicle. Oslo's ring roads encircle and tunnel under the city; if you follow the signs for "Ring 1" you'll be delivered right into the centre and emerge (eventually) at the Sentrum P-hus, a multistorey car park a short distance from Karl Johans gate.

You won't need your car to sightsee in Oslo, so you'd do best to use a designated **car park**. There are half a dozen **multistorey car parks** in the centre, though some of them operate restricted hours: both the Sentrum P-hus at CJ Hambros Plass 1, two blocks north of Karl Johans gate, and Aker Brygge P-hus, Sjøgata 4, are open 24 hours. Costs begin at 25kr for 30 minutes during the day (Mon–Sat 7am–7pm), up to a maximum of 240kr for 24 hours; Sunday, evening (after 7pm) and overnight rates are heavily discounted.

Alternatively, you can park in **pay-and-display car parks** and at **on-street metered spaces** around the city. Identified by blue "P" signs, these metered spaces are owned and operated by the municipality, and are usually free of charge from Monday to Friday between 6pm and 8am and over the weekend after 3pm on Saturday. There is usually a maximum two-hour stay in pay periods. **Charges** vary considerably: a prime on-street parking spot (if you can get one) costs 70kr for two hours, half that further out. Oslo Pass (see p.75) holders get free parking in all municipal parking spaces, but have to abide by the posted regulations. Holders must be sure to write the vehicle registration number, date and time on the card in the space provided.

Information

The main **tourist information office** (Oct–March Mon–Fri 9am–4pm; April–May & Sept Mon–Sat 9am–5pm; June–Aug daily 9am–7pm; ☎815 30 555, ⓦwww.visitoslo.com) is across from the Rådhus at Fridtjof Nansens plass 5. They have a full range of information about Oslo and its environs, and issue both free city maps and maps of the public transport system. They also sell the Oslo Pass (see below) and supply free copies of both the very thorough *Oslo Guide* and the listings brochure *What's On in Oslo*. They can also make reservations for guided tours and accommodation (see p.77). There's a second tourist office at the base of the distinctive Trafikanten tower in front of Oslo S on Jernbanetorget (May–Sept daily 8am–8pm; Oct–April Mon–Fri 8am–8pm, Sat & Sun 8am–6pm). This offers the same services as the other tourist office and shares its premises with the city's main public-transport information centre (see below). Oslo also has a youth information shop, **Ungdomsinformasjonen** or **Use-it**, a brief walk from Oslo S at Møllergata 3 (July–Aug Mon & Wed–Fri 9am–6pm, Tues 11am–6pm; Sept–June Mon–Fri 11am–5pm; ☎24 14 98 20, ⓦwww.use-it.no). They produce a free annual booklet, *Streetwise*, which gives a roundup of local bars and clubs and provides all sorts of advice and information about inexpensive food and accommodation. They also offer public internet access and carry all manner of fliers for gigs and concerts.

City transport

Oslo's safe and efficient public-transport system consists of buses, trams, a small underground rail system (the Tunnelbanen, or T-bane) and local ferries. It's run by Oslo Sporveier, whose information office, **Trafikanten**, is beneath the distinctive, transparent clocktower outside Oslo S, on the Jernbanetorget (May–Sept daily 8am–8pm; Oct–April Mon–Fri 8am–8pm, Sat & Sun 8am–6pm; ☎177, ⓦwww.trafikanten.no). The office, which shares its premises with one of the city's two tourist offices (see above), sells tickets and passes detailed below,

The Oslo Pass

The useful and money-saving **Oslo Pass** gives free admission to almost every museum in the city, unlimited free travel on the whole municipal transport system, and free parking in municipal car parks. It also provides some discounts in shops, hotels and restaurants, though in winter, when opening hours for many sights and museums are reduced, you may have to work hard to make the card pay for itself. Valid for 24, 48 or 72 hours, it costs 220kr, 320kr or 410kr respectively, with children aged four to fifteen charged 95kr, 115kr or 150kr. It's available at the city's two tourist offices and at most hotels and hostels. The card is valid for a set number of hours (rather than days) starting from the moment it is first used, at which time it should either be presented and stamped, or you should fill in the date and time yourself. A booklet detailing every advantage the Oslo Pass brings is issued when you buy one.

has racks of free timetables and gives away a useful **visitor's transit map**, the *Besøkskart*, though this is also available at the tourist office. Route plans for the buses and trams are also posted at most central stops.

Fares and passes

Flat-fare **one-way tickets** for all forms of city transport cost 24kr if purchased before the journey, or 34kr if purchased from a bus or tram driver or on a ferry. There are automatic ticket machines at all T-bane stations and ferry docks, many tram stops and some bus stops. Tickets are valid for unlimited travel within the city boundaries for one hour including transfers; seniors (67+) and children four to sixteen years old travel half-price, babies and toddlers free.

There are several ways to cut costs. The best is to buy an **Oslo Pass** (see p.75), which is valid on the whole network and on certain routes into the surrounding *kommunes* – but not on trains or buses to the airport. If you're not into museums, however, a straight **travel pass** might be a better buy. A 24hr pass (*Dagskort*) is valid for unlimited travel within the city limits and costs 60kr, while a seven-day pass costs 200kr. Alternatively, the Flexikort is valid for eight city trips and costs 160kr. All these passes and tickets can be bought at the automatic machines mentioned above, as well as from the Trafikanten office.

All tickets and passes must be **stamped** when they are first used: buses, trams and T-bane stations all have automatic stamping machines, but on ferries there's usually a conductor. Ticket inspectors roam around in mufti and if you haven't got a valid, stamped pass or ticket, you will receive a hefty on-the-spot fine of 750kr.

Buses

Many city **bus** services originate at – or pass through – Jernbanetorget, the square in front of Oslo S, while most suburban services depart from the Bussterminalen nearby. A second common port-of-call is Nationaltheatret further to the west near the harbour. Most buses stop running at around midnight, though on Friday and Saturday nights **night buses** (*nattbussen*) take over on certain major routes (flat-rate fare 50kr; Oslo Pass and other passes not valid).

Trams

The city's **trams** run on six routes through the city, crisscrossing the centre from east to west, and sometimes duplicating the bus routes. They are a bit slower than the buses, but are a rather more enjoyable and relaxing way of getting about. Major stops include Jernbanetorget, Nationaltheatret and Storgata. Most operate regularly – every ten or twenty minutes, from 6am to midnight.

Tunnelbanen and trains

The Tunnelbanen – **T-bane** – has six lines which converge to share a common slice of track crossing the city centre from Majorstua in the west to Tøyen in the east, with Nationaltheatret, Stortinget, Jernbanetorget/Oslo S and Grønland stations in between. From this central section, lines run west (*Vest*) and east (*Øst*) out into the suburbs. The system mainly serves commuters, but you may find it useful for hopping around the centre and for trips out into the forested hills of the Nordmarka, or to Frognerseteren, Holmenkollen and Sognsvannet. Apart from the central section, trains travel above ground. The system runs from around 6am until 12.30am.

A series of **local commuter trains**, run by NSB, links Oslo with Moss, Eidsvoll, Kongsberg, Drammen and other outlying towns; departures are from Oslo S, with many also stopping at Nationaltheatret.

For details of train services to and from Oslo Gardermoen airport, see p.71. see p.71

Ferries

Numerous **ferries** shuttle across the northern reaches of the Oslofjord to connect the city centre with the outlying district. As far as visitors are concerned, the most popular are the summertime ferries (mid-March to mid-Oct) that leave from Pier #3, immediately behind the Rådhus, bound for the museums of the Bygdøy peninsula. There are also all-year ferry services to a number of Oslofjord islets, including Hovedøya, and a June-to-August service to Langøyene, but these depart from the Vippetangen quay, 1300m south of Oslo S. To get to the Vippetangen quay by public transport, take bus #60 from Jernbanetorget.

Taxis

The speed and efficiency of Oslo's public transport system means that you should rarely have to resort to a **taxi**, which is probably just as well as they are very expensive. Taxi fares are regulated, with the tariff varying according to the time of day – night-times are about 25 percent more expensive than daytime – though on many longer routes there is a fixed tariff: central Oslo to Gardermoen airport, for instance, costs 650kr. Taxi ranks can be found round the city centre and outside all the big hotels. To call a cab, ring Oslo Taxi ℡02323 or Norgestaxi ℡08000.

Bicycles

Renting a **bicycle** is a pleasant way to get around Oslo, particularly as the city has a reasonable range of cycle tracks and many roads have cycle lanes; what's more, central Oslo is not engulfed by traffic thanks to its network of motorway tunnels. Even better, there is a **municipal bike rental scheme** (Easter to Nov) in which bikes are released like supermarket trolleys from racks all over the city. Visitors can join the scheme at the tourist office by paying 70kr for a 24hr cycling pass plus a refundable deposit of 500kr. Bikes can be used for up to three hours before they have to be dropped off (or swapped) at one of the bike racks to avoid a penalty; a map showing you the location of the racks and cycle lanes is provided by the tourist office – and city cycling maps are also available online at ⓦ www.oslosykkelkart.no (Norwegian only).

Accommodation

Oslo has the range of **hotels** you would expect of a capital city, as well as **B&Bs**, a smattering of **guesthouses** (*pensjonater*) and a trio of **youth hostels**. To appreciate the full flavour of the city, you're best off staying on or near the western reaches of Karl Johans gate – between the Stortinget and the Nationaltheatret – though the well-heeled area to the north and west of the Royal Palace (Det Kongelige Slott) is enjoyable too. Many of the less expensive lodgings are, however, to be found in the vicinity of Oslo S, a rather grimy district which – along with the grey suburbs to the north and east of the station – hardly sets the pulse racing. That said, if money is tight and you're here any time between June and August, your choice of location may well be very limited as the scramble for **budget beds** – sometimes any bed at all – becomes acute, or at least tight enough to make it well worth phoning ahead to check on space. For peace of mind, it is advisable to make an advance reservation, particularly for your first night, either direct or via the tourist office's website (ⓦ www.visitoslo.com).

If you don't want to reserve ahead, one way to cut the hassle after you arrive is to use the same-day and in-person **accommodation service** provided by the tourist office at both of their branches – one outside Oslo S train station (see p.75), the other near the Rådhus (see p.75). Each office has full accommodation lists and will make a reservation on your behalf for a minimal fee, altogether a real bargain when you consider that they often get discounted rates.

Hotels

At all but the busiest of times, you should be able to get a fairly small and simple, en-suite double room in a hotel in central Oslo for about 1000kr. You hit the comfort zone at about 1200kr, and luxury from around 1500kr. However, special offers and **weekend deals** often make the smarter hotels more affordable than this, with discounts of between thirty and forty percent commonplace. Also, most room rates are tempered by the inclusion of a good-to-excellent self-service buffet **breakfast**. The tourist office keeps lists of the day's best offers, or try the places in the following list – but always ring ahead first.

Central

Best Western Hotell Bondeheimen
Rosenkrantz gate 8 ☎ 23 21 41 00, ⓦ www .bondeheimen.com. One of Oslo's most enjoyable hotels, dating from 1913, the *Bondeheimen* is handily placed just 2min walk north of Karl Johans gate. Both the public areas and the comfortable bedrooms are attractively decorated in a modern, pan-Scandinavian style, with polished pine every-where. The inclusive buffet breakfast, served in the *Kaffistova* (see p.109), is substantial, and there's free internet access. The rack rate for a double is about 1300kr, but look out for weekend and summer discounts of up to thirty percent. ❺, sp/r ❹
Bristol Kristian IV's gate 7 ☎ 22 82 60 00, ⓦ www .bristol.no. Plush establishment distinguished by its sumptuous public areas with ornate nineteenth-century chandeliers, columns and fancifully carved arches. The 200-odd bedrooms are decorated in lavish period style. ❾, sp/r ❽
City Prinsensgate 6 ☎ 22 41 36 10, ⓦ www .cityhotel.no. This modest but pleasant hotel, a long-time favourite with budget travellers, is located above shops in a typical Oslo apartment block near Oslo S. The surroundings are a little seedy, but the hotel is cheerful enough, with small but perfectly adequate rooms. ❸
Continental Stortingsgata 24–26 ☎ 22 82 40 40, ⓦ www.hotel-continental.no. Arguably the classiest hotel in town, family-owned and with swish public areas that ooze an easy comfort, all pastel shades, flowers, and even some Munch paintings (or at least near-perfect copies of them). The bedrooms beyond are extremely comfortable and decorated in a fetching, modern style with delicate patterned wallpaper setting the tone. The hotel is also ideally located, a stone's throw from Karl Johans gate, and the breakfast is a veritable banquet. ❾, sp/r ❻
Grand Karl Johans gate 31 ☎ 23 21 20 00, ⓦ www.grand-hotel.no. Once Norway's most prestigious hotel, its café the haunt of Ibsen and his chums, the *Grand* remains one of Oslo's best hotels, its 300 guest rooms mostly decorated in a modern rendition of early twentieth-century style. Hefty weekend and summertime discounts make the *Grand* much more affordable than you might perhaps expect. Now a Rica hotel. ❾, sp/r ❻
Grims Grenka Kongens gate 5 ☎ 23 10 72 00, ⓦ www.grimsgrenka.no. Design hotel aimed firmly at the luxury end of the market with each of the 66 rooms and suites kitted out in true minimalist style with subdued back-lighting and an especially creative use of colours. Hard-to-beat location, metres from one of the city's prettiest squares, Bankplassen. ❾, sp/r ❽
Perminalen Øvre Slottsgate 2 ☎ 23 09 30 81, ⓦ www.perminalen.no. This hostel-like hotel has two things going for it – a central location and budget prices: a bed in a four-berth room costs just

345kr, singles 595kr, doubles 795kr. At these rates, it's hardly surprising that the guest rooms are frugal to positively spartan, though at least all the doubles and singles are en suite. ❷

Rica Holberg Holbergs plass 1 ☎23 15 72 00, ⓦ www.rica.no. This grand, nineteenth-century building has been creatively refurbished both inside and out, but still retains fragments of its historic atmosphere. The public rooms are pleasant and appealing, while the bedrooms are spick, span and modern, though one or two of them are too small for comfort. Overlooks Holbergs plass, a pint-sized square about 500m from the Slottsparken. ❼, sp/r ❹

Rica Victoria Rosenkrantz gate 13 ☎24 14 70 00, ⓦ www.rica.no. A large, modern hotel, just south of Karl Johans gate. Its two hundred spacious rooms have every convenience, and it's justifiably popular with visiting business folk. ❼, sp/r ❹

Scandic Edderkoppen St Olavs Plass 1 ☎23 15 56 00, ⓦ www.scandichotels.com. Overlooking one of the city's pleasanter, semi-pedestrianized squares, this *Scandic* hotel occupies a straightforward modern block, but the interior has been creatively remodelled in a bright and stylish modern manner, with spotlights, distinctive curved furniture and patterned carpets. ❻, sp/r ❸

Thon Hotel Europa St Olavs gate 31 ☎23 25 63 00, ⓦ www.thonhotels.no. Large, modern chain establishment that is perfectly adequate, even though it's in somewhat humdrum surroundings near the west end of St Olavs gate. ❼, sp/r ❹

Thon Hotel Stefan Rosenkrantz gate 1 ☎23 31 55 00, ⓦ www.thonhotels.no. Unremarkable but neat-and-tidy modern hotel above the street-level shops in a five-storey building. Handy location, just a couple of minutes' walk north of Karl Johans gate. Near the bottom of its price range, it's one of the city's better deals. ❻, sp/r ❹

Westside

Best Western West Hotel Skovveien 15 ☎22 54 21 60, ⓦ www.bestwestern.com/no. In one of Oslo's ritziest neighbourhoods, this pleasant hotel occupies a revamped nineteenth-century town house. Each of the comfortable bedrooms is decorated in an attractive contemporary manner. One kilometre west of the centre off Frognerveien; take tram #12 from the centre. ❺, sp/r ❹

Clarion Collection Hotel Gabelshus Gabels gate 16 ☎23 27 65 00, ⓦ www.gabelshus.no. This attractive, medium-sized hotel occupies an old villa dating from 1912 and stands in a smart residential area a couple of kilometres west of the city centre, off Drammensveien. The public areas are kitted out with antique furnishings, while the bedrooms are smart and well appointed. Tram #13 from the centre. ❽, sp/r ❹

Rica Hotel Bygdøy Allé Bygdøy allé 53 ☎23 08 58 00, ⓦ www.rica.no. With its forest of spiky, late nineteenth-century towers, this *Rica* possesses the most imposing hotel facade in the city. Inside, each of the rooms is individually decorated in tasteful retro style. The hotel is situated in a busy residential area about 2km west of the centre; to get there from the city centre, take bus #30 or #31 from Nationaltheatret. ❼, sp/r ❹

Eastside

Best Western Anker Hotel Storgata 55 ☎22 99 75 00, ⓦ www.anker.oslo.no. A large budget hotel in a glum high-rise block beside the Akerselva River at the east end of Storgata. The clientele is mainly Norwegian, and the facilities are adequate, if somewhat frugal. 15min walk from Oslo S or 5min by tram; the same block also houses the *Anker Hostel* (see p.80). ❻, sp/r ❸

Hostels, B&Bs and guesthouses

There are two very popular HI **hostels** in Oslo. Members get fifteen percent discount, and you can join on the spot at any hostel. Alternatively, the tourist office can book you into a **B&B**, which will cost in the region of 330kr for a single room, and 530–600kr for a double. This is something of a bargain especially as many B&Bs have cooking facilities, but they do tend to be out of the city centre, and there is often a minimum two–night stay; note also that the tourist office will only arrange them when you turn up at either of their offices (see p.75) in person. Another option is a **guesthouse**, or *pensjonater*, and these start at around 440kr for a single room, 650kr for a double. They offer basic but generally adequate accommodation, either with or without en-suite facilities, but breakfast is not included, and at some places you may need to supply your own sleeping bag. Unfortunately, there are very few guesthouses in Oslo, and only two near the city centre.

Anker Hostel Storgata 55 ☎ 22 99 72 10, ⓦ www.ankerhostel.no. This hostel occupies part of the same unappetizing modern block as the *Anker Hotel* (see p.79), and it's also in a cheerless neighbourhood at the east end of Storgata. More positively, the rooms are plain and simple, but perfectly adequate, with dorm beds at 225kr in a 4-bedded room, or 200kr in a 6-bedded room; double rooms go for 525kr, singles the same; breakfast costs an extra 85kr. Bed linen and towels are for hire, or bring your own; sleeping bags are not allowed. Breakfast is not included in the price. The hostel is 15min walk from Oslo S or 5min by tram #11, #12, #13 or #17. ❶

Cochs Pensjonat Parkveien 25 ☎ 23 33 24 00, ⓦ www.cochspensjonat.no. Friendly and engaging guesthouse occupying the upper floors of an old apartment block, in a handy location behind the Slottsparken. There are 88 rooms, each decorated in a frugal modern style – wood laminate floors and so on – and of three different types: those with shared facilities cost 620kr for a double (440kr single), en suite 720kr (540kr) and those with a kitchen unit 780kr (590kr). Breakfasts are served just along the street at *KafeCaffé*, Parkveien 21. ❷

MS Innvik Langkaia ☎ 22 41 95 00, ⓦ www.nordicblacktheatre.no. Owned by Nordic Black Theatre, *MS Innvik* is a 1980s ship that has been turned into – to quote the blurb – "a multi-cultural, cross-cultural, transcultural small ship". It is moored on Langkaia, near the new opera house, and a dozen or so of their two-berth, en-suite cabins are rented out for B&B. It's far from deluxe accommodation – the ship is really rather careworn – but it's certainly different. Breakfast is included in the price: 425kr for one person in a cabin, 750kr for two. ❷

Oslo Vandrerhjem Haraldsheim Haraldsheimveien 4, Grefsen ☎ 22 22 29 65, ⓦ www.haraldsheim.no. The pick of Oslo's HI youth hostels, 4km northeast of the centre, and open all year except Christmas week. The public areas are comfortable and attractively furnished in brisk, modern style and the bedrooms are frugal but clean. There are 270 beds in 70 rooms, most of which are four-bedded, and a good number have their own showers and WC. There are self-catering facilities, a restaurant, internet access and washing machines. The only downside can be parties of noisy schoolchildren. It's a very popular spot, so advance reservation is essential throughout summer. To get there, take tram #17 from Storgata, near the Domkirke, northeast to the Sinsenkrysset stop, from where it's a 5min (signposted) walk. By road, the hostel is close to – and signed from – Ring 3. The basic dorm bed price is 235kr, 260kr en suite; singles cost 395kr (450kr), doubles 520kr. Breakfast is included. ❶

Oslo Vandrerhjem Holtekilen Micheletsvei 55, Stabekk ☎ 67 51 80 40, ⓦ www.vandrerhjem.no. Much smaller than *Haraldsheim*, this HI hostel occupies part of a college building in its own grounds some 9km west of the city centre off the E18. There are kitchen facilities, an outdoor area and a laundry. To get there from Oslo Bussterminalen, take bus #151, #153, #161, #162 or #252 to the Kveldsroveien bus stop, from where it's a 200m walk. Open mid-April to Sept. Four-bed rooms cost 940kr, doubles 536kr, singles 385kr; breakfast is included. ❶

Residence Kristinelund Kristinelundsveien 2 ☎ 40 00 24 11, ⓦ www.kristinelund.no. Occupying a handsome nineteenth-century villa about 2km west of the city centre, this agreeable B&B, set in its own garden, is decorated in a pleasing approximation of period style. There are twenty rooms shoehorned into the house, all with shared facilities. To get there from the centre, take bus #30 or #31 and get off at Olav Kyrres plass: Kristinelundsveien is metres away, running north off Bygdøy Allé. ❶

Camping and cabins

The periphery of Oslo is dotted with campsites – a dozen or so are within a fifty-kilometre radius and the nearest is just 3km away. If you're out of luck with rooms in town, most sites also offer **cabins** (*hytter*), but be sure to ring ahead to check availability.

Bogstad Camping Ankerveien 117 ☎ 22 51 08 00, ⓦ www.bogstadcamping.no. Massive campsite on the edge of the Nordmarka (see p.104), about 9km north of the city centre. A good range of facilities, including kitchens, plus access to the Nordmarka's walking trails and ski slopes. They have forty or so cabins – from the simple to the deluxe – with prices starting at 460kr per night to accommodate two adults. The campsite is open all year. To get there by public transport, take bus #32 from Oslo S or the Nationaltheatret; the journey takes about 35min.

Ekeberg Camping Ekebergveien 65 ☎ 22 19 85 68, ⓦ www.ekebergcamping.no. Large, somewhat rudimentary but still popular campsite in a rocky, forested piece of parkland just 3km east of the city centre. To get there, take bus #34 from Jernbanetorget; it's a 10min journey. Open June–Aug.

Central Oslo

Despite the mammoth proportions of the Oslo conurbation, the **city centre** has remained surprisingly compact, and is easy to navigate by remembering a few simple landmarks. From the Oslo S train station, at the eastern end of the centre, the main thoroughfare, **Karl Johans gate**, heads directly up the hill, passing the **Domkirke** (Cathedral) and cutting a pedestrianized course until it reaches the **Stortinget** (Parliament building). From here it sweeps down past the **University** to **Det Kongelige Slott**, or Royal Palace, situated in parkland – the **Slottsparken** – at the western end of the centre. South of the palace, on the waterfront, sits the harbourside **Aker Brygge** shopping complex, across from which lies the distinctive twin-towered **Rådhus** (City Hall). South of the Rådhus, on the lumpy peninsula overlooking the harbour, rises the severe-looking castle, **Akershus Slott**. The castle, the Stortinget and Oslo S form a triangle enclosing a tight, rather gloomy grid of streets and high tenement buildings that was originally laid out by Christian IV in the seventeenth century. For many years this was the city's commercial hub, and although Oslo's burgeoning suburbs undermined its position in the 1960s, the district is currently making a comeback, reinventing itself with specialist shops and smart restaurants.

Along Karl Johans gate to the Domkirke

Heading west and uphill from Oslo S train station, **Karl Johans gate** begins unpromisingly with a clutter of tacky shops and hang-about junkies. But things soon pick up at the corner of Dronningens gate, where the curious **Basarhallene** is a circular, two-tiered building whose brick cloisters once housed the city's food market, but now hold shops and cafés. The adjacent **Domkirke** (Cathedral; daily 10am–4pm; free) dates from the late seventeenth century, though its heavyweight tower was remodelled in 1850. From the outside the cathedral appears plain and dour, but the elegantly restored interior is a delightful surprise, its homely, low-ceilinged nave and transepts awash with maroon, green and gold paintwork. At the central crossing, the flashy Baroque **pulpit**, where cherubs frolic among the foliage, faces a **royal box** that would look more at home at the opera. The **high altar** is Baroque too, its relief of the Last Supper featuring a very Nordic-looking sacrificial lamb. To either side are stained-glass **windows** created by Emanuel Vigeland in 1910 (for more on the Vigelands, see p.103). The brightly coloured **ceiling paintings** are also modern, with representations of God the Father above the high altar, Jesus in the north transept and the Holy Spirit in the south. Down below, the **crypt** is sometimes used for temporary exhibitions of religious fine and applied art.

Outside the cathedral, **Stortorvet** was once the main city square, but it's no longer of much account, its nineteenth-century **statue** of a portly Christian IV merely the somewhat forlorn guardian of a modest flower market.

The National Museum

Established in 2003, Norway's **Nasjonalmuseet** (National Museum; ⓦwww .nasjonalmuseet.no) is the collective name for four separate collections, the Nasjonalgalleriet (National Gallery; see p.88), the Kunstindustrimuseet (Museum of Applied Art; see p.90), the Museet for Samtidskunst (Contemporary Art Museum; see p.93) and the Arkitekturmuseet (Museum of Architecture; see p.94).

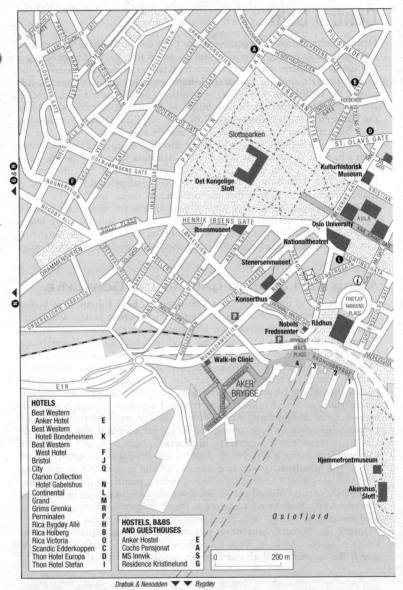

HOTELS

Best Western
  Anker Hotel   E
Best Western
  Hotell Bondeheimen   K
Best Western
  West Hotel   F
Bristol   J Q
City
Clarion Collection
  Hotel Gabelshus   N
Continental   L
Grand   M
Grims Grenka   R
Perminalen   P
Rica Bygdøy Allé   H
Rica Holberg   B
Rica Victoria   O
Scandic Edderkoppen   C
Thon Hotel Europa   D
Thon Hotel Stefan   I

HOSTELS, B&BS
AND GUESTHOUSES
Anker Hostel   E
Cochs Pensjonat   A
MS Innvik   S
Residence Kristinelund G

0   200 m

Drøbak & Nesodden ▼ ▼ Bygdøy

To the Stortinget and Nationaltheatret

Returning to Karl Johans gate, it's a brief stroll up to the **Stortinget** (Parliament building), an imposing chunk of neo-Romanesque architecture, whose stolid, sandy-coloured brickwork, dating from the 1860s, exudes bourgeois certainty. The Stortinget is open for guided tours (late June to late Aug 3 daily; Sept to late June Sat 3 daily; free; Ⓦwww.stortinget.no), but the interior is notably

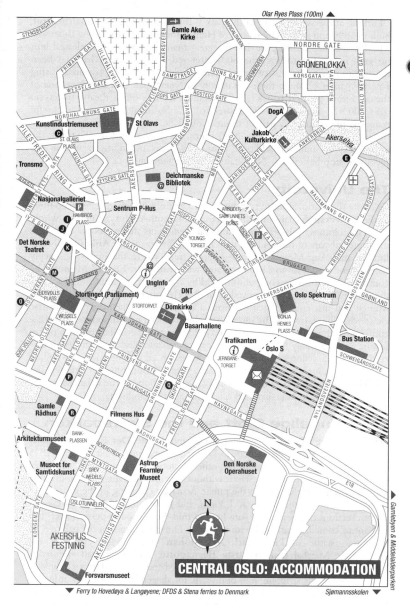

CENTRAL OSLO: ACCOMMODATION

▼ Ferry to Hovedøya & Langøyene; DFDS & Stena ferries to Denmark   Sjømannsskolen ▼

▶ Gamlebyen & Middelalderparken

unexciting. In front of the Parliament, a narrow **park-piazza** runs west to the Nationaltheatret, filling in the gap between Karl Johans gate and Stortingsgata. In summer, the park brims with promenading city folk, who dodge between the jewellery hawkers, ice-cream kiosks and street performers; in winter the magnet are the dinky little open-air and floodlit ice-skating rinks – where skates can be rented at minimal cost.

Lurking at the western end of the park is the Neoclassical **Nationaltheatret**, built in 1899 and fronted by statues of Henrik Ibsen and Bjørnstjerne Bjørnson. The Ibsen statue went up during the great man's lifetime, which pleased him no end. Inside the theatre, the 800-seater red-and-gold main hall has been restored to its turn-of-the-twentieth-century glory and can be savoured during a performance – though these are usually in Norwegian – or by taking one of the occasional **guided tours** (ask for details at the box office; theatre tickets on ☎815 00 811, ⊛www.nationaltheatret.no). The Nationaltheatret is also a useful transport interchange. A pair of tunnels round the back – one for points west, the other east – give access to NSB trains, the T-bane and the Flytoget, the airport express train. In addition, many city buses and trams as well as the Flybussen stop behind the Nationaltheatret, on Stortingsgata.

The University

Opposite the Nationaltheatret, at the western end of Karl Johans gate, stand three of the **University**'s main buildings, grand nineteenth-century structures whose classical columns, pilasters and imperial pediments fit perfectly with this monumental part of the centre. The middle of the trio is the **Aula** (usually late June to mid-Aug Mon–Fri 10am–2.45pm; free), where the imposing, deeply recessed entrance leads to a hall decorated with **murals** by **Edvard Munch**. The controversial result of a competition held by the university authorities in 1909, the murals weren't actually unveiled until 1916, after years of heated debate. Munch had just emerged (cured) from a winter in a Copenhagen psychiatric clinic when he started on the murals, and they reflect a new mood in his work – confident and in tune with the natural world they trumpet. All three main pieces feature a recognizably Norwegian landscape, harsh and bleak and painted in ice-cold blues and yellowy whites. *History* focuses on an old, bearded man telling stories to a young boy, and *Alma Mater* has a woman nourishing her children, but it is *The Sun* which takes the breath away, a searing globe of fire balanced on the horizon to shoot its laser-like rays out across a rocky landscape.

The Kongelige Slott and the Slottsparken

Standing on the hill at the west end of Karl Johans gate, **Det Kongelige Slott** (the Royal Palace) is a monument to Norwegian openness. Built between 1825 and 1848, when the monarchs of other European nations were nervously counting their friends, it now stands without railings and walls, its grounds – the **Slottsparken** – freely open to the public. A snappy changing of the guard takes place daily outside the palace at 1.30pm, and hour-long guided tours take in certain sections of the interior (late June to mid-Aug), though tickets (95kr) can be hard to come by – ask at the tourist office. Directly in front of the palace is an equestrian statue of king **Karl XIV Johan** (1763–1844). Formerly the Napoleonic Marshal **Jean-Baptiste Bernadotte**, Karl Johan had endured a turbulent relationship with Napoleon, who sacked and reinstated him a couple of times before finally stripping him of his rank for alleged lack of military ardour at the battle of Wagram, outside Vienna, in 1809. In a huff, Bernadotte stomped off back to Paris, where – much to his surprise – he was informed that the Swedish court had elected him as the heir to their king, the childless Charles XIII. This was not, however a quixotic gesture by the Swedes, but rather a desire to ensure that their next king was a good soldier able to protect them from their enemies, especially Russia. In the event, it worked out rather well: Bernadotte successfully steered the Swedes through the tail end of the Napoleonic Wars and, as king from 1818, proved popular and efficient, adding Norway to his future kingdom in 1814.

▲ Karl Johans gate

Not content, seemingly, with the terms of his motto (inscribed on the statue), "The people's love is my reward", Karl Johan had this whopping palace built for his further contentment, only to die before it was completed.

The Ibsen–museet

The grand, nineteenth-century mansions bordering the southern perimeter of the Slottsparken once housed Oslo's social elite. It was here, in a fourth-floor apartment at Arbins gate 1, on the corner of what is now Henrik Ibens gate, that Norway's most celebrated playwright Henrik Ibsen spent the last ten years of his life, strolling down to the *Grand Café* (see p.78) every day to hold court. Admirers did their best to hobnob with the great man as he took his daily walk, but Ibsen was unenthusiastic about being a tourist attraction in his own lifetime and mostly ignored all comers – no one could ever accuse him of being overly sociable. Ibsen's old apartment is now incorporated within the **Ibsen–museet**, whose entrance is just along the street at Henrik Ibsens gate 26 (Ibsen Museum; Tues– Sun: mid-May to mid-Sept 11am–6pm; mid-Sept to mid-May noon–3pm; 85kr; Ⓦwww.ibsenmuseet.no). The museum kicks off with a well-considered introduction to Ibsen and his plays, exploring, over two small floors, the themes that underpinned his work and his uneasy relationship with his home country. Beyond, Ibsen's apartment has been restored to its appearance in 1895, including many of the original furnishings, but it can only be visited on a guided tour (hourly; no extra charge). Both Ibsen and his wife died here: Ibsen breathed his last as he lay paralyzed in bed, but his wife, unwilling to expire in an undignified pose, dressed herself to die sitting upright in a chair in the library. Ibsen was argumentative to the end – famously, his final words were "To the contrary".

For more on Ibsen, see box on p.89 and Grimstad, p.139.

Stenersenmuseet

From the Ibsen Museum, it's a five-minute walk south to the **Stenersen museet**, Munkedamsveien 15 (Stenersen Museum; Tues & Thurs 11am–7pm; Wed, Fri, Sat & Sun 11am–5pm; 45kr; Ⓦwww.stenersen.museum.no), home to

Ibsen

Henrik Johan Ibsen (1828–1906), Norway's most famous and influential playwright, is generally regarded as one of the greatest dramatists of all time, and certainly his central themes have powerful modern resonances. In essence, these concern the alienation of the individual from an ethically bankrupt society, loss of religious faith and the yearning of women to transcend the confines of their roles as wives and mothers. Ibsen's central characters often speak evasively, mirroring the repression of their society and their own sense of confusion and guilt with venomous exchanges – a major characteristic of the playwright's dialogue – appearing whenever the underlying tensions break through. Ibsen's protagonists do things which are less than heroic, often incompetent, even malicious. Nevertheless, they aspire to *dåd*, the act of the hero/heroine, arguably a throwback to the old Norse sagas. These themes run right through Ibsen's plays, the first of which, *Catalina* (1850), was written while he was employed as an apothecary's assistant at Grimstad on the south coast (see p.139).

The alienation the plays reveal was undoubtedly spawned by Ibsen's troubled **childhood**: his father had gone bankrupt in 1836, and the disgrace – and poverty – weighed heavily on the whole family. More humiliation followed at Grimstad, where the shy, young Ibsen worked for a pittance and was obliged to share a bed with his boss and two maids, which resulted in one of them bearing him a child in 1846. Ibsen **escaped provincial Norway** in 1850, settling first in Oslo and then Bergen. But he remained deeply dissatisfied with Norwegian society, which he repeatedly decried as illiberal and small-minded. In 1864, he **left the country** and spent the next 27 years living in Germany and Italy. It was during his exile that Ibsen established his literary reputation – at first with the rhyming couplets of *Peer Gynt*, featuring the antics of the eponymous hero, a shambolic opportunist in the mould of Don Quixote, and then by a vicious attack on small-town values in *Pillars of Society*. It was, however, *A Doll's House* (1879) that really put him on the map, its controversial protagonist, Nora, making unwise financial decisions before walking out not only on her patronizing husband, Torvald, but also on her loving children – all in her desire to control her own destiny. *Ghosts* followed two years later, and its exploration of moral contamination through the metaphor of syphilis created an even greater furore, which Ibsen rebutted in his next work, *An Enemy of the People* (1882). Afterwards, Ibsen changed tack (if not theme), firstly with *The Wild Duck* (1884), a mournful tale of the effects of compulsive truth-telling, and then *Hedda Gabler* (1890), where the heroine is denied the ability to make or influence decisions, and so becomes perverse, manipulative and ultimately self-destructive.

Ibsen returned to Oslo in 1891. He was treated as a hero, and ironically – considering the length of his exile and his comments on his compatriots – as a symbol of Norwegian virtuosity. Indeed, the daily stroll he took from his apartment to the *Grand Hotel* on Karl Johans gate became something of a tourist attraction in its own right – not that Ibsen, who was notoriously grumpy, often wanted to talk to anyone. Ibsen was incapacitated by a heart attack in 1901 and died from the effects of another one five years later.

an eclectic collection of modern art, the bulk of which was gifted to the city in 1936 by the author and art collector Rolf Stenersen (the same man who gave a second collection to Bergen – see p.212). The museum's first-floor entrance, set beside the ugly concrete stairway across from the city's main concert hall, leads straight into the main exhibition area, which holds an enjoyable sample of early to mid-twentieth-century Scandinavian paintings. In particular, look out for the charming *Small Girl on a Sofa* by **Alex Revold** (1887–1962) and the aloof but finely observed *Two Children*, *Actress* and *Dressmaker* by **Per Krohg**

(1889–1965). Both Krohg and Revold were one-time pupils of Matisse and Revold spent a few months teaching **Arne Ekeland** (1908–94), though this later artist was much more influenced by German Expressionism and Cubism, which suited his leftist, class-conscious politics perfectly. Other highlights of the collection include the soft-hued Norwegian landscapes of **Amaldus Nielsen** (1838–1932) and the bright burlesques of Oslo life by **Ludvig Ravensberg** (1871–1958). There's also a lively programme of temporary exhibitions, but the Munch paintings that were once exhibited here were put in cold storage during the security panic that followed the theft of two of his paintings in 2004 (see p.105) – and there's no sign they will ever be returned.

Kulturhistorisk Museum

Returning to the west end of Karl Johans gate, follow Frederiks gate to get to Oslo's **Kulturhistorisk Museum** (Cultural History Museum; mid-May to mid-Sept Tues–Sun 10am–5pm; mid-Sept to mid-May Tues–Sun 11am–4pm; free), which occupies a handsome neo-Romanesque structure of imposing proportions. The capacious interior holds the university's hotchpotch historical and ethnographical collections, amongst which the undoubted highlight is the **Viking and early medieval** section, on the ground floor: in the rooms to the left of the entrance are several magnificent twelfth- and thirteenth-century stave-church portals, alive with dragons and beasts emerging from swirling, intricately carved backgrounds – for more on stave churches, see p.187. Here also are weapons, coins, drinking horns, runic stones, religious bric-a-brac and bits of clothing as well as a superb **vaulted ceiling** dating from the late thirteenth century and retrieved from the stave church in Ål, near Geilo. The room's brightly coloured wooden planks are painted in tempera – a technique where each pigment was mixed with glue, egg white and ground chalk – and feature a complicated biblical iconography, beginning at the apex with the Creation and Adam and Eve, followed, as you work your way down, by depictions of Christ's childhood and ultimately his death and resurrection. An English-language leaflet, available in the room, gives the full low down, but it's the dynamic forcefulness of these naive paintings, as well as the individuality of some of the detail, that really impresses – look out, in particular, for the nasty-looking Judas at the Last Supper, and the pair of amenable donkeys peeping into Christ's manger.

The rest of the ground floor is taken up by a pretty average **Viking Age** exhibition geared towards school parties. The tiny dioramas are downright silly, and detract from the exhibits, which attempt to illustrate various aspects of early Norwegian society, from religious beliefs and social structures through to military hardware, trade and craft. More positively, there is a fascinating sample of Viking decorative art, including the intensely flamboyant, ninth-century Oseberg and Borre styles and continuing into the Jellinge style, where greater emphasis was placed on line and composition. There's also a **skattkammeret** (treasure room) of precious objects – finger rings, crucifixes, pendants, brooches, buckles and suchlike – illustrating the sustained virtuosity of Norse goldsmiths and silversmiths.

On the floor above, the beginning of the **etnografiske utstillingene** (ethnographic exhibition; same times) is mostly devoted to the Arctic peoples and features an illuminating section on the Sami, who inhabit the northern reaches of Scandinavia. Incongruously, there's a **myntkabinettet** (coin collection) here as well, while the top two floors contain a diverse collection of African and Asiatic art and culture, from Samurai suits and African masks to Egyptian mummies, plus everything in between.

The Nasjonalgalleriet

From the Kulturhistorisk Museum, it's a couple of minutes' walk east to Norway's largest and most prestigious art gallery, the **Nasjonalgalleriet**, at Universitetsgata 13 (National Gallery; Tues, Wed & Fri 10am–6pm, Thurs 10am–7pm, Sat & Sun 10am–5pm; free; Ⓦ www.nationalmuseum.no). Housed in a whopping nineteenth-century building, the collection may be short on internationally famous painters – apart from a fine body of work by Edvard Munch – but there's compensation in the oodles of Norwegian art, including work by all the leading figures up until the end of World War II. The only irritation is the way the museum is organized: the kernel of the collection is displayed on the **first floor**, which is convenient enough, but paintings of individual artists tend to be displayed in several different rooms, which can be very frustrating. The **free plan** available at reception helps illuminate matters; the text below mentions room numbers where it's helpful, but note that locations are sometimes rotated.

Johan Christian Dahl and Thomas Fearnley

Near the top of the main staircase, Room 17 features the work of the country's most important nineteenth-century landscape painters, **Johan Christian Dahl** (1788–1857) and his pupil **Thomas Fearnley** (1802–42). The Romantic Naturalism of their finely detailed canvases expressed Norway's growing sense of nationhood after the break-up of the Dano–Norwegian union in 1814. In a clear rejection of Danish lowland civil-servant culture, Dahl and Fearnley asserted the beauty (and moral virtue) of Norway's wild landscapes, which had previously been seen as uncouth and barbaric. This reassessment was clearly influenced by the ideas of the Swiss-born philosopher Jean Jacques Rousseau (1712–78), who believed that the peoples of mountain regions possessed an intrinsic nobility precisely because they were remote from the corrupting influences of (lowland) civilization. Dahl, who was a professor at the Academy of Art in Dresden for many years, wrote to a friend in 1841: "Like a true Poet, a Painter must not be led by the prevailing, often corrupt Taste, but attempt to create … a landscape [that] … exposes the characteristics of this Country and its Nature – often idyllic, often historical, melancholic – what they have been and are."

Dahl's large 1842 canvas *Stalheim* is typical of his work, a mountain landscape rendered in soft and dappled hues, dotted with tiny figures and a sleepy village. Also in Room 17, his *Hjelle in Valdres* (1851) adopts the same approach, although here the artifice behind the naturalism is easier to detect. Dahl had completed another painting of Hjelle the year before; returning to the subject, he widened the valley and heightened the mountains, sprinkling them with snow. Fearnley often lived and worked abroad, but he always returned to Norwegian themes, painting no fewer than five versions of the moody *Labrofossen ved Kongsberg* (The Labro Waterfall at Kongsberg); his 1837 version is displayed in Room 17.

Late nineteenth- and early twentieth-century Norwegian paintings

Another Norwegian artist to seek out is **Adolph Tidemand** (1814–76), if not so much for the quality of his painting as for its content. Born in Mandal on the south coast, Tidemand went to art college in Denmark and taught art in Düsseldorf, but was firmly attached to his homeland, making a series of long research trips to study rural Norwegian folk customs and costumes. Tidemand's drawings were so precise that they are still used as a reference by students of traditional Norwegian dress, but his paintings are absurdly romantic, reflecting the bourgeois nationalism that swept Norway in the middle of the nineteenth century. The museum displays a whole batch of Tidemand's folkloric paintings in Room 21, but his most famous work is the *Bridal Voyage on the Hardanger Fjord* (Room 17), in which **Hans Frederik Gude** (1825–1903) painted the landscape and Tidemand filled in the figures. Gude was a great friend of Tidemand, sharing his romantic nationalism and being a fellow lecturer at the art academy in Düsseldorf.

In the 1880s, Norwegian landscape painting took on a mystical and spiritual dimension. Influenced by French painters such as Théodore Rousseau, Norwegian artists abandoned the naturalism of an earlier generation for more symbolic representations. **Gerhard Munthe** (1849–1929), for one, dipped into lyrical renditions of the Norwegian countryside (Room 23), and his cosy, folksy scenes were echoed in the paintings of **Erik Werenskiold** (1855–1938), who is well represented by *Peasant Burial* also in Room 23. Of a similar ilk was the work of the novelist, journalist and artist **Christian Krohg** (1852–1925), whose highly stylized paintings of the poor and destitute pricked many a middle-class conscience. It was, however, his sympathetic paintings of prostitutes that created the real brouhaha as exemplified by his tongue-in-cheek *Albertine at the Police Doctor's Surgery* in Room 23.

During this period, **Theodor Kittelsen** (1857–1914) defined the appearance of the country's trolls, sprites and sirens in his illustrations for Asbjørnsen and Moe's *Norwegian Folk Tales*, published in 1883. Six of Kittelsen's original paintings are displayed in Room 29 – and a splendid sample they are too, especially the one of a princess de-lousing a troll, a time-consuming job if ever there was one. In the same room are two examples of Kittelsen's other work – a self-portrait and a landscape – plus half a dozen panels illustrating a traditional folk song completed in an ersatz medieval style by **Gerhard Munthe**.

Moving on into Room 30 you encounter the works of **Harald Sohlberg** (1869–1935), who clarified the rather hazy vision of many of his Norwegian contemporaries, painting a series of sharply observed Røros streetscapes and expanding into more elemental themes with such stunning works as *En blomstereng nordpå* (A Northern Flower Meadow) and *Sommernatt* (Summer Night). These paintings are comparable with those of **Halfdan Egedius** (1877–99), as in *Opptrekkende uvaer* (The Approaching Storm) back in Room 29.

Edvard Munch

The Nasjonalgalleriet's star turn is its **Munch** collection. Representative works from the 1880s up to 1916 are gathered together in Room 24. His early work is very much in the Naturalist tradition of his mentor Christian Krohg, though by 1885 Munch was already pushing back the boundaries in *The Sick Child*, a heart-wrenching evocation of his sister Sophie's death from tuberculosis. Other works displaying this same sense of pain include *The Dance of Life*, *Madonna* and *The Scream*, a seminal canvas of 1893 whose swirling lines and rhythmic colours were to inspire the Expressionists. Munch painted several versions of *The Scream*, but this is the original, so it is hard to exaggerate the embarrassment felt by the museum when, in 1994, someone climbed in through the window and stole it. The painting was eventually recovered, but the thief was never caught. Consider Munch's words as you view it:

I was walking along a road with two friends. The sun set. I felt a tinge of melancholy. Suddenly the sky became blood red. I stopped and leaned against a railing feeling exhausted, and I looked at the flaming clouds that hung like blood and a sword over the blue-black fjord and the city. My friends walked on. I stood there trembling with fright. And I felt a loud unending scream piercing nature.

The gallery's sample of Munch's work serves as a good introduction to the artist, but for a more detailed appraisal – and a more comprehensive selection of his work – check out the Munch Museum (p.105).

Norwegian paintings from 1910

Munch aside, the general flow of Norwegian art was reinvigorated in the 1910s by a new band of artists who had trained in Paris under Matisse, whose emancipation of colour from Naturalist constraints inspired his Norwegian students. Among this group, **Henrik Sørensen** (1882–1962) is the outstanding figure. Sørensen summed up the Frenchman's influence on him thirty years later: "From Matisse, I learned more in fifteen minutes than from all the other teachers I have listened to" – lessons that inspired Sørensen's surging, earthy landscapes of the lowlands of eastern Norway (Room 33). **Axel Revold** (1887–1962) was trained by Matisse too, but also assimilated Cubist influences as in *The Fishing Fleet leaves the Harbour* (Room 39), whilst **Erling Enger** (1899–1990) maintained a gently lyrical, slightly whimsical approach to the landscape and its seasons. Look out also for the work of **Arne Ekeland** (1908–94), whose various World War II paintings are bleak and powerful in equal measure – as evidenced by the fractured, mosaic-like composition of *The Last Shots*.

Finally, the museum holds an enjoyable sample of work by the **Impressionists** and **Post-Impressionists**, with assorted bursts of colour from Manet, Monet, Degas and Cézanne, as well as a distant, piercing Van Gogh self-portrait. There is also a light scattering of early twentieth-century paintings by the likes of Picasso, Gris and Braque, but it must be said that for a national gallery there are few works of international significance, reflecting Norway's past poverty and its lack of an earlier royal or aristocratic collection to build upon.

The Kunstindustrimuseet

The **Kunstindustrimuseet** (Museum of Applied Art; Tues, Wed & Fri 11am–5pm, Thurs 11am–7pm, Sat & Sun noon–4pm; free, but admission charged for some exhibitions; Ⓦ www.nationalmuseum.no), at St Olavs gate 1, fills out an imposing nineteenth-century building some five minutes' walk from the Nasjonalgalleriet – continue to the far end of Universitetsgata, veer to the right and it's at the end of the street. Founded in 1876, it can lay claim to being one of the earliest applied-art museums in Europe and its multifaceted permanent collection is particularly strong on **furniture**, with examples of all the major styles – both domestic and imported – that have been popular in Norway from the medieval period to the present day.

The museum spreads over four floors with part of the ground floor devoted to a lively programme of temporary exhibitions. The next floor up focuses on the development of **Modernism**, casting a wide net to start in 1905 and end a century later. There are keynote displays on Art Deco and post-World War II Scandinavian design. The next floor up is devoted to the **History of Style 1100–1905**, and, in the first room to the right of the stairs, an engaging hotch-potch of **medieval** paraphernalia, from brooches and crosses through to portable altars, has been crammed into a glass cabinet. In the same room is the museum's most celebrated exhibit, the intricate and brightly coloured **Baldishol Tapestry**, one of the finest and earliest examples of woven tapestry in Europe, plus a charming selection of woven coverlets decorated with religious and folkloric motifs. Using skills distantly inherited from Flemish weavers, the Norwegians took to pictorial coverlets in a big way, their main modification being the elimination of perspective in the attempt to cover the seams. Of ceremonial significance, these items were brought out on all major occasions –

weddings and festivals in particular. The coverlets began as fairly crude affairs at the start of the seventeenth century, but achieved greater precision and detail throughout the eighteenth century, after which the art went into a slow decline. The two most popular subjects were the arrival of the Magi, and the Wise and Foolish Virgins, a suitably didactic subject for any newlyweds. Next on this floor is a sequence of **period interiors** illustrating foreign fashions from Renaissance and Baroque through to Rococo, Neoclassical and Art Nouveau.

The top floor holds a fashion gallery, one highlight here being the collection of extravagant **costumes** worn by Norway's royal family at the turn of the twentieth century. Dresses is too prosaic a word for the fairy-tale affairs favoured by Queen Maud, daughter of England's Edward VII and wife of Håkon VII, not to mention Crown Princess Sonja's consecratory robe from the 1930s.

East from the Kunstindustrimuseet to Grünerløkka

Heading east from the Kunstindustrimuseet, walk round the dull, brown-brick pile of **St Olavs kirke**, built for the city's Catholics in the middle of the nineteenth century, and follow Akersveien as far as the cemetery. There's a choice of routes here. If you keep straight, it's a short stroll up the slope to the **Gamle Aker Kirke** (May–Sept Tues–Fri noon–2pm; free), a sturdy stone building still in use as a Lutheran parish church. It dates from around 1100, which makes it the oldest stone church in Scandinavia, although most of what you see today is the result of a heavy-handed nineteenth-century refurbishment.

Alternatively, back at the cemetery, turn right down **Damstredet**, a steep cobbled lane flanked by early nineteenth-century clapboard houses built at all kinds of odd angles. These are some of the few wooden buildings to have survived Oslo's developers and they make the street a picturesque affair, a well-kept reminder of how the city once looked. At the bottom of Damstredet, there's another choice of routes. If you stroll south along **Fredensborgveien**, you'll thread your way past office blocks, regaining the city centre in around fifteen minutes. But if you head southeast for about five minutes along Iduns gate and then Hausmanns gate, you'll reach two cultural targets, the first one being **DogA Norsk Design og Arkitektursenter** (Mon, Tues & Fri 10am–5pm, Wed & Thurs 10am–8pm, Sat & Sun noon–5pm; free; ⓦwww.doga.no), the Norwegian Design and Architecture Centre, whose temporary displays, housed in a former electricity station, trumpet contemporary Norwegian design. A few metres away, the second target is the **Jakob Kulturkirke**, a disused church, which now accommodates a cultural centre where concerts, art exhibitions and theatre performances are held (ⓣ22 99 34 50, ⓦwww.kkv.no for details).

Behind the church is the **Ankerbrua** (Anker bridge), spanning the **River Akerselva**. Sporting sculptures by Norwegian sculptor Per Ung – look out for Peer Gynt and his reindeer – the bridge marks the main approach to **Grünerløkka**. Formerly a run-down working-class district, Grünerløkka's recent regeneration has turned it into one of the most fashionable parts of the city, particularly amongst artists and students. Turn left just beyond the bridge, and you'll find yourself on **Markveien**, which is dotted with boho cafés, bars, restaurants and eccentric, vaguely New Age designer shops. At Olav Ryes plass, the first splash of greenery, turn right to reach the liveliest part of Grünerløkka's other main drag, **Thorvald Meyers gate**, which runs north to **Birkelunden**, a grassy square that's especially popular for hanging out in the summer.

The quickest way to get back to the centre is on tram #11, #12 or #13, which all run along Thorvald Meyers gate.

❶ To the water: the Rådhus

From the Nationaltheatret (see p.84), it's just a couple of minutes' walk south to the **Rådhus** (City Hall; daily 9am–6pm; guided tours Mon–Fri 3 daily; free, but May–Aug 40kr), which rears high above the waterfront. Nearly twenty years in the making, Oslo's City Hall finally opened in 1950 to celebrate the city's nine-hundredth anniversary. Designed by Arnstein Arneberg and Manus Poulsson, this firmly Modernist, twin-towered building of dark brown brick was intended to be a grandiose statement of civic pride. At first, few locals had a good word for what they saw as an ugly and strikingly un-Norwegian addition to the city, but with the passing of time the obloquy has fallen on more recent additions to the skyline – such as Oslo S – and the Rådhus has become one of the city's more popular buildings.

Initially at least, the ornamentation was equally contentious. Many leading Norwegian painters and sculptors contributed to the decorations, which were designed to celebrate all things Norwegian, but the pagan themes chosen for much of the work gave many of the country's Protestants the hump. The **main approach** to the Rådhus is on its landward side via a wide ramp, whose side galleries are adorned by garish **wood panels** illustrating pagan Nordic myths with several featuring the Tree of the World, Yggdrasil or Yggdrask (see p.414). Inside, the principal hall – the **Rådhushallen** – is decorated with vast, stylized and very secular murals. On the north wall, Per Krohg's *From the Fishing Nets in the West to the Forests of the East* invokes the figures of polar explorer Fridtjof Nansen (on the left) and dramatist Bjørnstjerne Bjørnson (on the right) to symbolize, respectively, the nation's spirit of adventure and its intellectual development. On the south wall is the equally vivid *Work, Administration and Celebration*, which took Henrik Sørensen a decade to complete. The self-congratulatory nationalism of these two murals is hardly attractive, although the effect is partly offset by the forceful fresco in honour of the Norwegian Resistance of World War II, which runs along the east wall.

Outside, at the back of the Rådhus, a line of six muscular **bronzes** represents the trades – builders, bricklayers and so on – who worked on the building. Behind them stand four massive, granite female sculptures surrounding a fountain, and beyond is the busy central **harbour**, with the bumpy Akershus peninsula on the left and the islands of the Oslofjord filling out the backdrop. This is a delightful spot, one of the city's happiest moments, and a stone's throw away is the Nobels Fredssenter.

Nobels Fredssenter and Aker Brygge

The **Nobels Fredssenter** (Nobel Peace Centre; June–Aug daily 10am–6pm; Sept–Dec Tues–Sun 10am–6pm; Jan–May Tues–Fri 10am–4pm, Sat & Sun 11am–5pm; 80kr; ⓦ www.nobelpeacecenter.org) was founded to celebrate and publicize the Nobel Peace Prize. Born in Sweden, **Alfred Nobel** (1833–96) invented dynamite in his thirties and went on to become extraordinarily rich with factories in over twenty countries. In his will, Nobel established a fund to reward good works in five categories – physics, chemistry, medicine, literature and peace. The awards were to be made annually, based on the recommenda-tions of several Swedish institutions, with the exception of the Peace Prize, the recipient of which was to be selected by a committee of five, itself appointed by the Norwegian parliament.

Inside, the Peace Centre's ground floor features a series of temporary displays designed to get visitors into thinking about conflict and peace, poverty and wealth. Upstairs, there's a small display on the Nobel family; "wall papers" (broadly, information sheets) on all things to do with peace; and the so-called "Nobel Field", where each of the past holders of the Peace Prize is represented by a light bulb on a wispy stalk. With the overhead lights dimmed down, the stalks make a sort of miniature electrical forest, which really looks both effective and very engaging. As for the winners of the Peace Prize themselves, there are many outstanding individuals – Martin Luther King, Desmond Tutu, Nelson Mandela and Willy Brandt to name but four – but some real surprises too, especially Theodore Roosevelt, who was part of the American invasion of Cuba in the 1890s, and the USA's Henry Kissinger, who was widely blamed for destabilizing Cambodia in the 1970s. Indeed, despite its current exemplary image, the Nobel Prizes are in fact steeped in controversy: the writer and playwright Johan August Strindberg (1849–1912) was the pre-eminent literary figure in Sweden for several decades, but he was much too radical for the tastes of the prize givers and in 1911, after he had again failed to get one, the Swedish working class organized a whip-round and gave him a "Nobel Prize" themselves.

Behind the Peace Centre, the old Aker shipyard has been turned into the swish **Aker Brygge** shopping-cum-office complex, a gleaming concoction of walkways, circular staircases and glass lifts, all decked out with neon and plastic; the bars and restaurants here are some of the most popular in town.

East to Bankplassen

Running east from the Rådhus, **Rådhusgata** cuts off the spur of land dominated by the Akershus Castle (see p.96). For the most part the street is flanked by ponderous, late nineteenth-century high-rises, reminders of the time when this was the commercial heart of the city, but at the foot of Akersgata it bisects an elegant cobbled square framed by a handful of much older pastel-painted buildings, including the pint-sized **Gamle Rådhus**, Oslo's old town hall, though this was heavily restored after fire damage in 1996. It was here, in 1667, that Oslo's first theatrical performance took place, as recalled on the building's second floor in the mildly diverting Gamle Christiania og **Teatermuseet** (Old Oslo and Theatre Museum; June–Aug Tues–Sun 11am–4pm; Sept–Nov Sat & Sun 11am–4pm; free), with a short film on the history of the city along with theatrical posters, puppets and costumes.

Bankplassen, arguably the city's most attractive square, lies one block south of Rådhusgata, between Kongens gate and Kirkegata. Framed by Gothic Revival and Second Empire buildings, the square, with its trees and water fountain, is a perfect illustration of the grandiose tastes of the Dano-Norwegian elite who ran the country at the start of the twentieth century. The square's proudest building is the former Norges Bank headquarters of 1907, a redoubtable Art Nouveau-meets-Romanesque edifice that has been refurbished to house the **Museet for Samtidskunst** (Contemporary Art Museum).

The Museet for Samtidskunst

The enterprising **Museet for Samtidskunst** (Contemporary Art Museum; Tues, Wed & Fri 11am–5pm, Thurs 11am–7pm, Sat & Sun noon–5pm; free; Ⓦ www.nationalmuseum.no) owns work by every major post-World War II Norwegian artist and many leading foreign figures too, and for the most part the **displays** take the form of a series of temporary, thematic exhibitions spread over three floors. The works, some of which are massive, are each allowed a generous amount of space, so – given that the museum also hosts prestigious international exhibitions of contemporary art – only a fraction of the permanent collection can be shown at any one time. Nonetheless, Norwegian names to look out for include Bjørn Carlsen, Frans Widerberg, Erik Killi Olsen, Knut Rose, Snorre Ytterstad, Per Kleiva and Bjørn Ransve.

There are also two **permanent installations**, beginning with the weird *Inner Space V*, the fifth in a series of angst-rattling rooms made from recycled industrial junk by the Norwegian **Per Inge Bjørlo** (b.1952). The second, tucked away in a room of its own on the top floor, is the peculiar – and peculiarly engaging – *The Man Who Never Threw Anything Away*. This is the work of the Russian **Ilya Kabakov** (b.1933), who spent over a decade from 1983 collecting hundreds of discarded items from the recesses of his house – bits of toenail, string etc, etc – to assemble them here, each precisely labelled and neatly displayed. The installation occupies a sort of parallel reality that was originally a retreat from the bureaucratic illogicalities of the Soviet system, but is now a tribute to the anally retentive.

The museum's exhibits hang from every wall and offset every corner and stairwell, but it's still difficult not to be just as impressed by the building itself, its polished, echoing halls resplendent with gilt and marble, ornamental columns and banisters. The museum also does a good line in T-shirts – a recent offering was inscribed "Welcome foreigners – don't leave us alone with the Danes".

The Arkitekturmuseet

One of Oslo's four national museums, the **Arkitekturmuseet**, at Bankplassen 3 (Architecture Museum; Tues–Fri 11am–5pm, Thurs 11am–7pm, Sat & Sun noon–5pm; free; Ⓦ www.nationalmuseum.no), is a new and lavish development in which keynote architectural displays are laid out in a handsome modern pavilion at the back of an older structure, dating from 1830. Opened in 2008, the whole development cost millions of kroner and although the initial exhibitions have focused on Norwegian architects – and Norwegian design – international figures are destined to follow.

Astrup Fearnley Museet for Moderne Kunst

Opened in 1993, the **Astrup Fearnley Museet for Moderne Kunst**, about 200m to the east of Bankplassen at Dronningens gate 4 (Astrup Fearnley Modern Art Museum; Tues, Wed & Fri 11am–5pm, Thurs 11am–7pm, Sat & Sun noon–5pm; free; Ⓦ www.afmuseet.no), occupies a sharp modern building of brick and glass, with six-metre-high steel entrance doors. It's meant to impress – a suitably posh setting for the display of several private collections and for prestigious temporary exhibitions. The latter often leave little space for the permanent collection, which includes examples of the work of most major postwar Norwegian artists, as well as a smattering of foreign works by such celebrated figures as Francis Bacon, Damien Hirst, Jeff Koons and Anselm Kiefer.

The Akershus complex

Though very much part of central Oslo by location, the thumb of land that holds the sprawling fortifications of the **Akershus complex** (outdoor areas daily 6am–9pm; free) is quite separate from the city centre in feel. Built on a rocky knoll overlooking the harbour in around 1300, the original **Slott** (castle) was already the battered veteran of several unsuccessful sieges when Christian IV (1596–1648) took matters in hand. The king had a passion for building cities and took a keen interest in Norway – during his reign he visited the country about

Modern art in Norway

Norway has a well-organized, high-profile body of **professional artists** whose long-established commitment to encouraging artistic activity throughout the country has brought them respect, as well as state subsidies. In the 1960s, abstract and conceptual artists dominated the scene, but at the end of the 1970s there was a renewed interest in older art styles, particularly Expressionism, Surrealism and Cubism, plus a new emphasis on technique and materials. To a large degree these opposing impulses fused, or at least overlapped, but by the late 1980s several definable movements had emerged. One of the more popular trends was for artists to use beautiful colours to portray disquieting visions, a dissonance favoured by the likes of **Knut Rose** (b.1936) and **Bjørn Carlsen** (b.1945). The latter's ghoulish *Searching in a Dead Zebra* has been highly influential, and is now part of the Astrup Fearnley Museum's permanent collection. Other artists, the most distinguished of whom is Tore Hansen (b.1949), have developed a naive style. Their paintings, apparently clumsily drawn without thought for composition, are frequently reminiscent of Norwegian folk art, and constitute a highly personal response drawn from the artists' emotions and subconscious experiences.

Both of these trends embody a sincerity of expression that defines the bulk of contemporary Norwegian art. Whereas the prevailing mood in international art circles encourages detached irony, Norway's artists characteristically adhere to the view that their role is to interpret, or at least express, the poignant and personal for their audience. An important exception is **Bjørn Ransve** (b.1944), who creates sophisticated paintings in constantly changing styles, but always focused on the relationship between art and reality. Another exception is the small group of artists, such as **Bjørn Sigurd Tufta** (b.1956) and Sverre Wylier (b.1953), who have returned to non-figurative modernism to create works that explore the possibilities of the material, while the content plays no decisive role. An interest in materials has sparked a variety of experiments, particularly among the country's sculptors, whose **installations** incorporate everyday utensils, natural objects and pictorial art. These installations have developed their own momentum, pushing back the traditional limits of the visual arts in their use of many different media including photography, video, textiles and furniture. Leading an opposing faction is the painter **Odd Nerdrum** (b.1944), who has long spearheaded the figurative rebellion against the modernists, though some artists straddle the divide, such as Astrid Løvaas (b.1957) and Kirsten Wagle (b.1956), who work together to produce flower motifs in textiles. The most prominent Norwegian sculptor today is Bergen's own **Bård Breivik** (b.1948), who explores the dialogue between nature and humankind.

thirty times, more than all the other kings of the Dano–Norwegian union together. So, when Oslo was badly damaged by fire in 1624, he took his opportunity and simply ordered the town to be moved round the bay from its marshy location at the mouth of the River Alna beneath the Ekeberg heights. He had the town rebuilt in its present position, renamed it Christiania – a name which stuck until 1925 – and transformed the medieval Akershus castle into a Renaissance residence. Around the castle he also constructed a new fortress – the **Akershus Festning** – whose thick earth-and-stone walls and protruding bastions were designed to resist artillery bombardment. Refashioned and enlarged on several later occasions, and now bisected by Kongens gate, parts of the fortress have remained in military use until the present day.

There are several **entrances** to the Akershus complex, but the most appealing is at the west end of **Myntgata**, from where a footpath leads up to a side gate in the perimeter wall. Just beyond the gate is a dull museum-cum-information centre, which makes a strange attempt to tie in the history of the castle with modern environmental concerns. You're much better off keeping going along the signed **footpath** that twists its way up to the castle and the Resistance Museum, offering the possibility of heady views over the harbour on the way.

Hjemmefrontmuseum

The **Hjemmefrontmuseum** (Resistance Museum; June–Aug Mon–Sat 10am–5pm, Sun 11am–5pm; Sept–May Mon–Fri 10am–4pm, Sat & Sun 11am–4pm; 30kr; ⓦ www.mil.no/felles/nhm) occupies a separate building just outside the castle entrance, an apt location given that the Gestapo tortured and sometimes executed captured Resistance fighters in the castle. Labelled in English and Norwegian, the displays detail the history of the war in Norway, from defeat and occupation through resistance to final victory. There are tales of extraordinary heroism here – notably the determined resistance of hundreds of the country's teachers to Nazi instructions and the sabotaging of German attempts to produce heavy water for an atomic bomb deep in southern Norway, at Rjukan (see p.193). There's also the moving story of a certain Petter Moen, who was arrested by the Germans and imprisoned in the Akershus, where he kept a diary by using a nail to pick out letters on toilet paper; the diary survived, but he didn't. Another section deals with Norway's Jews, who numbered 1800 in 1939; the Germans captured 760, of whom 24 survived. There's also an impressively honest account of Norwegian collaboration: fascism struck a chord with the country's petit bourgeois, and hundreds of volunteers joined the Wehrmacht. The most notorious collaborator was **Vidkun Quisling**, who was executed by firing squad for his treachery in 1945. When the German army invaded in April 1940, Quisling assumed he would govern the country and made a radio announcement proclaiming his seizure of power. In the event, the Germans soon sidelined him, opting for military control instead, but Quisling's proclamation can be heard at the touch of a button in the museum.

Akershus Slott

Next door to the Resistance Museum, the severe stone walls and twin spires of the medieval **Akershus Slott** (Akershus Castle; May–Aug Mon–Sat 10am–4pm, Sun 12.30–4pm; 65kr including frequent guided tour, out of season 1 guided tour in English weekly, – call ☏ 22 41 25 21 for details) perch on a rocky ridge high above the zigzag fortifications added by Christian IV. The castle is approached through two narrow tunnel-gateways, which lead to a cobbled courtyard at the heart of the castle. So far so good, but thereafter the interior is a bit of a disappointment, mostly comprising a string of sparsely furnished rooms linked by bare-brick passageways. Nevertheless, there are one or two items of interest, primarily the royal crypt, holding the sarcophagi of Norway's current dynasty – not that there have been many of them, just two in fact, Håkon VII (1872–1957) and Olav V (1903–91) – and the royal chapel. Among the castle's assorted halls, the pick is the **Romerikssalen**, worth a few moments for its grand fireplace and Flemish tapestries.

It's also a real surprise to discover that the office of **Henrik Wergeland** (1808–45), who worked in the castle as a royal archivist for the last four years of his life, has survived pretty much undisturbed. Wergeland was one of the most prominent Norwegian poets and dramatists of his day and also an ardent campaigner for greater Norwegian independence. He was, therefore, roundly mocked for accepting the archivist's job – and pension – from the regime he had disparaged and ended up a bitter man: he kept a (fang-less) adder in his office to disconcert the unwary visitor, a not-so-playful reminder of one of his last works, *Vinaegers Fjeldeventyr*, in which the cruellest critic of a poet is so

▲ Akershus fortress

poisonous that a snake dies after it has bit him – and hence the plastic snake in the office today.

Back outside in the courtyard, walk through the first of the tunnel-gateways and then turn left along the **path** running down the side of the castle with the walls pressing in on one side and views out over the harbour on the other. At the foot of the castle, the path swings across a narrow promontory and soon reaches the **footbridge** over Kongens gate. Cross the footbridge for the Forsvarsmuseet (see below), or keep straight for the string of ochre-coloured barrack blocks that lead back to Myntgata (see p.95).

Forsvarsmuseet

On the far side of the Kongens gate footbridge, head southeast across the army parade ground to reach the **Forsvarsmuseet** (Armed Forces Museum; May–Aug Mon–Fri 10am–5pm, Sat & Sun 11am–5pm; Sept–April Mon–Fri 11am–4pm, Sat & Sun 11am–5pm; free), which tracks through Norwegian military history from the early Middle Ages to post war UN peace-keeping. The first floor sets a hectic pace, beginning with a surprisingly cursory look at the Vikings before ploughing on as far as the German invasion of 1940. There's a mildly interesting section on the country's early use of ski troops, but otherwise it's hard to get enthralled by the innumerable wars fought between the Scandinavian countries for obscure dynastic reasons. By contrast, the section on World War II is very detailed and the photographs chosen to illustrate the invasion and occupation are first-rate.

The Operahuset

From the Forsvarsmuseet, it's a short walk back to the main entrance of the Akershus complex at the foot of Kirkegata; keep going straight and after a couple of blocks turn right along Tollbugata to reach one of the elevated walkways that leads over to the waterside opera house, the **Operahuset** (ⓦ www.operaen.no), one of the city's proudest buildings. Home to Den Norske Opera and Ballet, this is a glassy, cubist structure, whose exterior ramps look like extended ski slopes, all to a loquacious design by the Norwegian company, Snøhetta. It is meant to impress, with no expense spared with the interior, and since its opening in 2008 Norwegians have visited in their thousands (Mon–Fri 10am–11pm, Sat 11am–11pm, Sun noon–10pm; free).

Southwest of the centre: the Bygdøy peninsula

Other than the city centre, the place where you're most likely to spend any time in Oslo is the **Bygdøy peninsula**, across the bay to the southwest of the main harbour, where **five museums** make for an absorbing cultural and historical excursion. Indeed, it's well worth spending a full day or, less wearyingly, two half-days here. The most enjoyable way to reach Bygdøy is by **ferry #91**. This leaves from the Rådhusbrygge (pier 3) behind the Rådhus every twenty to thirty minutes (mid-May to Aug daily 8.45am–8.45pm; mid-March to mid-May & Sept to mid-Oct daily 8.45am–6pm; 34kr), returning to a similar schedule. All ferries to the peninsula perform a loop, calling first at the **Dronningen** dock (10min from Rådhusbrygge) and then the **Bygdøynes** dock (15min) before returning to the Rådhusbrygge; note that the ferries only go **one-way** – so there is no service from Bygdøynes to Dronningen. The two most popular attractions – the Viking Ships and Folk museums – are within easy walking distance of the Dronningen dock; the other three are a stone's throw from Bygdøynes. If you decide to walk between the two groups of museums, allow about fifteen minutes: the route is well signposted but dull. The alternative to the ferry is **bus #30** (every 15–30min; 20min), which runs all year from Jernbanetorget and the Nationaltheatret to the Folk Museum and Viking Ships.

Norsk Folkemuseum

The **Norsk Folkemuseum**, about 700m uphill from the Dronningen dock at Museumsveien 10 (Norwegian Folk Museum; mid-May to mid-Sept daily 10am–6pm, 95kr; mid-Sept to mid-May Mon–Fri 11am–3pm, Sat & Sun 11am–4pm, 70kr; ⓦ www.norskfolkemuseum.no), combines indoor collections on folk art, furniture, dress and customs with an extensive open-air display of reassembled buildings, mostly wooden barns, stables, storehouses and dwellings from the seventeenth to the nineteenth centuries. Look out also for the imaginative temporary exhibitions, for which the museum has a well-deserved reputation. Pick up a free **map** of the museum at the entrance.

The complex of buildings just beyond the entry turnstiles holds the museum's indoor collections, both permanent and temporary. Of the former, the **folk art** section on the lower level (of Building B) is delightful, exhibiting samples of handsome carved and painted furniture from the sixteenth century onwards. It's here you'll spot the occasional fancily carved mangle board, whose significance is not at first apparent: these were in fact given by boys to girls as **love gifts** – though quite how a mangle board could be construed as romantic requires a leap of the imagination – and, if the attraction was mutual, the girls gave the boys mittens or gloves. In rural Norway, it was considered improper for courting couples to be seen together during the day, but acceptable (or at least tolerated) at night – and to assist the process parents usually moved girls of marrying age into one of the farm's outhouses, where tokens could be swapped without embarrassment.

On the next floor up, the **folk dress** section is excellent too. Rural customs specified the correct dress for every sort of social gathering, but it's the extravagant and brightly coloured bridal headdresses that grab the eye. The amount of work that went into the creation of the folk costumes was quite extraordinary, although it should be remembered that the exhibits were mostly owned by wealthier Norwegians – many others could barely avoid starvation, never mind indulge in fancy dress.

The **open-air collection** consists of more than 150 reconstructed buildings. Arranged geographically, they provide a marvellous sample of Norwegian rural architecture, somewhat marred by inadequate explanations. That said, it's still worth tracking down the **stave church** (see box, p.187), particularly if you don't plan to travel elsewhere in Norway. Dating from the early thirteenth century but extensively restored in the 1880s, when it was moved here from Gol, near Geilo, the church is a good example of its type, with steep, shingle-covered roofs, dragon finials, an outside gallery and fancily carved doorposts. The interior is cramped and gloomy, the nave preceding a tiny chancel painted with a floral design and sporting a striking *Last Supper* above and behind the altar. Elsewhere, the cluster of buildings from **Setesdal** in southern Norway holds some especially well-preserved dwellings and storehouses from the seventeenth century, while the **Numedal** section contains one of the museum's oldest buildings, a late thirteenth-century house from Rauland whose doorposts are embellished with Romanesque vine decoration.

In **summer**, many of the buildings are open for viewing, and costumed guides roam the site to both explain the vagaries of Norwegian rural life and demonstrate traditional skills, from spinning and carving to dancing and horn blowing.

Vikingskipshuset

From the Norsk Folkemuseum, it's a five-minute walk south along the main road to the **Vikingskipshuset** (Viking Ships Museum; daily: May–Sept 9am–6pm; Oct–April 11am–4pm; 50kr; ⓦwww.khm.uio.no), which occupies a large, cross-shaped hall specially constructed to house a trio of ninth-century Viking ships, with viewing platforms to enable you to see inside the hulls. The three oak vessels were retrieved from ritual burial mounds in southern Norway around the turn of the twentieth century, each embalmed in a subsoil of clay, which accounts for their excellent state of preservation. The size of a Viking **burial mound** denoted the dead person's rank and wealth, while the possessions buried with the body were designed to make the afterlife as comfortable as possible. Implicit was the assumption that a chieftain in this world would be a chieftain in the next – slaves, for example, were frequently killed and buried with their master or mistress – a belief that would subsequently give Christianity, with its alternative, less fatalistic vision, an immediate appeal to those at the bottom of the Viking pile. Quite how the Vikings saw the transfer to the afterlife taking place is less certain. The evidence is contradictory: sometimes the Vikings stuck the anchor on board the burial ship in preparation for the spiritual journey, but at other times the vessels were moored to large stones before burial. Neither was ship burial the only type of Viking funeral – far from it. The Vikings buried their dead in mounds and on level ground, with and without grave goods, in large and small coffins, both with and without boats – and they practised cremation too.

The museum's star exhibits are the Oseberg and Gokstad ships, named after the places on the west side of the Oslofjord where they were discovered in 1904 and 1880 respectively. The first ship you see as you enter the museum, the **Oseberg ship** is, at 22m long and 5m wide, representative of the type of vessel the Vikings used to navigate fjords and coastal waters. The ship has an ornately carved prow and stern, both of which rise high above the hull, where thirty oar-holes indicate the size of the crew. It is thought to be the burial ship of a Viking chieftain's wife and much of the treasure buried with it was retrieved and is now displayed just behind it. The grave goods reveal an attention to detail and a level of domestic sophistication not traditionally associated with the Vikings. There are marvellous decorative items like the fierce-looking animal-head posts and exuberantly carved ceremonial items, including a sled and a cart, plus a host of smaller, more mundane household items such as shoes, rattles, agricultural tools and cooking pots.

Here also are finds from the **Gokstad ship**, most memorably an ornate bridle and two dragonhead bedposts, though the Gokstad burial chamber was ransacked by grave robbers long ago and precious little has survived. The Gokstad ship itself is slightly longer and wider than the Oseberg vessel and is quite a bit sturdier too. Its seaworthiness was demonstrated in 1893 when a replica sailed across the Atlantic to the USA. The third vessel, the **Tune ship**, is the smallest of the nautical trio and only fragments survive; these are displayed unrestored, much as they were discovered in 1867 on the eastern side of the Oslofjord.

The Frammuseet

Just up from the Bygdøynes dock stands the **Gjøa**, the one-time sealing ship in which **Roald Amundsen** (1872–1928) made the first complete sailing of the Northwest Passage in 1906. By any measure, this was a remarkable achievement and the fulfilment of a nautical mission that had preoccupied sailors for several centuries. It took three years, with Amundsen and his crew surviving two ice-bound winters deep in the Arctic, but this epic journey was soon eclipsed when, in 1912, the Norwegian dashed to the South Pole famously just ahead of the ill-starred Captain Scott. The ship that carried Amundsen to within striking distance of the South Pole, the *Fram*, is displayed inside the mammoth triangular display hall that is the **Frammuseet** (Fram Museum; daily: March, April & Oct 10am–4pm, May & Sept 10am–5pm, June–Aug 9am–6pm, Nov–Feb 10am–3pm; 50kr; @www.fram.museum.no). Designed by Colin Archer, a Norwegian shipbuilder of Scots ancestry, and launched in 1892, the *Fram*'s design was unique, its sides made smooth to prevent ice from getting a firm grip on the hull, while inside a veritable maze of beams, braces and stanchions held it all together. Living quarters inside the ship were necessarily cramped, but – in true Edwardian style – the Norwegians found space for a piano.

Look out also for the assorted knick-knacks the explorers took with them, exhibited in the display cases on the uppermost of the **three galleries** that run along the museum's walls. There are maps, a drafts board, notebooks, snowshoes and surgical instruments – but this was as nothing to the equipment carted around by Scott, one of the reasons for his failure. Scott's main mistake, however, was to rely on Siberian ponies to transport his tackle. The animals were useless in Antarctic conditions and Scott and his men ended up pulling the sledges themselves, whereas Amundsen wisely brought a team of huskies. The galleries also detail a number of other polar expeditions and there's a fascinating display on one of Norway's most remarkable men, Fridtjof Nansen (1861–1930), an all-rounder who clocked up an extraordinary range of achievements. In 1895, Nansen made an unsuccessful attempt to reach the North Pole having previously hiked across Greenland. He then proceeded to publish six volumes of scientific observations on the Arctic before championing the cause of an independent Norway – and the break-up of the Norway–Sweden union. Later, he became a leading figure in the League of Nations, running their High

Commission for Refugees and organizing the vital supplies that saved literally millions of Russians from starvation during the famine of 1921–22. He was awarded the Nobel Peace Prize in 1922.

The Kon-Tiki Museet

Across from the Frammuseet, the **Kon-Tiki Museet** (Kon-Tiki Museum; daily: April–May & Sept 10am–5pm; June–Aug 9.30am–5.30pm; Oct–March 10.30am–3.30pm; 50kr; ⓦ www.kon-tiki.no) displays the eponymous balsawood raft on which, in 1947, the Norwegian **Thor Heyerdahl** (1914–2002) made his famous journey across the Pacific from Peru to Polynesia. Heyerdahl wanted to prove the trip could be done: he was convinced that the first Polynesian settlers had sailed from pre-Inca Peru, and rejected prevailing opinions that South American balsa rafts were unseaworthy. Looking at the flimsy raft, you could be forgiven for agreeing with Heyerdahl's doubters – and for wondering how the crew didn't murder each other after a day, never mind several weeks in such a confined space. The whole saga is outlined here in the museum, and if you're especially interested, the story is also told in his book *The Kon-Tiki Expedition*. Heyerdahl went on to attempt several other voyages, sailing across the Atlantic in a papyrus boat, *Ra II*, in 1970, to prove that there could have been contact between Egypt and South America. *Ra II* is also displayed here – indeed it's the first exhibit you come to – and the exploit is recorded in another of Heyerdahl's books, *The Ra Expeditions*. Preoccupied with transoceanic contact between prehistoric peoples, Heyerdahl organized two major archeological expeditions to Easter Island, one in 1955–56 and again in 1986–88. Heyerdahl was keen to demonstrate that there had been contact between the island and the mainland of South America and, although many still dispute his theory, it has now received a degree of acceptance. Perhaps more importantly, Heyerdahl undertook invaluable work in restoring the island's giant statues – the Moai – and the museum gives the low down.

Norsk Sjøfartsmuseum

Across from the Kon-Tiki Museet, the **Norsk Sjøfartsmuseum** (Norwegian Maritime Museum; mid-May to Aug daily 10am–6pm; Sept to mid-May Mon–Wed & Fri–Sun 10.30am–4pm, Thurs 10.30am–6pm; 40kr; ⓦ www .norsk-sjofartsmuseum.no) fills out two buildings, the larger of which is a well-appointed, modern brick structure holding a varied collection of all things nautical. Here, the museum's ground floor is given over to temporary exhibitions and the bulk of the permanent collection is shown on the two floors above. Among much else, the first floor holds pinpoint-accurate ship models, a peculiar-looking fog cannon dating to 1900, a section on shipwrecks, old passenger-ferry cabins, and even part of the deck of an old sailing ship from 1893. The top floor chimes in with more models and the so-called **Gibraltar boat**, a perilously fragile, canvas-and-board home-made craft on which a bunch of Norwegian sailors fled Morocco for British Gibraltar after their ship had been impounded by the Vichy French authorities. Here also is what is reputed to be the oldest surviving Norwegian boat, a **carved-out tree trunk** about two thousand years old.

The museum's second building, the **Båthallen** (boat hall), holds an extensive collection of small and medium-sized wooden boats from all over Norway, mostly inshore sailing and fishing craft from the nineteenth century though, frankly, non-sailors may find it all of limited interest.

West of the centre: the Henie-Onstad Kunstsenter

Overlooking the Oslofjord, some 15km west of the city centre in Høvikodden, the **Henie-Onstad Kunstsenter** (Henie-Onstad Art Centre; Tues–Thurs 11am–7pm & Fri–Sun 11am–5pm; 80kr but free on Wed; ☎67 80 48 80, ⓦwww.hok.no) is one of Norway's more prestigious modern-art centres. There's no false modesty here – it's all about art as an expression of wealth – and the low-slung, modernistic building is a glossy affair on a pretty, wooded headland landscaped to accommodate a smattering of sculptures. The centre was founded by the ice-skater-cum-movie-star **Sonja Henie** (1910–69) and her shipowner-cum-art-collector husband Niels Onstad in the 1960s. Henie won three Olympic gold medals (1928, 1932 and 1936) and went on to appear in a string of lightweight Hollywood musicals. Many of her accumulated cups and medals are displayed in a room of their own, and once prompted a critic to remark: "Sonja, you'll never go broke. All you have to do is hock your trophies." In the basement are the autographed photos of many of the leading celebrities of Sonja's day – though the good wishes of a youthful-looking Richard Milhous Nixon hardly inspire empathy.

The wealthy couple accumulated an extensive collection of twentieth-century painting and sculpture. Matisse, Miró and Picasso, post war French abstract painters, Expressionists and modern Norwegians all feature, but these now compete for gallery space with temporary exhibitions of contemporary art. It is, therefore, impossible to predict what will be on display at any one time – so call ahead for exhibition details. The centre also hosts regular concert and theatre performances. After the museum, be sure to spend a little time wandering the surrounding sculpture park, where you'll see work by the likes of Henry Moore and Arnold Haukeland; plans of the park are available at reception.

Getting there is easy by public transport: bus #151 leaves Oslo S bus terminal every fifteen minutes or so and the journey takes about 25 minutes. You will, however, need to ask the driver to let you off – at the Høvikodden bus stop – or else you'll go whistling past. The Høvikodden stop is beside the main road about five minutes' walk from the Centre. By car, the Kunstsenter is close to – and signposted from – the **E18** road to Drammen.

Northwest of the centre: Frognerparken

The green expanse of **Frognerparken** (Frogner Park), to the northwest of the city centre, incorporates one of Oslo's most celebrated and popular cultural targets, the open-air **Vigelandsparken** which, along with the nearby museum, commemorates a modern Norwegian sculptor of world renown, **Gustav Vigeland** (1869–1943). Between them, the park and the museum display a good proportion of his work, including over two hundred figures in bronze, granite and cast iron, all presented to the city in return for favours received by way of a studio and apartment during the years 1921–30. The park is also home to Frogner Manor, now housing the **Oslo Bymuseum**.

Frogner Park is readily reached from the centre on **tram #12**; one of the places it stops is Aker Brygge: get off at Vigelandsparken, the stop after Frogner plass.

The Vigelandsparken

A country boy, raised on a farm just outside Mandal, on the south coast, **Gustav Vigeland** began his career as a woodcarver but later, when studying in Paris, he fell under the influence of Rodin, and switched to stone, iron and bronze. He started work on the open-air **Vigelandsparken** (daylight hours; free) in 1924, and was still working on it when he died almost twenty years later. It's a literally fantastic concoction, medieval in spirit and complexity, and it was here that Vigeland had the chance to let his imagination run riot. Indeed, when the place was unveiled, many city folk were simply overwhelmed – and no wonder. From the monumental wrought-iron gates on Kirkeveien, the central path takes you to the footbridge over the river and a world of frowning, fighting and posturing bronze figures – the local favourite is *Sinnataggen* (The Angry child), who has been rubbed smooth by a thousand hands. Beyond, the **central fountain** is an enormous bowl representing the burden of life, supported by straining, sinewy bronze Goliaths, and with a cascade of water tumbling down into a pool flanked by figures engaged in play or talk, or simply resting or standing.

Yet it's the twenty-metre-high **obelisk** up on the stepped embankment just beyond that really takes the breath away. It's a deeply humanistic work, a writhing mass of sculpture which depicts the cycle of life as Vigeland saw it: a vision of humanity playing, fighting, teaching, loving, eating and sleeping – and clambering on and over each other to reach the top. The granite sculptures grouped around the obelisk are exquisite too, especially the toddlers, little pot-bellied figures who tumble over muscled adults, providing the perfect foil to the real Oslo children who splash around in the fountain down below.

The Vigeland-museet

From the obelisk, it's a five- to ten-minute walk south (head to the right) across the lawns of the Frognerpark – and over the river by a second footbridge – to the **Vigeland-museet** (Vigeland Museum; June–Aug Tues–Sun 10am–5pm, Sept–May Tues–Sun noon–4pm; 50kr, but free Oct–March; ⓦ www.vigeland .museum.no), on the far side of Halvdan Svartes gate. This was the artist's studio and home during the 1920s, built for him by the city, who let him live here rent free on condition that the building – and its contents – passed back to public ownership on his death. It's still stuffed with all sorts of items related to the sculpture park, including photographs of the workforce, discarded or unused sculptures, woodcuts, preparatory drawings, and scores of plaster casts. Vigeland was obsessed with his creations during his last decades, and you get the feeling that given half a chance he would have had himself cast and exhibited. As it is, his ashes were placed in the museum tower.

Emanuel Vigeland

Gustav Vigeland enthusiasts may be interested in the work of the great man's younger and lesser-known brother, **Emanuel Vigeland** (1875–1948), a respected artist in his own right. His stained-glass windows can be seen in Oslo's Domkirke (see p.81), while the Emanuel Vigeland Museum (Sun only noon–4pm; 30kr; ⓦ www .emanuelvigeland.museum.no), northwest of the city centre at Grimelundsveien 8 (T-bane #1 to Slemdal), has a collection of his frescoes, sculptures, paintings and drawings.

The Oslo Bymuseum

A couple of hundred metres north of the Vigeland-museet, back over Halvdan Svartes gate, the mildly diverting **Oslo Bymuseum** (City Museum; Tues–Sun 11am–4pm; free; Ⓦwww.oslobymuseum.no) is housed in the expansive, eighteenth-century **Frogner Manor**. The buildings are actually rather more interesting than the museum: a central courtyard is bounded on one side by the half-timbered Manor House, complete with its dinky little clocktower, and by antique agricultural buildings on the other three. The **museum** is in one of the latter – the renovated old barn – and it holds a sequence of thematic displays exploring the history of the city. Among many, there are sections on prisons, kitchens, the fire brigade and the police, but it's the paintings and photos of old Oslo and its people that catch the eye.

North of the centre: the Nordmarka

Crisscrossed by **hiking trails** and **cross-country ski routes**, the forested hills and lakes that comprise the **Nordmarka** occupy a tract of land which extends deep inland from central Oslo, but is still within the city limits for some 30km. A network of byroads provides dozens of access points to this wilderness, which is extremely popular with the capital's outdoor-minded citizens. **Den Norske Turistforening (DNT)**, the Norwegian hiking organization, maintains a handful of staffed and unstaffed huts here. Its Oslo branch, in the city centre at Storgata 3 (Mon–Fri 10am–5pm, Thurs 10am–6pm, Sat 10am–3pm; ☎22 82 28 22, Ⓦwww.dntoslo.no), has detailed **maps** and can sell a year's DNT member-ship for 480kr, which confers a substantial discount at its huts; see the *Hiking* colour section for more on DNT and hiking in general.

Frognerseteren and Holmenkollen

T-bane #1 delves deep into the Nordmarka, wriggling its way up into the hills to the **Frognerseteren terminus**, a thirty-minute ride north of the city centre. From the station, it's just a couple of hundred metres to **Frognerse-teren** (Mon–Sat 11am–10pm, Sun 11am–9pm; ☎22 92 40 40), a large and good-looking wooden lodge, where the views from the terrace out over Oslo and the Oslofjord are much more enjoyable than the food. From the T-bane terminus, there's also a choice of signposted trails across the surrounding countryside. **Forest footpaths** link Frognerseteren with Sognsvannet to the east (see p.103), an arduous and not especially rewarding trek over the hills of about 5km. Locals mostly shun this route in summer, but it's really popular in winter with parents teaching their children to cross-country ski. There is a longer and more interesting hiking route to Sognsvannet via **Ullevålseter**, where the lodge (Tues–Sun 9am–5pm, July Tues–Sun 10am–4pm; ☎22 14 35 58, Ⓦwww.ullevalseter.no) has a very good café serving excellent home-made apple cake. The whole route is about 9km long, and takes about three hours.

Alternatively, you can hop back onto the T-bane to make the five-stop return journey to the flashy chalets and hotels of the **Holmenkollen ski resort**, whose main claim to fame is its international **ski-jump** – a gargantuan affair that dwarfs its surroundings about 1km or so from the T-bane station. A mountain of metal steps leads up to the top of the ski-jump from where the view down is, for most people, horrifyingly steep. It seems impossible that the tiny bowl at the bottom could pull the skier up in time – or that anyone could possibly want to jump off in the first place. The bowl is also the finishing point for the 8000-strong cross-country skiing race that forms part of the Holmenkoll-rennene ski festival every March. Oslo's largest ski centre, the newly expanded **Tryvann Vinterpark** (Tryvann Winter Park; ⓦwww.tryvann.no), lies to the north of Holmenkollen – and to the northwest of the Frognerseteren T-bane terminus. It has no fewer than fourteen slopes and seven ski lifts, and its facilities are bang up to date; snow permitting, it's open from December to April.

From Holmenkollen T-bane station (line #1), it's a twenty-minute ride back to central Oslo.

Sognsvannet

It takes fifteen minutes for T-bane #3 to reach its northerly **Sognsvann terminus** from central Oslo. It's not as pleasant a journey as the T-bane trip to Frognerseteren (see p.104) – the landscape is flatter and you never really leave the city behind – but from the T-bane terminus, it's just five-minutes' walk straight ahead down the slope to **Sognsvannet**, an attractive loch flanked by forested hills and encircled by an easy four-kilometre hiking trail. The lake is iced over until the end of March or early April, but thereafter it's a perfect spot for swimming, though Norwegian assurances about the warmth of the water should be treated with caution. Forest footpaths link Sognsvannet with Frognerseteren (see p.104).

Northeast of the centre: the Munch-museet

Nearly everyone who visits Oslo makes time for the **Munch-museet** (Munch Museum; June–Aug daily 10am–6pm; Sept–May Tues–Fri 10am–4pm, Sat & Sun 11am–5pm; 75kr; ⓦwww.munch.museum.no) – and with good reason. In his will, Munch donated all the works in his possession to Oslo city council, a mighty bequest of several thousand paintings, prints, drawings, engravings and photographs, which took nearly twenty years to catalogue and organize before being displayed in this purpose-built gallery. The museum has, however, had its problems: in August 2004, two armed **robbers** marched into the museum and, in full view of dozens of bemused visitors, lifted two Munch paintings – the *Madonna* and *The Scream*, his most famous work, though fortunately Munch painted several versions (the earliest is in the Nasjonalgalleriet, see p.88). As if this wasn't bad enough, further embarrassments followed: it turned out that the paintings were not alarmed and neither were they especially secure, only being attached to the wall by a cord. The two works of art were finally recovered two years later and, in a classic case of closing the stable door after the horse has bolted, the gallery has beefed up its security, though plans are afoot to close it down and move the collection to central Oslo.

The museum is located to the northeast of the city centre in the workaday suburb of Tøyen, at Tøyengata 53. Getting there by public transport couldn't be easier: take the T-bane to Tøyen station and it's a signposted, five-minute walk.

The collection

The Munch-museet's **permanent collection** is huge, and only a small – but always significant – part can be shown at any one time. Consequently, the paintings are frequently rotated and the museum also sources a lively programme of temporary exhibitions concentrating on various aspects of Munch's work. Naturally, all this means that you can't be certain what will be displayed and when, but the key paintings mentioned below are almost bound to be on view. At the start of the museum, an illustrated, potted biography of Munch and a short film on his life and times sets the scene.

The landscapes and domestic scenes of Munch's **early paintings**, such as *Tête à Tête* and *At the Coffee Table*, reveal the perceptive if deeply pessimistic realism from which Munch's later work sprang. Even more riveting are the great works of the **1890s**, which form the core of the collection and are considered Munch's finest achievements. Among many, there's *Dagny Juel*, a portrait of the Berlin socialite Ducha Przybyszewska, with whom both Munch and Strindberg were infatuated; the searing representations of *Despair* and *Anxiety*; the chilling *Red Virginia Creeper*, a house being consumed by the plant; and, of course, *The Scream* – of which the museum holds several versions.

Munch's style was never static, however. **Later paintings** such as *Workers On Their Way Home* (1913), produced after he had recovered from his breakdown and had withdrawn to the tranquillity of the Oslofjord, reflect his renewed interest in nature and physical work. His technique also changed: in works like the *Death of Marat II* (1907) he began to use streaks of colour to represent points

Edvard Munch

Born in 1863, **Edvard Munch** had a melancholy childhood in what was then Christiania (Oslo). His early years were overshadowed by the early deaths of both his mother and a sister from tuberculosis, as well as the fierce Christian piety of his father. After some early works, including several self-portraits, he went on to study in **Paris**, a city he returned to again and again, and where he fell (fleetingly) under the sway of the Impressionists in general and Gauguin in particular, responding to his simplified forms and non-naturalistic colours. In 1892 he moved to **Berlin**, where his style developed and he produced some of his best and most famous work, though his first exhibition there was considered so outrageous it was closed after only a week – his painting was, a critic opined, "an insult to art": his recurrent themes, notably jealousy, sickness, alienation and the awakening of sexual desire, all of which he had extrapolated from his childhood, were simply too much for his early audience. Despite the initial criticism, Munch's work was subsequently exhibited in many of the leading galleries of the day. Generally considered the initiator of the **Expressionist** movement, Munch wandered Europe, painting and exhibiting prolifically. Meanwhile overwork, drink and problematic love affairs were fuelling an instability that culminated, in 1908, in a **nervous breakdown**. Munch spent six months in a Copenhagen clinic, after which his health improved greatly – and his paintings lost the hysterical edge characteristic of his most celebrated work – though he never dismissed the importance of his mental frailness to his art, writing, for example, "I would not cast off my illness, for there is much in my art that I owe to it."

Munch returned to Norway in 1909 and was based there until his death in 1944. He wasn't, however, a popular figure in his homeland despite – or perhaps because of – his high international profile and he was regularly criticized in the press for all manner of alleged faults, from miserliness to artistic arrogance. Neither was his posthumous reputation enhanced by the **state funeral** organized for him by the occupying Germans, his coffin paraded up Karl Johans gate in a cortege of guns, eagles and swastikas. To be fair, Munch had certainly not wanted a fascist funeral and neither was he sympathetic to the Germans, who he feared would end up confiscating his paintings and burning them as "degenerate" art – as they nearly did.

For an in-depth examination of Munch's life and times, read Sue Prideaux's comprehensive *Edvard Munch: Behind the Scream*.

of light. Later still, paintings such as *Winter in Kragerø* and *Model by the Wicker Chair*, with skin tones of pink, green and blue, begin to reveal a happier, if rather idealized, attitude to his surroundings, though this is most evident in works like *Spring Ploughing*, painted in 1919.

Look out also for Munch's **self-portraits**, which provide a graphic illustration of the artist's state of mind at various points in his life. There's a palpable sadness in his *Self-Portrait with Wine Bottle* (1906), along with obvious allusions to his heavy drinking, while the telling perturbation of *In Distress* (1919) and *The Night Wanderer* (1923) indicates that he remained a tormented, troubled man even in his later years. One of his last works, *Self-Portrait by the Window* (1940), shows a glum figure on the borderline between life and death, the strong red of his face and green of his clothing contrasted with the ice-white scene visible through the window.

Munch's **lithographs and woodcuts**, of which the museum owns several hundred, are a dark catalogue of swirls and fogs, technically brilliant pieces of work and often developments of his paintings rather than just simple copies. In these he pioneered a new medium of expression, experimenting with colour schemes and a huge variety of materials, which enhance the works' rawness: wood blocks show a heavy, distinct grain, while there are colours like rust and blue drawn from the Norwegian landscape. As well as the stark woodcuts on display, there are also sensuous, hand-coloured lithographs, many focusing on the theme of love (taking the form of a woman) bringing death.

East of the centre: medieval Oslo and prehistoric rock carvings

Founded in the middle of the eleventh century by Harald Hardrada (see p.397), **medieval Oslo** lay tucked beneath the Ekeberg heights at the mouth of the River Alna, some 3km round the fjord to the east of today's city centre. The old town, which had a population of around 3000 by the early fourteenth century, had two palaces – one for the bishop and one for the king – reflecting the uneasy division of responsibility that dogged its history. The settlement was also plagued by fires, which ripped through the wooden buildings with depressing regularity. After one such conflagration in 1624, **Christian IV** moved the city to its modern location and what remained of old Oslo became an insignificant outpost. In successive centuries the traces of the medieval town were almost entirely obliterated, and only recently has there been any attempt to identify the original layout of what is commonly called the **Gamlebyen** (Old Town). There are precious few fragments to see, but they're just about worth seeking out when combined with a peek at a group of nearby prehistoric **rock carvings**.

The rock carvings

From Jernbanetorget, it's a ten-minute tram ride (#18 or #19) east up to the old **Sjømannsskolen** (Merchant Marine Academy) – now a business school – housed in a large and conspicuous building perched high on a hill. The tram stops opposite the academy, whose fjord-facing terrace offers some of the most extensive views in Oslo, stretching all the way across the inner reaches of the Oslofjord to the Holmenkollen ski-jump. To the rear of the academy, a narrow drive – Karlsborgveien – leads downhill into a little dell. Here, a few metres down on the left-hand side, you'll spot a group of faded ochre **rock carvings** depicting elk, deer and matchstick people, around six thousand years old and the earliest evidence of settlement along the Oslofjord.

The Gamlebyen

Walking back down from the academy along Kongsveien and then Oslo gate, it takes about fifteen minutes to reach the junction of Bispegata at the heart of the **Gamlebyen**. On the corner is the **Ladegård**, a comely eighteenth-century mansion built on the site of the thirteenth-century Bishop's Palace, whose foundations are underneath. On the other side of Oslo gate are the battered foundations of St Hallvardskatedralen (St Halvard's Cathedral), with St Olavsklosteret (St Olav's Monastery) just behind.

South of the centre: the islands and beaches of the inner Oslofjord

The compact archipelago of low-lying, lightly forested **islands** to the south of the city centre in the **inner Oslofjord** is the capital's summer playground, and makes going to the **beach** a viable option, especially on warm summer evenings when the less populated islands become favourite party venues for the city's youth. **Ferries** to the islands leave from the Vippetangen quay, at the foot of Akershusstranda – a twenty-minute walk or a five-minute ride on bus #60 from Jernbanetorget. Ferry tickets cost 34kr each way, though Oslo Pass and all other transport passes are valid and there's also a ferry day-pass (Øybilletten) allowing unlimited inter-island travel for 40kr. There's an automatic ticket machine at the Vippetangen quay.

Hovedøya

Conveniently, **Hovedøya** (ferry #92; daily: late May to Aug 7.30am–11pm hourly; mid-March to late May & Sept to mid-Oct 7.30am–6.30pm, every hour to ninety minutes; Oct to mid-March 4–5 daily; 5min), the nearest island, is also the most interesting. Its rocky, rolling hills comprise both pastureland and deciduous woods as well as the substantial ruins of a **Cistercian monastery** built by English monks in the twelfth century. There are also incidental remains from the days when the island was garrisoned and armed to protect Oslo's harbour. A map of the island at the jetty helps with orientation, but on an islet of this size – it's just ten minutes' walk from one end to the other – getting lost is pretty much impossible. There are plenty of footpaths to wander, you can swim at the shingle beaches on the south shore, and there's a seasonal café opposite the monastery ruins. Camping, however, is not permitted as Hovedøya is a protected area, which is also why there are no summer homes.

Langøyene

The pick of the other islands is **Langøyene**, a pint-sized, H-shaped islet, just ten-minutes' walk or so from one side to the other, where a central meadow is flanked on either side by low, lightly forested rocky hills. There are no houses on the island and no roads to speak of, but there is a long and narrow sandy(ish) beach, plus a rudimentary café, though most visitors bring their own supplies, especially those who camp here – there's no campsite as such but wilderness camping is permitted and quite a few visitors do just that. To get to Langøyene, take ferry #94 (late May to Aug hourly 9am–7/8pm; 15min) from the Vippetangen quay.

Eating and drinking

There was a time when eating out in Oslo hardly set the pulse racing, but things are very different today. At the top end of the market, the city possesses dozens of fine **restaurants**, the pick of which feature Norwegian ingredients, especially fresh North Atlantic fish, but also more exotic dishes of elk, caribou and salted-and-dried cod – for centuries Norway's staple food. Many of these restaurants have also assimilated the tastes and **styles** of other cuisines and there is a reasonable selection of less-expensive foreign restaurants too, everything from Italian to Vietnamese.

Even more affordable – and more casual – are the city's **cafés and café-bars**. These run the gamut from homely family places, offering traditional Norwegian stand-bys, to student haunts and ultra-trendy joints. Nearly all serve inexpensive lunches, and many offer excellent, competitively priced evening meals as well, though some cafés close at around 5pm or 6pm as do the city's many **coffee houses**, where coffee is, as you might expect, the main deal alongside maybe a light snack. Downtown Oslo also boasts a vibrant **bar** scene, boisterous but generally good-natured and at its most frenetic at summer weekends, when the city is crowded with visitors from all over Norway.

Finally, those carefully counting the kroner will find it easy to buy bread, fruit, snacks and sandwiches from stalls, supermarkets and kiosks across the city centre, while fast-food joints offering hamburgers and *warme pølser* (hot dogs; 20–25kr) are legion. **Smoking** is forbidden inside every Norwegian bar, café and restaurant – hence the smoky huddles outside.

Cafés, café-bars and coffee houses

For sit-down food, **cafés** often represent the best value in town. Traditional *kafeterias* (usually self-service) offer substantial portions of Norwegian food in pleasant surroundings, though they are becoming thin on the ground. Oslo also has a slew of **café-bars** dishing up salads, pasta and the like in attractive, often modish premises. The best deals here are generally at lunchtime, when there's often a dish of the day. In addition, Oslo now holds dozens of specialist **coffee houses**, both independent and chains.

As for **opening hours**, most of the cafés listed below close between 5pm and 7pm, while the café-bars stay open much later, till midnight and often beyond. The coffee houses tend to close between 5pm and 7pm on weekdays, and around 5pm at weekends, though many are closed on Sundays altogether.

Downtown

Celsius Café Rådhusgata 19. Smashing café-bar occupying imaginatively refurbished old premises just off the cobbled square at the junction of Rådhusgata and Nedre Slottsgate. Especially attractive courtyard seating too – for either a drink or a light meal: the menu is strong on beef and seafood, with a home-made burger, for instance, costing 140kr. Daily 11am–midnight.

Kaffebrenneriet 45 Grensen at Akersgata. One of the most central branches of this popular Norwegian coffee-house chain. Serves particularly good espresso, as well as snacks and cakes. Bright, modern decor. Mon–Fri 7am–7pm, Sat 9am–5pm.

Kaffistova Rosenkrantz gate 8. Part of the *Hotell Bondeheimen* (see p.78), this spick-and-span self-service café serves quite tasty, traditional Norwegian cooking at very fair prices – reckon on

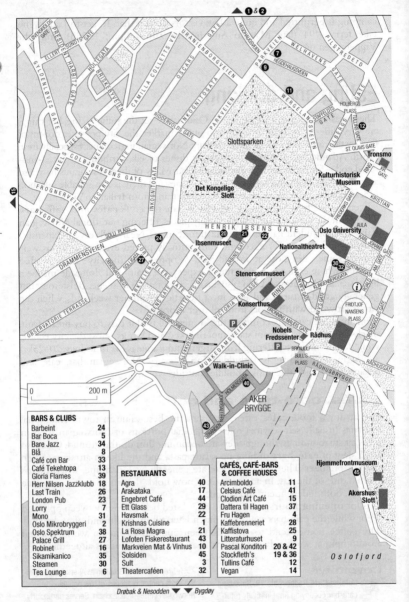

▲ **❶** & **❷**

Slottsparken

Det Kongelige
Slott

HENRIK IBSENS GATE

Ibsenmuseet

Stenersenmuseet

Konserthus

Nobels
Fredssenter

Walk-in-Clinic

AKER
BRYGGE

Kulturhistorisk
Museum

Tronsmo

Oslo University

AULA

Nationaltheatret

Rådhus

Hjemmefrontmuseum

Akershus
Slott

Oslofjord

0   200 m

BARS & CLUBS

Barbeint	24
Bar Boca	5
Bare Jazz	34
Blå	8
Café con Bar	33
Café Tekehtopa	13
Gloria Flames	39
Herr Nilsen Jazzklubb	18
Last Train	26
London Pub	23
Lorry	7
Mono	31
Oslo Mikrobryggeri	2
Oslo Spektrum	38
Palace Grill	27
Robinet	16
Sikamikanico	35
Steamen	30
Tea Lounge	6

RESTAURANTS

Agra	40
Arakataka	17
Engebret Café	44
Ett Glass	29
Havsmak	22
Krishnas Cuisine	1
La Rosa Magra	21
Lofoten Fiskerestaurant	43
Markveien Mat & Vinhus	10
Solsiden	45
Sult	3
Theatercaféen	32

**CAFÉS, CAFÉ-BARS
& COFFEE HOUSES**

Arcimboldo	11
Celsius Café	41
Clodion Art Café	15
Dattera til Hagen	37
Fru Hagen	4
Kaffebrenneriet	28
Kaffistova	25
Litteraturhuset	9
Pascal Konditori	20 & 42
Stockfleth's	19 & 36
Tullins Café	12
Vegan	14

Drøbak & Nesodden ▼ ▼ Bygdøy

130kr for a main course. Meatballs, gravy and
potatoes are the house speciality. There's usually a
vegetarian option, too. Mon–Fri 10am–9pm, Sat &
Sun 11am–7pm.

Pascal Konditori Tollbugata 11. Lovely little
café-patisserie comprising two rooms – one
pleasantly modern, the other in the original bakery,

which is decorated with ceramic tiles of cherubs
and fruit dating from the 1890s. Mouthwatering
pastries, great coffee and delicious, freshly-
prepared lunches – the fish soup is, for example,
first-rate and costs 120kr. Mon–Sat 10am–5pm.
Also in smart, modern premises at Henrik Ibsens
gate 36 (Mon–Sat 10am–5pm & Sun noon–5pm).

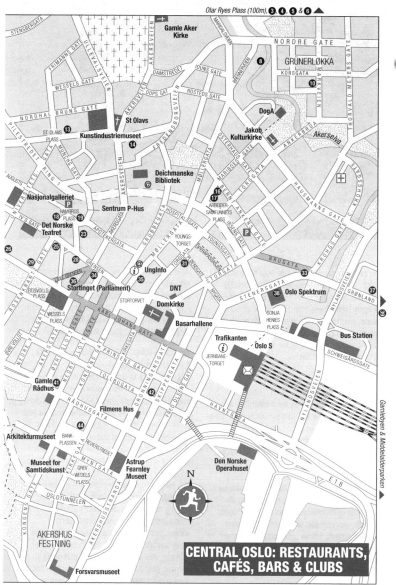

CENTRAL OSLO: RESTAURANTS, CAFÉS, BARS & CLUBS

▼ Ferry to Hovedøya & Langøyene; DFDS & Stena ferries to Denmark   Sjømannsskolen ▼

🏃 **Stockfleth's** Lille Grensen, off Karl Johans gate. With good reason, many locals swear by the coffee served at this small chain, which regularly wins awards for its brews. Also on CJ Hambros plass and at Prinsens gate 6. Lille Grensen hours: Mon–Fri 7am–7pm, Sat 10am–6pm & Sun noon–6pm.

Tullins Café Tullins gate 2. The building may be glum – it's a dull modern high-rise – but this ground-floor café-bar is painted in exuberant modern style and furnished with an idiosyncratic mix of bygones. Pasta dishes are the mainstay here – reckon on 100kr per main course – and there's inexpensive beer (at least inexpensive by Norwegian standards)

▲ Clodion Art Café

as the place morphs into a late-night bar. Handy central location too. Mon–Thurs 10am–2am, Fri 10am–3.30am, Sat noon–3.30am & Sun noon–1am.

Vegan Thor Olsens gate. Simple and straightforward, ground-floor café in an old Oslo apartment block with a good range of vegan dishes. Mains 100–130kr. Sun–Thurs 11am–9pm & Fri 11am–8pm; closed Sat.

Westside

Arcimboldo Wergelandsveien 17. Fashionable but unpretentious café-bar on the ground floor and adjoining terrace of the Kunstnernes Hus, an artist-run gallery whose Art Deco facade faces the Slottsparken. Offers good-quality food with a Norwegian slant, with main courses 140–240kr. Tues–Thurs 11am–11.30pm, Fri 11am–2.30am, Sat noon–1.30am & Sun noon–6pm.

Clodion Art Café Bygdøy Allé 63, but entrance round the corner on Thomas Heftyes gate. Well to the west of the city centre, not far from Frognerparken, this café-bar, with its brightly painted furniture, hosts regular art displays and serves good, basic food: pasta dishes at around 140kr, burgers 130kr. Open Mon–Sat 11am–midnight & Sun 11am–10.30pm, but kitchen closes about 9pm. Bus #30, or #31 from the centre.

Litteraturhuset Wergelandsveien 29. Opposite the tail end of the Slottsparken, this

most amenable café-bar-cum-bookshop spreads its net wide with poetry readings and book signings as well as a café and outside terrace. Light meals here – the salads are good – will cost you around 150kr. The café-bar is open Mon–Wed 10am–midnight, Thurs & Fri 10am–3.30am, Sun noon–8pm.

Eastside: Grønland and Grünerløkka

Dattera til Hagen Grønland 10. Extremely popular spin-off venture of *Fru Hagen* (see below), serving tasty snacks and light meals during the daytime (11am–4pm) and authentic tapas later on (4–10pm). Later still, the place turns into a happening bar with live DJs on the first floor (Mon–Sat). The outdoor area at the back is great on a hot summer's night. Mon–Thurs 11am–1am, Fri & Sat 11am–3am, Sun noon–1am.

Fru Hagen Thorvald Meyers gate 40, Grünerløkka. Long-standing, colourful joint; still trendy, and serving tasty snacks and meals from an inventive menu with a Mediterranean slant. Filling sandwiches, salads and wok-cooked dishes too. Main courses 100–150kr. The kitchen closes at 9.30pm, after which the drinking gets going in earnest, plus DJ guest spots Thurs through Sat. Very popular spot – so go early to be sure of a seat. Mon–Wed 11am–midnight, Thurs–Sat 11am–3am, Sun noon–midnight.

Restaurants

Dining out at one of Oslo's **restaurants** can make a sizeable dent in your wallet unless you exercise some restraint. In most places, a main course will set you back between 150kr and 240kr – not too steep until you add on a couple of beers or a bottle of wine. On a more positive note, Oslo's better restaurants have creative menus marrying Norwegian culinary traditions with those of the Mediterranean – and a lousy meal is a rarity. Restaurant decor is often a real feature too, ranging from fishing photos and nets to sharp modernist styles, all pastel walls and angular furnishings. Advance **reservations** are a good idea almost everywhere, especially at the weekend.

Downtown

Agra Holmens gate, Aker Brygge ☎22 83 07 12. Smart, North Indian restaurant serving all the classics – chicken tikka and so forth – with main courses averaging 210–250kr. Decorated in traditional style, from the Moghul prints to the mini-chandeliers. The only problem is that it is a little difficult to find: take the first right – Grundigen – go up the right-hand side of the Aker Brygge complex, turn left through the old factory gates and you are there. Mon–Sat 4–11pm, Sun 4–10pm.

Arakataka Mariboes gate 7 ☎23 32 83 00. This smart, modern bar and restaurant serves excellent food, mostly fish and meat, at unbeatable prices, both à la carte (mains average 180kr) and with a set three-course menu for just 290kr. Highly recommended, and a good place to sample that old Norwegian favourite, salted cod (bacalao), when it is on the menu, though the service can be a tad patchy. A 15min walk north of the Domkirke on the way to Grünerløkka. Sun–Thurs 4pm to midnight, Fri & Sat 4pm–3am.

Engebret Café Bankplassen 1 ☎22 82 25 25. Across from the Museum of Contemporary Art, this smart and fairly formal restaurant occupies a fetching old building with oodles of wood panelling and old oil paintings on the walls. Specializes in Norwegian delicacies such as reindeer and fish, with mouthwatering main courses in the region of 250–300kr, less at lunchtime, though the sauces can be a little heavy for some tastes. Reservations advised. In summer, there's seating outside on the pretty cobbled square. Mon–Fri 11am–11pm, Sat 1–10pm.

Havsmak Henrik Ibsens gate 4 ☎24 13 38 00. Smart, specialist seafood restaurant kitted out in cool modern style – and oodles of blue paint. First-rate range of fresh fish, albeit of minimalist portions, with main courses averaging 200kr. Set meals too – two courses for 300kr, 490kr with wine. Mon–Sat 11am–11pm & Sun noon–10pm.

La Rosa Magra Arbins gate 1 ☎22 56 14 00. Bright, modern and cheerful, this first-rate Italian restaurant has a short(ish) but well-chosen menu featuring fresh pastas (130–180kr) and a handful of meat and fish dishes (220–240kr). Exemplary service; delicious, unpretentious food; and no pizzas. On the corner of Henrik Ibsens gate. Mon–Sat 3–11pm & Sun 3–10pm.

Lofoten Fiskerestaurant Stranden 75, Aker Brygge ☎22 83 08 08. This smart, modern restaurant offers an outstanding selection of fish and shellfish, all immaculately prepared and served. It's beside the harbour at the far end of the Aker Brygge jetty, which makes it popular with locals and tourists alike. Mains kick off at around 260kr, but some of the more unusual fish – including the wonderfully textured cat fish (*steinbit*) cost another 90kr or so. Mon–Sat 11am–1am & Sun noon–midnight.

Solsiden Søndre Akershus Kai 34 ☎22 33 36 30. Tucked in below the Akershus castle, right on the harbourside, this lively and relaxed restaurant specializes in seafood, which is generally reckoned to be as good as anywhere in Oslo – try the turbot in a mustard purée. The emphasis is on natural, organic ingredients and the place has its own lobster tank. A three-course set meal costs 450kr, à la carte mains from 270kr. Open May–Aug only, daily 5–10pm.

Theatercaféen at The Hotel Continental Stortingsgata 24–26 ☎22 82 40 50. This handsome restaurant, with its long mirrors, vaulted ceiling and marble pillars, has been pulling in the city's movers and shakers for decades. The food is traditional Norwegian – nothing too fancy with main courses like reindeer with dauphinoise potatoes and broccoli costing 250–300kr. Mon–Sat noon–11pm & Sun 5–10pm.

Westside

Krishnas Cuisine Kirkeveien 59B ☎22 60 62 50. One of the city's best vegetarian restaurants, where the always tasty and filling *dagens rett* (daily special) costs a very economical 110kr. Just east of Bogstadveien and the briefest of walks from the Majorstuen T-bane station. Mon–Sat noon–8pm.

Eastside: Grønland and Grünerløkka

Markveien Mat & Vinhus Torvbakkgata 12, Grünerløkka ☎22 37 22 97. This popular, top-quality restaurant and wine bar serves up Mediterranean-inspired dishes as well as traditional Norwegian favourites. Main courses average 150–200kr in the restaurant, half that in the wine bar, and the service is excellent. Also boasts one of the best wine cellars in the city. The entrance is on Markveien. Restaurant:

113

Mon–Sat 5pm–12.30am, but kitchen closes at
11pm. Wine bar, Mon–Sat 4pm–1am.
Sult Thorvald Meyers gate 26, Grünerløkka
☏22 87 04 67. One of the city's most popular
restaurants – its name means "Hunger", after the
novel by Knut Hamsun – the informal, fashionable
but very relaxed *Sult* features a short but inventive

menu using only the freshest of (local) ingredients.
Main courses cost 180–200kr and star such
delights as Hardanger trout and chicken from
Stange. As if that wasn't enough, the adjacent bar
Tørst (Thirst) serves mouthwatering margaritas.
Sult kitchen open Tues–Thurs 4–10pm, Fri
4–11pm, Sat 1–11pm & Sun 1–10pm.

Bars

Bar-hopping in Oslo is an enjoyable affair. The more mainstream (meat-market) bars are in the centre along and around Karl Johans gate, while the sharper, more alternative spots are concentrated to the east in the Grønland and Grünerløkka districts. The westside of the city has its chic spots too, mostly along and around Hegdehaugsveien and Bogstadveien. Most city bars stay **open** until around 1am on weekdays, often 3–4am at the weekend, and almost all of them are open daily. Drinks are uniformly expensive, so if you're after a big night out, it's a good idea to follow Norwegian custom and have a few warm-up drinks at home before you set out (*vorspiel* in Norwegian). A number of bars feature **live music**, blurring the lines between the "bars" listed here and the "clubs" listed on p.115.

Central

Café Tekehtopa St Olavs plass 2. 'Tekehtopa' is
'Apotheket' (pharmacy) spelt backwards – an
appropriate little verbal play as this busy bar, which
attracts a student crew, occupies a former
pharmacy, complete with the original wooden
fittings. There's a wide range of beers on draft and
in bottles – look out for the ales of the microbrewery Nøgne Ø – plus inexpensive pizzas, salads,
omelettes and so forth. Mon–Thurs 10am–1am, Fri
10am–3am, Sat noon–3am & Sun noon–1am;
kitchen closes at 11pm.
Steamen Olavs gate 2. Owned by the *Hotel
Continental* (see p.78), this bright and lively sidewalk
bar, with its nautical paraphernalia, is popular with
the young(ish) and well-heeled. Mon noon–midnight,
Tues–Sat noon–2.30am, & Sun noon–midnight.

Westside

Lorry Parkveien 12. Popular and enjoyable bar with
old-fashioned (verging on the eccentric) fixtures
and fittings that attracts a mixed crowd. There's a
wide choice of beers – well over a hundred – and
outdoor seating in the summer. Also serves food. At
the corner of Hegdehaugsveien. Mon–Sat 11am–
3.30am, Sun noon–1.30am.
Oslo Mikrobryggeri Bogstadveien 6 – but
entrance on Holtegata. Dark, almost gloomy bar
with loud music and a dart board plus a tasty
range of ales, the pick of which are brewed on the
premises – the equipment is in full view. Mon–Sat
noon–3.30am, Sun noon–1.30am.

Palace Grill Solligata 2. Popular New Age-
meets-alternative café-bar with a roots, rock
and jazz soundtrack. Good food too. Mon 5pm–
12.30am, Tues–Sat 5pm–3am & Sun
5pm–12.30am. In summertime, there's an outside
bar, *Skaugum*, in the yard behind and beside the
Palace – and it heaves.

Eastside: Grønland and Grünerløkka

Bar Boca Thorvald Meyers gate 30, Grünerløkka.
Tiny 1950s retro-style bar serving some of the best
cocktails in town. The bartenders take their work
very seriously, and you need to get there early to
avoid the crush. Live jazz once or twice weekly.
Daily noon–3am.
Café con Bar Brugata 11, Grønland. Hip-as-you-
like with retro interior and a long bar that can
make buying a drink hard work. Good atmosphere,
loungy decor and unisex toilets for those surprise
meetings. Mon–Thurs 11am–11pm, Fri & Sat
11am–3am, Sun noon–11pm.
Robinet Mariboes gate 7. Possibly the smallest bar
in Oslo – 1950s retro kitsch combined with
excellent drinks and an intellectual crowd. Daily
noon–2am.
Tea Lounge Thorvald Meyers gate 33B. Lounge-
type café-bar with velvety red couches and big
windows. As you might guess from the name, tea
is a big deal here – all sorts and served to a soft
house backtrack. Cocktails also. Mon–Wed 11am–
1am, Thurs–Sat 11am–3pm & Sun noon–2am.

Entertainment and nightlife

With the city's bars staying open till the wee hours, Oslo's **nightclubs** struggle to make themselves heard – indeed there's often little distinction between the two – though there is still a reasonably good and varied nightclub scene. **Live music** is not perhaps Oslo's forte, and the domestic **rock** scene is far from inspiring, but **jazz** fans are well served, with a couple of first-rate venues in the city centre, and **classical music** enthusiasts benefit from an ambitious concert programme. Most **theatre** productions are in Norwegian, but English-language theatre companies visit often, and at the **cinema** films are shown in the original language with Norwegian subtitles.

For **entertainment listings** it's worth checking out *What's On Oslo*, a monthly English-language freebie produced by the tourist office. One other useful free publication is *Streetwise*, which is produced annually by Use-It, the city's youth information shop (see p.75); it carries descriptions of – amongst much else – the city's best bars and clubs. The nattiest website is ⓦwww .nattguiden.no, but it's only in Norwegian.

For **tickets**, contact the venue direct or try Billettservice (☏815 33 133, ⓦwww.billettservice.no), who use thirty of the city's post offices as outlets – details are on the website.

Nightclubs and live music

Oslo's hippest bars and **nightclubs** are located on the east side of the city, away from the centre in or near the Grønland and Grünerløkka districts, but there are also several clubs in the centre and out west. Nothing gets going much before 11pm and closing times are generally around 3.30am. Many nightclubs also host a variety of **live music**, ranging from local home-grown talent to big-name bands. Generally speaking, entry will set you back about 100kr and at the smarter places there's an informal dress code – go scruffy and you will be turned away.

Barbeint Henrik Ibsens gate 60 ☏95 06 46 86, ⓦwww.barbeint-oslo.no. If you're familiar with Scandinavian bands and films, you may recognize a few faces in this jam-packed, infinitely groovy bar with heavy drapes and mystery-making decor. Loud sounds – everything from rap to rock. On the west side of the city centre close to Parkveien. Thurs–Sat 11pm–3am.

Blå Brenneriveien 9C ☏40 00 42 77, ⓦwww .blx.no. Creative, cultural nightspot in Grünerløkka, featuring everything from live jazz and cabaret through to poetry readings. Also features some of the best DJs in town, keeping the crowd moving until 3.30am at the weekend. In summer, there's a pleasant riverside terrace too.

Gloria Flames Grønland 18 ☏22 17 16 00, ⓦwww.gloriaflames.no. Not the easiest bar-cum-club to find – there's just a small sign on the door – but worth searching out if you're into rock and rockabilly. Regular live acts and a summer rooftop bar. Mon–Thurs 4pm–1.30am, Fri & Sat 3pm–3.30am.

Last Train Karl Johans gate 45 ☏22 41 52 93, ⓦwww.lasttrain.no. The best rock-pub/club in town. Good old-style rock played at volume to a leather and jeans clientele. Entrance downtown on Universitetsgata. Mon–Fri 3pm–3.30am, Sat 6pm–3.30am.

Mono Pløens gate 4 ☏22 41 41 66, ⓦwww .cafemono.no. Darkly lit bar with retro fixtures and fittings that attracts a student crowd, who appreciate the live acts on several nights a week; diverse DJ sounds, too. Pløens gate is off Torggata, north of Oslo S. Mon–Sat 11pm–3am, Sun 6pm–3am.

Oslo Spektrum Sonja Henies plass 2 ☏815 11 211, ⓦwww.oslospektrum.no. Major venue, close to Olso S, showcasing big international acts, as well as small-fry local bands.

Sikamikanico Møllergata 2 ☏22 41 44 09, ⓦwww.sikamikanico.no. Hip-hop, drum'n'bass, jazz and house in heaving club near Oslo S. Great DJ nights too. Wed–Sun from 10pm.

Music festivals

Big-name rock bands often include Oslo on their tours, leavening what would otherwise be a pretty dull scene. The most prestigious annual event is **Norwegian Wood** (☎815 50 333, ⓦwww.norwegianwood.no), a four-day open-air rock festival held in June in the outdoor amphitheatre at Frogner Park, a ten-minute ride from the city centre on tram #12. Previous years have attracted the likes of Iggy Pop, Lou Reed, the Kinks and Van Morrison, and the festival continues to pull in some of the best international artists, supported by a variety of Norwegian acts. The arena holds around six thousand people, but tickets, costing around 400kr per day, sell out well in advance.

Oslo also hosts the more contemporary **Øyafestivalen** (☎815 33 133, ⓦwww .oyafestivalen.com), a four-day event held in August that showcases a wide range of artists, mostly Norwegian but with some imports too – 2008, for example, included Mogwai, Saviours, Dirty Pretty Things and Girl Talk. A club night traditionally kicks the whole thing off in style. The festival takes place in the open air in Middelalderparken, on the edge of Gamlebyen (the Old Town – see p.108) – a ten-minute walk from Oslo S or tram #18 or #19 from Jernbanetorget.

Jazz venues

Oslo has a strong **jazz** tradition, and in early or mid-August its week-long **Jazz Festival** attracts internationally renowned artists as well as showcasing local talent. The Festival Office, at Tollbugata 28 (☎22 42 91 20, ⓦwww.oslojazz.no), has full programme details of all the gigs, including those where there's an admission charge as well as the many free outdoor performances. At other times of the year, try one of the following for regular jazz acts.

Bare Jazz Grensen 8 ☎22 33 20 80, ⓦwww .barejazz.no. Split-level joint with a superb selection of jazz CDs for sale on the ground floor and a jazz café up above with frequent live sounds, both home-grown and imported. Mon & Tues 10am–6pm, Wed–Sat 10am–midnight.

Herr Nilsen Jazzklubb CJ Hambros plass 5 ☎22 33 54 05, ⓦwww.herrnilsen.no. Small and intimate bar whose brick walls are decorated with jazz memorabilia. Live jazz – often traditional and bebop – most nights. A/c; central location. Daily 2pm–2.30am.

Classical music and opera

Oslo's major orchestra, the **Oslo Filharmonien** (☎23 11 60 60, ⓦwww .oslofilharmonien.no), gives regular concerts in the city's Konserthus, at Munkedamsveien 14. As you might expect, programmes often include works by Norwegian and other Scandinavian composers. Tickets for most performances cost around 400kr. In August and September, the orchestra traditionally gives a couple of free evening concerts in the Vigeland sculpture park, as part of the city's summer entertainment programme, which also sees classical performances at a variety of other venues, including the Domkirke, the Munch-museet and the University Aula; for details of the summer programme, contact the tourist office (see p.75).

In October, the ten-day **Ultima Contemporary Music Festival** (☎22 40 18 90, ⓦwww.ultima.no) gathers together Scandinavian and international talent in an ambitious programme of concerts featuring everything from modern contemporary music to opera, ballet, classical and folk. The performances take place in a variety of venues throughout the city; for full details check Ultima's website or contact the tourist office.

Finally, **Den Norske Opera**, Norway's prolific opera company, offers a popular repertoire – Mozart, R. Strauss and the Italians – but also undertakes a number of contemporary works each year. Performances are held at the new, super-modern Operahuset (Opera House), on the waterfront near Oslo S at Kirsten Flagstads plass 1 (information ☎21 42 21 00, box office ☎815 444 88, ⓦ www.operaen.no).

Cinema

The facility with which most Norwegians tackle other languages is best demonstrated at the **cinema**, where films are shown in their original language with Norwegian subtitles. Given that American (and British) films are the most popular, this has obvious advantages for visiting English-speakers. Oslo has its share of mainstream multi-screens, as well as a good art-house cinema. Prices are surprisingly reasonable with tickets averaging 80–90kr.

Cinema listings – including information on late-night screenings – appear daily in the local press, and the tourist office has details too. All the main commercial cinemas share the **same telephone number** and website (☎820 50 001, ⓦ www.oslokino.no), and the following is a selection of central screens.

Eldorado Torggata 9. Mainstream cinema showing the usual blockbusters. Near the Domkirke.

Filmens Hus Dronningens gate 16 at Tollbugata. Art-house cinema with a varied and extremely enjoyable programme mixing mainstream and alternative/avant-garde films.

Gimle Bygdøy Allé 39. A sympathetically revamped old cinema with some of the most comfortable seats in town. A wine bar in the entrance adds a nice touch. Varied programme, mostly mainstream. One screen only.

Klingenberg Olav V's gate 4. Mainstream cinema with four screens. Central location, metres from the Nationaltheatret.

Saga Stortingsgata 28 at Olav V's gate. Mainstream cinema with six screens. Metres from the Nationaltheatret.

Theatre

Nearly all of Oslo's theatre productions are in Norwegian, making them of limited interest to (most) tourists, though there are occasional English-language performances by touring theatre companies. The principal venue is the **Nationaltheatret**, Stortingsgata 15 (☎815 00 811; ⓦ www.nationaltheatret .no), which hosts the prestigious, annual Ibsen Festival. Touring companies may also appear at the more adventurous **Det Norske Teatret**, Kristian IV's gate 8 (☎22 42 43 44, ⓦ www.detnorsketeatret.no).

Sports

Surrounded by forest and fjord, Oslo is very much an outdoor city, offering a wide range of **sports** and outdoor pursuits. In **summer**, locals take to the hills to hike the network of trails that lattice the forests and lakes of the Nordmarka (see p.104), where many also try their hand at a little freshwater fishing, while others head out to the offshore islets of the Oslofjord (see p.108) to sunbathe and swim. In **winter**, the cross-country ski routes of the Nordmarka are especially popular, as is downhill skiing. Indeed skiing is such an integral part of winter life here that the T-bane carriages all have ski racks. Sleigh-riding is possible too, and so is ice-skating, with the handiest rinks right in the middle of the city in front of the Stortinget (Parliament building).

Fishing

As regards **fishing**, the freshwater lakes of the Nordmarka are reasonably well stocked with such common species as trout, char, pike and perch. The Oslomarkas Fiskeadministrasjon, Sørkedalen 914 (☎40 00 67 68, ⓦwww.ofa .no) provides all the background information you need, though their website is only in Norwegian, so you may have to get the tourist office to help you out. In particular, they will advise about fishing areas and have lists of where local licences can be bought; see p.53 for general information about fishing in Norway. **Ice fishing** is another popular option, but do what the locals do (or even better, keep them company), as it can be dangerous.

Skiing

Skiing is extremely popular throughout Norway, and here in Oslo both cross-country and downhill enthusiasts might begin by calling in at either the tourist office or **Skiforeningen** (the Ski Association), at Kongeveien 5 (☎22 92 32 00, ⓦwww.skiforeningen.no), near the Holmenkollen ski-jump, on T-bane #1. They both have lots of information on Oslo's floodlit trails, cross-country routes, downhill and slalom slopes, ski schools (including one for children) and excursions to the nearest mountain resorts. Most Norwegians have their own skiing gear, but **equipment hire** is available – among several suppliers – from Skiservice Tomm Murstad, beside the Voksenkollen T-bane station (☎22 13 95 00, ⓦwww .skiservice.no). Oslo's largest and best downhill ski area is Tryvann Vinterpark (Tryvann Winter Park; ⓦwww.tryvann.no), located north of Holmenkollen and

---

Oslo with children

There's no shortage of things to do with young (pre-teen) children in Oslo, beginning with the enchanting, open-air **Vigelandsparken** (see p.103) and, if the weather is good, the **beaches** of the Oslofjord islands (see p.108). In wintertime, ice-skating, tobogganing and horse-drawn sleigh rides (see p.119) are also almost bound to appeal.

Few children will want to be dragged round Oslo's main museums, except perhaps for the **Frammuseet** (see p.100), but there are several museums geared up for youngsters. The most popular is the **Norsk Teknisk Museum**, at Kjelsåsveien 143 (Technology Museum; late June to late Aug daily 10am–6pm; late Aug to late June Tues–Fri 9am–4pm, Sat & Sun 11am–6pm; 80kr, children 40kr; ⓦwww .tekniskmuseum.no). Out to the north of the city, this is an interactive museum par excellence, equipped with working models and a galaxy of things to push and touch, as well as a café and picnic area. To get there from the city centre, take bus #54 from the Aker Brygge to Kjelsås station alongside the museum.

Alternatively, there's the rather more creative **Barnekunstmuseet** at Lille Frøens vei 4 (Children's Art Museum; mid-Jan to late June Tues–Thurs 9.30am–2pm, Sun 11am–4pm; late June to early Aug Tues–Thurs & Sun 11am–4pm; mid-Sept to early Dec Tues–Thurs 9.30am–2pm, Sun 11am–4pm; closed mid-Aug to mid-Sept; 50kr, children 30kr; T-bane to Frøen station). This has an international collection of children's art – drawings, paintings, sculpture and handicrafts – along with a children's workshop where painting, music and dancing are frequent activities; call ahead for details on ☎22 46 85 73 or check out the website ⓦwww.childrensart.com.

One bit of good news is that **discounts** for children are commonplace. Almost all sites and attractions let babies and toddlers in free, and charge half of the adult tariff for children between 4 and 16 years of age. It's the same on public transport, and hotels are usually very obliging too, adding camp beds of some description to their rooms with the minimum of fuss and expense.

northwest of the Frognerseteren T-bane terminus. There are fourteen ski slopes here and seven ski lifts, and its facilities include a ski school and ski equipment rental; snow permitting, the park is open from December to April.

Ice-skating and horse-drawn sleigh rides

Every winter, from November to March, a floodlit **skating rink**, Narvisen, is created in front of the Stortinget, beside Karl Johans gate. Admission is free and you can hire skates on the spot at reasonable rates. The tourist office also has the details of all sorts of other winter fun in the Nordmarka – from **tobogganing** and **horse-drawn sleigh rides** to guided **winter walks**.

Listings

Airlines British Airways ☎815 33 142; Brussels Airlines ☎23 16 25 68; Finnair ☎810 01 100; KLM ☎22 64 37 52; Norwegian Air Shuttle ☎815 21 815; SAS/Braathens ☎05400; Sterling ☎81 55 88 10; Widerøe's ☎810 01 200. For a comprehensive list, see under *Flyselskaper* in the *Yellow Pages*.
Banks and exchange ATMs are liberally distributed across the city centre and there are also ATMs at Gardermoen airport. Oslo has a plethora of banks, with normal banking hours being mid-May to mid-Sept Mon–Fri 8.30am–3pm, Thurs till 5pm; mid-Sept to mid-May Mon–Fri 8.30am–3.30pm, Thurs till 5pm. You can change money and traveller's cheques at banks and major post offices, where the rates are especially competitive. The money exchange company Forex has two outlets at Oslo S (Mon–Fri 7am–7pm & Sat 9am–4pm).
Books and maps The best independent bookshop in town, especially if you are politically left of centre, is ⚓Tronsmo, Kristian Augusts gate 19 (Mon–Wed 9am–5pm, Thurs & Fri 9am–6pm & Sat 10am–4pm; ☎22 99 03 99), where great care has been taken to select the best books on a wide range of subjects – both Norwegian and English titles. More mainstream is Tanum, inside the Paleet shopping complex, Karl Johans gate 37 at Universitetsgata (Mon–Fri 10am–8pm, Sat 10am–6pm; ☎22 41 11 00), which has the city's widest selection of English fiction. Norli has a competent range of English fiction too, and its biggest branch – of several – is at Universitetsgata 20–24 (Mon–Fri 9am–5pm, Sat 10am–5pm; ☎22 00 43 00). This particular branch has a separate – if small – section devoted to English translations of Norwegian writers. Norlis Antikvariat, opposite the National Gallery at Universitetsgata 18 (Mon–Fri 10am–5pm & Sat 10am–3pm; ☎22 20 01 40), sells second hand and some new English-language books. Nomaden, Uranienborgveien 4 (Mon–Fri

10am–6pm & Sat 10am–4pm; ☎23 13 14 15), just behind the Slottsparken, is Oslo's best shop for travel guides and maps, though maps of Oslo in particular and Norway in general are to be found in dozens of locations – the best are produced by Cappelen. Finally, Den Norske Turistforening (DNT), the Norwegian hiking organization, sell a comprehensive range of Norwegian hiking maps, covering every corner of the country, from their shop in the city centre at Storgata 3 (Mon–Fri 10am–5pm, Thurs 10am–6pm, Sat 10am–3pm; ☎22 82 28 22, ⓦ www.dntoslo.no).
Buses The main domestic carrier, Nor-Way Bussekspress, has an information desk at Oslo's main bus station in the Oslo S complex (☎81 54 44 44, ⓦ www.nor-way.no). A second information desk at the bus station covers several other companies, including Säfflebussen (☎815 66 010, ⓦ www.safflebussen.se), which operates international buses to Copenhagen and Stockholm; Swebuss (☎800 58 444, ⓦ www.swebusexpress .no), which covers much of Scandinavia; and Lavpriseksspressen (☎67 98 04 80, ⓦ www .lavpriseksspressen.no), which concentrates on long-distance Norwegian routes. For details of airport buses to and from Oslo, see p.71.
Car breakdown Each of the two major national breakdown companies has a 24hr helpline. They are Falken Redningskorps (☎02222) and Viking Redningstjeneste (☎06000).
Car rental Bislet Bilutleie, Pilestredet 70 (☎22 60 00 00, ⓦ www.bislet.no); Europcar, several downtown locations and at Gardermoen airport (☎64 81 05 60, ⓦ www.europcar.no); Hertz, several Oslo locations including Holbergs gate 30 (☎22 21 00 00), and at the airport (☎64 81 05 50, ⓦ www.hertz.no); National, at the airport (☎64 82 06 40, ⓦ www.nationalcar.no). See also under *Bilutleie* in the *Yellow Pages*.

Crafts One good bet for traditional and authentic Norwegian handicrafts is Heimen Husflid, Rosenkrantz gate 8 (Mon–Fri 10am–5pm, Thurs till 6pm, Sat 10am–3pm; ⊤23 21 42 00, ⓦwww .heimen.net). For more modern, pan-Scandinavian gear, try Norway Designs, Stortingsgata 28 (Mon–Fri 9am–5pm, Sat 10am–3pm; ⊤23 11 45 10, ⓦwww.norwaydesigns.no), which features an amazing glass castle every Christmas.

Cycling The Syklistenes Landsforening, in the Operapassasjen, at Storgata 23D (Norwegian Cyclist Association; Mon–Fri noon–3pm; ⊤22 47 30 42, ⓦwww.slf.no), gives advice and information on route planning and sells cycling maps. For bike hire in Oslo, see p.77.

Dentist Municipal dental information on ⊤22 67 30 00. Otherwise, see under *Tannleger* in the *Yellow Pages*.

Embassies and consulates Canada, Wergeland-veien 7 (⊤22 99 53 00); Ireland, Haakon VII's gate, 15 etg. (⊤22 01 72 00); Netherlands, Oscars gate 29 (⊤23 33 36 00); Poland, Olav Kyrres plass 1 (⊤24 11 08 50); UK, Thomas Heftyes gate 8 (⊤23 13 27 00); US, Henrik Ibsens gate 48 (⊤22 44 85 50). For others, look under *Ambassadeur og Legas-joner* in the *Yellow Pages*. There is no Australian or New Zealand consulate or embassy.

Emergencies Ambulance & medical assistance ⊤113; Police ⊤112; Fire brigade ⊤110.

Ferries DFDS Seaways (from Copenhagen), Vippetangen Utstikker (dock) #2, beside Akershusstranda (⊤21 62 13 40, ⓦwww.dfds.no); Stena Line (from Frederikshavn in Denmark), also from Vippetangen Utstikker #2 (⊤02010, ⓦwww.stenaline.no); and Color Line (from Kiel, Germany), Hjortneskaia (⊤810 00 811, ⓦwww.colorline.no). Tickets from the companies direct or travel agents.

Gay Oslo There's not much of a scene as such, primarily because Oslo's gays and lesbians are mostly content to share pubs and clubs with heteros. That said, gay men do congregate at the *London Pub*, CJ Hambros plass 5 (daily 3pm–3am; ⓦwww.londonpub.no), with a busy pub/bar on one floor and a disco on another; and at *Ett Glass*, a lively café-bar on Rosenkrantz gate, just up from Karl Johans gate 33 (daily 11am–1am, 3am at the weekend; kitchen closes at 10pm). The main gay event is the *Skeive Dager* (Queer Days; ⓦwww .skeivedager.no) festival usually held over ten days in late June with parties, parades, political meetings, a film festival and incorporating Gay Pride. Norway's national gay and lesbian organiza-tion is LLH (Landsforeningen for lesbisk og homofil frigjøring; ⓦwww.llh.no); their Oslo office is at Kongens gate 12.

Hiking Den Norske Turistforening (DNT; ⓦwww .turistforeningen.no), the Norwegian hiking organization, has its Oslo branch in the city centre at Storgata 3 (Mon–Fri 10am–5pm, Thurs 10am–6pm, Sat 10am–3pm; ⊤22 82 28 22; ⓦwww.dntoslo.no). It stocks a full range of Norwegian hiking maps, books and equipment plus DNT membership – a relative snip at 480kr per year. See the *Hiking* colour section for more on DNT and hiking in general.

Internet Almost all city hotels and hostels provide internet access for their guests either free or at (fairly) reasonable rates. Internet access is also available for free at the main city library, the Deichmanske bibliotek, at Arne Garborgs plass 4 (June–Aug Mon–Fri 10am–6pm, Sat 11am–2pm; Sept–May Mon–Fri 10am–7pm, Sat 10am–4pm; ⓦwww.deichman.no), and, if you are under 26, at Oslo's youth information shop, Use-it, Møllergata 3 (July–Aug Mon & Wed–Fri 9am–6pm, Tues 11am–6pm; Sept–June Mon–Fri 11am–5pm; ⊤24 14 98 20, ⓦwww.use-it.no). There's also an internet pit-stop, the Sidewalk Express, inside Oslo S (30kr for 1hr 30min).

Jewellery Juhl's Silver Gallery, Roald Amundsens gate 6 (⊤22 42 77 99, ⓦwww.juhls.no), is the Oslo outlet for the celebrated jewellers and silversmiths, who established their first workshop in remote Kautokeino (see p.367) forty years ago. Many of their designs are Sami-inspired. Mon–Fri 10am–6pm & Sat 10am–4pm.

Laundry Majorstua Myntvaskeri, Vibes gate 15 (⊤22 69 43 17); Snarvask, Thorvald Meyers gate 18, Grünerløkka (⊤22 37 57 70). See under *Vaskerier* in the *Yellow Pages*.

Left luggage Coin-operated lockers (24hr) and luggage office at Oslo S.

Lost credit cards American Express ⊤800 68 100; Diners Club ⊤21 01 50 00; MasterCard ⊤21 01 52 22; Visa ⊤800 12 052.

Lost property (*hittegods*) Trams, buses and T-bane at the Nationaltheatret station (⊤22 08 53 61). NSB railways, Oslo S (⊤81 56 83 40); police, call ⊤22 66 98 65.

Medical treatment For medical emergencies, call ⊤113. For lesser problems, either head for the nearest pharmacy (see "Pharmacy" below) or the Walk-In Clinic, to the rear of the Aker Brygge complex at the corner of Munkedamsveien and Sjøgata (⊤22 83 10 83, ⓦwww.walk-in-clinic .com). The clinic is fast, efficient, friendly – and expensive. For cheaper treatment, stick to the A&E department of the nearest hospital, at the north end of Storgata, beside the river.

Newspapers Many English and American newspapers and magazines are available in downtown Oslo's Narvesen kiosks and there's an especially wide selection at the newsagents in Oslo S train station. They don't come cheap: a British daily broadsheet costs 40kr, 70kr for weekend editions.

Pharmacy Oslo has scores of pharmacies – see under *Apotek* in the *Yellow Pages* or call the 24hr infoline, ☎23 35 81 00. See also "Medical treatment".

Police In an emergency, phone ☎112.

Post offices There are lots of post offices dotted across the city, including a branch in Oslo S. All post offices exchange currency and cash traveller's cheques at very reasonable rates. Normal opening hours are Mon–Fri 8am–5pm & Sat 9am–1pm.

Supermarkets There are lots of small supermarkets in central Oslo – Rimi, ICA and Kiwi are three of the larger chains. All of them sell at least a small selection of fresh fruit and veg. Rimi has a branch in Oslo S, ICA has one on Grensen near the corner with Akersgata 45. Opening hours are mostly Mon–Sat 9am–9pm, Sat 9am–6pm.

Taxis There are taxi ranks dotted all over the city centre. You can also telephone Oslo Taxi on ☎02323 or Norgestaxi on ☎08000.

Trains NSB (Norwegian State Railways) has two stations in central Oslo – Oslo S and Nationaltheatret. Enquiries and bookings on ☎815 00 888, ⓦwww.nsb.no.

Vinmonopolet There are lots of branches of this state-run liquor and wine store in Oslo, including one in Oslo S (Mon–Fri 10am–6pm, Sat 9am–6pm) and another at Rosenkrantz gate 11 (Mon–Fri 10am–6pm, Sat 9am–3pm). For a complete list of stores, with opening hours, consult ⓦwww .vinmonopolet.no.

Youth information Oslo's youth information shop, Ungdomsinformasjonen, or Use-it, is located a brief walk from Oslo S at Møllergata 3 (July–Aug Mon & Wed–Fri 9am–6pm, Tues 11am–6pm; Sept–June Mon–Fri 11am–5pm; ☎24 14 98 20, ⓦwww .use-it.no). It operates an advisory service on everything from sexual health to careers for the under-26s. This is also a good place to find out about live music and events, and it offers a free internet service too. It also produces a free annual booklet, *Streetwise*, which provides a review and round-up of all things Oslo, from bars and clubs to museums and cafés.

Around Oslo: the Oslofjord

Around 100km from top to bottom, the narrow straits and podgy basins of the **Oslofjord** link the capital with the open sea. This waterway has long been Norway's busiest, an islet-studded channel whose sheltered waters were once crowded with steamers shuttling passengers along the Norwegian coast. The young **Roald Dahl**, who spent his summer holidays here from 1920 to 1932, loved the area, writing in his autobiography entitled *Boy* "Unless you have sailed down the Oslofjord … on a tranquil summer's day, you cannot imagine the sensation of absolute peace and beauty that surrounds you." Even now, though industry has blighted the shoreline and cars have replaced the steamers, the Oslofjord makes for delightful sailing, and on a summer's day you can spy dozens of tiny craft scuttling round its nooks and crannies. The ferry ride from Oslo to Drøbak, a pretty village on the fjord's east shore, does provide a pleasant introduction, though it's not quite the same as having your own boat.

Both sides of the fjord are dotted with humdrum industrial towns, and frankly there's not much to tempt you out of Oslo if your time is limited – especially as several of the major city sights are half-day excursions in themselves. But if you have more time, there are several places on the train and bus routes out of the city that do warrant a stop. The pick of the crop is the town of **Fredrikstad**, down the fjord's eastern side on the train route to Sweden. The old part of Fredrikstad consists of a riverside fortress whose gridiron streets and earthen bastions, dating from the late sixteenth century, have survived in remarkably good condition. The fortress was built to defend the country from the Swedes, as was the imposing

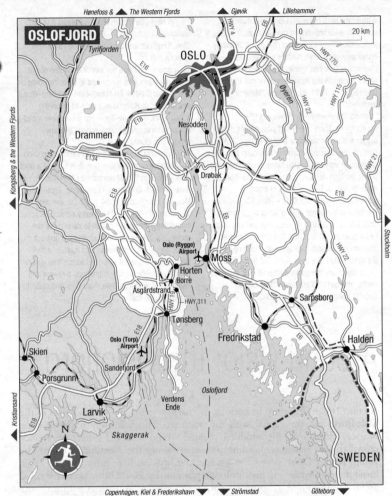

hilltop stronghold that rears up above **Halden**, an otherwise innocuous town further southeast, hard by the Swedish border. The highlight of the fjord's western shore is the cluster of Viking burial mounds at **Borre**, just outside the ferry port of **Horten**, while the breezy town of **Tønsberg** gives easy access to the shredded archipelago that pokes a rural finger out into the Skagerrak.

Motorways leave Oslo to strip along both sides of the Oslofjord – the E6 in the east, the E18 to the west – and there's a regular **train** service from Oslo S serving both sides too. On the east side, the train stops at Fredrikstad and Halden, but not Drøbak, which is best reached from Oslo by ferry. On the western side, trains run to Drammen and Tønsberg, but not Horten. To cross the Oslofjord, you can either use the seven-kilometre tunnel that runs west from Drøbak, or catch the **car ferry** (Mon–Fri 5.30am–midnight, Sat & Sun 7am–midnight, every 30min, 45 min at the weekend; 30min; driver & car 85kr each way; ⓦwww .basto-fosen.no) between Horten and **Moss**, about 60km south of Oslo.

The east shore: Drøbak, Fredrikstad and Halden

The first place of any real interest on the Oslofjord's eastern shore is **DRØBAK**, a tiny port that slopes along the shoreline about 40km from the capital. It's at its prettiest round the old harbour, where a cluster of white clapboard houses covers the headland and straggles up towards a handsome timber church dating from the early eighteenth century. Drøbak witnessed one of the few Norwegian successes during the German invasion of 1940, when the cruiser *Blucher* was sunk by artillery as it steamed towards Oslo. The gunners had no way of realizing just how important this was – the delay to the German flotilla gave the Norwegian king, Håkon VII, just enough time to escape the capital and avoid capture. Few commented upon it at the time, but the gun that did the damage was made in Germany by Krupp – a rich irony if ever there was one.

Drøbak's only other claim to fame comes from its specialist Christmas shop, the *Julehuset* (March–Oct Mon–Fri 10am–5pm Sat 10am–3pm, Nov to Dec 23 Mon–Fri 10am–7pm Sat 10am–3pm, also June to Dec 23 Sun noon–4pm; ⓦwww.julehus.no; ⓣ64 93 41 78), whose popularity is such that many Norwegian kids believe that Father Christmas actually lives here; he doesn't, of course, because his reindeer prefer Lapland. As for **cafés**, *Det Gamle Bakeri* (daily 11am–11pm) serves tasty snacks and light meals in an attractive wooden building with an open log fire, while the *Skipperstuen*, in the wooden house on the knoll next to the harbour (same times), does excellent sandwiches.

The most enjoyable way to get to Drøbak from Oslo is by **boat**. From mid-May to August, passenger ferries (ⓣ177, ⓦwww.nbds.no) depart Oslo's Aker Brygge pier for Drøbak five times weekly, clipping out across the islet-studded fjord and stopping off at a couple of small islands on the way. The journey takes about an hour and costs 75kr each way. The boat's timetable makes it possible to complete the return trip on the same day – though this isn't crucial as there's also a fast and frequent bus service between Drøbak and Oslo (hourly to Jernbanetorget and several other downtown bus stops).

Fredrikstad

It's an hour-long, ninety-kilometre train journey south from Oslo to **FREDRIKSTAD**, named after the Danish king Frederick II, who had the original fortified town built here at the mouth of the River Glomma in 1567. Danish kings ruled Norway from 1387 to 1814 and, with rare exceptions, the country's interests were systematically neglected in favour of Copenhagen. A major consequence was Norway's involvement in the bitter rivalry between the Swedish and Danish monarchies, which prompted a seemingly endless and particularly pointless sequence of wars lasting from the early sixteenth century until 1720. The eastern approaches to Oslo (then Christiania), along the Oslofjord, were especially vulnerable to attack from Sweden, and raiding parties ravaged the area on many occasions. Indeed, Frederick II's fortress only lasted three years before it was burnt to the ground, though it didn't take long for a replacement to be constructed – and for the whole process to be repeated again. Finally, in the middle of the seventeenth century, Fredrikstad's **fortifications** were considerably strengthened. The central gridiron of cobbled streets was encircled on three sides by zigzag bastions, which allowed the defenders to fire across and into any attacking force. In turn, these bastions were protected by a moat, concentric earthen banks and outlying redoubts. Armed with 130

cannon, Fredrikstad was by 1685 the strongest fortress in all of Norway – and it has remained in military use to this day, which partly accounts for its excellent state of preservation. The fort was also unaffected by the development of modern Fredrikstad, which grew up as a result of the timber industry: the new town was built on the west bank of the Glomma while the old fort – now known as the **Gamlebyen** (Old Town; ⓦwww.festningsbyen.no) – is on the east. Fredrikstad's other claim to fame is as the place where the last woman to be executed in Norway met her untimely end: the year was 1876 and the woman was a certain Sophie Johannesdatter, who had poisoned her husband.

The Town

From Fredrikstad's adjoining **train** and **bus** stations, located in the new part of town, it's a couple of minutes' walk to the river – head straight down Jernbanegata and take the first left along Ferjestedsveien. From the jetty, a passenger **ferry** (Mon–Thurs 5.30am–11pm, Fri 5.30am–1am, Sat 7am–1am, Sun 9.30am–11pm; every 15–30min; 5min; 10kr) shuttles over to the gated back wall of the Gamlebyen. Inside, the pastel-painted timber and stone houses of the old town, just three blocks deep and six blocks wide, make for a delightful stroll, especially as surprisingly few tourists venture this way except at the height of the season. It's the general appearance of the place that appeals rather than any specific sight, although the main square does hold an intriguingly unfortunate **statue** of Frederick II, who appears to have a serious problem with his pantaloons, and there's a **museum,** on Tøihusgaten (Tues–Sun 11am–4pm; 40kr), which dutifully outlines the history of the Old Town. Make sure also that you take in the most impressive of the town's outlying defences, the **Kongsten Fort**, about ten minutes' walk from the main fortress: go straight ahead from the main gate, take the first right along Heibergsgate and it's clearly visible on the left. Here, thick stone and earthen walls are moulded round a rocky knoll that offers wide views over the surrounding countryside – an agreeably quiet vantage point from where you can take in the lie of the land.

Back on the western side of the Glomma, a short walk along Ferjestedsveien away from the river brings you to a small park and the adjacent **Domkirke** (late June to mid-Aug Tues–Sat noon–3pm; free), a brown brick building with stained glass by Emanuel Vigeland (see p.103). Beyond the church is the centre of modern Fredrikstad, a humdrum place on a bend in the river.

Practicalities

Fredrikstad tourist office shares its premises with the museum (see p.124) in the Gamlebyen at Tøihusgaten 41 (June to late Aug Mon–Fri 9am–5pm, Sat & Sun 11am–4pm; late Aug to May Mon–Fri 9am–4.30pm; ☎69 30 46 00, ⓦwww .fredrikstad-hvaler.no). They have oodles of local information and a comprehensive list of places to stay, although it's actually best to see Fredrikstad as a day-trip. Amongst the town's handful of **hotels**, the most recommendable is the *Victoria*, Turngata 3 (☎69 38 58 00, ⓦwww.hotelvictoria.no; ❼, sp/r ❺), a comfortable, medium-sized place with period trimmings that dates back to the 1880s; it overlooks the park next to the Domkirke. Alternatively, the bargain basement *Fredrikstad Motel & Camping*, Torsnesveien 16 (☎69 32 03 15; ❶), is about 400m straight ahead outside the main gate of the Old Town; it provides tent space as well as inexpensive rooms.

As for **food**, the Gamlebyen is dotted with cafés and patisseries, the pick of which is *Café Balaklava*, in antique premises and with an outdoor terrace at Færgeportgata 78; the adjacent **restaurant**, *Balaklava Gjestgiveri* (☎69 32 30 40; Mon–Sat 6–11pm), also occupies period premises and specializes in seafood; main courses average around 160kr.

Halden

Just 3km from the Swedish border – and 40km from Fredrikstad – the workaday wood-processing town of **HALDEN** is bisected by the River Tista and hemmed in by steep forested hills, the closest of which is crowned by the commanding **Fredriksten Festning** (fortress). Work began on the stronghold in 1661 at the instigation of Frederick III, during a lull in the fighting between Sweden and Denmark. The stakes were high: the Swedes were determined to annihilate the Dano–Norwegian monarchy and had only just failed in their attempt to capture Oslo and Copenhagen. Consequently, Frederick was keen to build a fortress of immense strength to secure his northerly possessions. He called in Dutch engineers to design it and, after a decade, the result was a labyrinthine citadel whose thick perimeter walls, heavily protected gates, bastions and outlying forts were perfectly designed to suit the contours of the two steep, parallel ridges on which they were built. The proof of the pudding was in the eating. The Swedes besieged Fredriksten on several occasions, but without success, though the town itself suffered badly. In 1716, the Norwegians razed it to the ground, a scorched-earth policy that later prompted some nationalistic poppycock from the writer Bjørnstjerne Bjørnson: "We chose to burn our nation, ere we let it fall."

The Town

Halden **train station** abuts the south bank of the Tista and the **bus station** is close by on Jernbanegata. The **fortress** (mid-May to Aug daily 10am–5pm & Sept Sun noon–3pm; 50kr) is on the south side of the river too, its forested slopes climbed by several steep footpaths, the most enjoyable of which begins on **Peder Colbjørnsens gate** and leads up to the main gatehouse. Allow at least an hour for a thorough exploration of the fort, whose ingenuity and impregnability are its salient features. Although most of the buildings are labelled, only a handful are open to the public, most notably the **Krigshistorisk Utstilling** (Military History Exhibition) in the old prison in the eastern curtain wall. There are also hour-long guided tours (July–Aug 2–3 daily; 60kr), but you shouldn't require any help to absorb the obvious and powerful atmosphere. On the far side of the fortress, where the terrain is nowhere near as steep, you'll find a monument to the Swedish king Karl XII, who was killed by a bullet in the temple as he besieged the fort in 1718. An inveterate warmonger, Karl had exhausted the loyalty of his troops, and whether the bullet came from the fortress or one of his own men has been a matter of considerable Scandinavian speculation.

Practicalities

Despite its fortress, Halden is too routine a place to spend the night, but if you're marooned there's a reasonable range of accommodation. The **tourist office**, midway between the train station and the fortress at Torget 2 (late Aug to mid-June Mon–Fri 9am–3.30pm, late June to mid-Aug Mon–Fri 9am–4.30pm; ☎69 19 09 80, ⓦwww.visithalden.com), has a full list, but the pick of the **hotels** is the *Park Hotel*, Marcus Thranes gate 30 (☎69 21 15 00, ⓦwww.park-hotel .no; ❺, sp/r ❹), a neat, trim, modern place on the northwest edge of the town centre. Alternatively, Halden has a small, modern 32-bed HI **hostel** (late June to early Aug; ☎69 21 69 68, ⓦwww.vandrerhjem.no; dorm beds 150kr, doubles ❶), sited in a chalet-like school building on Flintveien, in the suburb of Gimle, 3km north of the train station and readily reached by several local buses.

The west shore: Drammen, Horten and Tønsberg

West of the city centre, Oslo's rangy suburbs curve round the final basin of the Oslofjord before bubbling up over the hills almost as far as **DRAMMEN**, a substantial industrial settlement some 40km southwest of the capital. Built on an arm of the Oslofjord, the town handles most of the vehicles imported into Norway. This is hardly a reason to visit, however, and nor do the modern office blocks and stuffy late nineteenth-century buildings of its centre conjure up much interest. From here, there's a **choice of routes**, with the E134 wriggling west through Kongsberg (see p.188) bound for the western fjords (see p.222), while the E18 presses on south down the Oslofjord.

The **E18** soon shoots past **HORTEN**, a small port and naval base from where a car ferry shuttles across the Oslofjord to Moss (Mon–Fri 5.30am–midnight, Sat & Sun 7am–midnight, every 30min, 45min at the weekend; 30min; driver & car 85kr each way; ⓦwww.basto-fosen.no). Horten is also just to the north of the Viking burial mounds at Borre (see p.128). After the Horten turning, the E18 pushes on down to the old port of Tønsberg.

Tønsberg

The last town of any size on the Oslofjord's western shore, **TØNSBERG**, some 100km from Oslo, was founded by Harald Hårfagre in the ninth century, and rose to prominence in the Middle Ages as a major ecclesiastical and trading centre. The sheltered sound made a safe harbour, the plain behind it was ideal for settlement, and, once they were built, the town's palace and fortress assured the patronage of successive monarchs. All of which sounds exciting, and you might expect Tønsberg to be one of the country's more important historical attractions. Sadly, though, precious little survives from the town's medieval heyday, the best of a decidedly poor hand being the renovated, nineteenth-century warehouses of the **Tønsberg Brygge**, a pedestrianized area whose narrow lanes, dotted with bars and restaurants, hug the waterfront in the centre of town.

As for the castle, the **Slottsfjellet**, only the foundations have survived, fragmentary ruins perched on a steep, wooded hill immediately to the north of the centre, though it takes little imagination to appreciate the castle's strategic and defensive virtues. The Swedes burned it down in 1503 and the place was never rebuilt – today's watchtower, the clumpy Slottsfjelltårnet (late May to late June Mon–Fri 10am–3pm, Sat & Sun noon–5pm; late June to mid-Aug daily noon–5pm; mid-Aug to late Sept Sat & Sun noon–5pm; late Sept to early Oct Sun noon–3pm; 20kr), was plonked on top in the nineteenth century.

Practicalities

From Tønsberg **train station**, it's a five- to ten-minute walk south to the main square, Torvet. From here, it's just a couple of hundred metres along Rådhusgaten to the waterfront Tønsberg Brygge, where you'll find the **tourist office** (late June to July Mon–Fri 10am–6pm, Sat & Sun 11am–4pm; Aug to late June Mon–Fri 10am–3pm; ☎33 35 45 20, ⓦwww.visittonsberg.com), which issues free town maps and carries all sorts of local information. Tønsberg has several central **hotels**, the most stylish of which is the *Quality Hotel Tønsberg*, right on the waterfront just metres from the tourist office at Ollebukta 3 (☎33 00 41 00, ⓦwww.quality hoteltonsberg.no; ❼, sp/r ❹). Part conference centre and including a concert hall, this modern hotel is handsomely built in the shape of a ship's bow and as such represents a striking addition to the town's skyline. It has over four hundred comfortable rooms with all mod-cons and most have harbour views. Rather more modest is the *Thon Hotel Brygga*, also on the waterfront near to the tourist office at Nedre Langgate 40 (☎33 34 49 00, ⓦwww.thonhotels.no; ❺, sp/r ❹). There are seventy cheerful guest rooms here in a modern building constructed in the style of an old warehouse. A third choice is Tønsberg's well-kept HI **hostel**, which occupies a chalet-like structure at Dronning Blancasgate 22 (☎33 31 21 75, ⓦwww.vandrerhjem.no; dorm beds 275kr, doubles ❶). The hostel is in a residential area beneath (and to the east of) the Slottsfjellet: turn right out of the train station and follow the signs for the five-minute walk.

For **food**, the Tønsberg Brygge is packed with café-bars and restaurants. One of the better options is the *Esmeralda*, an Italian restaurant with a good line in pizzas (110–150kr); it's open daily from 11am to late.

South from Tønsberg: Verdens Ende

The low-lying islands and skerries that nudge out into the Skagerrak to the south of Tønsberg are a popular holiday destination. By and large, people come here for the peace and quiet, with a bit of fishing and swimming thrown in, and the whole coast is dotted with summer homes. To the outsider, this is not especially stimulating, but there is one wonderfully scenic spot, **Verdens Ende** – "World's End" – about thirty-minutes' drive from Tønsberg, right at the southernmost tip of the southernmost island, **Tjöme**. In this blustery spot, rickety fishing jetties straggle across a cove whose blue-black waters are surrounded by bare, sea-smoothed rocks and miniature islets. It would be nice to think a wandering Viking gave the place its name, but in fact it was a romantic gesture by a visiting Victorian.

Verdens Ende apart, the most enjoyable way to see the archipelago is by **boat**, and the Tønsberg tourist office has information about island cruises departing from Honnørbryggen, the jetty just to the north of the tourist office.

North from Tønsberg: Åsgårdstrand and Borre's Viking burial mounds

Heading north from Tønsberg on Highway 311, it's a short drive to the seaside village of **ÅSGÅRDSTRAND**, where Edvard Munch spent many of his summers. Munch avoided the mountains of Norway whenever he could, sticking firmly to the country's flattest parts because of his agoraphobia – and the lightly forested shoreline here at Åsgårdstrand suited him just fine. The old, ochre-painted fisherman's **cottage** (June–Aug Tues–Sun 11am–6pm; May & Sept Sat & Sun 11am–6pm; free) Munch purchased in 1897 has survived and has been returned to its appearance when the artist lived and painted here, and the adjoining studio has been repaired and refurbished too. There are no Munch paintings on display, but there are a few Munch prints and bits and bobs of period furniture.

Just beyond Åsgårdstrand, Highway 311 intersects with Highway 19, which pushes on north to **BORRE**, a scattered hamlet that boasts one of the largest ensembles of extant **Viking burial mounds** (600–900 AD) in all of Scandinavia, the Borrehaugene. There are seven large and twenty-one small mounds in total, with the best-preserved being clustered together in the woods by the water's edge, a five-minute walk from the car park. These grassy bumps date from the seventh to the tenth century, when Borre was a royal burial ground and one of the wealthiest districts in southern Norway. The mounds are interesting in themselves but the setting is even better – in springtime wild flowers carpet the woods making this a perfect spot for a picnic. The area has been designated a national park and a visitor centre, the **Midgard Historisk Senter** (Historical Centre; May to mid-Sept daily 11am–4pm; Sept–April Wed–Fri 11am–2pm & Sun 11am–4pm; 50kr; Ⓦwww.midgardsenteret.no), stands beside the car park, but there's precious little actually in it – save yourself the entrance fee.

The Borre burial mounds are 4km south of Horten and 75km south of Oslo.

Travel details

Trains

Principal NSB train services (Ⓦwww.nsb.no)

Oslo to: Arendal (4–5 daily, change at Nelaug; 4hr 10min); Bergen (4 daily; 7hr 20min); Dombås (3–4 daily; 4hr); Drammen (4 daily; 40min); Fredrikstad (hourly; 1hr 10min); Geilo (3–4 daily; 3hr); Halden (hourly; 1hr 45min); Hamar (hourly; 1hr 30min); Hjerkinn (3–4 daily; 4hr 30min – request stop only); Kongsberg (4–5 daily; 1hr 10min); Kongsvoll (3–4 daily; 4hr 40min – request stop only); Kristiansand (4–5 daily; 4hr 30min); Lillehammer (hourly; 2hr); Myrdal (4 daily; 4hr 50min); Otta (6 daily; 3hr 30min); Røros (6 daily; 5hr); Sandefjord (every 1–2hr; 1hr 50min); Stavanger (4–5 daily; 8hr); Trondheim (3–4 daily; 6hr 40min); Tønsberg (every 1–2hr; 1hr 30min); Voss (4 daily; 6hr 40min); Åndalsnes (2–3 daily; 5hr 30min).

Oslo Gardermoen airport to: Kvam (1–2 daily; 3hr – request stop only).

Principal Nor-Way Bussekspress bus services (Ⓦwww.nor-way.no)

Oslo to: Balestrand (3 daily; 8hr 30min); Bergen (3 daily; 10hr 30min); Dombås (2 daily; 6hr 15min); Drøbak (hourly; 40min); Haugesund (3 daily; 8hr 45min); Kongsberg (3 daily; 1hr 30min); Kristiansand (6 daily; 5hr); Lillehammer (4 daily; 3hr); Lom (4 daily; 6hr 40min); Måløy (3 daily; 11hr); Odda (3 daily; 7hr); Otta (4 daily; 5hr 30min); Rjukan (3–4 daily; 3hr 30min); Sogndal (3 daily; 7hr); Stavanger (2–3 daily; 10hr); Stryn (3 daily; 8hr 40min); Trondheim (1–3 daily; 8hr); Ålesund (2 daily; 10hr); Åndalsnes (2 daily; 8hr).

Ferries (Ⓦwww.basto-fosen.no)

Horten to: Moss (Mon–Fri 5.30am–midnight, Sat & Sun 7am–midnight, every 30min, 45 min on the weekend; 30min).

2

The South

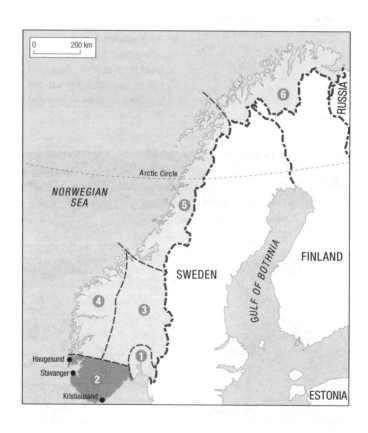

CHAPTER 2 # Highlights

* **The Clarion Hotel Tyholmen** Occupying a brace of handsome wooden buildings looking out to sea, Arendal's top-flight hotel is one of the finest places to stay on the whole of the south coast. **See p.138**

* **M/B Øya** Take a delightful three-hour cruise along the coast between Lillesand and Kristiansand on this pocket-sized ferryboat. **See p.140**

* **Mandal** One of the prettiest ports on the south coast, with the country's finest sandy beach. **See p.144**

* **Stay in a lighthouse** A string of south-coast lighthouses offer simple lodgings in wild locations – try Lindesnes, Hatholmen, Ryvingen or Ryvarden. **See p.146, p.145, p.145 & p.157**

* **Preikestolen** A geological oddity near Stavanger, this great hunk of rock offers staggering views down to the Lysefjord on three of its sides. **See p.156**

▲ Preikestolen (Pulpit Rock), Lysefjord

2

The South

A rcing out into the Skagerrak between the Oslofjord and Stavanger, Norway's **south coast** may have little of the imposing grandeur of other, wilder parts of the country, but its eastern half, running down to Kristiansand, is undeniably lovely. Speckled with islands and backed by forests, fells and lakes, it's this part of the coast that attracts Norwegians in droves, equipped not so much with bucket and spade as with boat and navigational aids – for these waters, with their narrow inlets, islands and skerries, make for particularly enjoyable **sailing**. Hundreds of Norwegians have summer cottages along this stretch of the coast and camping on the offshore islands is very popular too, especially as there are precious few restrictions: you can't stay in one spot for more than 48 hours, nor light a fire either on bare rock or among vegetation, and you must steer clear of anyone's home, but other than that you're pretty much free to go and come as you please. Leaflets detailing further coastal rules and regulations are available at any local tourist office.

The south coast down to Kristiansand is within easy striking distance of Denmark and as such it has always been important for Norway's international trade. Many of the region's larger towns, Larvik and Porsgrunn for instance, started out as timber ports, but are now humdrum, industrial centres in their own right, whereas several of their smaller neighbours – **Risør, Lillesand** and **Grimstad** are the prime examples – have dodged (nearly) all the industry to become pretty, pocket-sized resorts, whose white-painted clapboard houses provide an appropriately nautical, almost jaunty, air. Larger **Arendal** does something to bridge the gap between the resorts and the industrial towns and does so very nicely. There's also **Sandefjord**, an amenable if somewhat uninspiring place that may well be first up on your itinerary as it has its own international airport – **Oslo (Torp)** (see p.71 & p.134).

Anchoring the south coast is Norway's fifth largest city, **Kristiansand**, a bustling port and lively resort with enough sights, restaurants, bars and beaches to while away a night, maybe two. Beyond Kristiansand lies **Mandal**, an especially fetching holiday spot with a great beach, but thereafter the coast becomes harsher and less absorbing, heralding a lightly populated region with precious little to detain you before **Stavanger**, a burgeoning oil town and port with a clutch of historical sights and a full set of first-rate restaurants. Bergen (see pp.200–222) may lay claim to being the "Gateway to the Fjords", but actually Stavanger is closer with the splendid Lysefjord leading the scenic charge.

There are regular **trains** from Oslo to Kristiansand and Stavanger, but the rail line runs inland for most of its journey, only dipping down to the coast at the major resorts, which makes for a disappointing ride with the sea mostly shielded from view by the bony, forested hills. The same applies to the main **road and**

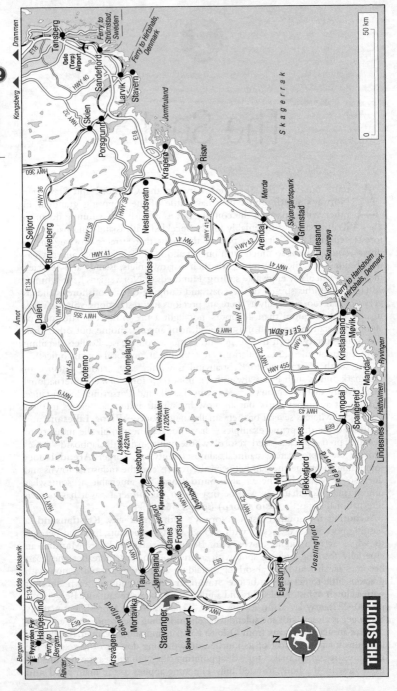

THE SOUTH

50 km

0

N

Skagerrak

Ferry to Strömstad, Sweden

Ferry to Hirtshals, Denmark

Drammen
Kongsberg
Åmot
Odda & Kinsarvik
Bergen
Rørvær

Tønsberg
Oslo (Torp) Airport
Sandefjord
Larvik
Stavern
E18
Skien
Porsgrunn
HWY 32
HWY 360
Seljord
Brunkeberg
HWY 36
HWY 38
Dalen
E134
HWY 355
HWY 38
HWY 45
Rotemo
HWY 41
HWY 41
Neslandsvatn
Tjønnefoss
Nomeland
HWY 9
HWY 41
HWY 41
HWY 415
HWY 42
Kragerø
Jomfruland
Risør
Merdo
Arendal
Skjærgårdspark
Grimstad
Lillesand
Skaurøya
HWY 42
E18
SETESDAL
HWY 9
HWY 2
HWY 455
HWY 43
Ferry to Hanstholm & Hirtshals, Denmark
Kristiansand
Møvik
Mandal
Ryvingen
Lyngdal
Spangereid
Lindesnes
Hatholmen
Hidra
HWY 43
Liknes
Moi
Flekkefjord
Fedafjord
E39
Egersund
Jøssingfjord
HWY 44
HWY 42
Hillekouten (1205m)
Lysekammen (1423m)
Lysebotn
HWY 13
Preikestolen
Lysefjord
Kjeragbolten
HWY 45
Øygardstøl
Oanes
Forsand
Jørpeland
Tau
Mortavika
Boknafjord
Stavanger
Sola Airport
Årsvågen
Haugesund
Hirvarden Fyr
E134
E39
Ferry to Bergen

bus route – the **E18/E39** – which also sticks stubbornly inland for most of the 330km from Oslo to Kristiansand (E18) and again for the 250km on to Stavanger (E39). Thanks to the E18/E39, even the tiniest of coastal villages is easy to reach, but you do need your own vehicle for most of the smaller places unless you are infinitely diligent with bus and rail timetables.

Right along the south coast, **accommodation** of one sort or another is legion, with all the larger towns having at least a couple of hotels and B&Bs, but if you're after a bit of social bounce bear in mind the **season** is short, running from the middle of June to August; outside this period many attractions are closed and local boat trips curtailed.

The E18 to Lillesand

The fretted shoreline that stretches the 200km southwest from Tønsberg (see p.126) to Lillesand is home to a series of small resorts that are particularly popular with weekenders from Oslo. The most interesting is **Grimstad**, with its Ibsen connections, the liveliest is **Arendal**, and the prettiest are **Lillesand** and **Risør**. All four have decent places to stay, but only a fifth resort, pint-sized **Kragerø**, has an HI hostel. Many of the resorts, including Lillesand, Kragerø and Arendal, offer **boat trips** out to the myriad islets that dot this coast, with trippers bent on a spot of swimming and beach – or at least rock – combing. The islands were once owned by local farmers, but many are now in public ownership, and zealously protected from any development. In addition, most of the resorts offer longer cruises along the coast during the summer, the prettiest being the delightful three-hour trip from Lillesand to Kristiansand.

Fast and frequent express **buses** scuttle along the **E18** from Oslo and/or Tønsberg to Kristiansand and these connect with local buses that run from the motorway to individual resorts – see "Travel details", p.159. A **train** line runs along the coast too, but it's not a particularly useful service – of the places described here only Arendal and Sandefjord have their own train stations. Kristiansand is also a major port with regular **ferries** arriving from Denmark.

Sandefjord

SANDEFJORD, some 120km south of Oslo, is best known as an international ferry port and as the site of **Oslo (Torp) airport**. It's an amiable, low-key kind of place, whose wide and open waterfront culminates in a spectacular water fountain – the **Hvalfangstmonumentet** (Whalers' Monument) – in which, amidst the billowing spray, a slender rowing boat and its crew ride the tail fluke of a whale. This is perhaps as good as it gets, but the town does rustle up a couple of other minor attractions, beginning with the nearby **Kurbadet**, the former thermal baths housed in a distinctive wooden complex built in a Viking-inspired dragon style in 1899; the baths closed at the beginning of World War II and have come close to being demolished on several occasions, but they have managed to hang on and are now in use as a cultural centre. The complex is located a couple of minutes' walk from the fountain – to the right as you face inland.

Behind the Kurbadet, cross Museumsgata and you'll soon stumble across the oldest and prettiest part of town, a narrow wedge of old clapboard buildings which ramble across what was once the foreshore focussed on **Bjerggata**. Just to the north, Museumsgata holds the town's best museum, another celebration of the town's whalers, the **Hvalfangstmuseet** (May–Aug daily 11am–5pm; Sept daily 11am–4pm; Oct–April Mon–Sat

11am–3pm & Sun noon–4pm; 50kr). The local whaling industry built up a head of steam at the end of the nineteenth century, peaking in the early 1950s, when as many as three thousand local men were dependent on whaling for their livelihoods. If the museum whets your interest, there's more whaling paraphernalia back down on the waterfront in the **Southern Actor**, a 1950s whaling vessel that managed to end up moored in the harbour (late June to Aug daily 11am–5pm; same ticket as Hvalfangstmuseet).

Finally, it's just a couple of kilometres north from the town centre along Highway 303 to the **Gokstadhaugen** (open access; free), the grassy mound which marks the spot where the **Gokstad Viking longship** was unearthed in 1880. The vessel is now on display in Oslo (see p.100), but information plaques displayed here add some context.

Practicalities

Oslo (Torp) airport is about 11km north of Sandefjord. The airport has expanded dramatically in recent years and now picks up a slew of domestic and international flights with Ryanair to the fore. The Torp-Ekspressen bus (see p.71) links the airport with Oslo and there are also airport buses to Sandefjord Torp train station, just one stop along the line from Sandefjord station (hourly; 3min; 33kr each way) – and a little under two hours from Oslo S (200kr each way).

From Sandefjord's **train** and neighbouring **bus station**, it's about 900m to the waterfront, straight down Jernbanealleen. The **tourist office** is just back from the waterfont, next to the Kurbadet at Thor Dahlsgate 7 (late June to late Aug Mon–Fri 9am–6pm, Sat 10am–4.30pm & Sun 12.30–4.30pm; rest of year Mon–Fri 9am–4pm; ☎33 46 05 90, ⓦwww.visitsandefjord.com). A few metres away is the Color Line quay (ⓦwww.colorline.com), where **car ferries** to and from Strömstad in Sweden arrive and depart (see "Travel details", p.159).

Of Sandefjord's several **hotels**, one of the more appealing is the large, plush *Rica Park Hotel Sandefjord*, in a big, modern tower block just back from the waterfront at Strandpromenaden 9 (☎33 44 74 00, ⓦwww.rica.no; ❽, sp/r ❻). Rather more distinctive – and a good bit more economical – is the *Hotel Kong Carl*, in an old timber building right in the centre of town at Torggata 9 (☎33 46 31 17, ⓦwww.kongcarl.no; ❸). The 25 rooms are each kitted out with a potpourri of old furnishings – pleasant if hardly stunning. There are also a couple of attractive B&Bs in the old part of town, notably *Lisbet's Guesthouse*, where there is one room to rent in the annexe with bunk beds and a shower (☎33 46 08 26, ⓔlisbe-ti@online.no; ❶).

For food, *Mathuset Solvold*, between the tourist office and the main square at Thor Dahlsgate 9, is a well-turned-out café-restaurant offering a wide-ranging menu – from pasta to mussels – with main courses 160–200kr.

Heading on to Kragerø

Pressing on along the E18, it's about 10km from Sandefjord to the turning for **Larvik**, where Color Line ferries arrive from Hirtshals in Denmark, and then another 25km to **Porsgrunn**, with a rare view of the sea as you cross the massive bridge spanning the fjord. After another 40km or so, you reach the first of several turns that lead down to the seashore at **KRAGERØ**, whose narrow harbour is spanned by a dinky little bridge. One of the busiest resorts on the coast, Kragerø has a tiny centre, with its cramped lanes and alleys rising steeply from the harbourfront, and makes a good living as a supply depot for the surrounding coves and islets, where the Norwegians hunker down in their summer cottages.

Founded as a timber port in the seventeenth century, Kragerø later boomed as a shipbuilding centre, its past importance recalled by its clutch of handsome old houses. The port was also a fashionable watering hole in the late nineteenth and early twentieth centuries. It was here that Edvard Munch produced some of his jollier paintings and where **Theodor Kittelsen** (1857–1914), a native of Kragerø, spent his summers. A middling painter but superb illustrator, Kittelsen defined the popular appearance of the country's folkloric creatures – from trolls through to sirens – in his illustrations for Asbjørnsen and Moe's *Norwegian Folk Tales*, published in 1883. Kittelsen's family home, the bright and breezy **Kittelsenhuset**, bang in the centre off Storgata at Theodor Kittelsens vei 5 (late June to Aug Tues–Sat noon–4pm; 30kr; Ⓦ www.kittelsenhuset.no), is now a lively little museum celebrating the artist's life and times with a smattering of his paintings and a few family knick-knacks. Kragerø's only other sight of note is its **church**, an imposing brown-brick structure perched on a hill on the north side of the centre.

By boat to Jomfruland

The most popular jaunt out from Kragerø is the **ferry to Jomfruland** (1–4 daily; 1hr; 60kr each way; Ⓣ 40 00 58 58, Ⓦ www.fjordbat.no), a long and slender island stuck out in the Skagerrak beyond the offshore skerries. The island, which is just 8km long and never more than 900m wide, is very different from its rocky neighbours, its fertile soils supporting deciduous woodland and providing good pastureland. The flatness of the terrain, plus the abundant bird life, attracts scores of walkers, who wander the island's network of footpaths. For many, the beach is the main target, rough and pebbly on the island's sea-facing side, more shingle and sand on its sheltered side with the best bit generally reckoned to be Øitangen in the north. The ferry docks at two places on the island; first stop is **Tårnbrygga**, about halfway along the island and an easy stroll from the island's two lighthouses – one old, from 1839, the other new, from 1937 – that stand side by side.

Practicalities

Long-distance express buses linking Oslo and Kristiansand stop at Tangen, from where there is a connecting local bus service on to Kragerø; the journey from Tangen takes 25 minutes. The nearest **train station** is at Neslandsvatn, where the Togbuss meets the Oslo–Kristiansand train for the 45-minute journey on to Kragerø. In Kragerø itself, the **bus station** and the **tourist office** (mid-June to mid-Aug Mon–Fri 9am–7pm, Sat 9am–6pm, Sun 10am–5pm; shorter hours rest of year; Ⓣ 35 98 23 88, Ⓦ www.visitkragero.no) are a stone's throw from the northern tip of the harbour. They are also just a couple of minutes' walk from the Jomfruland ferry dock.

Most visitors to Kragerø have their own summer homes, so although they stock up with provisions here, few actually **stay the night**. Nonetheless, the town does possess one very pleasant hotel, the *Victoria*, in a good-looking, brightly painted harbourside building at P. A. Heuchs gate 31 (Ⓣ 35 98 75 25, Ⓦ www.victoria-kragero.no; ❺, sp/r ❹). Each of the hotel's guest rooms are individually decorated in browns and creams and the best have balconies overlooking the harbour. Much less expensive is the HI **hostel**, the *Kragerø Vandrerhjem*, about 2km out of town along Highway 38 at Lovisenbergveien 20 (Ⓣ 35 98 57 00, Ⓦ www.vandrerhjem.no; dorm beds 325kr, doubles ❷; open late June to late Aug). The hostel occupies a rambling, chalet-like wooden building beside a pretty bay and rents out rowing boats. Breakfast is included in the price and the hostel also serves up filling evening **meals**; buses travelling into Kragerø on Highway 38 pass right by the hostel.

Kragerø's centre is crowded with cafés and café-bars with one of the best being *Dus Mat & Vinhus*, Storgata 1 (Mon–Sat 10am–11pm; ☎35 98 93 00), which does a good line in tapas as well as the more usual Norwegian offerings.

Risør

RISØR, spreading round the head of a gentle promontory about 45km from Kragerø, is a good-looking town, its genial array of old and white timber houses winkling back from its wide and deep harbour. The town rustles up a string of summer festivals, from Bluegrass in July to Chamber Music in June, and is something of a centre for arts and crafts, but it's the general flavour of the place that appeals rather than anything specific. Risør started out as a small fishing village, but the Dutch fleet began dropping by for timber in the 1570s and the port boomed until, by the 1880s, one hundred sailing vessels – and one thousand seamen – called the place home. A great fire destroyed the bulk of the town in 1861, but it was quickly rebuilt – and most of the wooden houses that survive date from this period. Risør's marine economy collapsed in the 1920s and today it looks like a rather conservative small town, but – surprise, surprise – the directly elected mayor, one Knut Henning Thygesen, is a member of the Red Party, a recent fusion of the Workers' Communist Party (AKP) and the Red Electoral Alliance (RV): he is the party's only mayor.

Practicalities

Risør **bus station** is on the main street just a few metres from the harbour, where the **tourist office** (early June & late Aug Mon–Sat 10am–4pm & Sun noon–4pm; mid-June to mid-Aug Mon–Fri 10am–6pm, Sat 10am–4pm & Sun noon–6pm; rest of year Mon–Fri 10am–3pm & Sat noon–2pm; ☎37 15 22 70, ⓦwww.risor.no) can advise on all things local. Among the town's several **hotels and guesthouses**, the most individual is *Det Lille Hotel*, whose twelve suites are distributed between two old buildings with one just by the harbour at Storgata 5 (☎37 15 14 95, ⓦwww.detlillehotel.no; ❼). For food, try the *Bakgården Café*, a cosy little place just back from the harbour on Kragsgata.

Arendal

Heading south from Risør, it's about 45km to the bustling town of **ARENDAL**, one of the most appealing places on the coast, its sheltered harbour curling right into the centre, which is further crimped by the forested hills pushing in from behind. The town's heyday was in the eighteenth century when its shipyards churned out dozens of the sleek wooden sailing ships that then dominated international trade. The shipyards faded away in the late nineteenth century, but there's an attractive reminder of the boom times in the striking medley of old timber buildings that make up the oldest part of town, **Tyholmen**, which rolls over the steep and bumpy promontory just to the southwest of the modern centre. The architectural highlight here is the Gamle **Rådhus** (Old Town Hall), Norway's tallest wooden house, a handsome, four-storey structure, whose classical symmetries overlook the Tyholmen waterfront. The house was built as a private residence in 1815, but the Danish merchant who owned the place died twelve years later and his widow sold it to the council, who turned it into the Town Hall, a role it performed until 2004. To explore Tyholmen's every nook and cranny, sign up at the tourist office (see p.138) for one of their guided **walking tours** (mid-June to early Aug 3 weekly; 1hr 30min; 60kr).

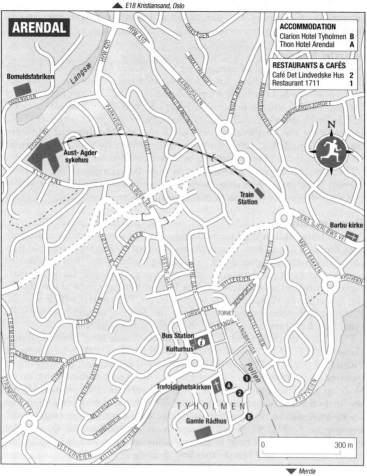

▼ Merdø

Perched on a rocky knoll at the northern edge of Tyholmen, the massive and massively ugly red-brick **Trefoldighetskirken** (Church of the Trinity) was meant to celebrate the town's economic success as well as its spirituality. Instead, it almost ended up being a total fiasco: Arendal hit the financial skids in 1886 and, although the church had been finished, there was no money to equip the interior and the altar was only installed twenty years later. The church overlooks the town centre, where the most conspicuous building is the glassy, modern **Kulturhus** (Ⓦ www.arendalkulturhus.no), which hosts conferences, public meetings, and concerts to suit (almost) every musical taste. From here, it's a couple of minute's, walk north to Pollen, the short, rectangular inner harbour, which is flanked by pavement cafés and bars.

Arendal's other key attraction is the region's largest contemporary-arts gallery, the **Bomuldsfabriken**, housed in a former textile factory a couple of kilometres north of the centre at Oddenveien 5 (Tues–Sun noon–3pm; free; Ⓦ www.bomuldsfabriken.no). The gallery hosts half a dozen exhibitions of contemporary art every year with Norwegian work to the fore; the gallery is signposted off Highway 410, one of the main approach roads into Arendal from the E18.

Merdø island

Amongst the scattering of islands lying just offshore from Arendal, the most diverting is **Merdø**, a fairly flat, lightly wooded islet, whose safe anchorages, orchards and fresh water made it a popular haven for sailing ships right up until the end of the nineteenth century. Footpaths network the island, there's a shingle beach and a café, and Merdø's one and only village is a pretty affair that spreads along the foreshore. It's here you'll find the **Merdøgaard Museum** (late June to mid-Aug daily noon–4pm; 20kr), a brightly painted eighteenth-century sea captain's house, complete with original fixtures and fittings.

The passenger ferry to **Merdø** departs from Pollen, right in the centre of Arendal (June to late Aug daily 10am–4pm every 30min to 1hr; 40kr; rest of year, sporadic service – details from the tourist office).

Practicalities

Arendal **train station** is on the north side of town, a five- to ten-minute walk from the main square, Torvet: go to the roundabout close to the station and then either proceed up and over the steep hill along Iuellsklev and then Bendiksklev, or (more easily) stroll through the tunnel (signed: P–Torget). Torvet is metres from the inner harbour, Pollen. The **bus station** is in the centre of town beside the Kulturhus on Vestre gate, just west of Torvet. The **tourist office** is in the Kulturhus (July Mon–Fri 9am–7pm, Sat & Sun 11am–6pm; Aug–June Mon–Fri 9am–7pm, Sat 11am–2pm; ⊕37 00 55 44, ⓦwww.arendal.com).

There's one smashing hotel in Arendal, the ⅉ *Clarion Hotel Tyholmen*, Teater-plassen 2 (⊕37 07 68 00, ⓦwww.choicehotels.no; ➏, sp/r ➍), which occupies a matching pair of buildings in the style of two old warehouses on the Tyholmen quayside. Full marks here to the architects, who designed the second, newer block to blend in seamlessly with its older neighbour. The guest rooms are resolutely modern, with blues and whites throughout, and most have splendid sea views. A second, very much more modest option is the *Thon Hotel Arendal*, Friergangen 1 (⊕37 05 21 50, ⓦwww.thonhotels.com/arendal; ➎, s/r ➍), a straightforward, modern hotel in the centre just off the west side of Pollen.

A string of **cafés and restaurants** line up along Pollen, with one of the best being *Restaurant 1711* (Mon–Sat 6–10.30pm; ⊕37 00 17 11), a smart and intimate little place in an old wooden building on the south side of the harbour. The house speciality is seafood and main courses cost 250–300kr. The grooviest place in town is *Café Det Lindvedske Hus* (Mon–Sat 11am–11pm, Sun noon–11pm), a laid-back, arty sort of place where they serve light meals – pastas, salads and so forth – upstairs in an old building just to the south of Pollen. Mains start at around 60kr and the kitchen closes at 9pm, whereupon it's over to the drinking. For a small town, Arendal has a lively drinking scene with a clutter of bars on and around Pollen keeping the punters going till the wee hours of the morning each and every weekend.

Grimstad

From Arendal, it's a short twenty-kilometre hop south along the E18 to **GRIMSTAD**, where a brisk huddle of white timber houses with orange- and black-tiled roofs is stacked up behind the harbour. Nowadays scores of yachts are moored in the harbour, but at the beginning of the nineteenth century the town had no fewer than forty shipyards and carried on a lucrative import-export trade with France. It was not particularly surprising, therefore, that when **Henrik Ibsen** (1828–1906) left his home in nearby Skien at the tender age of sixteen, he should come to Grimstad, where he worked as an apprentice pharmacist for the next six years. The ill-judged financial dealings of Ibsen's father had impoverished the family, and Henrik's already jaundiced view of Norway's provincial bourgeoisie was confirmed here in the port, whose worthies Ibsen mocked in poems like *Resignation*, and *The Corpse's Ball*. It was here too that Ibsen picked up first-hand news of the Paris Revolution of 1848, an event that radicalized him and inspired his paean to the insurrectionists of Budapest, *To Hungary*, written in 1849. Nonetheless, Ibsen's stay on the south coast is more usually recalled as providing the setting for some of his better-known plays, especially his *Pillars of Society*.

The small house where Ibsen lived and worked as a pharmacist is now the **Ibsen-museet** (Ibsen Museum; late May to Aug Mon–Sat 11am–5pm & Sun noon–5pm; 50kr, including optional guided tour) – and it's located just up from the harbour in the centre of town on Henrik Ibsens gate. The alley that serves as the entrance to the museum plus much of the ground floor beyond has been returned to an approximation of its appearance when Ibsen lived here, complete with its creaking wooden floors and narrow-beamed ceilings. Upstairs, there's a detailed display on Ibsen the dramatist plus an assortment of original letters and documents and, best of all, a glass cabinet of Ibsen memorabilia – his glasses and their case, an ink stand, a ruler and even a piece of the great man's hair. For more on Ibsen, see p.86.

From the museum, it's a couple of minutes' walk south to the pedestrianized part of Storgata, once the town's main street. Signposted off it near the harbourfront is the **Reimanngården**, four uninspiring replica eighteenth-century buildings, one of which is a reconstruction of another pharmacy where Ibsen worked – the original building was demolished in the 1950s; the Reimanngården is now home to the town's art society. In the opposite direction from the Ibsen house, it's a short, steep hike north up to **Grimstad Kirke**, a large, late nineteenth-century wooden church plonked on a hill high above the harbour. Inside, many of the original fittings have survived, including some heavy-duty wrought-iron lamps and candelabras, and there's a tapestry of the Resurrection by the font.

Practicalities

With regular services from Oslo, Arendal and Kristiansand, Grimstad **bus station** is at the south end of the harbour, a couple of hundred metres along from the **tourist office** (June–Aug Mon–Fri 9am–6pm, Sat 10am–4pm, plus Sun in July 10am–4pm; Sept–May Mon–Fri 8.30am–4pm; ℡37 25 01 68, ⓦwww.grimstad.net). They supply free town maps and have lots of information on the myriad islands that guard the seaward approaches to the town. Many of these islands are protected within the **Skjærgårdspark**, and have public access moorings, as well as picnic and bathing facilities. One or two of them can be reached by water taxi, but mostly you'll have to rent a boat – the tourist office will advise.

The best hotel in town is the *Rica Hotel Grimstad*, which occupies an old and cleverly converted clapboard complex among the narrow lanes near the Ibsen house at Kirkegaten 3 (℡37 25 25 25, ⓦwww.grimstadhotell.no; ❺, sp/rx❹). The best place to eat is the *Apotekergården*, a lively, informal café-restaurant also in the town centre at Skolegata 3 (daily noon–11pm; ℡37 04 50 25); their menu has a good range of meat and seafood dishes with mains around 220kr. While you're in town, look out for the locally made fruit wines – Fuhr Rhubarb and Fuhr Vermouth are the two to try.

Lillesand

Bright and cheery **LILLESAND**, just 20km south of Grimstad, is one of the
most popular holiday spots on the coast, the white clapboard houses of its tiny
centre draped prettily round the harbourfront. One or two of the buildings,
notably the sturdy **Rådhus** of 1734, are especially fetching, but it's the general
appearance of the place that appeals, best appreciated from the terrace of one of
the town's waterfront café-bars: the *Sjøbua*, midway round the harbour, does
very nicely.

To investigate Lillesand's architectural nooks and crannies, sign up at the
tourist office (see below) for one of their hour-long **guided walks** (1 daily
mid-June to Aug; 40kr). The tourist office also has information and sailing
schedules for a wide variety of local **boat trips**, from fishing trips and cruises
along the coast to the summertime *badeboot* (bathing boat), which shuttles across
to Hestholm bay on the island of **Skauerøya**, where swimmers don't seem to
notice just how cold the Skagerrak actually is. Perhaps better still is the three-
hour cruise aboard **M/B Øya** (July to early Aug Mon–Sat 1 daily; 225kr each
way; ☎95 93 58 55), a dinky little passenger ferry which wiggles south to
Kristiansand (see below) in part along a narrow channel separating the mainland
from the offshore islets. Sheltered from the full force of the ocean, this channel
– the **Blindleia** – was once a major trade route, but today it's trafficked by every
sort of pleasure craft imaginable, from replica three-mast sailing ships and
vintage tugboats to the sleekest of yachts. Other, faster, boats make the trip too,
but the M/B *Øya* is the most charming.

Practicalities

Lillesand is not on the train line and although some buses – principally those
from Arendal and Grimstad – halt at the **bus station** in the town centre, most
long-distance services pull into **Lillesand Borkedalen**, from where connecting
local buses proceed to Lillesand, a five-minute journey. Lillesand bus station is
at the southern end of the harbour footsteps from the **tourist office** (mid-June
to mid-Aug Mon–Fri 10am–6pm, Sat 10am–4pm & Sun noon–4pm; ☎93 01
17 81, ⓦwww.lillesand.com).

Lillesand has one central **hotel**, the first-rate ⚜ *Hotel Norge*, Strandgata 3 (☎37
27 01 44, ⓦwww.hotelnorge.no; ❼, sp/r ❻), which occupies a grand old wooden
building metres from the harbour. Refurbished in attractive period style, the
interior holds some charming stained-glass windows and the rooms are named
after some of the famous people who have stayed here – the novelist Knut
Hamsun and the Spanish king Alfonso XIII for starters. Alternatively, try *Tingsaker
Familiecamping* (☎37 27 04 21, ⓦwww.tingsakercamping.no), a well-equipped
and very busy seaside campsite with self-catering facilities, canoe hire, a pool and
cabins (850–1500kr), about 1km north of the centre on Øvre Tingsaker. To get
there, take Storgata and keep going. The *Hotel Norge* has an excellent **restaurant**,
but it's more expensive and formal than the harbourfront *Beddingen* (☎37 27 24
22), where you can sample excellent fish dishes for around 220kr.

Kristiansand

With 80,000 inhabitants, **KRISTIANSAND**, some 30km west along the E18
from Lillesand, is Norway's fifth-largest town and part-time holiday resort –
altogether a genial, energetic place which thrives on its ferry connections with
Denmark, its busy marinas, its passable sandy beaches and, last but not least, its

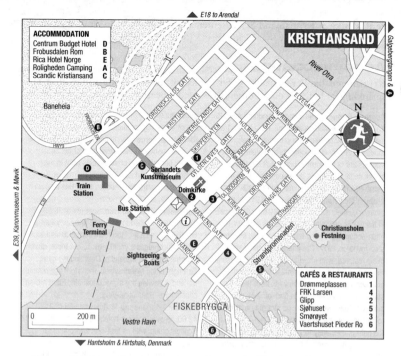

ACCOMMODATION
Centrum Budget Hotel **D**
Frobusdalen Rom **B**
Rica Hotel Norge **E**
Roligheden Camping **A**
Scandic Kristiansand **C**

KRISTIANSAND

River Otra

Baneheia

N

Train Station

Sørlandets Kunstmuseum

Domkirke

Bus Station

Ferry Terminal

Christiansholm Festning

Sightseeing Boats

0   200 m

FISKEBRYGGA

Vestre Havn

CAFÉS & RESTAURANTS
Drømmeplassen **1**
FRK Larsen **4**
Glipp **2**
Sjøhuset **5**
Smørøyet **3**
Vaertshuset Pieder Ro **6**

▼ Hantsholm & Hirtshals, Denmark

offshore oil industry. In summer, the seafront and adjoining streets are a frenetic bustle of bars, fast-food joints and flirting holidaymakers, and even in winter Norwegians even come here to live it up.

Like so many other Scandinavian towns, Kristiansand was founded by – and named after – **Christian IV**, who saw an opportunity to strengthen his coastal defences here. Building started in 1641, and the town has retained the spacious quadrant plan that characterized all Christian's projects. There are few specific sights as such, but the place is well worth a quick look around, especially when everyone else has gone to the beach and left the central pedestrianized streets relatively empty. The main historic attraction, however, is a few kilometres out of town at the **Kristiansand Kanonmuseum**, the forbidding remains of a large coastal gun battery built during the German occupation of World War II.

Arrival and information

Trains, **buses** and international **ferries** all arrive close to each other, beside Vestre Strandgate, on the edge of the town grid. The main regional **tourist office** is nearby, at Rådhusgaten 6 (mid-June to Aug Mon–Fri 8.30am–6pm, Sat 10am–6pm, Sun noon–6pm; Sept to mid-June Mon–Fri 8.30am–3.30pm; ☏38 12 13 14, ⓦwww.sorlandet.com). They issue free town maps and public transport timetables, will assist with accommodation and have information on local boat cruises, island bathing and beaches. The main car parks are along Vestre Strandgate and although spaces can be hard to find at the height of the season, they remain your best bet as on-street parking in the rest of the town centre is strictly limited. The best way to explore the town centre is on **foot** – it only takes about ten minutes to walk from one side to the other – but for the more outlying attractions, including the best beaches, you might want to

rent a bike at Kristiansand Sykkelsenter, about 800m northwest of the tourist office, just off Highway 9 at Grim Torv 3 (☎38 02 68 35).

Accommodation

Kristiansand has a reasonably good choice of **accommodation** with a fair sprinkling of hotels, a guesthouse or two, and a nearby campsite.

Centrum Budget Hotel Vestre Strandgate 49 ☎38 70 15 65, ⓦwww.budgethotel.no. Hard by the train station, this hostel-like hotel provides frugal, modern and very clean lodgings at budget prices. Doubles are in the form of bunk beds, and all rooms are en suite. Breakfasts is served close by at the *Jernbanekafeen* café and cost just 60kr. ❶

Frobusdalen Rom Frobusdalen 2 ☎91 12 99 06, ⓦwww.gjestehus.no. Undoubtedly the best place in town, this delightful guesthouse is a family-run affair occupying a good-looking mansion built for a ship-owner in 1917. The interior has been sensitively restored, with individually decorated en-suite rooms and public areas sprinkled with period antiques. It's just a 5–10min walk from the train station, but is a little hard to find: on foot, head north up Vestre Strandgate, go straight on at the roundabout by the flyover (signed Evje), then take the path immediately to your right; Frobusdalen is 10m along on the left. Drivers should head north along Festningsgata; turn left onto Tordenskjolds gate; and then watch for the short right turn that leads to a narrow bridge spanning the E18; the far side of the bridge is a few metres from the

guesthouse. Breakfast is not provided, but there are self-catering facilities. ❸

Rica Hotel Norge Dronningens gate 5 ☎38 17 40 00, ⓦwww.rica.no. No prizes for architectural charm, but this large chain hotel is right in the centre of town and its 170 guest rooms are decorated in attractive modern style. Has its own spa too. ❻, sp/r ❹

Rolighedan Camping Framnesveien ☎38 09 67 22, ⓦwww.roligheden.no. Large and fairly formal campsite 3km east of the town centre behind a car park, which edges a yacht jetty. To get there, drive over the bridge at the end of Dronningens gate, turn right along Marviksveien, then right again near the end, following the signs. Unusually, there are no cabins here. Open June–Aug.

Scandic Kristiansand Markensgate 39 ☎21 61 42 00, ⓦwww.scandic-hotels.com. The enterprising *Scandic* group, with its first-rate environmental policy, has about a dozen hotels in Norway and this one occupies a large modern block in the heart of downtown. The rooms are immaculate, all pastel shades and unfussy furnishings and fittings, and the breakfasts are top notch. ❼, sp/r ❹

The Town

Neat and trim, the gridiron streets that make up Kristiansand's compact centre hold one architectural high point, the **Domkirke** (late June to mid-Aug Mon–Fri 10am–4pm & Sat 10am–3pm; free), an imposing neo-Gothic edifice dating from the 1880s, whose spire pokes high into the sky at the corner of Kirkegata and Rådhusgaten. Its only rival is the **Christiansholm Festning**, on Strandpromenaden (mid-May to mid-Sept daily 9am–9pm; free), a squat fortress whose sturdy circular tower and zigzagging earth-and-stone ramparts overlook the marina in the east harbour. Built in 1672, the tower's walls are 5m thick, a defensive precaution that proved unnecessary since it never saw action. These days it houses various arts and crafts displays. The pick of the town's several museums is the **Sørlandets Kunstmuseum**, Skippergaten 24 (Sørlandet Art Museum; June–Aug Tues–Fri 11am–4pm, Sat & Sun noon–4pm; Sept–May Tues–Fri noon–5pm, Sat & Sun noon–4pm; free, exhibitions 40kr), which is best known for its temporary exhibitions of contemporary art, though it also rustles up a reasonable selection of Norwegian paintings from 1800 onwards.

If you fancy a **swim**, one option is to head off to **Galgebergtangen** (Gallows' Point), an attractive rocky cove with a small sandy beach, 2km east of the town centre. To get there, go over the bridge at the end of Dronningens gate, take the first major right at the lights – Kuholmsveien – and follow the signs.

Kristiansand Kanonmuseum

Despite the inveigling of the German admiralty, who feared the British would occupy Norway and thus trap their fleet in the Baltic, **Hitler** was lukewarm about invading Norway until he met **Vidkun Quisling** in Berlin in late 1939. Hitler took Quisling's assurances about his ability to stage a coup d'état at face value, no doubt encouraged by the Norwegian's virulent anti-Semitism, and was thereafter keen to proceed. In the event, the invasion went smoothly enough – even if Quisling was soon discarded – but for the rest of the war Hitler overestimated both Norway's strategic importance and the likelihood of an Allied counter-invasion in the north. These two errors of judgement prompted him both to garrison the country with nigh on half a million men and to build several hundred artillery batteries round the coast – a huge waste of resources even by his standards.

Work began on the coastal battery that is now conserved as the **Kristiansand Kanonmuseum** (mid-May to mid-June & mid-Aug to Sept Mon–Wed 11am–3pm & Thurs–Sun 11am–5pm; mid-June to mid-Aug daily 11am–6pm; Oct–Nov & Feb to mid-May Sun only noon–4pm; 60kr; ⓦ www .kanonmuseet.no) in 1941, using – like all equivalent emplacements in Norway – the forced labour of POWs. Around 1400 men worked on the project, which involved the installation of four big guns and the construction of protective concrete housings. The idea was to make the Skagerrak impassable for enemy warships at its narrowest part, and so complementary batteries were also installed opposite on the Danish shore; only a small zone in the middle was out of range, and this the Germans mined. The **Kristiansand** battery once covered 220 acres, but today the principal remains hog a narrow ridge, with a massive, empty artillery casement at one end, and a whopping 38cm-calibre **gun** in a concrete well at the other. The gun, which could fire a 500kg shell almost 55km, is in pristine condition, and visitors can explore the loading area, complete with the original ramrods, wedges, trolleys and pulleys. Below is the underground command post and soldiers' living quarters, again almost exactly as they were in the 1940s – including the odd bit of German graffiti.

The Kanonmuseum is situated an easy ten-kilometre drive south of Kristiansand, along the coast at **MØVIK**: take Highway 456 out of Kristiansand, turning down Highway 457 for the last 3km of the journey.

Eating and drinking

There are lots of **cafés and restaurants** in the centre of Kristiansand, with a particular concentration in the Fiskebrygga, a huddle of mostly modern timber houses set around a small harbour just off the eastern end of Vestre Strandgate. Standards are, however, very variable, so it pays to be selective – we've given a few of the choicer places below. Kristiansand also has a fairly active nightlife based around a handful of downtown **bars**, which stay open until 2 or 3am.

Drømmeplassen Corner of Skippergata and Kirkegata. Part clothes shop, part bakery, part café, this attractive little place sells an excellent range of bread as well as tasty coffee and the freshest of snacks. Mon–Fri 7am–7pm, Sat 9am–6pm & Sun 11am–4pm.

FRK Larsen Markensgate 5. It's something of a surprise to find that this resolutely alternative café-bar has survived for so long – but here it is in all its retro–New Age glory. Cocktails from 8pm and occasional live acts. Near the corner of Kongens-gate. Daily 11am–midnight, 3am at the weekend.

Glipp Rådhusgaten 11. Popular, sometimes slick café-bar that does a good line in tapas (40–80kr), though its main pull is perhaps its outside terrace, which looks out over the spacious main square. Daily 11am–11pm.

Sjøhuset Østre Strandgate 12a ☏38 02 62 60. In an old converted warehouse by the harbour at the east end of Markensgate, this

Moving on from Kristiansand

When it comes to **moving on from Kristiansand**, the obvious choice – the 250-kilometre trip west to Stavanger – is also the best. It's a journey that can be made by train as well as by bus or car along the E39, though both the railway line and the highway only afford glimpses of the coast, travelling for the most part a few kilometres inland. It may not be a gripping journey, but it's certainly a lot more pleasant than the dreary 240-kilometre haul north up **Setesdal** on Highway 9 to the E134. If, on the other hand, you're travelling north towards Oslo in July and early Aug, it might be worth considering the three-hour cruise up to Lillesand on the M/B Øya (see p.140).

Note the distinction between Kristiansund in the north and Kristiansand in the south: to make things easier, on timetables and in brochures they are often written as Kristiansund N and Kristiansand S.

excellent restaurant serves superb fish dishes from 250–300kr – less if you stick to the bar menu. Nautical fittings and wooden beams set the scene and there's an attractive outside terrace with sea views too. Daily 11am–11pm, restaurant 3–11pm. **Smørøyet Rådhusgaten 12.** Arguably better as a bar than as a restaurant, this imaginatively decorated, modern spot occupies an older building overlooking the main square. Attractive outside terrace. Daily 11am–11.30pm.

🏃 **Vaertshuset Pieder Ro** Gravane 10 ☎ 38 10 07 88. Many locals swear this is the best seafood restaurant in town and has the liveliest atmosphere. It occupies an ersatz traditional timber building down in the Fiskebrygga complex. Reservations advisable at all times, and essential for the herring buffet on Sat. Main courses average 250kr, though note that prices are a little less at lunchtime than they are in the evening. Lunch Mon–Fri 11.30am–6pm; dinner daily 4–11pm.

West from Kristiansand to Stavanger

West of Kristiansand lies a sparsely inhabited region, where the rough uplands and long valleys of the interior bounce down to a shoreline that is pierced by a string of inlets and fjords. The highlight is undoubtedly **Mandal**, a fetching seaside resort with probably the best sandy beach in the whole of Norway, but thereafter it's a struggle to find much inspiration. The best you'll do is the old harbour town of **Flekkefjord**, though frankly there's not much reason to pause anywhere between Mandal and Stavanger.

The **E39** weaves its way west for 250km from Kristiansand to Stavanger, staying inland for the most part and offering only the odd sight of the coast. The **train line** follows pretty much the same route – though it does, unlike the E39, bypass Flekkefjord – until it reaches **Egersund**, when it returns to the coast for the final 80km, slicing across long flat plains with the sea on one side and distant hills away to the east.

Mandal

Pocket-sized **MANDAL**, just 40km from Kristiansand along the E39, is Norway's southernmost town. This old timber port reached its heyday in the eighteenth century, when pines and oaks from the surrounding countryside were much sought after by the Dutch to support their canal houses and build their trading fleet. The timber boom dried up decades ago, but Mandal has preserved its quaint **old centre**, a narrow strip of white clapboard buildings spread along the north bank of the Mandalselva River just before it rolls into the sea. It's an attractive spot, well worth a stroll, and you can also drop by the municipal **museum** (late June to mid-Aug Mon–Fri 11am–5pm, Sat 11am–2pm & Sun noon–4pm; 20kr), whose rambling collection – from agricultural implements to seafaring tackle – occupies an antique merchant's house overlooking the river. Its exhibits also include a small but enjoyable collection of nautical paintings and outside, in the garden, stands a statue of the Viking chieftain Egil Skallagrimsson by the town's most famous son, **Gustav Vigeland** (see p.103). The central character of *Egil's Saga*, Skallagrimsson is a complex figure, sometimes wise and deliberate, at other times rash and violent. Vigeland has him putting on a horse's head, presumably a reference to his family's reputation as shape-shifters or shape-changers – the ability to change form and one that was shared with several Norse gods, including Odin himself.

Sjøsanden

It's not, however, its art that makes Mandal a popular holiday spot, but its fine beach, **Sjøsanden**. An 800-metre stretch of golden sand backed by pine trees and framed by rocky headlands, it's touted as Norway's best beach – and although this isn't saying a lot, it's a very enjoyable place to unwind for a few hours. The beach is about 1km from the town centre: walk along the harbour, past the tourist office to the end of the road and keep going through the woods on the signed footpath. You can also explore **Furulunden**, a tiny wooded peninsula directly to the west of the beach, where a network of paths winds through the trees and rocks to reveal hidden sand and shingle coves; pick up a map at the tourist office.

Practicalities

There are no trains to Mandal, but buses from Kristiansand (2–4 daily; 50min) and Stavanger (2–4 daily; 3hr 10min) pull in at the **bus station** by the bridge on the north bank of the Mandalselva River. From here, it's a brief walk west along the river bank to the old town centre and a couple of hundred metres more to the **tourist office**, facing the river at Bryggegata 10 (June–Aug Mon–Fri 9am–7pm, Sat & Sun 10am–4pm; Sept–May Mon–Fri 9am–4pm; ☎38 27 83 00, ⓦ www.visitregionmandal.com).

There are a couple of good places to **stay** in Mandal, beginning with the handy and economical *Kjøbmandsgaarden Hotel*, which occupies an old timber house in a street of such buildings, across from the bus station at Store Elvegate 57 (☎38 26 12 76, ⓦ www.kjobmandsgaarden.com; ❹). All the dozen or so rooms here are spick-and-span and the decor is bright and cheerful albeit a little staid. Much more up market is the *First Hotel Solborg*, Neseveien 1 (☎38 27 21 00, ⓦ www.firsthotels.com; ❺), an odd-looking but somehow rather fetching modern structure with every mod con, including a pool; it's on the west side of the town centre, a good ten-minute walk from the bus station, tight against a wooded escarpment. You can also **camp** or rent a cabin (❸) very close to the

Staying in a lighthouse

Mandal tourist office has the details of a couple of remote, offshore **lighthouses**, which offer simple accommodation during the summertime – **Hatholmen Fyr** (no contact details; ❶) and **Ryvingen Fyr** (ⓦ www.ryvingenfyr.no; ❶). Both lie out in the Skagerrak to the south of Mandal and in both cases you're responsible for your own food and bed linen. The biggest expense involved in staying at either is the return boat trip, which the tourist office will arrange on your behalf: it costs 750kr each way to Ryvingen, about half that to Hatholmen. It's also possible to stay at – and drive to – **Lindesnes Fyr** (see p.146).

western end of the **Sjøsanden** beach at the *Sjøsanden Feriesenter*, Sjøsandvei 1 (T38 26 10 94, W www.sjosanden-feriesenter.no; 850–1120kr for 6); note that the access road to the camp detours round the back of the woods, which back onto the beach; it's well signposted.

Among the cafés and restaurants in the town centre, nowhere really catches the eye, but *Jonas B Gundersen*, a popular pizzeria-restaurant across from the old water fountain at Store Elvegate 25 (Mon–Sat 11am–11pm, Sun 1–11pm), serves filling food at affordable prices with pizzas from 110kr. Alternatively, the café-restaurant of the *Kjøbmandsgaarden Hotel*, metres from the bus station at Store Elvegate 57 (Mon–Thurs 8am–9pm, Fri & Sat 8.30am–10pm & Sun 8.30am–6pm), takes a stab at more traditional Norwegian cuisine, offering a tasty range of dishes with mains averaging 220kr.

Lindesnes

Heading west from Mandal on the E39, it's about 12km to Highway 460, which snakes its way south to – and then along – **Lindesnes** (literally "where the land curves round"), a chubby, thirteen-kilometre-long promontory jutting out into the Skagerrak. Formidable seamen they may have been, but the Vikings feared the cape's treacherous waters to such an extent that they cut a canal across its base at **Spangereid** to avoid the vagaries of the open sea. In 2007, a replica canal was created along with a new attraction, **Vikingland** (mid-June to late Aug daily 11am–5pm; 80kr; W www.vikinglandspangereid.no), a sort of Viking theme park with axe-throwing, archery and boat trips on two motorized mock-ups of Viking longships.

Pushing on from Spangereid, it's a short drive to Norway's most southerly point, where a sturdy red-and-white lighthouse – **Lindesnes Fyr** – perches on a knobbly, lichen-stained headland. There has been a lighthouse here since the seventeenth century, but today's structure dates from 1916. The history of the lighthouse and its keepers is explored in a modest **museum**, which has been cut into the rock of the headland (May, June and mid-Aug to Sept daily 11am–5pm; July to mid-Aug daily 9am–9pm; Oct–April Sat & Sun 11am–5pm; 50kr), and the tower is open to the public too. The most dramatic time to visit is during bad weather: the headland is exposed to extraordinarily ferocious storms, when the warm westerly currents of the Skagerrak meet cold easterly winds. You can also overnight here, in some of the old lighthouse-keepers' quarters, which have been modernized in a pleasant manner (T38 25 88 51, W www .lindesnesfyr.no; ❸); reservations are essential.

Heading onto Flekkefjord

Moving on from Mandal, the **E39** hurries west, running past the turning for the Lindesnes lighthouse (see above) before proceeding over the hills to workaday **Lyngdal** and subsequently **LIKNES**, a fjordside village at the foot of Kvinesdal. Thereafter, the highway offers a rare glimpse of the ocean as it slips along the slender **Fedafjord** before turning inland again to snake over the hills to **FLEKKEFJORD**, 70km from Mandal. With a population of 6000, Flekke-fjord is the big deal hereabouts, the old and picturesque timber houses of its tiny centre strung along the banks of a short (500m) channel that connects the Lafjord and the Grisefjord. Flekkefjord boomed in the sixteenth century on the back of its trade with the Dutch, who purchased the town's timber for their houses and its granite for their dykes and harbours. Later, in the 1750s, the herring industry was the main money-spinner, along with shipbuilding and tanning, but the Flekkefjord economy had pretty much collapsed by the end of the nineteenth century when sailing ships gave way to steam. The oldest and prettiest part of Flekkefjord – known as **Hollenderbyen** after the town's Dutch connections – is on the west side of the channel, and only takes a few minutes to explore, though you can extend this pleasantly enough by visiting the nearby nineteenth-century period rooms of the **Flekkefjord Museum** (mid-June to Aug Mon–Fri noon–5pm, Sat & Sun noon–3pm; 20kr).

Practicalities

Buses pull in on Løvikgata, about 200m east of the central waterway; the **tourist office** is on the waterway's west side at Elvegata 9 (mid-June to mid-Aug Mon–Fri 9am–5pm, Sat & Sun 10am–3pm; mid-Aug to mid-June Mon–Fri 9am–4pm; ☎38 32 69 95, ⓦwww.visitsydvest.no). There's no pressing reason to overnight here, but if you do want **to stay**, the unassuming, fifty-room *Maritim Fjordhotell* (☎38 32 58 00, ⓦwww.fjordhotellene.no; ❺, sp/r ❸), overlooking the east side of the central waterway at Sundgata 9, is the best bet.

Egersund and the Jossingfjord

At Flekkefjord, the E39 turns inland, threading its way over the hills and down the dales bound for Stavanger, 120km away. Alternatively, you can take the more southerly, but slightly longer (30km or so), **Highway 44** which offers occasional glimpses of the sea, most memorably when it wiggles across the narrow **JOSSINGFJORD**, the scene of dramatic events in World War II. In February 1940, the German supply ship *Altmar* was transporting 300 Allied POWs to Germany, when it was spotted by a British destroyer, HMS *Cossack*. The destroyer gave chase, trapped the *Altmar* here in the Jossingfjord and freed the prisoners. At this time in the war, this was a rare British success and it prompted those Norwegians who were opposed to the Germans – the vast majority of the population – to call themselves "Jossings" throughout hostilities.

From the Jossingfjord, it's a further 35km or so to **EGERSUND**, a port and minor manufacturing centre that spreads over a jigsaw of bays and lakes at the end of a deep and sheltered ocean inlet. Apart from an assortment of old timber houses in the centre, along Strandgaten, Egersund's transport links are the main reason why you might pass through: the town is on the Kristiansand–Stavanger **train line**.

From Egersund, it's 10km north to the E39 and a further 65km to Stavanger.

Stavanger and around

STAVANGER is something of a survivor. While other Norwegian coastal towns have fallen foul of the precarious fortunes of fishing, Stavanger has diversified and is now the proud possessor of a dynamic economy, which has swelled the population to over 100,000. It was the herring fishery that first put money into the town, crowding its nineteenth-century wharves with coopers and smiths, net makers and menders. Then, when the fishing failed, the town moved into shipbuilding and now it's oil: nowadays Stavanger builds the rigs for Norway's offshore oilfields and refines the oil as well.

None of which sounds terribly enticing perhaps, but in fact Stavanger is an excellent place to start a visit to Norway: all the town's amenities are within easy walking distance of each other; it has excellent train, bus and ferry connections;

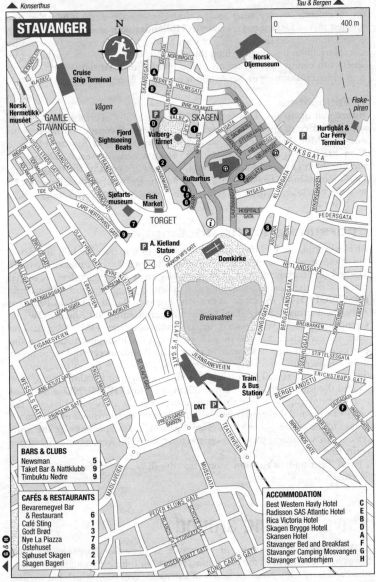

▲ Konserthus

Tau & Bergen ▲

STAVANGER

N

0   400 m

Cruise
Ship Terminal

Konserthus

Norsk
Oljemuseum

Fiske-
piren

Norsk
Hermetikk-
muséet

GAMLE
STAVANGER

Vågen

SKAGEN

Hurtigbåt &
Car Ferry
Terminal

Fjord
Sightseeing
Boats

Valberg-
tårnet

Kulturhus

Sjøfarts-
museum

Fish
Market

TORGET

A. Kielland
Statue

Domkirke

Breiavatnet

Train
& Bus
Station

DNT

BARS & CLUBS
Newsman	5
Taket Bar & Nattklubb	9
Timbuktu Nedre	9

CAFÉS & RESTAURANTS
Bevaremegvel Bar & Restaurant	6
Café Sting	1
Godt Brød	3
Nye La Piazza	7
Ostehuset	8
Sjøhuset Skagen	2
Skagen Bageri	4

ACCOMMODATION
Best Western Havly Hotel	C
Radisson SAS Atlantic Hotel	E
Rica Victoria Hotel	B
Skagen Brygge Hotell	D
Skansen Hotel	A
Stavanger Bed and Breakfast	F
Stavanger Camping Mosvangen	G
Stavanger Vandrerhjem	H

and it possesses an especially attractive harbour, a couple of enjoyable museums,
a raft of excellent restaurants plus several lively bars. The town is also – and this
comes as a surprise to many first-time visitors – nearer to the fjords than
Bergen, the self-proclaimed "Gateway to the Fjords". Within easy reach of
Stavanger are the **Lysefjord** and the dramatic rock formation of the
Preikestolen (see p.156).

Arrival

Stavanger's international **airport** is 14km southwest of the city centre at **Sola**. There's a Flybussen into Stavanger (Mon–Fri 8am–midnight, Sat 9am–10pm, Sun 10am–11pm; every 20–30min; 40min; 80kr each way) and this stops at major downtown hotels, the Fiskepiren ferry terminals and the bus and train stations. The **bus terminal** and the **train station** are adjacent to each other on the southern side of the **Breiavatnet**, a tiny lake that's the most obvious downtown landmark. Inside the bus station, Rogaland Kollektivtrafikk Kolumbus, an agency run collectively by several transport companies (Mon–Fri 7am–8pm, Sat 8am–3pm, Sun 11am–4pm; ☎177, ⓦwww.kolumbus.no), provides comprehensive details of buses, boats and trains in the city and surrounding area. There's a 13kr toll on all roads leading into Stavanger, but you won't be asked to stop – it is levied electronically.

Most **domestic ferries**, including Hurtigbåt passenger express boats and car ferries from the islands and fjords around Stavanger, dock at the Fiskepiren terminal, a short walk to the northeast of the central lake, Breiavatnet – and about 800m from the train and bus stations. There are no longer international ferries from the UK to and from Stavanger. On-street **parking** is difficult, but not impossible; central car parks include those behind the bus station and on Skagenkaien, beside the main harbour.

Information

Stavanger **tourist office** is opposite the cathedral, right in the centre of town at Domkirkeplassen 3 (June–Aug daily 7am–8pm; Sept–May Mon–Fri 9am–4pm, Sat 9am–2pm; ☎51 85 92 00, ⓦwww.visitstavanger.com). They publish a useful and free guide to Stavanger, provide local bus and ferry timetables, issue free cycling maps and make bookings on guided tours both on land and sea. The most popular excursions are to the Lysefjord and **Preikestolen** (see p.156) with some trips departing from the Fiskepiren terminal, others from Skagenkaien, beside the main harbour, Vågen.

Accommodation

There's no shortage of **accommodation** in Stavanger. Half a dozen **hotels** are dotted around the town's compact centre, each offering substantial weekend discounts. Alternatively, there are a couple of convenient, no-frills **guesthouses** and, further afield, an HI **hostel** and **campsite**.

Hotels and guesthouses

Best Western Havly Hotel Valberggata 1 ☎51 93 90 00, ⓦwww.havly-hotell.no. Unassuming, quiet hotel occupying a somewhat clumsy modern building squeezed into a narrow side-street off Skagenkaien. ❺, sp/r ❸

Radisson SAS Atlantic Hotel Olav V's gate 3 ☎51 76 10 00, ⓦwww.atlantic.stavanger .radissonsas.com. There was a time when this was the place to stay in Stavanger, hosting every celebrity who ever set foot in the place from Paul Gascoigne to Fats Domino. The hotel looks a tad jaded now – and it certainly occupies a big bruiser of a modern block – but the rooms are large and spacious and most offer attractive views over the central lake. ❽, sp/r ❹

Rica Victoria Hotel Skansegata 1 ☎51 86 70 00, ⓦwww.rica.no. This substantial hotel occupies a big old building, with a fancy portico, that peers out towards the east side of the main harbour. The interior has preserved a few period trimmings, but is mostly modern as are the bedrooms beyond. ❼, sp/r ❹

Skagen Brygge Hotell Skagenkaien 30 ☎51 85 00 00, ⓦwww.skagenbrygge hotell.no. A delightful quayside hotel, built in the style of an old warehouse but with lots of glass, and great views over the harbour. The rooms are modern and tastefully decorated, the buffet breakfast outstanding and delicious mid-afternoon nibbles are free. The only quibble concerns the noise from outside at summer weekends, when your best bet is probably to get a room at the back or on the top floor. ❼, sp/r ❹

Skansen Hotel Skansegata 7 ☎ 51 93 85 00, ⓦ www.skansenhotel.no. In a revamped and remodelled old building down by the main harbour, this unassuming place has about thirty hotel rooms decorated in brisk modern style plus sixteen guesthouse rooms that are somewhat plainer but still perfectly adequate. All rooms are en suite. Guesthouse ❹, sp/r ❷; hotel ❺, sp/r ❸

Stavanger Bed and Breakfast Vikedalsgata 1a ☎ 51 56 25 00, ⓦ www.stavangerbedandbreakfast .no. This friendly, hostel-like B&B has 22 simple and straightforward modern rooms, most of which have showers and sinks (but shared toilets). Every night at 9pm, guests gather in the dining room for the complimentary coffee and waffles – and a very sociable affair it is too. The B&B is in a residential area just 5min walk from the train station. A real snip at ❷.

Hostels and campsites

Stavanger Camping Mosvangen Tjensvollveien 1b ☎ 51 53 29 71, ⓦ www.stavangercamping.no. On the south bank of lake Mosvatnet, a 3km walk from the centre and metres from the HI hostel (see below), this large campsite has cabins (750–1500kr) as well as areas for tents and caravans. To get there, take Kannikgata/ Madlaveien west from near the station, continue along the north side of the lake and turn left just beyond it onto Tjensvollveien. Open mid-May to mid-Sept.

Stavanger Vandrerhjem Henrik Ibsens gate 19 ☎ 51 54 36 36, ⓦ www.vandrerhjem.no. This no-frills HI hostel stands on the south side of lake Mosvatnet, a 3km walk from the centre – directions are as for *Stavanger Camping* (see above), with Henrik Ibsens gate being a continuation of Tjensvollveien. The hostel has self-catering and laundry facilities; advance reservations are advised. Open early June to late Aug. Dorm beds 280kr, doubles ❷

The City

Much of **central Stavanger** is strikingly modern, a flashy but surprisingly likeable ensemble of mini-tower blocks that spreads over the hilly ground which abuts the main harbour and surrounds the decorative, central lake, **Breiavatnet**. The principal relic of the medieval city is the **Domkirke** (June–Aug daily 11am–7pm; Sept–May Tues–Thurs & Sat 11am–4pm; free), whose pointed-hat towers signal a Romanesque church dating from the early twelfth century, though it has been modified on several occasions. Inside, the squat pillars and rough stonework of the narrow, three-aisled nave are the Romanesque heart of the church, but the choir beyond, with its curling tracery and pointed windows, is Gothic, the work of English masons who were brought here in the 1270s. This was far from unusual: the Norwegians had no experience of building in stone, so whenever they decided to build a stone church they imported skilled craftsmen, mainly from England and

Antony Gormley in Stavanger

Stavanger has no fewer than 23 sculptures by the contemporary British sculptor **Antony Gormley** (best known for his *Angel of the North* in England): together they constitute *Broken Column*, whose aim is to illustrate the many facets of the city and, for that matter, life (and death) itself. Each and every sculpture is a blank-faced human figure made of cast iron and 195cm high, the same height as – and apparently modelled on – Gormley himself, though some are partly sunk into the ground. This sinking is, as you might expect from Gormley, not at random: each location has a predetermined height quota and the last one in the series, which is stuck out on a rock in the harbour, is mostly (149cm) under water. Work began on *Broken Column* in 1999 and the project was completed four years later. One of the sculptures is beside the Domkirke, a second is beside Torget's covered fish market.

Germany. The ornate seventeenth-century pulpit is the most distinctive feature of the church's nave along with the five conspicuous memorial tablets that hang on its walls – a jumble of richly carved cherubs, crucifixes and apostles.

Torget

From the Domkirke, it's a few metres to the top of **Torget**, the main square, from where there is a fine view of Stavanger's principal harbour, Vågan, a tapering finger of water that buzzes with cruise ships, yachts, ferryboats and catamarans. Sharing the view is a **statue** of the author Alexander Kielland (1849–1906), one of the city's most famous sons, looking decidedly pleased with himself in his top hat and cape. Born into a rich merchant family, Kielland was a popular figure hereabouts, praised for his novels and plays and for his (relatively) generous treatment of the workers in his factory. He also set about building a political career, becoming burgomaster of Stavanger in 1891, but it was food – not his political rivals – that did for him: Kielland loved eating and, to all intents and purposes, died of obesity.

At the foot of Torget, beyond the flower and knick-knack vendors, is the covered **fish market** (Mon–Fri 9.30am–4pm & Sat 9am–3pm), where half a dozen stalls sell a wide range of seafood, including hot fish cakes and the west coast's traditional staple, *klippfisk*, dried and salted cod, sometimes – depending on how it is cured – known by its Spanish name, *bacalao*.

Gamle Stavanger

On the western side of the main harbour is the city's star turn, **Gamle Stavanger** (Old Stavanger). Though very different in appearance from the modern structures back in the centre, the buildings here were also the product of a boom. From 1810 until around 1870, herring turned up just offshore in their millions, and Stavanger took advantage of this slice of luck.

▲ Gamle Stavanger

The town flourished and expanded, with the number of merchants and shipowners increasing dramatically. Huge profits were made from the exported fish, which were salted and later, as the technology improved, canned. Today, some of the wooden stores and warehouses flanking the western quayside hint at their nineteenth-century pedigree, but it's the succession of narrow, cobbled lanes behind them that shows Gamle Stavanger to best advantage. Formerly home to local seafarers, craftsmen and cannery workers, the area has been maintained as a residential quarter, mercifully free of tourist tat; the long rows of white-painted, clapboard houses are immaculately maintained, complete with gas lamps, picket fences and tiny terraced gardens. There's little architectural pretension, but here and there flashes of fancy wooden scrollwork must once have had the curtains twitching amongst the staunchly Lutheran population.

The Norsk Hermetikkmuséet

In the heart of Gamle Stavanger at Øvre Strandgate 88, the **Norsk Hermetikkmuséet** (Canning Museum; mid-June to mid-Aug daily 11am–4pm; mid-Aug to mid-June Tues–Sun 11am–4pm; 60kr) occupies an old **sardine-canning factory** and gives a glimpse of the industry that saved Stavanger from collapse at the end of the nineteenth century. When the herring vanished from local waters in the 1870s, the canning factories switched to imported fish, thereby keeping the local economy afloat. They remained Stavanger's main source of employment until as late as 1960: in the 1920s there were seventy canneries in the town, and the last one only closed down in 1983.

A visit to an old canning factory may not seem too enticing, but the museum is actually very good, mainly because of its collection of **sardine tin labels**, called *iddis* in these parts from the local pronunciation of *etikett*, the Norwegian for label. Several hundred labels have survived, in part because they were avidly collected by the town's children, though this harmless hobby seems to have worried the town's adults no end – "Label thefts – an unfortunate collection craze", ran a 1915 headline in the *Stavanger Aftenblad* newspaper. The variety of label design is extraordinary – anything and everything from representations of the Norwegian royal family to surrealistic fish with human qualities. Spare a thought also for a Scottish seaman by the name of **William Anderson**: it was his face, copied from a photograph, that beamed out from millions of Skippers' sardine tins, a celebrity status so frowned upon by shipowners that Anderson couldn't find work, though fortunately the story ended happily: Anderson wrote to the cannery concerned to complain and they put him on the payroll for the remainder of his working life.

You can watch the museum **smoking its own sardines** on the first Sunday of every month and every Tuesday and Thursday from mid-June to mid-August, and then munch away to your heart's content.

The Sjøfartsmuseum

Walk back through Gamle Stavanger towards the centre and you'll soon come to the **Sjøfartsmuseum** (Maritime Museum; mid-June to mid-Aug daily 11am–4pm; mid-Aug to mid-June Sun only 11am–4pm; 60kr), sited in two old and adjacent warehouses at Nedre Strandgate 17 and 19. The museum's interior is jam-packed with all things nautical, from charts and drawings and replica workshops, through to archeological finds, paintings of ships, model boats and, perhaps best of the lot, scores of old photos.

Hiking

Home to some of the world's most magnificently scenic wildernesses, Norway seems almost made for hiking. From top to bottom, the country is traversed by a sequence of wondrously rugged mountain ranges, accentuated by icy glaciers, rocky spires and deep green fjords. Great chunks of this wild terrain have been incorporated into national parks that are magnets for hikers in search of everything from easy rambles to full-scale expeditions along clearly marked trails, served by an excellent network of huts.

Walking up to Briksdalbreen glacier, near Olden ▲

Jotunheimen Nasjonalpark ▼

Hiking trails and maps

Norway's **hiking trails** are typically marked at regular intervals by **cairns** (piles of stones). Most junctions are marked by **signposts**, some of which have stood for many years and are on the small side, making them hard to spot. There are also **red "T"** symbols painted on rocks – welcome route markers when the weather is poor, as they're visible from farther away than the signposts. Although waymarking is quite good, you should always purchase **hiking maps**. The entire country has been accurately mapped by the Norwegian highways department – their *Statens Kartverk M711 Norge 1:50,000* series, with red-and-white covers, are the most detailed, while their maroon-covered maps cover all the more popular hiking areas at the scale of 1:100,000. You can buy hiking maps at DNT outlets (see box opposite) most tourist offices and at many bookshops.

Overnighting in the wilds

Staffed mountain lodges, found mainly in the southern part of the country, provide meals and lodging, often accommodating over a hundred. They are clean, friendly and well-run, usually by DNT staff – although there are some private lodges where prices are slightly higher (discounts apply for DNT members). **Self-service huts**, with twenty to forty beds, are also concentrated in the mountains of southern Norway and offer lodging with bedding, a shop selling groceries and a well-equipped kitchen. **Unstaffed huts**, often with fewer than twenty beds, are mostly in the north. They provide bedding, stoves for heating and cooking and kitchen equipment; you must bring and prepare your own food.

Finding out more

Den Norske Turistforening (Norwegian Mountain Touring Association) plays an active part in managing all aspects of hiking in Norway. As well as selling maps, giving advice on equipment and organizing all-inclusive tours, it takes care of trails and waymarking and co-ordinates local hiking associations, which run over 300 mountain lodges. If you stay at a hut, DNT membership gives you about a fifty percent saving. It costs 480kr per annum (19–26-year-olds 270kr, 13–18 years 160kr, 67-plus 365kr, under 12 100kr): join at any of their offices or staffed mountain lodges.

DNT's main office in Oslo is at Storgata 7 (☎22 82 28 22); its postal address is Postboks 7, Sentrum, 0101 Oslo. The website – ⓦwww.turistforeningen.no – gives details of suggested hikes, and opening times and contact numbers for every DNT and affiliate hut (*hytter*), but some information is only in Norwegian.

▲ Coastal hiking

▼ Mountain hut for hikers

Reservations are accepted at staffed lodges for stays of more than two nights, though the lodges are primarily for guests in transit. Otherwise, beds are provided on a first-come, first-served basis. Lodges can get full in high season. If beds are not available, you are given a mattress and blankets for sleeping in a common area. DNT members over 50 years of age are always guaranteed a bed. No one is ever turned away.

Rough camping is allowed freely throughout Norway, although campfires are prohibited from April 15 to September 15. You may camp for one night only anywhere more than 150 metres from a building. In some national parks and other walking areas, you must move a bit further away from a hut, or stay near to the hut in a designated camping area. Camping may be the only option in remoter regions.

▼ Rough camping

Hardangervidda Nasjonalpark ▲

High level in the Dovrefjell Nasjonalpark ▼

Mountain scenery, Jotunheimen Nasjonalpark ▼

Best national parks for hiking

▶▶ **Jotunheimen Nasjonalpark** Near the east end of the Sognefjord, 300km from Oslo, Norway's most famous hiking area has a heady concentration of towering, ice-tipped peaks, many exceeding 1900m and including northern Europe's two highest. See p.117.

▶▶ **Rondane Nasjonalpark** The Rondane comprises both a high alpine zone, with ten peaks exceeding the 2000-metre mark, and a much gentler upland area of rounded, treeless hills. It is on the E6 between Oslo and Trondheim and is especially popular with families. See p.176.

▶▶ **Hardangervidda Nasjonalpark** Europe's largest mountain plateau stretches east from the Hardangerfjord to Finse in the north and Rjukan in the east. Its bare, almost lunar-like rocks and myriad lakes make for some spectacular hiking. The Hardangervidda begins about 130km east of Bergen. See p.231.

▶▶ **Dovrefjell Nasjonalpark** Bisected by the E6 and the Dombås–Trondheim railway, the Dovrefjell is one of the most accessible of Norway's national parks, about 400km north of Oslo. In the east, there are marshes and open moors with rounded ridges, but as you hike west the serrated alpine peaks of the Romsdal hove into view. See p.182.

Hiking season

The short **hiking season**, loosely defined by the opening and closing of the mountain lodges, runs from early July (mid-June in some areas) through to late September. This coincides with mild weather – daytime mountain temperatures of between 20°C and 25°C – ideal for hiking. And, of course, it's daylight for most of the time.

Skagen

Skagen, the bumpy promontory on the east side of the main harbour, is an oddly discordant district, a sometimes clumsy, sometimes charming mixture of the old and new, and it incorporates a busy shopping zone, whose mazey street plan is the only legacy of the original Viking settlement. The spiky **Valbergtårnet** (Valberg tower), sitting atop Skagen's highest point and guarded by three rusty cannons, is the one specific sight, a nineteenth-century firewatch offering sweeping views of the city and its industry.

The Norsk Oljemuseum

The intricate workings of the offshore oil industry are explored in depth at the excellent **Norsk Oljemuseum** (Norwegian Petroleum Museum; June–Aug daily 10am–7pm; Sept–May Mon–Sat 10am–4pm & Sun 10am–6pm; 80kr; ⓦ www.norskolje.museum.no), in a sleek modern building beside the waterfront on the far side of Skagen. The first tentative searches for oil beneath the North Sea began in the early 1960s and the first strike was made in 1969. Production started two years later and has continued ever since with Norway owning about half of western Europe's oil and gas reserves – enough to transform what had once been one of the poorer countries on the continent to one of the richest. The museum is not especially large, but it is a little confusing, so be sure to pick up a free plan at reception.

There are introductory displays on North Sea geology, explaining how the oil was created, but you're soon into the offshore section with scale models of oil rigs, explanations as to how oil wells are sunk, and a few mechanical bits and pieces – drill bits, diving bells and so forth. There's also a section on the **Alexander Kielland disaster** of 1980, when the eponymous oil rig collapsed in heavy seas, killing 123 oil workers, Norway's worst offshore disaster by a mile. The museum has a mini-cinema, showing a film about the industry, plus several hands-on exhibits, notably a mock-up of a drilling platform. Embedded in the museum are nuggets of social commentary: women were only allowed to work offshore from the late 1970s and soon after their arrival the oil companies had to bring in more toiletries for the men, who suddenly started to shower more. Incidentally, the large yellow bridge-like structure outside the museum was retrieved from the Frigg oilfield, when it closed down in 2004 after 27 years of production. Frigg was a joint operation between the UK and Norway and this particular piece of kit, built to link two oil installations far out in the ocean, actually crossed the international frontier – as the surviving signage illustrates.

The most agreeable way to return to the centre is by walking northwest along the waterfront, which is lined with old ferries and schooners.

Eating and drinking

Although prices are marginally inflated by the oil industry, Stavanger is a great place to **eat**, with a gaggle of first-rate restaurants on the east side of the main harbour along and around Skagenkaien. Alternatively, if your pocket book won't stretch that far, there are several inexpensive cafés in the vicinity of the Kulturhus, in the heart of the Skagen shopping area, and you can often buy fresh prawns from the fishing smacks that dock on the waterfront to the west of the Fiskepiren.

Stavanger is lively at night, particularly at weekends when a rum assortment of oil workers, sailors, fishermen, executives, tourists and office workers gathers in the **bars and clubs** on Skagen and Skagenkaien to live (or rather drink) it up. Most places stay open until 2am or later, with rowdy – but usually amiable – revellers lurching from one bar to the next.

Cafés and restaurants

Bevaremegvel Bar & Restaurant Skagen 12 ☏51 84 38 60. Bistro-style restaurant – with an adjoining bar – where the wide-ranging menu covers everything from burgers (155kr) to seafood (270kr). Better to go early in the evening before the place gets too packed (and the service slows down). Mon–Wed 11am–midnight, Thurs–Sat 11am–1am & Sun 4pm–midnight; kitchen closes at 11pm.

Café Sting Valberget 3 ☏51 89 38 78, ⓦwww .cafe-sting.no. Right next to the Valbergtårnet tower, this laid-back café-bar is the coolest spot in town in a young, arty sort of way. The food is filling and inexpensive and the place also doubles as an art gallery and live-music venue, hosting anything from indie to rock. Mon–Thurs noon–midnight, Fri & Sat noon–3am & Sun 3pm–midnight.

Godt Brød Sølvberggata. Inexpensive, modern café that sells a good range of freshly baked bread as well as inexpensive sandwiches. Opposite the Kulturhus. Mon–Sat 7am–6pm.

Nye La Piazza Rosenkildetorget 1. By the main harbour, just off Torget, this smart Italian restaurant serves delicious pizzas, pasta and more. Pizzas begin at 140kr, other main courses 250kr. Mon–Sat noon–midnight, Sun noon to 10pm.

🏃 **Ostehuset** Klubbgata 3. Attractive modern café, where the speciality is pizza: the basic pizza costs 100kr and then you customize by selecting from a delicious range of extra toppings for 25–30kr each. There's also a daily menu featuring the freshest of local ingredients with mains from about 120kr plus sandwiches and

baguettes. Tastiest coffee in town too. Mon–Fri 8am–9pm, Sat 8am–6pm.

Sjøhuset Skagen Skagenkaien 16 ☏51 89 51 80. Popular restaurant in an antique harbourside building, whose dark timber interior, with its several small storeys, resembles an old warehouse. The fish dishes are the tastiest items on the menu; main courses cost 260–290kr. Mon–Sat 11.30am–midnight & Sun 1–11pm.

Skagen Bageri Skagen 18. This pleasantly old-fashioned coffee house, with its dinky wooden furniture, occupies the prettiest of the old timber buildings on Skagen – note the finely carved antique door and lintel. Serves tasty pastries, cakes and snacks at reasonable prices. Mon–Fri 7am–3.30pm & Sat 8am–3.30pm.

Bars and clubs

Newsman Skagen 14. One block back from the east side of the harbour, this dark and boisterous English-style pub heaves at the weekend. Open Mon–Fri noon–1.30am, Sat 11am–1.30am & Sun 3pm–midnight.

Taket Bar & Nattklubb Nedre Strandgate 15 ☏51 84 37 00, ⓦwww.herlige-restauranter.com. The best club in town, strong on house music with special DJ nights; don't be surprised if you have to queue; above *Timbuktu* (see below), just west of Torget, the main square. Open Tues–Thurs midnight–3am, Fri & Sat 10pm–3am & Sun midnight–3am.

Timbuktu Nedre Strandgate 15. Flashy café-bar noted for its imaginative modern decor and trendy atmosphere; beneath *Taket* (see above). Mon–Sat 6pm–12.30am.

Entertainment

The **Stavanger Konserthus** (Concert Hall; ☏51 53 70 00, ⓦwww.stavanger -konserthus.no) is north of the centre beyond Gamle Stavanger in Bjergsted park. It features regular concerts by visiting artists and is home to the Stavanger Symphony Orchestra (ⓦwww.sso.no). Among several central cinemas, the eight-screen Kino 1 is inside the Kulturhus, at Sølvberggata 2 (☏51 51 07 00, ⓦwww.kino1.no).

Listings

Airlines Norwegian Air Shuttle (☏815 21 815); SAS/Braathens (☏05400); Widerøe (☏810 01 200).
Car rental Hertz, Olav V's gate 13 (☏51 52 00 00). For a comprehensive list, see under *Bilutleie* in the *Yellow Pages*.
Emergencies Fire ☏110; Police ☏112; Ambulance ☏113.

Ferries Domestic: Rogaland Kollektivtrafikk Kolumbus for regional bus, boat and train enquiries (☏177, ⓦwww.kolumbus.no); Flaggruten (☏53 40 91 20, ⓦwww.flaggruten.no) for Hurtigbåt passenger express boat services to Haugesund and Bergen.
Hiking The DNT-affiliated Stavanger Turist-forening, in the underpass at the top of Olav V's

gate (Mon–Wed & Fri 10am–5pm, Thurs 10am–6pm, Sat 10am–2pm; ☎51 84 02 00, ⓦwww.stavanger-turistforening.no), will advise on local hiking routes and sells a comprehensive range of hiking maps. It maintains around 900km of hiking trails and runs more than thirty cabins in the mountains east of Stavanger, as well as organizing ski schools at winter weekends. It also offers general advice about local conditions, weather, etc, and you can obtain DNT membership here too.

Internet Internet access is free at the main library, inside the Kulturhus at Sølvberggata 2 (Mon–Wed & Fri 10am–5pm, Thurs 10am–7pm & Sat 10am–3pm). There's also an internet café, Café Com, close by at Sølvberggata 15 (Mon–Sat 11am–9pm, Sun noon–9pm; ☎51 55 41 20); they charge 20kr for the first 20min.

Laundry Renseriet, Kongsgata 40, by Breiavatnet. Coin-operated machines (☎51 89 56 53).

Left luggage Coin-operated lockers at the Fiskepiren terminal (Mon–Fri 6.30am–11.15pm, Sat 6.30am–8pm, Sun 8am–10pm); at the train station (Sun–Fri 6am–11pm, Sat 6am–6pm); and at the bus station (daily 7am–10pm).

Pharmacy Vitusapotek, Olav V's gate 11 (daily 9am–11pm).

Post office The main post office is on Lars Hertevigs gate, just a few metres from Haakon VII's gate (Mon–Fri 9am–6pm & Sat 10am–3pm).

Taxis Norgestaxi (☎08000).

Vinmonopolet State-run liquor and wine outlet in the Straensenteret shopping centre, just west of Torget at Lars Hertevigs gate 6 (Mon–Fri 10am–6pm & Sat 10am–3pm).

Around Stavanger: Lysefjord

Stavanger sits on a long promontory that pokes a knobbly head north towards the **Boknafjord**, whose wide waters form a deep indentation in the coast and lap against a confetti of islets and islands. To the east of Stavanger, longer, narrower fjords drill far inland, the most diverting being the blue-black **Lysefjord**, famous for its precipitous cliffs and an especially striking rock formation, the **Preikestolen**. This distinctive 25-metre-square table of rock boasts a sheer 600-metre drop to the fjord down below on three of its sides. There are regular summertime boat cruises to the Lysefjord, and Preikestolen can be reached by ferry and bus.

Boat trips along the Lysefjord

There are no roads along the length of the **Lysefjord**, so although the fjord can be reached by car at three points – one at the west end, one at the east and one in the middle – you'll need to take a **boat trip** to appreciate its full dimensions. The fastest trips are by **Hurtigbåt passenger express boat** (June–Aug 1 daily, May & Sept 1 weekly; 3hr 30min; 320kr), but these excursions, which depart from the Skagenkaien, only go halfway up along the Lysefjord and the views from the boat are not nearly as good as they are from a normal car ferry. A second, better option is to take the **ferry** (late May to mid-Sept 1 daily; 9hr; passengers 270kr) from the Fiskepiren terminal in Stavanger to Lysebotn, at the east end of the Lysefjord, and then come back along the same route, though the return ferry journey can be a bit of a drag. You can liven up this itinerary by opting for a "**Fjord and Mountain**"excursion (late June to mid-Aug 1 daily; 7hr; 490kr), which includes a bus ride to Lauvvik, the ferry onto Lysebotn and then the dramatic bus trip up and over the mountains and back to Stavanger. Another permutation is the "**Hike to Kjerag**" tour (late June to mid-Aug 1 daily; 14hr; 490kr), which follows the same itinerary as the "Fjord and Mountain" trip except that you get off the bus at **Øygardstøl** for a guided hike to the **Kjeragbolten** and then round off the day with the bus back to Lysebotn and the ferry. Finally, if you have your own vehicle, then you can catch the Lysefjord ferry from the Fiskepiren terminal in Stavanger to Lysebotn (late May to mid-Sept 1 daily; car & driver 375kr) and then follow whatever itinerary you want, but note that advance ferry reservations for the car are essential. Foot passengers travelling independently pay 195kr each way for this same ferry – and an extra 85kr to get up to Øygardstøl by bus or taxi.

Several companies offer Lysefjord excursions, but the main provider is **Veteran Fjord Cruise** (T51 86 87 88, Wwww.vfc.no); trips can be booked direct with the company or at Stavanger tourist office (see p.149).

Lysefjord, Lysebotn and Kjeragbolten

Heading out from Stavanger, the **Lysefjord ferry** (see p.155) chops through raggle-taggle islands before turning into the Lysefjord between Oanes, on its northern shore, and Forsand to the south. Before long the ferry passes the base of Preikestolen (see below), though from this angle the rock hardly makes any impression at all. It then nudges on up the fjord with mighty cliffs to either side before reaching the first of several request stops, **Flørli**, where a scattering of houses hugs the shore in sight of the old power station – the new one is actually inside the mountain. A remarkably long wooden stairway leads up the mountainside here and, even more remarkably, the occasional visitor actually gets off the boat to clamber up it.

Lysebotn, at the far end of the Lysefjord, is the neatest of villages, a tiny little place built to house hydroelectric workers in the middle of the twentieth century. It's also extremely popular with Base-jumpers, who hunker down at the village's simple campsite (T90 83 20 35, Wwww.lysebotn-touristcamp .com) before heading off to the mountains nearby.

The narrow **road up from Lysebotn**, which is closed during the winter, offers spectacular views as it wiggles and wriggles its way up the mountainside. Eventually, after 7km, just above the last hairpin, the road arrives at the **Øygardstøl** café, which has panoramic views back down towards the fjord. Øygardstøl is also the starting point for the **hiking trail** which leads west to the **Kjeragbolten**, a much-photographed boulder wedged between two cliff faces high above the ground. It's a tough route, so allow six hours for the round trip – and steel your nerves for the dizzying drops down to the fjord below. For guided hikes to Kjeragbolten, see p.155.

Beyond Øygardstøl, the road crosses a stunningly beautiful mountain plateau, a barren, treeless expanse of boulder and loch whose wide vistas are intercepted by the occasional cabin. Eventually, the road meets Highway 45, which slices west between the bulging mountains of **Øvstabødal** on its way back to Stavanger.

Preikestolen

Lysefjord's most celebrated vantage point, **Preikestolen** (Pulpit Rock), offers superlative views, though on sunny summer days you'll be sharing them with lots and lots of others. To get to the rock, take the **ferry** east from Stavanger to **Tau** (every 30min–1hr; 40min; passengers 39kr, car & driver 116kr) and then drive south along Highway 13 until, after about 14km, you reach the signed side road leading to Preikestolen. A local **bus** covers the Tau–Preikestolen road too (mid-May to mid-Sept 3–6 daily; 35min), but you'll need to check with the tourist office as to which of the ferries connects with the bus. From the car park at the end of the road, it's a four-hour **hike** there and back to Preikestolen along a clearly marked trail. The first half is steep in parts and paved with uneven stones, while the second half – over bedrock – is a good bit easier. The change in elevation is 350m and you should take food and water; the hike is not feasible in winter.

Back at the Preikestolen car park, a short sharp hike leads down to **Refsvatn**, a small lake encircled by a footpath which takes three hours to negotiate, passing

From Stavanger to Bergen

With great ingenuity, Norway's road builders have cobbled together the **E39** coastal road, the **Kystvegen** (ⓦ www.kystvegen.no), which traverses the west coast from Stavanger to Haugesund, Bergen and ultimately Trondheim with eight ferry trips breaking up the journey. The first part of the trek, the 190-kilometre haul up to Bergen, includes two ferry trips and sees the highway slipping across a string of islands, which provide a pleasant introduction to the scenic charms of western Norway – and hint at the sterner beauty of the fjords beyond. Perhaps surprisingly, this region is primarily agricultural: the intricacies of the shoreline, together with the prevailing westerlies, made the seas so treacherous that locals mostly stuck to the land, eking out a precarious existence from the thin soils that had accumulated on the leeward sides of some of the islands.

By **car**, it takes between five and six hours to get from Stavanger to Bergen. En route, the first of the two E39 **ferries** shuttles across the Boknafjord from **Mortavika to Arsvågen**, about 30km out of Stavanger (24hr service, every 30min–1hr; 25min; car & passengers 143kr; ⓦ www.fjord1.no); the second, another 120km beyond, links **Sandvikvåg with Halhjem** (daily 7am–11pm every 30min to 1hr; 40min; car & driver 177kr; ⓦ www.fjord1.no), 40km short of Bergen. A fast and frequent **bus** service – the **Kystbussen** – plies the E39 too, taking a little under six hours to get from Stavanger to Bergen (Mon–Fri hourly, Sat & Sun every 1–2hr); it's slower, but more economical (450kr one-way) and offers much better views than the **Hurtigbåt** passenger express boat which plies the same route (720kr one-way). The obvious place to break the journey is Haugesund (see below), though the town is of only mild interest, and you might opt instead for **Ryvarden Fyr** (☏ 53 74 80 00; ⓦ www.ryvarden.no; ❸ full board), where the old lighthouse stands glued to the rocks on the edge of the ocean. There's a café and an art gallery here (early July to early Aug Tues–Sat noon–4pm, Sun 11am–5pm) and the old lighthousemen's quarters have been attractively equipped in pleasant, modern style. Ryvarden is about 20km north of Haugesund and 15km west of the E39 along narrow byroads; reservations are essential.

birch and pine woods, marshes, narrow ridges and bare stretches of rock. It also threads through **Torsnes**, an isolated farm that was inhabited until 1962. The lake footpath connects with a rough path that careers down to the **Refsa quay** on the Lysefjord. For further details of these and other local hikes, consult the DNT-affiliated Stavanger Turistforening (see p.154), who sell an excellent English-language hiking guide to the area.

Also by the car park is a first-rate HI **hostel**, *Preikestolen Vandrerhjem* (☏ 51 74 52 51, ⓦ www.vandrerhjem.no; dorm beds 250kr, doubles ❷; June–Aug), perched high on the hillside with great views over the surrounding mountains. Built on the site of an old mountain farm, the hostel comprises a small complex of turf-roofed lodges, each of which has a spick-and-span pine interior. There are self-catering facilities, a laundry and boat rental as well as a café serving breakfasts and simple evening meals; reservations are advised as the place is popular with school groups.

Haugesund

There is no strong reason to break your journey between Stavanger and Bergen, but **HAUGESUND**, a workaday industrial town 90km north of Stavanger – via the E39 and the Mortavika–Arsvågen ferry (see box, above) – has its moments. A small but lively port that thrived on the herring fisheries in the nineteenth century, Haugesund now booms as a major player in the North Sea oil industry, though the appearance of **Smedasundet**, its bustling main harbour and the effective centre of town, is largely unaffected. It's flanked by a hotch-potch of big, old stone buildings dating from the early twentieth century. Specific sights are thin on the ground here, but a stroll along the harbourfront is an amiable way to spend half an hour and the tumbling water fountains of the adjacent **Torggata** lead up towards the town's prettiest church, Vår Frelsers Kirke, a slender brick affair of 1901 whose neo-Gothic design is enlivened by some Jugenstil flourishes. Haugesund may be light on sights, but it does do well for **festivals**, the prime examples being the **Sildajazz Festival** (ⓦwww .sildajazz.no) and the **Norwegian International Film Festival** (ⓦwww .filmweb.no/filmfestivalen2009), both of which are held in August. The town's other claim to fame is as the hometown of the baker Edward Mortenson, who emigrated to the USA, where he almost certainly fathered Norma Jean, otherwise Marilyn Monroe, who was born in 1926.

Haraldshaugen

The first ruler of a united Norway, **Harald Hårfagre** (Harald Fair Hair; c.880–930), is thought to have been buried up along the coast just 2km to the north of Haugesund – and a grand granite obelisk, the **Haraldshaugen**, now marks his presumed resting place. **Hårfagri** defeated a coalition of local chieftains at the battle of Hafrsfjord just south of Stavanger in about 885, thereby cementing his control of the fjordland, an achievement that, according to legend, released him from a ten-year vow not to cut his hair until he had united the country. In a nationalist flush, the Norwegians erected the **Haraldshaugen monument** to celebrate **Hårfagri** in 1872, but very little is known about Hårfagri's rule or the extent of his real power. The most detailed evidence comes from several of the sagas, which insist that Harald "kept a sharp eye on the landed men and rich farmers", so much so that many fled west to settle in Iceland and the Faroes, though this does not entirely match with the facts – the move west began earlier.

Arrival and information

Haugesund's **international airport** is some 14km southwest of town. From the airport, there is a regular bus service to Haugesund (25min 60kr), with departure times linked to flight arrivals. Passengers are dropped at Haugesund **bus station**, the arrival point for all long-distance buses. The bus station is an inconvenient twenty-minute walk from the harbourfront and, even worse, the chronic shortage of signs makes it hard to find your way; the taxi fare to the harbour is 75kr. **Hurtigbåt** passenger express ferries from Bergen and Stavanger stop on the harbourfront right in the centre of town. Haugesund **tourist office** is one block in from the main harbour at Strandgata 171 (May–Aug Mon–Fri 9am–5pm, Sat & Sun 10am–3pm; Sept–April Mon–Fri 10am–4.30pm; ☎52 01 08 30, ⓦwww.haugesund.net).

Accommodation, eating and drinking

The town's plushest **hotel** is the *Rica Maritim*, in a large, ultra-modern block on the harbourfront at Åsbygaten 3 (☎52 86 30 00, ⓦwww.rica.no; ❽, sp/r ❻); all the rooms here are decorated in crisp, modern style and most have harbour views. A good reserve option is the nearby *Clarion Hotel Amanda*, also on the main harbourfront at Smedasundet 93 (☎52 80 82 00, ⓦwww.choicehotels .no; ❼, sp/r ❹). This hotel occupies a substantial stone building dating back to the early twentieth century; the rooms are large and comfortable, if a little decoratively staid, and most unusually an evening buffet meal is included in the

From Haugesund, you can either continue north on the E39 to Bergen (see box, p.157), or branch off east along the E134 towards Lofthus (see p.229) and Kinsarvik (see p.228), on the Hardangerfjord.

price. For something a tad more distinctive, take the passenger ferry (6–8 daily; 30min; 42kr each way; ⓦwww.visitrovar.no) from the harbourfront to car-free **Røvær** (ⓦwww.visitrovar.no), a green and fairly flat little island 10km to the west of Haugesund. The boat docks a short walk from the main village, there's easy rambling and a beach or two plus a no-frills HI **hostel**, *Røvær Vandrerhjem* (late June to late Aug; ☎52 71 80 35,ⓦwww.vandrerhjem.no; dorm beds 200kr, doubles ❶), in a distinctive timber building metres from the ferry dock.

The best **café** in Haugesund by a long chalk is *Café Moody*, one block up from the harbourfront, near the corner of Torggata, at Strandgata 152 (Mon–Sat 11am to midnight, Sun 1pm to midnight). A laid-back sort of place, with secondhand furniture and modern art on the walls, the café attracts a student crew and serves up tasty, filling sandwiches and snacks from 60kr and up. The pick of the town's several **restaurants** is *Lothes Mat & Vinhus*, in a cosy huddle of old timber buildings just up from the harbourfront at Skippergata 4 (daily 11am–1am, restaurant Mon–Sat 6–11pm; ☎52 71 22 01); the wide-ranging menu features a whole raft of Norwegian favourites, with main courses costing in the region of 300kr.

Travel details

Principal trains (ⓦwww.nsb.no)

Kristiansand to: Oslo (4–5 daily; 4hr 30min); Stavanger (4–5 daily; 3hr).
Oslo to: Arendal (4–5 daily, change at Nelaug; 4hr 10min); Egersund (4–5 daily; 7hr); Kristiansand (4–5 daily; 4hr 30min); Kragerø for (4–5 daily, change at Neslandsvatn; 2hr 40min); Sandefjord (every 1–2hr; 1hr 50min); Stavanger (4–5 daily; 8hr); Tønsberg (every 1–2hr; 1hr 30min).
Sandefjord to: Oslo (every 1–2hr; 1hr 50min); Tønsberg (every 1–2hr; 20min).
Stavanger to: Kristiansand (4–5 daily; 3hr); Oslo (4–5 daily; 8hr).

Principal Nor-Way Bussekspress bus services (ⓦwww.nor-way.no)

Arendal to: Kristiansand (7 daily, local bus to Harebakken bussterminalen, then change; 1hr 30min); Oslo (7 daily, local bus to Harebakken bussterminalen, then change; 4hr 10min).
Grimstad to: Kristiansand (7 daily; 50min); Lillesand (7 daily, change at Lillesand Borkedalen for the last 5min of the journey by local bus; 20min); Oslo (7 daily; 4hr 15min).

Kristiansand to: Flekkefjord (3–4 daily; 2hr); Mandal (3–4 daily; 50min); Oslo (7 daily; 5hr 10min); Stavanger (3–4 daily; 4hr).
Lillesand to: Kristiansand (7 daily, local bus to Lillesand Borkedalen, then change; 30min); Oslo (7 daily, local bus to Lillesand Borkedalen, then change; 4hr 45min).
Mandal to: Kristiansand (3–4 daily; 50min); Stavanger (3–4 daily; 3hr 10min).
Oslo to: Arendal (7 daily, change at Harebakken bussterminalen for the last 10min of the journey by local bus; 4hr 10min); Grimstad (7 daily; 4hr 15min); Kragerø (7 daily, change at Tangen for the last 25min of the journey by local bus; 4hr 45min); Kristiansand (7 daily; 5hr 10min); Lillesand (7 daily, change at Lillesand Borkedalen for the last 5min of the journey by local bus; 4hr 45min); Risor (7 daily, change at Vinterkjaer for the last 20min of the journey by local bus; 4hr); Stavanger (2–3 daily; 10hr).
Stavanger to: Bergen (Mon–Fri hourly, Sat & Sun every 1–2hr; 5hr to 6hr); Haugesund (Mon–Fri hourly, Sat & Sun every 1–2hr; 2hr 15min); Kristiansand (3–4 daily; 4hr); Mandal (3–4 daily; 3hr 10min).

Principal Nettbuss buses (ⓦwww.nettbuss.no)

Arendal to: Grimstad (hourly; 30min); Kristiansand (hourly; 1hr 30min); Lillesand (hourly; 50min).
Grimstad to: Arendal (hourly; 30min); Kristiansand (hourly; 1hr); Lillesand (hourly; 25min).
Lillesand to: Arendal (hourly; 50min); Grimstad (hourly; 25min).

International car ferries

Hirstshals (Denmark) to: Stavanger/Bergen (3–5 weekly; 12hr/19hr; ⓦwww.fjordline.com).
Hirtshals (Denmark) to: Kristiansand (1–2 daily; 3hr 30min; ⓦwww.colorline.com); Larvik (1–2 daily; 4hr; ⓦwww.colorline.com).
Strömstad (Sweden) to: Sandefjord (4–6 daily; 2hr 30min; ⓦwww.colorline.com).

Domestic car ferries (ⓦwww.fjord1.no)

Mortavika to: Arsvågen, about 30km north of Stavanger on the E39 (24hr service, every 30min–1hr; 25min).
Sandvikvåg to: Halhjem, about 150 north of Stavanger on the E39 (daily 7am–11pm every 30min– 1hr; 40min).

Principal Flaggruten Hurtigbåt passenger express boats (ⓦwww.flaggruten.no)

Stavanger to: Bergen (1–2 daily; 4hr 30min); Haugesund (2–4 daily; 1hr 20min; Flaggruten Hurtigbåt passenger express boat).

Central Norway

CHAPTER 3 **Highlights**

✳ **Whitewater rafting** Brave some of Norway's most exciting whitewater-rafting runs on the River Sjoa. **See p.174**

✳ **Lake Gjende** A boat trip along one of Norway's most beautiful lakes provides a scenic introduction to the mighty Jotunheimen mountains. **See p.178**

✳ **Kongsvold Fjeldstue** This lovely hotel occupies a tastefully restored complex of old timber buildings, and is convenient for exploring the Dovrefjell National Park. **See p.181**

✳ **Borgund stave church** One of the best-preserved and most harmonious of Norway's 29 remaining stave churches. **See p.187**

✳ **Dalen Hotel** Immaculately restored 1890s hotel in a quiet country town halfway between the fjords and Oslo. **See p.195**

▲ Whitewater kayaking

Central Norway

reoccupied by the fjords and the long road to Nordkapp, few tourists
are tempted to explore **central Norway**. The Norwegians know
better. Trapped between Sweden and the fjords, this great chunk of
land boasts some of the country's finest scenery, with the forested
dales that trail north and west from Oslo heralding the region's rearing peaks.
It's here, within shouting distance of the country's principal train line and the
E6 – long the main line of communication between Oslo, Trondheim and
the north – that you'll find three of Norway's prime **hiking areas**. These
comprise a trio of mountain ranges, each partly contained within a national
park – from south to north, Jotunheimen, Rondane and the Dovrefjell.
Of the three, **Jotunheimen** is the harshest and most stunning, with its string
of icy, jagged peaks; the **Dovrefjell** is more varied with severe mountains
in the west and open moors and rounded ridges in the east; while **Rondane**,
a high alpine zone, has more accessible mountains and low vegetation.
Each of the parks is equipped with well-maintained walking trails and
DNT huts, and **Kongsvoll**, on both the E6 and the train line, makes a
particularly good starting-point for hiking expeditions into one of them, the
Dovrefjell.

Despite these attractions, it's easy to think of the whole region as little more
than a **transport corridor** whose four main highways rush from Oslo across
the interior heading north and west. Of these, the **E6** is perhaps the most interesting, as it runs up the **Gudbrandsdal** valley past several historic sights en
route to the Jotunheimen and Dovrefjell parks. The E6 also passes within
comfortable striking distance of the intriguing old iron-town of **Røros** and,
even better, it's the starting point for **Highway 15** and the **E136**, two wonderful
roads that thread through the mountains to the fjords: the first goes to Lom (see
p.251) and Geiranger (see p.262), the second to Åndalsnes (see p.267). To the
west of Oslo, the **E16** is the fastest of the three main roads to the fjords, as it
bangs across to Lærdal and through the series of tunnels that enable it to fast
track to Bergen. It has much to recommend it west of Flåm (see p.239), but its
dull eastern reaches are enlivened only by the handsome **Borgund stave
church**. Further south, the easterly section of **Highway 7** to Flåm via Highway
50 or Eidfjord (see p.229) is also pretty routine, but further west beyond Geilo
the road traverses the wonderfully wild Hardangervidda mountain plateau (see
p.230), passing several useful trail-heads such as Halne (see p.231). Finally, there's
the **E134** to Lofthus (see p.229), which has the advantage of passing through
the attractive former silver-town of **Kongsberg** and within a whisker of
Dalen, with its excellent hotel, before making a dramatic defile over the
Hardangervidda.

CENTRAL NORWAY

0   30 km

N

◄ Trondheim

SWEDEN

FEMUNDSMARKA
NASJONAL PARK

Lake Femund

Synnervika

HWY 28

Olavsgruva
Røros

HWY 31

GAULDAL

HWY 30

HWY 30

HWY 30

HWY 3

HWY 3

HWY 3

HWY 3

Alvdal

HWY 29

HWY 27

HWY 21

Ringebu

HWY 254

E6

Støren

E6

Oppdal

DOVREFJELL
NASJONALPARK

Kongsvoll

Hjerkinn

HWY 29

RONDANE
NASJONALPARK

Mysuseter

GUDBRANDSDAL

Kvam

Hundorp

E6

▲ Snøhetta
(2286m)

Dombås

E6

E6

Otta

HWY 257

Sjoa

HEIDAL

HWY 70

E136

Lom

HWY 15

Galdhøpiggen
(2469m)

▲

Glittertind
(2470m)

▲

HWY 51

Gjendesheim

Lake Gjende

JOTUNHEIMEN

Lake Bygdin

Andalsnes

Marstein

Kylling
Bru

TROLLVEGGEN

Kristiansund

TROLLSTIGEN

Geiranger

Grotli

HWY 15

HWY 55

SOGNEFJELLSVEG

Turtagrø

Stryn

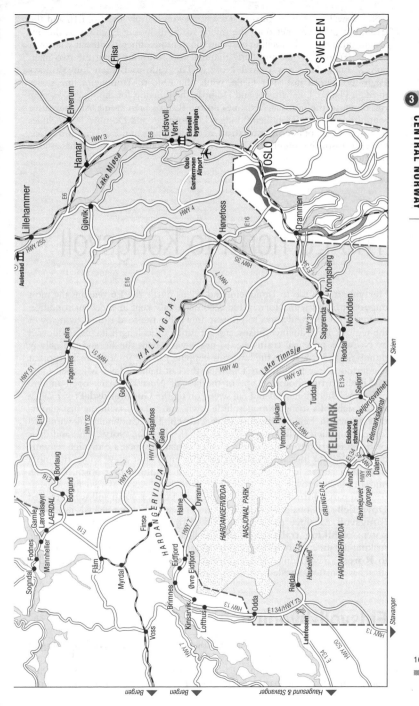

Nor-Way Bussekspress **buses** (Ⓦ www.nor-way.no) ply the E6, E16 and the E134, but once you get onto the minor roads, including Highway 7, the bus system thins out and travelling becomes much more difficult without your own vehicle. **Trains** are fast and fairly frequent too, shuttling along the two main railway lines that cross central Norway. The Oslo-to-Bergen line shadows Highway 7 until just after Geilo, while the Oslo-to-Trondheim line passes through Hamar, Lillehammer and Dombås, the junction for the superbly scenic run down to the fjords at Åndalsnes on the Rauma branch line. An alternative route from Oslo to Trondheim dodges Lillehammer and Dombås, but includes Røros. In terms of **accommodation**, roadside campgrounds are commonplace, there's a reasonable supply of HI hostels, and every town and village has at least one hotel or guesthouse.

The E6 north to Kongsvoll

Hurrying from Oslo to Trondheim and points north, the **E6** remains the most important highway in Norway, and is consequently kept in excellent condition – often with the roadworks to prove it. Inevitably, the road is used by many of the region's long-distance **buses**, and for much of its length it's also shadowed by Norway's principal **train** line. To begin with, both the E6 and the railway thump northwards across the lowlands, clipping past the international airport at Gardermoen (see p.70) before following the east bank of Lake Mjøsa en route to **Lillehammer**, home to one of the best of Norway's many open-air folk museums. Thereafter, road and rail sweep on up the **Gudbrandsdal** river valley, within sight of a string of modest little towns and villages, with the first significant attraction being **Ringebu stave church**. The Gudbrandsdal witnessed some of the fiercest fighting of World War II when the Norwegians and their British allies tried to stem the northward German advance, a campaign remembered at the war museum in **Kvam**. Pushing on, it's just a few kilometres more to **Sjoa**, a centre for whitewater rafting, and a little further north, **Otta**, an undistinguished town but one that is within easy reach of two magnificent national parks, **Jotunheimen** and **Rondane**. Further north still is the rugged **Dovrefjell** Nasjonalpark, which is most pleasingly approached from tiny **Kongsvoll**. All three parks are networked by an extensive and well-planned system of **hiking trails**. From Kongsvoll, Trondheim is within comfortable striking distance; alternatively, you can detour east via either Highway 29 or 30 to **Røros**, a fascinating old iron-mining town on the mountain plateau that stretches across to Sweden.

Eidsvoll-bygningen

Clearly signposted off the E6 about 70km from Oslo, **Eidsvoll-bygningen** (45min guided tours: May–Aug daily 10am–5pm; Sept & April Tues–Fri 10am–3pm, Sat & Sun noon–5pm; Oct–March Wed–Fri 10am–3pm, Sat & Sun noon–5pm; 70kr) is a charming and spacious old manor house that gives a real insight into the tastes of Norway's early nineteenth-century upper class. In its own little park with the river down below, this two-storey timber house has just over thirty rooms, with what were once the owners' living areas on the first floor, beneath the servants' quarters and above the basement kitchens. The main entrance hall is in the Neoclassical style much favoured by the Dano–Norwegian elite, its columns a suitably formal introduction to the spacious suites that lie beyond. The library is well stocked, there's a billiard room and a smoking room, and a string of elegant dining rooms and bedrooms. Oriental knick-knacks and English furniture appear throughout, and the occasional mural depicts Greek mythological figures. There's also an obsession with symmetry: doors were camouflaged and false windows created to avoid breaking up the architectural regularity whenever it was threatened. The house was owned by the Ankers family, who made their money from the local iron works – hence the splendid cast-iron stoves.

It's a delightful ensemble, but the house owes its preservation to its historical significance rather than its aesthetics. One of the Ankers, Carsten, was a close friend and ally of the Danish crown prince **Christian Frederik**, and this connection has given the house national importance. Towards the end of the Napoleonic Wars, the Russians and British insisted the Danes be punished for their alliance with the French, and proposed taking Norway from Denmark and handing it over to Sweden. In an attempt to forestall these territorial shenanigans, the Danes dispatched Christian Frederik to Norway, where he set up home in Carsten Ankers' house in 1813, and proceeded to lobby for Norwegian support. In April of the following year more than a hundred of the country's leading citizens gathered here at Eidsvoll to decide whether to accept union with Sweden or go for independence with Christian Frederik on the throne. The majority of this **National Assembly** chose independence, and set about drafting a liberal constitution based on those of France and the United States. Predictably, the Swedes would have none of this. Four years earlier, the Swedes had picked one of Napoleon's marshals, **Jean-Baptiste Bernadotte** (see p.84), to succeed their previous king who had died without an heir. As King Karl Johan, Bernadotte was keen to flex his military muscles and, irritated by the putative National Assembly, he invaded Norway in July 1814. Frederik was soon forced to abdicate and the Norwegians were pressed into union, though Karl Johan did head off much of the opposition by guaranteeing the Norwegians a new constitution and parliament, the Storting.

Carsten Ankers converted the upper storey of his home into premises for the National Assembly, comprising a handful of administrative offices plus the Room for the Constitutional Committee, where the original wooden benches have survived along with various landscape paintings. There's a rusticated modesty to it all which is really rather charming, and a painting of Venus has been put back in the room after years of being shunted up and down the adjoining corridors: after prolonged discussion, it had originally been removed because the representatives considered it an erotic distraction. For more on the evolution of democracy in general and the Norwegian Constitution in particular, drop by the visitor centre (same times; no extra charge) just down from the house near the river.

The house is in the country just to the south of the industrial town of **Eidsvoll Verk**: it's signed off the E6, 2km down a byroad.

Hamar

Just beyond Eidsvoll Verk, the E6 curves round the eastern shore of Norway's largest lake, **Lake Mjøsa**, a favourite retreat for Norwegian families, whose second homes dot the surrounding farmland, woods and pastures. Before the railroad arrived in the 1880s, the lake was an important transport route, crossed by boats in summer and by horse and sleigh in winter. It's also halfway country: the quiet settlements around the lake give a taste of small-town southern Norway before the E6 plunges into the wilder regions further north.

Midway round the lake, some 130km from Oslo, lies **HAMAR**, a modest little place of 27,000 souls, whose long, straggly waterfront is at its prettiest down by the marina, where a couple of cafés make a gallant attempt to sustain a nautical air. Unlikely though it may seem today, Hamar was once the seat of an important medieval bishopric, and the battered remains of its Romanesque-Gothic **Domkirke (cathedral)**, now protected by a glass and steel superstructure – the Hamardomen – are stuck out on the Domkirkeodden (cathedral point), a low, leafy headland about 2km west of the centre. The cathedral is thought to have been built by the "English pope" Nicholas Breakspear, who spent a couple of years in Norway as the papal legate before becoming Adrian IV in 1154, but the building, along with the surrounding episcopal complex, was ransacked during the Reformation, and local road-builders subsequently helped themselves to the stone. The ruins have now been incorporated into the rambling **Hedmarksmuseet** (late May to mid-June Tues–Sun 10am–4pm; mid-June to mid-Aug daily 10am–5pm; mid-Aug to early Sept Tues–Sun 10am–4pm; 75kr; ⓦwww.hedmarksmuseet.no), which contains an archeological museum and an open-air folk museum. The latter holds around fifty buildings collected from across the region and, although it's not as comprehensive as the one in Lillehammer (see p.171), it does contain several particularly fine buildings, the oldest of which are clustered in the Hedmarkstunet section. The most scenic approach to the headland is along the pleasant lakeshore footpath that stretches 2km north from the train station.

DS Skibladner

Hamar is as good a place as any to pick up the 130-year-old **paddle steamer**, the DS *Skibladner* (Ⓣ61 14 40 80, ⓦwww.skiblander.no), which shuttles up and down **Lake Mjøsa** between late June and mid-August. On Tuesdays, Thursdays and Saturdays the boat makes the return trip across the lake from Hamar to Gjøvik and on up to Lillehammer; on Mondays, Wednesdays and Fridays it chugs south down to Eidsvoll and back; there's no Sunday service. Sailing times are available direct or at any local tourist office. Tickets are bought on board: return trips from Hamar to Eidsvoll cost 280kr and last two-and-a-half hours, those to Lillehammer cost 320kr and last eight hours. One-way fares cost a little over half these rates. Travellers heading north may find the trip to Lillehammer tempting at first sight, but the lake is not particularly scenic, and after four hours on the boat you may well feel like jumping overboard. The best bet is to take the shorter ride to Eidsvoll instead.

Practicalities

Hamar's **train station** is just to the east of the town centre beside the lake; **buses** stop outside. Some trains from Oslo pause here before heading up the branch line to Røros (see p.183), a fine three-and-a-half-hour ride over hills and through huge forests. The jetty for the DS *Skibladner* is about 600m to the west of the train station along the lakeshore.

There's no pressing reason to overnight in Hamar, but the town does have a fair choice of central **accommodation**. Cream of the hotel crop is the *Scandic Hamar*, in a large modern block on the northeast edge of the town centre at Vangsvegen 121 (☎21 61 40 00, ⓦwww.scandichotels.com; ❺, sp/r ❹). The hotel may not be especially prepossessing from the outside, but the interior has been kitted out in a bright and well-conceived modern/minimalist style as have the spacious bedrooms, some of which – on the top floors – have wide views over town; breakfasts here are first-rate too. To get here from the train station, walk west along Strandgata, turn right up Vangsvegen and keep going – an easy twenty-minute walk. Alternatively, Hamar's all-year HI **hostel**, part of the *Vikingskipet Motell* at Åkersvikvegen 21 (☎62 52 60 60, ⓦwww.vandrerhjem.no; dorm beds 410kr, doubles ❸), occupies a modern, two-storey, motel-style timber building about 2km south along the lakeshore from the train station. It's in the middle of nowhere, just across from the massive skating arena, the Vikingskipet, built for the 1994 Winter Olympics in the shape of an upturned Viking ship.

Among Hamar's clutch of downtown cafés and restaurants, two deserve a mention, kicking off with *Hot & Spicy*, a cheerfully decorated, Chinese–Thai restaurant at Torggata 21 (daily except Tues 3–11pm). The service here in this informal, family-run place is fast and efficient and main courses are priced between 120–160kr. The second option is the much slicker and smarter *Victoria Haven*, beside the main city park just back from the lakeshore on Strandgata (daily 11am–11pm). They serve coffee and cakes here in the morning, and a range of Norwegian dishes at lunch and dinner with mains averaging 180kr.

Lillehammer and around

LILLEHAMMER (literally "Little Hammer"), 60km north of Hamar and 190km from Oslo, is Lake Mjøsa's most worthwhile destination. In **winter**, it's one of Norway's top ski centres, a young and vibrant place whose rural lakeside setting and extensive cross-country ski trails contributed to its selection as host of the 1994 Olympic Winter Games. In preparation for the games, the Norwegian government spent a massive two billion kroner on the town's **sporting facilities**, which are now among the best in the country. Spread along the hillsides above and near the town, they include several dozen downhill ski trails catering for everyone from beginner to expert, floodlit slopes for night skiing, ski-jumping towers and multiple chair lifts, an ice hockey arena, and a bobsleigh track. There is even a special stadium – the Birkebeiner – where skiers can hone their skills before setting off into the mountains, which are criss-crossed by 350km of cross-country ski trails. As you would expect, most Norwegians arriving here in winter come fully equipped, but it's possible to rent or buy equipment locally – the tourist office (see p.170) will advise.

Lillehammer is a popular **summer** holiday spot too. As soon as the weather picks up, hundreds of Norwegians hunker down in their second homes in the hills that flank the town, popping into the centre for a drink or a meal. Cycling, walking, fishing and canoeing are popular pastimes at this time of year, with all sorts of possibilities for guided tours. Yet, however appealing the area may be to Norwegians, the countryside hereabouts has little of the wonderful wildness of other parts of Norway, and unless you're someone's guest or bring your own family, you'll probably feel rather out on a limb. That said, Lillehammer is not a bad place to break your journey, and there are a couple of attractions to keep you busy for a day or two – principally the **Maihaugen** open-air museum, and **Aulestad**, the country home of Norwegian author Bjørnstjerne Bjørnson, about thirty minutes' drive away.

Arrival, information and orientation

The E6 runs along the lakeshore about 500m below the centre of Lillehammer, where the ultramodern **Skysstasjon**, on Jernbanetorget at the bottom of Jernbanegata, incorporates the **train station** and the **bus terminal**. The **tourist office** is also here (late June Mon–Sat 9am–6pm & Sun noon–5pm; July Mon–Sat 9am–8pm & Sun 11am–6pm; rest of year Mon–Fri 9am–4pm & Sat 10am–2pm; ☎61 28 98 00, ⊛www.lillehammer.com). Staff have information on local events and activities, and will help with finding accommodation. **Orientation** couldn't be easier, with all activity focused on the pedestrianized part of Storgata, which runs north from Bankgata, across Jernbanegata to the tumbling River Mesnaelva; Anders Sandvigsgate and Kirkegata run parallel on either side to east and west respectively.

Accommodation

Lillehammer is a tad light on top-rate hotels, but it does have an HI hostel and several central guesthouses.

First Hotell Breiseth Jernbanegata 1 ☎61 24 77 77, ⊛www.firsthotels.com. Metres from the train station, the *Breiseth* dates back to the late nineteenth century – as evidenced by parts of the facade – but the interior is minimalist-modern give or take the odd rhetorical flourish (like the wing-back chairs). There are ninety-odd comfortable rooms here, mostly in browns and creams. ❺, sp/r ❹

Lillehammer Vandrerhjem Jernbanetorget 2 ☎61 26 00 24, ⊛www.vandrerhjem.no. All-year HI hostel in the same block as the train station. Has a good range of facilities, from a self-catering kitchen and a café through to internet access, a laundry, free parking and common grounds. The rooms themselves are fairly spartan, but they are perfectly adequate and most are en suite. Dorm beds 325kr, doubles ❸

Suttestad Gård Suttestådvegen 17 ☎61 25 04 44, ⊛www.lillehammerturist.no/suttestad.htm. Large former farmhouse with eight modern guest rooms, most of which are en suite and have views down towards the lake. It's 1.5km south of the train station; take Kirkegata – Suttestådvegen is a turning on the right. ❷

The town centre

Lillehammer's briskly efficient centre, just a few-minutes' walk from one end to the other, is tucked into the hillside above the lake, the E6 and the railway. It has just one really notable attraction, the **Kunstmuseum** at Stortorget 2 (Art Museum; late June to late Aug daily 11am–5pm; rest of year Tues–Sun 11am–4pm; 60kr). Housed in two adjacent buildings, one a municipal structure from the 1960s, the other a flashy modern edifice added thirty years later, the gallery is renowned for its temporary exhibitions of contemporary art (which often carry an extra admission charge), but the small permanent collection (in the older building) is also very worthwhile, comprising a representative sample of the works of most major Norwegian painters, from Johan Dahl and Christian Krohg to Munch and Erik Werenskiold. In particular, look out for the striking landscapes painted by one of the less familiar Norwegian artists, **Axel Revold** (1887–1962). A student of Matisse and an admirer of Cézanne, Revold spent years working abroad before returning home and applying the techniques he had learned to his favourite subject, northern Norway: his beautifully composed and brightly coloured *Nordland* is typical. Revold also dabbled in the bizarre, as in the bold Expressionism of *A Sailor's Dream*.

After you've visited the art museum, the obvious target is Maihaugen (see below), though you might wander up along the river on the west side of the centre or stroll down to the lake to take a ride on the antique **DS Skibladner** paddle steamer as it shuttles up and down Lake Mjøsa: the jetty is about 800m south of the centre (see p.168 for further details).

Maihaugen

The much-vaunted **Maihaugen** open-air folk museum – the largest of its type in northern Europe – is a twenty-minute walk southeast from the town centre along Anders Sandvigsgate (mid-May to Sept daily 10am–5pm; Oct to mid-May Tues–Sun 11am–4pm; 80kr, mid-May to Sept 100kr; Ⓦ www.maihaugen .no). Incredibly, the bulk of the collection represents the lifetime's work of one man, a magpie-ish dentist by the name of Anders Sandvig (1862–1950), who only ended up here in Lillehammer by accident: he contracted tuberculosis and moved here from Oslo to recuperate in the clear mountain air. Since Sandvig's death, the city have augmented the original collection and Maihaugen now holds around 200 relocated buildings, brought here from all over the region and including several real treasures such as a charming seventeenth-century presbytery (*prestegårdshagen*) and a thirteenth-century stave church from Garmo.

The key exhibits, however, are the two **farms** from Bjørnstad and Øygarden, dating from the late seventeenth century. Complete with their various outhouses and living areas, the two comprise 36 buildings, each with a specific function, such as food store, sheep-shed, hay barn, stable and bathhouse. This setup may have worked, and it certainly looks quaint, but it was, in fact, forced upon farmers by their tried-and-tested method of construction, **laft**. Based on the use of pine logs notched together at right angles, the technique strictly limited the dimensions of every building, as the usable part of the pine tree was rarely more than 8m long. Indeed, it seems likely that many farmers would have preferred to keep their winter supplies in the main farmhouse rather than in a separate store, as implied by a draconian medieval law that stated, "When a man discovers another in his storehouse … then he may kill the man if he so wishes."

In the summertime, costumed guides give the lowdown on traditional rural life and there's often the chance to have a go at domestic activities such as spinning, baking, weaving and pottery – good, wholesome fun. You can spend time too in the main museum building, which features temporary exhibitions on folkloric themes. Allow a good half-day for a visit and take advantage of the free forty-minute English-language guided tour (June to mid-Aug only; every other hour, on the hour, until 2hr before closing).

To get to the museum from the train station, walk up Jernbanegata, turn right onto Anders Sandvigsgate, and keep going; all in all, it's about 1.5km.

Eating and drinking

Downtown Lillehammer has a reasonably good supply of **cafés** and **restaurants**. One good choice is the *Blåmann Restaurant & Bar*, off the pedestrianized part of Storgata at Lilletorvet 1, which has a leafy terrace suspended over the cascading river below and has a wide-ranging menu with the likes of *klippfisk*, Mexican dishes, crab and moussaka; main courses are around 230–250kr. There's also *Svare & Berg*, in old timber premises by the river on Elvegata, where they serve first-rate snacks and light meals – try the meatballs (120kr).

The town has an animated **nightlife**, with bars clustered around the western end of Storgata – try *Nikkers* at Elvegata 18 for lively low-key drinks, or *Brenneriet*, just over the road, a swanky nightclub-and-restaurant combo.

Around Lillehammer: Aulestad

Eighteen kilometres northwest of Lillehammer, in the hamlet of Follebu, is **Aulestad** (daily: mid-May & Sept 11am–4pm; June–Aug 10am–5pm; 75kr), a good-looking villa perched on a leafy knoll, and packed with mementoes of its former owner **Bjørnstjerne Bjørnson** (1832–1910). Little known outside Norway today, Bjørnson was a major figure in the literary and cultural revival that swept the country at the end of the nineteenth century. Bjørnson made his name with the peasant tales of *Synnøve Solbakken* in 1857 and thereafter he churned out a veritable flood of novels, stories, poems and plays, many of which romanticized Norwegian country folk and, unusually for the time, were written in Norwegian, rather than the traditional Danish. He also championed all sorts of progressive causes, from Norwegian independence through to equality of the sexes and crofters' rights, albeit from a liberal (as distinct from leftist) viewpoint. Nowadays, however, his main claim to fame is as author of the poem that became the national anthem. Bjørnson moved to Aulestad in 1875, and an audiovisual display inside the house gives further details on the man and his times.

To get to Aulestad, head north from Lillehammer on the E6 and turn onto Highway 255 after about 4km. To get back onto the E6 heading north, follow Highway 255 from the Bjørnson house, then turn onto Highway 254: this brings you out on the E6 halfway between Lillehammer and the Ringebu church (see p.172).

The Gudbrandsdal

Heading north from Lillehammer, the E6 and the railway leave the shores of Lake Mjøsa to run along the **Gudbrandsdal**, a 160-kilometre river valley, which was for centuries the main route between Oslo and Trondheim. Enclosed by mountain ranges, the valley has a comparatively dry and mild climate, and its fertile soils have nourished a string of farming villages since Viking times, though today the **Gudbrandsdal** is partially blotched by light industry.

Ringebu stave church

The Gudbrandsdal begins pleasantly enough, the easy sweep of its forested hills interrupted by rocky outcrops and patches of farmland dotted with brightly coloured farmsteads. After about 60km, the E6 swings past the turning to **Ringebu stave church** (daily: late May to June & Aug 9am–5pm; July 8am–6pm; 40kr, 60kr including Weidemann exhibition, see below), whose distinctive maroon spire stands on a hill 1km off the E6 – and a couple of kilometres south of Ringebu village. Dating from the thirteenth century, the original church was modified and enlarged in the 1630s, reflecting both an increase in the local population and the new religious practices introduced after the Reformation. At this time, the nave was broadened, the chancel replaced and an over-large tower and spire plonked on top. The exterior is rather glum, but the western **entrance portal** sports some superb if badly weathered zoomorphic carvings from the original church. **Inside**, the highlights are mainly eighteenth-century Baroque – from the florid pulpit and altar panel through to a memorial to the Irgens family, complete with trumpeting cherubs and intricate ruffs.

The old vicarage behind the church was in ecclesiastical hands until the 1990s, but it now holds the **Weidemannsamlingen** (late May to Aug Tues–Sun 10am–5pm; 40kr, 60kr including church) featuring a selection of paintings by the prolific **Jacob Weidemann** (1923–2001), one of Norway's most talented modern artists. Many of Weidemann's works were inspired by the Norwegian landscape, but he eschewed realism for deeply coloured abstract canvases of great emotional intensity. His liking for strong colours is often tied to an accident that befell him during World War II. Active in the Resistance, Weidemann was forced to escape to neutral Sweden, where he lost an eye when an explosive charge was accidentally detonated.

Hundorp and Sygard Grytting

From Ringebu church, it's about 12km to the straggling village of **HUNDORP**, whose southern peripheries hold a neat little quadrangle of old farm buildings tastefully turned into a roadside tourist stop, with a café, art gallery, shop and **hotel**. This hotel, the *Hundorp Dale-Gudbrands gard* (☎61 29 71 11, ⊛www .hundorp.no; ❹), has twelve comfortable rooms decorated in traditional Norwegian country style and occupying an attractive two-storey building of ancient provenance – with timber planking on top of a stone cellar. There has been a farm here since prehistoric times, its most famous owner being a Viking warrior by the name of Dalegudbrand, who became a bitter enemy of St Olav after his enforced baptism in 1021.

With a little time to spare, you could ramble down towards the river to explore the complex's immediate surroundings, where there are six small but distinct **Viking burial mounds**, as well as a rough circle of standing stones – a plaque shows how to get to them all. The stones, which date from around 700 AD, mark the spot where freemen gathered in the *allting* to discuss issues of local importance – such meetings were nearly always held in the open air. The most powerful local chieftain presided over the *allting* with the assistance of a "law speaker", who was able to recite existing law and memorize new decisions. Theoretically at least, it was one man, one vote, but in practice the more powerful landowners usually had their own way with the assembled freemen showing their consent by brandishing their weapons and/or banging on their shields. There is no **train station** at Hundorp – the nearest is at Ringebu – but buses stop in front of the hotel on the E6.

A further 6km to the north, overlooking the E6, the ancient farmstead of ⚒ **Sygard Grytting** (☎61 29 85 88, ⊛www.grytting.com; July to early Aug) nestles among the orchards, providing some of the region's most distinctive lodgings. The eighteenth-century farm buildings are in an almost perfect state of preservation, a beautiful ensemble with the assorted barns, outhouses and main house facing onto a tiny courtyard. One of these building is even older, dating from the fourteenth century, and its upper storey was used to shelter pilgrims on the long haul north to Trondheim cathedral (p.288). **Dormitory** accommodation (325–360kr per person including breakfast) is on offer here once again. Most of the **double rooms** are in the main farmhouse (❹), which has been superbly renovated to provide extremely comfortable lodgings amid antique furnishings, faded oil paintings and open fires. Breakfast is splendid too – the bread is baked on the premises – and dinner is available by prior arrangement (at 7pm).

The nearest you'll get by bus is the *Dale-Gudbrands gard* hotel in Hundorp, 6km away.

Kvam

Pressing on, the E6 weaves its way north following the course of the river to reach, after about 20km, **KVAM**, a modest chipboard-producing town that witnessed some of the worst fighting of World War II. Once the Germans had occupied Norway's main towns in the spring of 1940, they set about extending their control of the main roads and railways, marching up the Gudbrandsdal in quick fashion. At Kvam, they were opposed by a scratch force of Norwegian and British soldiers, who delayed their progress despite being poorly equipped – the captain in charge of the British anti-tank guns had to borrow a bicycle to patrol his defences. The battle for the Gudbrandsdal lasted for two weeks (April 14–30, 1940) and is commemorated at the **Gudbrandsdal Krigsminnesamling** (War Museum; late June to July daily 10am–5pm; early Aug Wed–Sun 10am–4pm; 40kr; ⓦwww.krigsminne.no), in the centre of Kvam beside the E6. In the museum, a series of excellent multilingual displays runs through the campaign, supported by a substantial collection of military mementoes and lots of fascinating photographs. There are also informative sections on the rise of Fascism and the Norwegian Resistance, plus a modest display on the role played by the villagers of Otta in the Kalmar War of 1611–13 (see p.175). Across the main street from the museum, in the **church graveyard**, is a Cross of Sacrifice, honouring the 54 British soldiers who died here while trying to halt the German advance in 1940.

Buses travel through Kvam on the E6 and there's a request stop metres from the museum; Kvam train station, also a request stop, is about 200m south of the museum.

Sjoa

From Kvam, it's 9km further up the valley to **SJOA**, a scattered hamlet set beside the junction of the E6 and Highway 257. The latter cuts west along the **Heidal valley**, where the River Sjoa boasts some of the country's most exciting **whitewater rafting**. If you want to come to grips with the river's gorges and rapids, contact the local specialists, Heidal Rafting (☎61 23 60 37, ⓦwww .heidalrafting.no). An all-inclusive, one-day rafting excursion costs around 1000kr, 800kr for half a day; a more strenuous two-day expedition inclusive of meals and lodgings will set you back around 2000kr. The season lasts from May to October and reservations are recommended, though there's a reasonably good chance of being able to sign up at the last minute. Heidal Rafting is based at the HI **hostel**, *Sjoa Vandrerhjem* (☎61 23 62 00, ⓦwww.vandrerhjem.no; dorm beds 270kr, chalets ❶–❷; mid-May to Sept), which is itself worth a second look. Perched on a wooded hillside high above the river, the main building is a charming log farmhouse dating from 1747 and, although visitors sleep in more modern quarters, this is where you eat. Breakfasts are banquet-like, and dinners (by prior arrangement only) are reasonably priced if rather less spectacular. The hostel offers two types of accommodation: there's a no-frills dormitory block at the bottom of the slope and a handful of spacious and comfortable chalets up above. Reservations are advisable for the chalets at weekends. The hostel is just off Highway 257, about 1500m west of the E6. There's no train station – the nearest is at Otta 10km to the north – but buses stop on the E6 near the Highway 257 intersection.

Beyond the Heidal valley, Highway 257 continues west to meet Highway 51, the main access road to the east side of the Jotunheimen National Park at Gjendesheim (see p.178).

Otta

OTTA, just 10km beyond Sjoa, is an unassuming and unexciting little town at the confluence of the rivers Otta and Lågen. It may be dull, but Otta does make a handy base for hiking in the nearby Rondane national park (see p.176), especially if you're reliant on public transport – though staying in one of the park's mountain lodges is much to be preferred. The town is also within easy driving distance of the Jotunheimen (see p.177). In Otta itself, everything you need is within easy reach: the E6 passes within 300m of the town centre, sweeping along the east bank of the Lågen, while Highway 15 bisects the town from east to west with the few gridiron streets that pass for the centre lying a few metres to the south.

There are no sights as such, but the **statue** outside the Skysstasjon, just north of Highway 15, commemorates a certain **Pillarguri**, whose alertness made her an overnight sensation. During the Kalmar War of 1611–13, one of many wars between Sweden and Denmark, a band of Scottish mercenaries hired by the king of Sweden landed in the Romsdalsfjord, intent on crossing Norway to join the Swedish army. The Norwegians – Danish subjects at that time – were fearful of the Scots, and when Pillarguri spotted them nearing Otta she dashed to the top of the nearest hill and blew her birch-bark horn to sound the alarm. The locals hastily arranged an ambush at one of the narrowest points of the trail and all but wiped the Scots out – a rare victory for peasants over professionals. One of Pillarguri's rewards was to have a hill named after her, and today the stiff hike along the footpath up the forested slopes to the summit, **Pillarguritoppen** (853m), across the River Otta south of the centre, is a popular outing; free trail maps are available at the tourist office (see below).

Practicalities

Clumped together in the Skysstasjon on the north side of Highway 15 are the **train station**, **bus terminal** and **tourist office** (late June to mid-Aug daily 8.30am–4pm; mid-Aug to late June Mon–Fri 8.30am–4pm; ☎61 23 66 70, ⓦwww.visittrondane.com). The latter can provide local bus timetables, book accommodation and reserve Lake Gjende boat tickets; they also sell fishing licences and local hiking maps. **Accommodation** is thin on the ground, but the *Norlandia Otta Hotell*, in the centre on Ola Dahls gate (☎61 21 08 00, ⓦwww .norlandia.no; ❹) makes a reasonable hand of its uninspiring modern premises. The nearest **campsite**, *Otta Camping* (☎61 23 03 09, ⓦwww.ottacamping.no; May to mid-Oct), lies about 1500m from the town centre on the wooded banks of the River Otta, with cabins (350–750kr for 4–5 persons, with facilities) and

Moving on from Otta to the western fjords

Running west from Otta, **Highway 15** sweeps along wide river valleys bound for **Lom** (see p.251), where there's a choice of wonderful routes on into the western fjords: you can either carry on along Highway 15 towards Stryn (see p.257) and Loen (see p.256), or branch off north onto the rattling **Ørnevegen** (Eagle's Highway; Highway 63) to Geiranger (see p.262). Alternatively, you can turn off Highway 15 at Lom, onto the **Sognefjellsveg** (Highway 55) which climbs steeply to the south, travelling along the western flank of the Jotunheimen national park and offering breathtaking views of its jagged peaks before careering down to Sogndal (see p.247).

The Nor-Way Bussekspress (ⓦwww.nor-way.no) Oslo–Måløy **service** (3 daily) runs along Highway 15 from Otta to Lom, Langvatn and Stryn. The journey time from Otta to Lom is one hour, three hours to Stryn. From mid-June to August, a twice-daily local bus links Langvatn with Geiranger and ultimately Åndalsnes. From late June to August, there's also a twice-daily bus from Otta and Lom to Sogndal via the Sognefjellsveg, Highway 55.

Most fjordland bus and ferry services are provided by either Tide (ⓦwww.tide.no) or Fjord1 (ⓦwww.fjord1.no); both websites carry timetables.

space for tents: to get there, cross the bridge on the southwest side of the centre, turn right and keep going.

Otta's choice of **places to eat** is also constrained, but there is one recommendable spot, the *Pillarguri*, Storgata 7 (℡61 23 01 04), a café–restaurant, offering a good range of traditional Norwegian dishes with mains about 150kr; it's normally open daily from noon to 10pm.

From Otta to the Rondane and Jotunheimen national parks

From Otta, it's about 20km east to **Rondane** Nasjonalpark: take the byroad to the sprawling chalet settlement of **Mysuseter** and keep going a further 5km to the **Spranghaugen car park**, right on the edge of the park itself and an easy ninety-minute walk from the *Rondvassbu* mountain lodge (see p.176). In the summertime, a local bus plies this route, but it is a very limited service (late Aug only, Sat & Sun 1–2 daily; 1hr; ⓦwww.fjord1.no); the alternative is to go by taxi – try Otta Taxi (℡61 23 05 01). There's currently no bus service from Otta to Gjendesheim (see p.178) in Jotunheimen Nasjonalpark, but it only takes an hour or two to drive the 100km along Highway 15 and then 51.

Rondane Nasjonalpark

Spreading north and east from Otta, **Rondane Nasjonalpark** was established in 1962 as Norway's first national park and is now one of the country's most popular hiking areas. Its 527 square kilometres, one third of which is in the high alpine zone, appeal to walkers of all ages and abilities. The soil is poor, so vegetation is sparse and lichens, especially reindeer moss, predominate, but the views across this bare landscape are serenely beautiful, and a handful of lakes and rivers plus patches of dwarf birch forest provide some variety. Wild mountain peaks divide the Rondane into three distinct areas. To the west of **Rondvatnet**, a centrally located lake, are the wild cirques and jagged peaks of Storsmeden (2017m), Sagtinden (2018m) and Veslesmeden (2015m), while to the east of the lake rise Rondslottet (2178m), Vinjeronden (2044m) and Storronden (2138m). Further east still, Høgronden (2115m) dominates the landscape. The mountains, ten of which exceed the 2000-metre mark, are mostly accessible to any reasonably fit and eager walker, thanks to a dense network of trails and hiking huts/lodges.

From the **Spranghaugen car park**, where the bus from Otta terminates (see above), it's a ninety-minute level walk northeast along the service road to the southern tip of lake **Rondvatnet** with the bleak and bare peaks of the Rondane slowly revealing themselves – a dozen peaks in all, surrounding the lake's shadowy waters. At the southern tip of the lake is the DNT ♣ **Rondvassbu lodge** (late June to early Oct; ℡61 23 18 66, ⓦwww.rondvassbu.com; dorm beds for DNT members 180kr, 250kr for non members, doubles ❶), the most accessible of the park's several huts and lodges. It's a typical staffed DNT lodge, with more than one hundred beds, filling meals and pleasant service. For all but the briefest of hikes, it's best to arrive at the lodge the day before to have a chance of starting first thing the next morning. If, however, visibility is poor or you don't fancy a climb, there is a delightful summer **boat service** (July–Aug 2–3 daily; 30min each way; 100kr return) to the far end of Rondvatnet, from where it takes about two and a half hours to walk back to *Rondvassbu* along the lake's steep western shore.

Among the many other **hiking** possibilities, one popular choice is the haul up from *Rondvassbu* to the top of **Storronden** (2138m), the first peak to the right

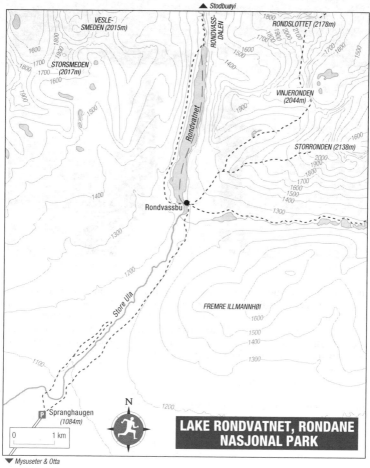

▲ *Stodbuøyi*

VESLE-
SMEDEN (2015m)

RONDVASS-
DALEN

RONDSLOTTET (2178m)

STORSMEDEN
(2017m)

Rondvatnet

VINJERONDEN
(2044m)

STORRONDEN (2138m)

Rondvassbu

Store Ula

FREMRE ILLMANNHØI

N

P Spranghaugen
(1084m)

0   1 km

**LAKE RONDVATNET, RONDANE
NASJONAL PARK**

▼ *Mysuseter & Otta*

of the lake. This makes a fine excursion for the beginner, since – except for a short steep and exposed section just below the summit – there is no really difficult terrain to negotiate and the trail is clearly signed; the round trip takes about five hours – three up and two down. Neighbouring peaks involve more arduous mountain hiking, with the finest views over the range generally reckoned to be from **Vinjeronden** and nearby **Rondslottet**, both to the north of Storronden. Finally, note that parts of the park are out of bounds during the reindeer calving season, from early May to the middle of June.

Jotunheimen Nasjonalpark

Norway's most celebrated hiking area, **Jotunheimen Nasjonalpark** ("Home of the Giants" National Park) lives up to its name: pointed summits and undulating glaciers dominate the skyline, soaring high above river valleys and lake-studded plateaux. Covering only 3900 square kilometres, the park offers an

▲ Cross-country skiing, Rondane National Park

amazing concentration of high peaks, more than two hundred of which rise above 1900m, including Norway's (and northern Europe's) two highest mountains, Galdhøpiggen (2469m) and Glittertind (2464m). Here also is Norway's highest waterfall, **Vettisfossen**, boasting a 275-metre drop and located a short walk from the Vetti lodge on the west side of the park. A network of footpaths and mountain lodges lattices the Jotunheimen, but be warned that the weather is very unpredictable and the winds can be bitingly cold – take care and always come well equipped.

There are no public/asphalted roads into the park; visitors usually hike or ski into the interior from the Sognefjellsveg (Highway 55) in the west (see p.250) or make the slightly easier approach from the east, driving to **Gjendesheim**, 2km off Highway 51 and some 90km from Otta. The only half-reasonable bus service to Gjendesheim is provided by Nor-Way Bussekspress (Ⓦ www .nor-way.no): their Valdresekspressen bus (4–6 daily) links Oslo with Fagernes (see p.186), where you change for Beitostølen (2–4 daily), changing again for Gjendesheim (late June to early Sept 1–2 daily; 40min). Gjendesheim has long been a popular base for exploring the Jotunheimen – the first mountain hut was built here in the 1870s – but it is still no more than a ferry dock and a couple of buildings, one of which is the excellent, staffed DNT 🏃 *Gjendesheim* lodge (mid-Feb to March & mid-June to early Oct; ☎61 23 89 10, Ⓦ www.gjendesheim.no; dorm beds for DNT members 220kr, non members 285kr, doubles ❶), at the eastern tip of long and slender **Lake Gjende**. Some 18km long and 146m deep, the lake is one of Norway's most beautiful, its glacially-fed waters tinted green by myriad clay particles; it was also here that Ibsen had his Peer Gynt tumble into the water from the back of a reindeer. Boats (mid-June to mid-Sept 1–3 daily; ☎61 23 85 09, Ⓦ www.gjende.no) travel the length of the lake, connecting with mountain trails and dropping by two more lodges. These are the privately owned lodge at **Memurubu** (mid-June to mid-Sept; ☎61 23 89 99, Ⓦ www.memurubu .no; ❷), halfway along the lake's north shore; and **Gjendebu**, a staffed DNT lodge (early to late March & late June to late Sept ☎61 23 89 44, Ⓦ www.gjendebu .com; dorm beds for DNT members 220kr, non members 285kr, doubles ❶),

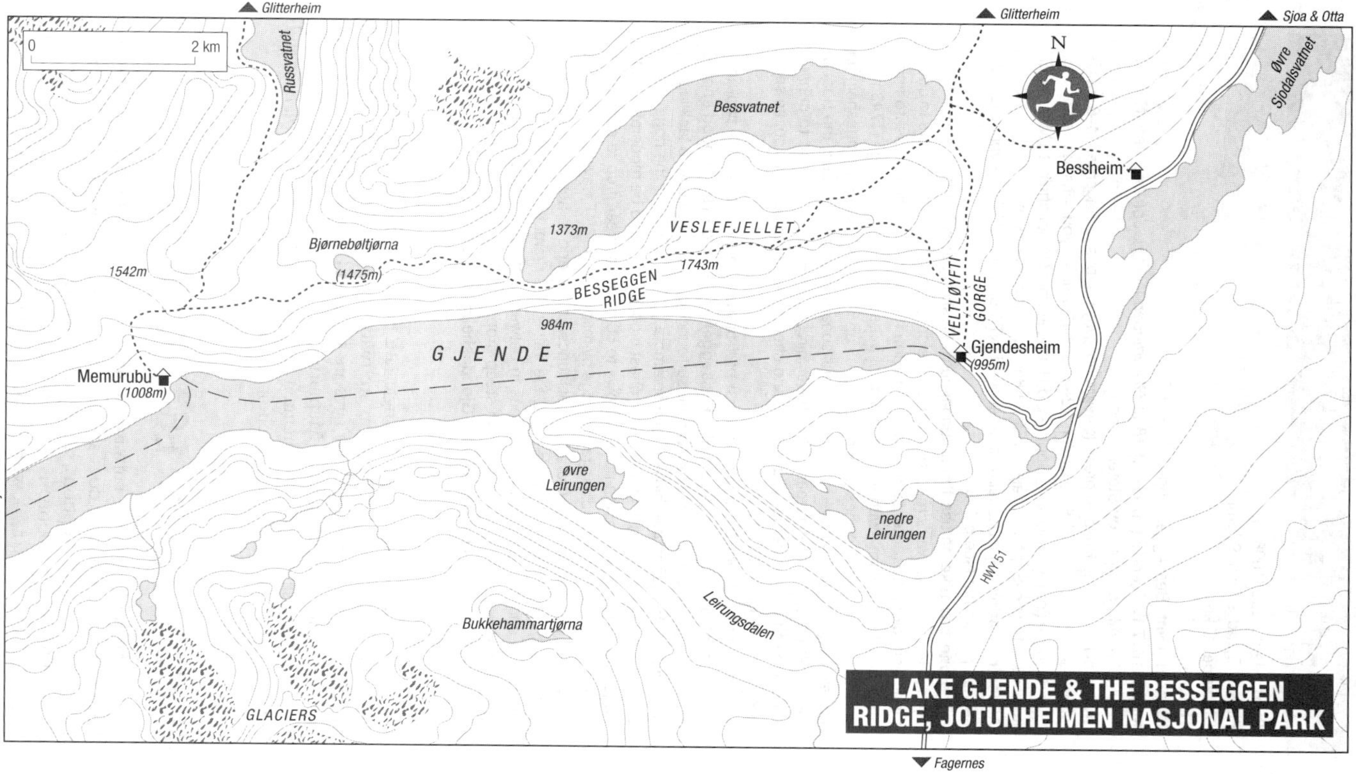

LAKE GJENDE & THE BESSEGGEN
RIDGE, JOTUNHEIMEN NASJONAL PARK

N

▲ Spa & Otta

Øvre Sjodalsvatnet

▲ Glitterheim

Bessheim ■

Gjendesheim ■
(995m)

VELTLØYFTI GORGE

nedre
Leirungen

Bessvatnet

VESLEFJELLET
1743m

1373m

BESSEGGEN
RIDGE

994m

G J E N D E

Leirungsdalen

øvre
Leirungen

HWY 51

Bukkehammartjørna

▲ Glitterheim

Russvatnet

Bjørnebeltjørna
(1475m)

1542m

Memurubu ■
(1008m)

GLACIERS

2 km

0

▲ Gjendebu

A day's hike in the Jotunheimen Nasjonalpark – the Besseggen ridge

Start: Memurubu (1008m).
Finish: Gjendesheim (995m).
Distance: 15km.
Time: 6hr.
Highest point: Besseggen ridge (1743m).
Maps: 1617 IV *Gjende* (M711); 1618 III *Glittertinden* (M711). *Jotunheimen* (No. 45) 1:100,000. All produced by Statens Kartverk.
Transport: Nor-Way Bussekspress (ⓦwww.nor-way.no) bus to Fagernes (4–6 daily), where you change for Beitostølen (2–4 daily), where you change again for Gjendesheim (late June to early Sept 1–2 daily); boat from Gjendesheim to Memurubu (mid-June to mid-Sept 1–3 daily; ⓣ61 23 85 09, ⓦwww.gjende.no).
Accommodation: *Gjendesheim*, full-service DNT hut (see p.178); *Memurubu*, full-service private hut (see p.178).

The **one-day hike** across the Jotunheimen's **Besseggen ridge** high above Lake Gjende is one of Norway's most popular excursions; it takes about six hours to cover the fifteen-kilometre route, starting at Memurubu (1008m) and heading east to finish at Gjendesheim (995m), with the highest point in between being the ridge (1743m). If you do the hike in the opposite direction, you can return by boat to Gjendesheim in the evening, but you'll have to calculate your speed accurately to meet the boat at Memurubu – and that isn't easy. Whichever direction you take, be sure to confirm boat departure times before you set out, and check weather conditions too, as snow and ice can linger well into July.

Starting at the **Memurubu** jetty, the first part of the hike involves a stiff, two-and-a-half-hour haul up to the base of the **Besseggen ridge**, and this is a good spot to take a break and enjoy the views over the surrounding wilderness before tackling the ridge itself. Thereafter, the thirty-minute scramble up to the peak of the ridge is very steep, with ledges that are, on occasion, chest high; you need to be moderately fit to negotiate them. In places, the ridge narrows to 50m with a sheer drop to either side, but you can avoid straying close to the edge by following the DNT waymark "T"s. The views are superlative, but the drops disconcerting – and a head for heights is essential. Beyond the peak of the ridge, the trail is less dramatic, crossing a couple of plateau and clambering up the slopes in between before reaching the **Veltløyfti gorge**, where a slippery scramble with steep drops requires care, though the trail is well marked and the final destination, **Gjendesheim**, is clearly visible.

right at the lake's western end. A single fare from Gjendesheim to Memurubu costs 100kr, Gjendebu 130kr; returns are twice that unless you make the round trip on the same day, in which case fares are 130kr and 160kr respectively. It takes the boat twenty minutes to reach Memurubu, forty-five for Gjendebu. Naturally, you get to see a slice of the Jotunheimen and avoid a hike by riding the boat and sleeping at the lodges – a prudent choice in bad weather.

North along the E6 to Kongsvoll

From Otta, the E6 and the railway lead 45km north to **DOMBÅS**, a mundane crossroads settlement that does at least have a couple of good **places to stay**. The better of the two options, situated close to the train and bus station as well as the E6/E136 junction, is the *Dombås Hotell* (ⓣ61 24 10 01, ⓦwww .rica-hotels.com; ❻, s/r ❹), whose main building, with its high gables and smart public rooms, looks back down the valley. This is a hotel of two halves, with most of the bedrooms tucked away in the modern annexe round the back, but the main building does hold a few guest rooms and some of these enjoy valley views too. A cheaper choice, but also with good views, is Dombås' HI **hostel** (☎61 24 09 60, ⓦwww.vandrerhjem.no; all year; dorm beds 250kr, doubles ❷), a comfortable complex of mountain huts way up on the hillside above the E6. To get there, head north out of town along the E6 for around 1km and follow the signs up the hill (a further 0.5km).

Beyond Dombås, the E6 and the main train line head north through the mountains towards Hjerkinn, Kongsvoll (see p.181) and ultimately Trondheim, whilst the E136 and the dramatic Rauma branch line lead west to the port of Åndalsnes (see box, p.182).

Hjerkinn

Staying on the E6 north of Dombås, it's just 30km to the outpost of **HJERKINN**, stuck out on bare and desolate moorland, its pint-sized military base battened down against the wind and snow of winter. The base overlooks the E6/Highway 29 junction, as does the adjacent **train station** (request stop only), a perky wooden affair with brightly painted window frames. There's been a mountain inn here since medieval times, a staging post on the long trail to Trondheim, now just 170km away. The present inn, the *Hjerkinn Fjellstue* (☎61 21 51 00, ⓦwww.hjerkinn.no; ❹), is a fitting successor, its two expansive wooden buildings featuring big open fires and breezy pine furniture. The restaurant is good, too – try the reindeer culled from local herds – and there's horseriding from the stables next door. The inn is set on a hill overlooking the moors just over 2km from the train station beside Highway 29.

If you're travelling north to Røros (see p.183), then Highway 29, which branches off the E6 at Hjerkinn, is the shortest route, but Highway 30, further north (see p.182), is a much more scenic approach.

Kongsvoll

Beyond Hjerkinn, the E6 slices across barren uplands before descending into a narrow ravine, the **Drivdal**. Hidden away here, just 12km from Hjerkinn, is **KONGSVOLL**, home to a tiny train station and the delightful ⚑ *Kongsvold Fjeldstue* (☎72 40 43 40, ⓦwww.kongsvold.no; shared facilities ❹, en suite ❺), which provides some of the most charming accommodation in the whole of Norway. As at Hjerkinn, an inn has stood here since medieval times and the present complex, a huddle of tastefully restored timber buildings with sun-bleached reindeer antlers tacked onto the outside walls, dates back to the eighteenth century. Once a farm as well as an inn, its agricultural days are recalled by several outbuildings: there are the little turf-roofed storehouses (*stabbur*), the lodgings for farmhands (*karstuggu*) and the barn (*låve*), atop which is a bell that was rung to summon the hands from the fields. The main building retains many of its original features and also holds an eclectic sample of antiques. The bedrooms, dotted round the compound, are of the same high standard – and the old vagabonds' hut (*fantstuggu*), built outside the white picket fence that once defined the physical limits of social respectability, contains the cosiest family rooms imaginable. Dinner is served in the excellent **restaurant**, with mains averaging 220kr, and the complex also includes a **café** and a small Dovrefjell Nasjonalpark **information centre**. The inn makes a lovely spot to break your journey and an ideal base

The E136 and the Rauma branch line to Åndalsnes

Dombås is where the **E136** and the **Rauma train line** (2–3 daily; 1hr 45min) branch west for the thrilling 110-kilometre rattle down to Åndalsnes. The journey begins innocuously enough with road and rail slipping along a ridge high above a wide, grassy valley, but soon the landscape gets wilder as both nip into the hills. After 65km, they reach **Kylling bru**, an ambitious stone railway bridge, 56m high and 76m long, which spans the Rauma river. Pressing on, it's a further 20km to the shadowy hamlet of **Marstein** with the grey, cold mass of the Trollveggen ("Troll's Wall") rising straight ahead. At around 1100m, the **Trollveggen** incorporates the highest vertical overhanging mountain wall in Europe and as such is a favourite with experienced mountaineers, though it wasn't actually scaled until 1967. Somehow, the E136 and the railway manage to squeeze through the mountains and soon afterwards they slide down to the attractive little town of Åndalsnes (see p.267), the fjord glistening beyond.

for hiking into the park, which extends to the east and west. If you're arriving by **train**, note that only some services stop at Kongsvoll station, 500m down the valley from the inn – and then only by prior arrangement with the conductor.

From Kongsvoll, it's about 40km to **Oppdal**, an uninspiring crossroads town where the Kristiansund road (Highway 70) meets the E6. Moving on, it's another 70km north to **Støren**, just 50km short of Trondheim, where you can turn off onto Highway 30 for the 100-kilometre drive along the picturesque **Gauldal** valley to Røros (see p.183).

Dovrefjell Nasjonalpark

Bisected by the railway and the E6, **Dovrefjell Nasjonalpark** is one of the more accessible of Norway's national parks. A comparative minnow at just 265 square kilometres, it comprises two distinct zones: spreading east from the E6 are the marshes, open moors and rounded peaks that characterize much of eastern Norway, while to the west the mountains become increasingly steep and serrated as they approach the jagged spires backing onto Åndalsnes (see p.267).

Hiking trails and **huts** are scattered across the western part of the Dovrefjell. **Kongsvoll** (see p.181) makes an ideal starting point: it's possible to hike all the way from here to the coast, but this takes all of nine or ten days. A more feasible expedition for most visitors is the two-hour circular walk up to the mountain plateau, or a two-day, round-trip hike to one of the four ice-tipped peaks of mighty **Snøhetta**, at 2286m. There's accommodation five-hours' walk west from Kongsvoll at the unstaffed **Reinheim hut** (all year). On the first part of any of these hikes, you're likely to spot **musk ox**, the descendants of animals imported from Greenland in the 1950s. Conventional wisdom is that these chunky beasts will ignore you if you ignore them and keep at a distance of at least 100m. They are, however, not afraid of humans and will charge if irritated – retreat as quickly and quietly as possible if one starts snorting and scraping. Further hiking details and maps are available at the park **information centre** in the *Kongsvold Fjeldstue* (see p.181).

Røros and around

RØROS, glued to a treeless mountain plateau some 160km northeast of Kongsvoll, is a blustery place even on a summer's afternoon, when it's full of day-tripping tourists surveying the old part of town, little changed since its days as a copper-mining centre. Mining was the basis of life here from the seventeenth century onwards and although the mining company finally went bust in 1977, its assorted industrial remains were never bulldozed, making Røros a unique and remarkable survivor of the resource towns that once littered Norway's more isolated regions. Copper mining was dirty and dangerous work and even if the locals supplemented their incomes with a little farming and hunting, life for the average villager can't have been anything but hard. Remarkably, Røros' wooden houses, some of them 300 years old, have escaped the fires which have devastated so many of Norway's timber-built towns, and as a consequence the town is on UNESCO's World Heritage list. Firm regulations now protect this rare townscape and changes to its grass-roofed cottages are strictly regulated. Film companies regularly use the town as a backdrop for their productions: as early as 1971, it featured as a Soviet labour camp in the film version of Alexander Solzhenitsyn's *One Day in the Life of Ivan Denisovich*, a choice of location that gives something of the flavour of the place.

The town centre

In the town centre, **Røros kirke** (early to mid-June & mid-Aug to mid-Sept Mon–Sat 11am–1pm; mid-June to mid-Aug Mon–Sat 10am–5pm, Sun 1–3pm; mid-Sept to May Sat 11am–1pm; 25kr) is the most obvious target for a stroll, its heavy-duty tower reflecting the wealth of the early mine-owners. Built in 1784, and once the only stone building in Røros, the church is a massive structure designed – like the church at Kongsberg (see p.188) – to overawe rather than inspire. The most notable feature of the interior, which looks more like a theatre than a place of worship, is the two-tiered gallery running around the nave. Mine labourers were accommodated in the gallery's lower level, while "undesirables" were compelled to sit above, and even had to enter via a separate, external staircase. Down below, the nave exhibited even finer distinctions: every pew nearer the front was a step up the social ladder, while mine managers vied for the curtained boxes, each of which had a well-publicized annual rent. The monarch (or royal representative) had a private box commanding views from the back and the pulpit was placed directly over the altar to emphasize the importance of the priest. These byzantine social arrangements are explained in depth during the **guided tour** (mid-June to mid-Aug, 1–2 daily in English), the cost of which is included in the admission fee.

Immediately below the church, on either side of the river, lies the oldest part of Røros, a huddle of sturdy cross-timbered smelters' cottages, storehouses and workshops squatting in the shadow of the **slegghaugan** (slagheaps) – more tourist attraction than eyesore, and providing fine views over the town and beyond. Here also, next to the river, are the rambling main works, the **Smelthytta** (literally "melting hut"; early to mid-June & mid-Aug to mid-Sept Mon–Fri 11am–4pm, Sat & Sun 11am–3pm; mid-June to mid-Aug daily 10am–6pm; mid-Sept to May Mon–Fri 11am–3pm, Sat & Sun 11am–2pm; 60kr; ⓦwww .rorosmuseet.no), which has been tidily restored and turned into a museum. This is a large three-storey affair whose most interesting section, set in the cavernous hall that once housed the smelter, explains the intricacies of copper production. Dioramas illuminate every part of the process, and there are production charts,

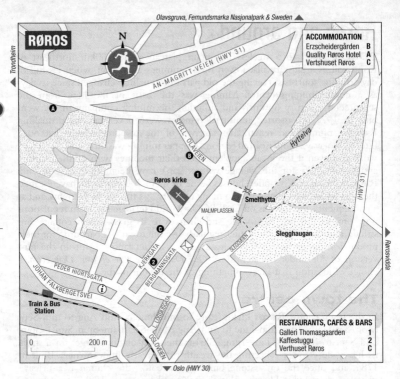

samples of ore and a potted history of the company – pick up the comprehensive English-language leaflet available free at reception. All that said, there's actually not that much to look at – the building was gutted by fire in 1975 – and so the museum is perhaps for genuine mining enthusiasts only.

The Smelthytta faces on to **Malmplassen** ("ore-place"), the wide earthen square where the ore drivers arrived from across the mountains to have their cartloads of ore weighed on the outdoor scales. In the square too, hung in a rickety little tower, is the smelters' bell, which used to be rung at the start of each shift. Malmplassen is at the top of Bergmannsgata which, together with parallel Kjerkgata, forms the heart of today's Røros. Conspicuously, the smaller artisans' dwellings, some of which have become art and craft shops, are set near the works, away from the rather more spacious dwellings once occupied by the owners and overseers, which cluster round the church.

Arrival and accommodation

Røros **train** and **bus** stations are at the foot of the town centre, a couple of minutes' walk from the **tourist office** on Peder Hiortsgata (mid-June to late Aug Mon–Sat 9am–6pm & Sun 10am–4pm; late Aug to mid-June Mon–Fri 9am–3pm & Sat 10.30am–12.30pm; ☎72 41 11 65, ⓦwww.rorosinfo.com), where you can pick up a comprehensive booklet on Røros and the surrounding region. They also have details of local **hikes** across the uplands that encircle the town, one of the more popular being the five-hour trek east to the self-service DNT hut at Marenvollen. In winter, the uplands are popular with **cross-country skiers** and the tourist office also has a leaflet mapping out several possible skiing routes.

Røros makes for a pleasant overnight stay, which is just as well given its solitary location. Even better, there's a good supply of central **accommodation** with the best deal in town being the ⚑ *Erzscheidergården* guesthouse, Spell-Olaveien 6 (☎72 41 11 94, ⓦwww.erzscheidergaarden.com; ❸, sp/r ❹), where there are some charming, unassuming rooms in its wooden main building. Some rooms also have fine views over town, and there's an attractive subterranean breakfast area and a cosy lounge. A second good choice is *Vertshuset Røros*, Kjerkgata 34 (☎72 41 93 50, ⓦwww.vertshusetroros.no; ❹), a guesthouse that has been dovetailed into an old timber building (1914) bang in the centre of town; there are fifteen guest rooms here, half with their own kitchenette, and each is decorated in cheerful, modern style. A third option is the *Quality Røros Hotel*, An-Magritt veien (☎72 40 80 00, ⓦwww.choicehotels .no; ❼, sp/r ❺), a big, modern chain hotel on the northern edge of the centre, about 1.3km from the train station.

Eating and drinking

When it comes to **food**, Røros may not be a gourmet's paradise, but there's just enough choice to get by. The unfussy homeliness of the restaurant at the *Vertshuset Røros*, Kjerkgata 34 (daily 4–10pm), makes it a good spot to enjoy an evening meal – choose from traditional Norwegian dishes like *kjøttkaker i brun saus* (meatballs in brown sauce) at around 220kr. For a quicker bite, *Kaffestuggu*, Bergmannsgata 18 (Mon–Sat 10am–5pm, Sun 11am–5pm), has a suntrap of a courtyard and a series of elegant, panelled little rooms where you can sample their cakes, sandwiches and reasonably priced daily specials. Finally, tucked away at Kjerkgata 48, is *Galleri Thomasgaarden*, a ceramics gallery that also houses the cosiest café in town, where you can avoid the crowds and get tasty home-cooked snacks (Mon–Sat 11am–4pm, Sun noon–4pm).

Around Røros: Olavsgruva copper mine and Femundsmarka Nasjonalpark

Some 13km east of Røros off Highway 31, one of the old copper mines, the **Olavsgruva**, has been kept open as a museum, and there are daily guided tours of its workings throughout the summer – make reservations at Røros tourist office (early to mid-June & late Aug to early Sept Mon–Sat 2 daily, Sun 1 daily; late June to mid-Aug 5 daily; early Sept to May Sat 1 daily; 80kr; ⓦwww .rorosmuseet.no). The temperature down the mine is a constant 5°C, so remember to take something warm to wear – you'll need sturdy shoes too.

Further afield still, around 35km southeast of Røros, tucked in tight between the Swedish border and the elongated Lake Femund, is the remote **Femunds-marka Nasjonalpark**, whose 385 square kilometres encompass a wide variety of terrains. In the north are pine forests, marshes, lakes and rivers, which give way in the south to bare mountains and plateaux. There is no road access into the Femundsmarka, but a minor road leads from Røros to **Synnervika**, on the west side of **Lake Femund**, from where a **passenger boat**, the M/S *Fæmund* (early June to mid-Aug 1 daily; mid-Aug to mid-Sept 3 weekly; ☎93 69 20 17, ⓦwww.femund.no), shuttles around the lake, stopping at several remote outposts and jetties. Among the latter, several give access to the limited network of unstaffed DNT huts and **hiking trails** that cross the park; the jetties at **Røa** (30min from Synnervika; 125kr each way) and **Haugen** (1hr 15min; 155kr each way) are perhaps the handiest. Sailing schedules are available from Røros tourist office, which also has details of connecting buses from town to the jetty. Several Røros-based operators run canoeing and fishing expeditions into the park.

From Oslo to the western fjords

The forested dales and uplands that fill out much of central Norway between Oslo and the western fjords rarely inspire: in almost any other European country, these elongated valleys would be attractions in their own right, but here in Norway they simply can't compare with the mountains and fjords of the north and west. Furthermore, almost everywhere the architecture is routinely modern and most of the old timber buildings, which once lined the valleys, are long gone – except in the ten-a-penny open-air museums that are a feature of nearly every town. Neither does it help that the towns and villages of the region almost invariably string along the roads in long, seemingly aimless ribbons.

Of the three major trunk roads crossing the region, the **E16** is the fastest and least scenic, a quick 350-kilometre gallop up from Oslo to both the fjord ferry near Sogndal (see p.247) and the colossal 24-kilometre tunnel leading to Flåm (see p.238). Otherwise, the E16's nearest rival, the slower and much prettier **Highway 7**, branches off the E16 at Hønefoss to weave its way up Hallingdal before slicing across the wild wastes of the Hardangervidda plateau en route to the fjords at Eidfjord near Hardangerfjord, a distance of 350km; Highway 7 also intersects with **Highway 50**, offering another possible route to Flåm. For most of its length, Highway 7 is shadowed by the **Oslo–Bergen railway**, though they part company when the train swings north for its spectacular traverse of the mountains. The third road, the **E134**, covers the 417km from Drammen near Oslo to Haugesund, passing near Odda on the Sørfjord after 310km. Again, it's a slower route, but it has the advantage of passing through the attractive town of **Kongsberg** and within earshot of Dalen, the sight of the region's most enjoyable hotel. The E134 also inches its way over the southern reaches of the Hardangervidda plateau and crosses one of the country's highest mountain passes, the dramatic Haukelifjell.

Regular long-distance **buses** serve all three of the major roads, but the train is quicker albeit more limited in its range of destinations: Oslo to Bergen by train takes about seven hours with stops at Finse on the Hardangervidda (see p.230) and Voss, near the Hardangerfjord (see p.224); the bus takes about three hours more.

The E16 to Fagernes and Borgund stave church

Clipping along the **E16** from Oslo, it's about 190km up through a series of river valleys to ribbon-like **FAGERNES**, where you can break your journey in some comfort at the amenable *Quality Hotel Fagernes* (☎61 35 80 00, ⓦwww .choice.no; doubles ❻, sp/r ❹), which occupies a large lakeside complex with every facility and some lushly traditional public rooms. Fagernes is also where Highway 51 branches north to run along the eastern edge of the Jotunheimen Nasjonalpark, passing near Gjendesheim and its lodge (see p.178) before finally joining Highway 15 west of Otta (see p.174). In summertime, Nor-Way Bussekspress buses (🌐www.nor-way.no) depart from Fagernes (2–4 daily) for Beitostølen, where you change for Gjendesheim (late June to early Sept 1–2 daily; 40min).

About 30km west of Fagernes along the E16, the scenery begins to improve as you approach the coast. The road dips and weaves from dale to dale, slipping between the hills until it reaches the **Lærdal valley**, whose wooded slopes shelter the stepped roofs and angular gables of the **Borgund stave church** (daily: May to mid-June & late Aug to Sept 10am–5pm; mid-June to late Aug 8am–8pm; 65kr). One of the best-preserved stave churches in Norway, this was built beside what was one of the major pack roads between east and west until bubonic plague wiped out most of the local population in the fourteenth century. Much of the church's medieval appearance has been preserved, its tiered exterior protected by shingles and decorated with finials in the shape of dragons and Christian crosses, the whole caboodle culminating in a slender ridge turret. A rickety wooden gallery runs round the outside of the church, and the doors sport an intense swirl of carved animals and foliage. Inside, the dark, pine-scented nave is framed by the upright wooden posts that define this style of church architecture, and the adjacent visitor centre fills in some of the historical and architectural background.

Beyond the church, the valley grows wilder as the E16 travels the 40km down to **Fodnes**, where a 24-hour car ferry zips over to **Mannheller** (every 20min, hourly midnight to 6am; 10min; car & driver 103kr, including a road toll of 48kr), some 19km from Sogndal (see p.247). En route, you'll pass the entrance

Stave churches

The majority of Norway's 29 surviving stave churches (🌐www.stavechurch.com) are inland in the south and centre of the country, but taken together they represent the nation's most distinctive architectural legacy. The key feature of their design is that their timbers are placed vertically into the ground – in contrast to the log-bonding technique used by the Norwegians for everything else. Thus, a stave wall consists of vertical planks slotted into sills above and below, with the sills connected to upright posts – or **staves**, hence the name – at each corner. The general design seems to have been worked out in the twelfth century and common features include external wooden galleries, shingles and finials. There are, however, variations: in some churches, nave and chancel form a single rectangle, in others the chancel is narrower than, and tacked on to, the nave. The most fetching stave churches are those where the central section of the nave has been raised above the aisles to create – from the outside – a distinctive, almost pagoda-like effect. In virtually all the stave churches, the **door frames** (where they survive) are decorated from top to bottom with surging, intricate carvings that clearly hark back to Viking design, most memorably fantastical long-limbed dragons entwined in vine tendrils.

The origins of stave churches have attracted an inordinate amount of academic debate. Some scholars argue that they were originally pagan temples, converted to Christian use by the addition of a chancel, while others are convinced that they were inspired by Russian churches. In the nineteenth century, they also acquired symbolic importance as reminders of the time when Norway was independent. Many had fallen into a dreadful state of repair and were clumsily renovated – or even remodelled – by enthusiastic medievalists with a nationalist agenda. Undoing this repair work has been a major operation, and one that continues today. For most visitors, seeing one or two will suffice – and three of the finest are those at Heddal (see p.191), Borgund (see above) and Urnes (see p.249).

to the 24-kilometre tunnel that extends the E16 to Flåm (see p.238) – for the fastest route to Bergen. Just beyond the tunnel entrance, you'll also zip past **GAMLE LÆRDALSØYRI** – or simply **Lærdal** – an old fjordside settlement where many of the early timber buildings have survived and are now rigorously protected. The most important – and interesting – string along the main drag, Øyragata, including the old telegraph station, savings bank and general store.

Highway 7 to Geilo and the fjords

Highway 7 branches off the E16 about 70km from Oslo at **Hønefoss**, and then cuts an unexciting course along the **Hallingdal valley**, shadowed by the main Oslo–Bergen railway. Some 180km from Hønefoss, the road forks at **Hagafoss**, with Highway 50 descending the dales to reach, after 100km, the Aurlandsfjord just round the coast from Flåm (see p.238). Meanwhile, Highway 7 presses on west to the winter ski resort of **GEILO**, 250km from Oslo. Frankly, Geilo is a boring town out of the skiing season, but it does have several inexpensive places to stay, including an HI **hostel** (☎32 08 70 60, ⓦ www.vandrerhjem.no; all year; dorm beds 275kr, doubles ❷), housed in two large mountain lodge–style buildings in the town centre just off the main drag. Details of other accommodation are available from the **tourist office** (June & late Aug Mon–Fri 8.30am–5pm, Sat 9am–3pm; July to mid-Aug Mon–Fri 8.30am–9pm, Sat 9am–5pm & Sun 11am–5pm; Sept–May Mon–Fri 8.30am–4pm & Sat 9am–2pm; ☎32 09 59 00, ⓦ www.geilo.no).

Just beyond Geilo, the rail line stops following the road, breaking off to barrel its way over the mountains to Finse, Myrdal (where you change for the scenic branch line down to Flåm; see p.235) and points to Bergen. Highway 7, meanwhile, continues west for a further 100km, slicing across the Hardangervidda mountain plateau (see p.230). It's a lonely, handsome road that passes several places – such as **Halne** (see p.231) and **Dyranut** – where you can pick up the Hardangervidda's network of hiking trails. On the far side of the plateau, Highway 7 rushes down a steep valley, passing the Vøringsfossen waterfall (see p.230) en route to the fjords at Eidfjord (see p.229).

The E134 – west to Kongsberg

Stuck up in the hills some 80km from Oslo, **KONGSBERG** is one of the most interesting towns in the region and a key attraction along the **E134**, the third main road linking Oslo with the western fjords. A local story claims that the **silver** responsible for Kongsberg's existence was discovered by two goatherds, who stumbled across a vein of the metal laid bare by the scratchings of an ox. True or not, Christian IV (1577–1648), with his eye on the main chance, was quick to exploit the find, sponsoring the development of mining here – the town's name means "King's Mountain" – at the start of a silver rush that boosted his coffers no end. In the event, it turned out that Kongsberg was the only place in the world where silver could be found in its pure form, and there was enough of it to sustain the town for a couple of centuries. By the 1750s, it was the largest town in Norway, with half its 8000 inhabitants employed in and around the 300-odd mine shafts that dotted the area. The silver works closed in 1805, but by this time Kongsberg was also the site of a royal mint, which still employs people to this day.

Downtown Kongsberg

To appreciate the full economic and political clout of the mine owners, it's necessary to visit the church they funded – **Kongsberg kirke** (mid-May to mid-Aug Mon–Fri 10am–4pm, Sat 10am–1pm & Sun 2–4pm; mid- to late Aug Mon–Fri 10am–noon; Sept to mid-May Tues–Thurs 10am–noon; 30kr), the largest and arguably most beautiful Baroque church in Norway. It dates from 1761, when the mines were at the peak of their prosperity, its ruddy-brown brickwork and copper-green spire shadowing a large square, whose other three sides are flanked by period wooden buildings. The interior is a grand affair too, with its enormous and showy mock-marble western wall incorporating the altar, pulpit and organ. This arrangement was dictated by political considerations: the pulpit is actually above the altar to ram home the point that the priest's stern injunctions to work harder were an expression of God's will. The

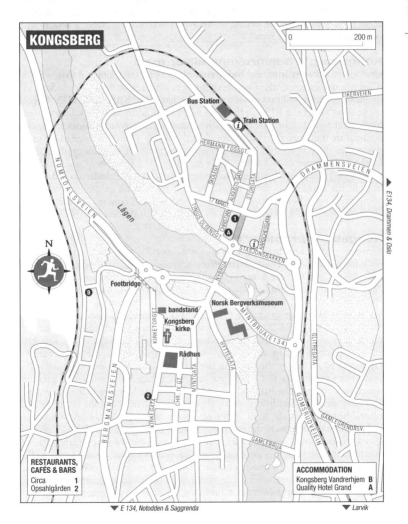

KONGSBERG

0   200 m

Bus Station
Train Station

EIKERVEIEN

HERMANN FOSSGT.

DRAMMENSVEIEN

NUMEDALSVEIEN

SKOLEGT.
AUGUSTS GATE
STORGATA
17. MAIGT.
CHRISTIAN
KIRKEGÅRDSGATA
CHRISTIAN AUGUSTS GT.

Lågen

1
A

STASJONSBAKKEN

N

NYBRUA

Footbridge

B

bandstand

Norsk Bergverksmuseum

MYNTBRUA (E134)

GLITREGATA

KIRKETORGET

Kongsberg kirke

Rådhus

HYTTEGATA

BERGMANNSVEIEN

2

CHR. IV GT.
MYNTGATA
KIRKEGATA

GOMSRUDVEIEN

GAMLEGRENDÅSV.

GAMLEBRUA

RESTAURANTS, CAFÉS & BARS	
Circa	**1**
Opsahlgården	**2**

ACCOMMODATION	
Kongsberg Vandrerhjem	**B**
Quality Hotel Grand	**A**

▼ E 134, Notodden & Saggrenda

▼ Larvik

seating arrangements were rigidly and hierarchically defined, and determined the church's principal fixtures. Facing the pulpit are the King's Box and boxes for the silver-works' managers, while other officials sat in the glass enclosures. The pews on the ground floor were reserved for their womenfolk, while the sweeping balcony was divided into three tiers to accommodate the Kongsberg petite bourgeoisie, the workers and, squeezing in at the top and the back, the lumpen proletariat.

As for the rest of Kongsberg, it's an amenable if quiet little town with plenty of green spaces. The **River Lågen** tumbles through the centre, and statues on the town bridge at the foot of Storgata, commemorate various local activities, including foolhardy attempts to locate new finds of silver – one of which involved the use of divining rods. Mining enthusiasts will enjoy the **Norsk Bergverksmuseum**, Hyttegata 3 (Mining Museum; daily: mid-May to Aug 10am–5pm; Sept to mid-May noon–4pm; 60kr), housed in the old smelting works near the river and sharing its premises with a tiny ski museum and coin collection, but merely wandering around the town is as enjoyable a way as any of spending an hour or two.

Kongsberg's Sølvgruvene silver mine

One set of **silver mines**, the **Sølvgruvene**, is open for tours and makes for a good excursion, especially if you have pre-teen children to amuse. It's hidden in green surroundings 8km west of town in the hamlet of **SAGGRENDA**. To get there, drive along the E134 in the direction of Notodden and look for the sign leading off to the right. The informative ninety-minute tour includes a ride on a miniature train into the shafts through dark tunnels. There are three to six tour departures daily from mid-May to August and two weekly in September and October; the **tour** costs 140kr – 80kr for kids – and Kongsberg tourist office (see below) has the schedule; take a sweater, as it's cold underground. Back outside the mine, just 350m down the hill, the old ochre-painted workers' compound – the *Sakkerhusene* – has been restored and contains a **café** as well as some rather half-hearted displays on the history of the mines.

Kongsberg practicalities

Kongsberg **train and bus stations** are on the north side of town, a five-minute walk from the centre. The **tourist office** is inside the train station (May to late June & late Aug to Sept Mon–Fri 9am–4pm, Sat 10am–2pm; late June to late Aug Mon–Fri 9am–7pm, Sat & Sun 10am–2pm; Oct–April Mon–Fri 9am–4pm; ☎32 29 90 50, ⓦwww.visitkongsberg.no) and can help with accommodation – not that there's much to choose from. The HI ⚑ **hostel**, *Kongsberg Vandrerhjem*, Vinjesgate 1 (☎32 73 20 24, ⓦwww.vandrerhjem.no), is the place to stay if you've an eye on your expenses, with both dorm beds (270kr) and comfortable en-suite doubles (❷) in an attractive timber lodge close to the town centre. Drivers need to follow the signs on the E134; train and bus users should walk south from the station along Storgata, cross the bridge, walk round the back of the church on the right-hand side, then head down the lane beside the bandstand and cross over the footbridge – it's about a fifteen-minute walk in all. As for central **hotels**, easily the most appealing option is the *Quality Hotel Grand*, in a modern block down near the river at Christian Augusts gate 2 (☎32 77 28 00, ⓦwww.choicehotels.no ❺, sp/r ❹). From the outside, the hotel is undistinguished, but the interior, which is decorated in crisp modern style, is extremely well-maintained and the 175 guest rooms are large and extremely comfortable; the best, on the top floors, offer wide views over the churning, tumbling River Lågen. The only disappointment is breakfast, which is very average.

Circa, at Storgata 13, serves the best coffee in town as well as sandwiches, snacks and light lunches; in the evening, it morphs into a very pleasant, laid-back bar (Mon & Tues 10am–5pm, Wed & Thurs 10am–11.30pm, Fri & Sat 10am–3am; Sun noon–5pm). The pick of the town's several **restaurants** is the *Opsahlgården*, a smart and cosy little place near the church at Kirkegata 10 (Mon–Fri 3–10pm & Sat 5–10pm; ☎32 76 45 00). They do a particularly good line in seafood here with main courses averaging just 100kr.

The E134 west of Kongsberg – Heddal stave church

A few kilometres west of Kongsberg, the **E134** slips into **Telemark** (Ⓦwww .visittelemark.no), a county that covers a great forested chunk of southern Norway. In a country where the fjords are the apple of the tourist industry's eye, Telemark is often neglected, but it can be stunningly beautiful, its deep valleys, blue-black lochs and bulging forested hills intercepted by tiny villages in a manner that resembles the Swiss Alps. Heading into the county on the E134, things begin inauspiciously with **Notodden**, a workaday industrial town, but from here it's just 5km to the delightful **stave church of Heddal** (late May to late June & late Aug to mid-Sept Mon–Sat 10am–5pm, Sun 1–5pm; late June to late Aug Mon–Sat 9am–7pm, Sun 1–7pm; 50kr; Ⓦwww.heddalstavkirke.no), which stands beside the road fronted by the neatest of cemeteries. The largest surviving stave church in Norway, it has a pretty tumble of shingle-clad roofs which was restored to something like its medieval appearance in 1955, recti-fying a heavy-handed nineteenth-century remodelling. The crosses atop the church's gables alternate with dragon-head gargoyles, a mix of Christian and pagan symbolism typical of many stave churches (see box, p.187). Inside, the twenty masts of the nave are surmounted by masks, and there's some attractive seventeenth-century wall decoration in light blues, browns and whites. Pride of place, however, goes to the ancient **bishop's chair** in the chancel. Dating from around 1250, the chair carries a relief retelling the saga of Sigurd the

▲ Telemarkskanal ferry

Dragonslayer, a pagan story that Christians turned to their advantage by recasting the Viking as Jesus and the dragon as the Devil. Across from the church, there's a **café** and a modest museum illustrating further aspects of the church's history.

Seljord

Pushing on west, the E134 rattles up the valley, passing the first (and quickest) turning to Rjukan (see p.193), before making a dramatic passage over the mountains on its way to **SELJORD**, a small but straggly industrial town at the head of Seljordsvatnet lake, about 55km from Heddal. Modest it may be, but Seljord seems to have attracted more than its fair share of "Believe It or Not" stories: a monster is supposed to lurk in the depths of the lake; elves are alleged to gather here for some of their soirees; and the medieval stone church, with its whitewashed walls and dinky little spire, was, so the story goes, built by a goblin. Beside the church are two more curiosities: the nearer is a large granite slab carved with a picture of the Norwegian pastor Magnus Brostrup Landstad (1802–80), shown mounted on his horse with an open hymn book in his hand. Landstad, who was briefly a minister here in Seljord, made his name among the Norwegian nationalists of his day by collecting traditional country ballads and by creating the *Landstad Hymnbook*, which discarded the Danish of its predecessors for Norwegian; it was in use until 1985. A few metres away, stuck in the ground, is the 570-kilogram stone, which was lifted for the first and last time by a Telemark strongman, one Nils Langedal (1722–1800), who, according to local legend, was reared on mare's milk.

To Røldal and Odda

Beyond Seljord, it's a further 34km west along the E134 to Highway 45, the first of the two turnings to Dalen (see p.195), and 16km more to the **Åmot crossroads**, where roads lead north to Rjukan (Highway 37; see p.193) and south to Dalen (Highway 38; see p.195). Continuing west, the E134 zigzags across hill and dale before beginning its long climb up to the bare and bleak wastes of the Hardangervidda plateau (see p.230) via **Haukelifjell**, one of Europe's highest mountain passes. The road cuts a nervous course across the plateau, diving into a series of tunnels before slipping down into the hamlet of **RØLDAL**, a remote little place nestled in the greenest of valleys. Røldal has its own stave **church** (mid-May to mid-Sept daily 10am–5pm; 30kr), a trim, rusticated affair dating from the twelfth century but much amended. In medieval times, the church was a major point of pilgrimage on account of the crucifix with healing powers that still hangs above the altar and it was then that the elaborate wall paintings were added.

After Røldal, the E134 makes another stirring climb to reach its junction with Highway 13, the road to Stavanger (see p.147). The E134 – combined with the northerly extension of Highway 13 – then plunges across the Hardangervidda on its way to another crossroads, where you either keep going on the E134 to Haugesund (see p.157), 140km away, or stay on Highway 13 for Odda and Lofthus (see p.229). The latter road drops down a severe, boulder-strewn river valley, passing, in 5km, the **Latefossen** waterfall, where two huge torrents empty into the river with a deafening roar. From the waterfall, it's a short drive north to **ODDA**, an unappetizing industrial town and an unfortunate introduction to the fjords: try to allow enough time to avoid the place altogether and carry on to the much more appealing hamlet of Lofthus (see p.229); Odda is 43km from Røldal – allow an hour, more in poor weather.

Rjukan

From the E134, there are two roads to **RJUKAN** – one from a point west of Heddal stave church (see p.191), the other from the Åmot crossroads (see p.192). The first is 55km long and fairly fast, the second is about 65km long and quite slow. Rjukan itself spreads out along the bottom of the Vestfjorddalen valley, its oldest buildings dating from its foundation as a saltpetre manufacturing centre at the start of the twentieth century. Saltpetre needed power and Rjukan had plenty of that in the form of the water that tumbles down into the valley from the mountains up above and this was harnessed to create a reliable source of electricity. Nowadays, the town still produces hydroelectricity, but it has diversified into tourism, taking advantage of its proximity to the Hardangervidda mountain plateau, while its first power station, Vemork, has become an industrial museum of some repute.

The Town

Rjukan may have an impressive river-valley setting with a backdrop of harsh, rough mountains, but it is itself really rather humdrum, its six thousand inhabitants sharing a modest gridiron town centre originally assembled by the Norsk Hydro power company at the start of the twentieth century. More positively, the town is a useful base for hiking the Hardangervidda mountain plateau (see p.230), whose southeast corner rises above the town. Easy access to the Hardangervidda is provided by Rjukan's **Krossobanen cable car** (daily: late June to Aug 9am–8pm, rest of year 10am–4pm, 6pm in Sept; 40kr each way; ⓦ www.krossobanen.no), which carries passengers up to the plateau from a station about 2km from the train station, at the west end of town. For details of Hardangervidda hiking trails, enquire at the tourist office. Built in 1928, the Krossobanen was the first cable car to be built in northern Europe and Norsk Hydro stumped up the money, curiously enough because they wanted their workers to be able to see the sun in winter. Rjukan also boasts a funicular railway, but there was no philanthropic motive here – it was built for the military in the 1950s. This railway, the **Gaustabanen**, goes 860m into the heart of Mount Gausta, where you change for the kilometre-long journey up to the top of the mountain. By means of the railway, Norwegian soldiers could maintain their mountain-top, radio-listening gear with the greatest of ease and, now that the army has gone, it's open to tourists (late June to mid-Aug daily 10am–4pm; 350kr return; ⓦ www.gaustabanen.no); the Gaustabanen terminal is 14km east of Rjukan.

The Norsk Industriarbeidermuseum

Rjukan's key attraction is the **Norsk Industriarbeidermuseum** (Norwegian Industrial Workers' Museum; May to mid-June & mid-Aug to Sept daily 10am–4pm; mid-June to mid-Aug daily 10am–6pm; Oct–April Tues–Fri noon–3pm, Sat & Sun 11am–4pm; 70kr; ⓦ www.visitvemork.com), housed in the former **Vemork hydroelectric station**, some 7km to the west of Rjukan. When it was opened in 1911, Vemork had the greatest generating capacity in the world – its ten turbines provided a combined output of 108 megawatts – and it remains a fine example of industrial architecture pretending to be something else: with its high gables and symmetrical windows it looks more like a country mansion. Inside, the museum explores the effects of industrialization on what was then a profoundly rural region, has displays on hydroelectric power and the development of the trade unions, and features a gallery of propagandist paintings about workers and the class struggle by Arne Ekeland. Yet, most foreigners come here because of the plant's role in – and excellent displays on – World War II, when it was the site chosen by the Germans for the manufacture of **heavy water** – necessary for regulating nuclear reactions in the creation of a nuclear bomb. Aware of the plant's importance, the Americans bombed it on several occasions and the Norwegian Resistance mounted a string of guerrilla attacks; as a result, the Nazis decided to move the heavy water they had made to Germany. The only way they could do this was by train, and part of the journey was across Lake Tinnsjø just east of Rjukan – ingeniously the ferry was fitted with a set of railway tracks. This was the scene of one of the most spectacular escapades of the war, when the Norwegian Resistance sunk ferry and train on January 20, 1944. All the heavy water was lost, but so were the fourteen Norwegian passengers – a story recounted in the 1965 film *The Heroes of Telemark*, in which Kirk Douglas played the cinematic stereotype of the Norwegian: an earnest man with an honest face, wearing a big pullover.

Visitors to the museum have to park on the far side of the suspension bridge and walk the last 700m, which takes about fifteen minutes – grim if it's raining, though there is a minibus service in summer (mid-June to mid-Aug; 25kr).

Rjukan practicalities

Long-distance **buses** to Rjukan from Oslo and Kongsberg pull in at the **bus station** on the south side of the river. The town centre is a couple of minutes' walk away, across the bridge on the north side of the river, and it's here you'll find the **tourist office**, at Torget 2 (mid-June to early Sept Mon–Fri 9am–7pm, Sat & Sun 10am–6pm; early Sept to mid-June Mon–Fri 9am–3.30pm; ☎ 35 08 05 50, Ⓦ www.visitrjukan.com). They carry local bus timetables, sell maps and will provide advice on hiking the Hardangervidda. They also have details of local **accommodation** with one of the better bets being *Rjukan Hytteby* (☎ 35 09 01 22, Ⓦ www.rjukan-hytteby.no; 750kr for 1–2 persons, linen an extra 90kr per person), where ten modern cottages, built in the style of the original workers' houses of the 1910s, string along the south side of the river about 800m east of the centre. There's also an HI **hostel**, *Rjukan Vandrerhjem* (☎ 35 09 20 40, Ⓦ www.vandrerhjem.no; mid-June to Sept; doubles ●), in a set of three modern cabins up in the hills about 12km to the southeast of town along a wiggly mountain byroad.

As for **food**, there's a very good café-restaurant at the Norsk Industriarbeider-museum, and *Rjukan Hytteby* has a competent café.

South to Dalen – Ravnejuvet and Eidsborg stavkirke

From the E134, there are two roads south to the sleepy little town of Dalen – Highway 45 and, further to the west from the Åmot crossroads, Highway 38; both are around 20km long. Highway 38 has the more imperious scenery as it inches its way along the edge of the **Ravnejuvet** (Raven Gorge), a severe gash in the landscape whose sheer dark walls are no less than 350m high. According to the local tourist brochure, the gorge's unusual air currents mean you can throw a banknote over the edge and it will come back to you – but most people experiment with ordinary bits of paper instead.

The contrasting Highway 45 threads its way over forested hills before nipping through a series of alpine-like valleys, where old farmsteads hug the hillsides flanked by bright-green pastureland. This is fine scenery indeed and here also, just 5km short of Dalen, is **Eidsborg Stavkirke**, whose tightly-packed roofs, decorative finials and cedar shingles date back to the thirteenth century. The church has been renovated on several occasions, but it remains one of the best preserved in the country and its interior sports some fascinating if faded water-colour friezes of Biblical scenes. Given its remote location, it's not surprising that the church has attracted more than its fair share of legend with one of the most charming relating to the adjacent graveyard: digging graves was so difficult in this rocky plot of land that a local magistrate offered mercy to a pair of condemned women if they could rectify matters; they solved the problem by carrying sand here in their aprons and were promptly pardoned. The church is dedicated to St Nicholas of Bari (aka Santa Claus) and, in an echo of a pagan past, a wooden image of the saint was carried round the lake below the church three times once every year and then ceremonially washed, right up until the 1850s. The church is part of the open-air **Vest-Telemark Museum** comprising thirty old timber buildings (June–Aug daily 10am–5pm; 60kr). Finally, there's an excellent two-hour (4km) forest walk along a well-marked trail from the church to the edge of Ravnejuvet (see p.194); maps of local hiking trails are available at Dalen tourist office (see below).

Dalen

Trailing along the valley between steep forested hills, **DALEN** is a pleasant place in a pleasant setting, its string of modern houses somewhat reminiscent of small-town USA. Dalen's four hundred inhabitants mostly work in the hydro and timber industries, but a fair few of them are reliant on the town's main claim to fame, the 🍴 *Dalen Hotel* (ⓣ35 07 90 00, ⓦwww.dalenhotel.no; ❽; mid-May–Oct), right at the end of town facing the lake. In the 1890s, the opening of the **Telemarkskanal** (see below) made Dalen an important transit point. It was then that a group of businessmen decided to build the lavish *Dalen Hotel*, which soon became one of the most fashionable spots in the country. After World War II, however, the hotel hit the skids as the development of the road system began to undermine its importance and in the 1960s it went to wrack and ruin. At this point, it looked as if the hotel would be demolished, but luckily it was picked up and expertly restored in the 1990s. Returned to its full splendour, the hotel's main facade is an imposing affair, whose twin towers are topped by finials in a permutation of Viking style. Inside, pride of place goes to the galleried hall with its huge stained-glass ceiling, open fireplace and carved woodwork. The 35 very comfortable guest rooms, which are in the hotel's two wings, have been returned to an approximation of their original appearance too, and the pick have balconies overlooking the hotel gardens, which stretch down to the lake. The hotel dining room is also very grand with its acres of wood panelling and the food – traditional Norwegian – is top-notch with main courses averaging 300kr.

If your budget won't stretch as far as the *Dalen Hotel*, then the all-year *Dalen Bed & Breakfast* (ⓣ35 07 70 80, ⓦwww.dalenbb.com; ❷), in an attractive, modern chalet-like house just a few metres away is a good alternative; there are eleven rooms here and most are en suite. For other options, pop into the **tourist office** (mid-June to mid-Aug Mon–Fri 9am–7pm, Sat & Sun 10am–5pm; rest of year Mon–Fri 9am–3.30pm; ⓣ35 07 70 65, ⓦwww.visitdalen.com), also a few metres from the *Dalen Hotel*.

The Telemarkskanal

Dalen is the terminus of the passenger ferry that wends its way southeast along the **Telemarkskanal** to **Skien**, a journey that takes a little under eleven hours. Extending 105km, the canal links a string of lakes and rivers by means of eighteen locks that negotiate a difference in water levels of 72m. Completed in 1892, the canal was once an important trade route into the interior, but today it's mainly used by pleasure craft and four vintage **passenger ferries** (☎35 90 00 30, ⓦwww.telemarkskanalen.no), which make the trip daily from late June to mid-Aug, less frequently in the shoulder seasons (late May to late June & mid-August to early Sept). Ferries leave Dalen at 8.20am in the morning and the one-way fare to Skien is 420kr; it's also possible to make shorter excursions out by boat and back by bus. The jetty is 750m beyond the *Dalen Hotel*.

Travel details

Principal NSB train services (ⓦwww.nsb.no)

Dombås to: Oslo (3–4 daily; 4hr); Åndalsnes (2–3 daily; 1hr 45min).

Geilo to: Oslo (3–4 daily; 3hr).

Hamar to: Oslo (hourly; 1hr 30min); Røros (4–6 daily; 3hr 20min).

Hjerkinn to: Oslo (3–4 daily; 4hr 30min – request stop only).

Kongsberg to: Oslo (4–5 daily; 1hr 10min).

Lillehammer to: Oslo (hourly; 2hr); Trondheim (3–4 daily; 4hr 40min).

Oslo to: Bergen (4 daily; 7hr 20min); Dombås (3–4 daily; 4hr); Drammen (4 daily; 40min); Geilo (3–4 daily; 3hr); Hamar (hourly; 1hr 30min); Hjerkinn (3–4 daily; 4hr 30min – request stop only); Kongsberg (4–5 daily; 1hr 10min); Kongsvoll (3–4 daily; 4hr 40min – request stop only); Kvam (1–2 daily; 3hr 30min – request stop only); Lillehammer (hourly; 2hr); Myrdal (4 daily; 4hr 50min); Otta (6 daily; 3hr 30min); Røros (4–6 daily; 5hr); Trondheim (3–4 daily; 6hr 40min); Voss (4 daily; 6hr 40min); Åndalsnes (2–3 daily; 5hr 30min).

Oslo Gardermoen airport to: Dombås (3–4 daily; 3hr 30min); Hamar (hourly; 1hr); Hjerkinn (3–4 daily; 4hr – request stop only); Kongsvoll (3–4 daily; 4hr 10min – request stop only); Kvam (1–2 daily; 3hr – request stop only); Lillehammer (hourly; 1hr 30min); Otta (6 daily; 3hr); Røros (4–6 daily; 4hr 30min); Trondheim (3–4 daily; 6hr 10min); Åndalsnes (2–3 daily; 5hr).

Otta to: Oslo (6 daily; 3hr 30min).

Røros to: Hamar (2–4 daily; 3hr 30min); Oslo (6 daily; 5hr); Trondheim (2–4 daily; 2hr 30min).

Åndalsnes to: Dombås (2–3 daily; 1hr 45min); Oslo (2–3 daily; 5hr 30min).

Principal Nor-Way Bussekspress bus services (ⓦwww.nor-way.no)

Kongsberg to: Haugesund (3 daily; 7hr 30min); Oslo (3 daily; 1hr 30min); Rjukan (3–4 daily; 2hr).

Lillehammer to: Bergen (1 daily; 9hr); Flåm (1 daily; 5hr 30min); Lom (3 daily; 3hr 40min); Oslo (4 daily; 3hr); Otta (3 daily; 2hr 30min); Stryn (3 daily; 5hr 40min).

Oslo to: Beitostølen (3–4 daily; 4hr, change at Fagernes); Bergen (3 daily; 10hr 30min); Dombås (2 daily; 6hr 15min); Fagernes (6–8 daily; 3hr); Gjendesheim in the Jotunheimen (late June to early Sept 2 daily; 5hr, changing at Fagernes and then Beitostølen); Hjerkinn (1–2 daily; 6hr 45min); Hundorp (1 daily; 4hr); Kongsberg (3 daily; 1hr 30min); Kongsvoll (1 daily; 7hr); Kvam (Mon–Fri 1 daily; 4hr 45min); Lillehammer (4 daily; 3hr); Lom (4 daily; 6hr 40min); Odda (3 daily; 7hr); Otta (4 daily; 5hr 30min); Rjukan (3–4 daily; 3hr 30min); Røros (1 daily; 7hr); Sjoa (Mon–Fri 1 daily; 4hr 45min); Sogndal (3 daily; 7hr); Stryn (3 daily; 8hr 40min); Trondheim (1–3 daily; 8hr); Ålesund (2 daily; 10hr); Åndalsnes (2 daily; 8hr).

Rjukan to: Kongsberg (3–4 daily; 2hr); Oslo (3–4 daily; 3hr 30min).

Røros to: Oslo (1 daily; 7hr); Trondheim (4 daily; 3hr 10min).

Bergen and the western fjords

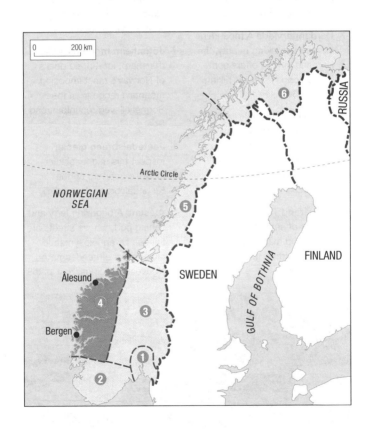

0   200 km

NORWEGIAN
SEA

Arctic Circle

RUSSIA

FINLAND

SWEDEN

GULF OF BOTHNIA

Ålesund

Bergen

CHAPTER 4

Highlights

✳ **Bergen's Fløibanen** This must be Europe's quaintest funicular railway and there are wonderful views over the city at the top. **See p.211**

✳ **Troldhaugen** Visit the delightful fjordside home and studio of Edvard Grieg, Norway's foremost composer. **See p.216**

✳ **Hardangervidda** A mountain plateau of striking beauty, the Hardangervidda offers some of the country's finest hiking. **See p.230**

✳ **The Flåmsbana** Take a trip on the exhilarating Flåm railway, which careers down the mountainside with the fjords waiting down below. **See p.235**

✳ **Balestrand** The relaxing charms of small-town Balestrand make it a fine base for further fjordland explorations. **See p.243**

✳ **The Fjærlandsfjord** The once-remote Fjærlandsfjord offers wonderful scenery, country hikes and a couple of first-rate hotels. **See p.245**

✳ **Urnes stave church** The oldest stave church in Norway is renowned for its exquisite, almost frenzied, Viking woodcarvings. **See p.249**

✳ **Jotunheim mountains** View the sharp, ice-tipped peaks of Norway's most imposing mountain range from the Sognefjellsveg mountain road. **See p.250**

✳ **Jostedalsbreen glacier** Inspect this mighty glacier at close quarters on the Kjenndalsbreen. **See p.257**

✳ **Ålesund** A beguiling ferry and fishing port, whose streets are flanked by an idiosyncratic assortment of handsome Art Nouveau buildings. **See p.269**

▲ Ålesund harbour

Bergen and the western fjords

I f there's one familiar and enticing image of Norway it's the **fjords**, giant clefts in the landscape running from the coast deep into the interior. Rugged yet serene, these huge, wedge-shaped inlets are visually stunning; indeed, the entire fjord region elicits inordinate amounts of purple prose from tourist-office handouts, and for once it's rarely overstated. The fjords are undeniably beautiful, especially around early May, after the brief Norwegian spring has brought colour to the landscape; but winter, when all is unerringly quiet, has its charms too, the blue-black waters of the fjords contrasting with the blinding white of the snow that blankets the hills, valleys and mountains. In summer, the wilds are filled with hikers and the waters patrolled by a steady flotilla of bright-white ferries, but don't let that put you off: the tourists are rarely in such numbers as to be intrusive, and even in the most popular districts, a brief walk off the beaten track will bring solitude in abundance.

The fjords run all the way up the coast from Stavanger to the Russian border, but are most easily – and impressively – seen on the west coast near **Bergen**, the self-proclaimed "Capital of the Fjords". Norway's second-largest city, Bergen is a welcoming place with an atmospheric old warehouse quarter, a relic of the days when it was the northernmost port of the Hanseatic trade alliance. It's also – as its tag suggests – a handy springboard for the nearby fjords, beginning with the gentle charms of the **Hardangerfjord** and the Flåmsdal valley, where the inspiring **Flåmsbana** mountain railway trundles down to the Aurlandsfjord, a small arm of the mighty **Sognefjord**. Dotted with pretty village resorts, the Sognefjord is the longest and deepest of the country's fjords and is perhaps the most beguiling, rather more so than the **Nordfjord**, lying parallel to the north. Between the Sognefjord and Nordfjord lies the **Jostedals-breen glacier**, mainland Europe's largest ice-sheet, while north of the Nordfjord is the narrow, S-shaped **Geirangerfjord**, a rugged gash in the landscape that is both the most celebrated and the most visited of the fjords. Further north still, the scenery becomes even more extreme, reaching pinnacles of isolation in the splendid **Trollstigen** mountain highway, a stunning prelude to both the amenable town of **Åndalsnes** and the ferry port of **Ålesund**, with its attractive Art Nouveau buildings.

Bergen

As it has been raining ever since she arrived in the city, a tourist stops a young boy and asks if it always rains here. "I don't know," he replies, "I'm only thirteen." The joke isn't brilliant, but it does contain a grain of truth. Of all the things to contend with in **BERGEN**, the weather is the most predictable: it rains on average 260 days a year, often relentlessly even in summer, and its forested surroundings are often shrouded in mist. Yet, despite its dampness, Bergen is one of Norway's most enjoyable cities. Its setting – amidst seven hills and sheltered to the north, south and west by a series of straggling islands – is spectacular. There's plenty to see in town too, from sturdy old stone buildings and terraces of tiny wooden houses to a veritable raft of **museums**, and just outside the city limits are Edvard Grieg's home, **Troldhaugen**, as well as the charming open-air **Gamle Bergen** (Old Bergen) museum.

More than anything else, though, it's the general flavour of the place that appeals. Although Bergen has become a major port and something of an industrial centre in recent years, it remains a laid-back, easy-going town with a firmly nautical air. Fish and fishing may no longer be Bergen's economic lynchpins, but the bustling main harbour, **Vågen**, is still very much the focus of attention. If you stay more than a day or two – perhaps using Bergen as a base for viewing the nearer **fjords** – you'll soon discover that the city also has the region's best choice of **restaurants**, some impressive **art** galleries and a decent nightlife.

Arrival

Bergen's sturdy stone **train station** (local ☎55 96 69 00, national ☎815 00 888) is located on Strømgaten, just along from the entrance to the Bergen Storsenter shopping mall, within which is the **bus station**. From Strømgaten, it's a five- to ten-minute walk west to the most interesting part of the city, on and around Bergen's main harbour, **Vågen**, via the pedestrianized shopping street, Marken. The **airport** is 20km south of the city at Flesland and it's connected to the centre by **Flybussen** (Mon–Fri & Sun 5am–9pm, Sat 5am–5pm, every 15–30min; 45min; 80kr one-way). These Flybussen pull in at the bus station, the *SAS Hotel Norge*, on Ole Bulls plass, and the tourist office before proceeding to the harbourfront *SAS Royal Hotel*, on the Bryggen. **Taxis** from the rank outside the airport arrivals hall charge around 350–400kr for the same trip.

By boat

Fjord Line (☎815 33 500, ⓦwww.fjordline.com) international car ferries from Egersund, Haugesund and Hantsholm in Denmark dock at the Skoltegrunnskaien, at the tip of the main harbour, Vågen, as do Smyril Line (☎55 59 65 20, ⓦwww.smyril-line.com) ferries from Scotland via Iceland and the Faroes. Bergen is also the home port of the Hurtigrute coastal boat (☎81 03 00 00, ⓦwww.hurtigruten.com), which docks at the Hurtigrute-terminalen, on the south side of the city centre, off Nøstegaten, about 900m

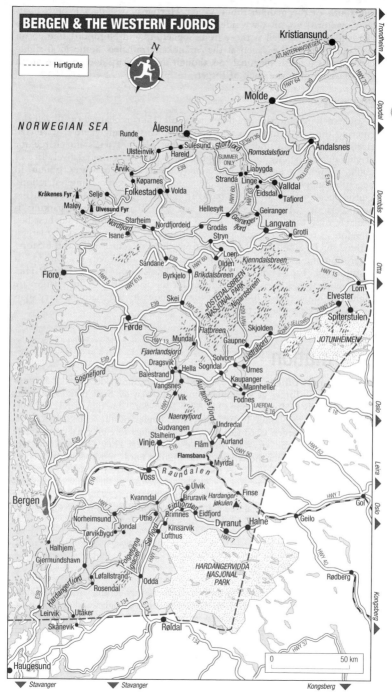

BERGEN & THE WESTERN FJORDS

- - - - Hurtigrute

NORWEGIAN SEA

Trondheim

Oppdal

Dombås

Otta

Oslo

Leira

Oslo

Kongsberg

Kristiansund

ATLANTERHAVSVEGEN

Molde

HWY 64

E39

HWY 70

Åndalsnes

Romsdalsfjord

E39/136

TROLLSTIGEN

E136

Ålesund

Runde

Storfjord

Ulsteinvik

Sulesund

SUMMER
ONLY

Hareid

Liabygda

Årvik

Stranda

Linge

Valldal

Køparnes

HWY 60

Eidsdal

Tafjord

Folkestad

Volda

Hellesylt

Geiranger

Geirangerfjord

Langvatn

Kråkenes Fyr

Selje

Starheim

Grodås

Stryn

Grotli

Måløy

Ulvesund Fyr

Nordfjordeid

Nordfjord

Loen

Isane

Olden

Kjenndalsbreen

HWY 15

Sandane

Brikdalsbreen

JOSTEDALSBREEN

Lom

Florø

Byrkjelo

E39

NASJONAL PARK

HWY 615

Skei

Nigardsbreen

Elvester

HWY 5

HWY 604

Spiterstulen

HWY 55

SOGNEFJELLVN.

Førde

Flatbreen

Skjolden

HWY 13

Mundal

Gaupne

JOTUNHEIMEN

Fjaerlandsfjord

Solvorn

Dragsvik

Hella

Sogndal

Urnes

Balestrand

Kaupanger

Mannheller

Sognefjord

Vangsnes

Fodnes

Vik

Aurlandsfjord

HWY 13

LAERDAL

E16

Naerøyfjord

Undredal

Gudvangen

Stalheim

Aurland

Vinje

Flåm

HWY 50

E16

Flamsbana

E18

HWY 52

Myrdal

Voss

Raundalen

Ulvik

Finse

Kvanndal

Hardanger-
jøkulen

Bruravik

HWY 7

HWY 7

Bergen

Eidfjorden

Brimnes

Gol

Norheimsund

Uthe

Eidfjord

Halne

Geilo

Torvikbygd

Jondal

Kinsarvik

Dyranut

HWY 7

Lofthus

HWY 7

Halhjem

HWY 40

Gjermundshavn

HARDANGERVIDDA
NASJONAL
PARK

Hardangerfjord

Folgefonna

Løfallstrand

Odda

Rødberg

Rosendal

Kongsberg

Leirvik

Utåker

E134

E134

Skånevik

Røldal

E134

0   50 km

Haugesund

201

Stavanger

Stavanger

Kongsberg

due south of the main harbour, Vågen. Hurtigbåt passenger express boats (Ⓦwww.fjord1.no or www.tide.no) from Haugesund, Stavanger and the Hardangerfjord, as well as those from Sognefjord and Nordfjord, line up on the south side of the Vågen at the Strandkaiterminalen. Some local sight-seeing boats use this terminal too, though the majority dock on the north side of Vågen or at the back of Torget.

By car

If you're driving into Bergen, note that a **toll** (15kr) is charged on all vehicles entering the city centre, but you don't have to stop anywhere – it's levied electronically with cameras reading number plates. There's no charge for driving out of the city. In an attempt to keep the city centre relatively free of traffic, there's a confusing and none-too-successful one-way system in operation, supplemented by rigorously enforced on-street parking restrictions. Outside peak periods, on-street **parking** is relatively easy and free, but during peak periods (Mon–Fri 8am–5pm, Sat 8am–10am) metered parking is available only, for a maximum of two hours at 15kr an hour. Your best bet, therefore, is to make straight for one of the four central car parks: the largest is the 24hr Bygarasjen, a short walk from the city centre, behind the Stors-enter shopping mall and bus station. Charges here are heavily discounted – it costs just 90kr for 24 hours, 30kr overnight. The 24-hour Rosenkrantz P-Hus, on Rosenkrantzgaten, is much handier for the harbourfront, but charges are higher: 24 hours costs 170kr. To get there, follow the international ferry signs until you pick up the car park signs.

Information

Bergen **tourist office** is handily located in a large, mural-decorated hall across the road from Torget at Vågsallmenningen 1 (May & Sept daily 9am–8pm; June–Aug daily 8.30am–10pm; Oct–April Mon–Sat 9am–4pm; ℡55 55 20 00, Ⓦwww.visitbergen.com). They supply free copies of the exhaustive *Bergen Guide*, sell the Bergen Card (see box, p.204), change foreign currency, arrange car hire, and sell train, city-tour and fjord-tour tickets. They also have oodles of free information about the whole of the western fjords and operate an accom-modation service, booking hotel rooms and rooms in private houses (see p.204). In high season, expect long queues. Available here too, and in many other places across the city centre, is (the Bergen version of) *Natt & Dag*, a free monthly **magazine**, containing local news, entertainment listings and reviews. Naturally enough, it's in Norwegian, but the listings are still easy(ish) to use.

City transport

Most of Bergen's key attractions are located in the city centre, which is compact enough to be readily explored **on foot**. For outlying sights and accommoda-tion, however, you may well need to take a city **bus**. These are operated by tide (℡177, Ⓦwww.tide.no), who provide a dense network of local services that reaches every corner of Bergen and its environs; the hub of the network is the **bus station**, in the Storsenter shopping mall on Strømgaten. Flat-fare tickets for travel within the city limits cost 23kr; they are available from the driver.

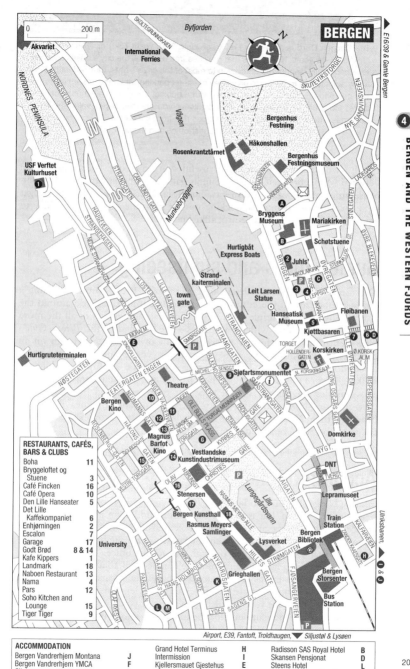

BERGEN

Byfjorden

E16/39 & Gamle Bergen

Akvariet

International Ferries

Skoltegrunnskaien

Skutevikstorget

N

NYE SANDVIKSVEIEN

NORDNESVEIEN

NORDNES PENINSULA

Vågen

Bergenhus Festning

Håkonshallen

Rosenkrantztårnet

Bergenhus Festningsmuseum

USF Verftet Kulturhuset ①

CARL SUNDTS GATE

STRANDGATEN

Munkebryggen

SANDBRUGATEN

SANDBRUGATEN

Ⓐ

Bryggens Museum

Mariakirken

STOLEGATEN

ØVRE BLEKEVEIEN

LADEGÅRDS. GT.

HAUGEVEIEN

STRANGEHAGEN

NEDRE STRANDGATEN

Ⓑ

Juhls' ②

Schøtstuene

BRYGGEN

NIKOLAIKIRK.

ØVREGATEN

STEINKJELLER

Hurtigbåt Express Boats

③ ④

Ⓒ

LEPPSGT.

IMRANT.

KLOSTERGATEN

LILLE MARKEVEIEN

Strand-kaiterminalen

Leit Larsen Statue

Fløibanen

town gate

Hanseatisk Museum

⑤

Kjøttbasaren

Ⓓ

Ⓓ

Hurtigruteterminalen

NØSTEGATEN

L. MURALM.

DOMKIRKEGATEN

SMØRSGATE

STRANDKAIEN

STRANDGATEN

TORGET

HOLLENDER-GATEN

Korskirken

⑦

L.L. ØVREGATEN

Ø.K.KORSK. ALM.

Ⓔ

ENGEN

P

VALKENDORFSGT.

SENSGT.

Sjøfartsmonumentet ⑨

Ⓕ

⑧

N. KORSKIRKEALM.

ⓘ

KONG OSCARS GATE

BISPENGSGATEN

Theatre

TEATERGATEN

ENGEN

HAKONS. GT.

VÅGSALLM.

MARKEVEIEN

Bergen Kino

⑩

OLE BULLS PLASS

TORGALLMENNINGEN

RÅDHUSGT.

STRANDGATEN

C. MICHEL SENSGT.

KLOSTEGATEN

ENGEN

VASKE- ELV. SM.

TORGGATA.

KYRRESG.

NYGT.

Domkirke

VEITERGATEN

Magnus Barfot Kino

⑫

⑬

⑪

Vestlandske Kunstindustrimuseum

⑭

KAIGATEN

DNT

TVERGT.

Lepramuseet

ROSENBERGSGATEN

SIG. BRODSG.

ØSTRE TORGGATE

OLAV

NEDRES.

CHRISTIES

RASMUS MEYERS ALLÉ

Lille Lungegårdsvann

Stenersen

⑰

⑮

⑯

KAIGATEN

Bergen Kunsthall ⑱

University

HARALD HÅRFAGRES. GT.

ROSSMK. G.

Rasmus Meyers Samlinger

L. HILLES GATE

Lysverket

Bergen Bibliotek

Ⓗ

NYGÅRDSGATEN

STRØMGATEN

FJØSANGERVEIEN

Bergen Storsenter

Ulriksbanen, ▼ ① & ②

L. HILLES GATE

Grieghallen

NYGÅRDSGATEN

Ⓚ

Train Station

JANSEN KAISSERG.

KALFARVEIEN

FOSSWINCKELS GATE

HANS HOLMBOES GATE

Ⓛ Ⓜ

OLAF FROS.

PARKVEIEN

LYDER SAGENS GT.

Bus Station

P

0   200 m

RESTAURANTS, CAFÉS, BARS & CLUBS

Boha	11
Bryggeloftet og Stuene	3
Café Fincken	16
Café Opera	10
Den Lille Hanseater	5
Det Lille Kaffekompaniet	6
Enhjørningen	2
Escalon	7
Garage	17
Godt Brød	8 & 14
Kafe Kippers	1
Landmark	18
Naboen Restaurant	13
Nama	4
Pars	12
Soho Kitchen and Lounge	15
Tiger Tiger	9

Airport, E39, Fantoft, Troldhaugen, ▼ Siljustøl & Lysøen

ACCOMMODATION

Bergen Vandrerhjem Montana	J	Grand Hotel Terminus	H	Radisson SAS Royal Hotel	B
Bergen Vandrerhjem YMCA	F	Intermission	I	Skansen Pensjonat	D
Citybox	K	Kjellersmauet Gjestehus	E	Steens Hotel	L
Clarion Collection Havnekontoret	A	Park	M	Thon Hotel Rosenkrantz	C
		Radisson SAS Hotel Norge	G		

The Bergen Card

The **Bergen Card** is a 24-hour (190kr; children 3–15 years 75kr) or 48-hour (250kr; children 3–15 years 100kr) pass that provides free use of all the city's buses and free or substantially discounted admission to most of the city's sights, plus reductions on many sightseeing trips. It also gives free on-street parking within the posted limits – if you can find a space. The pass comes with a booklet listing all the various concessions. Obviously, the more diligent a sightseer you are, the better value the card becomes – doubly so if you're staying a bus ride from the centre. The card is sold at a wide range of outlets, including the tourist office and major hotels.

Finally, two passenger **ferries** offer useful short cuts: one bobs across Vågen between Munkebryggen, on Carl Sundts gate, and a point near the Bryggens Museum on the Bryggen (Mon–Fri 7am–4pm; 15kr); the second links Torget with the Nordnes peninsula, docking not far from the Akvariet (late May to Aug daily 10am–6pm; 60kr return, 40kr one-way).

Guided tours and sightseeing

The tourist office has the details of a plethora of **local tours**, including a quick gambol round the city by bus, an electric mini-train ride around the city's environs and multiple fjord sightseeing trips; itineraries of all the more popular tours – along with some prices – are detailed in the *Bergen Guide*. However, it's usually cheaper to arrange your own visits than to go on an organized tour and details as to how to get where and when are given throughout this chapter. That said, one tour to be recommended is the walking tour of the **Bryggen** (see box, p.207) and, if time is short, you might also consider one of the several excellent tours organized by Fjord Tours (ⓦ www.fjord-tours.com; and see p.32), most notably the heavily trailed **Norway in a Nutshell** tour to Flåm, which involves a quick zip through the fjords by train, boat and bus (see p.224).

Accommodation

Finding budget **accommodation** in Bergen can be a bit of a problem at the height of the season, but is usually straightforward. There are three hostels, a choice of guesthouses, and some of the central hotels are surprisingly good value. Also among the better deals are the **rooms** in private houses – or "private rooms" – that can be reserved through the tourist office. The vast majority provide self-catering facilities and some are fairly central, though most are stuck out in the suburbs. Prices are at a fixed nightly rate – currently 430kr for a double room without en-suite facilities (300kr single), and 500kr for en suite (350kr single). They are very popular, so in summer you'll need to arrive at the tourist office early to secure one for the night. The tourist office makes a small supplementary charge (of 30kr, 50kr in advance) for making a booking, as it does for hotel and guesthouse reservations.

Hotels

Citybox Nygårdsgaten 31 ☎55 31 25 00, ⓦwww.citybox.no. Great emphasis here on economy prices in return for what you actually need – a brightly decorated, albeit rather spartan room – as distinct from what you can manage without, for instance a mini-bar and room service. Rooms are either en suite (an extra 100kr) or with shared facilities. Internet access. Central location. ❶

🏃 **Clarion Collection** Havnekontoret Slottsgaten 1 ☎55 60 11 00, ⓦwww .choicehotels.no. Prestige development in which Bergen's former harbour office has been tastefully converted into a deluxe hotel. The handsome public areas are capacious and although the emphasis is on the modern, the original 1920s stone archways and vaulted side-rooms, with their intricate murals, have been preserved. The best of the guest rooms, where browns and creams predominate, have harbour views. ❼, sp/r ❺

Grand Hotel Terminus Zander Kaaes gate 6 ☎55 21 25 00, ⓦwww.ght.no. There was a time when the tweed-jacketed visitors from pre war England headed straight for the *Grand* as soon as they arrived in Bergen – and not just because the hotel is next door to the train station. Those ritzy days are long gone, but the hotel has reinvented itself, making the most of its quasi-baronial flour-ishes, notably its extensive wood panelling, chandeliers and stained glass. Breakfasts are superb and the bedrooms attractive and quiet, though some are rather pokey: if you can, have a look before you commit. ❼, sp/r ❺

🏃 **Park** Harald Hårfagres gate 35 ☎55 54 44 00, ⓦwww.parkhotel.no. This excellent, family-run hotel occupies two handsome, late nineteenth-century town houses on the edge of the town centre near the univer-sity. The charming interior is painted in soft pastel colours and the public areas are dotted with antiques. The bedrooms are smart, neat and appealing. It's very popular, so reservations are advised. ❺, sp/r ❹

Radisson SAS Hotel Norge Ole Bulls plass 4 ☎55 57 30 00, ⓦwww.radissonsas.com. Demure and reassuring top-flight hotel with a foyer of classic postwar design, whose rectangular lines are broken up by the most appealing of balconies. The rooms beyond are comfortable and engaging and there's a full range of facilities from bar to heated swimming pool. Ole Bulls plass is in the thick of things too. ❽, sp/r ❻

Radisson SAS Royal Hotel Bryggen ☎55 54 30 00, ⓦwww.radissonsas.com. Full marks here to the architects, who have built an extremely

smart, first-rate hotel behind a brick facade that mirrors the style of the old timber buildings that surround it. All facilities – pool, health club and so forth, plus attractively appointed rooms. ❽, sp/r ❻

Steens Hotel Parkveien 22 ☎55 30 88 88, ⓦwww.steenshotel.no. In a good-looking, late nineteenth-century villa, this well-established hotel boasts all sorts of period detail, from the bygones in the foyer through to the neo-Baronial touches – and stained-glass windows – in the dining room. The guest rooms are well-kept if a little spartan, and the hotel overlooks the miniature lake and parklet that form the western tip of the green and leafy Nygardsparken. 10min walk from Vågen. ❼, sp/r ❻

Thon Hotel Rosenkrantz Rosenkrantzgaten 7 ☎55 30 14 00, ⓦwww.thonhotels.com. Proficient, mid-range chain hotel in an oldish building just behind the Bryggen. Has everything you'll need, including free coffee and internet access in the foyer, though the rooms could do with a re-fit (one is promised) and it's worth avoiding the ones that face the interior courtyard, insisting instead on a room that overlooks the Bryggen and, on the top floors, the harbour; there's no extra charge. Better-than-average buffet breakfast too. Shame about the aluminium window-frames stuck in the old facade. ❻, sp/r ❺

Guesthouses

Kjellersmauet Gjestehus Kjellersmauet 22 ☎55 96 26 08, ⓦwww.gjestehuset.com. Immaculately maintained 1880s timber house whose interior has been turned into three en-suite apartments of varying size but all with kitchenettes. On a narrow alley off a busy main street – Jonsvollsgaten – about 10min walk west from Ole Bulls plass. ❸

🏃 **Skansen Pensjonat** Vetrlidsallmenningen 29 ☎55 31 90 80, ⓦwww.skansen -pensjonat.no. This pleasant little guesthouse occupies a nineteenth-century stone house of elegant proportions just above – up the steps and hairpins from – the terminus of the Fløibanen funicular railway, near Torget: it's a great location, in one of the most beguiling parts of town. The pension has eleven guest rooms, most of which are en suite, and all are very homely. A real snip at ❷.

Hostels

Bergen Vandrerhjem Montana Johan Blyttsveien 30, Landås ☎55 20 80 70, ⓦwww .montana.no. This large and comfortable HI hostel occupies lodge-like premises in the hills

overlooking the city. Great views and great breakfasts, plus self-catering facilities, a café, a laundry and internet access. Has dorm accommodation, family rooms and doubles – almost all of which are en suite. The hostel is 6km east of the centre, 15min on bus #31 (stop Montana) from the train station. Popular with school parties, who are (usually) housed in a separate wing. Dorm beds 180–200kr, doubles **②**
Bergen Vandrerhjem YMCA Nedre Korskirkealmenning 4 ☎ 55 60 60 55, ⓦ www.vandrerhjem.no. No-frills HI hostel in the city centre, a short walk from Torget. Has room for 170 guests, but fills up fast in summer. Facilities include self-catering and a laundry. Open May–Sept. Breakfast 55kr. Dorm beds 155kr, doubles **③**
Intermission Kalfarveien 8 ☎ 55 30 04 00, ⓦ www.intermissionhostel.no. Christian-run, private hostel in a two-storey, oldish wooden building, a 5min walk from the train station – just beyond one of the old city gates. Open mid-June to mid-Aug. Breakfast 25kr, dorm beds 150kr.

The City

Founded in 1070 by King Olav Kyrre ("the Peaceful"), a Norwegian survivor from the battle of Stamford Bridge in 1066, **Bergen** was the largest and most important town in medieval Norway and a regular residence of the country's kings and queens. In the fourteenth century Bergen also became an ecclesiastical centre, supporting no fewer than thirty churches and monasteries, and a member of the **Hanseatic League**, confirmation of its status as a prosperous port linked to other European cities by a vigorous trading life. The League was, however, controlled by German merchants and, after Hansa and local interests started to diverge, the Germans came to dominate the region's economy, reducing the locals to a state of dependency. Neither could the people of Bergen expect help from their kings and queens. Indeed it was the reverse: in return for easily collected taxes from the Hansa merchants, Norway's medieval monarchs compelled west-coast fishermen to sell their catch to the merchants – and at prices the merchants set themselves. As a result, the German trading station that flourished on the Bryggen, Bergen's main wharf, became wealthy and hated in equal measure, a self-regulating trading station with its own laws and an administration that was profoundly indifferent to local sentiment.

In the 1550s, with Hansa power finally evaporating, a local lord – one **Kristoffer Valkendorf** – reasserted Norwegian control, but not out of the goodness of his heart. Valkendorf and his cronies simply took over the monopolies that had enriched their German predecessors, and continued to operate this iniquitous system, which so pauperized the region's fishermen, right up to the late nineteenth century. In fact, it's only after World War II that local fishermen started to receive their financial dues, a prerequisite of the economic boom that has, since the 1960s, transformed Bergen from a fish-dependent backwater to the lively city of today.

Orientation

Very little of medieval Bergen has survived, although parts of the fortress, the **Bergenhus Festning** – which commands the entrance to the harbour – date from the thirteenth century. The rest of the city centre divides into several distinct parts, the most interesting being the harbourside **Bryggen**, which accommodates an attractive ensemble of stone and timber eighteenth- and nineteenth-century merchants' trading houses. The Bryggen ends at the head of the harbour, where Bergen's main square, the **Torget**, features an open-air fish market. East of here, stretching up towards the train station, is one of the older districts, a mainly nineteenth-century quarter that's at its prettiest along and around **Lille Øvregaten**. The main thoroughfare of this quarter, **Kong Oscars gate**, has been roughly treated by the developers, but it does lead to the city's most endearing museum, the **Lepramuseet** (Leprosy Museum). A stone's throw from here, the modern concrete blocks surrounding the central **lake**, Lille Lungegårdsvann, form the cultural focus of the city, holding Bergen's art galleries and main concert hall, while the chief commercial area is a few metres to the west along the wide and airy **Torgalmenningen**. The steep hill to the south of the central lake is topped by the **university**.

Most of the main sights and museums are concentrated in these areas, but no tour of the city is complete without a stroll out along the **Nordnes peninsula**, where fine timber houses pepper the bumpy terrain and the old USF sardine factory now contains a lively and very fashionable arts complex and café.

Torget

In 1890, Lilian Leland, author of *Traveling Alone: A Woman's Journey Around the World*, complained of Bergen that "Everything is fishy. You eat fish and drink fish and smell fish and breathe fish." Those days are long gone, but now that Bergen is every inch a go-ahead, modern city, tourists in search of all things piscine flock to **Torget**'s open-air **fish market** (June–Aug daily 7am–5pm; Sept–May Mon–Sat 7am–4pm). It's not a patch on the days when scores of fishing vessels crowded the quayside to empty their bulging holds, but the stalls still display mounds of prawns and crab-claws, dried cod, buckets of herring and a hundred other varieties of marine life on slabs, in tanks, under the knife, and in packets. Fruit, vegetables and flowers – as well as souvenirs – have a place in today's market too, and there's easily enough variety to assemble an excellent picnic lunch, so load up or eat up. At the end of the jetty behind Torget, also take a peek at the **statue** of Leif Andreas Larsen, aka Shetlands Larsen, one of Norway's most renowned World War II heroes; for more on the man, see p.299.

Bryggen

Spearing down the north side of Vågen, **Bryggen** is the obvious historical and cultural target after Torget. The site of the original settlement, Bryggen recalls its medieval provenance by a string of wooden and stone warehouses, whose distinctive gable ends face out to the waterfront. The whole area between the Bryggen and Øvregaten just to the rear was once known as Tyskebryggen, or "German Quay", after the **Hanseatic** merchants who operated their **trading station** here, but the name was unceremoniously dumped after World War II. Hansa influence dated back to the thirteenth century, and was derived from trading grain and beer for fish shipped here from northern Norway. Only later did the Germans come to dominate local affairs, much to the consternation of local landowners. By the middle of the sixteenth century, however, the

Guided tours of Bryggen

Informative and amusingly anecdotal English-language **guided tours** of the Bryggen start from the tourist office (see p.202) daily from June to August at 3pm, and take roughly an hour and a half. They are popular, so it's a good idea to book ahead – tickets (95kr) from the tourist office.

Hanseatic League was in decline; the last German merchant hung on here till 1764, but by then economic power had long since passed to the Norwegian bourgeoisie.

The Hanseatisk Museum

The **medieval buildings** of the Bryggen were destroyed by fire in 1702, to be replaced by another set of wooden warehouses. In turn, many of these were later demolished to make way for brick-and-stone warehouses built in a style modelled on – and sympathetic to – that of the Hansa period. Nevertheless, a significant number of early eighteenth-century timber buildings have survived, though the first you'll come to, at the north end of Torget, has brick-and-stone neighbours. This is the **Hanseatisk Museum** (Hanseatic Museum; mid-May to mid-Sept daily 9am–5pm; mid-Sept to mid-May Tues–Sat 11am–2pm & Sun 11am–4pm; 50kr, includes Schøtstuene), a delightfully well-preserved, early eighteenth-century merchants' dwelling, kitted out in late Hansa style. As per standard Hansa format, it was a rabbit warren of a place in which the trading area occupied the ground floor and the junior staff the top, with the merchants in between. There was, predictably enough, a considerable difference in the comfort afforded to the juniors as distinct from the merchants, but everyone hunkered down in the panelled bunk beds that survive to this day. Also of particular interest is the building's **painted woodwork**, with broad, bold and colourful floral designs in many of the working areas and more formal, Italianate scenes in the merchants' quarters – though the exact provenance of these designs has been the subject of much debate. Dotted throughout the museum is an idiosyncratic assortment of bygones, including the possessions of contemporary families, a medley of indeterminate portraits, several fine pieces of furniture, and an ancient and much-used fish press.

The rest of the Bryggen

A few metres further on from the Hanseatisk Museum is the main block of old **timber buildings**, now housing souvenir shops, restaurants and bars. Despite the crowds of tourists, it's well worth nosing around here, wandering down the passageways wherever you can. Interestingly, these eighteenth-century buildings carefully follow the original building line: the governing body of the Hansa trading station stipulated the exact depth and width of each merchant's building, and the width of the passage separating them – a regularity that's actually best observed from Øvregaten (see p.209). The planning regulations didn't end there: trade had to be carried out in the front section of the building, with storage rooms at the back; above were the merchant's office, bedroom and dining room. Up above those, on the top floor, were the living quarters of the employees, grouped into rooms by rank – junior merchants, journeymen/clerks and foremen, wharf hands and, last (and least), errand boys. Every activity in this rigidly hierarchical, all-male society was tightly controlled – employees were forbidden to fraternize with the locals and stiff fines were imposed for hundreds of "offences" including swearing, waking up the master and singing at work.

The Bryggens Museum

Just off the Bryggen, beside the *SAS Royal Hotel*, stands the lumpily modern **Bryggens Museum** (mid-May to Aug daily 10am–5pm; Sept to mid-May Mon–Fri 11am–3pm, Sat noon–3pm & Sun noon–4pm; 50kr), where a visit begins in the basement, which exhibits all manner of things dug up in the archeological excavations of the Bryggen in the 1950s. A wide range of items was unearthed, from domestic implements like combs and pots through to shoes, buckles and trade goods plus several runic sticks – perhaps surprisingly, Norwegians were laboriously carving runes (see p.392) onto their sticks well into medieval times. The museum displays these finds thematically both to illustrate the city's early history and provide the backcloth to a set of twelfth-century foundations at the back of the basement, left *in situ* where they were unearthed. The museum's two upper floors are given over to temporary exhibitions exploring other aspects of Bergen's past.

Mariakirken

Behind the museum, the perky twin towers of the **Mariakirken** (St Mary's Church; late June to late Aug Mon–Fri 9–11am & 1–4pm; late Aug to late June Tues–Fri 11am–12.30pm; 20kr, free in winter) are the most distinctive feature of what is Bergen's oldest extant building, a Romanesque-Gothic church dating from the twelfth century. Still used as a place of worship, Mariakirken is now firmly Norwegian, but from 1408 to 1706 it was the church of the Hanseatic League merchants, who purchased it lock, stock and barrel. The merchants installed the church's ostentatious Baroque pulpit and its gaudy North German altarpiece, a fifteenth-century triptych, whose exquisite framing is really rather wasted on the sentimental carvings of saints and apostles it surrounds. The walls of the Mariakirken are hung with old commemorative paintings, an insipid lot for the most part with the exception of a finely detailed portrait of *Pastor Lammer, his wife and six children*, looking suitably serious in their Sunday best. The painting is by Lambert von Haven, a seventeenth-century Dutch artist, who went on to greater things at the royal court in Copenhagen; it hangs above the side door on the right-hand side of the nave.

Schøtstuene and Øvregaten

At the back of the Mariakirken, at Øvregaten 50, the **Schøtstuene** (mid-May to mid-Sept daily 10am–5pm; mid-Sept to mid-May Sun only 11am–2pm; 50kr, includes Hanseatisk Museum) comprises the old Hanseatic assembly rooms, where the merchants would meet to lay down the law or just relax – it was the only building in the whole trading post allowed heating and so it was here that they held their feasts, ceremonies and celebrations. As you explore the comfortable and commodious rooms, it's hard not to conclude that the merchants cared not a jot for their employees shivering away nearby – though, to be fair, their bunk beds weren't much fun either.

Saving the mildly interesting Bergenhus fortress for later (see p.210), stroll east from the Schøtstuene along **Øvregaten**, an attractive cobbled street which has marked the boundary of the Bryggen for the last eight hundred years and was once, despite the fulminations of the Hansa merchants, the haunt of the city's prostitutes. From Øvregaten, it's still possible to discern the **layout** of the old trading station, a warren of narrow passages separating warped and crooked buildings surmounted by their hat-like, high-pitched roofs. On the upper levels, the eighteenth-century loading bays, staircases and higgledy-piggledy living quarters are still much in evidence, while the overhanging eaves of the passageways were designed to shelter trade goods.

At the eastern end of Bryggen's timber houses, cobbled Nikolaikirkeallmenningen leaves Øvregaten to run down to the harbourfront, where you turn right for the Bergenhus; if you stay on Øvregaten, it's a couple of minutes to the lower terminus of the Fløibanen (see p.211).

Bergenhus Festning

Overlooking the mouth of the harbour, the **Bergenhus Festning** (Bergen Fortress) is a large and roughly star-shaped fortification now used mostly as a park (daily 6.30am–11pm; free). The fort's thick stone-and-earth walls date from the nineteenth century, but they enclose the remnants of earlier strongholds – or rather their copies: the Bergenhus was wrecked when a German ammunition ship exploded just below the walls in 1944. Of the two main medieval replicas, the more diverting is the forbidding **Rosenkrantztårnet** (Rosenkrantz Tower; mid-May to Aug daily 10am–4pm; Sept to mid-May Sun noon–3pm; 40kr), whose spiral staircases, medieval rooms and low rough corridors make an enjoyable gambol. It's also possible to walk out onto the rooftop battlements, from where there is a wide view over the harbour. The tower is named after a certain **Erik Rosenkrantz**, governor of Bergen from 1560 to 1568, who turned his draughty medieval quarters into a grand fortified residence, equipping his own chamber with fine large windows and a handsome Renaissance chimneypiece, both of which have survived in good condition. This room also has a copy of Rosenkrantz's gravestone, a somewhat ill-balanced but still strikingly realistic work depicting his wife in a long flowing dress and him in a suit of armour with a codpiece that would bring tears to most men's eyes. Rosenkrantz was known principally as the architect of a new law under which anyone found guilty of an illegitimate sexual affair had to confess to a priest before being fined. The law applied initially to men and women in equal measure, but by the 1590s women bore the brunt of any punishment. In Bergen, for example, women who could not pay the fine had to stand naked at the entrance to a church before being thrown out of town – the men just got exiled.

Metres from the tower is the entrance to a large cobbled courtyard, which is flanked by nineteenth-century officers' quarters and the **Håkonshallen** (mid-May to Aug daily 10am–4pm; Sept to mid-May daily noon–3pm, Thurs 3–6pm; 40kr), a careful reconstruction of the Gothic ceremonial hall built for King Håkon Håkonsson in the middle of the thirteenth century. After Norway lost its independence, the capacious hall became surplus to requirements and no one knew quite what to do with it for several centuries, but it was revamped in 1910 and rebuilt after the 1944 explosion and is now in use once again for public ceremonies.

Frequent **guided tours** of both the Rosenkrantztårnet and the Håkonshallen start at the Håkonshallen; there's no extra charge.

Bergenhus Festningsmuseum

From the entrance to the Bergenhus Festning, it's a couple of minutes' walk to the **Bergenhus Festningsmuseum** (Bergenhus Fortress Museum; Tues–Sun 11am–5pm; free), on Øvre Dreggsallmenningen, where, on the first floor, several displays explore the effects of World War II on Bergen. There's a detailed account of the German naval attack on Bergen in 1940 and on the development of the Resistance thereafter. Bergen had long-standing seafaring links with Great Britain and had also suffered grievously from U-boat attacks on Norwegian shipping in World War I, and as a result the Resistance to the occupation was particularly strong here. Unfortunately, the Germans proved adept at tracking down their enemies, and time and again they broke the back of the main Resistance groups, though they were flummoxed by the explosion which levelled much of the Bergenhus on Hitler's birthday in 1944: they thought it was sabotage, but in fact it was an accident. The museum's second floor is far less interesting, being given over to a detailed exploration of the history of the Bergenhus fortress; the ground floor is for temporary displays.

From the museum, it's a few-minutes' walk back along Bryggen to Torget and the Fløibanen funicular railway.

The Fløibanen funicular railway

At the east end of Øvregaten, back near Torget, stands the distinctly Ruritanian lower terminus of the **Fløibanen funicular railway** (May–Aug Mon–Sat 8am–midnight & Sun 9am–midnight; Sept–April same details, but only until 11pm; departures every 15–30min; return fare 70kr), which shuttles up to the top of **Mount Fløyen** – "The Vane" – at 320m above sea level. When the weather is fine, you get a bird's-eye view of Bergen and its surroundings from the plateau-summit, and here also is a large and popular café-restaurant. Afterwards, you can walk back down to the city in about 45 minutes, or push on into the woods along several well-marked, colour-coded footpaths. The shortest and one of the more enjoyable is the 1.6km-loop trail to Skomakerdiket lake and back. Pick up free trail maps at the lower terminal.

Lille Øvregaten to the Lepramuseet

Running east from the lower Fløibanen terminal, **Lille Øvregaten** is lined by an appealing mix of expansive nineteenth-century villas and dinky timber houses, all bright-white clapboard and angular gables. There are more old timber houses up above too, and these are, if anything, even quainter, pressing in against the steep cobbled lanes that steer and veer around hunks of stone which were, at the time, simply too bothersome to move: to explore the area, take the first left up the hillside from Lille Øvregaten and follow your nose. Meanwhile, back down below, Lille Øvregaten curves round to the **Domkirke** (Cathedral; late June to late Aug Mon–Fri 11am–4pm; late Aug to late June Tues–Fri 11am–12.30pm; free), a heavy-duty edifice whose stern exterior has been restored and rebuilt several times since its original construction in the thirteenth century. Neither does the interior set the pulse racing, though there's a noticeable penchant for fancy wooden staircases – two leading to the organ and one to the pulpit – which can't help but seem a little flippant given the dourness of their surroundings.

Rather more promising is the fascinating **Lepramuseet** (Leprosy Museum; mid-May to Aug daily 11am–4pm; 40kr), just up from the Domkirke at Kong Oscars gate 59. The museum is housed in the charming, eighteenth-century buildings of **St Jørgens Hospital** (St George's Hospital), whose assorted dwellings are ranged around a paved courtyard, and it tells the tale of the Norwegian fight against leprosy. The disease first appeared in Scandinavia in Viking times and became especially prevalent in the coastal districts of western Norway, with around three percent of the population classified as lepers in the early nineteenth century. The hospital specialized in the care of lepers, assuming a more proactive role from 1830, when a series of Norwegian medics tried to find a cure for the disease. The most successful of them was **Armauer Hansen**, who in 1873 was the first person to identify the leprosy bacillus. The last lepers left St Jørgens in 1946 and the hospital has been left untouched, the small rooms off the central gallery revealing the patients' humble living quarters. Also on display are medical implements and a few gruesome sketches and paintings of sufferers alongside their desperate life stories. Dating from 1702, the adjoining hospital **chapel** is delightfully homely, its rickety, creaking timbers holding a domineering pulpit topped off by half a dozen folksy cherubs and an altarpiece decorated with yet more cherubs and some dainty scrollwork. The two altar paintings are crude but appropriate – *Jesus and the Ten Lepers* and *The Canaanite's Daughter Healed*.

Lille Lungegårdsvann: Bergen's art galleries

Bergen's attractively landscaped central lake, **Lille Lungegårdsvann**, is a focus for summertime festivals and parades, and its southern side is flanked by the city's five main art galleries, three of which comprise the **Bergen Kunstmuseum** (Bergen Art Museum; Ⓦ www.kunstmuseene.no). These three galleries have the same opening hours and a common admission fee (50kr covers all), but the other two – one devoted to decorative art, the other to temporary exhibitions of contemporary art – are separate.

Many of the twentieth-century paintings in the Bergen Kunstmuseum collection were bequeathed to the city by **Rolf Stenersen** (1899–1978), who donated his first art collection to his hometown of Oslo in 1936 (see p.85) and was in a similar giving mood 35 years later, the beneficiary being his adopted town of Bergen. Something of a Renaissance man, Stenersen – one-time athlete, financier and chum of Munch – seems to have had a successful stab at almost everything, even writing some highly acclaimed short stories in the 1930s.

Also on the southern side of the lake, behind the galleries on Nygårdsgaten, is the **Grieghallen** concert hall, a large modern edifice that serves as the main venue for the annual Bergen International Festival (see p.220).

Bergen Kunstmuseum - Lysverket

The easternmost of the five lakeside galleries is **Lysverket**, Rasmus Meyers Allé 9 (mid-May to mid-Sept daily 11am–5pm; mid-Sept to mid-May Tues–Sun 11am–5pm), which occupies a distinctive Art Deco/Functionalist building, complete with its own mini-rotunda, that started out as offices for a power company. The gallery spreads over three floors with the ground floor divided between temporary exhibitions and modern art from the 1950s onwards. It's here you'll find a selection of watercolours and oils by the versatile Norwegian JaCob Weidemann (1923–2001), whose work was much influenced by French Cubists during the 1940s, though he is now associated with the shimmering, pastel-painted abstracts he churned out in the 1960s.

The next floor up has a whole room devoted to **Johan Christian Dahl** (1788–1857; see p.88), one of Norway's finest landscape painters. Several of Dahl's early sketches are exhibited here, but these are crude affairs executed before he hit his artistic stride, whereas his *Bergen Harbour* and *Nordic Landscape with a River* reveal Dahl at his most accomplished. A neighbouring room has several examples of the work of **Adolph Tidemand** (1814–76) and **Hans Gude** (1825–1903), both of whom specialized in rural scenes populated by idealized versions of Norwegian country folk. There are also several minor Munchs as well as a proselytizing canvas by **Christian Krohg** (1852–1925) entitled *Fight for Survival*, which rails against urban poverty. The third room on this floor holds the Kunstmuseum's modest selection of old masters, mostly Dutch and Italian paintings, plus an engaging miscellany of medieval Greek and Russian icons.

The top floor has one room devoted to twentieth-century Norwegian art with more JaCob Weidemann, a delightful *Four Sisters* by Alf Rolfsen (1895–1979) and a searing *Sisters of Liberty* by **Arne Ekeland** (1908–1994). A self-taught painter from Eidsvoll, near Oslo, Ekeland was a committed leftist whose paintings either protest the oppression of the working class or portray a vision of a Socialist utopia – though some do both at the same time. A further room on this floor features the paintings of **Nikolai Astrup** (1880–1929), generally regarded as the last of the Norwegian Romantics – or at least neo-Romantics: sometimes

Astrup's paintings portray a benign rural idyll, at other times – as in *Kollen* – the Norwegian landscape appears dangerous and malevolent. A final room holds a small selection of twentieth-century international works, most notably from Picasso, Braque, Ernst, Rivera and the Bauhaus painter Paul Klee.

Bergen Kunstmuseum – Rasmus Meyers Samlinger

The **Rasmus Meyers Samlinger** (Rasmus Meyer Collection; mid-May to mid-Sept daily 11am–5pm; mid-Sept to mid-May Tues–Sun 11am–5pm) is housed in a large and distinctive building with a pagoda-like roof at Rasmus Meyers Allé 7. It boasts a superb survey of Norwegian art from 1815 to 1915, gifted to the city by one of its old merchant families – the Meyers – and now displayed broadly chronologically on two easily absorbed and well-organized floors. On the ground floor, the first rooms concentrate on Norwegian Romanticism, with Dahl, Thomas Fearnley and Tidemand much in evidence. This is followed by several period rooms, most memorably the Rococo excesses of the **Blumenthal room**, whose fancy stucco work and allegorical wall and ceiling paintings were knocked up in the 1750s for a Bergen merchant by an itinerant Danish artist, one Mathias Blumenthal. Up above, the first floor moves on to the decorative medievalism of Gerhard Munthe (1849–1929) and the work of Erik Werenskiold (1855–1938), who is best known for his colourful illustrations of the folk stories collected by Asbjørnsen and Moe in rural Norway. The stories had already been published several times when Werenskiold and his accomplice Theodor Kittelsen (1857–1914) got working on them, but it was they who effectively defined the appearance of the country's various folkloric figures – from trolls onwards – in the popular imagination.

It is, however, for its large sample of the work of **Edvard Munch** (1863–1944) that the museum is best known – if you missed out in Oslo (see p.89 & p.105), this is the place to make amends. There are examples from all Munch's major periods, with the disturbing – and disturbed – works of the 1890s inevitably stealing the spotlight, especially the searing and unsettling *Jealousy* and the fractured *Woman in Three Stages*.

Bergen Kunsthall and the Stenersen gallery

Just along the street from the Rasmus Meyer Collection is the **Bergen Kunsthall**, Rasmus Meyers Allé 5 (Tues–Sun noon–5pm; 40kr; ⓦwww .kunsthall.no), which has developed into the city's most imaginative contemporary arts venue with up to three separate exhibitions at any one time. It's all very hit and miss – banal at worst, stunning at best – but no one could say the exhibitions were predictable.

Next door, in a glum concrete block, the **Stenersen** (mid-May to mid-Sept daily 11am–5pm; mid-Sept to mid-May Tues–Sun 11am–5pm) specializes in temporary exhibitions of contemporary art, mostly international but with a strong Norwegian showing. The gallery occupies two smallish floors above the ground-floor shop and coffee bar.

Vestlandske Kunstindustrimuseum

Across the road from the Stenersen, the **Vestlandske Kunstindustrimuseum**, at the corner of Christies gate and Nordahl Bruns gate (West Norway Decorative Art Museum; mid-May to mid-Sept daily 11am–5pm; mid-Sept to mid-May Tues–Sun noon–4pm; 50kr; ⓦwww.kunstmuseene.no), occupies the Permanenten building, a whopping neo-Gothic structure built as a cultural centre in the 1890s. A lively exhibition programme with the focus on contemporary craft and design brings in the crowds, and some of the displays are very good indeed – which is perhaps more than can be said for much of the permanent collection, a hotch-potch of everything from chests and cupboards to jewellery and porcelain. Fans of Ole Bull (see p.217) will, however, be keen to gawp at one of the great man's violins, made in 1562 by the Italian Salò.

Torgalmenningen

The broad sweep of pedestrianized **Torgalmenningen** is a suitably handsome setting for the commercial heart of modern Bergen, lined with arcaded shops and department stores and decorated at its Torget end by the vigorous large-scale granite and bronze **Sjøfartsmonumentet** (Seafarers' Monument), celebrating the city's seafaring traditions. Unveiled in 1950, it sports twelve sculptures on its lower section with two sets of reliefs up above. Its southeast side – nearest the Galleriet shopping centre – bears the inscription Tiende Århundre (Tenth Century), the theme being the Vikings' semi-legendary voyages to Vinland (North America). The reliefs depict a Viking ship with its sails hoisted and a meeting between the Norsemen and American Indians; down below there is a Norwegian chieftain with a spear, a skald (Norse bard) wearing sheepskin clothing, and a berserker (warrior) with a shield on his back. On the monument's southwest side, inscribed Attende Århundre (Eighteenth Century), the theme is the re-discovery of Greenland by Bergen seamen with reliefs of the Norwegian missionary Hans Egede preaching to the Eskimos (Inuit) and a ship being launched while a huge sea serpent writhes in the water beneath it. The northwest side of the monument is dedicated to Bergen's mercantile success in the Nittende Århundre (Nineteenth Century). There are sculptures of a wealthy ship-owner with a tricorn hat, a rookie merchant seaman and a pilot; the reliefs above show whaling and a scene from a shipyard. The fourth and final side, facing the fish market, and inscribed Tjuende Århundre (Twentieth Century), has the theme of Carrying Oil and the sculptures depict a young deckhand, a first mate with binoculars and a ship's engineer with a spanner – respectively symbolizing loyalty, daring and watchfulness. One relief up above has a ship with the rising sun behind it (symbolizing hope) and the other depicts the Resurrection in which the drowned souls on the left are resurrected to eternal life by an angel.

Ole Bulls plass and around

At the far end of Torgalmenningen is **Ole Bulls plass**, also pedestrianized and sporting a rock pool and fountain, above which stands a jaunty statue of local lad Ole Bull, the nineteenth-century virtuoso violinist and heart-throb – his island villa just outside Bergen is a popular day-trip (see p.217). Ole Bulls plass stretches up to the municipal **theatre**, Den Nationale Scene, at the top of the hill, worth the short walk for a look at the fearsome, saucer-eyed statue of Henrik Ibsen that stands guard in front. Near here too, just down Smørsgate at the back of the theatre on Strandgaten, is an old **town gate**, built in 1628 to control access to the city but soon used by the authorities to increase their revenues by the imposition of a toll.

The Nordnes peninsula

Beyond the theatre, the hilly **Nordnes peninsula** juts out into the fjord, its western tip accommodating the large **Akvariet** (Aquarium; May–Aug daily 9am–7pm, 150kr; Sept–April daily 10am–6pm, 100kr; bus #11; Ⓦwww .akvariet.no) and a pleasant park. It takes about fifteen minutes to walk there from Ole Bulls plass – via Klostergaten/Haugeveien – but the effort is perhaps better spent in choosing a different, more southerly, route along the peninsula. This takes you past the charming timber houses and nineteenth-century stone villas of Skottegaten and Nedre Strangehagen before it cuts through the bluff leading to the old, waterside United Sardine Factories, imaginatively converted into an arts complex, the **USF Verftet Kulturhuset** (ⓦwww.usf.no); this incorporates a groovy, harbourside café-bar, *Kafe Kippers* (see p.219). From here, it takes about ten minutes to get to the aquarium.

Out from the centre

The lochs, fjords and rocky wooded hills surrounding central Bergen have channelled the city's **suburbs** into long ribbons, which trail off in every direction. These urban outskirts are not in themselves appealing, though they are extraordinarily handsome when viewed from either Mount Fløyen (see p.211) or the highest of the seven hills around town, the 642-metre **Mount Ulriken**. The **Ulriksbanen cable car** (daily: June–Aug 9am–9pm, April–May & Sept–Oct 10am–5pm; Nov–March Sat & Sun 10am–4pm weather permitting; 95kr return; ⓦwww.ulriken.no) whisks up most of the mountain. Its lower terminal is behind the Haukeland Sykehus (hospital) and near the *Montana* youth hostel, about 6km east of the centre; there are walks and a café at the top too. To get to the cable car by public transport, take city bus #2 (Mon–Fri every 10–20min, Sat & Sun every 30min–1hr) from Strandkaiterminalen.

Elsewhere, tucked away among the city's surroundings, are five attractions, two of which – **Troldhaugen**, Edvard Grieg's home, and **Lysøen**, Ole Bull's island villa – could happily occupy you for half a day. These two lie to the south of the city as does Harald Sæverud's former home at Siljustøl, whereas the open-air **Gamle Bergen** (Old Bergen) is just to the north. A trip to the Troldhaugen is often combined with a quick visit to **Fantoft stave church**, which you can pass en route. There are organized excursions to Troldhaugen and Gamle Bergen – tickets and details from the tourist office – and all five attractions are accessible by **public transport** with varying degrees of ease, but the special bus which went direct from the city centre to Fantoft, Troldhaugen and Gamle Bergen no longer runs; there is a possibility it will be revived – check at the tourist office.

Fantoft stave church

Fantoft stave church (mid-May to mid-Sept daily 10.30am–2pm & 2.30–6pm; 30kr), clearly signposted off the E39 about 5km south of downtown Bergen, was actually moved here from a tiny village on the Sognefjord in the 1880s. The first owner, a government official, had the structure revamped along the lines of the Borgund stave church (see p.187), complete with dragon finials, high-pitched roofs and an outside gallery. In fact, it's unlikely that the original version looked much like Borgund, though this is somewhat irrelevant considering the Fantoft church got burnt to the ground in 1992. Extraordinarily, the then owner didn't surrender, but had a replica of the destroyed church built instead and it stands today, a finely carved affair with disconcertingly fresh timbers, set among beech and pine trees just 600m from the main road.

The same buses that head to Troldhaugen (see p.216) pass the stop for Fantoft stave church – cross the road (Highway 582) from the bus stop, turn right and walk up the hill along Fantoftveien, a ten-minute stroll.

Troldhaugen

Back on the E39, it's a couple of kilometres south to the signed turning for **Troldhaugen** (Hill of the Trolls; May–Sept daily 9am–6pm; Oct & Nov Mon–Fri 10am–2pm, Sat & Sun noon–4pm; mid-Jan to April Mon–Fri 10am–4pm, daily; 60kr; ⓦ www.kunstmuseene.no), the lakeside home of **Edvard Grieg** (see box below) for the last 22 years of his life – though "home" is something of an exaggeration, as he spent several months every year touring the concert halls of Europe. Norway's only composer of world renown, Grieg has a good share of commemorative monuments in Bergen – a statue in the city park and the Grieghallen concert hall to name but two – but it's here that you get a sense of the man, an immensely likeable and much-loved figure of leftish opinions and disarming modesty: "I make no pretensions of being in the class with Bach, Mozart and Beethoven," he once wrote. "Their works are eternal, while I wrote for my day and generation."

Edvard Grieg

The composer of some of the most popular works in the standard orchestral reper-toire, **Edvard Grieg** (1843–1907) was born in Bergen, the son of a salt-fish merchant – which was, considering the region's historical dependence on the product, an appropriate background for a man whose romantic compositions have come to epitomize western Norway, or at least an idealized version of it. Certainly, Grieg was quite happy to accept the connection, and as late as 1903 he commented that "I am sure my music has the taste of codfish in it." In part this was sincere, but Grieg had an overt political agenda too. Norway had not been independent since 1380, and, after centuries of Danish and Swedish rule, its population lacked political and cultural self-confidence – a situation which the Norwegian nationalists of the day, including Ibsen and Grieg, were determined to change. Such was their success that they played a key preparatory role in the build-up to the dissolution of the union with Sweden, and the creation of an independent Norway in 1905.

Musically, it was Grieg's mother, a one-time professional pianist, who egged him on, and at the tender age of 15 he was packed off to the Leipzig Conservatoire to study music, much to the delight of his mentor, **Ole Bull** (see p.217). In 1863, Grieg was on the move again, transferring to Copenhagen for another three-year study stint and ultimately returning to Norway an accomplished performer and composer in 1866. The following year he married the Norwegian soprano Nina Hagerup, helped to found a musical academy in Oslo and produced the first of ten collections of folk-based *Lyric Pieces* for piano. In 1868, Grieg completed his best-known work, the *Piano Concerto in A minor*, and, in 1869, his *25 Norwegian Folk Songs and Dances*. Thereafter, the composer's output remained mainly songs and solo piano pieces with a strong folkloric influence, even incorporating snatches of traditional songs.

During the 1870s Grieg collaborated with a number of Norwegian writers, including **Bjørnstjerne Bjørnson** and **Henrik Ibsen**, one of the results being his much acclaimed *Peer Gynt Suites*, and, in 1884, he composed the *Holberg Suite*, written to commemorate the Dano-Norwegian philosopher and playwright, Ludvig Holberg. It is these orchestral suites, along with the piano concerto, for which he is best remembered today. In 1885, now well-heeled and well-known, Grieg and his family moved into **Troldhaugen** (see above), the house they had built for them near Bergen. By that time, Grieg had established a pattern of composing during the spring and summer, and undertaking extended performance tours around Europe with his wife during the autumn and winter. This gruelling schedule continued until – and contrib-uted to – his death in Bergen in 1907.

A visit begins at the **museum**, where Grieg's life and times are exhaustively chronicled, and a short film provides yet further insights. From here, it's a brief walk to the **house** (guided tours only), a pleasant and unassuming villa built in 1885, and still pretty much as Grieg left it, with a jumble of photos, manuscripts and period furniture. Grieg didn't, in fact, compose much in the house, but preferred to walk round to a tiny **hut** he had built just along the shore. The hut has survived, but today it stands beside a modern concert hall, the **Troldsalen**, where there are **recitals** of Grieg's works from mid-June through to October. Recital tickets (160–220kr) can be bought from Bergen tourist office; free buses for these concerts leave from near the tourist office one hour before the concert begins. The bodies of Grieg and his wife – the singer Nina Hagerup – are inside a curious **tomb** blasted into a rock face overlooking the lake, and sealed with twin memorial stones; it's only a couple of minutes' walk off from the main footpath, but few people venture out to this beautiful, melancholic spot.

To get to Troldhaugen by public transport, take **bus** #20 #21 #22 #23 or #24 from the city bus station (every 10–20min; 23kr each way) and ask the driver to drop you off; from the bus stop, it's a stiff and dull twenty-minute walk along Troldhaugensveien.

Ole Bull's villa on Lysøen

Around 25km south of Bergen, the leafy, hilly little island of **Lysøen** boasts the eccentrically ornate summer **villa** of the violinist **Ole Bull** (1810–80), which, like Grieg's home, has been turned into a museum packed with biographical bits and pieces. With its onion dome and frilly trelliswork, Bull's villa was supposed to break with what the man felt to be the dour architectural tradi-tions of Norway, but whether it works or not is difficult to say – for one thing, the arabesque columns and scrollwork of the capacious music hall-cum-main room look muddled rather than inventive. Bull may have chosen to build in a foreign style, but he was a prominent member of that group of nineteenth-century artists and writers, the **Norwegian Romanticists**, who were determined to revive the country's traditions – his special contribution being the promulgation of its folk music. He toured America and Europe for several decades, his popularity as a sort of Victorian Mantovani dented neither by his fervent utopian socialism, nor by some of his eccentric remarks: asked who taught him to play the violin, he replied "The mountains of Norway". Then again, people were inclined to overlook his faults because of his engaging manner and stunning good looks – smelling salts were kept on hand during his concerts to revive swooning women; they were much in use. The hourly **guided tour** of the house (mid-May to Aug Mon–Sat noon–4pm, Sun 11am–5pm; Sept Sun noon–4pm; 30kr; Ⓦwww.kunstmuseene.no) is a little too reverential for its own good and could do with a bit more pace, but the island's wooded footpaths, laid out by Bull himself, make for some energetic walks afterwards. Maps of the island are given away free at the house, from where it's a stiff, steep but short walk over the hill to **Lysevågen**, a sheltered cove where you can go for a dip.

To reach the villa from Bergen, take the Lysefjord-ruta **bus** #566 from the main bus station (Mon–Fri 5 daily; 46kr each way; Ⓦwww.tide.no). After about fifty minutes, you'll reach Buena Kai, from where a **passenger ferry** makes the ten-minute crossing to Lysøen (hourly, on the hour, when the villa is open; last ferry back from the island at 4.30pm, 5.30pm on Sun; 50kr return). There are also cruises to the villa from Bergen on the M/S *Bruvik* (July to mid-Aug 1 daily; 5hrs; 430kr round trip), a pleasant albeit expensive way to reach the villa and see a slice of the coastline at the same time. The M/S *Bruvik* leaves from the Dreggekaien quay, on the Bryggen, metres from the *Radisson SAS Royal Hotel.*

Harald Sæverud's Siljustøl

Bergen's own Harald Sæverud (1897–1992) was a classical composer of some international renown, whose oeuvre included a hatful of symphonies and concertos. Among Norwegians he was, however, more popular for the anti-Nazi music he wrote during the German occupation of World War II and his gallows humour. After his death, his old home and studio at Siljustøl were turned into the Siljustøl Museum (mid-June to mid-Sept Sun noon–4pm; 60kr; Ⓦ www.kunstmuseene.no), where you can nose around his life and musical times. Sæverud's music is showcased in a series of summer concerts (150kr; tickets from the tourist office) and the house, a large stone structure dating from the 1930s, is surrounded by wooded parkland, crisscrossed by footpaths.

Siljustøl is 12km south of downtown Bergen, off Highway 580 – take **bus** #30 from the bus station.

Gamle Bergen

Gamle Bergen (Old Bergen), located just off the E16/39 4km north of the city centre, is an open-air complex comprising forty wooden houses representative of eighteenth- and nineteenth-century Norwegian architecture. Entry to the site as well as the adjacent park, which stretches down to the water's edge, is free and there's open access, but the **buildings** can only be visited on a **guided tour** (early May to early Sept daily 9am–5pm; 50kr; tours every hour on the hour from 10am–4pm). Immaculately maintained, the interiors give a real idea of small-town life, and although the site, with its careful cobbled paths and trim gardens, is a little too cutesy, the anecdotal tour is bound to make you grin. The enduring impression is one of social claustrophobia: everyone knew everyone else's business – grim or scandalous, mundane or bizarre. It was this enforced uniformity that Ibsen loathed and William Heinesen explored in *The Black Cauldron* – see "Books", p.433.

Gamle Bergen is served by several buses, including **bus** #9 (Mon–Sat every 30min, Sun 3 daily) from Torget.

Eating, drinking and nightlife

Bergen has a first-rate supply of **restaurants**, the pick of which focus on seafood – the city's main gastronomic asset. The pricier tourist haunts are concentrated on the Bryggen, but these should not be dismissed out of hand – several are very good indeed. Other, marginally less expensive, restaurants dot the side streets behind the Bryggen and there's another cluster on and around Engen. But many locals tend to eat more economically and informally at the city's many **café–bars** and these are dotted all over the city centre as are the city's coffee houses, where the big deal – as you might expect – is coffee in its many different guises. The busiest late-night **bars** are gathered in the vicinity of Ole Bulls plass, which is also the heart of Bergen's fairly limited club scene. As regards **opening hours**, the city's restaurants mostly open daily from noon to 10 or 11pm, though some don't open their doors until 4pm and others close one day a week; it's a very informal scene, so reservations aren't essential, though they are, of course, a good idea at the more popular places and at the weekend. Café-bars stay open much longer than restaurants, often till the early hours of the morning, whereas the coffee houses start early and close early, usually from 8 or 9am to 5, 6 or 7pm.

For **picnics**, the **fish market** on the Torget (June–Aug daily 7am–5pm; Sept–May Mon–Sat 7am–4pm) offers everything from dressed crab, prawn rolls and smoked-salmon sandwiches to pickled herring and canned caviar. There's also a covered market, the **Kjøttbasaren** (Mon–Fri 10am–5pm & Sat 9am–4pm), where half a dozen stalls sell all manner of fresh produce and freshly baked breads. The covered market is in the long and narrow, fancily gabled building at the Torget end of the Bryggen.

Cafés, coffee houses and café-bars

Café Opera Engen 24, near Ole Bulls plass. Inside a white wooden building with plant-filled windows, a fashionable crowd gathers to drink beer and good coffee. Tasty, filling snacks from as little as 60kr. DJ sounds – mostly house – at the weekend. Mon 11am–12.30am, Tues–Sat 11am–3am & Sun noon–12.30am.

Godt Brød Nedre Korskirkealmenning 12. Eco-bakery and café (in that order), with great bread and good pastries, plus coffee and made-to-order sandwiches too. Mon–Fri 7am–6pm, Sat 7am–4.30pm & Sun 10am–5pm. Also at Vestre Torggate 2 (Mon–Fri 7am–6pm, Sat 8am–5pm & Sun 10am–5pm), though here the order is reversed – it's a café first and then a bakery.

Kafe Kippers USF Verftet Kulturhuset, Georgernes Verft ⓦ www.usf.no. Part of the city's leading contemporary arts complex (see p.215) on the Nordnes peninsula, this laid-back café-bar serves inexpensive, canteen-style food, with mains about 100–120kr; occasionally rustles up great barbecues too. With its sea views and terrace, this is *the* place to come on a sunny evening when the crowds gather, especially when there's some live music or DJ sounds. Mon–Fri 11am–11.30pm, Sat & Sun noon–11pm.

🏃 **Det Lille Kaffekompaniet** Nedre Fjellsmug 2. Many locals swear by the coffee here, reckoning it to be the best north of the Alps. Great selection of teas too, plus delicious cakes and funky premises – just one medium-sized room in an old building, two flights of steps above the Fløibanen funicular terminal. Mon–Fri 10am–10pm, Sat noon–6pm, Sun noon–10pm.

Restaurants

Boha Vaskerelveien 6 ⓣ 55 31 31 60. Smart and popular restaurant kitted out in attractive modern style and offering a small(ish) but well-chosen menu. Main courses – for example chicken in

pancetta with paprika – hover around 240kr. Mon–Thurs 4–10pm, Fri 4–11pm & Sat 5–11pm.

🏃 **Bryggeloftet og Stuene** Bryggen 11 ⓣ 55 30 20 70. A tourist favourite, this restaurant may be a little old-fashioned – the decor is too folksy for its own good – but they do serve a very good range of seafood here: delicious, plainly served meals usually with a good wallop of potatoes. Elk, reindeer and other Nordic beasts too. Main courses around 220kr, much less at lunchtime. Mon–Sat 11am–11pm, Sun 1–11.30pm.

Enhjørningen Bryggen ⓣ 55 30 69 50. Smart and fairly formal second-floor restaurant in wonderful premises – all low beams, creaking floors and old oil paintings on the walls. The prices match the decor, with most main courses approaching 300kr, but the seafood is indeed outstanding. A tourist favourite. Daily 4–11pm, but closed Sun Sept–May.

Escalon Vetrlidsallmenningen 21 ⓣ 55 32 90 99. Cheery basement tapas-bar-cum-restaurant, where they serve authentic Spanish food at competitive prices – tapas cost 60–100kr. Metres from the lower terminus of the Fløibanen. Daily 3–11.30pm.

Den Lille Hanseater Kjøttbasaren. The Kjøttbasaren, the covered market where the Torget meets the Bryggen, has a clutch of food stalls and this pleasant café-restaurant, where they serve tasty, straightforward food at reasonable prices – try the meatballs at 150kr. Café: Mon–Fri 8am–5pm, Sat 9am–4pm & Sun 10am–4pm; restaurant: daily 4–10pm.

🏃 **Naboen Restaurant** Sigurdsgate 4 ⓣ 55 90 02 90. Easy-going, pleasantly presented restaurant featuring a lively, inventive menu – including Swedish specialities and, on occasion, the likes of kangaroo and ostrich. Offers a good range of fish dishes, including unusual offerings such as sea bass with blood-orange sauce; the cod is especially good. When you've finished eating, you can venture down to the basement bar. Reckon on 200–220kr for a main course. Restaurant: Mon–Sat 4pm–11pm, Sun 4pm–10pm.

4

Nama Lodin Lepps gate 2b ⊕55 32 20 10. Behind the Bryggen, this popular sushi and noodle restaurant is a modern affair, crisply decorated with pastel-painted walls and angular furniture. Their noodle dishes are a (relative) snip at 150kr and otherwise each piece of sushi will set you back around 15kr. Mon–Sat 3pm–midnight, Sun 2–11pm.

Pars Sigurdsgate 5 ⊕55 56 37 22. First-rate Persian food in pleasantly kitsch surroundings. A good range of vegetarian dishes – aubergine casserole with rice, for instance, at 110kr; meat dishes in the region of 160kr. Open Tues–Thurs 4–11pm, Fri & Sat 4pm–midnight, Sun 3–10pm.

Soho Kitchen and Lounge Håkonsgaten 27 ⊕55 90 19 60. A place of two halves. One is a chic and ultra-modern restaurant with a creative menu, including a great line in traditional Norwegian dishes – try the *klippfisk* (dried and salted fish), if it's on. Main courses average around 230kr; open Mon–Sat 5–10.30pm. The other is the **Soho Sushi**, equally chic and open later (Mon–Fri 4pm till late, Sat & Sun 2.30pm till late).

Late-night bars and clubs

Garage at the corner of Nygårdsgaten and Christies gate ⊕55 32 19 80, ⓦwww.garage.no. Very busy place catering to a mixed crowd. Two bars on the ground floor, and a live music area in the basement – mostly rock and pop. Packed at the weekend.

Landmark Rasmus Meyers Allé 5. Club/pub with an arty atmosphere and a student scene; occasional live music and DJ sounds. In the same building as the Bergen Kunsthall gallery (see p.213). Open Tues–Thurs noon–1.30am, Fri & Sat noon–3.30am & Sun noon–6pm.

Tiger Tiger Christian Michelsensgate 4 ⓦwww .bergen.tigertiger.no. Immensely popular club with house the big deal and the city's best DJ rosta. Occasional live bands too. Thurs through Sat from 10pm till the wee hours.

Festivals and the performing arts

Bergen takes justifiable pride in its **performing arts**, especially during the **Festspillene i Bergen** (Bergen International Festival; ⊕55 21 06 30, ⓦwww .festspillene.no), held over twelve days at the end of May and the beginning of June and presenting an extensive programme of music, ballet, folklore and drama. The principal venue for the festival is the **Grieghallen**, on Lars Hilles gate (⊕55 21 61 50, ⓦwww.grieghallen.no), where you can pick up programmes, tickets and information, as you can at the tourist office. The city's contemporary arts centre, the **USF Verftet Kulturhuset**, down on the Nordnes peninsula (⊕55 30 74 10, ⓦwww.usf.no), contributes to the festival by hosting **Nattjazz** (⊕55 30 72 50, ⓦwww.nattjazz.no), a prestigious and long-established international jazz festival held over the same period.

The Bergen International Festival is also the main player in the wide-ranging programme of cultural events that is coordinated by the tourist office in their **Sommer Bergen** programme (ⓦwww.visitbergen.com). Part of this summer programme is devoted to **folk music** and **folk events** – singing, dancing and costumed goings-on of all kinds. Catch folk dancing at either the Schøtstuene (June to mid-Aug; 100kr; ⊕55 55 20 06) or at **Fana Folklore**'s "country festivals" (⊕55 91 52 40, ⓦwww.folklore.no), a mix of Norwegian music, food and dancing held on a private estate outside the city. These take place at 7pm a couple of times a week from June to August and cost 300kr per person, including meal and transport; tickets for both from the tourist office. There are also **chamber music and organ recitals** at the Mariakirken in June, July and August, and **Grieg recitals** at Grieg's home, Troldhaugen, from mid-June to October.

Outside the summer season, the **USF Verftet Kulturhuset** (see p.215) puts on an ambitious programme of concerts, art-house films and contemporary plays; the **Bergen Philharmonic** performs regularly in the Grieghallen (tickets on ⊕55 21 61 50, ⓦwww.harmonien.no); and Bergen's main

theatre, Den Nationale Scene, on Engen (☎55 60 70 80, ⊕www.dns.no), offers a wide range of performances on several stages. Most productions are, of course, in Norwegian, but there are occasional appearances by English-speaking troupes.

The **tourist office** (see p.202) has all the details of up-and-coming events and performances – and they are available on their website too.

Listings

Airlines Norwegian (☎815 21 815); SAS/ Braathens (☎815 20 400); Sterling (☎815 58 810); Widerøe (☎810 01 200).

Bookshop Norli (⊕www.norli.no), right in the city centre at Torgalmenningen 7, is easily the best bookshop in town, with a good range of English titles as well as a wide selection of Norwegian hiking and road maps. Very competitive prices also. Mon–Fri 9am–8pm, Sat 9am–4pm. There's also a smaller branch across the street at Torgalmenningen 4.

Bus enquiries Timetable information on ☎177, ⊕www.tide.no.

Car rental All the major international car-rental companies have offices in town and/or at the airport, including Hertz, Nygårdsgaten 59 (☎55 96 08 20); Avis at Lars Hilles gate 20 (☎55 55 39 55); and National, at the airport (☎55 22 81 66). For the full list see under *Bilutleie* in the *Yellow Pages*.

Cinema Bergen has two large city-centre cinemas and both are on Neumannsgate, a 5min walk southwest of Ole Bulls plass. They are Bergen Kino, Konsertpaleet, with 13 screens (☎82 05 00 05, ⊕www.filmweb.no/bergenkino) and Magnus Barfot Kino with 5 screens (same details).

Consulates Netherlands, Kalfarveien 76 (☎55 56 06 20); UK, Ole Bulls Plass 1 (☎55 36 78 10).

Dentists Emergency dental care is available at Vestre Strømkai 19 (Mon–Fri 6–8.30pm, Sat & Sun 3.30–8.30pm; ☎55 56 87 17).

Emergencies Ambulance ☎113; Fire ☎110; Police ☎112.

Ferries domestic: Hurtigbåt passenger express boats depart from the Strandkaiterminalen. Tide's Flaggruten (⊕www.tide.no) service links Bergen with Haugesund and Stavanger (1–2 daily; 4hr/5hr 30min). Tide also operates Hurtigbåt services east to the Hardangerfjord (May–Sept 1 daily), whilst Fjord1 (⊕www.fjord1.no) links the city with both the Sognefjord (1–2 daily) and the Nordfjord (1–2 daily). The **Hurtigrute** coastal boat sails north from Bergen daily either at 8pm (mid-April to mid-Sept) or 10.30pm (mid-Sept to mid-April). Departures are from the Hurtigruteterminalen, on the south side of the city centre, about 900m due south of the main harbour, Vågen. Hurtigrute tickets can be purchased from local travel agents or direct from the company (☎81 03 00 00, ⊕www.hurtigruten.com).

Ferries international: Fjord Line (☎815 33 500, ⊕www.fjordline.com) operates a car ferry service from Bergen to Haugesund, Egersund and Hantsholm in Denmark. Sailings are from the Skoltegrunnskaien at the tip of the main harbour, Vågen.

Gay scene Bergen's low-key gay scene is focused on its main gay café-bar, *Café Fincken*, Nygårdsgaten 2a (☎55 32 13 16, ⊕www.fincken.no). It's open Wed–Fri & Sun 7pm–1.30am, Sat 8am–2.30am.

Hiking The DNT-affiliated Bergen Turlag, Tverrgaten 4–6 (Mon–Fri 10am–4pm, Thurs till 6pm, Sat 10am–2pm; ☎55 33 58 10, ⊕www.bergen-turlag.no), will advise on hiking trails in the region, sells hiking maps and arranges guided walks.

Internet Many of Bergen's hotels and hostels now provide free internet access for their guests and there's also free access at the main city library, Bergen Bibliotek (Mon–Thurs 10am–8pm, Fri 10am–4.30pm & Sat 10am–4pm), on Strømgaten, immediately in front of the Bergen Storsenter shopping centre.

Juhls' Silvergallery Bryggen 39 (☎55 32 47 40, ⊕www.juhls.no). Bergen outlet for these nationally famous, Sami-influenced jewellers, whose base is away in the north in Kautokeino (see p.367).

Laundry Coin-operated and service wash at Jarlens Vaskoteque, Lille Øvregate 17, near the funicular (☎55 32 55 04).

Pharmacy Vitusapotek, in Bergen Storsenter, by the bus station (Mon–Sat 8am–11pm, Sun 10am–11pm).

Post office Bergen's main post office is in the Xhibition shopping centre at the junction of Olav Kyrresgate and Småstrandgaten (Mon–Fri 9am–8pm & Sat 9am–6pm). Also a handy branch just off the Bryggen, opposite the

Cathedral at Dreggsallmenningen 20 (Mon–Fri
8.30am–5pm & Sat 10am–2pm).
Taxi Bergen Taxi ℡07000.
Trains National timetable information on
℡81 50 08 88.

Vinmonopolet There is a branch of this
state-owned liquor store in the Bergen
Storsenter, Strømgarten (Mon–Thurs 10am–6pm,
Fri 9am–6pm & Sat 9am–3pm).

The western fjords

From Bergen, it's a hop, skip and jump over the mountains to the **western fjords**. The most popular initial target is the **Hardangerfjord**, a delightful and comparatively gentle introduction to the wilder terrain that lies beyond, but similarly popular is **Voss**, inland perhaps, but still an outdoor sports centre of some renown. Voss is also a halfway house on the way to the **Sognefjord** by train, bus or car. By **train**, it's a short journey from Voss east to **Myrdal**, at the start of a spectacularly dramatic train ride down the Flåmsdal valley to **Flåm**, sitting pretty against the severe shores of the **Aurlandsfjord**, one of the Sognefjord's many subsidiaries; by **road**, you can head north direct to Flåm along the E16 or stick to Highway 13 as it careers over the mountains bound for Vik and Vangsnes. Both of these little towns are on the Sognefjord and it's this fjord, perhaps above all others, that captivates visitors, its stirring beauty amplified by its sheer size, stretching inland from the coast for some 200km. Beyond, and running parallel, lies the **Nordfjord**, smaller at 120-kilometer long and less intrinsically enticing, though its surroundings are more varied with hunks and chunks of the **Jostedalsbreen glacier** visible and visitable nearby. From here, it's another short journey to the splendid **Geirangerfjord** – narrow, sheer and rugged – as well as the forbidding **Norangsdal** valley, with the wild and beautiful **Hjørundfjord** beyond. Skip over a mountain range or two, via the dramatic **Trollstigen**, and you'll soon reach the town of **Åndalsnes**, which boasts an exquisite setting with rearing peaks behind and the tentacular Romsdalsfjord in front. At the western end of the Romsdalsfjord is the region's prettiest

Fjord ferries

Throughout this chapter there are numerous mentions of fjord **car ferries** and **Hurtigbåt passenger express boats**. The details given in parenthesis concern the frequency of operation, the duration of the crossing and the price. Hurtigbåt services are usually fairly infrequent – three a day at most – whereas many car ferries shuttle back and forth every hour or two, if not more, from around 7am in the morning until 10pm at night every day of the week. **Hurtigbåt fares** are fixed individually with prices starting at around 100kr for every hour travelled: the four-hour trip from Bergen to Balestrand, for example, costs 455kr, 625kr to Flåm. Rail-pass holders are often entitled to discounts of up to fifty percent and on some routes there are special excursion deals – always ask. **Car ferry fares**, on the other hand, are priced according to a nationally agreed sliding scale, with ten-minute crossings running at around 24kr per person and 60kr per car and driver, 29kr and 80kr respectively for a 25-minute trip.

All the region's **public transport timetables** are available on the internet, but the problem is that there's no guarantee the companies running the routes one year will be the same the next: the whole network is subject to competitive tendering. At time of writing, most car ferries and Hurtigbåt passenger boats are operated by either **Fjord 1** (ⓦ www.fjord1.no) or Tide (ⓦ www.tide.no). Fjord 1 also operates a large number of bus routes, but not in and around the Hardangerfjord, which is pretty much the preserve of Skyss (ⓦ www.skyss.no).

More secure are the positions of **Nor-way Bussekspress** (ⓦ www.nor-way.no), who handle all long-distance bus routes; NSB, which operates the trains (ⓦ www .nsb.no); and the Hurtigrute coastal boat (ⓦ www.hurtigruten.com). Any tourist office in the fjords can help with public transport timetables.

④

BERGEN AND THE WESTERN FJORDS | The western fjords

town, **Ålesund**, whose centre is liberally sprinkled with charming Art Nouveau buildings, courtesy of Kaiser Wilhelm II.

This is not a landscape to be hurried – there's little point in dashing from fjord to fjord. Stay put for a while, go for at least one hike or cycle ride, and it's then that you'll really appreciate the western fjords in all their grandeur. The sheer size is breathtaking – but then the **geological movements** that shaped the fjords were on a grand scale. During the Ice Age, around three million years ago, the whole of Scandinavia was covered in ice, the weight of which pushed the existing river valleys deeper and deeper to depths well below that of the ocean floor – the Sognefjord, for example, descends to 1250m, ten times deeper than most of the Norwegian Sea. Later, as the ice retreated, it left huge coastal basins that filled with seawater to become the fjords, which the warm Gulf Stream keeps ice-free.

Getting around the fjords

The convoluted topography of the western fjords has produced a dense and complex public-transport system that is designed to reach all the larger villages and towns at least once every weekday, whether by train, bus, car ferry, Hurtigrute coastal boat or Hurtigbåt passenger express boat. By **train**, you can reach Bergen, Finse and Flåm in the south and Åndalsnes in the north. For everything in between – the Nordfjord, Jostedalsbreen glacier and Sognefjord – you're confined to **buses** and **ferries**, although (mercifully) virtually all services connect up with each other so at least you shouldn't get stranded anywhere. General travel details for this chapter are given on p.277, and in the chapter itself we've detailed local connections where they are especially useful; this information should be used in conjunction with the **timetables** that are widely available across the region and on the internet (see box above). Bear in mind also that although there may be a transport connection to the town or village you want to go to, many Norwegian settlements are scattered and you may be in for a long walk after you've arrived – a particularly dispiriting experience if it's raining.

We've covered the region **south to north** – from the Hardangerfjord to Sognefjord, Nordfjord, Geirangerfjord, Åndalsnes and Ålesund. There are certain obvious connections – from Bergen to Flåm, and from Geiranger over the Trollstigen to Åndalsnes, for example – but otherwise routes are really a matter of personal choice; the text lists the options. Note also that the **E39**, which cuts an ingenious north–south route across the western edge of the fjord region, is potentially useful as a quick way of getting between Bergen and Ålesund, as is the Hurtigrute coastal boat.

Of all the myriad excursions organized by fjordland tour operators, the most trumpeted is the whistle-stop **Norway in a Nutshell**, which can be booked at any tourist office in the region or online at Ⓦ www.norwaynutshell.com. The full trip takes seven hours, and is an exhausting but exhilarating romp that gives you a taste of the fjords in one day. The tour starts in Bergen with a train ride to Voss and Myrdal, where you change for the dramatic Flåmsbana branch line down to Flåm. Here, a two-hour cruise heads along the Aurlandsfjord and then the Nærøyfjord to Gudvangen, where you get a bus back to Voss, and the train again to Bergen. You can pick up the tour in Voss for an affordable 595kr: the full excursion from Bergen costs 895kr.

Where to stay in the fjords

Bergen advertises itself as the "Gateway to the Fjords" and the city's tourist office does indeed carry the details of a barrage of fjordland excursions – most famously the much-touted "Norway in a Nutshell" tour (see above). These are, however, expensive options and you'll save money, and keep more control, if you organize your own itinerary. Also, as Bergen is in fact on the western edge of the fjords, the bulk of the day-trips from that city involve more travelling than is really comfortable. This is doubly true as the main road east from Bergen – the **E16** – is prone to congestion and possesses over twenty tunnels, many of which are horribly noxious. Avoid the E16 east of Bergen if you can, and certainly aim to branch off onto the relatively tunnel-free and much more scenic **Highway 7** the first chance you get – about 30km east of the city. For all these reasons, the small towns that dot the fjords are far better as bases than Bergen, especially as distances once you're actually amidst the fjords are – at least by Norwegian standards – quite modest. As for specific targets, **Ulvik** and **Lofthus** are the most appealing bases in the Hardangerfjord; Sognefjord has **Mundal** and **Balestrand**; and further north the cream of the crop are **Loen** and **Ålesund**.

At the height of the season, say late June to August, vacant rooms can get very thin on the ground and prices start to climb. Therefore, both for peace of mind and to save money, you're far better making reservations either direct or, even better, through Fjord Tours, the company which operates the **Fjord Pass** scheme (Ⓦ www.fjord-pass.com; see p.43). At other times of the year, you can pretty much come and go as you please, but note that many hotels and nearly all hostels close for winter – from October, sometimes November, to April or more likely May.

The Hardangerfjord

To the east of Bergen, the most inviting target is the hundred-kilometre-long **Hardangerfjord** (Ⓦ www.hardangerfjord.com), whose wide waters are overlooked by a rough, craggy shoreline and a scattering of tiny settlements. At its eastern end the Hardangerfjord divides into several lesser fjords, and it's here you'll find the district's most appealing villages, **Utne**, **Lofthus** and **Ulvik**, each of which has an attractive fjordside setting and at least one an especially good place to stay. To the east of these tributary fjords rises the **Hardangervidda**, a mountain plateau of remarkable, lunar-like beauty and a favourite with Norwegian hikers. The plateau can be reached from almost any direction, but one popular starting–point for the extremely fit is **Kinsarvik**, with this approach involving a stiff day-long climb up from the fjord.

▲ Hardangerfjord

Of the two principal **car ferries** negotiating the Hardangerfjord, one shuttles between Kvanndal, Utne and Kinsarvik, the other links Brimnes with Bruravik, though this is scheduled to be replaced by a bridge in the near future. There are no trains in the Hardangerfjord area, but **buses** are fairly frequent, allowing you to savour the scenery and get to the three key villages without too much difficulty, except possibly on Sundays when services are reduced. The buses are operated by Skyss (ⓦwww.skyss.no), the ferries by **Tide** (ⓦwww.tide.no).

Finally, if you're planning to travel south along Highway 13 from Kinsarvik bound for either Oslo or Stavanger – or the other way round – be sure your itinerary does not involve an overnight stay in the eminently missable industrial town of **Odda**, at the head of the Storfjord. Note also that if you are going to, or coming from, Oslo along the E134, you'll climb onto, or come down from, the Hardangervidda plateau via Haukelifjell, one of the region's bleakest and windiest approaches.

East from Bergen to Norheimsund and the Kvanndal ferry

Heading east from Bergen en route to the Hardangerfjord by bus or car, the **E16** begins by travelling through a string of polluted tunnels, an unpleasant thirty-kilometre journey before you can fork off along **Highway 7**. By contrast, this is a rattlingly good trip, with the road twisting over the mountains and down the valleys, gliding past thundering waterfalls and around tight bends before racing down to **NORHEIMSUND** on the Hardangerfjord. A small-time port and furniture-making town, Norheimsund makes a gallant effort to bill itself as a gateway to the fjords, but in truth it's a modest, middling sort of place and there's precious little reason to hang around: like many fjord settlements, it's the journey to get there that is the main attraction. From June to August, Norheimsund does, however, have its uses as a minor transport hub, principally for its once-daily **Hurtigbåt passenger express boat** service to Utne, Lofthus, Kinsarvik, Ulvik and Eidfjord, operated by Tide.

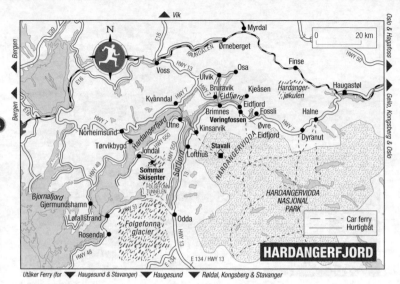

Utåker Ferry (for ▼ Haugesund & Stavanger) ▼ Haugesund ▼ Røldal, Kongsberg & Stavanger

Leaving Norheimsund by road, Highway 7 sticks to the rugged shoreline as it travels east to the ferry dock at **Kvanndal**, another pleasant journey with every turning bringing fresh mountain and fjord views as the Hardangerfjord begins to split into its various subsidiaries. There's a choice of routes from Kvanndal: you can either press on down the northern shore of the Hardangerfjord towards Ulvik and Voss (see p.231 & p.233), or take the Tide **ferry** over from Kvanndal to Utne and/or Kinsarvik (1 or 2 hourly; 20min/50min). Kvanndal to Utne costs 27kr per passenger, 71kr car and driver, 36kr and 107kr respectively to Kinsarvik. There are **buses** from Bergen to Norheimsund every couple of hours and most continue on to the Kvanndal ferry; the whole journey takes two hours and twenty minutes, ninety minutes to Norheimsund.

Utne

The tiny hamlet of **UTNE**, the Kvanndal ferry's midway point, occupies a splendid location, its huddle of houses and perky country church overlooking the fjord from the tip of the rearing peninsula that divides the Hardangerfjord from the Sørfjord. Utne was long dependent on the orchards that still trail along the Sørfjord's sheltered slopes, its inhabitants making enough of a living to support themselves in some comfort, especially when supplemented by fishing and furniture-making: the brightly painted furniture that once hailed from the district made a popular export. Classic examples of this distinctive furniture are on display in the public rooms of the *Utne Hotel* (℡53 66 64 00, Ⓦ www.utnehotel.no; ❹, en suite ❻), whose 26 rooms, the majority of which are en suite, mostly occupy a sympathetically updated, clapboard hotel dating from 1722, though nine are in the neighbouring annexe. Straight opposite the ferry dock, the hotel is a very relaxing spot, though the walls of the rooms in the main house, which are reached by an unusual spiral staircase, are paper-thin – hard luck if you are billeted next to a champion snorer. The hotel restaurant is first-rate, focusing on local, seasonal ingredients, all served amid the ancient panelling of the dining room; their three-course set dinner costs 400kr.

Hardanger Folkemuseum

Utne's heritage is celebrated at the **Hardanger Folkemuseum** (daily: May–June 10am–4pm, July–Aug 10am–5pm; Sept–April Mon–Fri 10am–3pm; 50kr; ⓦ www.hardanger.museum.no), a five-minute walk north along the fjord from the hotel. One of the largest and best-appointed folk museums in the region, its collection features a wide range of displays on various aspects of traditional Hardanger life, from fishing and farming through to fruit-growing and trade. A particular highlight is the large display of local **folk costume** – the women's headdresses hereabouts were among the most elaborate in Norway and a popular subject for the romantic painters of the nineteenth century, notably Adolph Tidemand and Hans Frederik Gude. There are also some fine examples of the Hardanger fiddle, an instrument much loved by both Ole Bull (see p.217) and Grieg (see p.216). Outside, an assortment of old wooden buildings – farmhouses, cottages, store houses and so forth – rambles over the steep and rocky hillside behind the museum. The logic of this open-air section is hard to fathom, but in summertime, when there are demonstrations of farming and craft skills, things make much more sense. One of the more intriguing buildings is a sixteenth-century dwelling, known as an **Ulgenesløa**, whose dark and dingy interior is encased by roughly hewn log walls. When the museum is closed, you can still wander round the open-air section to your heart's content.

Southwest of Utne: Jondal and the Folgefonna glacier

South of Utne, the peninsula separating the Hardangerfjord from the Sørfjord widens and heightens, its upper reaches dominated by the sprawling **Folgefonna** glacier. Conditions on the glacier are well-nigh perfect for **summer skiing**, both Alpine and Telemark, as well as snowboarding, and there's even a purpose-built sledge run. The place to head for is the Folgefonn Sommar Skisenter (early May to late Sept daily 9am–4pm; ☎53 66 80 28, ⓦwww .folgefonn.no), on the edge of the glacier at 1200m above sea level, where there is ski rental, a ski school, a café and a ski lift to the slopes. From here also, between May and late August, Folgefonni Breførarlag (☎95 11 77 92, ⓦwww .folgefonni-breforarlag.no) runs a programme of guided glacier hikes and climbs with the cheaper/shorter excursions beginning at about 350kr per person including equipment.

To get to the ski centre from Utne, head southwest along Highway 550 as far as tiny **Jondal**, 36km away, and then turn east up the signposted, mountain toll-road for the bumpy nineteen-kilometre ride up to the glacier. In high summer, it's also possible to do the trip from Jondal by Skyss **bus** (mid-June to mid-Aug 1 daily each way; 45min; ⓦwww.skyss.no), which will give you five hours up there. Buses from Utne to Jondal connect with the glacier bus – check times at your hotel or the nearest tourist office. Jondal has its own tourist office (late June & early Aug daily 9.30am–4pm; July daily 9.30am–5.30pm; ☎53 66 85 31, ⓦwww.hardangerfjord.com) and a Tide **car ferry** connection over the Hardangerfjord to Tørvikbygd (hourly; 20min; passengers 27kr, car & driver 71kr), 13km south of Norheimsund (see p.225).

South of Utne: Odda and the Baroniet Rosendal

South of Utne, Highway 550 runs along the shore of the Sørfjord bound for the unprepossessing industrial town of **ODDA**, a journey of 45km. Just before Odda, the highway passes the entrance to the eleven-kilometre-long **Folgefonntun-nelen** (60kr toll), which bores west beneath the Folgefonna glacier as it crosses the peninsula. When you emerge from the tunnel, it's 35km or so south along the fjord to **ROSENDAL**, the location of one of Norway's few country houses – the Norwegian landowning aristocracy has always been too thin on the ground to build more than a hatful. Dating from the seventeenth century, the **house and estate of the Baroniet Rosendal** (guided tours: early May to late June & mid-Aug to early Sept daily 11am–3pm; late June to mid-Aug daily 10am–5pm; 100kr, 75kr in shoulder seasons; Ⓦ www.baroniet.no) were in private hands until 1927, when the last owner bequeathed the whole lot to the University of Oslo. By comparison with country houses in other European countries, the house is really quite modest, but it does hold a string of period rooms, amongst which the Baroque library and the Neoclassical "yellow room" are the most diverting. Afterwards, you can stroll out into the surrounding gardens and **park**, with its ponds, bridges and views out across the fjord. There's **B&B accommodation** (Ⓣ53 48 29 99, Ⓦ www.baroniet.no; ❸; early May to Aug) here too, in the estate's old farmhouses, a couple of which have been pleasantly modernized to hold two dozen guest rooms; it's a popular spot, so reserve ahead.

From Rosendal, you can continue south by road and ferry to Haugesund and Stavanger or double back a handful of kilometres to **Løfallstrand** for the **Tide car ferry** (every 30min–1hr; 25min; passengers 29kr, car & driver 80kr) ride over the Sidafjord to **Gjermundshamn** and Highway 49 for Norheim-sund or Bergen.

Kinsarvik

From Utne, the Tide car ferry (every 1–1hr 30min; 25min; passengers 29kr, car & driver 80kr; Ⓦ www.tide.no) bobs over the mouth of the Sørfjord to **KINSARVIK**, a tiny settlement, which was once an important Viking market-place. It was just the sort of spot the Vikings liked. The foreshore was gentle, making it easy for them to ground their ships, and it was buried deep in the fjords, making it difficult for any enemy to approach unseen. Nothing now remains from that period, but the sturdy, whitewashed stone **church** (late May Tues–Fri 10am–3pm; June to mid-Aug daily 10am–7pm; free) lurking on the foreshore dates back as far as the middle of the twelfth century and constructed with defence in mind: throughout the Middle Ages, the sails and assorted tackle of the village's *leidangskipet* (defence ship) were stored in its ample loft. Twelfth-century Norwegians knew little of building in stone and the church would seem to have been the work of British masons, but it was clumsily renovated in the 1880s. Today the most interesting hints of its medieval past are the hooped windows and a series of faint, chalk wall paintings.

Kinsarvik lies at the mouth of the forested **Husedalen valley**, with its four crashing waterfalls. The valley makes an enjoyable hike with most visitors choosing to drive up to the first cascade before proceeding on foot – the road beyond the first waterfall is really too difficult for ordinary vehicles. The valley is also used as an access route up to the Hardangervidda plateau. From Kinsarvik, it takes six hours to reach the nearest DNT hut, the self-service **Stavali** (at 1024m), but the route up to the plateau is very steep and in rainy conditions very slippery. Hiking maps can be purchased and hiking advice is dispensed at Kinsarvik **tourist office** near the ferry jetty (late June to late Aug daily 9am–7pm; late Aug Mon–Fri 9am–5pm; Sept to late June Mon–Fri 9am–4pm; Ⓣ53 66 31 12, Ⓦ www.visitullensvang.no). For more on the **Hardangervidda** and its various access routes, see pp.230–231.

As for a place **to stay**, the obvious choice is the *Best Western Kinsarvik Fjord Hotel* (☎53 66 74 00, ⓦwww.kinsarvikfjordhotel.no; ❻, sp/r ❺), in a well-kept and reasonably attractive modern block down by the fjord, metres from the ferry dock. Skyss **buses** link Kinsarvik with Eidfjord, Lofthus and Odda (2–4 daily).

Lofthus

In a fine location, **LOFTHUS** strings along the Sørfjord, beginning about 10km to the south of Kinsarvik, with the Folgefonna glacier glinting in the distance. The first part of the village – around the *Hotel Ullensvang* – is somewhat routine, but the second is an idyllic place of narrow lanes and mellow stone walls, where a scattering of timber houses sits among the orchards, pinky-white with blossom in the springtime. It's the overall impression that counts, though the **Ullensvang church** (May Tues–Fri 10am–3pm; June–Aug daily 10am–7pm; free), which dates from 1250 and is named after the district not the village, is a good-looking stone structure with immensely thick walls; below it is a pebble beach and a miniature jetty, where the brave propel themselves into the waters of the fjord. A stream gushes through the village, tumbling down the steep escarpment behind Lofthus to bubble past the delightful *Ullensvang Gjesteheim* (☎53 66 12 36, ⓦwww.ullensvang-gjesteheim.no; ❸), a huddle of antique wooden buildings with thirteen cosy and unassuming rooms. There are other places to stay too – the plush *Hotel Ullensvang* (☎53 67 00 00, ⓦwww .hotel-ullensvang.no; ❼, sp/r ❻), a sprawling affair plonked on the water's edge in a building that mixes modern and traditional Norwegian design in a (fairly) successful manner; and an HI hostel, *Hardanger Vandrerhjem* (☎53 67 14 00, ⓦwww.vandrerhjem.no; June to early Aug), about 500 metres up the slope from the fjord in a residential rural high school, a Folkehøgskule. The hostel has a café, self-catering facilities and a laundry; dorm beds cost 235kr, double rooms ❶. Both the *Ullensvang Gjesteheim* and the *Hotel Ullensvang* serve evening meals.

As at Kinsarvik, a steep **hiking trail** leads up from Lofthus to the Hardangervidda plateau; part of the trail includes the **Munketreppene**, stone steps laid by the monks who farmed this remote spot in medieval times. It takes about four hours to reach the plateau at Nosi (959m), and about seven or eight hours to reach the Stavali self-service DNT hut. For more on access to the **Hardangervidda**, see pp.230–231.

Skyss (ⓦwww.skyss.no) operates a **bus** service between Kinsarvik and Lofthus (2–4 daily), part of a longer route from Eidfjord to Odda.

Eidfjord

Heading north from Kinsarvik, **Highway 13** fidgets its way along the coastline to reach, after 19km, **Brimnes**, from where a Tide **car ferry** (1–2 hourly; passengers 28kr, car & driver 75kr 10min; ⓦwww.tide.no) shuttles over the fjord to **Bruravik**, for Ulvik (see p.231) and Voss (see p.233), though plans are afoot to span the water with a bridge. Beyond Brimnes, Highway 13 becomes **Highway 7**, whose first significant port of call, after another 11km or so, is the large village of **EIDFJORD**, which straggles over a neck of land facing the fjord with a lake, the Eidfjordvatnet, just inland. There's been a settlement here since prehistoric times and for centuries the village prospered as a trading centre at the end of one of the main routes over the Hardangervidda – though this was very much a two-edged sword: traditionally, the villagers were obliged to build and repair foot and cart tracks up to the plateau, forced labour for which they were not paid.

Nowadays, Eidfjord and its environs rustle up a trio of attractions, beginning with the **Kjeåsen mountain farm**, a lonely complex of old farm buildings, from where you'll be rewarded with spectacular views over the tapering Simadalsfjord. To get there, head northeast from Eidfjord for 14km along the narrow byroad that hugs the Simadalsfjord to reach the tortuous, five-kilometre lane that wriggles up to the farm – it's signed. The lane is much too narrow to take two-way traffic and half the road goes through a tunnel without any lights, but drivers can relax (a little): you can only drive up to the farm on the hour and descend on the half-hour. Secondly, the **Hardangervidda Natursenter** (daily: April–May & Sept–Oct 10am–6pm; June–Aug 9am–8pm; 80kr), in a glassy modern structure 7km southeast of Eidfjord along Highway 7 in **ØVRE EIDFJORD**, tells you all you ever wanted to know about the Hardangervidda, including its natural history and geology. Staff also dispense hiking advice and sell hiking maps; one popular local walk is the twenty-minute haul up from Eidfjord up to the Hæreid plateau, which has the region's greatest concentration of Viking burial mounds.

Practicalities

Skyss buses (ⓦ www.skyss.no) from Odda and Kinsarvik (2–4 daily) pull in beside Highway 7 just to the east of the **tourist office** (May Mon–Fri 9am–6pm; early June & late Aug Mon–Sat 9am–6pm; mid-June to mid-Aug Mon–Fri 9am–7pm, Sat & Sun 10am–6pm; Sept–April Mon–Fri 9am–4pm; ⓣ 53 67 34 00, ⓦ www.visiteidfjord.no). There are two recommendable **hotels** in Eidfjord, the grander of which is the fjordside *Quality Hotel & Resort Vøringfoss* (ⓣ 53 67 41 00, ⓦ www.choicehotels.no; ❺), a large, modern complex built in a (relatively) pleasing version of traditional style with mini-towers and decorative gable ends. The second is the *Eidfjord Fjell og Fjord Hotel* (ⓣ 53 66 52 64, ⓦ www.effh.no; ❺), a crisply designed, medium-sized modern place with attractively furnished rooms that perches on a knoll high above the fjord. The *Vøringfoss* has the better restaurant. If these hotels don't suit, the tourist office has the details of a handful of private rooms (❷–❸).

The Vøringfossen waterfalls

Heading southeast from Eidfjord, Highway 7 clips past the **Hardangervidda Natursenter** (see above) before starting its long climb up to the Hardangervidda plateau. After 20km, the road passes the mighty, 145m-high **Vøringfossen waterfalls**, which are best viewed from the hamlet/hotel of **FOSSLI**, perched on a cliff-top, about 1km off Highway 7. Inevitably, the main pull here at the hotel (ⓣ 53 66 57 77, ⓦ www.fossli-hotel.com; mid-May to mid-Sept; ❹) is the view of the waterfall, but the place also chips in with 21 plain but perfectly adequate bedrooms and a better-than-average restaurant.

Beyond the waterfalls, Highway 7 creeps its way up through the mountains to finally emerge on the Hardangervidda plateau.

The Hardangervidda plateau

The **Hardangervidda** is Europe's largest mountain plateau, occupying a one-hundred-kilometre-square slab of land east of the Hardangerfjord and broadly south of the Oslo–Bergen railway. The plateau is characterized by rolling fells and wide stretches of level ground, its rocky surfaces strewn with pools, ponds and rivers. The whole plateau is above the tree line, and in places has an almost lunar-like appearance, although even within this elemental landscape there are variations. To the north, in the vicinity of Finse, there are mountains and a glacier, the **Hardangerjøkulen**, while the west is wetter – and the flora somewhat richer – than the barer moorland to the east. The lichen that covers the rocks is savoured by herds of reindeer, who leave their winter grazing lands on the east side of the plateau in the spring, chewing their way west to their breeding grounds before returning east again after the autumn rutting season.

Stone Age hunters once followed the reindeer on their migrations, and traces of their presence – arrowheads, pit-traps, etc – have been discovered over much of the plateau. Later, the Hardangervidda became one of the main crossing points between east and west Norway, with horse traders, cattle drivers and Danish dignitaries all cutting across the plateau along cairned paths, many of which are still in use as part of a dense network of trails and tourist huts that has been developed by several DNT affiliates. Roughly one third of the plateau has been incorporated within the **Hardangervidda Nasjonalpark**, but much of the rest is protected too, so hikers won't notice a great deal of difference between the park and its immediate surroundings. The entire plateau is also popular for winter cross-country, hut-to-hut skiing. Many hikers and skiers are content with a day on the Hardangervidda, but some find the wide-skied, lichen-dappled scenery particularly enchanting and travel from one end of the plateau to the other, a seven- or eight-day expedition.

Approaches to the Hardangervidda

Access to the Hardangervidda can be gained from the **Oslo–Bergen train line** which calls at Finse (see p.235), from where hikers and skiers head off across the plateau in all directions. Finse is not, however, reachable by road, so motorists (and bus travellers) mostly use **Highway 7**, which runs across the plateau between Eidfjord (see p.229) and Geilo (see p.188). There's precious little in the way of human habitation on this lonely hundred-kilometre stretch of road, but you can pick up the plateau's hiking trails easily enough at several points. **Dyranut** and **Halne** are two such places, respectively 39km and 47km from Eidfjord. Some hikers prefer to walk eastwards onto the Hardangervidda from Kinsarvik and Lofthus (see p.229), an arduous day-long trek up from the fjord, or from Rjukan (see p.193), to the southeast of the plateau, where a cable car eases the uphill part of the trek. Local tourist offices all carry hiking maps and will advise about hiking routes as will the **Hardangervidda Natursenter** (see p.230). If all that sounds too arduous, there are also **boat trips** (late June to early Sept; 1–3 daily; 1hr) from Halne along the Halnefjord, which cuts across the Hardangervidda for around 15km. For times of departure, consult Eidfjord tourist office (see p.230).

Ulvik

Tucked away in a snug corner of the Hardangerfjord, the pocket-sized village of **ULVIK** strings prettily along the shoreline with orchards dusting the green, forested hills behind. This is one of the gentlest of fjord landscapes, with little of the harsh beauty of many of its neighbours, and although there's nothing specific to see, Ulvik does have one or two claims to fame: this is the place where potatoes were first grown in Norway (in 1765) and it took a pummelling during World War II. The Germans invaded Norway on April 9, 1940, and during the next couple of weeks, before the Norwegians threw in the towel, there were several naval skirmishes in the Hardangerfjord. In one of them, the so-called **Battle of Ulvik**, the German navy shelled the centre of the village to smithereens after being shot at from the shore. Also during the battle, the Norwegian navy scuttled the *Afrika*, a German merchant ship they had previously captured; the wreck remains in Ulvik harbour today. They also scuttled a neutral ship, the *San Miguel*, which had taken refuge here, thereby – in a true *Whisky Galore* moment – releasing the ship's cargo, thousands of oranges, which bobbed around the harbour, much to the amazement of the locals, for whom fresh fruit was a real treat.

Nowadays, Ulvik is an excellent place to unwind, and the favourite pastime is walking. **Hiking trails** lattice the rough uplands behind Ulvik and also explore the surrounding coastline. The tourist office (see below) produces a detailed guide to the *Heritage Trails of Ulvik* (15kr) and a series of excellent A4 (10kr) sheets describing particular mapped walks that can be done inside a day. One of the most enjoyable is the three-hour round-trip up into the hills to the east of Ulvik, which takes in a set of Iron Age burial mounds and the **Ljonakleiv crofter's farm**, an old farmstead from where there are splendid views over the fjord. A second option is to walk or drive along the nine-kilometre country road that leads east from Ulvik, across the adjacent promontory and up along the Osafjord to the smattering of farmsteads that constitutes **OSA**. Here, in the forested hills about 1km above the fjord, is one of the region's more unusual sights, the timber-and-brick **Stream Nest sculpture** (mid-May to Aug daily 10am–4pm; 40kr), resembling a gigantic bird's nest and perched above a green river valley framed by stern hills. The sculpture was constructed by Takamasa Kuniyasu for the 1994 Lillehammer Winter Olympics, and moved here afterwards. As you near the site of the sculpture, the road passes the **Hjadlane Gallery for Samtidskunst** (Gallery of Contemporary Art; May–Aug daily 11am–6pm; free), which has a programme of temporary exhibitions.

Practicalities

Ulvik is off the main bus routes, but there is a **Skyss bus** service here from Voss (2–6 daily; 1hr; @www.skyss.no); this is routed via Bruravik to pick up passengers who've arrived on the Brimnes–Bruravik ferry (see p.229). From May to September, there are also **Tide Hurtigbåt passenger express boat** services to Ulvik from Norheimsund via Utne, Lofthus and Kinsarvik (1 daily; 2hr 15min; @www.tide.no); the same service continues onto Eidfjord. Buses pull into the centre of the village, metres from the jetty and the waterfront **tourist office** (mid-May to mid-Sept Mon–Sat 8.30am–5pm & Sun 1–5pm; Jan to mid-May Mon–Fri 8.30am–1.30pm; @56 52 63 60, @www.visitulvik.com). Staff here issue all the usual information, including bus and ferry timetables, sell detailed hiking maps and rent out bikes.

Among the **hotels**, the big deal hereabouts is the *Brakanes* (@56 52 61 05, @www.brakanes-hotel.no; @), a large, modern place hogging the waterfront in the centre of the village. The *Brakanes* has all the facilities you would expect of a big hotel, including a fitness centre, and is popular as a conference centre. If that sounds a bit too predictable, the *Rica Ulvik Hotel* (@56 52 62 00, @www.rica.no; @), a couple of minutes' walk east along the waterfront, is a good deal less overpowering. Again, it's the setting rather than the architecture that appeals, with the fjord stretching out in front of the hotel, overlooked by the balconies of the fifty-odd modern bedrooms. Different again is the fjordside ✷ *Ulvik Fjord Hotel* (@56 52 61 70, @www.ulvikfjordpensjonat.no; late May to Sept; @), a well-maintained and very appealing **hotel** situated at the beginning of the village, an easy ten-minute walk west from the centre along the waterfront. It has nineteen guest rooms, some in the main house, an attractive wooden, two-storey building dating from the 1940s, and some in the modern annexe, where most of the rooms have their own outside area beside a babbling brook. It's not a luxury res – and makes no claim to be so – but it is very comfortable and the family who own and run the place are the friendliest of hosts. Breakfasts are first-rate and home-made evening meals, which come recommended by several of our readers, are available by prior arrangement; their three-course set-menu dinner costs 250kr.

Voss

Travelling east from Bergen on the E16 or by train, you first have to clear some markedly polluted tunnels, but thereafter it's an enjoyable jaunt over the hills and round the mountains to **VOSS**, which, at 100km from Bergen, has an attractive lakeside setting and a splendid thirteenth-century church. Voss is, however, best known as an adventure-sports and winter-skiing centre, with everything from skiing and snowboarding through to summertime rafting, kayaking and horseriding. Consequently, unless you're here for a sweat, your best bet is to have a quick look round and then move on, though there is a caveat: Voss is the ideal base for a **day-trip by train** east up the Raundal valley, an especially scenic part of the Bergen–Oslo rail line. The most popular target on this stretch of the line is the Myrdal junction, where you change for the dramatic train ride down to Flåm (see box, p.235).

Arrival, information and accommodation

Buses stop outside the **train station** at the western end of the town centre. From here, it's a five-minute walk to the **tourist office** (June–Aug Mon–Fri 8am–7pm, Sat 9am–7pm & Sun 2–7pm; Sept–May Mon–Fri 8.30am–3.30pm; ☏56 52 08 00, ⓦwww.visitvoss.no) on the main street, Uttrågata – veer right round the Vangskyrkja church and it's on the right.

Voss sports

Every **summer**, hundreds of Norwegians make a beeline for Voss on account of its **watersports**. The rivers near the town offer a wide range of conditions, suitable for everything from a quiet paddle to a finger-chewing whitewater ride. There are several operators, but **Voss Rafting Senter** (☏56 51 05 25, ⓦwww.vossrafting.no) sets the benchmark. Their four-hour whitewater-rafting trips venture out onto two rivers – the Stranda and Raun; the price, including a swimming test and a snack, is 820kr. Other options with the same operator and at about the same price include river-boarding (5hr), sports rafting, which is akin to canoeing (4hr), and whitewater rappelling (4hr). In addition, Nordic Ventures (☏56 51 00 17, ⓦwww.nordicventures.com) offers all sorts of **kayaking** excursions as well as **tandem paragliding and parasailing**; and Voss Fjellhest (☏56 51 91 66, ⓦwww.vossfjellhest.no) specializes in mountain **horseback riding**.

In **winter**, **skiing** in Voss starts in mid-December and continues until mid-April – nothing fancy, but good for an enjoyable few days. From behind and above the train station, a **cable car** – the Hangursbanen – climbs 700m to give access to several short runs as well as the first of three chair lifts that take you up another 300m. In January and February some trails are floodlit. There's a choice of red, green and black downhill ski routes, and among the greens is a long and fairly gentle route through the hills above town; cross-country skiing here is limited to 20km of tracks. Full **equipment** for both downhill and cross-country skiing can be rented by the day from Voss Ski, at the upper Hangursbanen station (ⓦwww.vossresort.no). They also offer lessons in skiing and snowboarding techniques.

They have oodles of information on hiking, rafting, skiing and local touring, the bones of which are detailed in the free *Voss Guide*; they also operate an accommodation booking service.

To cater for all the visiting sportsfolk, Voss has lots of inexpensive **accommodation**, from guesthouses through to camping. The best budget bet is the excellent HI **hostel** (T 56 51 20 17, W www.vandrerhjem.no; Jan–Sept), which has both double rooms (❷) and dorm beds (260kr), and is in a modern lodge overlooking the water about 700m from the train station. To get there, turn right outside the station building and head along the lake away from the town centre – a ten-minute walk. The hostel serves good breakfasts and inexpensive evening meals – though these need to be pre-booked – and has self-catering facilities; it also has its own laundry and internet access, and rents out bikes and canoes. Reservation is strongly recommended. A second inexpensive option is the rudimentary *Voss Camping* (T 56 51 15 97, W www.vosscamping.no; 500–700kr for 5 persons), a short walk south of the Vangskyrkja church: turn left from the train station, take the right fork at the church and then turn right again, along the Prestegardsalléen footpath. It's open all year and has a few cabins (❷), an outside pool and washing machines. As for the town's **hotels**, one or two barely pass muster and the pick by a long chalk is *Fleischer's* (T 56 52 05 00, W www.fleischers.no; ❻, sp/r ❺), next door to the train station. Dating from the 1880s, the hotel's high-gabled and towered facade overlooks the lake and consists of the original building and a modern wing built in the same style. Parts of the hotel – and many of the bedrooms – have the whiff of real luxury, but others are more mundane. The **restaurant** serves the best food in town and there's a terrace bar as well. Their all-inclusive food-and-lodging deals offer substantial savings on the normal rate.

The Town

With the lake on one side and the River Vosso on the other, **Voss** has long been a trading centre of some importance, though you'd barely guess this from the

---

Moving on from Voss

When it comes to **moving on from Voss**, there are three obvious routes to choose from – one by train and two by road. **By train**, Voss is on the main Bergen–Oslo rail line and from here it's a short haul east up the Raundal valley (3–4 trains daily; W www.nsb.no) to the **Myrdal junction**, where you change for the world-famous train ride down to Flåm on the **Flåmsbana** (see p.235). You can, however, choose instead to disembark two stops further down the line at **Finse**, an isolated outpost on the Hardangervidda plateau (see p.235), which offers a bevy of hiking and skiing routes amid stirring scenery. Incidentally, drivers should note that Myrdal and Finse cannot be reached by car.

Alternatively, it's a quick and easy 65km north from Voss along the **E16** to the village of **Flåm**, a pleasant and much-visited little place amid magnificent fjordland scenery. The E16 is the main road between Bergen and Oslo and you can, as a third possibility, dodge most of the traffic by forking off the E16 at **Vinje**, some 20km north of Voss, to take scenic **Highway 13** down the dales and over the mountains to **Vik**, where there's a fine stave church, and **Vangsnes**, on the Sognefjord. There are **buses** along both routes: **Nor-Way Bussekspress buses** (2–6 daily; W www.nor-way.no) link Voss with Flåm and points east, and a local bus runs from Voss to Vangsnes (1–2 daily except Sat; 1hr 30min/1hr 40min), connecting with the ferry over the Sognefjord to Hella and Dragsvik for Balestrand (see p.243).

4

The Flåm railway – the Flåmsbana

Lonely **Myrdal**, just forty minutes by train from Voss, is the start of one of Europe's most celebrated branch rail lines, the **Flåmsbana** (ⓦ www.flaamsbana.no), a twenty-kilometre, nine-hundred-metre plummet down the Flåmsdal valley to **Flåm** – a fifty-minute train ride that should not be missed if at all possible; it is part of the "Norway in a Nutshell" route (see box, p.224). The track, which took four years to lay in the 1920s, spirals down the mountainside, passing through hand-dug tunnels and, at one point, actually travelling through a hairpin tunnel to drop nearly 300m. The gradient of the line is one of the steepest anywhere in the world, and as the tiny train squeals its way down the mountain, past cascading waterfalls, it's reassuring to know that it has five separate sets of brakes, each capable of bringing it to a stop. The service runs all year round, a local lifeline during the deep winter months. There are ten departures daily from mid-June to late September, between four and eight the rest of the year; Myrdal–Flåm fares are 210kr single, 310kr return.

In the past, the athletic have risen to the challenge and undertaken the five-hour **walk** from the railway junction at Myrdal down the old road into the valley, instead of taking the train, but much the better option is to disembark about halfway down and walk in from there. **Berekvam** station, at an altitude of 345m, will do very nicely, leaving an enthralling two- to three-hour hike through changing mountain scenery down to Flåm. **Cycling** down the valley road is also perfectly feasible, though it's much too steep to be relaxing.

modern appearance of the town centre. In 1023, King Olav visited to check that the population had all converted to Christianity, and stuck a big stone cross here to ram home his point. Two centuries later another king, Magnus Lagabøte, built a church in Voss to act as the religious focal point for the whole region. The church, the **Vangskyrkja** (June–Aug Mon–Sat 10am–4pm & Sun 1–4pm; 15kr), still stands, its eccentric octagonal spire rising above stone walls which are up to two-metres-thick. The interior is splendid, a surprisingly flamboyant and colourful affair with a Baroque reredos and a folksy rood screen showing a crucified Jesus attended by two cherubs. The ceiling is even more unusual, its timbers painted in 1696 with a cotton-wool cloudy sky inhabited by flying angels – and the nearer you approach the high altar, the more angels there are. That's pretty much it as far as specific sights go, though you could take a stroll along the leafy Prestegardsalléen footpath, which heads south along the shore of lake **Vangsvatnet** from opposite the church; or wander the central shops and cafés – if you've come from the hamlets and villages further north, the shopping might seem something of a treat.

East from Voss by train: Myrdal and Finse

Trains pulling east out of Voss head up the Raundal valley before climbing up to the bare but eerily beautiful wastes of the Hardangervidda plateau. All trains stop at **MYRDAL**, a remote railway junction where you change for the extraordinary train ride down to Flåm (see box, above), and then proceed onto **FINSE**, just half an hour by train from Myrdal and the highest point on the Bergen–Oslo railway line. A solitary lakeside outpost on the northern peripheries of the plateau, Finse comprises nothing more than its station and a few isolated buildings, hunkered down against the howling winds that rip across the Hardangervidda in wintertime. There's snow here from the beginning of November until well into June, and the **cross-country skiing** is particularly enthusiastic, with locals skiing off from the station in every direction. You can rent cross-country ski equipment at the *Finse 1222 Hotel* (see below), but you'll need to reserve. After the snow has melted, cycling (see below) and **hiking** take over, with one especially popular hike being the four-hour round trip to the northeast edge of the **Hardangerjøkulen glacier**. Other, longer hiking trails skirt the glacier to traverse the main body of the Hardangervidda plateau. From Finse, it's an eleven-hour haul to Highway 7 at Dyranut (see p.231), so most hikers overnight after around eight hours at the self-catering **Kjeldebu** DNT hut (March to mid-Oct). Finse has scope for more specialist activities too, most notably **guided glacier walks** on the Hardangerjøkulen. These guided walks take place between July and September, last around seven hours and cost in the region of 500kr including equipment hire – contact *Finse 1222 Hotel* for further details.

If all this sounds much too energetic, you can content yourself with Finse's **Rallarmuseet** (Navvy Museum; Jan to early Oct Mon–Fri 10am–10pm; 30kr), which holds a pictorial record of the planning and construction of the Oslo–Bergen railway, whose final piece of track was laid in 1909. The old black-and-white photos are the most interesting exhibits and a well-earned tribute to the navvies who survived such grim conditions.

Cycling from Finse

Cycling from Finse is made possible by the **Rallarvegen** ("The Navvy Road"), which was originally built to allow men and materials to be brought up to the railway during its construction. Now surfaced with gravel and sometimes asphalt, the Rallarvegen begins in Haugastøl beside Highway 7, runs west to Finse and then continues to Myrdal, from where you can cycle or take the Flåmsbana down to Flåm. It's 27km by bicycle from Haugastøl to Finse, 37km from Finse to Myrdal and another 16km to Flåm. The Finse-to-Flåm section, which passes through fine upland scenery before descending the Flåmsdal, is the most popular part of the Rallarvegen. Most cyclists travel east to west as Finse is a good deal higher than Myrdal, and the whole journey from Finse to Flåm takes around nine hours; the return trip is usually made by train, with NSB railways transporting bikes for 100kr. Locals reckon that the best time to cycle the Rallarvegen is usually from mid-July to late September. However, snow is not cleared from the route and its highest section – between Finse and Myrdal – can be blocked by snow until very late in summer, so check conditions locally before you set out. **Mountain-bike rental** is available from the *Finse 1222 Hotel* (see below), but advance reservations are required.

Finse practicalities

Finse has two **places to stay**: both are chalet complexes, geared up for hikers, cyclists and skiers. Of the two, the *Finse 1222 Hotel* (☎56 52 71 00, ⓦwww .finse1222.no; ❻ including meals; Jan to late May & mid-July to Oct) is the more comfortable, with pleasant rooms, a good restaurant and a sauna. The more frugal option is DNT's fully staffed *Finsehytta* (☎56 52 67 32, ⓦwww .finsehytta.no; mid-March to late May & July to mid-Sept; dorm beds 180–220kr, doubles ❶), which sleeps up to 150.

From Finse, the train takes an hour to reach Geilo (see p.188), three and a half hours more to Oslo.

North from Voss to Vik and Vangsnes

From Voss, it's about 20km north to **VINJE**, where **Highway 13** begins its 60-kilometre trek over to Vik and Vangsnes on the Sognefjord. A quintessential fjordland journey, the road begins by clambering up the Myrkdal valley, passing waterfalls and wild ravines before cutting an improbable route across the bleak and icy wastes of **Vikafjell mountain** – so improbable indeed that the highway is closed in winter, usually from November to April, and snow is piled high on either side of the road until at least the end of May. Beyond the mountain, the road slips down into **VIK**, a rather half-hearted village that sprawls up a wide valley. The only reason to stop here is to take a peek at **Hopperstad stave church** (mid-May to mid-June & mid-Aug to Sept daily 10am–5pm; mid-June to mid-Aug daily 9am–7pm; 45kr; Ⓦwww .stavechurch.com), sat on a hillock just off Highway 13, about 1500m from the fjord. In the 1880s the locals were about to knock it down, but a visiting architect and his antiquarian chum persuaded them to change their minds. The pair promptly set about repairing the place and they did a good job. Today the church is one of the best examples of its type, its angular roofing surmounted by a long and slender tower. The interior has its moments too, with a Gothic side-altar canopy, parts of which may have been swiped from France by the Vikings, and a so-called lepers' window through which the afflicted listened to church services.

Vangsnes

From Vik, it's a straight 11km north along the fjord to **VANGSNES**, where local farmers must have had a real shock when, in 1913, Kaiser Wilhelm erected a twelve-metre-high **statue** of the legendary Viking chief Fridtjof the Bold on the hilltop above their jetty. The **Fridtjovstatuen** still stands, an eccentric and vaguely unpleasant monument to the Kaiser's fascination with Nordic mythology – Fridtjof the Bold was in love with Ingebjorg, daughter of King Bele, whose statue, also commissioned by the Kaiser, is back across the fjord at Balestrand (see p.243). You can walk the 500m up from the jetty to take a closer look at Fridtjof and enjoy the fjord views from here too.

There are **car ferries** (Ⓦwww.fjord1.no) from Vangsnes north across the Sognefjord to both **Hella** on Highway 55 (every 40min–1hr; 15min; passengers 25kr, car & driver 65kr) and **Dragsvik** (every 40min–1hr; 30min; passengers 28kr, car & driver 76kr), which is just a few kilometres from Balestrand (see p.243); local buses run from Voss to Vangsnes (1–2 daily except Sat; 1hr 30min/1hr 40min).

North from Voss to Flåm

Heading north along the **E16** from Voss, it's a short, scenic hop to **Flåm**, one of the region's most visited villages and justifiably famous for its railway, the **Flåmsbana** (see p.235). Flåm is also an excellent base for further explorations, whether it be the ferry trip up along the **Nærøyfjord** or a day-long hike in the surrounding mountains. Nearing Flåm you'll pass through two spirited pieces of tunnelling, with stretches of 11km and 5km bored through the mountainside at colossal expense. Yet, these are but pip squeaks when compared with the 24-kilometre-long **tunnel** that links Aurlandsdal – from a point just east of

Flåm – with Lærdal and, more importantly, completes the fast road, the E16, from Bergen to Oslo. Even better, there are no tolls (hurrah). En route to Flåm, **Stalheim** boasts one of the region's most superbly sited hotels, **Undredal** is the quaintest of villages, and Gudvangen contrives to be really dreary despite its fjordside setting.

As for public transport, **Nor-way Bussekspress** (ⓦwww.nor-way.no) operates the **Sognebussen express bus** service, which begins in Bergen and passes through Voss bound for Flåm, the Fodnes–Mannheller ferry and ultimately Sogndal (2–6 daily).

Stalheim and Gudvangen

From Voss, it's 20km north to Vinje and another 16km or so to the scattered hamlet of **STALHEIM**, which plays host to the first-rate ⚐ *Stalheim Hotel* (ⓣ56 52 01 22, ⓦwww.stalheim.com; May to mid-Oct; ❻, sp/r ❺). The original hotel was built here on a mini-mountain plateau in the late nineteenth century, but today's building, a large and chunky structure short of grace, dates from the 1960s and is the hotel's fourth incarnation. All is redeemed inside, where the large and spacious public rooms have been kitted out in an endearing version of antique Norwegian style, all heirlooms and bygones plus a few landscape paintings to boot. The bedrooms are large and modern if a tad plain, but really who's bothered when the highlight is the view – a simply breathtaking vista down along the Nærøydal valley, so stunning, in fact, that the British artist **David Hockney** came and painted it. The hotel serves a top-notch breakfast and an excellent buffet dinner – all you can eat for 335kr – and is popular with tour groups. The hotel is located up a twisty byroad, just 1.5km from the E16 on what was once the main road until they tunnelled through the mountain below.

From Stalheim, it's a further 13km to the mini-port of **GUDVANGEN**, a forlorn little place at the southern tip of the Nærøyfjord. In the summertime, hundreds of tourists pour through here partly on account of the car-ferry connections to Kaupanger, but mainly because it's on the "Norway in a Nutshell" itinerary (see box, p.224). A modern complex down by the jetty incorporates souvenir shops, a café and a **hotel** of unusual design, the *Gudvangen Fjordtell* (ⓣ57 63 39 29, ⓦwww.gudvangen.com; May–Sept; ❹), consisting of a series of hut-like structures with turf roofs.

Undredal

Just beyond Gudvangen, the E16 disappears into an eleven-kilometre tunnel to emerge a few kilometres short of Flåm – and a few hundred metres short of the byroad leading north to **UNDREDAL**. Just 6km long, this byroad cuts an attractive route, romping along a boulder-strewn valley to reach the village, which perches right on the edge of the Aurlandsfjord, its narrow, meandering lanes overshadowed by the severity of the surrounding mountains. There's been a settlement here since Viking times, and for much of its history the village has been reliant on the export of its goat's cheese, now produced in Undredal's two surviving dairies – there were once a dozen. The main item of interest here is the **church** (late June to mid–Aug daily 11am–6pm; 30kr), parts of which date back to the twelfth century. A tiny affair – it's one of the smallest churches in the whole of Norway – it's decorated in fine folkloric style, from the floral patterns on the walls through to the crucified Christ above the high altar and the stylized stars and naive figures on the ceiling.

Flåm

Fringed by meadows and orchards, **FLÅM** village sits beside the Aurlandsfjord, a slender branch of the Sognefjord, with the mountains glowering behind. It's a splendid setting, but otherwise first impressions are poor: the fjordside complex adjoining the train station is crass and commercial – souvenir trolls and the like – and on summer days the place heaves with tourists, who pour off the train, have lunch, and then promptly head out by bus and ferry. But a brief stroll is enough to leave the crowds behind at the harbourside, while out of season or in the evenings, when the day-trippers have all moved on, Flåm is a pleasant spot – and an eminently agreeable place to spend the night. If you're prepared to risk the weather, late September is perhaps the best time to visit: the peaks already have a covering of snow and the vegetation is just turning its autumnal golden brown.

Not only is Flåm the terminus for the Flåmsbana (see box, p.235), but it's also the starting point for one of the most stupendous **ferry trips** in the fjords, the two-hour cruise up the **Aurlandsfjord** and down its narrow offshoot, the **Nærøyfjord** (1–5 daily; 2hr; 235kr one-way, 325kr return; Ⓦwww.fjord1.no) to Gudvangen (see p.238). With high and broody cliffs keeping out the sun throughout the winter, Nærøyfjord is the narrowest fjord in Europe, and its stern beauty makes for a magnificent excursion. This forms part of the "Norway in a Nutshell" itinerary (see box, p.224).

Practicalities

Flåm's harbourside complex may be ugly, but it is convenient, holding a super-market, public-access computers, a train station and the **tourist office** (daily: May & Sept 8.30am–4pm; June–Aug 8.30am–8pm; Ⓣ91 35 16 72, Ⓦwww.alr .no), where you can pick up a very useful free booklet on Aurland, Flåm and Lærdal that includes all sorts of local information. Staff also have details on local hiking routes, sell hiking maps and rent mountain bikes. You can also go **fjord kayaking** with Flåm-based Njord (Ⓣ97 19 45 11, Ⓦwww.njord.as/no), who offer an interesting range of tours, the shortest and cheapest of which is their two-hour Aurlandsfjord paddle for 350kr per person.

If you decide to overnight here, there's inexpensive **accommodation** at *Flåm Camping og Vandrerhjem*, which has tent spaces and cabins (750–1000kr) and incorporates a small and well-kept HI **hostel** (May to mid-Sept; Ⓣ57 63 21 21, Ⓦwww.vandrerhjem.no; dorm beds 170k, doubles ❶). It's about 300m from the train station towards the back of the village by the stream.

Moving on from Flåm

From May to September, daily **Hurtigbåt passenger express boats** (Ⓦwww.fjord1 .no) leave Flåm to travel up the Aurlandsfjord and along the Sognefjord to Balestrand and Bergen. The one-way trip to Bergen takes five and a half hours and costs 625kr; Balestrand is an hour and a half away and costs 215kr. By **train** (Ⓦwww.nsb.no), Myrdal, at the top of the Flåmsbana (see box, p.235), is on the main Oslo–Bergen line, while **Nor-way Bussekspress** (Ⓦwww.nor-way.no) operates the **Sognebussen express bus** service, which begins in Bergen and passes through Voss, Flåm and Fodnes en route to Sogndal (2–6 daily). Heading east by car, it's tempting to use the enormous, 24-kilometre-long – and free – tunnel through to Lærdal (see p.187), but the 48-kilometre **mountain road** the tunnel replaced – the **Aurlandsvegen** – has survived to provide splendid views and some hair-raising moments; it's open from the beginning of June to around the middle of October.

Alternatively, the *Heimly Pensjonat* (☎57 63 23 00, ⓦwww.heimly.no; ❹) provides simple but perfectly adequate lodgings in a modern block about 450m east of the train station along the shore; it's a friendly place and the views down the fjord are charming. A third choice, about 200m back from the station, is the *Fretheim Hotel* (☎57 63 63 00, ⓦwww.fretheim-hotel .no; ❼, sp/r ❺), a rambling structure whose attractive older part, with its high-pitched roofs and white-painted clapboard, is now joined to a flashy glass structure that is, in its turn, attached to a matching, modern wing whose well-appointed rooms are furnished in brisk modern style. The hotel is the best place to **eat** in the village, with a banquet-like buffet every night; go early to get the pick of the buffet crop.

The Aurlandsdal valley

From Flåm, it's 10km north along the fjord to the hamlet of **AURLAND**, which strings along the water at the foot of the **Aurlandsdal valley** – and near the entrance to the whopping Lærdal tunnel. The valley was once the final part of one of Norway's most celebrated **hikes**, a classic two- or three-day expedition that began at Finse train station (see p.235), from where the trail crossed the northern peripheries of the Hardangervidda plateau before descending the Aurlandsdal, with hikers then pushing on to Flåm to get the train back again. The trail incorporated an extravagant range of scenery, from upland plateau to plunging ravines, and parts of it followed an old cattle-drovers' route that once linked eastern and western Norway. The trail lost much of its allure – and some of its beauty – when **Highway 50**, which links Highway 7 near Geilo (see p.188) with Aurland, was rammed through the Aurlandsdal as part of a hydroelectricity generation scheme in the 1970s, but sections of the old trail still provide some excellent hiking. Perhaps the most scenic section today is the 21-kilometre stretch between Østerbø (820m) and Vassbygdi (94m), which takes between six and seven hours to complete. The trail threads its way through the woods and farms of the Aurlandsdal, passing crashing waterfalls and offering handsome valley views as well as one or two tight and steep scrambles. **Østerbø**, the starting point, comprises a pair of lonely mountain lodges (see below), located about 800m off Highway 50 about 43km from Flåm; **Vassbygdi** is a dull hamlet where the trail ends at the car park and bus stop.

The **local bus** service from Flåm to Østerbø (June to late Sept 2 daily; 1hr; ⓦwww.fjord1.no) isn't great, but timetables are such that it is usually possible to catch the bus, make the hike to Vassbygdi then return to Flåm by bus the same day. However, this does mean you'll be hiking against the clock, which can be avoided by booking a taxi for the return leg or by overnighting in Østerbø at either of its two privately owned **mountain lodges** – *Østerbø Fjellstove* (☎57 63 11 77, ⓦwww.aurlandsdalen.com; late May to Sept; dorm beds from 200kr, hotel ❹) or the adjacent and more spartan *Østerbø Turisthytte* (☎57 63 11 41, ⓦwww.osterbo-turisthytte.no; dorm beds from 345kr, cabins 600–700kr for two persons; late May to Sept).

The Sognefjord

Profoundly beautiful, the **Sognefjord** (ⓦwww.sognefjord.no) drills in from the coast for some 200km, its inner recesses splintering into half a dozen subsidiary fjords. Perhaps inevitably, none of the villages and small towns that dot the fjord quite lives up to the splendid setting, but **Balestrand** and **Mundal**, on the

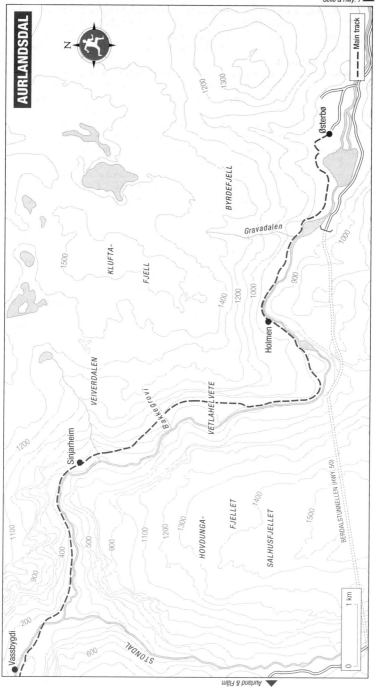

AURLANDSDAL

N

Geilo & Hwy. 7 ▲

- - - - Main track

Østerbø

BYRDEFJELL

Gravadalen

KLUFTA-

FJELL

Holmen

VEIVERDALEN

Bakkegrovi

VETLAHELVETE

Sinjarheim

HOVDUNGA-

FJELLET

SALHUSFJELLET

BERDALSTUNNELEN (HWY. 50)

Vassbygdi

STØNDAL

1300

1200

1500

1400

1200

1000

900

1000

1200

1400

1500

1100

1200

1300

1100

900

500

400

200

600

600

1000

1 km

0

4

▲ Aurland & Flåm

Fjærlandsfjord, come mighty close and are easily the best bases. Both are on the north side of the fjord which, given the lack of roads on the south side, is where you want (or pretty much have) to be – Flåm (see p.238) apart. Mundal is also near two southerly tentacles of the Jostedalsbreen glacier: **Flatbreen** and easy-to-reach **Bøyabreen**.

Highway 55 hugs the Sognefjord's north bank for much of its length, but at **Sogndal** it slices northeast to clip along the lustrous **Lustrafjord**, which boasts a top-notch attraction in **Urnes stave church**, reached via a quick ferry ride from **Solvorn**. Further north, a side road leaves Highway 55 to clamber up from the Lustrafjord to the east side of the Jostedalsbreen glacier at the **Nigardsbreen nodule**, arguably the glacier's finest vantage point. Thereafter Highway 55 – as the **Sognefjellsveg** – climbs steeply to run along the western side of the **Jotunheimen mountains**, an extraordinarily beautiful journey even by Norwegian standards and one which culminates with the road thumping down to **Lom** on the flatlands beside Highway 15.

Public transport to and around the Sognefjord is generally excellent, its assorted car ferries, buses and Hurtigbåt express passenger boats mostly run by Fjord 1 (Ⓦwww.fjord1.no). Operating about halfway along the fjord, perhaps the most useful of the **car ferries** plies between Vangsnes (see p.237), Hella and Dragsvik (for Balestrand), and in the east another useful link is the 24-hour ferry shuttle between Mannheller and Fodnes. Among a number of **Hurtigbåt passenger express boat** services, one handy route connects Bergen, Vik, Balestrand and Sogndal, another links Balestrand with Flåm (May–Sept only). These services are supplemented by Nor-Way Bussekspress **long-distance buses** (Ⓦwww.nor-way.no), which depart Bergen for Sogndal, arriving via Voss, Flåm and the Fodnes–Mannheller ferry; others arrive in Sogndal from Oslo and

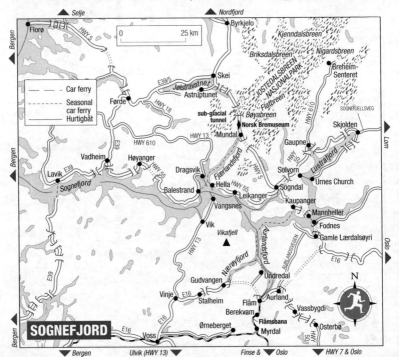

points east before proceeding onto Balestrand. Sogndal is something of a transport hub with buses leaving here to travel northwest to Mundal and the Nordfjord (see p.253); and, in the summertime only, north to the Nigardsbreen glacier arm and Lom, which is reached along the stirring Sognefjellsveg (Highway 55).

Balestrand

BALESTRAND, an appealing first stop on the Sognefjord, has been a tourist destination since the middle of the nineteenth century, when it was discovered by European travellers in search of cool, clear air and picturesque mountain scenery. Kaiser Wilhelm II got in on the act too, becoming a frequent visitor and sharing his holiday spot with the tweeds and bustles of the British bourgeoisie. These days, the village is used as a touring base for the immediate area, as the battery of small hotels above the quay testifies, but it's all very small-scale, and among the thousand-strong population, farming remains the principal livelihood.

An hour or so will suffice to take a peek at Balestrand's several low-profile attractions. Lining up along the harbour are the old post office, which features temporary displays on the town and its environs; a brace of art galleries; and an aquarium, the Sognefjord Akvarium. From the harbour, it's a couple of minutes' walk to the **English church of St Olav** (May–Sept daily 10am–10pm; free), a spiky brown-and-beige wooden structure of 1897, built in the general style of a stave church at the behest of a British émigré, a certain Margaret Kvikne, who moved here after she married a local curate. The Germans have left their mark, too. About 300m south of the church along the fjord are two humpy **Viking burial mounds**, supposedly the tombs of King Bele and his wife, who both appear in the Sagas. On the larger of them is a statue of the king in heroic pose, plonked there by the Kaiser in 1913 to match the statue of Bele's son-in-law that stands across the fjord in Vangsnes (see p.237).

Several **hiking trails** ascend the rocky slopes immediately to the west of the village, clambering up to the peaks and lakes of the plateau beyond. None of them is easy – all begin with a short, stiff climb and pass through boggy ground, and several have steep drops too – but the scenery is splendid. Balestrand tourist office (see below) sells a detailed hiking map with multilingual trail descriptions. If you want to avoid the initial slog – and have a vehicle – drive south out of Balestrand along Highway 55 for 7km, then turn up the narrow road that leads, after 6km or so, to **Saurdal**, where a particularly pleasant circular walk can be made round the lake and across the uplands with the Sognefjord visible way down below.

Practicalities

The only **car ferry** direct to Balestrand is the summertime service south from Mundal, on the Fjærlandsfjord (see box, p.244); otherwise, the nearest you'll get is Dragsvik, 9km along the fjord to the north of Balestrand, and reached by ferry from either Hella to the east or Vangsnes on the fjord's south shore (for details, see p.237). Both the Mundal ferry and **Hurtigbåt passenger express boat** services (from Bergen and Vik to the west, and Flåm and Sogndal to the east) dock at the village quayside, plumb in the centre. **Buses** stop beside the quayside too and this is also where you will find the **tourist office** at the back of a shop (May & Sept Mon–Sat 10.30am–5pm; June–Aug Mon–Sat 8am–6pm & Sun 10am–5pm; ☎57 69 12 55, ⓦ www.sognefjord.no). Staff hand out a wide range of fjord leaflets, sell local hiking maps, issue bus and ferry timetables and rent out bicycles.

For **accommodation**, the all-year *Midtnes Pensjonat* (T 57 69 11 33, W www
.midtnes.no; ❸), about 300m from the dock behind the English church, is a
low-key, pleasantly sedate affair with a few workaday but spacious rooms in a
modern wing adjoining the original clapboard house; make sure to get a room
with a fjord view. Close by, the *Balestrand Hotell* (T 57 69 11 38, W www
.balestrand.com; mid-May to mid-Sept; ❹) is comparable, with thirty
unassuming rooms kitted out in modern, modest style. A third choice, just
150m uphill from the dock, is the HI **hostel** (T 57 69 13 03, W www
.vandrerhjem.no; late June to mid-Aug; dorm beds 225kr, doubles ❷), which
is part of the neat and trim *Kringsjå Hotell* (same number; W www.kringsja.no;
late June to mid-Aug; ❸). This complex occupies an attractive timber building,
whose long verandah overlooks the fjord; there's a communal kitchen, a more-
than-competent café-restaurant and a laundry. The big cheese hereabouts,
though, is *Kviknes Hotel* (T 57 69 42 00, W www.kviknes.no; May–Sept ❼,
sp/r ❻;), whose various buildings – some old, some new – dominate much of
the waterfront. It's worth popping into the hotel's main building for a look at
the fancy furnishings and fittings, from the Norwegian landscape and seascape
paintings to the sort of neo-Viking baronial carving and the coffered timber
ceilings. If you do decide to stay here, don't take a room without having a
gander first: the best and most expensive overlook the fjord, but some are at
the back in the modern annexe. Finally, the town **campsite**, *Sjøtun Camping*
(T 57 69 12 23, W www.sjotun.com; June to mid-Sept), occupies a treeless field
just beyond the burial mounds, 1km or so south of the dock; there are cabins
(250kr for 4 persons) as well as tent and caravan pitches.

For **food**, the *Midtnes* serves tasty, excellent-value dinners (at 235kr) and there
are competent snacks and light lunches at *Gekkens Café*, to the rear of the

Moving on from Balestrand

When it comes to **moving on from Balestrand**, you're spoilt for choice. In the
summertime, one especially tempting proposition is the **car ferry** (May–Sept 4 daily;
1hr 30min; passengers 195kr one-way, 290kr return; car & driver 350kr each way;
W www.fjord1.no) north up along the stunningly beautiful Fjærlandsfjord to the
eminently appealing hamlet of Mundal (see p.245). There is also a **Hurtigbåt
passenger express boat** service linking Balestrand with Bergen and Vik in one
direction, Sogndal in the other (1 daily), and another to Flåm (May–Sept 1–2 daily; 1hr
30min; W www.fjord1.no). **Driving** north from Balestrand, **Highway 13** cuts a scenic
route over the mountains on its way to its junction with the E39 (near Førde), which
itself proceeds north to the Nordfjord (see p.253), but **Highway 55** to Sogndal and
the eastern reaches of the Sognefjord has much more to offer – not least the
wondrous Sognefjellsveg mountain road (see p.250). To get to Sogndal from
Balestrand, it's necessary to cross the mouth of the Fjærlandsfjord by ferry from
Dragsvik, 9km up along the coast to the north of Balestrand. This **Dragsvik car ferry**
operates a triangular service shuttling both east across the fjord to Hella on Highway
55 (15min) and south to Vangsnes (30min); see p.237 for prices and sailing details.
The other significant cost for drivers is the 175kr toll payable as you approach
Mundal from the south on Highway 5.

As for **buses**, Nor-Way Bussekspress **express buses** travel west from Balestrand
to Vadheim, where you change for services along the E39 (3 daily; 2hr; W www
.nor-way.no). The same company also operates a service east from Balestrand to
Sogndal and ultimately Oslo (3 daily). At Sogndal, passengers change for Mundal and
Lom (see p.251). Note, however, that connecting services can be few and far between
– mostly you'll have to hang around for an hour or two (at least) between buses.

building that holds the tourist office. The cream of the gastronomic crop is the restaurant at *Kvikne's Hotel*, which serves up a banquet-sized, help-yourself buffet (440kr) every night – go early to get the pick and be sure to leave room for the ground-moving, earth-shattering mousse. The hotel also has a small and separate, à la carte restaurant – but stick to the buffet.

North to the Fjærlandsfjord and Mundal

To the north of Balestrand, the **Fjærlandsfjord** is a wild place, its flanks blanketed by a thick covering of trees that extends down to the water's edge, with a succession of thundering waterfalls tumbling down vast clefts in the rock up above. The village of **MUNDAL** – sometimes inaccurately referred to as Fjærland – matches its surroundings perfectly, a gentle ribbon of old wooden houses edging the fjord, with the mountains as a louring backcloth. It's one of the region's most picturesque places, saved from the developers by its isolation: it was one of the last settlements on the Sognefjord to be connected to the road system, with Highway 5 from Sogndal only being completed in 1986. Moreover, Mundal has eschewed the crasser forms of commercialism to become the self-styled "Norwegian Book Town" (Den Norske Bokbyen; ⓦ www.bokbyen.no), with a dozen rustic buildings accommodating antiquarian and second hand **bookshops**. Naturally enough, most of the books are in Norwegian, but there's a liberal sprinkling of English titles too. The bookselling season runs from May to September and the bookshops are mostly open daily from 10am to 6pm.

Bookshops aside, the village has two good-looking buildings, the first of which is the **Hotel Mundal** (see p.247), whose cream-painted, nineteenth-century high-pitched roofs, turrets and verandahs overlook the fjord from among the handful of buildings which amount to the village centre. Next door, the maroon **church** (June–Sept daily 10am–6pm; free), which dates from 1861, lacks ornamentation but is immaculately maintained and its graveyard hints at the hard but healthy life of the district's farmers – most of them seem to have lived to a ripe old age. One man who didn't make it that far was the German officer, buried here after a climbing accident in 1910: his family donated the modest painted, baptismal font.

▲ Mundal – "Norwegian Book Town"

Many locals are still farmers, but in summer few herd their cattle up to the mountain pastures, as was the custom until the 1960s. The disused tracks to these summer farms (*støls*) now serve as **hiking trails** of varying length and difficulty – the tourist office (see below) will advise, but one of the easier routes is the two-hour (each way) jaunt west from the village up the country lane that follows **Mundalsdal** to **Fjellstølen**, at 350m.

Much easier is the 2.5km stroll north along the quiet byroad that slips prettily along the fjord to link the village with Highway 5. Just before you get to the main road, you'll spy a bird hide that overlooks the protected wetlands at the tip of the Fjærlandsfjord. These wetlands, **Bøyaøri**, attract over one hundred species of bird with mallard, oystercatcher, heron and lapwing, among many others, all making their appearance.

Around Mundal: Flatbreen and Bøyabreen

Just beyond the Bøyaøri wetlands (see above) is the **Norsk Bremuseum** (Norwegian Glacier Museum; daily: April, May, Sept & Oct 10am–4pm; June–Aug 9am–7pm; information free but displays 110kr; ☏57 69 32 88, ⊛www.bre .museum.no), which tells you more than you ever wanted to know about glaciers and then some. It features several lavish hands-on displays and screens films about glaciers; package tourists turn up in droves.

The museum is one of the **Jostedalsbreen Nasjonalpark**'s three information centres (see p.255 for details of the others), and as such has the details of all the various **guided glacier walks** on offer across the park as outlined in their *Breturar* (glacier walks) leaflet; this same leaflet is also available at Mundal tourist office (see below). The usual target from Mundal is the **Supphellebreen**, the Jostedalsbreen's nearest hikeable arm, or, to be precise, that part of it called **Flatbreen**, though this is a challenging albeit beautiful part of the glacier and neither is it easy to get to. Flatbreen excursions take between seven and nine hours and the season runs from late June to early September. Advance reservations, at least a day beforehand, are essential – in the first instance contact Mundal tourist office. The cost is 650kr per person including special equipment and you get two to three hours on the ice.

At the other extreme, you can get close to the glacier without breaking sweat just 10km north of Mundal on Highway 5. Here, just before you enter the tunnel, look out for the signposted, dirt and gravel side-road on the right that leads to the Bøyabreen, just 800m away. You can drive the first 600m, to the café and car park, and from here it's an easy stroll to the slender glacial lake that is fed by the sooty shank of the **Bøyabreen** glacier arm up above.

Mundal practicalities

Arriving **by car** from the south on Highway 5, there's a whopping 175kr toll to pay just before you reach the turning for Mundal. **Car ferries** from Balestrand (May–Sept 4 daily; 1hr 30min; passengers 195kr one-way, 290kr return; car & driver 350kr each way; ⊛www.fjord1.no) dock a couple of minutes' walk from the centre of the village. Drivers should note that by using the ferry, they can avoid the toll providing, that is, they are continuing north from Mundal. The nearest you'll get to Mundal by **bus** is the Norsk Bremuseum on Highway 5, from where it's an easy 2.5-kilometre stroll south along the fjord to the village. Mundal **tourist office**, about 300m from the boat dock (May–Sept daily 10am–6pm; ☏57 69 32 33, ⊛www .fjaerland.org), advises on local hiking routes, sells hiking maps and has bus and ferry timetables. **Cycle rental** is available from them too, at 140kr per day.

There are two fjordside **hotels** in Mundal. The obvious choice is the splendid
⚹ *Hotel Mundal* (℡57 69 31 01, ⓦwww.hotelmundal.no; May–Sept; ❻), a
quirky sort of place whose public rooms, which date back to 1891, display
many original features, from the parquet floors and fancy wooden scrollwork
through to the old-fashioned sliding doors of the expansive dining room. The
rooms are perhaps a tad frugal, but somehow it doesn't matter much. If you do
stay, look out for the old photos on the walls of men in plus-fours and hobnail
boots clambering round the glaciers – only softies bothered with gloves. As
usual, the overnight rate includes breakfast, but given that Mundal hardly
heaves with restaurants, you'll probably want dinner at the hotel too – the
four-course set menu costs 500kr. A second choice, the *Fjærland Fjordstue Hotell*
(℡57 69 32 00, ⓦwww.fjaerland.no; mid-May to mid-Sept; ❹, ❺ with fjord
view) is very different – a well-tended family hotel with smart modern
furnishings and a conservatory overlooking the fjord. They offer dinners too at
a cost of 360kr. The third option is *Bøyum Camping* (℡57 69 32 52, ⓦwww
.fjaerland.org/boyumcamping) near the Bremuseum, which has cabins
(550–980kr) as well as spaces for tents.

East to Sogndal

From Balestrand, it's 9km north along the fjord to **Dragsvik**, where ferries
shuttle over to the jetty at **Hella**, which is itself 40km from **SOGNDAL** –
bigger and livelier than Balestrand, but still hardly a major metropolis, with a
population of just six thousand. Neither is Sogndal as appealing: it has,
admittedly, a pleasant fjord setting in a broad valley, surrounded by low, green
hills dotted with apple and pear trees, but its centre is a rash of modern concrete
and glass. Frankly, there are other much more agreeable spots within a few
kilometres' radius and your best option is to keep going.

    Buses drop passengers at the **bus station** on the west side of the town centre
near the end of Gravensteinsgata, the long main drag. From the bus station, it's
about 600m east along Gravensteinsgata to the **tourist office** (May to mid-
June Mon–Fri 10am–4pm; mid-June to mid-Aug Mon–Fri 9am–6pm & Sat
10am–4pm; mid-Aug to Sept Mon–Fri 10am–4pm; ℡97 60 04 43, ⓦwww
.sognefjorden.no), housed in the town's large and modern Kulturhus. Staff issue
bus and ferry timetables, and have a list of local **accommodation**, but pickings
are fairly slim.

    The nicest place to stay is the *Hofslund Fjord Hotel*, down on the fjord, a stone's
throw from the tourist office (℡57 62 76 00, ⓦwww.hofslund-hotel.no; ❹).
This comprises an older wooden building and a modern annexe, but the setting
– with the main road to one side and the dreary town centre on the other –
hardly fires the soul. Another palatable and certainly more economical option is
the HI **hostel** (℡57 62 75 75, ⓦwww.vandrerhjem.no; mid-June to mid-Aug;
dorm beds 200kr, doubles ❶), which actually manages to feel quite homely
despite being housed in a residential rural high school, a Folkehøgskule. Finding
the place is straightforward too: approaching Sogndal from the southeast on

Moving on from Sogndal

From Sogndal, there is a **Hurtigbåt passenger express boat** service **along the Sognefjord** to Balestrand, Vik and Bergen (May–Sept 1–2 daily; ⓦwww.fjord1.no). Sogndal is also on the route of the long-distance **Sogn og Fjordane ekspressen bus** (3 daily; ⓦwww.nor-way.no) services west to Langva, which – among several permutations – links Oslo with Gol, the Fodnes–Mannheller ferry, Kaupanger, Sogndal, Mundal on the Fjærlandsfjord, Skei (for Stryn), Førde and Florø. **Local buses** from Sogndal include a limited service north to Lom up along the Sognefjellsveg, the highest parts of which are closed by snow throughout the winter (late June to Aug; 2 daily). There are also local bus services to Solvorn (July & Aug 1–3 daily; rest of year 2–3 daily, but no Sat service) and the Nigardsbreen glacier nodule (July & Aug 1 daily).

Finally, **drivers** should remember that the road to Oslo, Bergen and Flåm is interrupted some 18km southeast of Sogndal by the round-the-clock Mannheller–Fodnes **car ferry** (every 20min, hourly midnight–6am; 10min; car & driver 103kr, including a road toll of 48kr).

Highway 5, the hostel is clearly signposted from the main drag, just beyond the bridge at the east end of town; in the opposite direction, coming from the bus station, it's about 400m beyond the roundabout at the east end of Gravensteinsgata.

This same roundabout, which is just 50m from the tourist office, marks the start of **Fjøravegen**, the town's other main drag, which cuts through the commercial heart of Sogndal.

Southeast from Sogndal to Kaupanger

Highway 5 cuts a breezy course as it travels southeast from Sogndal, offering wide views over the Sognefjord. After about six kilometres, you'll pass the roadside **De Heibergske Samlinger – Sogn Folkmuseum** (Heiberg Collections of the Sogn Folk Museum; daily: May & Sept 10am–3pm; June–Aug 10am–5pm; 60kr, including Sogn Fjordmuseum, see p.249; ⓦwww.dhs .museum.no), named after a Mr Heiberg, an avid collector of – and expert in – old Norwegian agricultural tools. If that sounds like he may not have gone down a storm at dinner parties, his legacy, this Folk Museum, is pleasant enough, its thirty-odd relocated buildings, which mostly date from the nineteenth century, rolling down the bumpy hillside. Together, they give something of the flavour of an older rural Norway, especially when the animals are knocking around in the summer months. Speaking of flavours, the staff bake their own cakes and sell them at the café – and very tasty they are, too.

Pushing on, it's about four kilometres to the village and miniature port of **KAUPANGER**. Here, the red and white timber houses of the old part of the village slope up from the harbour towards the **stave church** (daily: late May to late Aug 9.30am–5.30pm; late Aug to Sept 10.30am–5.30pm; 35kr; ⓦwww .stavechurch.com), a much-modified thirteenth-century structure whose dourness is offset by its situation: the church stands on a hillside amid buttercup meadows with views of the fjord on one side and forested hills on the other. The interior has several unusual features, most memorably a musical score painted on one of the walls. No one is quite sure if the score was meant to be purely decorative or had some musical function, but it does appear to be a (rough) copy of a hymn traditionally sung on Ascension Day. The church also has two sad portraits of Danish bailiffs and their families: one is pictured with three stillborn babies, the other with one young son, who has a tiny red cross (for death) above his head.

Afterwards, you might want to head down to the dock to visit the **Sogn Fjordmuseum** (daily: May & Sept 10am–3pm; June–Aug 10am–5pm; 60kr, including Folkmuseum – see p.248), which holds an assortment of old wooden boats. Exhibits range from sturdy inshore fishing boats and ice boats (fitted with runners for use on frozen fjord inlets) to daintier, faster craft used by Danish dignitaries.

Northeast from Sogndal: Solvorn and Urnes stave church

Travelling northeast from Sogndal, it's about 13km up along Highway 55 to the steep 3km-long side road that threads its way down to **SOLVORN**, an immaculate hamlet of bright-white timber houses clustering the sheltered foreshore of the **Lustrafjord** with the mountains louring behind. Solvorn is a lovely little place, both a quick boat ride from one of the region's star attractions – Urnes stave church (see below) – and the site of two really good places to stay. First up is the harbourside *Walaker Hotell* (⊤57 68 20 80, ⓦwww.walaker .com; ❺), the prettiest part of which is the old house, a comely, pastel-painted, two-storey building whose porch is supported by a pair of columns, a Neoclassical extravagance that must have once amazed the locals. The hotel has a lovely garden and first-rate period bedrooms, although most of the guest rooms are in the modern annexe, a low-slung really rather successful building that also looks out at the fjord. The second option is the distinctive *Eplet Bed & Apple* (⊤41 64 94 69, ⓦwww.eplet.net; May–Sept), a self-styled "Modern Guest House & Apple Juice Farm" in the village about 300m back up the road from the dock – just watch for the sign. The host, a long-distance cyclist and traveller, seems to have been just about everywhere and he has created a laid-back, easy-going place with dormitory accommodation (140kr) and a few neat, trim, modern guest rooms (❹). You can camp in the grounds, mountain-bike hire is free for guests, and there's internet access. The juice factory is in the basement and the house is surrounded by an orchard which has its own complement of sheep.

Urnes stave church

From Solvorn, a local **car ferry** (June–Aug daily 10am–4pm, hourly; Sept–May Mon–Fri 4–5 daily, no Sat & Sun service; 20min; passengers 28kr, car & driver 76kr; ⊤91 79 42 11, ⓦwww.urnesferry.com) shuttles across the Lustrafjord to the hamlet of **Ornes**, from where it's a stiff, ten-minute hike up the hill to **Urnes stave church** (June–Aug daily 10.30am–5.30pm; 45kr; ⓦwww .stavechurch.com). Magnificently sited with the fjord and the snow-dusted mountains as its backdrop, this is the oldest and most celebrated stave church in Norway. Parts of the building date back to the twelfth century, and its most remarkable feature is its wonderful medieval **carvings**. On the outside, incorporated into the north wall, are two exquisite door panels, the remains of an earlier church dating from around 1070 and alive with a swirling filigree of strange beasts and delicate vegetation. These forceful, superbly crafted panels bear witness to the sophistication of Viking woodcarving – indeed, the church has given its name to this distinctively Nordic art form, found in many countries where Viking influence was felt and now generally known as the "Urnes" style. Most of the interior is seventeenth-century – including some splendidly bulbous pomegranates – but there is Viking woodcarving here too, notably the strange-looking figures and beasts carved on the capitals of the staves and the sacred-heart bench-ends. A small display in the neighbouring house-cum-ticket-office fills in all the details and has photographic enlargements of carvings that are hard to decipher inside the (poorly lit) church.

If you're driving, there's a choice of routes on from the church. You can head north along the minor road that tracks along the east shore of the Lustrafjord to rejoin Highway 55 at Skjolden (see below), or retrace your steps back to Highway 55 via Solvorn. The latter is the route you'll need to take if you're heading to the Nigardsbreen arm of the Jostedalsbreen glacier.

North to the Nigardsbreen

North from the Solvorn turning, it's about 13km along Highway 55 to **Gaupne**, where **Highway 604** forks north for the delightful 34-kilometre trip up the wild, forested river valley that leads to the **Breheimsenteret Jostedalsbreen Nasjonalpark information centre** (daily: May to late June & late Aug to Sept 10am–5pm; late June to late Aug 9am–7pm; displays 50kr; ⊤57 68 32 50, ⓦwww.jostedal.com). This angular, ultramodern structure fits in well with the bare peaks that surround it and, as you sip a coffee on the terrace, you can admire the glistening glacier dead ahead – the **Nigardsbreen**, an eastern arm of the Jostedalsbreen. From the centre, it's an easy three-kilometre drive or walk along the toll road (25kr) to the shores of an icy green lake, where a tiny **boat** (mid-June to early Sept daily 10am–6pm; 30kr return) shuttles across to the bare rock slope beside the glacier, a great rumpled and seamed wall of ice that sweeps between high peaks. It's a magnificent spectacle and most visitors are satisfied with the short hike up from the jetty to the glacier's shaggy flanks, but others plump for a **guided glacier walk**. There is a plethora to choose from, beginning with a quick and easy one- to two-hour jaunt suitable for children over six (daily July to late Aug; 200kr, children 100kr), through to much tougher seven-hour excursions (July to late Aug 4 weekly; 675kr). Prices include equipment.

The guided glacier-walk season lasts from mid-May to mid-September. Tickets for the family walks can be purchased direct from the guides at the glacier (cash only), but longer excursions need to be pre-booked and pre-paid with the Breheimsenteret at least one hour before departure. Advance reservations for overnight trips must be made at least four weeks beforehand. For more on the Jostedalsbreen glacier, see pp.253–255; further information on glacier walks is given on p.255.

Along the Sognefjellsveg

Back at Gaupne, Highway 55 continues 26km northeast to **SKJOLDEN**, a dull little town that is both at the head of the Lustrafjord and the start of the hundred-kilometre **Sognefjellsveg** road over the mountains to Lom. Despite the difficulty of the terrain, the Sognefjellsveg – which is closed from late October to May depending on conditions – marks the course of one of the oldest trading routes in Norway, with locals transporting goods by mule or, amazingly enough, on their shoulders: salt and fish went northeast, hides, butter, tar and iron went southwest. That portion of the road that clambers over the highest part of the mountains – no less than 1434m above sea level – was only completed in 1938 under a Great Depression "make-work" scheme, which kept a couple of hundred young men busy for two years. Tourist literature hereabouts refers to the lads' "motivation and drive", but considering the harshness of the conditions and the crudeness of their equipment – pickaxes, spades and wheelbarrows – their purported enthusiasm seems unlikely.

Beyond Skjolden, the Sognefjellsveg worms its way up the Bergsdal valley to a mountain plateau which it proceeds to traverse, providing absolutely stunning views of the jagged, ice-crusted **Jotunheimen** peaks to the east. En route are several roadside **lodges**, easily the best of which is the comfortable and very modern *Turtagrø Hotel* (☎57 68 08 00, ⓦwww.turtagro.no; dorm bunks 340kr, 470kr with breakfast, hotel rooms ❼; Easter–Oct), just 15km out from Skjolden. There's been a hotel here since 1888, but the present structure, a large and attractive red-timber building, was only constructed in 2001, after fire destroyed its predecessor. The interior is very Scandinavian, with spacious public rooms and even a library, and the food is first-rate, with a three-course midday meal costing 400kr. The hotel is a favourite haunt for **mountaineers**, but it also provides ready access to the **hiking trails** that network the Jotunheimen national park (see p.177), though the terrain is unforgiving and the weather unpredictable, so novice hikers beware.

One tough hike from the hotel is the six-hour, round-trip haul southeast along the well-worn (but not especially well-signed) path up the **Skagastølsdal valley** to DNT's self-service **Skagastølsbu** hut, though you can of course make the hike shorter by only going some of the way. The valley is divided into a number of steps, each preceded by a short, steep ascent; the hotel is 884m above sea level, the hut, a small stone affair surrounded by a staggering confusion of ice caps, mini-glaciers and craggy ridges, is at 1758m. If you'd rather have a guide, the *Turtagrø* is a base for mountain guides, who offer an extensive programme of guided mountain and glacier walks as well as **summer cross-country skiing** – the hotel will help to sort things out; the season begins at Easter and extends until October.

On to Elveseter and Spiterstulen

On the far side of the plateau, the Sognefjellsveg clips down through forested **Leirdal**, passing the old farmstead of **ELVESETER**, some 45km from the *Turtagrø*. Here, a complex of old timber buildings has been turned into a hotel-cum-mini-historical-theme-park, its proudest possession being a bizarre 33-metre-high plaster and cyanite column, the **Sagasøyla**. On top of the column is the figure of that redoubtable Viking Harald Hardrada and down below is carved a romantic interpretation of Norwegian history. Dating from the 1830s, the column was brought to this remote place because no one else would have it – not too surprising really.

Elveseter is near the northern end of the Leirdal valley, from where it's a short hop over the hills to **Bøverdal**, which runs down into the crossroads settlement of **Lom**. En route, you'll pass the start of the narrow, eighteen-kilometre-long mountain road that sneaks up the **Visdal valley** to the *Spiterstulen* lodge and chalet complex at 1100m (☎61 21 94 00, ⓦwww.spiterstulen.no; March to mid-Oct). A wide range of accommodation is available, from the bunk beds of the youth section (250kr) to small cottages (❸), and there's a café-restaurant; for part of the season the lodge becomes an Outdoor Pursuits Centre – the lodge is within a day's hike of no fewer than seventeen peaks.

Lom

A long time trading and transport centre, **LOM** benefits – in a modest sort of way – from the farms that dot the surrounding valleys. It also makes a comfortable living from the passing tourist trade, with motorists pausing here before the last thump down Highway 15 to the Geirangerfjord. Even so, with a population of just 2000, it could hardly be described as a boom town. Lom's two thousand eighteenth-century heyday is recalled by its **stave church** (mid-June to mid-Aug daily 9am–8pm; 45kr), a strikingly attractive structure perched on a grassy knoll above the river. The original church was built here about 1200, but it was remodelled and enlarged after the Reformation, when the spire and transepts were added and the flashy altar and pulpit installed. Its most attractive features are the dinky, shingle-clad roofs, adorned by dragon finials, and the Baroque acanthus-vine decoration inside.

Nearby – up behind the tourist office – is the town's open-air museum, the **Lom Bygdamuseum** (late June to mid-Aug daily 11am–4pm; 40kr), a surprisingly enjoyable collection of old log buildings in a forest setting. Norway teems with this type of museum – stay in the country long enough and the very sight of one will make you want to scream – but Lom's is better than most, though you wouldn't think so from the ticket office: it's in what must be the biggest and ugliest late-medieval *storstabburet* (large storehouse) in the country. Persevere. The old wooden buildings in the woods beyond are a delight and one of them, the **Olavsstugu**, is a modest hut where St Olav, otherwise King Olav Haraldsson, is said to have spent a night as he beetled his way north to Trondheim. When the museum is closed, you can still wander round the site, though of course all the buildings are locked up.

Museum enthusiasts will also want to visit Lom's **Norsk Fjellmuseum** (Norwegian Mountain Museum; mid-June to mid-Aug Mon–Fri 9am–7pm, Sat & Sun 10am–7pm; May to mid-June & mid-Aug to Sept Mon–Fri 9am–4pm, Sat & Sun 11am–5pm; Oct–April Mon–Fri 10am–3pm; 50kr), a modern place that focuses on the Jotunheimen mountains. It's all here in admirable detail, from the fauna and the flora to the landscapes, farmers and past mountaineers, who scaled the peaks in tweeds and hobnail boots.

Practicalities

Buses to Lom pull in a few metres west of the main crossroads, and most of what you're likely to need is within easy walking distance of here. The church and the open-air museum are across the bridge on the other side of the river, as is the mountain museum, which shares its premises – and opening times – with the **tourist office** (T 61 21 29 90, W www .visitjotunheimen.com).

Car and bus routes on from Lom

Heading west from Lom along **Highway 15**, you are within comfortable driving distance of either the Geirangerfjord (see p.259) or Stryn and the western flanks of the Jostedalsbreen glacier (see p.256). Lom is also at the northern end of the wondrous Sognefjellsveg (Highway 55), running over the Jotunheimen mountains before proceeding down to the Sognefjord (see p.240). In the opposite direction, also along Highway 15, it's another very manageable drive to Otta (see p.174) and the main E6 highway between Oslo and Trondheim.

By **bus** from Lom, there are fast and frequent **Nor-Way Bussekspress** (W www.nor-way.no) services west to Langvatn, Stryn and ultimately Bergen, and east to Otta, Lillehammer and Oslo or Trondheim. From mid-June to the end of August, you can change onto a local bus at Langvatn for the Geirangerfjord – but check connections with Lom tourist office before you depart. There is also a local bus service south from Lom along the Sognefjellsveg (Highway 55) to Turtagrø, Solvorn and Sogndal (late June to Aug 1–2 daily).

The choicest **accommodation** is the ⚑ *Fossheim Turisthotell* (☎61 21 95 00, ⓦ www.fossheimhotel.no; ❺), about 300m east of the crossroads along Highway 15. The main lodge here has been added to over the years and the guest rooms, which are at the back, have a real rural feel with their timber walls, floors and ceilings. It's all very cosy and so are the delightful little wooden cabins (1000–1200kr) that trail up the wooded hillside beside the main building; some of them are very old and all are en suite. The hotel **restaurant** is outstanding and wherever possible features local ingredients. They serve set meals with three courses costing 350kr, four courses 500kr – try the beef in a rosemary jus with broad beans. A second good place to stay is the *Fossberg Hotel* (☎61 21 22 50, ⓦ www.fossberg.no; ❹), a chalet-like modern place made mostly of timber and a few metres from the town crossroads. For bargain-basement lodgings, the nearest HI **hostel**, *Bøverdalen Vandrerhjem* (☎61 21 20 64, ⓦ www.vandrerhjem .no; late May to early Oct; dorm beds 160kr, doubles ❶), is about 20km back down Highway 55 (the Sognefjellsveg) and occupies a series of glum modern buildings right by the roadside.

Nordfjord and the Jostedalsbreen glacier

The most direct way to get from the Sognefjord to the **Nordfjord**, the next great fjord system to the north, is to travel north from Mundal (see p.245) on Highway 5 as it tunnels beneath an arm of the vast **Jostedalsbreen glacier**, though this somehow seems a bit of a cheek. With the glacier left behind, Highway 5 then presses on past the turning for the **Astruptunet**, one-time home of the artist Nikolai Astrup, before proceeding on to the inner recesses of the Nordfjord. These recesses are readily explored along **Highway 60**, which weaves a pleasant, albeit tortuous, course through a string of unexciting

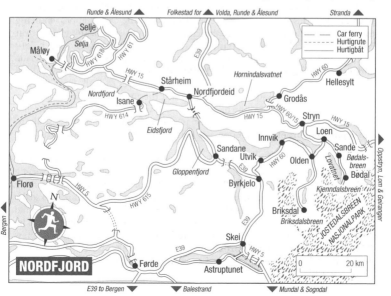

little towns between the fjord and the glacier's west side. Amongst them, **Loen** is easily the best base for further explorations, including the glacier, though humdrum **Stryn** is larger and more important. Stryn is also where Highway 60 meets **Highway 15**. The former presses on north to **Grodås**, home of the Anders Svor Museum, and Hellesylt on the Geirangerfjord (see p.259), while the latter runs west along the Nordfjord, with the road dipping and diving along the northern shore in between deep-green reflective waters and bulging peaks. It's a pleasant enough journey, but the Nordfjord doesn't have the severe allure of its more famous neighbours, at least in part because its roadside hamlets lack much appeal. Indeed, the only real reason to head this way is to make the time-consuming trek to the solitary monastic remains of **Selja island**, about 130km from Stryn.

High up in the mountains, dominating the whole of the inner Nordfjord region, lurks the **Jostedalsbreen glacier**, a five-hundred-kilometre-square ice plateau that creaks, grumbles and moans out towards the Sognefjord, the Nordfjord and the Jotunheim mountains. The glacier stretches northeast in a lumpy mass from Highway 5, its myriad arms – or "**nodules**" – nudging down into the nearby valleys, the clay particles of its meltwater giving the local rivers and lakes their distinctive light-green colouring. Catching sight of the ice nestling between peaks and ridges can be unnerving – the overwhelming feeling being that somehow it shouldn't really be there. As the poet **Norman Nicholson** had it: "A malevolent, rock-crystal/ Precipitate of lava,/Corroded with acid,/Inch by inch erupting/ From volcanoes of cold."

For centuries, the glacier presented an impenetrable east–west barrier, crossed only at certain points by determined farmers and adventurers. It's no less daunting today, but access is much freer, a corollary of the creation of the **Jostedalsbreen Nasjonalpark** in 1991. Since then, roads have been driven deep into the glacier's flanks, the comings (but mostly goings) of the ice have been closely monitored and there has been a proliferation of officially licensed **guided glacier walks** (*breturar*) on its various arms (see box, p.255). If that sounds too energetic and all you're after is a **close look at the glacier**, then this is possible at several places, with the easiest approach being the five-minute stroll to the Bøyabreen on the south side of the glacier near Mundal (see p.246). By contrast, the east side's Nigardsbreen (see p.250) requires much more commitment – getting to the ice involves a boat ride and a short, stiff hike – as does the **Briksdalsbreen**, here on the west side of the glacier, off Highway 60. It takes about 45 minutes to walk from the end of the road to the Briksdalsbreen, but it's still the most visited approach by a long chalk, partly on account of its pony-and-trap rides up towards the ice. Much less crowded and far prettier is the easy twenty-minute walk to the **Kjenndalsbreen**, near Loen – a delightful way to spend a morning or afternoon.

Travelling around the Nordfjord region by **bus** presents few problems if you stick to the main highways, but services from Highway 60 to the glacier are limited. There are no buses at all to Kjenndalsbreen and an infrequent service (June–Aug 1 daily) from Stryn, Loen and Olden to Briksdal (for Briksdalsbreen). The good news is that the times of the Briksdal buses are coordinated so you get three hours at Briksdalsbreen between arrival and departure. The most useful long-distance bus service hereabouts is the Nor-way Bussekspress (ⓦ www.nor-way.no) **Nordfjordekspressen**, which links Stryn with Nordfjordeid and Måløy in one direction, Langvatn (for Geiranger), Lom, Otta and ultimately Oslo in the other.

Guided glacier walks and national park information centres

Most **guided glacier walks** on the Jostedalsbreen are scheduled between late June and early September, though on some arms of the glacier the season extends from May until late September. The walks range from two-hour excursions to five-day expeditions. Day-trip prices start at 500–600kr per person for a two- to four-hour gambol, rising to 700kr for six to eight hours. A comprehensive leaflet detailing all the various walks is widely available across the region and at the national park's three **information centres**. These are the **Norsk Bremuseum**, on the south side of the glacier near Mundal (see p.246); the **Breheimsenteret Jostedal** on the east side at the Nigardsbreen (see p.250); and the **Jostedalsbreen Nasjonalparksenter** (daily: May & early Sept noon–4pm; June & Aug 10am–4pm; July 10am–6pm; exhibitions 70kr; ☎57 87 72 00, ⊛www.jostedalsbre.no) in Oppstryn, 20km east of Stryn on Highway 15. Each of the centres has displays on all things glacial and sells books, souvenirs and hiking maps.

Booking arrangements for the shorter glacier walks vary considerably. On some of the trips – for example those at the Nigardsbreen – it's sufficient to turn up at the information centre an hour or two beforehand, but in general it's a good idea to make a reservation at least a day ahead. Sometimes this is best done through the information centre, sometimes direct with the tour operator. In the case of the overnight trips, however, you must reserve generally at least four weeks beforehand. In all cases, basic **equipment** is provided, though you'll need to take good boots, waterproofs, warm clothes, gloves, hat, sunglasses – and sometimes your own **food** and **drink** too.

North from Mundal to Astruptunet and Skei

Heading north from Mundal on Highway 5, it's about 30km to the Kjøsnes junction, where two long and slender lakes intersect. Turn left here, over the bridge, and it's an eleven-kilometre detour west along the southern shore of one of these lakes, Jølstravatnet, to **Astruptunet** (late May to late June daily 11am–4pm; late June to mid-Aug daily 10am–6pm; mid-Aug to mid-Sept Thurs, Sat & Sun 11am–4pm; 50kr; ⊛www.astruptunet.com), the one-time farmstead home and studio of Nikolai Astrup (1880–1928). On the steep slope above the lake, this huddle of old turf-roofed timber buildings looks pretty much the same as it did during the artist's lifetime, though the old barn has been replaced by a modern gallery, used for temporary exhibitions of modern art. A versatile artist, Astrup's work included paintings, sketches, prints and woodcuts, of which a good selection is on display here. However, the bulk of the collection consists of his landscape paintings, characteristically romanticized rural scenes in bright colours, with soft, flowing forms. Unlike many of his contemporaries, Astrup eschewed Realism in favour of Neo-Impressionism and, as such, he bridged the gap between his generation of Norwegian painters and the Matisse-inspired artists who followed.

Back on Highway 5, the Kjøsnes junction is just a couple of kilometres short of **SKEI**, where you can either head west for the hundred-kilometre journey to the coast at Florø (see p.274), or turn north for the twenty-kilometre yomp up the valley to the **Byrkjelo crossroads**. From here, it's a further 55km over the mountains and along the Nordfjord to Olden, where you turn off for the Briksdalsbreen (see p.256), and 7km more to Loen, at the start of the road to the Kjenndalsbreen (see p.257).

Olden and the Briksdalsbreen

Hard by the Nordfjord, the hamlet of **OLDEN** doesn't have much going for it, but it is at the start of the 24km-long byroad south to **BRIKSDAL**, a scattering of mountain chalets that serves as the starting point for the easy 45-minute (2–3km) walk to the **Briksdalsbreen glacier arm**. The path skirts waterfalls and weaves up the river until you finally reach the glacier, surprisingly blue except for streaks of dirt. It's a simple matter to get close to the ice as the only precaution is a flimsy rope barrier with a small warning sign – but do be careful. Alternatively, you can hop on a twee-looking **battery-driven golf cart** at the café area for the twenty-minute drive up to the glacier. Several operators offer **guided glacier walks** on the Briksdalsbreen and the adjacent Brenndalsbreen: Olden Aktiv (ⓣ57 87 38 88, Ⓦwww.oldenaktiv.no) is as good as any.

A local **bus** service connects Stryn, Loen and Olden with Briksdal (June–Aug 1 daily); schedules mean that passengers get three hours at Briksdal before the departure of the return service.

Loen and the Kjenndalsbreen

LOEN spreads ribbon-like along the Nordfjord's low-lying, grassy foreshore, with ice-capped mountains breathing down its neck. The village is home to one of Norway's most famous hotels, the outstanding, family-run ⚞ *Alexandra* (ⓣ57 87 50 00, Ⓦwww.alexandra.no; ❽), whose exterior hardly does it justice. The hotel occupies a large and fairly undistinguished modern block overlooking the fjord, but inside the lodge-like public rooms are splendid – wide, open and extremely well appointed. There's every convenience, including a sauna and solarium, while the bedrooms are spacious, infinitely comfortable and furnished in bright modern style. Breakfasts are banquet-like, but the evening **buffets** (from 7pm; 470kr, 250kr for hotel guests) are even better, a wonderful selection that lays fair claim to being the best in the fjords. The *Alexandra* is, of course, fairly pricey, but across the road and right on the water's edge, the *Hotel Loenfjord* (ⓣ57 87 57 00, Ⓦwww.loenfjord.no; ❻, sp/r ❺) is an excellent and less-expensive second choice. A happy cross between a motel and a lodge, the *Loenfjord* comprises a long and low modern building in a vernacular version of traditional Norwegian style. The public rooms are expansive, and the evening buffet very good. More of a bargain still is *Loen Pensjonat* (ⓣ57 87 76 24, Ⓦwww.loen-pensjonat.com; ❶), in a chalet-like, modern house about 500m inland from the *Alexandra* – and across from the church in the old village.

Loen kyrkje

Both of Loen's hotels are located on land reclaimed from the fjord and the handful of dwellings that make up the old village are located about 500m inland. Here, perched on top of a gentle ridge, is **Loen kyrkje**, a tidy structure dating from 1837. Its interior is unremarkable, though the folksy furnishings and fittings are pretty enough, but the views from outside over the fjord are delightful. Its churchyard and precincts also hold a couple of items of interest, namely a stone Celtic cross that is at least a thousand years old, and a pair of **memorial plinths** to the villagers who were drowned in the disasters of 1905 and 1936. On both occasions, a great hunk of the Ramnefjell mountain fell into lake Lovatnet behind the village and the ensuing **tidal wave** swept dozens of local farmsteads away. The second disaster was particularly tragic as the government had only just persuaded many of the villagers to return home after the first trauma.

To the Kjenndalsbreen

From beside the *Hotel Alexandra*, a 21-kilometre byroad leads south to the **Kjenndalsbreen** arm of the Jostedalsbreen glacier. The road starts by slipping up the river valley past lush meadows, before threading along the northerly shore of **Lovatnet**, a long and thin lake of glacial blue. After 4.4km, the byroad reaches the ferry point for boat cruises along the lake (see box below) and then scuttles on to the hamlet of **BØDAL**, whose grassy foreshore marks the sight of the village that bore the brunt of the two tidal waves (see p.256): today's houses perch cautiously on the ridge well above the water. There are guided glacier walks near Bødal on the **Bødalsbreen** with the main operator being Briksdal Breføring (☎57 87 68 00, ⓦwww.briksdal-adventure.com) (mid-June to mid-Sept; ☎57 87 68 00). Their standard offering lasts five to six hours, including three hours on the ice, and costs 500kr; there are no guided glacier walks on the Kjenndalsbreen itself.

Pushing on along the Kjenndalsbreen road, it's a further 3km or so to a toll post (30kr) and a couple of hundred metres more to the **café** (May–Sept) at the very end of the Lovatnet – and the spot where the boat docks. From here, it's 5km more to the car park and then an easy and very pleasant twenty-minute ramble through rocky terrain to the **ice**, whose fissured, blancmange-like blue-and-white folds tumble down the rock face, with a furious white-green river, fed by plummeting meltwater, flowing underneath. If the weather holds, it's a lovely spot for a picnic.

There are no **buses** from Loen to the Kjenndalsbreen.

Around Loen: Mount Skåla

Loen is also the starting point of a popular five-hour hike east up to the plateau-top of **Mount Skåla** (1848m), from where the fjord and mountain views are fantastic. The path is clearly marked, but you'll have to be in good physical condition and have proper walking gear to undertake the trek: also, check locally for snow and ice conditions at the summit before setting out. The hike back down again takes about three hours, or you can overnight in the circular stone tower at the summit, the **Skålatårnet**, which serves as a self-service DNT hut with twenty beds and a kitchen. Curiously, the tower was built in 1891 at the behest of a local doctor – one Dr Kloumann – as a recuperation centre for tuberculosis sufferers.

Stryn

STRYN, merely 12km around the Nordfjord from Loen, is the biggest town hereabouts, though with a population of just 1600 that's hardly a major boast. For the most part, it's a humdrum modern sprawl straggling beside its long main

---

By boat from Loen to the Kjenndalsbreen

From June to August, a small **passenger boat** (1 daily) weaves a leisurely course from one end of lake **Lovatnet** to the other, a delightful cruise through beguiling scenery. The departure point is the pint-sized **Sande jetty**, 4.4km down the Kjenndalsbreen road from the *Hotel Alexandra* in Loen, and the boat docks about 5km from the Kjenndalsbreen ice face. The excursion costs 180kr, including onward transportation by bus from the dock to the car park at the end of the Kjenndalsbreen road and the return journey – again by bus and boat – back to Sande; in total the round trip takes four hours. The *Hotel Alexandra* (see p.256) issues tickets and takes bookings and will, at a pinch, give you a lift down to Sande if required.

street, but there is a pleasant pocket of antique **timber houses** huddled round the old bridge, down by the river near the tourist office and just to the south of the main drag; take a few moments to have a look.

Stryn **bus station** is beside the river to the west of the town centre on Highway 15/60 (the road to Nordfjordeid). From here, it's a 600m walk to the **tourist office**, in the centre just off the main street, Tonningsgata (early June & late Aug Mon–Fri 8.30am–6pm & Sat 9.30am–5pm; late June & early Aug Mon–Fri 8.30am–6pm, Sat & Sun 9.30am–5pm; July daily 8.30am–8pm; Sept–May Mon–Fri 8.30am–3.30pm; ☎57 87 40 40, ⓦwww.nordfjord.no). Staff issue free town maps, rent mountain bikes, have a wide range of local brochures and sell hiking maps. There's no strong reason to overnight here, but Stryn does possess one excellent **hotel**, the *Visnes*, Prestestegen 1 (☎57 87 10 87, ⓦwww .visnes.no; ❺), an extremely comfortable, family-run place, which occupies a pair of handsome – and handsomely restored – old villas, one of which comes complete with Viking-style dragon finials and wedding-cake-like balconies. In total, the hotel has fifteen suites and doubles, each of which is decorated in vintage style, and one of the two buildings – Villa Visnes – boasts a splendid, timber-clad Grand Hall. The hotel is a couple of kilometres west of centre on the hilly promontory above the road to Loen (Highway 60). Stryn also has a better-than-average HI **hostel** (☎57 87 11 06, ⓦwww.vandrerhjem.no; all year; dorm beds 245kr, doubles ❶), perched high above the centre at Geilevegen 14. This lodge-style building has self-catering facilities, a laundry and internet access plus splendid views over Stryn and its surroundings – compensation for the lung-wrenching one-kilometre trek up here. The hostel is signposted from the main drag – north up Bøavegen – on the east side of the centre. Four-star *Stryn Camping* (☎57 87 11 36, ⓦwww.stryn-camping.no) is handier, just a couple of hundred metres up Bøavegen; it's well equipped and has tent pitches as well as cabins (600–700kr for two persons).

Heading west out of Stryn, highways 15 and 60 share the same stretch of road for 16km before they separate: Highway 60 then spears north to reach, after another 35km, Hellesylt, on the Geirangerfjord (see p.261), while Highway 15 continues west to the village of **Nordfjordeid** before travelling along the northern shore of the **Nordfjord** bound for Måløy and **Selje** (see below), just over an hour's drive away.

West from Stryn to the islet of Selja

Travelling west from Stryn, it's 45km to dreary, small-town **Nordfjordeid** and a further 30km along the bare and bleak northern shore of the **Nordfjord** to Highway 61. This minor road then leads the final 30km up and over the hills to **SELJE village**, a light scattering of houses straggling along a wide bay. Selje has a long sandy beach, but more importantly is the starting point for two-hour guided tours of the nearby **islet of Selja** (May Sun 1 daily; June–Sept 1–3 daily; 150kr including the 15min boat ride; ⓦwww.seljekloster.no). The islet is the site of several medieval remains, easily the most significant of which are the ruins of **Selja Kloster**, a monastery built in the tenth century by Benedictine monks. It was originally named after the legendary St Sunniva, an Irish princess who refused to marry the pagan selected by her father. Royal blood, chastity and loyalty to the Catholic faith were key ingredients for beatification and sure enough Sunniva eventually got her saintly reward, but only after spending the rest of her life hidden away in a cave here on this island. The best-preserved part of the monastery is the church tower, but otherwise the dilapidated masonry is rather less impressive than the setting.

For details of boat times and to make a reservation, contact the **tourist office** in Selje village (early June & late Aug daily 9am–4pm; late June & early Aug daily 9am–5pm; July daily 9am–7pm; Sept & Jan–May Mon–Fri 8am–3.30pm; ☎57 85 66 06, ⓦwww.nordfjord.no). The village has one **hotel**, the *Selje* (☎57 85 88 80, ⓦwww.seljehotel.no; ⑥, sp/r ❹), a large, modern lodge right behind the beach, which specializes in health treatments, and comes complete with indoor and outdoor pools, massage facilities and jacuzzi.

Driving on from Selje, you can push north along the coast to the delightful town of Ålesund (see p.269), 120km away. This involves two **car ferry** crossings, one from **Koparneset to Årvik** (every 30min–1hr; 15min; passengers 23kr, car & driver 55kr; ⓦwww.tide.no), the other from **Hareid to Sulesund** (every 30min to 1hr; 25min; passengers 29kr, car & driver 80kr; ⓦwww.tide.no). On the way, you'll pass within easy striking distance of the bird island of Runde (see p.273). In the opposite direction, it's 50km south along the coast to the fishing port of Måloy (see p.274).

North from Stryn: Grodås and Hellesylt

From Stryn, it's about 20km on Highway 60 to the town of **GRODÅS**, which curves round the eastern tip of the **Hornindalsvatnet**, at 514m Europe's deepest and Norway's clearest lake. A straggly little place, **Grodås** is distinguished mainly by the **Anders Svor Museum** (late June to mid-Aug daily 11am–6pm; late May to late June & mid-Aug to mid-Sept Thurs, Sat & Sun noon–3pm; 30kr), which inhabits a sweet-looking Neoclassical structure built beside the lake in 1953. Hardly a household name today, Svor (1864–1929) was a native of Grodås, who established something of an international reputation as a sculptor of those highly stylized, romantic figures much admired by the European bourgeoisie of the late nineteenth and early twentieth centuries. Some of the more clichéd pieces on display here, such as *Bøn* (Prayer), *Sorg* (Grief) and *Lita jente* (A Small Girl), are typical of his work, though busts of his family and friends, in particular those of his wife, Brit, and his mother, reveal much more originality and talent. Svor's career is typical of his generation, too: like other Norwegian artists, he was keen to escape the backwoods, moving to Kristiania (Oslo) in 1881 and four years later to Copenhagen, the start of an extended exile that only ended after Norway won independence in 1905.

There's no strong reason to overnight in Grodås, but the town does have an agreeable **hotel**, the *Best Western Raftevolds* (☎57 87 96 05, ⓦwww.raftevold .no; ⑤), a modern place whose well-proportioned concrete and timber lines work quite well; the hotel backs directly onto the lake. Otherwise, Highway 60 continues beyond Grodås, clipping up the valley and over the hills to reach, after 25km, the turning for the Norangsdal valley (see p.261) and shortly afterwards **Hellesylt**, on the Geirangerfjord (see p.261).

The Geirangerfjord and Norangsdal

The **Geirangerfjord** is one of the region's smallest fjords, but also one of its most breathtaking. A convoluted branch of the Storfjord, the Geirangerfjord cuts deep inland and is marked by impressive waterfalls, with a village at either end of its snake-like profile – **Hellesylt** in the west and **Geiranger** in the east. Of the two, Geiranger has the smarter hotels as well as the tourist crowds, Hellesylt is tiny and dull, but it is but a troll's throw from the magnificent **Norangsdal valley**, where the hamlet of **Øye** boasts one of the region's most enjoyable hotels.

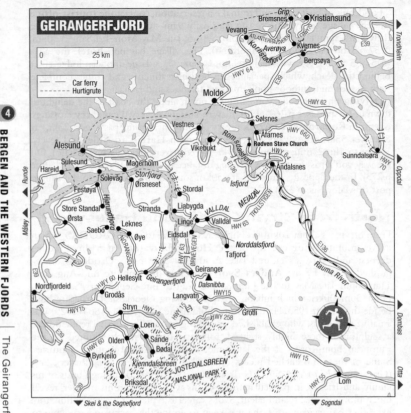

You can reach Geiranger in dramatic style from both north and south along the rip-roaring, nerve-jangling Highway 63, the aptly named **Ørnevegen** ("Eagle's Highway"). The approach to Hellesylt along Highway 60 is comparatively demure, though taken as a whole this highway is an especially appealing route between the Nordfjord and Ålesund.

In the summertime, **car ferries** link Hellesylt and Geiranger in what is one of the most celebrated trips in the entire region (May to mid-Oct 4–8 daily; 1hr; passengers 110kr one-way, 140kr return; car & driver 230kr each way; Ⓦ www.fjord1.no). With rearing cliffs to either side, the ferry follows the S-shaped profile of the fjord, whose cold waters are about 300m deep and fed by a series of plunging waterfalls up to 250m in height. The falls are all named, and the multilingual commentary aboard the ferry does its best to ensure that you become familiar with every stream and rivulet. More interesting are the scattered ruins of abandoned farms, built along the fjord's sixteen-kilometre length by fanatically optimistic settlers during the eighteenth and nineteenth centuries. The cliffs backing the fjord are almost uniformly sheer, making farming of any description a short-lived and back-breaking occupation – and not much fun for the children either: when they went out to play, they were roped to the nearest boulder to stop them dropping off.

Long-distance **Nor-Way Bussekspress buses** travelling west along Highway 15 link Otta (see p.174) and Lom (see p.251) with Stryn (see p.257) via Langvatn, where you change for the **local bus** north to Geiranger, though note that this onward, connecting service only operates from mid-June to August. This same local bus pushes on from Geiranger to Åndalsnes (see p.267). Hellesylt is on the main Bergen–Ålesund bus route operated by **Nor-Way Bussekspress**. This service connects, among many other places, Skei, Olden, Loen, Stryn, Grodås and Hellesylt. Finally, there's a limited **local bus** service from Hellesylt down along the Norangsdal valley to Øye and Leknes (late June to mid-Aug Mon–Fri 1 daily); it leaves at lunchtimes, whereas the bus from Leknes leaves mid-morning. For bus frequencies, see "Travel details", p.277.

Hellesylt

Tiny, inconsequential **HELLESYLT** is now little more than a stop-off on tourist itineraries, with most visitors staying just long enough to catch the ferry down the fjord to Geiranger (see p.262) or scuttle off along Highway 60. For daytime entertainment, there is a tiny beach beyond the mini-marina near the ferry quay, the prelude to some very cold swimming, or you can watch the waterfall crashing down the cliffs a few metres from the dock. Otherwise, the place seems more than a little down-at-the-mouth: the old dockside Hotel Grand is empty and other houses are boarded up too. The main dampener has been Mount Åknes, a great chunk of which is eroding away from the rest of the mountain, threatening to collapse into the Storfjord and create a tsunami which will hit Hellesylt in six minutes; experts are monitoring the mountain closely, but of course no one knows if or when it will go, but it's a very real danger – see Tafjord, p.266.

The **tourist office** (June–Aug daily 11am–7pm; Sept Sat & Sun 11am–7pm; ☎94 81 13 32, ⓦwww.hellesylt.no) is a five-minute walk from the jetty in a modern building that doubles as the Peer Gynt Galleriet (same timings; 50kr). On display is a set of kitsch-meets-Baroque woodcarvings illustrating Ibsen's *Peer Gynt* by a certain Oddvin Parr from Ålesund. It's all rather strange, but good(ish) fun all the same. Hellesylt's HI **hostel** (☎70 26 51 28, ⓦwww .vandrerhjem.no; mid-May to late Sept) is pleasantly positioned on the hillside above the village beside Highway 60 – and a steep 350-metre walk up the signed footpath from the jetty. They have cabins (600–700kr for two persons) as well as both double rooms (❶) and dorm beds (210kr); facilities include self-catering, a café and a bike store.

The Norangsdal valley

A century ago, pony and trap took cruise-ship tourists from Hellesylt down through the majestic **Norangsdal valley** to what was then the remote hamlet of **Øye**, a distance of 24km. By car, it's a simple journey today, but the scene appears not to have changed at all: steep, snow-tipped peaks rise up on either side of a wide, boulder-strewn and scree-slashed valley, dented by a thousand rock falls – all in all some of the wildest scenery imaginable. Near the top of the valley, the road slips through mountain pastures, where local women once spent every summer with their cows. The women slept in spartan timber cabins and today a roadside **plaque** at a set of five surviving cabins fleshes out the details of life on these mountain pastures. Further along, the road runs besides lake **Lyngstøylvatnet**, created when a large rock-slide dammed the valley's stream in 1908; the lake covers the remains of a group of shacks and the water is so clear that you can still make out their outlines – again, you will spot the plaque.

Further on, the road soon dips down into **ØYE**, at the eastern tip of the Norangsfjord. The village's pride and joy is the splendid ✈ *Hotel Union* (☎70 06 21 00, ⓦwww.unionoye.no; April–Oct; ❼), whose handsome, high-gabled exterior of 1891 was designed to appeal to touring gentry. The hotel's interior is crammed with period antiques and bygones seemingly hunted down from every corner of the globe. Each of the 27 bedrooms is individually decorated in elaborate style and most celebrate the famous people who have stayed here, like King Hakon VII and Kaiser Wilhelm II, not to mention the Danish author Karen "*Out Of Africa*" Blixen. It's a great place to spend the night – though you do have to turn a blind eye to the occasional period excesses, like the four-posters – and the food is first-rate, too. Telephones are banned, which is inducement enough to sit on the terrace and watch the weather fronts sweeping in off the glassy green **Norangsfjord**, or have a day's fishing – the hotel sells licences and dispenses advice; they also offer bike rental and will arrange guided mountain walks.

Hjørundfjord

No ferries dock at Øye itself, but they do use the jetty just 8km away to the west at **LEKNES**. This minuscule port occupies a magnificent location at the point where the Norangsfjord meets the **Hjørundfjord**, whose blue-black waters stretch away to the north hemmed in by jagged, pyramid-shaped peaks. Only 40km long, the Hjørundfjord is one of the most visually impressive fjords in the whole of the country, a stirringly melancholic place of almost intimidating beauty. Perhaps appropriately, it takes its name from the terrible times when the Black Death swept Norway, leaving the fjord with just one inhabitant, a woman called **Hjørund**, who wandered its peaks crying out at the heavens. The best way to see more of the fjord is to leave your car at Leknes and take a **round trip** on the ferry (1–3 daily) that shuttles along the shores of the Hjørundfjord, visiting several of its tiny settlements; the whole trip takes a couple of hours and costs passengers 64kr.

It's also possible to use the ferry from Leknes to go straight to the main coastal highway, the **E39**, which runs from Bergen to Ålesund. There are two possibilities: take the ferry from Leknes to **Saebo** (every 1–2hr; 15min; passengers 24kr, car & driver 60kr) and then drive 25km west to **Ørsta** on the E39; or catch the boat to **Store Standal** (1–3 daily; 40min; passengers 32kr, car & driver 91kr), from where it's 14km north to the **Festøya–Solevåg ferry** (every 30min; 20min; passengers 25kr, car & driver 65kr) on the E39. If you're heading north to Ålesund (see p.269), the second option is a good shortcut. All the Hjørundfjord ferries are operated by Fjord1 (ⓦwww.fjord1.no).

Geiranger

Any approach to **GEIRANGER** is spectacular. Arriving by ferry reveals the village tucked away in a hollow at the eastern end of the fjord, while approaching from the north by road involves thundering along a fearsome set of switchbacks on the **Ørnevegen** (Highway 63) for a first view of the village and the fjord glinting in the distance. Similarly, the road in from Highway 15 to the south squeezes through the mountains before squirming down the zigzags to arrive in Geiranger from behind, passing two celebrated vantage points, **Flydalsjuvet** (see p.264) and **Dalsnibba** (see p.264), on the way; note, however, that both approaches are closed as soon as the snow comes.

Geiranger boasts a beautiful setting, one of the most magnificent in western Norway, the only fly in the ointment being the excessive number of tourists at the peak of the season. That said, the congestion is limited to the centre of the village and it's easy enough to slip away to appreciate the true character of the fjord, hemmed in by sheer rock walls interspersed with hairline waterfalls, with tiny-looking ferries and cruise ships bobbing about on its blue-green waters.

Early tourism to Geiranger

The **cruise ships** are a constant feature of the Geirangerfjord, sailing here from every part of northern Europe. The first one arrived in Geiranger in 1869, but this was packed with Quakers bearing tracts – much to the surprise of the locals, who thought themselves good Lutheran Christians already. The Quakers may not have had much luck converting the locals, but they were certainly taken with the beauty of the Geirangerfjord and spread the word on their return home: within twenty years the village was receiving a regular supply of visitors. Seizing their chance, local farmers mortgaged, sold and borrowed anything they could to buy ponies and traps, and by the end of the century tourists were being carted up from the jetty to the mountains by the score. In 1919, the horse was usurped when a group of farmer-cum-trap-owners clubbed together to import cars, which they kitted out with a municipal livery – the region's first taxi service. The present owner of the *Union Hotel* (see p.264) has restored a dozen or so of these **classic cars**, including a 1922 Hudson, a 1932 Studebaker and a 1931 Nash, and garaged them at the hotel: they can be admired for free most afternoons – ask at the hotel reception.

Arrival and information

Buses to Geiranger stop a stone's throw from the waterfront and the **ferry terminal**. The latter is used by both the ferry from Hellesylt (see p.261) and the **Hurtigrute coastal boat**, which detours from – and returns to – Ålesund on its northbound route between the middle of April and the middle of September only; it leaves Geiranger at 1.30pm. The **tourist office** is also on the waterfront, a couple of minutes' walk away, beside the sightseeing boat dock (mid-June to mid-Aug daily 9am–7pm; mid-May to mid-June & mid-Aug to mid-Sept daily 9am–5pm; ☎70 26 30 99, ⓦwww.visitgeiranger.no). Staff here issue bus and ferry timetables, sell hiking maps and supply free village maps, which usefully outline local hiking routes. They also promote expensive boat tours of the fjord, though the car ferry from Hellesylt is perfectly adequate.

From mid-June to August, local **buses** run north into Geiranger from Langvatn on Highway 15. There are two buses daily. One goes straight from Langvatn to Geiranger (45min), the other makes the detour to the **Dalsnibba viewpoint** (1hr 15min; see p.264). After Geiranger, both these local buses push to Åndalsnes (see p.267) via the Trollstigen (see p.266). The journey from Geiranger to Åndalsnes takes about three hours. Two buses daily complete the same route from north to south, again from mid-June to August. **Nor-Way Bussekspress** long-distance buses travelling along Highway 15 connect with these local services to and from Geiranger, but check connections before you set out.

Accommodation

Considering its popularity, Geiranger doesn't have many hotels, so vacant rooms are at a premium during the high season, when you should always reserve ahead. The village does better for campsites, the main one being *Geiranger Camping* (☎70 26 31 20; late May to early Sept), which sprawls along the fjordside fields a couple of hundred metres to the east of the tourist office. In summer it's jam-packed with caravans, cars and motorbikes – frankly not much fun at all. Rather more comfortable – and usually a good bit quieter – are the two fjordside campsites a couple of kilometres north of the village on the road to Eidsdal. These are the *Geirangerfjorden Feriesenter* (☎95 10 75 27, ⓦwww.geirangerfjorden.net; cabin 600–1000kr; May–Sept) and the *Grande Hytteutleige og Camping* (☎70 26 30 68, ⓦwww.grande-hytteutleige.no; May to mid-Sept; cabins 400–750kr).

Grande Fjordhotell ☎70 26 94 90, ⓦwww .grandefjordhotel.com. Ultramodern, timber-built hotel with few architectural surprises, but a pleasing fjordside location about 2km north of the centre on the Eidsdal road. The hotel is adjacent to the *Geirangerfjorden Feriesenter* (see above). ❹

🏃 **Hotel Union** ☎70 26 83 00, ⓦwww .union-hotel.no. Cream of the Geiranger crop, this large and lavish hotel perches high on the hillside about 500m up the road from the jetty. There's been a hotel here since 1891, and although the present building is firmly modern, it's an attractive structure and the public rooms are spacious and eminently comfortable. The bedrooms are pleasantly furnished in modern style and the best have fjord-facing balconies; those on the fourth floor are the pick. Open March to mid-Dec. ❽, sp/r ❻

Villa Utsikten ☎70 26 96 60, ⓦwww .villautsikten.no. On the south side of Geiranger, high up on the hill beside the main approach road, the family-run *Utsikten* offers simply wonderful views across the fjord and its surrounding mountains. There's been a hotel here since the 1890s, but today's building is resolutely modern, the public areas a tad retro. The thirty-odd bedrooms are decorated in a simple, modern manner, but the pick look out over the fjord. Open May–Sept. ❺, with fjord view ❻

The Village

Geiranger's principal man-made attraction is the **Norsk Fjordsenter** (daily: May to mid-June 9am–4pm; late June and early Aug 9am–6pm; July 9am–10pm; mid-Aug to mid-Sept 9am–4pm; 85kr; ⓦwww.fjordsenter.info), just across from the *Union Hotel* (see above). The centre follows the usual pattern of purpose-built museums, with separate sections exploring different aspects of the region's history from communications and transportation through to fjord farms and the evolution of tourism. Perhaps the most interesting display examines the problem of fjordland avalanches – whenever there's a major rock fall into a fjord, the resulting tidal wave threatens disaster.

Hiking trails and viewpoints

The Norsk Fjordsenter is, however, small beer when compared with the scenery. A network of **hiking trails** lattices the mountains that crimp and crowd Geiranger: some make their way to thundering waterfalls, yet others visit abandoned mountain farmsteads or venture up to vantage points where the views over the fjord are exhilarating if not downright scary. One popular and very enjoyable excursion involves both a boat ride and a four-hour hike. It begins with a short cruise along the fjord on the *MS Geirangerfjord* (mid-to late May & early Sept 1 daily; June–Aug 4–6 daily; 135kr) to a small jetty, from where it's a stiff, one-hour walk up to the mountain farm of **Skageflå**, followed by a three-hour trek back to Geiranger. If that sounds too much like hard work, speak to the crew about picking you up again at the jetty.

There's also the short but precarious trail to the **Flydalsjuvet**, an overhanging rock high above the Geirangerfjord that features in a thousand leaflets. To get there, drive south from the Geiranger jetty on Highway 63 and watch for the sign after about 5km; the car park offers extravagant views, but the Flydalsjuvet is about 200m away, out at the end of a slippery and somewhat indistinct track. A second famous viewpoint, **Dalsnibba**, at 1476m, is another 12km or so to the south along Highway 63 and then up a clearly signed, five-kilometre mountain toll-road. Remarkably enough, two of the four local buses that run into Geiranger from north and south make the detour (mid-June to Aug).

Eating

As for **food**, it's got to be the *Hotel Union* (see p.264), who do a magnificent, help-yourself buffet dinner for 435kr; check with the hotel to see when things get started as it's best to get there early before the munching starts in earnest. The restaurant also does an à la carte menu with mains costing around 250kr. The main competitor is the *Aida Restaurant* at *Villa Utsikten* (see p.264), where they focus on local, seasonal ingredients – and traditional Norwegian cuisine; mains hover around 220kr.

North to Åndalsnes via the Trollstigen

Promoted as the "Golden Route", the ninety-kilometre journey **from Geiranger to Åndalsnes** along Highway 63 is famous for its mountain scenery – no wonder. Even by Norwegian standards, the route is of outstanding beauty, the road bobbing past a whole army of austere peaks whose cold severity is daunting. The journey also incorporates a ferry ride across the Norddalsfjord, a shaggy arm of the Storfjord, and can include a couple of brief but enjoyable detours – one west along the Norddalsfjord to **Stordal**, home to an especially fine church, the other east to the intriguing village of **Tafjord**. Yet, the most memorable section is undoubtedly the **Trollstigen**, a mountain road that cuts an improbable course between the Valldal valley and **Åndalsnes**, which is itself a useful base for further fjordland explorations and has a couple of pleasant places to stay. Åndalsnes is also the northern terminus of the dramatic **Rauma train line** (see p.182) from Dombås to the east.

Twice daily from mid-June to August, a **local bus** travels the length of the Golden Route, taking the sweat out of driving round its hairpins and hairy-scary corners; the trip takes three hours and includes one ferry ride. Drivers should note that the higher parts of the road are generally closed from early October to mid-May – earlier/later if the snows have been particularly heavy.

Over the Ørnevegen to Linge – and Stordal

Heading north from Geiranger, the first part of the Golden Route is the 26-kilometre jaunt up and over the **Ørnevegen** (Highway 63) mountain road to **Eidsdal** on the Norddalsfjord. From here, a **car ferry** (every 20–45min; 10min; passengers 23kr, car & driver 55kr) shuttles over to the **Linge jetty**, where there's a choice of routes: travel east for the Trollstigen and Tafjord (see p.266), or head west for the 21-kilometre detour along Highway 650 to **STORDAL**, a workaday furniture-making town in a genial valley setting. Stordal may not fire the soul, but it is on the way to Ålesund (see p.269) and it does possess the remarkable **Rosekyrkja** (Rose Church; late June to mid-Aug daily 11am–4pm; 30kr), standing right beside the main road. Dating from the 1780s, the church has a modest exterior, with oodles of whitewashed clapboard, but the interior is awash with floral decoration, swirling round the pillars, across the ceiling and down the walls. There's an intensity of religious feeling here that clearly demonstrates the importance of Christianity to Norway's country folk, an effect amplified by a whole series of naive, almost abstract paintings with biblical connotations.

Valldal and Tafjord

Back at the Linge jetty, it's just 4km east to **VALLDAL**, a shadowy, half-hearted village that straggles along the fjord at the foot of the **Valldal valley**, which marks the start of the Trollstigen (see below). Valldal is also where a narrow byroad branches off Highway 63 to follow the fjord round to the remote, back-of-beyond village of **TAFJORD**, just 14km away to the east. Ignore the old power station at the entrance to the village, but keep going over the river to the pint-sized **harbour**, notable only for its complete lack of old buildings: they were swept away in 1934, when a great hunk of mountain dropped into the Norddalsfjord, creating a sixteen-metre tidal wave that smashed into the place, killing 23 locals in the process. Safe just 400m up the slope from the harbour, the upper part of Tafjord did survive and, unlike most of its neighbours, seems to have dodged postwar development almost completely. Here, a string of old houses and barns, with their cairn-like chimneys, picket fences and clapboard walls, ramble round twisty lanes demonstrating what these fjord villages looked like as late as the 1950s; it makes for a fascinating hour or so's wander.

A local **bus** makes the twenty-minute journey between Valldal and Tafjord twice daily on weekdays only.

Over the Trollstigen

The alarming heights of the **Trollstigen** ("Troll's Ladder"), a trans-mountain route between Valldal and Åndalsnes, are equally compelling in either direction. The road negotiates the mountains by means of eleven hairpins with a maximum gradient of 1:12, but it's still a pretty straightforward drive until, that is, you meet a tour bus coming the other way – followed by a bit of nervous backing up and repositioning. Drivers (and cyclists) should also be particularly careful in wet weather.

From Valldal, the southern end of the Trollstigen starts gently enough with the road rambling up the **Valldal valley**, passing dozens of fresh strawberry stalls in June and July – many Norwegians reckon these are the best strawberries in the country, some say the world. Thereafter, the road swings north, building up a head of steam as it bowls up the **Meiadal valley** bound for the barren mountains beyond. It's here that the road starts to climb in earnest, clambering up towards the bleak and icy plateau-pass, the **Trollstigplatået**, which marks its high point. In recent years, the assorted cafés and souvenir shops on the Trollstigplatået had begun to look rather tired, so the Norwegians are in the process of bringing it all bang up to date with a brand-new complex for completion in 2010. They have installed enhanced observation points and a new footbridge over the fast-flowing river that rushes off the plateau to barrel down the mountain below. From the main **Utsikten** (viewing point), there is now a magnificent panorama over the surrounding mountains and valleys. Clearly visible to the west are some of the region's most famous mountains with Bispen and Kongen (the "Bishop" and the "King") being the nearest two, at 1462m and 1614m respectively. From here also, the sheer audacity of the road becomes apparent, zigzagging across the face of the mountain and somehow managing to wriggle round the tumultuous, 180-metre **Stigfossen falls**.

The road was completed in 1936 to replace the **Kløvstien**, the original drovers' track that cut an equally improbable course over the mountains. Most of the track has disappeared, but you can pick it up at Slettvikane, from where it's a one-hour walk north across a barren mountain plateau to Stigøra on the Trollstigplatået. The Kløvstien then proceeds down the mountains as far as Bosetra, passing the Stigfossen falls on the way, but although this stretch only takes an hour, it's very steep and exposed, with chains to assist. Both of these one-hour hikes are, of course, linear, which is one reason why most hikers prefer

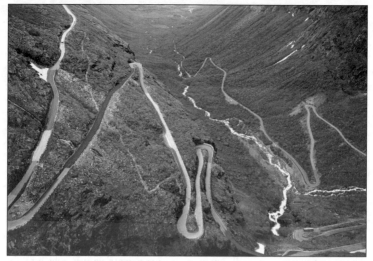
▲ Trollstigen (Trolls' Ladder)

to undertake less demanding, circular outings among the peaks and mountain lakes to the west. By contrast, the mountains to the east are part of the **Trollveggen** mountain wall and remain the preserve of climbers. As usual, prospective hikers should come properly equipped and watch for sudden weather changes.

Beyond the hairpins on the northern part of the Trollstigen, the road resumes its easy ramblings, scuttling along the **Isterdal** to meet the **E136** just 6km from Åndalsnes.

Åndalsnes

At the end of the splendid Rauma train line from Dombås (see p.182), **ÅNDALSNES** is for many travellers their first – and sometimes only – contact with the fjord country, a distinction it suits well enough. Damaged during World War II, the town centre may be modern and mundane, but it does possess a wonderful setting between lofty peaks and chill waters and, with a population of just 3500, it's small and restfully quiet. Åndalsnes is also an excellent place to start a visit to the fjordland: everything you're likely to need is near at hand, there's some economical accommodation, and the town is within easy reach by ferry, bus and/or car of some wonderful scenery, from the stern peaks that bump and hump away inland through to the fretted fjords that stretch towards the open sea.

There's also the matter of **Rødven stave church** (late June to late Aug daily 10am–4pm; 30kr), just half an hour's drive away – from Åndalsnes, head east round the Isfjord and after 22km take the signed turning which covers the final 10km. In an idyllic setting amid meadows, by a stream and overlooking a slender arm of the Romsdalsfjord, the church dates from around 1300, though its distinctive wooden supports may have been added in 1712 during the first of several subsequent remodellings. Every inch a country church, the place's creaky interior holds boxed pews, a painted pulpit and a large medieval crucifix, but it's the bucolic setting that most catches the eye.

Arrival and information

Buses to Åndalsnes all stop outside the **train station**, where you'll also find the **tourist office** (mid-June to mid-Aug Mon–Fri 9am–6pm, Sat & Sun 11am–4pm; mid-Aug to mid-June Mon–Fri 9am–3.30pm; ☎71 22 16 22, ⓦwww.visitandalsnes.com). Staff here provide bus and train timetables, rent mountain bikes at 180kr per day, issue regional guides and carry a wide range of local information geared to make you use Åndalsnes as a base. Their free *Dagsturer* (day-trips) booklet gives details of all sorts of motoring excursions in which most of their recommendations include a short hike. They also have details of local day-long hikes, fishing trips out on the fjord and guided climbs, not to mention fixed-rate sightseeing expeditions with Åndalsnes Taxisentral (☎71 22 15 55), who charge, for example, 800kr for a brief scoot down the Trollstigen, or 750kr for the return trip to Rødven church. This is, however, hardly a bargain when you consider the special deals offered by local car-hire firms with 24-hour rentals sometimes going for as little as 550kr – the tourist office has the details. Local **hiking maps** are sold at Romsdal Libris (Mon–Fri 9.30am–5pm & Sat 10am–3pm), a couple of minutes' walk northwest from the tourist office in the centre of town.

Accommodation

The tourist office has a small supply of en-suite **private rooms**, which go for 350–450kr per double per night, with self-catering facilities often provided, though most are a good walk from the town centre. Alternatively, Åndalsnes has a delightful ⚵ HI **hostel** (late May to Aug; ☎71 22 13 82, ⓦwww.vandrerhjem .no; dorm beds 260kr, doubles ❷, both including breakfast), a two-kilometre hike west out of town on the E136. To get there, head up the hill out of the centre to the roundabout, where you veer right (signed "E136 Dombås") under the flyover; keep going to the junction, where you keep straight, following the E136 in the direction of Ålesund – not Dombås; shortly afterwards, beyond the river, you'll see the sign on the right. The hostel has an attractive rural setting with open views down to the fjord and its simple rooms, set in a group of antique wooden buildings, are extremely popular, making reservations pretty much essential. The buffet-style **breakfast**, with its fresh fish, is one of the best hostellers are likely to get in the whole country, but note that the hostel doesn't do evening meals, though there are self-catering facilities. There is cycle storage, common rooms and a laundry; reception is closed from 11am to 4pm. There's one good hotel in the centre, the *Grand Hotel Bellevue* (☎71 22 75 00, ⓦwww .grandhotel.no; ❻, sp/r ❸), which occupies a large whitewashed block with a distinctive, pagoda-like roof on a hillock just up from the train station. The third hotel on this site – the second was bombed to bits in World War II – the *Grand* has a distinguished pedigree as evidenced by the old photographs opposite the reception desk: King Håkon spoke to the assembled locals from its entrance way; assorted ambassadors and bigwigs hunkered down here for a touch of R&R; and, most important of all, a young and distinctly modish Cliff Richard once stayed here – there's a picture of him skittling down the entrance steps. The hotel is now attached to the ultra modern Rauma Kulturhus, a combined library and theatre, which detracts from the atmosphere of the place, but the rooms are perfectly adequate in a plain sort of way and those on the top floors – four and five – have great fjord views. Among several local **campsites**, *Åndalsnes Camping og Motell* (☎71 22 16 29, ⓦwww.andalsnescamp.no) has a fine riverside setting about 3km from the town centre – follow the route to the youth hostel but turn first left immediately after the river. It's a well-equipped site with cabins (475–550kr for 4 persons) and it does bicycle and boat rental.

Eating

Åndalsnes is short of places to eat. The restaurant at the *Grand Hotel Bellevue* is really rather ordinary, offering standard Norwegian dishes – salad and poached salmon for example – for around 220kr per main course. Alternatively, you might try the *China House*, just up from the centre and below the *Grand*, where they serve all the Chinese classics from 130kr and up; it's open daily from noon to 10pm.

Ålesund

On the coast at the end of the E136, about 120km west of Åndalsnes, the fishing and ferry port of **ÅLESUND** is immediately – and distinctively – different from any other Norwegian town. Neither old clapboard houses nor functional concrete and glass is much in evidence, but instead the centre boasts a proud conglomeration of stone and brick, three-storey buildings, whose pastel-painted facades are lavishly decorated and topped off by a forest of towers and turrets. There are dragons and human faces, Neoclassical and mock-Gothic facades, decorative flowers and even a pharaoh or two, the whole ensemble ambling round the town's several harbours. These architectural eccentricities sprang from disaster: in 1904, a dreadful **fire** left ten thousand people homeless and the town centre destroyed, but within three years a hectic reconstruction programme saw almost the entire area rebuilt in an idiosyncratic **Art Nouveau** style, which borrowed heavily from the German Jugendstil movement. Many of the Norwegian architects who undertook the work had been trained in Germany, so the Jugendstil influence is hardly surprising, but this was no simple act of plagiarism: the Norwegians added all sorts of whimsical, often folkloric flourishes to the Ålesund stew. The result was

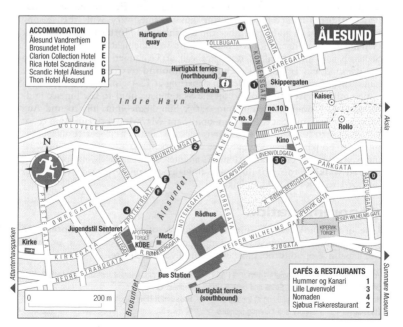

ÅLESUND

ACCOMMODATION
Ålesund Vandrerhjem	D
Brosundet Hotel	F
Clarion Collection Hotel	E
Rica Hotel Scandinavie	C
Scandic Hotel Ålesund	B
Thon Hotel Ålesund	A

CAFÉS & RESTAURANTS
Hummer og Kanari	1
Lille Løvenvold	3
Nomaden	4
Sjøbua Fiskerestaurant	2

0   200 m

Moving on from Åndalsnes

Travelling on from Åndalsnes, there are regular **Nor-Way Bussekspress buses** west along the E136 to Ålesund (2 daily; 2hr 10min) and northwest along Highway 64 to Molde (2 daily; 1hr 20min). The journey to Molde involves a short **ferry** trip from Åfarnes to Sølsnes (every 30min to 1hr; 15min; passengers 24kr, car & driver 60kr). Both Ålesund and Molde have good bus and ferry connections along the coast south to Bergen and north to Kristiansund and Trondheim; both are also ports of call for the **Hurtigrute coastal boat** (see p.278). Heading southwest from Åndalsnes, a **local bus** (mid-June to Aug 2 daily; 3hr; ⓦ www.fjord1.no) negotiates the so-called "Golden Route" over the Trollstigen mountain road to Geiranger.

Incidentally, be careful to distinguish between Kristiansund (see p.276) and the southern coastal town of Kristiansand (see p.140): to save confusion, on timetables and in brochures they are often written as Kristiansund N and Kristiansand S.

– and remains – an especially engaging stylistic hybrid, and Kaiser Wilhelm II, who footed the bill, was mightily pleased.

Art Nouveau aside, Ålesund has a couple of other mild attractions – the **Atlanterhavsparken**, a sort of glorified aquarium, and the old buildings of the open-air **Sunnmøre Museum**; the town also makes a good base from which to day-trip out to the bird cliffs of the island of **Runde**.

Arrival and information

From north to south, Ålesund's town centre is about 700m wide. The **bus station** is situated on the southern waterfront and from beside it **Hurtigbåt passenger express boats** depart for points south on the coast; northbound Hurtigbåt services leave from the Skateflukaia quay on the other side of the town centre, just metres from the quay for the **Hurtigrute coastal boat** (ⓦ www.hurtigruten.com). Hurtigrute sailing times vary with the seasons. From mid-April to mid-September, the **northbound** Hurtigrute sails daily for Geiranger at 9.30am and for Kristiansund and Trondheim at 6.45pm; from mid-September to mid-April, it does not call at Geiranger, but sails north to Kristiansund and Trondheim at 3pm. **Southbound** services are, however, the same all year, with sailings to Bergen departing at 12.45am.

Ålesund's **tourist office** is also on the Skateflukaia (mid-to late June & mid-to late Aug Mon–Fri 8.30am–7pm, Sat & Sun 11am–4pm; July to mid-Aug Mon–Fri 8am–7pm, Sat & Sun 8am–6pm; Sept–May Mon–Fri 9am–4pm & Sat 10am–2pm; ☎70 15 76 00, ⓦ www.visitalesund.com). They operate an accommodation booking service, supply free town brochures, issue a free if somewhat unrevealing leaflet describing Ålesund's architectural attractions, and coordinate **guided walking tours** of the centre (mid-June to mid-Aug 1 daily; shoulder seasons 1 weekly; 1hr 30min; 75kr).

Accommodation

One of Ålesund's real pleasures is the quality of its downtown **hotels** and **guesthouses**. If your purse is showing signs of strain, however, there are other, less expensive options too, most economically an HI **hostel**.

Ålesund Vandrerhjem Parkgata 14 ☎70 11 58 30, ⓦ www.vandrerhjem.no. Small and central HI hostel in a pleasant 1920s building at the top of Rådstugata. Has a laundry, self-catering facilities and a café plus internet access. Dorm beds 245kr, doubles ❷

Brosundet Hotel Apotekergata 5 ☎70 11 45 00, ⓦ www.brosundet.no. An excellent hotel occupying an attractively converted, waterside warehouse right in the centre of town. ❻, sp/r ❹

Clarion Collection Hotel Bryggen Apotekergata 1 ☎70 12 64 00, ⓦwww.choicehotels.no. Smart hotel in a carefully modernized, old waterside warehouse, where the public areas are kitted out with all sorts of nautical knick-knacks. The guest rooms are set out around three internal galleries that overlook the public areas in the manner of a cruise ship – and it all works very well. ❽, sp/r ❹

🏃 **Rica Hotel Scandinavie** Løvenvoldgata 8 ☎70 15 78 00, ⓦwww.rica.no. Exemplary chain hotel inhabiting a grand Art Nouveau edifice, which has been sympathetically modernized, from the handsome wrought-iron work of the main doors through to the intricate friezes and medallion frescoes beyond. Has the real sniff of luxury, but

unlike several of its rivals is not down by the water. ❻, sp/r ❹

🏃 **Scandic Hotel Ålesund** Molovegen 6 ☎21 61 45 00, ⓦwww.scandichotels.com. It may be one of a chain and occupy a routine modern block, but there's something very appealing about this relaxed and friendly hotel, not least its sea and harbour views. The breakfasts are excellent – and the breakfast room overlooks the ocean – and the rooms are bright and cheerful, each comfortably furnished in contemporary style with the pick – once again – offering charming sea views. ❻, sp/r ❺

Thon Hotel Ålesund Kongensgate 27 ☎70 12 29 38, ⓦwww.thonhotels.no. Suffers by comparison with its more atmospheric rivals, but this modern block is right in the centre and the rooms are perfectly adequate. ❺, sp/r ❹

The town centre

To get better acquainted with Ålesund's architectural peccadilloes, you might begin by visiting the **Jugendstil Senteret**, bang in the centre of town at Apotekergata 16 (Art Nouveau Centre; June–Aug daily 10am–5pm; Sept Mon–Fri 11am–5pm, Sat 11am–4pm & Sun noon–4pm; Oct–May Tues–Fri 11am–5pm, Sat 11am–4pm & Sun noon–4pm; 50kr, 70kr for joint ticket with KUBE, see below; ⓦwww .jugendstilsenteret.no). The Centre occupies one of the town's proudest Art Nouveau buildings, the old **Apothek** (pharmacy), whose spiky tower and heavy-duty stonework lend it a decidedly neo-baronial appearance. Inside, the ground floor is dominated by the ornate wood display cabinets of the former pharmacy and here also is a rather gimmicky "Time Machine" in which visitors are "beamed back" to 1904 to watch a short film on the fire that ripped through Ålesund and the reconstruction that followed. As the film explains, the fire happened when Norway's construction industry was in the doldrums, so skilled men turned up here looking for work from all over the country. This pleased the city's burghers no end, but they were frightened half to death when these same men turned out to be unionized, demanding a fair wage for a fair day's work – very different from the more placid country folk who made up the local workforce beforehand.

Approached via a handsome corkscrew staircase, the Centre's first floor holds a modest assortment of Art Nouveau pieces – vases, plates, furniture, jewellery and so forth – plus a magnificent, panelled dining room original to the house. Also on this floor are two more film shows, one on Art Nouveau as art, the other providing its international and socio political context.

KUBE and kirke

Adjoining the Jugendstil Senteret, in what was formerly a bank, is the town's top art gallery, **KUBE** (June–Aug daily 10am–5pm; Sept–May Tues–Fri 11am–5pm, Sat 11am–4pm & Sun noon–4pm; 50kr, 70kr joint ticket with Jugendstil Senteret), whose temporary displays focus on contemporary art, architecture and design.

From KUBE, it's just a few metres to Kirkegata, probably Ålesund's most harmonious street, its long line of Art Nouveau houses decorated with playful turrets and towers reminiscent of a Ruritanian film set. Up along this street stands the town's finest building, its **kirke** (church; June–Aug Tues–Sun 10am– 2pm; free), completed in 1909 to a decidedly Romanesque design, from the hooped windows through to the roughly dressed stone blocks and the clunky tower. Inside, the high altar is flanked by the most wonderful frescoes, a blaze of colour that fair takes the breath away. They were the work of a certain **Enevold Thømt** in the 1920s and are both keenly religious and startlingly original in their amalgamation of Art Nouveau and Arts and Crafts influences. The left-hand wall carries an image of the birth of Christ, the right the Ascension, while the vaulting of the arch above displays a variety of religious symbols – for baptism, communion, and so forth.

Kongensgate and around

From the church, it's a few-minutes' walk across town to Ålesund's main drag, pedestrianized **Kongensgate**, which is flanked by a string of Art Nouveau buildings. It's the whole ensemble that impresses most, but one or two are of special note, beginning with the whimsical medieval tower, hooped windows and geometrical friezes of the Skippergaten, at no. 18. Nearby, no. 10b is the narrowest house in Ålesund, its rough neo-Romanesque stonework contrasting with the polished tiles and wrought-iron grilles of no. 9 just across the street. There's more ersatz medievalism round the corner on Løvenvoldgata, where the Kino (cinema) is housed in a large and lugubrious stone tower topped by a cutesy cupola.

Architecture aside, the other obvious objectives in the town centre are the main harbour, with its assorted ferries and yachts coming and going, and the pretty little park at the top of Lihauggata, which runs up from Kongensgata. It's a surprise to find monkey puzzle and copper beech trees here, as well as a large statue of **Rollo**, a Viking chieftain born and raised in Ålesund, who seized Normandy and became its first duke in 911. Rollo was an ancestor of William the Conqueror, the epitome of the Norman baron and thus evidence of the speed with which the Vikings were absorbed into their host communities. Near to Rollo, up a short flight of steps on top of a little hillock, is a rough, stone column whose bronze plaque commemorates the town's benefactor, the **Kaiser**, looking suitably proud and noble. From the park, several hundred steps lead to the top of the **Aksla hill**, where the view out along the coast and its islands is nothing short of fabulous.

The Sunnmøre Museum

The **Sunnmøre Museum** (late May to late June Mon–Fri 11am–4pm & Sun noon–4pm; late June to late Aug Mon–Sat 11am–5pm & Sun noon–5pm; late Aug to mid-Sept Mon–Fri 11am–4pm & Sun noon–4pm; mid-Sept to late May Mon–Fri 11am–3pm & Sun noon–4pm; 65kr), about 4km east of the town centre just off the E136, is one of the region's more ambitious heritage museums. It may not be especially large, but everything is well presented and the location is really striking, spreading as it does over the lightly wooded hills of a tiny headland with water to either side. Inside the main building, a series of displays explores various aspects of local life from medieval times onwards and moored outside is an assortment of old and replica **boats** typical of vessels used hereabouts from the seventh century onwards. From beside the main building, a walking trail heads off over the hills to thread its way past fifty-odd antique **timber buildings** moved here from other parts of the Sunnmøre district. The buildings include assorted cowsheds, storehouses, stables and dwellings, as well as a row of eighteenth-century *kyrkjebuer* (church shacks), where local country folk once holed up before attending Sunday service. By law, Norwegians had to go to church, and as this involved many of them in long and arduous journeys, *kyrkjebuer* were built next to parish churches, so the peasantry could rest and change into their Sunday best. The *kyrkjebuer* also played a romantic role: it was here that many a Norwegian caught the eye of their future wife or husband.

The Atlanterhavsparken

Ålesund also possesses one of those prestige tourist attractions so beloved of development boards and local councillors. It's the **Atlanterhavsparken** (Atlantic Sea Park; June–Aug Mon–Fri & Sun 10am–7pm, Sat 10am–4pm; Sept–May daily 11am–4pm; 120kr; ⓦ www.atlanterhavsparken.no), a large-scale re-creation of the Atlantic marine environment that includes several enormous fish tanks; there's also an outside area with easy footpaths and bathing sites. The sea park is on a low-lying headland 3km west of the town centre.

Eating and drinking

For a town of just 40,000, Ålesund does well for cafés and restaurants, with the pick all within a stone's throw of the main harbour. If it's hot, anyone and everyone heads down to the harbourside terrace of the *Metz* pub.

Hummer og Kanari Kongens gate 19 ⓣ70 12 80 08. Relaxed and amenable café-restaurant, where they serve up a good line in seafood at around 220–280kr per main course. Also a good place to try a Norwegian favourite, klippfisk (salted and dried cod) cooked every which way and costing about 250kr. After the kitchen closes down – at about 9.30pm – the place turns into one of the grooviest bars in town. Mon–Fri 4pm till late, Sat & Sun from 2pm.

Lille Løvenvold Løvenvoldgata 2. Grooviest café in town, attracting a mixed but (nearly always) cool crew, who sip away at the best coffee in town. New Age-meets-lighter-shade-of-Goth decor in a rabbit warren of rooms. Mon–Sat 11am–11pm, sometimes later, Sun 2–11pm.

Nomaden Apotekergata 10. Tasty sandwiches, light meals, coffees and cakes in this cosy little café, where the decor is vaguely Edwardian – antique cupboards and so forth – with prints and paintings on the walls. Smooth, jazzy background music too. Great cheesecake. Mon–Sat 11am–4pm.

Sjøbua Fiskerestaurant Brunholmgata 1 ⓣ70 12 71 00. Smart, fairly formal restaurant serving an outstanding range of seafood from its harbourside, cellar premises. They even have their own lobster tank – something of a rarity in Norway. It's expensive, with main courses hovering around 300kr, but very popular, so reservations are advised. Mon–Fri 4–11pm.

Around Ålesund: birdwatching on Runde

The steep and craggy cliffs on the pocket-sized island of **Runde** are the summer haunt of several hundred thousand **sea birds**. Common species include gannet, kittiwake, fulmar, razorbill and guillemot, but the most numerous of all is the **puffin**, whose breeding holes honeycomb the island's higher ground. Most species congregate here between mid-April and August, though some – like the grey heron and the velvet scoter – are all-year residents. A network of hiking trails provides access to a number of birdwatching vantage points, though these invariably involve a fair climb up from the foreshore. One of the more popular hikes is the stiff forty-minute hoof up to the sea cliffs on the island's north shore from the car park at the end of the road. The island is connected to the mainland by bridge and this, its one and only road, slips along both the south and east shores. En route, it passes Runde's simple hostel (see p.274). For more detailed advice about hiking routes on Runde, ask at the hostel and/or consult ⓦ www.runde.no.

The easiest way to get to Runde is to **drive** the 70km from Ålesund. Allow two hours: Runde is itself connected to the mainland by bridge, but the journey still involves the car ferry ride from Sulesund to Hareid (every 30min–1hr;

If you're heading back to Bergen from Ålesund, the best bet is the relaxing thirteen-hour cruise on the **Hurtigrute coastal boat** as it weaves its way south along the mountainous, fjord-shredded coastline. An Ålesund-to-Bergen port-to-port ticket will cost in the region of 1100kr (770kr off-season), which bears comparison with the cost of the ten-hour, 380km **Nor-Way Bussekspress** bus journey (600kr). Express buses use the main coastal highway, the E39, which is by far the fastest route and covers some fine coastal scenery, with one particularly handsome stretch being between Folkestad and Nordfjordeid (see p.258). Nonetheless, the highway manages to miss almost every town and village of any real interest and only a major detour – to the likes of Florø and perhaps Måloy – turns up trumps. **Car drivers** will find the E39 fairly expensive too, as it includes four ferry trips at a combined cost of around 300kr per car and driver; be sure to pick up ferry timetables from Ålesund tourist office before you set out.

The Hurtigrute stops at three ports between Bergen and Ålesund, the most interesting of which is **FLORØ**, Norway's westernmost town. Florø has much in common with its west-coast neighbours: it boasts a blustery island setting; its economy has been boosted by the oil industry; it offers sea-fishing trips and excursions to a whole string of offshore islands; and its mostly modern centre is wrapped around the traditional focus of coastal town life, the harbour. More distinctively, Florø was once an important Viking centre and its early days are recalled on the offshore islet of **Kinn**, where the stone **Kinnakyrkja** (church), with its intriguing carvings and Baroque altarpiece, is a much-modified Romanesque structure dating from the twelfth century. **Passenger boats** to Kinn leave from Florø harbour once or twice daily except Sundays from late June to mid-August and the journey takes thirty minutes; boat timetables are available at the **tourist office**, by the harbour at Strandgata 30 (℡57 74 75 05, ⓦwww.fjordkysten.no). The tourist office also has a list of local **accommodation**, with one good option being the waterfront *Quality Hotel Florø*, Hamnegata 7 (℡57 75 75 75, ⓦwww.choicehotels.no; ❺, sp/r ❹), a smart chain hotel built in the style of an old warehouse; ask for a room with a sea view.

The second port of some interest is **MÅLOY**, an unassuming fishing village, which strings along the rugged foreshore of Vågsøy island. Måloy doesn't have too much to offer itself, but it is a short drive from **Kråkenes Fyr**, where the old lighthouse and the adjacent quarters offer pleasant accommodation in a wonderfully wild setting on a shank of rock that pokes out into the ocean (℡57 85 55 27, ⓦwww.krakenesfyr.no; Easter to early Oct; ❷, en suite ❹). Måloy is also just fifteen-minutes' drive from a second lighthouse, **Ulvesund Fyr** (℡57 85 17 77, ⓦwww.ulvesundfyr.no; ❹), which has a more sheltered if still profoundly isolated location and a handful of guest rooms in the three old buildings that once housed the lighthouseman and his family.

25min; passengers 29kr, car & driver 80kr; ⓦwww.tide.no). Runde is best visited on a day-trip, but there is a somewhat frugal HI **hostel** (℡90 74 43 43, ⓦwww.vandrerhjem.no; dorm beds 200kr, doubles ❶; May–Sept), in the southeast corner of the island right by the water.

North to Kristiansund

Ålesund is within easy striking distance of the next major towns up along the coast – **Molde** and **Kristiansund**, at 80km and 150km respectively. Neither is especially riveting, but Molde does put on a first-rate annual jazz festival and Kristiansund boasts a handsome coastal location plus a handful of mildly interesting sights recalling its heyday as a centre of the *klippfisk* (salted, dried cod) industry. The main road from Ålesund to Molde – the **E39** – is a pleasant coastal run culminating in a ferry crossing of the Romsdalsfjord. From Molde, there's a choice of routes to Kristiansund: the scenic **Highway 64**, incorporating the **Atlanterhavsvegen**, a short but dramatic stretch of highway that hops from islet to islet on the very edge of the ocean; and the faster, but more mundane, continuation of the E39.

As regards public transport, **Nor-Way Bussekspress buses** (Ⓦwww .nor-way.no) connect Ålesund with Molde and Trondheim (Mon–Fri 3 daily; 2hr/7hr 30min). En route, these buses pass through Bergsøya, where passengers change onto a local bus bound for Kristiansund, just 25km away (Mon–Sat hourly, Sun 4 daily; 40min; Ⓦwww.fjord1.no); be sure to check the Bergsøya connection before you set out. The **Hurtigrute coastal boat** (Ⓦwww .hurtigruten.com) also links Ålesund with Molde, Kristiansund and Trondheim, taking three hours to reach Molde, seven to Kristiansund, and thirteen and a half hours to Trondheim.

Molde

From Ålesund, it's about 80km along the E39 to the **Vestnes ferry** (every 30min–1hr; 35min; passengers 35kr, car & driver 101kr; Ⓦwww.fjord1.no), which scuttles over the Romsdalsfjord to **MOLDE**, an industrial town that sprawls along the seashore with a ridge of steep, green hills behind. Despite its modern appearance, Molde is one of the region's older towns, but it was blown to pieces by the Luftwaffe in 1940, an act of destruction watched by King Håkon from these very same hills just weeks before he was forced into exile in England. The new town that grew up in its stead is unremarkable, but it does host the week-long **Molde Jazz Festival**, held annually in the middle of July. Programme details are widely available across the region and tickets can be purchased both online and in person from the Molde ticket office (Ⓣ71 20 31 50, Ⓦwww.moldejazz.no). Naturally enough, the big-name concerts are sold out months in advance and accommodation is impossible to find during the festival, but the authorities do operate a large official campsite, **Jazzcampen**, for the duration. Festival apart, there's no strong reason to overnight here despite the sterling efforts of the *Rica Seilet Hotel*, which occupies a striking, sail-shaped glass tower on the fjord about 800m west of the centre at Gideonvegen 2 (Ⓣ71 11 40 00, Ⓦwww.rica.no; ❼, sp/r ❺).

All of Molde's amenities are within easy reach of each other: the Vestnes–Molde **ferry terminal** is on the east side of the centre, about 500m from the **bus station**, which is itself close to the **tourist office** at Torget 4 (mid-June to Aug Mon–Fri 9am–6pm, Sat 9am–3pm & Sun noon–5pm; Sept to mid-June Mon–Fri 8.30am–3.30pm; Ⓣ71 20 10 00, Ⓦwww.visitmolde.com).

From Molde to Kristiansund

There are two possible routes north from Molde to Kristiansund. The quicker, but less interesting, option is the **E39**, which begins with a fifty-kilometre canter northeast to a massive suspension **bridge**, which spans the straits between the mainland and the islet of **Bergsøya**. Here, **Highway 70** spears north for the 25-kilometre trip to Kristiansund via the five-kilometre Freifjord tunnel, while the E39 continues on to Trondheim, another 170km away to the east (see p.284).

The second, and far more picturesque route, is to take **Highway 64**, which forks north off the E39 just to the east of Molde. This highway starts off by tunnelling through the mountains, before rounding the head of the slender Malmefjord. Afterwards, it rattles over the hills, down the valley and along the edge of the **Kornstadfjord** to reach the coast at the start of the **Atlanterhavsveien** (Atlantic Highway), some 50km from Molde. A spirited piece of engineering, the Atlanterhavsvegen is a scenic eight-kilometre stretch of road that negotiates the mouth of the Kornstadfjord, manoeuvring from islet to islet by a sequence of bridges and causeways. In calm conditions, it's an attractive run, but in blustery weather it's exhilarating with the wind whistling round the car, the surf roaring and pounding but a stone's throw away.

Beyond, Highway 64 ploughs on across the island of **Averøy**, a twenty-kilometre run that ends at the **Bremsnes car ferry** to Kristiansund (every 30min–1hr; 20min; passengers 29kr, car & driver 80kr; ⓦ www.fjord1.no). On Averøy, the **Kvernes stavkirke** (late June to late Aug Mon–Sat 10am–5pm & Sun 11am–4pm; late Aug to mid-Sept Sun only 11am–4pm; 30kr) merits a brief detour – it's 10km south of Highway 64, along the island's eastern shore. Dating from the thirteenth century, the church was built on what had previously been a pagan ceremonial site, as proved by the discovery here of a Viking phallus stone. Much modified over the centuries, the church is a simple barn-like affair distinguished by its biblical wall paintings, added in the 1630s.

Kristiansund

Despite **KRISTIANSUND**'s attractive coastal setting, straddling three rocky islets and the enormous channel-cum-harbour that they create, the town somehow manages to look quite dull. The Luftwaffe is at least partly to blame as it polished off most of the old town in 1940, and, although Kristiansund dates back to the eighteenth century, precious little remains from pre war days. One minor exception is the handful of antique clapboard houses that string along **Fosnagata**, immediately to the north of the main quay, but otherwise the gridiron of streets that now serves as the town centre – just up the slope to the west of the main quay – is resolutely modern. At the south end of the main quay is the **klippfiskkjerringa statue** of a woman carrying a fish. The statue recalls the days when salted cod was laid out along the seashore to dry, producing the *klippfisk* that was the main source of income in these parts until well into the 1950s. Appropriately, therefore, the town is also home to the **Norsk klippfiskmuseum** (late June to early Aug daily noon–5pm; 50kr), housed in an old and well-worn warehouse, the **Milnbrygga**, across the harbour to the east of the main quay. The most pleasant way to reach the museum is by a small passenger boat, the **Sundbåten** (Mon–Fri 7.30am–7pm & Sat 9.30am–4.30pm; 2 hourly; 20kr one-way ticket, day-ticket 50kr), which leaves from beside the statue to call at each of the town's three islets. The service was once crucial for getting around Kristiansund, but the islands are now connected by bridge and the boats are, essentially, an exercise in nostalgia. The other noteworthy target is the handful of venerable timber houses that make up the **Gamle Byen** (Old Town), situated on the smallest of the three islets, **Innlandet** – south across the harbour from the main quay. Look out here also for the distinctive **Lossius-gården**, a large and handsome house that belonged to an eighteenth-century merchant; unfortunately, you can't go inside.

Around Kristiansund – Grip

Kristiansund's most popular attraction by a long chalk is **Grip**, a tiny, low-lying islet just 14km offshore. Grip is dotted with brightly painted timber homes, possesses an appealing assortment of antique boathouses, and comes complete with a much-modified medieval church, where the islanders once took refuge whenever they were threatened by a storm, as they often were – indeed, when you look at the place, it's amazing anyone ever lived here at all: there's a real touch of claustrophobia here even on a calm day, and when the weather's up the effects can be quite overpowering. There are no permanent residents now – the last ones left in 1964 – but in the summertime fishermen dock in the sliver of a harbour and there are even some basic guesthouse-style **lodgings** (❶); reservations are advised, and can be made via the Kristiansund tourist office (see below).

In summer, a daily **boat** links Kristiansund with Grip (mid-June to mid-Aug 1–2 daily; early June & late Aug Wed–Sun 1–2 daily; 30min; 190kr return; ⓦwww.gripskyss.no), and again reservations should be made at the tourist office.

Practicalities

Buses to Kristiansund pull in beside the Nordmørskaia quay at the north end of the main **town quay**, which is where the boat for Grip (see p.276) and the Sundbåt city boat (see p.276) depart, as does the **Hurtigbåt passenger express boat** service to Trondheim (1–3 daily; 3hr 15min; ⓦwww.fjord1.no). The **Hurtigrute** coastal boat docks at Holmakaia, a few metres to the east of the bus station. From the town quay, it's a short stroll up Kaibakken to the **tourist office** at Kongens plass 1 (mid-June to mid-Aug Mon–Fri 9am–6pm, Sat 10am–3pm & Sun 11am–4pm; mid-Aug to mid-June Mon–Fri 9am–4pm; ☎71 58 54 54, ⓦwww.visitkristiansund.com).

Kristiansund's first choice for **accommodation** is the sprightly *Quality Hotel Grand*, Bernstorrfstredet 1 (☎71 57 13 00, ⓦwww.choicehotels.no; ❺, sp/r ❸), whose one hundred or so rooms are comfortable and well appointed; Bernstorrfstredet is just to the south of Kaibakken, the short street linking the south end of the town quay with the main square, Kongens plass. Alternatively, there's the *Rica Hotel Kristiansund*, a smart and very modern chain hotel a short walk south from the main town quay at Storgata 41 (☎71 57 12 00, ⓦwww.rica.no; ❼, sp/r ❸). For **food**, the *Smia* restaurant, at Fosnagata 30 (☎71 67 11 70; Mon–Fri 4–11pm, Sat 3–11pm & Sun 3–9pm), stands head and shoulders above its competitors. Housed in a converted boat shed metres from the north end of the town quay, it serves superb fish dishes from around 140kr.

Travel details

Principal NSB train services (ⓦwww.nsb.no)

Åndalsnes to: Dombås (2–4 daily; 1hr 20min); Oslo (2–3 daily; 5hr 30min).
Ålesund to: Åndalsnes (2 daily; 2hr 10min); Bergen (1–2 daily; 10hr 30min); Hellesylt (1–2 daily; 2hr 45min); Oslo (2 daily; 10hr); Stryn (2–3 daily; 3hr 20min); Trondheim (3 daily; 7hr).
Bergen to: Finse (4 daily; 2hr 15min); Geilo (4 daily; 3hr 10min); Myrdal (4 daily; 2hr); Oslo (4 daily; 7hr 20min); Voss (4 daily; 1hr 10min).
Dombås to: Åndalsnes (2–4 daily; 1hr 20min); Trondheim (2–4 daily; 2hr 40min).

Myrdal to: Flåm (mid-June to late Sept 10 daily; mid-Sept to mid-June 4–8 daily; 50min).
Voss to: Bergen (4 daily; 1hr 10min); Myrdal (4 daily; 45min); Oslo (4 trains daily; 6hr).

Principal Nor-Way Bussekspress bus services (ⓦwww.nor-way.no)

Balestrand to: Oslo (3 daily; 8hr 30min); Sogndal (3 daily; 1hr 30min).
Bergen to: Flåm (4–5 daily; 3hr); Hellesylt (1–2 daily; 7hr 45min); Langvatn (2 daily; 8hr); Loen (3–4 daily; 6hr 30min); Lom (2 daily; 9hr); Norheimsund (1–3 daily; 1hr 30min); Odda (1–3 daily; 3hr 30min); Oslo (3 daily; 10hr 30min);

Otta (3 daily; 10hr); Skei (3–5 daily; 5hr 15min); Sogndal (4–5 daily; 4hr 30min); Stavanger (every 1–2hr; 5hr, 5hr 45min via Haugesund); Stryn (3–4 daily; 7hr); Trondheim (1 daily; 14hr); Utne (1–3 daily; 2hr 50min); Voss (4–5 daily; 1hr 50min); Ålesund (1–2 daily; 10hr 30min).
Kristiansund to: Oslo (1 daily; 11hr).
Mundal to: Oslo (3 daily; 7hr 50min); Sogndal (3 daily; 30min).
Sogndal to: Balestrand (3 daily; 1hr 15min); Bergen (4–5 daily; 4hr 30min); Mundal (3 daily; 30min); Oslo (3 daily; 7hr); Voss (4–5 daily; 2hr 40min).
Stryn to: Bergen (3–4 daily; 7hr); Hellesylt (1–2 daily; 1hr); Oslo (3 daily; 9hr); Trondheim (1 daily; 7hr 30min).
Voss to: Bergen (4–5 daily; 1hr 50min); Flåm (4–5 daily 1hr); Sogndal (4–5 daily; 2hr 50min).

Principal local bus services

Åndalsnes to: Geiranger (mid-June to Aug 2 daily; 3hr).
Geiranger to: Åndalsnes (mid-June to Aug 2 daily; 3hr).
Hellesylt to: Øye (late June to mid-Aug 1 daily; 45min).
Lom to: Sogndal (late June to Aug 2 daily; 3hr 30min); Turtagrø (late June to Aug 2 daily; 1hr 45min).
Sogndal to: Lom (late June to Aug 2 daily; 3hr 30min); Nigardsbreen glacier nodule (July & Aug 1 daily; 2hr); Otta (late June to Aug 2 daily; 5hr); Solvorn (July & Aug 1–3 daily; rest of year 2–3 daily, but no Sat service; 30min); Turtagrø (late June to Aug 2 daily; 1hr 50min).
Øye to: Hellesylt (late June to mid-Aug 1 daily; 45min); Leknes ferry quay (Mon–Fri 3–5 daily; 15min).

Car ferries

There are two main operators – Tide (ⓦ www .tide.no) and Fjord 1 (ⓦ www.fjord1.no). Principal services include:
Balestrand to: Mundal on the Fjærlandsfjord (May to Sept 4 daily; 1hr 30min).
Bruravik to: Brimnes (1–2 hourly; 10min).
Dragsvik to: Hella (every 40min to hourly; 15min); Vangsnes (every 40min to hourly; 30min).
Flåm to: Gudvangen (1–4 daily; 2hr).
Fodnes to: Mannheller (every 20min, hourly midnight to 6am; 10min).
Geiranger to: Hellesylt (May to mid-Oct 4–8 daily; 1hr).

Gudvangen to: Flåm (1–4 daily; 2hr).
Hella to: Dragsvik (every 40min to hourly; 15min); Vangsnes (every 40min to hourly; 30min).
Hellesylt to: Geiranger (May to mid-Oct 4–8 daily; 1hr).
Kvanndal to: Kinsarvik (1 or 2 hourly; 50min); Utne (1 or 2 hourly; 20min).
Utne to: Kinsarvik (1 or 2 hourly; 30min).

Principal Hurtigbåt passenger express boats

There are two main operators – Tide (ⓦ www .tide.no) and Fjord 1 (ⓦ www.fjord1.no). Principal services include:
Balestrand to: Bergen (1–3 daily; 4hr); Flåm (May–Sept 1–2 daily; 1hr 30min).
Bergen to: Ålesund (Mon–Fri 1 daily; 8hr 30min); Balestrand (1–3 daily; 4hr); Flåm (May–Sept 1–2 daily; 5hr 40min); Florø (1–2 daily; 3hr); Haugesund (1–2 daily; 4hr); Selje (1–2 daily; 5hr); Sogndal (1–3 daily; 5hr); Stavanger (1–2 daily; 5hr 30min).
Flåm to: Balestrand (May–Sept 1–2 daily; 1hr 30min).
Norheimsund to: Eidfjord (May–Sept 1 daily; 2hr 45min); Kinsarvik (May–Sept 1 daily; 1hr 30min); Lofthus (May–Sept 1 daily; 1hr 10min); Utne (May–Sept 1 daily; 50min).

Hurtigrute coastal boat

Summertime (mid-April to mid-Sept)
Northbound departures: daily from Bergen at 8pm; Florø at 2.15am; Måløy 4.30am; Ålesund at 9.30am for Geiranger & 6.45pm for Molde; Geiranger at 1.30pm; Molde at 10pm; Kristiansund at 1.45am; arrives Trondheim at 8.15am.
Southbound departures: daily from Trondheim at 10am; Kristiansund at 5pm; Molde at 9.30pm; Ålesund at 12.45am; Måløy 5.45am; Florø at 8.15am; arrives Bergen, where the service terminates, at 2.30pm.
Wintertime (mid-Sept to mid-April):
Northbound departures: daily from Bergen at 10.30pm; Florø at 4.45am; Måløy 7.30am; Ålesund at 3pm; Molde at 6.30pm; Kristiansund at 11pm; arrives Trondheim at 6am.
Southbound departures: daily from Trondheim at 10am; Kristiansund at 5pm; Molde at 9.30pm; Ålesund at 12.45am; Måløy 5.45am; Florø at 8.15am; arrives Bergen, where the service terminates, at 2.30pm.
Note: that it's only the northbound, summertime Hurtigrute service that detours to Geiranger.

Trondheim to the Lofoten islands

0   200 km

RUSSIA

Narvik

Lofoten

Bodø

Arctic Circle

NORWEGIAN SEA

5

FINLAND

Trondheim

SWEDEN

GULF OF BOTHNIA

4

3

1

2

ESTONIA

CHAPTER 5 # Highlights

✻ **Trondheim cathedral**
Scandinavia's largest
medieval building makes and
marks a stirring focal-point for
the city. See p.288

✻ **Bakklandet** The bars,
cafés and restaurants of
this attractive old district in
Trondheim are a great place for
a lively night out. See p.296

✻ **Ofotbanen railway** A
dramatic train ride from
Narvik over the Swedish
border through stunningly
beautiful mountain scenery.
The adventurous can walk
back. See p.317

✻ **Whale-watching at Andenes**
From late May to mid-
September, whale-watching
safaris from this remote port
almost guarantee a sighting.
See p.327

✻ **Henningsvær** One of the
Lofoten islands' most
picturesque fishing villages,
with brightly painted wooden
houses framing the dinkiest of
harbours. See p.338

✻ **Norwegian Fishing Museum**
Fishy history combines with a
stunning setting at Å's Fishing
Village Museum. See p.344

▲ Whale-watching

Trondheim to the Lofoten islands

arking the transition from the rural south to the blustery north is the 900-kilometre-long stretch of Norway that extends from **Trondheim** to the island-studded coast near Narvik. Easily the biggest town hereabouts is Trondheim, Norway's third city, a charming place of character and vitality, which boasts an imposing cathedral – the finest medieval building in the country. Trondheim is also the capital of the **Trøndelag** province, whose sweeping valleys are – by Norwegian standards at least – very fertile and profitable: indeed the region's landowners acted as a counter weight to the power of the south for hundreds of years and, when the country regained its independence in 1905, it seemed logical for the new dynasty to hold their coronations here in Trondheim. The city is also readily accessible by train, plane and bus from Oslo, but push on north and you begin to feel far removed from the capital and the more intimate, forested south. Distances between places grow ever greater, travelling becomes more of a slog, and as Trøndelag gives way to the province of **Nordland** the scenery becomes ever wilder and more forbidding – "Arthurian", thought Evelyn Waugh. The **E6** and the railway thrash north from Trondheim over the hills and down the dales, but with the exception of the rugged landscape there's not much to detain you until you reach the modest little industrial town of **Mosjøen** and nearby **Mo-i-Rana**, also industrial but attractively sited beside the Ranafjord and partly rejigged to attract passing tourists. Just north of Mo-i-Rana on the E6, you cross the **Arctic Circle** – one of the principal targets for many travellers – at a point where the cruel and barren scenery seems strikingly appropriate. On the Arctic Circle, the midnight sun and 24-hour polar night occur once a year, at the summer and winter solstices respectively; the further north you go from here, the longer these two phenomena last (see box, p.354).

Beyond the Arctic Circle, the mountains of the interior lead down to a fretted, craggy coastline, and even the towns, the largest of which is the port of **Bodø**, have a feral quality about them. The iron-ore port of **Narvik**, in the far north of Nordland, has perhaps the wildest setting of them all, and was the scene of some of the fiercest fighting between the Allied and Axis forces in World War II. To the west lies the offshore archipelago that makes up the **Vesterålen** and **Lofoten islands**. In the north of the Vesterålen, between **Harstad** and **Andenes**, the coastline of this island chain is mauled by massive fjords, whereas

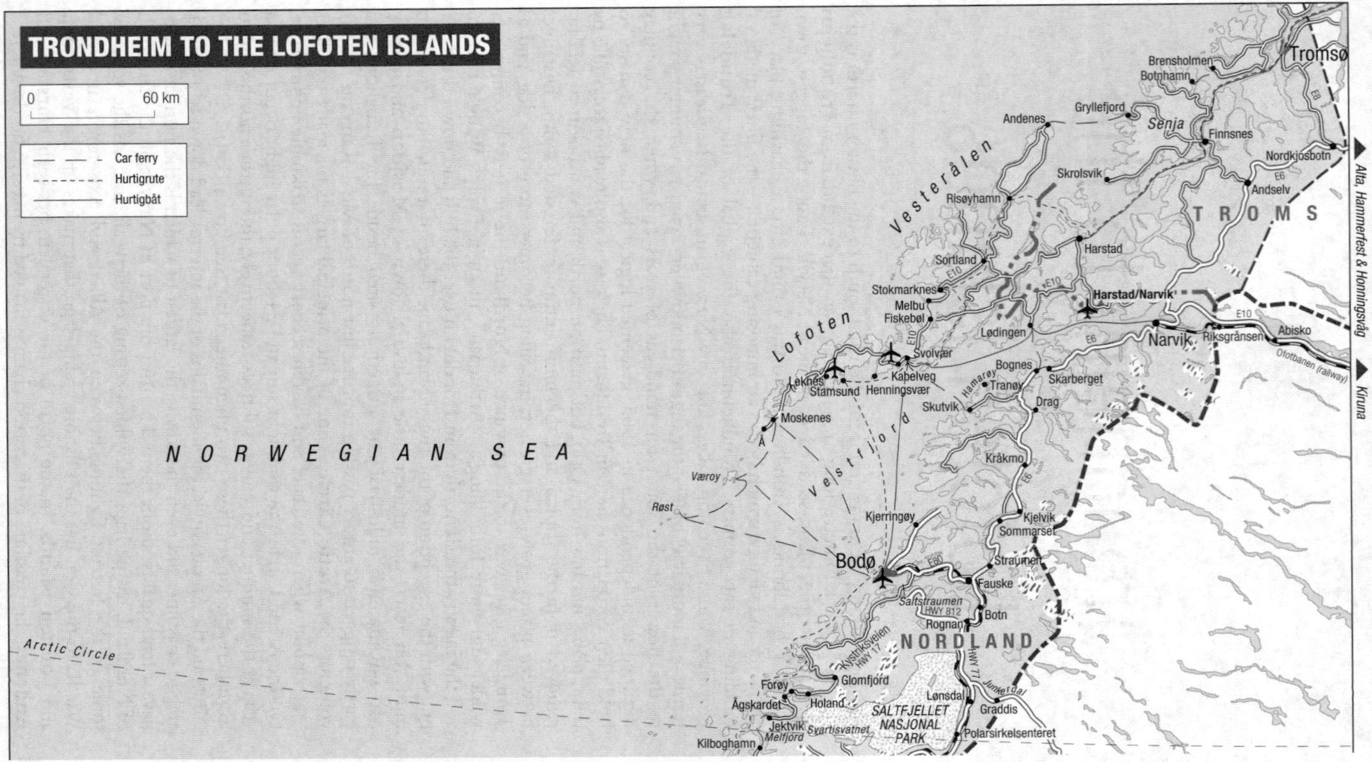

TRONDHEIM TO THE LOFOTEN ISLANDS
0 60 km
Car ferry
Hurtigrute
Hurtigbåt
Hammerfest & Honningsvåg
Alta, Hammerfest & Honningsvåg
Kiruna
NORWEGIAN SEA
Vesterålen
Lofoten
Vestfjord
TROMS
NORDLAND
Tromsø
Brensholmen
Botnhamn
Gryllefjord
Senja
Finnsnes
Andenes
Nordkjosbotn
Skrolsvik
Andselv
Risøyhamn
Harstad
Sortland
Harstad/Narvik
Stokmarknes
Melbu
Fiskebøl
Lødingen
Narvik
Riksgränsen
Abisko
Ofotbanen (railway)
Svolvær
Kabelveg
Henningsvær
Stamsund
Leknes
Bognes
Hamarøy
Tranøy
Skarberget
Skutvik
Drag
Moskenes
Å
Værøy
Røst
Kråkmo
Kjerringøy
Kjelvik
Sommarset
Bodø
Straumen
Fauske
Saltstraumen
HWY 812
Botn
Rognan
Kystriksveien
HWY 17
HWY 77
Junkerdal
Glomfjord
Forøy
Ågskardet
Holand
Lønsdal
Graddis
SALTFJELLET NASJONAL PARK
Jektvik
Melfjord
Svartisvatnet
Polarsirkelsenteret
Kilboghamn
Arctic Circle
E6
E8
E10
E80

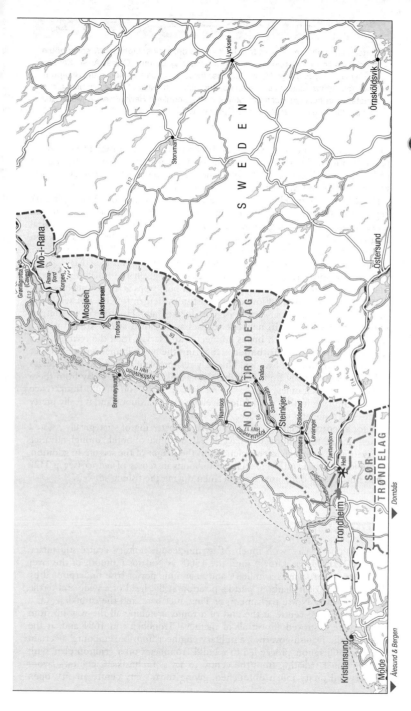

Lycksele

Örnsköldsvik

S W E D E N

Storuman

Østersund

Grønligrotta
(Caves)
Mo-i-Rana
Rana-
fjord
Korgen
Mosjøen
Laksforsen
Trofors
Brønnøysund
Kystriksveien HWY 17
Snåsa
Vannsøy
Kystriksveien HWY 17
Snåsavatn
Steinkjer
Verdalsøra
Levanger
Stiklestad
Fjættenfjord
Hell
NORD-TRØNDELAG
SØR-
TRØNDELAG
Trondheim
E14
E12
E6
Kristiansund

Ålesund & Bergen

Molde

▼ Dombås

Dotted across the province of Nordland are 33 open-air **sculptures** by some of the world's leading contemporary sculptors, including Dorothy Cross, Anish Kapoor, Antony Gormley and Inge Mahn. Together these sculptures comprise the **Skulptur-landskap** (Ⓦ www.skulpturlandskap.no) and although many of the sculptures are in remote, even obscure locations, others – like Gormley's *Havmannen* in Mo-i-Rana (see p.303) – are more likely to come your way.

to the south, the Lofoten islands are backboned by a mighty and ravishingly beautiful mountain wall – a highlight of any itinerary. Among a handful of idyllic fishing villages in the Lofoten the pick is the tersely named **Å**, though **Henningsvær** and **Stamsund** come a very close second.

The **E6**, or "Arctic Highway", is the main road north from Trondheim: it's kept in excellent condition, though in summer motor-homes and caravans can make the going frustratingly slow. Slower still, but stunningly scenic, the coastal **Highway 17**, or "**Kystriksveien**", utilizes road, tunnels, bridges and seven ferries to run the 700km from Steinkjer, just north of Trondheim, up to Bodø, though its most picturesque stretch by a long chalk is north of Mo-i-Rana. **Public transport** is good, which is just as well given the isolated nature of much of the region. The **Hurtigrute** coastal boat stops at all the major settlements on its route up the Norwegian coast from Bergen to Kirkenes, while the islands are accessed by a variety of **car ferries** and **Hurtigbåt passenger express boats**. The **train** network reaches as far north as Fauske and nearby Bodø, from both of which **buses** connect with Narvik, itself the terminal of a separate rail line – the **Ofotbanen** – that runs the few kilometres to the border and then south through Sweden. The only real problem is likely to be **time**: it's a day or two's journey from Trondheim to Fauske, and another day from there to Narvik. In fact, unless you've several days to spare, you should think twice before venturing further north: the travelling can be arduous, and is really pretty pointless if done at a hectic pace.

As for **accommodation**, the region has a smattering of strategically located hostels, and all the major towns have at least a couple of hotels, though advance reservations are strongly recommended in the height of the season. In addition, the Lofoten islands offer inexpensive lodgings in scores of *rorbuer* (see p.332), small huts/cabins once used by fishermen during the fishing season.

Trondheim

An atmospheric city with much of its nineteenth-century centre still intact, **TRONDHEIM** was known until the 1500s as Nidaros ("mouth of the river Nid"), its importance as a military and economic power base underpinned by the excellence of its harbour and its position at the head of a wide and fertile valley. The early Norse parliament, or Ting, met here, and the cathedral was a major pilgrimage centre at the end of a route stretching all the way up from Oslo. A fire destroyed almost all of medieval Trondheim in 1681 and, at the behest of the Danish governor, a military engineer from Luxembourg, a certain Caspar de Cicignon, proceeded to rebuild Trondheim on a gridiron plan, with broad avenues radiating from the centre to act as firebreaks. Cicignon's layout has survived pretty much untouched, giving today's city centre an airy, open feel, though the buildings themselves mostly date from the commercial boom of the late nineteenth century. Among them are scores of doughty stone structures that were built to impress and a handsome set of old timber warehouses that line up along the river. Together, they provide a suitably expansive setting for the **cathedral**, one of Scandinavia's finest medieval structures.

With a population of around 160,000, Trondheim is now Norway's third city, but the pace of life here is slow and easy, and the main **sights** are best appreciated in leisurely fashion over a couple of days. Genial and eminently likeable, Trondheim is also a pleasant place to wave goodbye to city life before heading for the wilds of the north.

Arrival

Trondheim is on the E6 highway, a seven- or eight-hour drive (500km) from Oslo. In the city centre, on-street **parking** during restricted periods (Mon–Fri 8am–8pm, Sat 8am–3pm) is expensive (20kr per hour) and hard to find, but is otherwise free with spaces commonplace. During restricted periods, you're best off heading for a car park: try the handy Torget P-hus, in the centre at Erling Skakkes gate 16 (Mon–Fri 7am–9pm & Sat 7am–7pm); or the Bakke P-hus, east across the bridge from the centre at Nedre Bakklandet 60 (Mon–Fri 6.30am–11pm & Sat 6.30am–9pm). Car-park rates are 15kr per hour up to a maximum of 150kr in any 24hr period.

The city's combined bus and train terminal, **Sentralstasjon**, is on the northern edge of the centre, a ten-minute walk from the main square, Torvet. Inside, an **information** kiosk (☎177) deals with all local transport enquiries. The all-year **Kystekspressen** (ⓦwww.kystekspressen.no) passenger express boat from Kristiansund docks at the Pirterminalen, from where it's a dull fifteen-minute walk south to Sentralstasjon. The quay for the **Hurtigrute coastal boat** (ⓦwww.hurtigruten.no) is near the Pirterminalen, another 300m or so away to the north. Local buses #2 and #46 run from the Pirabadet swimming pool, in between the two quays, to **Sentralstasjon**.

Trondheim **airport** is 35km northeast of the city centre at Værnes. From here, Flybussen (Mon–Fri 4am–8.30pm every 15min; Sat 4am–6pm every 30min; Sun 4am–9pm every 15–30min; 45min; 90kr) run to Sentralstasjon and various points in the city centre, including the *SAS Royal Garden Hotel*.

Information

Trondheim **tourist office** is bang in the centre of town on the edge of Torvet at Munkegata 19 (late May to late June & late Aug Mon–Fri 8.30am–6pm, Sat & Sun 10am–4pm; late June to mid-Aug Mon–Fri 8.30am–8pm, Sat & Sun 10am–6pm; early Aug Mon–Fri 8.30am–10pm, Sat & Sun 10am–8pm; Sept to late May Mon–Fri 9am–4pm, Sat 10am–2pm; ☎73 80 76 60, ⓦwww.trondheim.no). Staff here issue the free and very useful *Trondheim Guide* (also available from information racks at Sentralstasjon) as well as a wide range of other tourist literature, including a cycle map of the city and its surroundings. They also sell hiking maps, change money and have a limited supply of private rooms (see p.287).

City transport

The best way to explore the city centre is **on foot** – it only takes about ten minutes to walk from one end to the other. If, however, you want to travel outside the centre, to one of the outlying museums or the hostel for example, you'll need

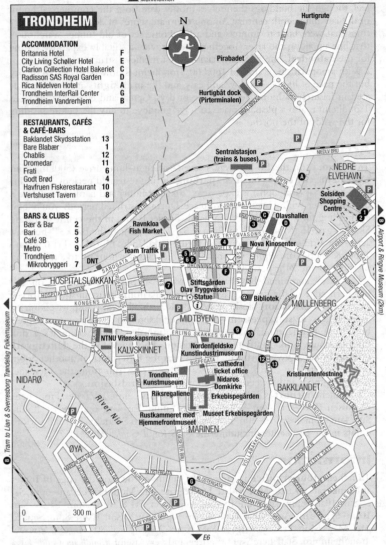

to use a city **tram** or **bus**. These are operated by **Team Trafikk** (☎177, ⓦwww
.team-trafikk.no), with flat-fare single tickets, purchased from the driver, costing
30kr (exact change only). There's also an unlimited 24-hour bus ticket, the
døgnbillet, which costs 70kr – and again this can be bought from the driver. The
hub of the system is the bus stops around the Munkegata/Dronningens gate intersection. There's also a Team Trafikk travel office in the centre at Dronningens gate
40 (Mon–Fri 8am–6pm & Sat 10am–3pm). Finally, Trondheim has a summertime
public bike scheme with over one hundred bikes in ten bike racks dotted across
the city centre. The bikes are released just like supermarket trolleys, and you can
get your access card at the tourist office for 70kr.

Accommodation

Accommodation is plentiful in Trondheim, with a choice of private rooms, two hostels, and a selection of reasonably priced hotels. What's more, most of the more appealing places are dotted round the city centre, which is precisely where you want to be. The exception is the private rooms booked via the tourist office, which are usually out in the suburbs. These **private rooms** are good value at around 500–600kr per double per night (400–500kr single), plus a small booking fee.

Hotels

Britannia Hotel Dronningens gate 5 ⊕73 80 08 00, ⓦwww.britannia.no. Right in the middle of town, this long-established hotel has a splendid, bright-white facade that dates back to the nineteenth century. Inside, a couple of the public rooms have splendid wood panelling and the breakfast room comes complete with a Moorish fountain, Egyptian-style murals and Corinthian columns. The well-appointed bedrooms manage to be both unfussy and cosy with browns and creams to the fore. ❽, sp/r ❻

City Living Schøller Hotel Dronningens gate 26 ⊕73 87 08 00, ⓦwww.cityliving.no. Economy chain hotel above shops in the centre of the city. The modern rooms are spick-and-span verging on the spartan, but the price is right. ❷–❸

Clarion Collection Hotel Bakeriet Brattørgata 2 ⊕73 99 10 00, ⓦwww.choicehotels.no. Competent chain hotel in an intelligently revamped former bakery. The guest rooms, which were once occupied by the bakery workers, are kitted out in standard modern style. Central location. ❻, sp/r ❹

Radisson SAS Royal Garden Kjøpmannsgata 73 ⊕73 80 30 00, ⓦwww.radissonsas.com. Full marks to the architects here, who have designed this large, modern, riverside hotel in the style of the old timber warehouses it replaced. Lots of glass – indeed the interior of the hotel looks a bit like a series of enormous greenhouses – but the rooms themselves can feel a bit frumpy. Banquet-like breakfasts. ❻, sp/r ❹

🏃 **Rica Nidelven Hotel** Havnegata 1–3 ⊕73 56 80 00, ⓦwww.rica.no. Large and flashy chain hotel nudging out into the river with lots of glass to maximize views. The public areas are bold and expansive – modernism at its most decisive – but the guest rooms are not perhaps quite as distinctive as they could be. Every facility. ❽, sp/r ❺

Guesthouses, hostels and camping

Trondheim InterRail Center Elgeseter gate 1 ⊕73 89 95 38, ⓦwww.tirc.no. Bargain-basement lodgings in the unusual, big, red and round building – the Studentersamfundet (university student centre) – that stands just over the bridge at the south end of Prinsens gate, a 5min walk from the cathedral. Offers basic mixed-dorm accommodation at 150kr per person per night and breakfast is served in the downstairs café. No curfew, and Internet access. Open early July to mid-Aug only.

Trondheim Vandrerhjem Weidemannsveien 41 ⊕73 87 44 50, ⓦwww.trondheim-vandrerhjem .no. This large, well-equipped hostel is mostly parcelled up into four-bed dorm rooms, only a few of which are en suite. Looks more like a hospital than somewhere you'd want to stay from the outside, but the interior is pleasant enough – especially the comfortable, newer rooms. It has self-catering facilities, a laundry and a canteen. A 20min, 2km hike east from the centre: cross the Bakke bru (bridge) onto busy Innherredsveien (the E6) and walk uphill; turn right onto Wessels gate and hang a left at the fourth crossroads. To save your legs, take any bus up Innherredsveien and ask the driver to let you off as close as possible. Open all year. Dorm beds 230kr, doubles ❷

The city centre

The historic **centre of Trondheim** sits on a small triangle of land bordered by a loop of the River Nid, with the sweep of the long and slender Trondheims-fjord beyond. **Torvet** is the main city square, a spacious open area anchored by a statue of Olav Tryggvason perched high on the top of his column. The broad avenues that radiate out from here were once flanked by long rows of wooden buildings, which served all the needs of a small town and administrative centre.

Most of these older structures are long gone, replaced for the most part by uninspiring modern buildings, though one notable survivor is the **Stiftsgården**, a fine timber mansion erected in 1774. Nonetheless, this is small beer when compared with the **Nidaros Domkirke** (cathedral), an imposing, largely medieval structure that is the city's architectural high point. The cathedral dominates the southern part of the centre and close by is the much-restored **Erkebispegården** (Archbishop's Palace) as well as the pick of Trondheim's several museums, the **Nordenfjeldske Kunstindustrimuseum** (Museum of Decorative Arts) and the **Trondheim Kunstmuseum** (Trondheim Art Museum). Near here too, on the far side of the **Gamle Bybro** – the old town bridge – is the clutter of old warehouses and timber dwellings that comprises the prettiest and most fashionable part of town, **Bakklandet**, home to some of its best bars and restaurants.

Nidaros Domkirke

The goal of Trondheim's pilgrims in times past was the rambling **Nidaros Domkirke**, Scandinavia's largest medieval building, whose copper-green spire and multiple roofs lord it over the south end of Munkegata (Cathedral; May to early June & mid-Aug to mid-Sept Mon–Fri 9am–3pm, Sat 9am–2pm & Sun 1–4pm; early June to mid-Aug Mon–Fri 9am–6pm, Sat 9am–2pm & Sun 1–4pm; mid-Sept to April Mon–Fri noon–2.30pm, Sat 11.30am–2pm & Sun 1–3pm; 50kr, combined ticket with Erkebispegården 100kr; Ⓦ www .nidarosdomen.no). Gloriously restored following several fires and the upheavals of the Reformation, the cathedral, which is dedicated to St Olav (see box, p.289), remains the focal point of any visit to the city and is best explored in the early morning, when it's reasonably free of tour groups. In the summertime, there are free English-language **guided tours** (mid-June to mid-Aug 4 daily; 30min) and you can climb the cathedral tower for a panoramic view over the city and its surroundings (mid-June to mid-Aug Mon–Fri 10am–5pm, Sat 10am–12.30pm, Sun 1–3.30pm).

The crowning glory of this magnificent blue- and green-grey soapstone edifice is its west facade, a soaring cliff-face of finely worked stone sporting a magnificent rose window, rank after rank of pointed arches, biblical, religious and royal figures by the dozen and a fancy set of gargoyles. The west facade and the nave behind may look medieval, but date from the nineteenth century: the originals were erected in the early Gothic style of the early thirteenth century, but they were destroyed by fire in 1719 and what you see today is a painstakingly accurate reconstruction. The fire did not, however, raze the Romanesque transepts, whose heavy hooped windows and dog-tooth decoration were the work of English stonemasons in the twelfth century. English workmen also leant a hand in the thirteenth-century choir, where the arches, flying buttresses and intricate tracery are the epitome of early Gothic – and are reminiscent of contemporaneous churches in England.

The interior

Inside, the gloomy half-light hides much of the lofty decorative work, but it is possible to examine the strikingly ascetic early twentieth-century **choir screen**, whose wooden figures are the work of Gustav Vigeland (see p.103). Vigeland was also responsible for the adjacent soapstone **font**, a superb piece of medievalism sporting four bas-reliefs depicting Adam and Eve, John the Baptist baptizing the Christ, the Resurrection and a beguiling Noah and the Ark: Noah peers apprehensively out of his boat, not realizing that the dove, with the tell-tale branch, is up above. The other item of particular interest is

St Olav

Born in 995, **Olav Haraldsson** followed the traditional life of the Viking chieftain from the tender age of 12, "rousing the steel-storm" as the saga writers put it, from Finland to Ireland. He also served as a mercenary to both the duke of Normandy and King Ethelred of England, and it was during this time that he was converted to Christianity. In 1015, he invaded Norway, defeated his enemies and became king, his military success built upon the support of the more prosperous farmers of the Trøndelag, an emergent class of yeomen who were less capricious than the coastal chieftains of Viking fame. However, Olav's zealous **imposition of Christianity** – he ordered the desecration of pagan sites and the execution of those who refused baptism – alienated many of his followers and the bribes of Olav's rival Knut (Canute), king of England and Denmark, did the rest: Olav's retainers deserted him, and he was forced into exile in 1028. Two years later, he was back in the Trøndelag, but the army he had raised was far too weak to defeat his enemies, and Olav was killed near Trondheim at the **battle of Stiklestad** (see p.300).

Olav might have lost his kingdom, but the nationwide Church he founded had no intention of losing ground. Needing a local **saint** to consolidate its position, the Church carefully nurtured the myth of Olav, a process of sanctification assisted by the oppressive rule of Olav's successor, the "foreigner" Knut. After the battle of Stiklestad, Olav's body had been spirited away and buried on the banks of the River Nid at what is today Trondheim. There were rumours of miracles in the vicinity of the grave, and when the bishop arrived to investigate these strange goings-on, he exhumed the body and found it, lo and behold, perfectly uncorrupted. Olav was declared a saint, his body placed in a silver casket and when, in 1066, Olav Kyrre, son of Olav's half-brother Harald the Fair-Haired, became king of Norway, he ordered work to begin on a grand church to house the remains in appropriate style. Over the years the church was altered and enlarged to accommodate the growing bands of medieval pilgrims; it achieved cathedral status in 1152, when Trondheim became the seat of an archbishopric whose authority extended as far as Orkney and the Isle of Man.

a famous fourteenth-century **altar frontal** (front panel of an altar painting) displayed in a chapel off the ambulatory, directly behind the high altar. At a time when few Norwegians could read or write, the cult of St Olav had to be promoted visually, and the frontal is the earliest surviving representation of Olav's life and times. In its centre, Olav looks suitably beatific holding his axe and orb; the top left-hand corner shows the dream Olav had before the battle of Stiklestad (see p.300), with Jesus dropping a ladder down to him from heaven. In the next panel down, Olav and his men are shown at prayer before the battle and, in the bottom right-hand corner, Olav meets a sticky end, speared and stabbed by three cruel-looking soldiers. The final panel shows church officials exhuming Olav's uncorrupted body and declaring his sainthood.

What you won't see now is the object of the medieval pilgrims' veneration: St Olav's silver casket-coffin was taken to Denmark and unceremoniously melted down for coinage in 1537.

Erkebispegården

Behind the cathedral stands the heavily restored **Erkebispegården** (Archbishop's Palace), a courtyard complex that was originally built in the twelfth century for the third archbishop, Øystein, though two stone-and-brick wings are all that survive of the medieval quadrangle – the other two wings were added later.

After the archbishops were kicked out during the Reformation, the palace became the residence of the Danish governors. It was subsequently used as the city armoury, and many of the old weapons are now displayed in the **west wing** in the **Rustkammeret med Hjemmefrontmuseet**, though the museum's most interesting displays deal with the German occupation of World War II. Next door, also in the west wing, the Norwegian crown jewels are exhibited in the **Riksregaliene**, not that there's actually much to see, while the south wing chips in with the medieval sculptures of the **Museet Erkebispegården**.

After you've finished with the museums, you can leave the Erkebispegården to the south, strolling out onto the grassy **lawns** which flank the River Nid. A trio of earthen bastions are reminders of the military defences that once protected this side of town, but they have worn low with time, and you'll soon reach the dignified old tombstones and wildflowers of the cathedral **graveyard**, just to the east of the church's main entrance.

The Riksregaliene

Norway's crown jewels, the **Riksregaliene** (National Regalia; May to early June & early Aug to mid-Sept Mon–Sat 10am–3pm & Sun noon–4pm; early June to early Aug Mon–Fri 10am–5pm, Sat 10am–3pm & Sun noon–4pm; mid-Sept to April Tues–Sat 11am–3pm & Sun noon–4pm; 70kr, combined ticket for cathedral & Erkebispegården 100k), are displayed in the basement of the first part of the Erkebispegården's west wing. At the end of the Napoleonic Wars, Britain and her allies forced Denmark to cede Norway to Sweden (see p.403). The Swedish king was himself new to the throne – oddly enough he had previously been one of Napoleon's generals, Jean-Baptiste Bernadotte – and although he received Norway as a welcome bonus, he was deemed to be a ruler of two kingdoms rather than one. Sweden already had its own crown jewels, but Norway, which hadn't been independent for centuries, had nothing at all. As a consequence, Bernadotte, now Karl IV Johan, scuttled around Stockholm ordering a new set of crown jewels in preparation for his coronation in Trondheim. The results are on display here, principally a crown, a sceptre, an orb and a tiny anointing horn, all made in the 1810s. Another set of ceremonial gear was made for the queen, but it's still a very thin collection and the Sword of State was actually recycled: it had originally been given to Bernadotte by Napoleon in return for military services rendered. The last Norwegian coronation took place here in Trondheim cathedral in 1906 on the accession of Håkon VII, but his successors – Olav V and Harald V – elected for benedictions instead, in 1958 and 1991 respectively.

The Rustkammeret med Hjemmefrontmuseet

The extensive **Rustkammeret med Hjemmefrontmuseet** (Armoury and Resistance Museum; June–Aug Mon–Fri 9am–3pm, Sat & Sun 11am–4pm; free) spreads over two main floors. The **first floor** gives the broad details of Norway's involvement in the interminable **Dano–Swedish Wars** that racked Scandinavia from the fifteenth to the nineteenth centuries. As part of the Danish state, Norway was frequently attacked from the east along the Halden–Oslo corridor, the most memorable incursions being by that most bellicose of Swedish kings, Karl XII. Much to the Danish king's surprise, Karl came a cropper in Norway: it was here that he was defeated for the first time and, when he came back for more, shot (possibly by one of his own men) while besieging Fredriksten fortress in 1718 (see p.125).

Of more general interest, the **second floor** describes the German invasion and occupation of **World War II**, dealing honestly with the sensitive issue of collaboration. In particular, you can hear **Vidkun Quisling**'s broadcast announcing – in a disarmingly squeaky voice – his coup d'état of April 9, 1940. There are also some intriguing displays on the daring antics of the Norwegian Resistance, notably an extraordinary – perhaps hare-brained – attempt to sink the battleship *Tirpitz* as it lay moored in an inlet of the Trondheimsfjord in 1942 (see box, p.299). This escapade, like so many others, involved **Leif Larsen**, the Resistance hero who is commemorated by a statue on the Torget in Bergen. Larsen worked closely with the Royal Navy, organizing covert operations in occupied Norway from the RN base in the Shetlands. Supplies and personnel were transported across the North Sea by Norwegian fishing boats – a lifeline known, in that classically understated British (and Norwegian) way, as the "Shetland bus"; the book of the same name by David Howarth (see p.429) tells the tale of this remarkable enterprise.

Museet Erkebispegården

The **south wing** of the old Archbishop's Palace holds the **Museet Erkebispegården** (Archbishop's Palace Museum; May to early June & early Aug to mid-Sept Mon–Sat 10am–3pm & Sun noon–4pm; early June to early Aug Mon–Fri 10am–5pm, Sat 10am–3pm & Sun noon–4pm; mid-Sept to April Tues–Sat 11am–3pm & Sun noon–4pm; 50kr, combined ticket for cathedral & Erkebispegården 100k), which is largely devoted to a few dozen medieval statues retrieved and put away for safekeeping during the nineteenth-century reconstruction of the cathedral's nave and west facade. Many of the statues are too battered and bruised to be engaging, but they are well displayed and several are finely carved. In particular, look out for a life-sized sculpture of **St Denis**, his head in his hands (literally) in accordance with the legend that he was beheaded, but then proceeded to irritate his executioners no end by carrying his head to his grave. Downstairs in the basement, an assortment of artefacts unearthed during a lengthy 1990s archeological investigation of the palace demonstrates the economic power of the archbishops: they employed all manner of skilled artisans – from glaziers and shoemakers to rope-makers, armourers and silversmiths – and even minted their own coins.

Trondheim Kunstmuseum

Metres from the cathedral, at Bispegata 7b, the **Trondheim Kunstmuseum** (Trondheim Art Museum; June to late Aug daily 10am–5pm; rest of year Tues–Sun 11am–4pm; 50kr; Ⓦwww.tkm.museum.no) is perhaps best known for its temporary exhibitions of contemporary art. The downside is that these exhibitions often leave little space for the museum's permanent collection, which features a particularly enjoyable selection of Norwegian paintings from 1850 onwards. Highlights of the permanent collection include several works by Johan Dahl and Thomas Fearnley, the leading figures of nineteenth-century Norwegian landscape painting, as well as the romantic canvases of Hans Gude and his chum Adolph Tidemand. The museum also owns the first overtly political work by a Norwegian artist, *The Strike* (*Streik*), painted in 1877 by the radical Theodor Kittelsen (1857–1914), who is better known for his illustrations of the folk tales collected by Jorgen Moe and Peder Asbjørnsen. Additionally, the museum possesses a substantial selection of Munch woodcuts, sketches and lithographs, including several of those disturbing, erotically charged personifications of emotions – *Lust*, *Fear* and *Jealousy* – that are so characteristic of his oeuvre. However, after the theft of the Munch paintings in Oslo (see p.105), the museum has become notably chary about displaying its Munch pieces, so you'll never see many at any one time.

The Nordenfjeldske Kunstindustrimuseum

The delightful **Nordenfjeldske Kunstindustrimuseum** is a couple of minutes' walk north from the cathedral at Munkegata 5 (National Museum of Decorative Arts; June to late Aug Mon–Sat 10am–5pm, Sun noon–5pm; late Aug to May Tues–Wed, Fri & Sat 10am–3pm, Thurs 10am–5pm, Sun noon–4pm; 60kr; ⓦwww.nkim.museum.no). The museum has a wide-ranging permanent collection, but it's too extensive to be shown in its entirety at any one time and so the exhibits are regularly rotated, especially as there is also an ambitious programme of special exhibitions: nevertheless, you can expect to see most of the pieces mentioned below. Start in the **basement**, where the historical collection illustrates bourgeois life in Trøndelag from 1500 to 1900 by means of an eclectic assemblage of furniture, faïence, glassware and silver. The modern collection follows on, featuring a small but well-chosen international selection of Arts & Crafts and Art Nouveau pieces, from glass, ceramics and textiles through to furniture – there's even an immaculate William Morris chair. The domestic theme is developed on the **ground floor**, where one small room has been kitted out with early 1950s furnishings and fittings by the Danish designer Finn Juhl and a second room does the same with the work of the Belgian designer and architect **Henri van de Velde** (1863–1957).

On the **first floor**, fourteen wonderful tapestries by **Hannah Ryggen** occupy an entire room. Born in Malmö in 1894, Ryggen moved to the Trondheim area in the early 1920s and stayed until her death in 1970. Her tapestries are classically naive, the forceful colours and absence of perspective emphasizing the feeling behind them. This is committed art at its best, railing in the 1930s and 1940s against Hitler and Fascism, later moving on to more disparate targets such as the atom bomb and social conformism. But Ryggen still made time to celebrate the things she cherished: *Yes, we love this country* (tapestry no. 11) is as evocative a portrayal of her adopted land as you're likely to find.

NTNU Vitenskapsmuseet

From the Nordenfjeldske Kunstindustrimuseum, it's a five- to ten-minute walk west to the **NTNU Vitenskapsmuseet**, Erling Skakkes gate 47 (Museum of Natural History and Archeology; May to mid-Sept Mon–Fri 9am–4pm, Sat & Sun 11am–4pm; mid-Sept to April Tues–Fri 9am–2pm, Sat & Sun noon–4pm; 25kr), which has several collections gathered together by the university. Entrance is at the side, a few metres along Gunnerus gate, and the large building at the front holds a substantial rocks-and-minerals section, stuffed animals in its nature exhibition and a series of temporary displays devoted to all things Norwegian. Rather more interesting, however, is the **Middelalder i Trondheim** (medieval exhibition), in the old **suhmhuset** (hay storehouse), a low, long building to the rear of the main entrance. This tracks the development of Trondheim from its foundation in the tenth century to the great fire of 1681. The thoroughly researched, multilingual text is supported by an excellent range of archeological finds, and departs from the predictable "Kings and Queens" approach, investigating everything from sanitary towels and reliquary jars to popular games and attitudes to life and death. One of the more remarkable exhibits is the **Kulisteinen** (Kuli stone), which is carved with both a Christian cross and a runic inscription. Found near Trondheim and dated to around 1034, it's a very rare illustration of the transitional period between a pagan and a Christian Norway.

Equally interesting is the **Kirkeutstilling** (church exhibition) in the building across from the main entrance, though it's normally kept locked and you'll need to ask at reception to gain access. Among the assorted ecclesiastical knick-knacks, there are pulpits and fonts, processional crosses and statues of the saints, plus religious paintings galore. By and large, the workmanship is crude and the painting garish, but there is a raw, naïve vitality to many of the earlier pieces which is really rather delightful. Highlights include several fancily carved stave-church portals and an idiosyncratic, seventeenth-century Adam & Eve, whose belly buttons look like eyes.

Torvet

Back in the centre, near the Kunstindustrimuseum, **Torvet** is the main city square, a spacious open area anchored by a statue of **Olav Tryggvason** (c.968–1000), Trondheim's founder, perched on a tall stone pillar like some medieval Nelson. Tryggvason is kitted out in a full set of chain mail with helmet and sword, and has one arm outstretched presenting an orb, the symbol of monarchical power. One of the most spectacular Vikings of his time, Tryggvason is surrounded by myth and legend, but it does seem likely that his mother fled Norway with her son when he was about three years old, ending up in exile in Sweden and ultimately Russia. Thereafter, Tryggvason cut his Viking spurs in a series of piratical raids, before leading a Viking fleet in an attack on England in 991. The English bought him off, a pattern repeated three years later, and the two payments of this "Danegeld" made him extremely rich. Part of the deal for the second payment was that he become a Christian and, against all expectations, the Viking chieftain seems to have taken his new faith seriously. Tryggvason then hot-footed it back to Norway, where he quickly wrested control of most of the country, though his brutal imposition of Christianity infuriated many of his subjects and few mourned when, after just five years as king, he was ambushed and killed. One of his feats was to found Trondheim in 997, but ironically – considering the statue that dominates Torvet – the Tronders were determined to hang on to their pagan gods and were especially hacked off by Olav's bloody attempts to force them to be Christians. On the other hand, the statue depicts a very taciturn-looking Tryggvason, apt when you consider the Tronders' reputation for taciturnity. There's an old joke that sums it up: two Tronder brothers once rowed from Trondheim to Bergen some five hundred kilometres down the coast. Going on board in Trondheim, one of the brothers fell into the water. "I fell in", he exclaimed. Jumping ashore in Bergen, the other brother fell in. "I too", he said.

Kongens gate's medieval church ruins

From Torvet, it's a couple of minutes' walk to the **bibliotek** (library) at the east end of Kongens gate. The library was built on top of some **medieval church ruins** and these are now in full view. A twelfth-century relic of the days when Trondheim had fifteen or more religious buildings, the ruins are thought to be those of a chapel dedicated to St Olav, although the evidence for this is a bit shaky. Excavations revealed nearly five hundres bodies in the immediate area, which was once the church graveyard, and a pair of skeletons are now neatly displayed under glass. The site is accessible during library opening hours (Mon–Thurs 9am–7pm, Fri 9am–4pm & Sat 10am–3pm; also Sept–April Sun noon–4pm; free).

The Stiftsgården

One conspicuous remnant of old timber-town Trondheim survives in the city centre – the **Stiftsgården**, which stretches out along Munkegata just north of Torvet (guided tours every hour on the hour till 1hr before closing: June to late Aug Mon–Sat 10am–5pm, Sun noon–5pm; 60kr). Built in 1774–78, this good-looking yellow structure is claimed to be the largest wooden building in northern Europe. These days it serves as an official royal residence, a marked social improvement on its original function as the home of the provincial governor. Inside, a long string of period rooms illustrates the genteel tastes of the mansion's late eighteenth- to early nineteenth-century occupants with a wide range of styles, from Rococo to Biedermeier, but it's the fanciful Italianate wall paintings that steal the decorative show. The obligatory anecdotal guided tour brings a smile or two – but not perhaps 60kr wide.

North to the Ravnkloa

If the **Stiftsgården** has wetted your appetite for old wooden buildings, then you'll enjoy the tangle of narrow alleys and pastel-painted clapboard frontages that fills out the side streets just **north of Kongens gate** and west of Prinsens gate. There's nothing special to look at, but it's a pleasant area for a stroll, after which you can wander over to **Ravnkloa**, the jetty at the north end of Munkegata and the site of the fish market (Mon–Fri 10am–5pm & Sat 10am–4pm). This is also where ferries leave for Munkholmen (see p.295).

To Nedre Elvehavn, Bakklandet and the Kristianstenfestning fortress

From **Ravnkloa**, it's a few-minutes' walk east to the slender footbridge that spans the river to link Havnegata with Nedre Elvehavn, where the former shipyard has been turned into a leisure and shopping complex that trundles along beside the old quays. This is one of the busiest parts of the city, thronged with revellers every summer weekend, and from here you can stroll along the east side of the river down to the next bridge along, Bakke bru. Beyond this second bridge is tiny **Bakklandet**, Trondheim's own "Left Bank", a one-time working-class district of brightly painted timber houses that now holds a battery of cafés and restaurants, including some of the best in town. Bakklandet abuts the **Gamle Bybro** (Old Town Bridge), a quaint wooden structure offering splendid views over **Kjøpmannsgata**'s eighteenth-century gabled and

▲ Bakklandet, Trondheim

timbered warehouses, now mostly restaurants and offices. In the opposite direction from the bridge, Brubakken leads up the hill from Bakklandet to Kristianstensbakken and the **Kristianstenfestning** fortress (June–Aug daily 11am–4pm; free), dating from 1681 and providing wide views back over Trondheim. The earth and stone fortifications have survived in reasonably good condition here as have several of the old buildings. During the war, this was where the Germans tortured their prisoners, many of whom had been betrayed by Arthur Rinnan, a clever and sadistic Norwegian collaborator who was executed in 1947.

From the Gamle Bybro, it's a couple of minutes' walk back to the cathedral.

Out from the centre

All of Trondheim's key attractions are neatly packed within walking distance of each other, on or around the city's central island, but there are nevertheless one or two additional sights that may lure you out of the centre. The historic **Munkholmen island** is an easy ten-minute ferry ride away, while a couple of museums – the **Ringve**, to the northeast of the centre, and the **Sverresborg Trøndelag Folkemuseum** in the southwest – both have merit.

Munkholmen island

Poking up out of the Trondheimsfjord just 2km offshore, the tiny islet of **Munkholmen** is easily reached by **boat** from the Ravnkloa jetty (every hour on the hour: late May & late Aug to early Sept 10am–4pm; June to late Aug 10am–6pm; 55kr return). The island has an eventful history. In Viking times it was used as the city's execution ground, and St Olav went to the added trouble of displaying the head of one of his enemies on a pike here, which must have made approaching mariners a tad nervous. In the eleventh century, the Benedictines founded a monastery on the island – hence its name – but it was not one of their more successful ventures: the archbishop received dozens of complaints about, of all things, the amount of noise the monks made, not to mention alleged heavy drinking and womanizing. After the Reformation, the island was converted into a prison, which doubled as a fortress designed to protect the seaward approaches to the city; later still it became a customs house. The longest-serving prisoner was the Danish count **Peder Griffenfeld** (1635–99), who spent eighteen years cooped up here until his eventual release in 1698. One of the most powerful men in Denmark, Griffenfeld played a leading role in the assumption of absolute power by King Frederick III (see p.401), but was outmanoeuvred and imprisoned by his rivals after the king's death.

Sturdy stone walls encircle almost the entire island, and behind them, sunk in a circular dip, is a set of quaint, almost cottage-like, **prison buildings** surrounding a cobbled courtyard. There are thirty-minute guided tours of the central part of the **fortress** (late May to early Sept hourly; 30kr), a cheerful romp through its galleries and corridors. The tour includes a visit to the spacious cell occupied by Griffenfeld, and a glimpse of the gun emplacement the Germans installed during World War II. After the tour you can wander over to the **café** or scramble along outside the walls and round the rocks beneath to either of a couple of rough, pebbly beaches.

The Ringve Museum

The **Ringve Museum** (mid-April to mid-May Mon–Fri 11am–3pm & Sun 11am–4pm; mid-May to late June & mid-Aug to mid-Sept daily 11am–3pm; late June to mid-Aug daily 11am–5pm; mid-Sept to mid-May Sun only

11am–4pm; 75kr; ⓦwww.ringve.no) occupies a delightful eighteenth-century country house and courtyard complex on the hilly Lade peninsula, some 4km northeast of the city centre. Devoted to musical history and to musical instruments from all over the world, the museum is divided into two sections. In the main building, the collection focuses on antique European instruments in period settings, with several demonstrations included in a lengthy – and obligatory – guided tour. The second section, in the old barn, contains an international selection of musical instruments and offers a self-guided zip through some of the key moments and movements of musical history. There are themes like "the invention of the piano" and "pop and rock", as well as the real humdinger, "the marching band movement in Norway". Immaculately maintained, the surrounding **botanical gardens** (daily; free) make the most of the scenic setting. To get there, take bus #3 or #4 to Lade from Munkegata.

The Sverresborg Trøndelag Folkemuseum

Three kilometres southwest of the city centre lies one of Norway's best folk museums, the **Sverresborg Trøndelag Folkemuseum** (June–Aug daily 11am–6pm, 80kr; Sept–May Mon–Fri 10am–3pm, Sat & Sun noon–4pm, 50kr; ⓦwww.sverresborg.no). In a pleasant rural setting, with views over the city, the museum's indoor section kicks off with some well-presented displays tracing everyday life in the Trøndelag from the eighteenth century onwards. Outside, you'll see sixty relocated Trøndelag timber buildings, including a post office, grocery store, stave church and all sorts of farmhouses and outhouses, built for a variety of purposes from curing meat to drying hay. Finally, it's worth staying for lunch here at the museum's *Vertshuset Tavern*, which serves up traditional Norwegian dishes at affordable prices (and see p.297). To get here, take bus #8 (direction Stavset) from Dronningens gate.

Eating and drinking

As befits Norway's third city, Trondheim has a good selection of first-rate **restaurants** serving a variety of cuisines, though the Norwegian places almost always have the gastronomic edge. In particular, there's a couple of especially fine restaurants in the **Bakklandet** district, by the eastern end of Gamle Bybro, and a third at the south end of neighbouring Kjøpmannsgata. Bars are dotted all over the city centre, but the weekend scene is at its liveliest on and around Brattørgata and in the **Nedre Elvehavn** district, where the former municipal shipyard has been turned into a large leisure complex of shops, bars and restaurants. Finally – if needs must – the city's mobile fast-food stalls are concentrated around Sentralstasjon and along Kongens gate, on either side of Torvet.

As for **opening hours**, some restaurants open for a couple of hours at lunchtime and then in the evening, but many just stick to the evenings; many also close one day a week. Café-bars and bars almost invariably open from around 11am until the early hours of the morning – or at least until there's no one left (standing) – while coffee bars open around 9am and close at 6/7pm.

Cafés and café-bars

🏃 **Dromedar** Nedre Bakklandet 3a. Laid-back, cosy-cramped coffee bar in antique wooden premises a few metres north of the Gamle Bybro. Arguably the best coffee in town plus snacks and light meals – filled bagels, sandwiches, etc – at bargain prices. One of a small chain. Mon–Fri 7am–7pm, Sat 10am–7pm & Sun 11am–7pm.

Godt Brød Thomas Angells gate 16. The aroma of baking bread, rolls and pastries, all organic, wafts around this cosy little café-cum-bakery, where the coffee is good and the breads and pastries even better. Sandwiches made to order too. Daily except Sun 6am–6pm.

Restaurants

Baklandet Skydsstation Øvre Bakklandet 33 ☎73 92 10 44. Friendly, intimate former coaching inn with a warren of homely dining rooms and a small courtyard. A reasonably priced menu with mains from as little as 200kr features home-cooked staples such as that old Norwegian favourite, *bacalao* (dried and salted cod fish), and an earth-moving cheesecake. Daily noon–1am.

Bare Blabær Innherredsveien 16, Nedre Elvehavn. The excellent-value, stone-baked pizzas at this fast-moving café-restaurant make it very popular with a youthful clientele. Pizzas from 90kr. Daily 11am–1am.

Chablis Øvre Bakklandet 66 ☎73 87 42 50. Just metres from the Gamle Bybro, this polished restaurant, with its modish furnishings and fittings, features a creative menu in which traditional Norwegian ingredients – fish, pork and so forth – are served with the unexpected, like cod with a lentil-and-bacon ragout. In summertime, you can eat outside on a floating pontoon that's moored on the river. Main courses hover around 290kr. Open Mon–Sat 5–11pm.

Frati Munkegata 25 ☎73 52 57 33. Much favoured by locals, this traditional, family-run Italian restaurant serves all the classics in plentiful and authentic portions. Above a bar. Main courses from 140kr. Mon–Fri 3–11pm, Sat & Sun 2–11pm.

Havfruen Fiskerestaurant Kjøpmannsgata 7 ☎73 87 40 70. In an old and cleverly refashioned riverside warehouse, this smart and extremely popular seafood restaurant is one of the best in town with main courses – cod, coalfish, char and so forth – averaging around 290kr. Mon–Sat 6–11.30pm.

Vertshuset Tavern Sverresborg allé 7 ☎73 87 80 70. In business since 1739, this restaurant-tavern used to be in the town centre, but it was moved lock, stock and barrel to the Sverresborg Folkemuseum (see p.296) several years ago. Its low-ceilinged timber rooms are furnished in appropriate period style and the food is traditional Norwegian *husmannskost* (working-class fare) at its best: the *Kjøttkaker i brun saus med erterstuing* (meatballs in brown gravy served with pea stew) is hard to beat, closely followed by the *spekemat* (cured meat), the *rømmegrøt* (sourcream porridge) and the *fiskekaker* (fish cakes). Mains from 120–260kr. Bus #8 from Dronningens gate. Mon–Fri 4pm–midnight, Sat & Sun 2pm–midnight.

Bars and nightclubs

Bær & Bar Innherredsveien 16. Managing to straddle that fine line between trendy and pretentious, this is the pick of the bars along the Nedre Elvehavn dockside strip. The sister of the neighbouring Bare Blabær restaurant (see opposite), *Bær & Bar* has house and electro until 3am at the weekend, fresh fruit cocktails and outdoor seating. Daily from 11am.

Bari Munkegata 26. Smooth and polished bar-restaurant, all dark-stained wood and soft lighting. Attracts an older/smarter crew, who sip wine and cocktails (rather then downing litres of ale). Below the *Frati* restaurant (see opposite). Daily from 10.30am–1am, 2.30am at the weekend.

Café 3B Brattørgata 3B. Rock and roll and indie club-cum-bar, where you can drink well into the wee hours. One of the grooviest places in town. Tues–Fri 8pm–2.30am, Sat 4pm–2.30pm & Sun 10pm–2.30am.

Metro Kjøpmannsgata 12 ⓦwww.gaytrondheim .com. Trondheim's principal gay and lesbian bar, tastefully decorated and with DJ sounds at the weekend. Wed 9pm–1am, Fri & Sat 10pm–2am.

Trondhjem Mikrobryggeri Prinsens gate 39. Mainstream bar serving up its own microbrewery brews. In a pleasant little courtyard just off Prinsens gate. Filling pub food too. Mon 5–10pm, Tues–Fri 3pm–2am, Sat noon–2am.

Listings

Airlines Norwegian ☎815 21 815; SAS ☎74 80 41 00; Widerøe ☎74 80 41 00.

Banks & exchange ATMs are liberally distributed across the city centre. The main post office (see p.298), most banks and the tourist office change currency.

Car rental Avis, Kjøpmannsgata 34 (☎73 84 17 90) and at the airport (☎74 84 01 00); Europcar, at the airport (☎74 82 29 90); Hertz, Innherredsveien 103 (☎73 50 35 00) and at the airport (☎74 80 16 60).

Cinema Nova Kinosenter, Cicignons plass (☎820 54 333, ⓦwww.trondheimkino.no), shows all the blockbusters on its eleven screens.

Consulates UK, Beddingen 8 (☎73 60 02 00); Poland, TMV-kaia 23 (☎73 87 69 00).

Dentists Dental emergencies ☎73 50 55 00.

DNT Trondhjems Turistforening, just west of the centre at Sandgata 30 (May–Sept Mon–Fri 8am–4pm, Thurs till 6pm; Oct–April Mon–Fri 8am–4pm, Thurs 10am–4pm; ☏73 92 42 00, ⓦwww.tt.no), is DNT's local branch, offering advice on the region's hiking trails and huts. It also organizes a variety of guided walks and cross-country skiing trips, with activities concentrated in the mountains to the south and east of the city. There are one-day excursions and longer expeditions to suit different levels of skill and fitness.

Emergencies Ambulance ☏113; Fire ☏110; Police ☏112.

Internet There's free internet access at the library, Kongens gate (Mon–Thurs 9am–7pm, Fri 9am–4pm & Sat 10am–3pm; also Sept–April Sun noon–4pm).

Performing arts Olavshallen, Kjøpmannsgata 44 (☏73 99 40 50, ⓦwww.olavshallen.no), is the city's main concert hall, offering everything from opera to rock, comedy and musicals. It's also home to the city's symphony orchestra.

Pharmacy Vaktapoteket St Olav, Solsiden, Beddingen 4 (Mon–Sat 8.30am–midnight, Sun 10am–midnight; ☏73 88 37 38). Vitusapotek Løven, Olav Tryggvasonsgate 28 (Mon–Fri 9am–6pm & Sat 9am–3pm; ☏73 83 32 83).

Post office Main office at Dronningens gate 10 (Mon–Fri 8am–5pm & Sat 9am–2pm, though hours are reduced somewhat in the summer).

Taxis Eight ranks in and around the city centre including ranks at Torvet, Sentralstasjon and the *Radisson SAS Royal Garden Hotel*, or call Trønder Taxi (☏073 73).

Vinmonopolet Among several city-centre branches of Vinmonopolet, the government-run liquor and wine store, there's one just off Torvet at Munkegata 30 (Mon–Wed 10am–5pm, Thurs & Fri 10am–6pm & Sat 9am–3pm).

North from Trondheim to Bodø

North of Trondheim, it's a long haul up the coast to the next major places of interest: Bodø, the main ferry port for the Lofoten, and the gritty but likeable port of Narvik – respectively 720km and 910km distant. The easiest way to make the bulk of the trip is by **train**, a rattling good journey on the Nordlandsbanen (Nordland Line) with the scenery becoming wilder and bleaker the further north you go – and you usually get a blast from the whistle as you cross the Arctic Circle – but be sure to sit on the left of the carriage going north as the views are much better. The train takes nine hours to reach **Fauske**, where the line reaches its northern limit and turns west for the final 60-kilometre dash to Bodø. There's precious little to detain you in Fauske, but there are **bus** connections north to Narvik, a five-hour drive away, and many travellers take an overnight break here, though in fact nearby Bodø makes a far more pleasant stopover; there are buses to Narvik from here too.

If you're **driving**, you'll find the main highway, the **E6**, which runs all the way from Trondheim to Narvik and points north, too slow to cover more than three or four hundred kilometres comfortably in a day. Fortunately, there are several pleasant places to stop, beginning with **Steinkjer** and **Snåsa** in the province of Trøndelag. Steinkjer is a modest little town with a couple of good hotels, Snåsa, a relaxed – and relaxing – village, again with somewhere good to stay. Further north, in Nordland, the next province up, **Mosjøen** and **Mo-i-Rana**, two rejigged and revamped former industrial towns, make pleasant pit-stops, with Mo-i-Rana serving as a handy starting-point for a visit to the **Svartisen glacier**, crowning the coastal peaks close by. The glacier is on the western rim of the **Saltfjellet Nasjonalpark**, a wild and windswept mountain plateau that extends east towards the Swedish border. The E6 and the railway cut through the park, giving ready access, but although this is a popular destination for experienced hikers, it's too fierce an environment for the novice or the lightly equipped.

The main alternative to the E6 is the coastal **Highway 17**, the Kystriksveien (ⓦwww.rv17.no), an ingenious and extremely scenic cobbling together of road, tunnel, bridge and car ferry that negotiates the shredded shoreline from

Steinkjer, just north of Trondheim, all the way up to Bodø, a distance of nigh on 700km. It's a slow route – there are no fewer than seven ferry crossings – but if you can't spare the time or money to do the whole thing, you could join Highway 17 to the west of Mo-i-Rana, cutting out five ferries and the first 420km, yet still taking in the most dramatic part of the journey, including fabulous views of the **Melfjord** and the Svartisen glacier.

The E6 north to Hell and Verdal

Leaving Trondheim, the **E6** tunnels and twists its way round the Trondheims-fjord to **HELL**, a busy rail junction, where one train line forks north to slice through the dales and hills of Trøndelag en route to Fauske, while the other branches east for the seventy-kilometre haul to the Swedish frontier, with Östersund beckoning beyond. Hell itself has nothing to recommend it except its name, though paradoxically *hell* in Norwegian means good fortune: don't

---

Leif Larsen and the attack on the Tirpitz

Commissioned in 1941, the German battleship **Tirpitz** spent most of its three-year existence hidden away in the **Fjættenfjord** (see p.300), where it was protected from air attack by the mountains and from naval attack by a string of coastal gun emplacements. With the fjord as its base, the *Tirpitz* was able to sally forth to attack Allied convoys bound for Russia and as such was a major irritant to the Royal Navy, who dreamt up a remarkable scheme to sink it. The navy had just perfected a submersible craft called the **Chariot**, which was 6m long, powered by electric motors, and armed with a torpedo. A crew of two volunteer divers manned the craft, sitting astride it at the rear – which must amount to some kind of definition of bravery.

The plan was to transport two of these Chariots across from Shetland to Norway in a Norwegian fishing boat and then, just before the first German checkpoint, to hide them by attaching them to the outside of the boat's hull. Equipped with false papers and a diversionary load of peat, the fishing boat would, it was thought, stand a good chance of slipping through the German defences. Thereafter, as soon as the boat got within reasonable striking distance, the Chariots could be launched towards the *Tirpitz* and, once they got very close to the ship, their torpedoes would be fired.

The boat selected was the *Arthur*, skippered by the redoubtable **Leif Larsen**, a modest man of extraordinary courage, who, over the course of the war, ran over fifty trips to Norway from the Shetlands. The *Arthur* had a crew of four Norwegian and six British seamen – four to pilot the Chariots and two to help them get into their diving suits. At first the trip went well. As soon as they reached Norway's coastal waters, the crew moved the Chariots from their hiding place in the hold and attached them to the hull. They then fooled the Germans and were allowed into the Trondheimsfjord, but here the weather deteriorated and the Chariots broke loose from the boat, falling to the bottom of the ocean before they could be used. There was, therefore, no choice but to abort the mission, scuttle the *Arthur* and row ashore in the hope that the crew could escape over the mountains to neutral Sweden. They divided into two parties of five, one of which made it without mishap – except for a few lost toes from frostbite – but the other group, led by Larsen, ran into a patrol. In the skirmish that ensued, one of the Englishmen, a certain A.B. Evans, was wounded and had to be left behind; the Germans polished him off.

On September 11, 1944, the *Tirpitz* was caught napping in the **Kåfjord** (see p.362) by Allied bombers, which flew in from a Russian airfield to the east, screened by the mountains edging the fjord. The *Tirpitz* was badly damaged in the attack and although it managed to limp off to Tromsø the warship was finally sunk just outside that city on November 12 by a combined bombing-and-torpedo attack.

despair, the locals still sell postcards of the train station's freight depot tagged "Hell – gods ekspedisjon" ("have a good journey"). Just beyond Hell, the road forks too, with the E6 nudging north and the E14 travelling east to Sweden. Continuing along the E6, it's about 20km to the **Fjættenfjord**, a narrow inlet of the Trondheimsfjord and one-time hideout of the battleship *Tirpitz* (see box, p.299). Beyond the Fjættenfjord, the E6 clips past the tedious little towns of **Levanger** and **Verdal**, a centre for the fabrication of offshore oil platforms.

Stiklestad

From Verdal, it's just 6km inland along Highway 757 to **STIKLESTAD**, one of Norway's most celebrated villages. It was here in 1030 that Olav Haraldsson, later St Olav (see p.289), was killed in battle, his death now commemorated by the **Stiklestad Nasjonale Kultursenter** (Stiklestad National Culture Centre; mid-June to mid-Aug daily 9am–8pm; mid-Aug to mid-June daily 11am–5.30pm; ⓣ74 04 42 00, ⓦwww.stiklestad.no), whose assorted museums and open-air amphitheatre are spread out over a pastoral landscape. A descendant of Harald Hårfagre (the Fair-Haired), **Olav Haraldsson** was one of Norway's most important medieval kings, a Viking warrior turned resolute Christian monarch whose misfortune it was to be the enemy of the powerful and shrewd King Knut of England and Denmark. It was Knut's bribes that did for Olav, persuading all but his most loyal supporters to change allegiance – as a Norse poet commented in the cautionary *Håvamål* (the Sayings of Odin), "I have never found a man so generous and hospitable that he would not take a present." Dislodged from the throne, Olav returned from exile in Sweden in 1030, but was defeated and killed here at the **Battle of Stiklestad**. His role as founder of the Norwegian Church prompted his subsequent canonization, and his cult flourished at Trondheim until the Reformation.

Stiklestad is difficult to reach without your own transport, and there's nowhere to stay when you get there. A twice-daily **train** from Trondheim runs to Verdal, 6km away, from where you have to walk, or use one of the taxis that usually wait outside the station. During the St Olav Festival, however, special trains and buses take visitors to the site from Trondheim – details from Trondheim tourist office.

The sights

The government has spent millions of kroner developing the Stiklestad Nasjonale Kultursenter, one of the results being the broad-beamed **Kulturhus**, whose prime attraction is a pleasingly melodramatic **museum** (95kr) that uses shadowy dioramas and a ghoulish soundtrack to chronicle the events leading up to Olav's death. Nonetheless, the dioramas contain few artefacts of note, other than one or two bits of armour and jewellery dating from the period, and neither is the text particularly revealing, which is a pity, since something more could have been made of Olav's position in medieval Christian folklore. One such tale, passed down through the generations, relates how Olav spent the night on a remote Norwegian farm, only to discover the family praying over a pickled horse's penis. Expressing some irritation – but no surprise – at this pagan ceremony, Olav threw the phallus to the family dog and took the opportunity to explain some of the finer tenets of Christianity to his hosts. There's a second display on St Olav upstairs in the museum, focusing on his cult and how it spread across western Europe.

Across from the Kulturhus, the much modified, twelfth-century stone **kirke** (church) reputedly marks the spot where Olav was stabbed to death. Claims that the stone on which the body was first laid out had been incorporated into the church's high altar were abandoned during the Reformation, in case of damage by Protestants. Just up the hill from the Kulturhus, a five-minute walk away, is the open-air **amfiteater** (amphitheatre), where the colourful Olsok-spelet (St Olav's Play), a costume drama, is performed each year as part of the **St Olav Festival**. This is held over several days either side of the anniversary of the battle, July 29, and thousands of Norwegians make the trek here; tickets need to be booked months in advance via the Kultursenter website. The amphitheatre also adjoins an open-air **folkemuseum** (folk museum), containing a few indoor exhibits, and some thirty seventeenth- to nineteenth-century buildings moved here from all over rural Trøndelag.

To Steinkjer

Back on the **E6** just to the west of Stiklestad, it's a further 30km north to **STEINKJER**, a pleasant, unassuming town that sits in the shadow of wooded hills, at the point where the river that gave the place its name empties into the fjord. The Germans bombed the town to bits in 1940 because it was the site of an infantry training camp, and the modern replacement is a tidy, appealing ensemble that fans out from the long main street, Kongens gate. The E6 bypasses Steinkjer town centre, running parallel to – and about 400m to the west of – Kongens gate, with the train station in between. The E6 also passes the tourist office (late June to mid-Aug Mon–Fri 9am–8pm, Sat 10am–7pm & Sun noon–7pm; mid-Aug to late June Mon–Fri 9am–4pm; ☎74 40 17 16, Ⓦwww.visitinnherred.com). Right in the centre of town across from the train station is the *Quality Hotel Grand Steinkjer*, Kongens gate 37 (☎74 16 47 00, Ⓦwww.choicehotels.no; ❻, sp/r ❹), which occupies a clumpy modern tower block, though the rooms on the upper floors more than redeem matters by having splendid views out along the coast.

Among Steinkjer's assorted cafés and restaurants, one of the best is *Café Madam Brix*, Kirkegata 7 (Mon–Sat 11am–11pm, Sun 1–8pm; ☎74 16 74 60), a cosy café-restaurant, which takes its name from the redoubtable widow who founded an inn here in 1722; mains hover around 200kr, less at lunchtimes. A good second choice is the bright and inviting *Brod & Circus*, Kongens gate 40 (Mon–Fri 11am–5pm & Sat noon–4pm), a small local chain where a range of bread, freshly baked on the premises, serves as a sound basis for a Mediterranean-inspired menu with main courses from 140kr.

North to Snåsa

Six kilometres north of Steinkjer is the point where the Krystiksveien (Highway 17; see p.306) branches off the E6 to begin its scenic 700-kilometre journey north to Bodø. Alternatively, there's a choice of routes north to Snåsa: you can either take the E6 along the northern shore of the long and slender Lake Snåsavatn, or opt for the more agreeable (and slower) Highway 763, which meanders along the southern side of the lake through farmland and wooded hills.

Taking the faster E6, it's 60km from Steinkjer to the far end of the lake and the sleepy, scattered hamlet of **SNÅSA**, a fine example of a Trøndelag rural community. It looks as if nothing much has happened here for decades, but there is one sight of note, a pretty little hilltop **church** of softly hued grey stone, dating from the Middle Ages and very much in the English style. On the west side of the village – and 6km from the E6 – is the *Snåsa Hotell* (☎74 15 10 57, Ⓦwww.snasahotell.no; ❹, sp/r ❸), a modern place in a lovely setting overlooking the lake; the decor is somewhat dated, but the bedrooms are comfortable and it's a peaceful spot, ideal if you want to rest after a long drive. The hotel also operates a small **campsite** (same number; all year) with huts (❶) as well as spaces for tents and caravans. There's a restaurant here too, serving humdrum but filling Norwegian staples, but if you're likely to arrive after 7pm, you should telephone ahead to check it will still be open.

Into Nordland: Mosjøen

Beyond Snåsa, the E6 leaves the wooded valleys of the Trøndelag for the wider, harsher landscapes of the province of Nordland (ⓦwww.visitnordland.no). The road bobs across bleak plateaux and scuttles along rangy river valleys before reaching, after about 190km, the short (700m), signposted side-road that leads to the **Laksforsen** waterfalls, a well-known beauty spot where the River Vefsna takes a 17-metre tumble. The café here offers a grand view of the falls, which were once much favoured by British aristocrats for their salmon fishing.

Back on the E6 from the waterfalls, it's another 30km to the town of **MOSJØEN**, where first impressions are not especially favourable. The setting is handsome enough, with the town wedged amid fjord, river and mountain, but a huge aluminium plant dominates, hogging the north side of the waterfront. Persevere, for Mosjøen was a small-time trading centre long before the factory arrived, and **Sjøgata**, down by the river just to the south of the plant, is lined by attractive old timber dwellings, warehouses and shops dating from the early nineteenth century. It's an appealing streetscape, especially since the buildings are still in everyday use. It only takes a few minutes to walk from one end of Sjøgata to the other, and on the way you'll encounter (the main part of) the mildly diverting **Vefsn Museum**, Sjøgata 31b (mid-June to mid-Aug Mon–Fri 10am–6pm, except Thurs noon–8pm, & Sat 10am–3pm; 30kr), which has displays on life in old Mosjøen and exhibits some interesting work by contemporary Nordland artists.

Mosjøen practicalities

Mosjøen train station is beside the E6 on the north side of town, in front of the aluminium plant. From here, it's about 1100m to the east end of Sjøgata – just follow the signs. The bus station is about 100m beyond the west end of Sjøgata, on Strandgata, and from here it's a few metres to the tourist office at C.M. Havigsgate 39 (late June to July Mon–Fri 9am–6pm, Sat & Sun 11am–4pm; early Aug Mon–Fri 9am–5pm; late Aug to late June Mon–Fri 9am–3.30pm; ☏75 11 12 40, ⓦwww.visithelgeland.com).

The pick of the town's several **hotels** is *Fru Haugans*, also metres from the tourist office at Strandgata 39 (☏75 11 41 00, ⓦwww.fruhaugans.no; ❺, sp/r ❹). There's been an inn here since the eighteenth century and the present building is a well-judged amalgamation of the old and the new. Rather more unusual is the accommodation offered by the *Kulturverkstedet*, a local heritage organization that has refurbished a couple of old wooden houses at Sjøgata 22–24 and rents them out as the *Gjestehusene i Sjøgata* (☏75 17 27 60, ⓦwww.alrunen.no; 800kr for two people for first night, 500kr thereafter). They are simple but eminently appealing lodgings, with or without bed linen.

Kulturverkstedet also operates a charming old-fashioned **café**, serving coffee and traditional Nordland pastries, but the best **restaurant** in town is *Ellenstuen* (Mon–Sat 5–10.30pm), at the *Fru Haugans* hotel, which provides tasty, mainly Norwegian dishes from a seasonal menu that makes the most of local ingredients; main courses start at around 240kr. Otherwise, for a daytime coffee or an evening **drink**, *Lilletorget*, at Strandgata 42, is the liveliest spot in town.

To Korgen

Beyond Mosjøen, the E6 cuts inland to weave across the mountains of the interior, while the railway stays glued to the seashore down below. Either way, it's an enjoyable journey, though the E6 has the scenic edge even if it now tunnels through the flanks of **Korgfjellet** rather than going over the top. The old road is, however, still open, offering panoramic views, its highest point marked by a motel and a monument honouring the 550 Yugoslav prisoners of war who built this section of the road during World War II. Just beyond Korgfjellet is **Korgen**, sitting pretty beneath the mountains in the bend of a river. From here, the E6 slips down a river valley and sidles along the fjord to Mo-i-Rana, 90km from Mosjøen.

Mo-i-Rana

Hugging the head of the Ranfjord, **MO-I-RANA**, or more usually "**Mo**", was a minor port and market town until World War II, after which its fortunes, and appearance, were transformed by the construction of a steel plant. The plant dominated proceedings until the 1980s, when there was some economic diversification and the town began to clean itself up: the fjord shore was cleared of its industrial clutter and the E6 re-routed to create the pleasantly spacious, surprisingly leafy town centre of today. Most of Mo is resolutely modern, but look out for **Mo kirke**, a good-looking structure of 1832, with a high-pitched roof and onion dome, perched on a hill on the eastern edge of the centre. Enclosed by a mossy stone wall, the well-tended graveyard contains a communal tomb for unidentified Russian prisoners of war and the graves of six Scots Guards killed hereabouts in May 1940. In front of the church is a bust commemorating Thomas van Westen, an eighteenth-century evangelist-missionary who spearheaded early attempts to convert the Sámi. Otherwise, Mo is first and foremost a handy base for visiting the east side of the **Svartisen glacier** (see p.305) and/or exploring the region's lakes, caves, fjords and mountains, though it does possess one real surprise: here, standing in the shallows, is an **Antony Gormley** sculpture, **Havmannen** (Man of the Sea), a large and stern-looking figure, which gazes determinedly down the fjord.

Arrival, information and transport

Mo's **bus and train stations** are close together, down by the fjord on Ole Tobias Olsens gate. The compact town centre lies east of this street, with the foot of the main pedestrianized drag, Jernbanegata, opposite the bus station. The tourist office is about 300m to the south of the bus and train stations, also on Ole Tobias Olsens gate (mid-June to mid-Aug Mon–Fri 9am–8pm, Sat 9am–4pm & Sun 1–7pm; mid-Aug to mid-June Mon–Fri 9am–4pm; ☎75 13 92 00, ⓦwww.arctic-circle.no). They have the usual local leaflets, provide free town

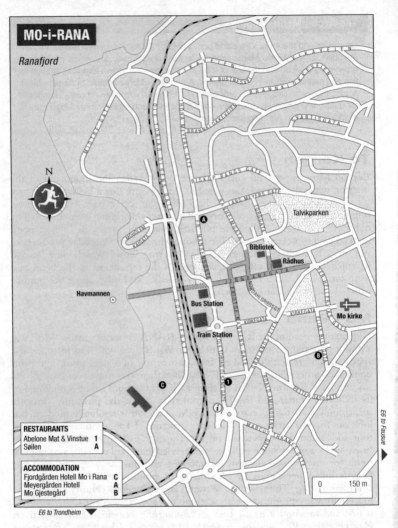

maps and issue a free booklet detailing the Highway 17 Coastal Route (see box, p.306). Bus timetables are available too, but local services are much too patchy for any serious exploration of the town's environs without your own transport. In this regard, car rental is available from a couple of outlets, including Hertz, in the town centre on Gjennomgangen (℡75 15 22 55), for around 750kr a day. If that looks too expensive, the tourist office rents out **bikes**, though you have to be pretty fit to reach most local points of interest – and just forget it altogether if it's raining. The tourist office can arrange a shared taxi ride to the Svartisen glacier (see p.305) and will check that the boats that give access to the glacier are running. The staff will also make reservations for a wide range of guided excursions, from rafting, kayaking and fishing through to caving, climbing and trekking.

Accommodation

The pick of the town's several hotels is the excellently run and very comfortable
𝄞 *Meyergården Hotell*, a short walk north of the train station, off Ole Tobias
Olsens gate at Fridtjof Nansensgate 28 (☎75 13 40 00, ⓦwww.meyergarden
.no; ❻, sp/r ❹). Most of the hotel is modern, but the original lodge has survived
and is maintained in period style, with stuffed animal heads on the wall and
elegant panelled doorways. A less expensive, but much plainer, alternative is the
Fjordgården Hotell Mo i Rana, a tour-group favourite down by the waterfront at
Søndregate 9 (☎75 15 28 00, ⓦwww.fjordgarden.no; May to Aug; ❹). A third
option is *Mo Gjestegård*, tucked into the backstreets near the church at Elias Blix
gata 5 (☎75 15 22 11, ⓦwww.mo-gjestegaard.no; ❷). This family-run guesthouse is a little heavy on the pine finishings, but it's quiet and peaceful and the
rooms are pleasantly homely.

Cafés and restaurants

Mo's best **restaurant** is the *Søilen* (daily from 1–10pm; ☎75 13 40 80) at the
Meyergården Hotell, where you can sample an excellent range of Norwegian
dishes featuring local ingredients; main courses here average around 220kr. A
second choice is the *Abelone mat & vinstue*, Ole Tobias Olsens gate 6 (daily
2–9pm; ☎75 15 38 88), which serves competent pizzas and steaks from
around 170kr.

Around Mo: Grønligrotta and the Svartisen glacier

The limestone and marble mountains to the north of Mo are pocked by caves.
The most accessible is the limestone **Grønligrotta** (mid-June to mid-Aug daily
10am–7pm; 100kr; ⓦwww.gronligrotta.no), where an easy 35-minute guided
tour follows a subterranean river and takes in a 400-metre-long underground
chamber. Grønligrotta is lit by electric lights – it's the only illuminated cave in
Scandinavia – and it's located 25km from Mo: head north out of town along
the E6 and follow the signs along the same minor road that leads to the most
accessible part of the Svartisen glacier.

Svartisen glacier

Norway's second largest glacier, **Svartisen** – literally "Black Ice" – covers
roughly 375 square kilometres of mountain and valley between the E6 and the
coast to the northwest of Mo. The glacier is actually divided into two sections
– east and west – by the Vesterdal valley, though this cleft is a recent phenomenon: when it was surveyed in 1905, the glacier was one giant block, about 25
percent bigger than it is today; the reasons for this change are still obscure. The
highest parts of the glacier lie at around 1500m, but its tentacles reach down to
about 170m – the lowest-lying glacial arms in mainland Europe. Mo-i-Rana is
within easy reach of one of the glacier's **eastern nodules**: to get there, drive
north from Mo on the E6 for about 12km and then take the signed byroad to
the glacier, a straightforward 23-kilometre trip running past the Grønligrotta
caves (see above) and ending beside the ice-green, glacial lake **Svartisvatnet**.
Here, **boats** (early June & late Aug 2 daily; late June to mid-Aug hourly 10am–
4pm; 20min each way; 90kr return) shuttle across the lake, though services can't
begin until the ice has melted – usually by late June – so check with the tourist
office in Mo before you set out. Viewed from the boat, the great convoluted
folds of the glacier look rather like bluish-white custard, but close up, after a stiff
three-kilometre hike past the rocky detritus left by the retreating ice, the sheer
size of the glacier becomes apparent – a mighty grinding and groaning wall of
ice edged by a jumble of ice chunks, columns and boulders.

The Kystriksveien Coastal Route on Highway 17

Branching off the E6 just beyond Steinkjer (see p.301), the tortuous **Kystriksveien** (Ⓦ www.rv17.no) – the **coastal route** along Highway 17 – threads its way up the west coast, linking many villages that could formerly only be reached by sea. This is an obscure and remote corner of the country, but apart from the lovely scenery there's little of special appeal, and the seven ferry trips that interrupt the 688-kilometre drive north to Bodø (there are no through buses) make it expensive and time-consuming in equal measure. A free **booklet** describing the route can be obtained at tourist offices throughout the region – including Mo – and it contains all Highway 17's car-ferry timetables.

Conveniently, the stretch of Highway 17 between **Mo-i-Rana** and **Bodø** takes in most of the **scenic highlights**, can be negotiated in a day, and cuts out five of the ferry trips. To sample this part of the route, drive 35km west from Mo along Highway 12 to the Highway 17 crossroads, from where it's some 60km north to the **Kilboghamn–Jektvik** ferry (June–Aug every 1–2hr, Sept–May 3–10 daily; 1hr; driver and car 143kr; Ⓦ www.hurtigruten.no) and a further 30km to the ferry linking **Ågskardet** with **Forøy** (every 1hr–1hr 30min; 10min; driver and car 55kr). On the first ferry you cross the Arctic Circle with great views down and along the beautiful **Melfjord**, and on the second, after arriving at Forøy, you get a chance to see a westerly arm of the **Svartisen** glacier (see p.305), viewed across the slender Holandsfjord. For an even closer look at the glacier, stop at the information centre in **HOLAND**, 12km beyond Forøy, and catch the **passenger boat** (late May to early Sept Mon–Fri 8am–9pm, Sat & Sun 11am–5.30pm, every 1hr–1hr 30min; 10min; 60kr return; ☏99 40 30 00), which zips across the fjord to meet a connecting bus; this travels the kilometre or so up to the *Svartisen Turistsenter* (☏75 75 11 00, Ⓦ www.svartisen.no), from where it's another 2km to the glacier. The **Turistsenter** has a café, rents cabins from 990kr a night, and is the base for four-hour guided **glacier walks** (mid-June to mid-Aug only; prior booking is essential; 600kr).

From Holand, it's 140km to the Saltstraumen (see p.312) and 30km more to Bodø (see p.308).

The west side of the Svartisen glacier can be seen – and accessed – from the "Kystriksveien" Coastal Route along Highway 17 (see box above); it can also be visited on **organized bus and ferry trips** from Bodø (see pp.308–311).

The Arctic Circle

Given its appeal as a travellers' totem, and considering the amount of effort it takes to actually get here, crossing the Arctic Circle, about 80km north of Mo, is a bit of a disappointment. Uninhabited for the most part, the landscape is undeniably bleak, but the gleaming **Polarsirkelsenteret** (Arctic Circle Centre; daily: May 10am–6pm; June to mid-July 9am–8pm; late July to late Aug 8am–10pm; late Aug 9am–8pm; early Sept 10am–6pm; Ⓦ www.polarsirkelsenteret .no) only serves to disfigure the scene – it's a giant lampshade of a building plonked by the roadside and stuffed with every sort of tourist bauble imaginable. You'll whizz by on the bus, the train toots its whistle, and drivers can, of course, shoot past too, though the temptation to brave the crowds is strong. Inside, you should be able to resist the Arctic exhibition, but you'll probably get snared by either the "Polarsirkelen" certificate, or the specially stamped postcards. Less tackily, there are poignant reminders of crueller times back outside, where a couple of simple stone memorials pay tribute to the Yugoslav and Soviet POWs who laboured under terrible conditions to build the Arctic railroad – the Nordlandsbanen – to Narvik for the Germans in World War II.

Saltfjellet Nasjonalpark: Lønsdal and Graddis

The louring mountains in the vicinity of the Polarsirkelsenteret are part of the **Saltfjellet**, a vast mountain plateau whose spindly pines, stern snow-tipped peaks and rippling moors extend west from the Swedish border to the Svartisen glacier. The E6 and the railway cut inland across this range between Mo-i-Rana and Rognan (see below), providing access to the cairned hiking trails that lattice the Saltfjellet, part of which – to the immediate west of the E6 – has been protected as the **Saltfjellet Nasjonalpark**. You can also reach the trails from Highway 77, which forks east off the E6 down the **Junkerdal**, a remote and rather unwelcoming river valley that leads to the Swedish border. The region is, however, largely the preserve of experienced hikers: the trails are not sufficiently clear to dispense with a compass, weather conditions can be treacherous and, although there's a good network of DNT-affiliated huts, none is staffed, nor do any of them supply provisions. Keys to these huts (most of which are owned by BOT, Bodø's hiking association; see p.310) are available locally, but clearly you have to sort this out with BOT before you set off.

Among several possible bases for venturing into the Saltfjellet, **LØNSDAL**, around 100km north of Mo and 20km beyond the Arctic Circle, is the most easily reached either on the E6 or by train from Trondheim, Mo or Bodø (1–3 daily, but some trains only stop here by request; check with the conductor). Not that there's actually much to reach: a kilometre-long turning off the E6 leads first to the *Polarsirkelen Høysfjellshotell* (☎75 69 41 22, ⓦ www.polarhotell.no; ❸), a long wooden building in a sheltered location and with a cosy modern interior, and then to the lonely train station; the hotel has the only restaurant for miles around.

From Lønsdal, **hiking trails** lead off into the Saltfjellet. One of the more manageable options is the four-hour hike east (away from the national park) to **GRADDIS**, a tiny hamlet situated beside Highway 77, 18km east of the E6. Graddis has a **guesthouse** and **camping**, the *Graddis Fjellstue og Camping* (☎75 69 43 41, ⓔgraddis@c2i.net; March to mid-Sept), which has double rooms (❸), and rudimentary cabins (❷) as well as tent pitches all on a farmstead on the wooded slopes of the Junkerdal. Despite its gloominess, the Junkerdal is a favourite spot from which to explore the Saltfjellet, not least because it's easy to reach by road from Sweden.

Botn

Some 45km north of Lønsdal, the E6 regains the coast at **Rognan**, from where it pushes along the east side of the Saltdalsfjord. About 5km from Rognan, at **BOTN**, keep your eyes peeled for the signposted, kilometre-long road up to the Krigskirkegården, truly one of Nordland's most mournful and moving places. Buried here, in a wooded glade high above the fjord, are the Yugoslav prisoners of war and their German captors who died in the district during World War II. The men are interred in two separate graveyards – both immaculately maintained, though, unlike the plainer Yugoslav cemetery, the German graveyard is entered by a sturdy granite gateway. Mostly captured Tito partisans, the Yugoslavs died in their hundreds from disease, cold and malnutrition, as well as torture and random murder, during the construction of the **Arctic railroad** to the iron-ore port of Narvik. When the Germans occupied Norway in 1940, the railway ended at Mosjøen, but they soon decided to push it north so that their cargo ships might avoid the dangerous voyage along the coast. This line, the **Nordlandsbanen**, involved the labour of 13,000 POWs, but the Germans failed to complete it, and it was not until 1962 that the railway finally reached Bodø.

Fauske

From Botn, it's another 30km up the E6 to **FAUSKE**, which, but for a brief stretch of line from Narvik into Sweden, marks the northernmost point of the Norwegian rail network and is, consequently, an important transport hub. Along with nearby Bodø, the town is a departure point of the twice-daily Nord-Norgeekspressen (Ⓦwww.nor-way.no), the express **bus** service that carries passengers to Narvik, where you change for either the bus to Tromsø or the Nordkappekspressen bus, which covers the next leg of the journey up to Alta (for Honningsvåg and Nordkapp). It takes about five and a half hours to get from Fauske to Narvik, a gorgeous run with the E6 careering round the mountains and along a series of blue-black fjords, but if you are aiming for Alta, you'll have to overnight in Narvik – which is no hardship at all (see p.316). In Fauske, the Nord-Norgeekspressen leaves from beside the **train station** and tickets can be purchased from the driver or in advance at any bus station.

Fauske practicalities

From Fauske's train and long-distance bus station, it's a five- to ten-minute walk down the hill and left at the T-junction to the local bus station and a few metres more to the main drag, **Storgata**, which doubles as the E6. Storgata runs parallel to the fjord and holds the handful of shops that passes for the town centre. There's certainly no strong reason to linger here – nearby Bodø is a much more palatable place to stay, never mind Narvik – but Fauske can still be a handy if unexciting place to break your journey. Of the town's **hotels**, the pick is the *Fauske Hotell*, Storgata 82 (Ⓣ75 60 20 00, Ⓦwww .fauskehotell.no; Ⓞ, sp/r Ⓞ), a chunky square, block whose interior is made slightly sickly by a surfeit of salmon-coloured streaky marble. Quarried locally, the marble is exported all over the world, but is something of an acquired taste. Marble apart, the hotel rooms are comfortable enough and the breakfasts are large and tasty. Otherwise, the best bet is the *Lundhøgda* campsite (Ⓣ75 64 39 66, Ⓦwww.lundhogdacamping.no; May–Sept). This occupies a splendid location about 3km west of the town centre, overlooking the mountains and the fjord: head out of town along the E80 (the Bodø road), and turn off down a signposted country lane, ablaze with wild flowers in the summertime and flanked by old timber buildings. The campsite takes caravans, has spaces for tents and also offers cabins from 490kr a night.

Bodø and around

BODØ, some 65km west of Fauske along the E80, is the terminus of the Trondheim train line and the starting point of the Nord-Norgeekspressen express bus to points north. Founded in 1816, the town struggled to survive in its early years, but was saved from insignificance by the herring boom of the 1860s, a time when the town's harbourfront was crowded with the net-menders, coopers, oilskin-makers and canneries that kept the fleet at sea. Later, it accrued several industrial plants and became an important regional centre, but was then heavily bombed during World War II and today there's precious little left of the proud, nineteenth-century buildings that once flanked the

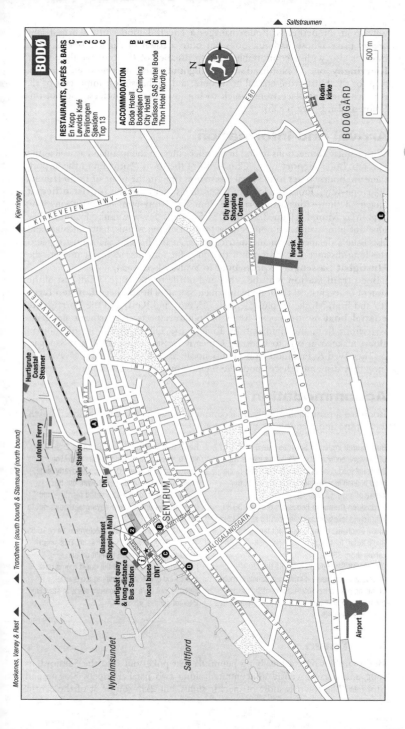

Moskenes, Værøy & Røst ◀   ◀ *Trondheim (south bound) & Stamsund (north bound)*   *Kjerringøy* ◀   ▲ *Saltstraumen*

BODØ

RESTAURANTS, CAFÉS & BARS

En Kopp	C
Løvolds Kafé	1
Paviljongen	2
Sjøsiden	C
Top 13	C

ACCOMMODATION

Bodø Hotell	B
Bodøsjøen Camping	E
City Hotel	A
Radisson SAS Hotel Bodø	C
Thon Hotel Nordlys	D

Nyholmsundet

Saltfjord

SENTRUM

BODØGÅRD

Bodin kirke

City Nord Shopping Centre

Norsk Luftfartsmuseum

Hurtigrute Coastal Steamer

Lofoten Ferry

Train Station

Hurtigbåt quay & long-distance Bus Station

Glasshuset (Shopping Mall)

local buses

Airport

KIRKEVEIEN HWY. 834

RØNVIKVEIEN

E 80

GAMLE RIKSVEI

PLASSMYRA

HÅLOGALANDSGATA

OLAV V GATE

DRONNINGENSGATE

PRINSENSGATE

TORGGATA

HAAKON VII GATE

OLAV V GATE

HERNESVEIEN

0   500 m

N

5

TRONDHEIM TO THE LOFOTEN ISLANDS

309

waterfront. Nonetheless, Bodø manages a cheerful modernity, a bright and breezy place whose harbour looks out onto a batch of rugged, treeless hills. Bodø is also within comfortable striking distance of the old trading post of **Kjerringøy**, one of Nordland's most delightful spots; has long been a regular stop for the Hurtigrute coastal boat route; and, perhaps most important of all, is much the best place from which to hop over to the choicest parts of the Lofoten islands (see p.333).

Arrival and information

With regular connections to and from other cities on the mainland as well as the Lofoten, Bodø **airport** is just 2km south of the town centre. From the airport, there are hourly buses to the local bus station right in the heart of Bodø (10min; 30kr one-way). From the local bus station, it's metres to the **tourist office**, at Sjøgata 3 (June–Aug Mon–Fri 9am–8pm, Sat 10am–6pm & Sun noon–8pm; Sept–May Mon–Fri 9am–3.30pm; ℡75 54 80 00, @www.visitbodo.com). They give out information on connections to the Lofoten islands, rent out bikes and also issue a detailed town and district guide. At the back of the tourist office is the long-distance bus station and the quay for local ferries, most usefully the **Hurtigbåt passenger express boat** to Svolvær (see p.334).

Bodø **train station** is at the other end of the town centre, 700m east of the tourist office, just off the long main street, Sjøgata. The southern **Lofoten ferry** (to and from Moskenes plus the islets of Værøy and Røst) and the **Hurtigrute coastal boat** use the docks 400m and 600m respectively northeast along the waterfront from the train station. To join the **DNT** hiking organization in Bodø, make your way to Bodø og Omegns Turistforening (BOT), at Sandgata 3 (Tues, Wed & Fri noon–3pm, Thurs noon–5pm; ℡75 52 14 13, @www.bot .no); they dispense advice about the region's hiking trails and cabins.

Accommodation

Bodø has a reasonable supply of accommodation, including half a dozen hotels, a campsite and a couple of guesthouses.

Bodø Hotell Professor Schyttes gate 5 ℡75 54 77 00, @www.bodohotell.no. Well-kept rooms with all the usual mod cons in this mid-sized, mid-range hotel housed in a five-storey block right in the centre of town. ❺, sp/r ❹

Bodøsjøen Camping Bodøsjøen ℡75 56 36 80. Year-round lakeside campsite located about 3.5km to the southeast of the centre, not far from the Bodin kirke. Tent pitches, caravan hook-ups and cabins (from 55kr).

City Hotell Storgata 39 ℡75 52 04 02, @johansst@online.no. Simple, unassuming rooms at this bargain-price hotel-cum-guesthouse near the train station. Twenty-three en-suite rooms; free internet access. ❷

Radisson SAS Hotel Bodø Storgata 2 ℡75 51 90 00, @www.bodo.radissonsas.com. The biggest hotel in town. Occupies an overly large, modern concrete-and-glass tower, but has commodious and well-appointed rooms – and those on the upper floors have great views out to sea. ❼, sp/r ❹

Thon Hotel Nordlys Moloveien 14 ℡75 53 19 00, @www.thonhotels.no. This smart, very modern chain hotel is right on the harbourfront, and most of the guest rooms have some kind of sea view. Nothing too special perhaps, but it's a very pleasant place to stay. Free internet access. ❼, sp/r ❺

The Town

Bodø rambles over a low-lying peninsula that pokes out into the Saltfjord, its long and narrow centre concentrated along two parallel streets, Sjøgata and Storgata. The town is short of specific sights, but 2km southeast of the centre, on Olav V's gate, is its most popular attraction, the imaginative **Norsk Luftfartsmuseum** (Norwegian Aviation Museum; mid-June to mid-Aug daily 10am–6pm; mid-Aug to mid-June Mon–Fri 10am–4pm, Sat & Sun 11am–5pm; Ⓦwww.luftfart.museum.no; 90kr), which tracks through the general history of Norwegian aviation. It adopts an imaginative approach to the subject and even the building itself is constructed in the shape of a two-bladed propeller: one "blade" houses air force and defence exhibits, the other civilian displays. The spot where the two blades meet straddles the ring road – Olav V's gate – and is topped by part of the old Bodø airport control tower. Among the planes to look out for are a Spitfire, a reminder that two RAF squadrons were manned by Norwegians during World War II, and a rare Norwegian-made Hønningstad C-5 Polar seaplane. Bodø was used by the US Air Force throughout the Cold War, and you can also see one of their U2 spy planes.

From the museum, it's a short drive east along the ring road to the Gamle riksvei roundabout, where you turn right for the one-kilometre detour to the onion-domed **Bodin kirke** (late June to mid-Aug Mon–Fri 10am–3pm; free), a pretty little stone church sitting snugly among clover meadows. Dating from the thirteenth century, the church was modified after the Reformation by the addition of a tower and the widening of its windows – the Protestants associated dark, gloomy churches with Catholic superstition. It is, however, the colourful seventeenth-century fixtures that catch the eye, plus the lovingly carved Baroque altarboard and pulpit, both painted in the eighteenth century by an itinerant German artist called Gottfried Ezechiel.

Eating and drinking

Bodø is hardly a gourmet's paradise, but there are one or two competent cafés and restaurants, kicking off with the traditional and inexpensive Norwegian menu of the canteen-style *Løvolds Kafé* (Mon–Fri 9am–6pm & Sat 9am–3pm), down by the quay at Tollbugata 9; main courses here feature local ingredients and average around 120kr. More upmarket is the wood-panelled *Sjøsiden* restaurant (daily 5–11pm; ☏75 51 90 00) upstairs in the *Radisson SAS Hotel*; they do a good line in local fish here with mains averaging 250–300kr. Also in the *Radisson SAS* tower block is the ground-floor *En Kopp* coffee bar, which serves the best coffee in town, and the bar with the best view, the rooftop *Top 13*. There's also the amenable *Paviljongen* café-bar in the distinctive glass chalet at the east end of the Glasshuset shopping mall (Mon–Sat 10am–11.30pm & Sun 12.30–11.30pm). A nice way to fill up cheaply is to buy a big bag of prawns (40–50kr) from one of the fishing boats along the quayside and eat al fresco at the water's edge.

Out from Bodø: Kjerringøy, Saltstraumen and the Svartisen glacier

There are three obvious excursions from Bodø: one northeast to the old trading station at **Kjerringøy**, another southeast to the tidal phenomenon known as the **Saltstraumen**, and a third, the longest, the 170-kilometre trip south to Holand (see p.306) for the **Svartisen glacier**. All three places can be reached by car or bike, Kjerringøy along Highway 834 and the other two via Highway 17 – the Kystriksveien – between Bodø and Mo-i-Rana (see p.306). As for **public transport**, Kjerringøy is reachable by bus and ferry, the Saltstraumen by bus, and the glacier is best seen on a guided tour. Bodø tourist office coordinates glacier tours and the most straightforward last around twelve hours, include bus and ferry transport, and cost in the region of 600kr, though that doesn't cover food. Reservation – at least a day ahead – is advised, and be sure to have warm clothing. For longer excursions onto the glacier, contact the local specialist Nordland Turselskap direct (☎ 90 63 60 86, ⓦ www.nordlandturselskap .no), though their trips are necessarily more expensive, beginning at about 800kr excluding transport.

Kjerringøy

The **KJERRINGØY trading post** (mid–May to Aug daily 11am–5pm; 60kr; ☎ 75 55 77 41, ⓦ www.kjerringoy.no), just 40km north along the coast from Bodø by road and ferry, has a superbly preserved collection of nineteenth-century timber buildings set beside a slender, islet-sheltered channel. This was once the domain of the **Zahl family**, merchants who supplied the fishermen of Lofoten with every-thing from manufactured goods and clothes to farmyard foodstuffs in return for fish. It was not, however, an equal relationship: the Zahls, who operated a local monopoly until the 1910s, could dictate the price they paid for the fish, and many of the islanders were permanently indebted to them. This social division is still very much in evidence at the trading post, where there's a marked distinction between the guest rooms of the main house and the fishermen's bunk beds in the boat- and cookhouses. Indeed, the **family house** is remarkably fastidious, with its Italianate busts and embroidered curtains – even the medicine cabinet is well stocked with formidable Victorian remedies like the bottle of "Sicilian Hair Renewer". Also of interest is the old barn, the Zahlfjøsen (same times), where there is a display on the life and work of the novelist Knut Hamsun (also see p.315).

There are enjoyable, hour-long **guided tours** around the main house throughout the summer (daily, every hour on the hour; 40kr), and afterwards you can nose around the reconstructed general store, drop in at the café and stroll the fine sandy beach. Taken altogether, it's an especially peaceful and picturesque spot and one that film-goers may recognize from the movie *I am Dina*, based on *Dina's Book*, by the Norwegian author Herbjørg Wassmo, which was filmed here.

Practicalities

Getting here from Bodø **by car** is easy enough – a straightforward coastal drive north along Highway 834 with the added treat of a ferry ride from Festvåg to Misten (every 30min to 1hr 30min, less frequently on Sun; 10min; passengers 23kr, car & driver 55kr return; ☎ 177, ⓦ www.177nordland.com). Things are more complicated **by bus**, but a day-return trip beginning at Bodø bus station is possible on Saturday; pick up a combined bus-and-ferry timetable at Bodø tourist office. More generally, there are one or two buses daily from Bodø to Kjerringøy, where there's **accommodation** at both the new *Kjerringøy Brygge Hotell* at the trading post (☎ 75 52 54 00, ❺) and the old parsonage, *Kjerringøy Prestegård*, about 700m north of the trading post along the main road (☎ 75 51 11 14, ⓦ www .kjerringoy.no). The latter has simple double rooms in the main building (❷) and slightly pleasanter ones in the renovated cowshed next door (❸).

Saltstraumen

Less interesting than Kjerringøy, but more widely publicized, is the maelstrom known as the **Saltstraumen**, 33km east of Bodø round the bay on Highway 17. Here, billions of gallons of water are forced through a narrow, 150m-wide channel four times daily, making a headlong dash between the inner and outer fjord. The whirling creamy water is at its most turbulent at high tide, and its most violent when the moon is new or full – and a timetable is available from Bodø tourist office. However, although scores of tourists troop here every high tide, you can't help but feel they wish they were somewhere else – the scenery is, in

Norwegian terms at least, flat and dull, and the view from the bridge which spans the channel unexciting. That said, fishing enthusiasts will be impressed by the force of the water which pulls in all sorts of fish: cod, catfish and coley are common catches – one coley caught here weighed a remarkable 22.7 kilos (or so they say). Rods can be hired at several places, including the **Saltstraumen Opplevelsessenter** (Saltstraumen Adventure Centre), housed in two adjoining buildings near the eastern end of the bridge.

It takes about fifty minutes to **drive** from Bodø to the Saltstraumen, or you could take a local **bus** from the bus station (Mon–Sat 4–6 daily, Sun 1 daily; 1hr; Ⓦwww.nbuss.no), though its times rarely coincide with high tide. In this case, you can kill a couple of hours very pleasantly at *Kafé Kjelen*, a little red house on the west side of the bridge, whose terrace offers views over the maelstrom – don't miss its *møsprumlefse*, a traditional, burrito-like pancake stuffed with a mix of sweet brown-cheese sauce, sour cream and melted butter.

North to Narvik

The 240-kilometre journey north from Fauske to Narvik is spectacular, with the **E6** rounding the fjords, twisting and tunnelling through the mountains and rushing over high, pine-dusted plateaux. The scenery is the main event hereabouts, and there's little to merit a stop, with two notable exceptions – the fascinating old farmstead at **Kjelvik**, where the hardship of rural life in Norway is revealed in idyllic surroundings, and the remote former trading post of **Tranøy**, a thirty-kilometre detour west of the E6 via Highway 81. At the end of the journey, **Narvik** is an eminently likeable industrial town that witnessed some especially fierce fighting during the German invasion of 1940. It's a good place for an overnight stop and a useful launching pad for the long haul to the far north, or a visit to the Vesterålen and Lofoten islands.

En route between Fauske and Narvik, the E6 presents two opportunities to catch a **car ferry** to Lofoten – one at Skutvik, the other at Bognes. The more

▲ Ski hut on Fagernesfjellet, near Narvik

southerly of the two is **Skutvik**, 35km to the west of the E6, with ferries to Svolvær. At **Bognes**, where the E6 is interrupted by the Tysfjord, there's a choice of ferries. One sails to Lødingen and the E10 on Lofoten, while a second hops across the Tysfjord to **Skarberget** to pick up the E6, just 80km south of Narvik. All these ferries are operated by Hurtigruten (Ⓦwww.hurtigruten.no), the same company that operates the Hurtigrute coastal boat, and work on a first-come, first-served basis, though reservations can be made – and are strongly advised – on the once-daily Skutvik-to-Svolvær ferry (see below). Long-distance **buses** link Bodø, Fauske and Narvik twice daily; the bus journey from Fauske to Narvik takes five and a half hours.

The E6 north to Kråkmo

Beyond Fauske, the E6 scuttles over the hills to the small industrial town of **Straumen** and then threads along the coast to **Sommarset**, an old ferry point where boats crossed the **Leirfjord** until a new stretch of road was built around the fjord in 1986. This new section is an ambitious affair that drills through the mountains with the fjord glistening below. It also passes within 250m of the old farmstead of **KJELVIK**, 56km from Fauske, where a scattering of old wooden buildings, including a cottage, woodshed, forge and mill, nestle in a green, wooded valley. It's a beautiful spot, but the tenant farmers who worked the land finally gave up the battle against their harsh isolation in 1967. There was no electricity, no water, the soil was thin, and the only contact with the outside world was by boat – supply vessels would come up the Leirfjord to the Kjelvik jetty, from where it was a steep two-kilometre hike to the farm, 200m above the fjord. Today, there's **open access** to the farm, which is kept in good condition, and wandering around is a delight: you can also follow the old footpath down to the Kjelvik jetty. **Guided tours** of Kjelvik are available in the summer (late June to mid-Aug daily 11am–5pm; 35kr; Ⓦwww.saltenmuseum.no) and, on the last Saturday of the season, the **Kjelvik festival** sees the old buildings put to their original uses. Griddle-cakes are cooked on the wood stove, and dollops of sour cream and porridge are doled out to visitors.

After Kjelvik, the E6 bores through the mountains to reach, after about 40km, the couple of houses that make up **KRÅKMO**, with the lake on one side and the domineering mass of a mighty mountain, Kråkmotind, on the other. This was once a favourite haunt of that crusty old reactionary Knut Hamsun, for more on whom, see p.315.

North to Bognes

From Kråkmo, it's around 50km to the point where Highway 81 branches off for Skutvik and the Svolvær car ferry (see below) and another scenic 20km or so up the E6 to **Bognes**. Here, one ferry heads west to **Lødingen** on the Vesterålen islands (late June to mid-Aug 16 daily, mid-Aug to late June 13 daily; 1hr; passengers 51kr, car & driver 163kr; Ⓦwww.hurtigruten.no), while a second travels to **Skarberget** for the E6 and the remaining 80km to Narvik (every 1hr–1hr 30min; 25min; passengers 31kr, car & driver 87kr; Ⓦwww.hurtigruten.no). In summer, it's worth arriving two hours before departure to be sure of a space.

West off the E6: Tranøy, Hamsund and Skutvik (for Svolvær)

Spearing off the E6 20km before Bognes, **Highway 81** wriggles its way west across the islet-shredded coastline bound for the **Skutvik car ferry** over to

Svolvær, on the Lofoten (1 daily; 2hr; passengers 76kr, car & driver 262kr; reservations advised: ⊤177 in Nordland, otherwise ⊤75 77 24 10, Ⓦwww .hurtigruten.no). The road is only 35km long, but it takes a good hour to drive and en route it threads through some dramatic scenery, all craggy shorelines and imposing peaks. About 15km from the E6, the highway spans a narrow channel to reach the island of **Hamarøy**, noteworthy as the boyhood home of the writer **Knut Hamsun** (1859–1952). Long a leading literary light, Hamsun blotted his Norwegian copybook with his admiration for Hitler and the Nazis before and during the occupation, though his culpability has been the subject of much heated debate. Whatever the truth, Hamsun remained something of a hate figure for several decades and only recently has there been a degree of rehabilitation – as witnessed by the opening of several Hamsun-related sites on this, his home island.

Tranøy

Just after Highway 81 crosses onto **Hamarøy**, a side road cuts north to make the fourteen-kilometre journey to the old trading post of **TRANØY**, in stern and bleak surroundings on the island's northern shore. Here you'll find two art galleries celebrating Hamsun's work, beginning with the **Tranøy Galleri** (mid-June to mid-Aug daily 11am–6pm; free; Ⓦwww.tranoy-galleri.com), which features illustrations of Hamsun's books by Tor Arne Moen as well as the work of local artists, much of it for sale. Nearby, the **Hamsungalleriet på Tranøy** (Hamsun Gallery; mid-June to mid-Aug 11am–6pm; 30kr; Ⓦwww .hamsungalleriet.no), in the old general store where Hamsun worked as a youth, also concentrates on Hamsun-related paintings. Perhaps even more impressive, however, is the permanent open-air exhibition out on the rocks just a short stroll from the gallery, showing blow-ups of nature-related pictures in a stunning setting.

Tranøy has a couple of excellent **places to stay**. First up is the *Edvardas hus* (⊤75 77 21 82, Ⓦwww.edvardashus.no; ❻; mid-June to mid-Aug), which occupies two old buildings set a couple of hundred metres apart, one a merchant's house dating back to the 1910s, the other a former bank built a decade later; there are nine impeccably stylish, extremely comfortable bedrooms here and the food is outstanding – both at breakfast and at the pocket-sized restaurant, where reservations are strongly advised. Alternatively, *Tranøy Fyr* (⊤90 60 46 95, Ⓦwww.tranoyfyr.no; June–Aug) has a dozen straightforward rooms in the old lighthousemen's quarters, on the edge of the ocean beneath the lighthouse. *Tranøy Fyr* also has its own **café–restaurant** with outdoor seating in the summertime, although the place could do with a lick of fresh paint. Another enjoyable option is staying at the *Tranøy Galleri* (⊤47 02 92 08, Ⓦwww.tranoy-galleri.com; ❸) right next to the gallery and with two comfortably decorated apartments with an indoor sauna. From here it's a short stroll to the best spot for a **drink** in the old whaling-boat-turned-pub overlooking the harbour at the end of the road.

Hamsund and Skutvik

Doubling back to Highway 81, it's a brief drive west to the hamlet of **HAMSUND**, the site of Knut Hamsun's boyhood home, now the tiny and very modest **Hamsuns barndomshjem** (late June to late Aug daily 11am–6pm; 35kr), though the foundations have already been laid for something far more substantial – the **Knut Hamsun Centre**, which, designed by Steven Holl, is scheduled to be opened in August 2009, exactly 150 years after Hamsun's birth. From here, it's another short haul to the Skutvik ferry.

Narvik

A relatively modern town, **NARVIK** was established just a century ago as an ice-free port to handle the iron ore brought here by train from the mines in northern Sweden. Neither does it make any bones about what is still its main function: the **iron-ore docks** are immediately conspicuous, slap-bang in the centre of town, the rust-coloured machinery overwhelming much of the waterfront. Yet, for all the mess, the industrial complex is strangely impressive, its cat's cradle of walkways, conveyor belts, cranes and funnels oddly beguiling and giving the town a frontier, very Arctic, feel. Not content with its iron, Narvik has also had a fair old stab at reinventing itself as an **adventure sports** centre, becoming a popular destination for skiers, paraglidlers and scuba-divers – and developing a good range of guesthouses to match.

Arrival and information

Fifteen-minutes' walk from one end to the other, Narvik's sloping centre straggles along the main street, **Kongens gate**, which doubles as the E6. The **train station** is at the north end of town and from here it's a five- to ten-minute walk along Kongens gate to the **tourist office**, at Kongens gate 57 (June to mid-Aug Mon–Fri 9am–7pm, Sat & Sun 10am–5pm; mid-Aug to Sept Mon–Fri 9am–5pm & Sat 10am–2pm; Oct–May Mon–Fri 9am–4pm; ☏76 96 56 00, ⓦwww.destinationnarvik.com). The staff issue free town maps, provide lots of information on outdoor pursuits and have the full range of bus and ferry

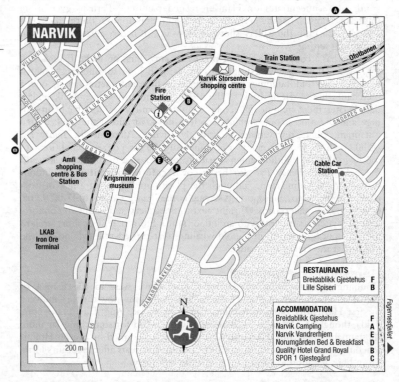

The Ofotbanen

One of the real treats of a visit to Narvik is the **train ride** into the mountains that rear up behind the town and spread east across the Swedish border. Completed in 1903, this railway line – the **Ofotbanen** – was, by any standard, a remarkable achievement and the hundreds of navvies that made up the work force endured astounding hardships during its construction. The line passes through some wonderful scenery, slipping between hostile peaks before reaching the rocky, barren and loch-studded mountain plateaux beyond. **SJ** (ⓦ www.sj.se), a Swedish company, now operates the **Ofotbanen** and trains arrive and depart **Narvik train station** two or three times daily, shuttling to and from Kiruna, three hours away in northern Sweden. The times of the trains mean that a short day-trip into the mountains behind Narvik is easy enough, and the obvious target is **RIKSGRÄNSEN**, a pleasant hiking and skiing centre just over the border in Sweden – so take your passport. The journey from Narvik to Riksgränsen takes fifty minutes and costs 33kr each way. Most train travellers nose around Riksgränsen for a few hours before returning to Narvik, but the more adventurous can **hike** at least a part of the way back on the **Rallarveien**, the old and refurbished trail originally built for the railway workers. This extends west for 15km from Riksgränsen to the **Rombaksbotn**, a deep and narrow inlet where the navvies once started their strenuous haul up into the mountains; the trail also heads east deeper into Sweden, to Abisko and Kiruna. A favourite option is to walk from Riksgränsen back towards the coast, picking up the return train at one of the several Norwegian stations on the way.

The area around the Ofotbanen isn't nearly as remote now that the **E10** crosses the mountains to the north of the railway, but the terrain is difficult and weather unpredictable, so hikers will need to be well equipped. For details of other **trails** hereabouts, as well as **cabins**, contact Narvik tourist office and/or the DNT affiliate Narvik og Omegn Turistforening (ⓦ www.narvikfjell.no). Hiking **maps** are available from the tourist office too.

timetables; they will also assist with ferry and activity reservations. The **bus station** is a little further to the south in the basement of the Amfi shopping centre, on the west side of the main drag.

As regards adventure sports, a number of operators combine to offer everything from hang- and para-gliding through to **mountain climbing**, caving, canoeing and **glacier walking**. There's also **scuba diving** amid the wreck-studded waters around Narvik with Divenarvik (ⓣ 99 51 22 05, ⓦ www .divenarvik.com). Most operators rent out the appropriate specialist tackle – but check when you reserve.

Accommodation

Narvik is a tad short of **hotels**, but it does have several very recommendable **guesthouses**, an **HI hostel** and a reasonably convenient **campsite**, *Narvik Camping*, about 2km north of the centre on the E6 at Rombaksveien 75 (ⓣ 76 94 58 10, ⓦ www.narvikcamping.com). It's open all year and has tent and caravan pitches, hook-ups and cabins (from 650kr).

Hotels and guesthouses

Breidablikk Gjestehus Tore Hunds gate 41 ⓣ 76 94 14 18, ⓦ www.breidablikk.no. This pleasant, unassuming guesthouse is neat and trim, with homely en-suite rooms. Those on the upper floors have attractive views over town, and a good,

hearty breakfast is included in the room rate. It's located at the top of the steps at the end of Kinobakken, a side road leading east off Kongens gate, just up from the main town square. ❹

Narvik Vandrerhjem Dronningensgate 58 ⓣ 76 96 22 00, ⓦ www.vandrerhjem.no. Part of a larger hotel, the hostel rooms are plain and pretty frugal, but at least you're in the town centre. Free internet access, a laundry, a café and a self-catering kitchen. Some of our readers have complained about the noise from the neighbouring nightclub at the weekend. Dorm beds 270kr, doubles ❷

🏃 **Norumgården Bed & Breakfast** Framnesveien 127 ☎76 94 48 57, ⓦwww .norumgaarden.narviknett.no. Lavish but good-value B&B in a 1920s timber villa. The Germans used the place as an officers' mess during the war and today, tastefully restored, it holds three large guest rooms, two of which have kitchenettes. Antiques are liberally distributed across the house and breakfast is included. A snip at ❶

Quality Hotel Grand Royal Kongens gate 64 ☎76 97 70 00, ⓦwww.choicehotels.no. Some of Narvik's hotels have seen better days, but the *Grand*, just down from the train station, is well kept and well maintained; its public rooms are wood-panelled and appealing, while the bedrooms are perfectly adequate albeit in standard chain style. ❼, sp/r ❺

SPOR 1 Gjestegård Brugata 2a ☎76 94 60 20, ⓦwww.spor1.no. This spick-and-span place is the pick of the budget/backpacker options with clean if spartan modern rooms. Doubles, quads and a larger dorm plus kitchen facilities, a sauna and a bar. Occupies a creatively recycled former railway building, a simple one-storey block just below the main town bridge. Dorm beds from 200kr, doubles ❶

The Town

Narvik's first modern settlers were the navvies who built the railway line, the **Ofotbanen** (see box, p.317), to the mines in Kiruna, over the border in Sweden at the end of the nineteenth century – a herculean task commemorated every March by a week of singing, dancing and drinking, when the locals dress up in period costume. The town grew steadily up until World War II, when it was demolished during ferocious fighting for control of the harbour and its iron-ore supply. Perhaps inevitably, the rebuilt town centre is rather lacking in appeal, with modern concrete buildings replacing the wooden houses that went before, but it still musters a breezy northern charm. It also possesses the fascinating **Nordland Røde Kors Krigsminnemuseum** (Red Cross War Memorial Museum; May to early June Mon–Sat 10am–4pm & Sun noon–4pm; early June to late Aug Mon–Sat 10am–9pm & Sun noon–6pm; late Aug to mid-Sept Mon–Sat 10am–4pm & Sun noon–4pm; rest of year Mon–Fri 11am–3pm; 50kr; ⓦwww.warmuseum.no), just down from the tourist office. Run by the Red Cross, the museum documents the wartime German saturation bombing of the town, and the bitter and bloody sea and air battles in which hundreds of foreign servicemen died alongside a swathe of the local population. It was a complicated campaign, with the German invasion of April 1940 followed by an Allied counterattack spearheaded by the Royal Navy. The Allies actually recaptured Narvik, driving the Germans into the mountains, but were hurriedly evacuated when Hitler launched his invasion of France. The fight for Narvik lasted two months and the German commander wrote of the sea change among his Norwegian adversaries, who toughened up to become much more determined soldiers, and skilled ones at that: many were crack shots from their hunting days and all could ski. In the short term, this change of attitude prefigured the formation of the Resistance; in the long term it pretty much put paid to Norway's traditional isolationism. The museum gives a thoroughly moving and thoughtfully presented account of the battle for Narvik and then tracks through the German occupation of Norway until liberation in 1945.

Narvik also offers **guided tours** of the LKAB mining company's ore-terminal complex (mid-June to mid-Aug 3pm daily; 50kr), interesting if only for the opportunity to spend ninety minutes amid such giant, ore-stained contraptions. After its arrival by train, the ore is carried on the various conveyor belts to the quayside, from where some thirty million tons of it are shipped out each year. Sign up for the tours at the tourist office.

Moving on from Narvik

There's a choice of routes on from Narvik. The **Nordkappekspressen bus** (1 daily except Sat; ⓦwww.nor-way.no) shoots north along the E6 to Alta (see p.362), a journey of ten hours, while the **Nord-Norgeekspressen bus** (1–3 daily; ⓦwww .nor-way.no) makes the four-hour hop north to Tromsø (see p.354). Both trips give sight of some wonderfully wild and diverse scenery, from craggy mountains and blue-black fjords to gentle, forested valleys – though it's not perhaps quite as scenic a journey as the E6 from Fauske to Narvik. A third bus service, the **Lofoten Ekspressen** (1 daily; ⓦwww.nor-way.no) runs west from Narvik to Fiskebol, Svolvær, Kabelvåg and Leknes in the Lofoten islands (see p.334). There are no buses direct to the Vesterålen.

Ofotbanen trains (see box, p.317) run east from Narvik to Kiruna and Luleå in Sweden; the ride to Luleå takes around six and a half hours.

Fagernesfjellet

Narvik's **cable car** (daily: early June & Aug 1–9pm; late June 1pm–1am; 80kr single, 100kr return), a stiff fifteen-minute walk up from the town and behind the train station, is the easiest way to reach the town's mountainous environs, whisking passengers up the first 650m of the mighty **Fagernesfjellet**. There's a café and viewing point at the top of the cable car, and from here, on a clear day, you can see the Lofoten islands and experience the midnight sun in all its glory (end of May to mid-July). In addition, **hiking trails** delve further into the mountains, and in the winter season, from late November to early May, the cable car provides a shuttle service for **skiers and snowboarders**. The network of skiing amenities includes six ski lifts, nine prepared slopes and unlimited off-piste skiing, with some floodlit areas; for further details contact the tourist office or ⓦwww.narvikfjellet.no. The cable car stops running in windy or foggy conditions, so – if you're walking there – you might want to check it's operating with the tourist office before setting out.

Eating

Narvik is short of recommendable **cafés** and **restaurants**. Easily the best of the bunch is the *Lille Spiseri*, a smart restaurant in the *Quality Hotel Grand Royal* (see p.318), where they specialize in local ingredients with main courses averaging around 200kr; it's a member of the Arctic Menu scheme (see p.303). Alternatively, guests can pre-book filling, home-made dinners at the *Breidablikk Gjestehus* (see p.317).

The Vesterålen islands

A raggle-taggle archipelago nudging into the Norwegian Sea, the **Vesterålen islands**, and their southerly neighbours the Lofoten, are like western Norway in miniature: the terrain is hard and unyielding, the sea boisterous and fretful, and the main – often the only – industry is fishing. The weather is temperate but wet, and the islanders' historic isolation has bred a distinctive culture based, in equal measure, on Protestantism, the extended family and respect for the ocean.

The archipelago was first settled by semi-nomadic hunter-agriculturalists some 6000 years ago, and it was they and their Iron-Age successors who chopped down the birch and pine forests that once covered the coasts. It was

LOFOTEN & VESTERÅLEN ISLANDS

Car ferries
Hurtigrute
Hurtigbåt

Tromsø & Alta ◄

Finnsnes & Tromsø ◄

Gryllefjord (late May–late August) ◄

Riksgränsen ▲ ▲ Riksgränsen

E6

E6/E10

E6/E10

Rombaksbotn

OFOTBANEN

Narvik

E6

T R O M S

Harstad/
Narvik ✈

Skarberget

Bognes

HWY 83

E10

Lødingen

H i n n ø y a

Harstad

Gullesfjordbotn

Andenes

Bleik

Stave

Nordmela

HWY 82

Andøya

Risøyhamn

HWY 82

Sortland

Langøya

E10

Raftsundet

Trollfjord

LOFAST

E10

Stokmarknes

Melbu

Fiskebøl

Hadseløya

Austvågøya

N O R D L A N D

V e s t e r å l e n

N O R W E G I A N

S E A

N

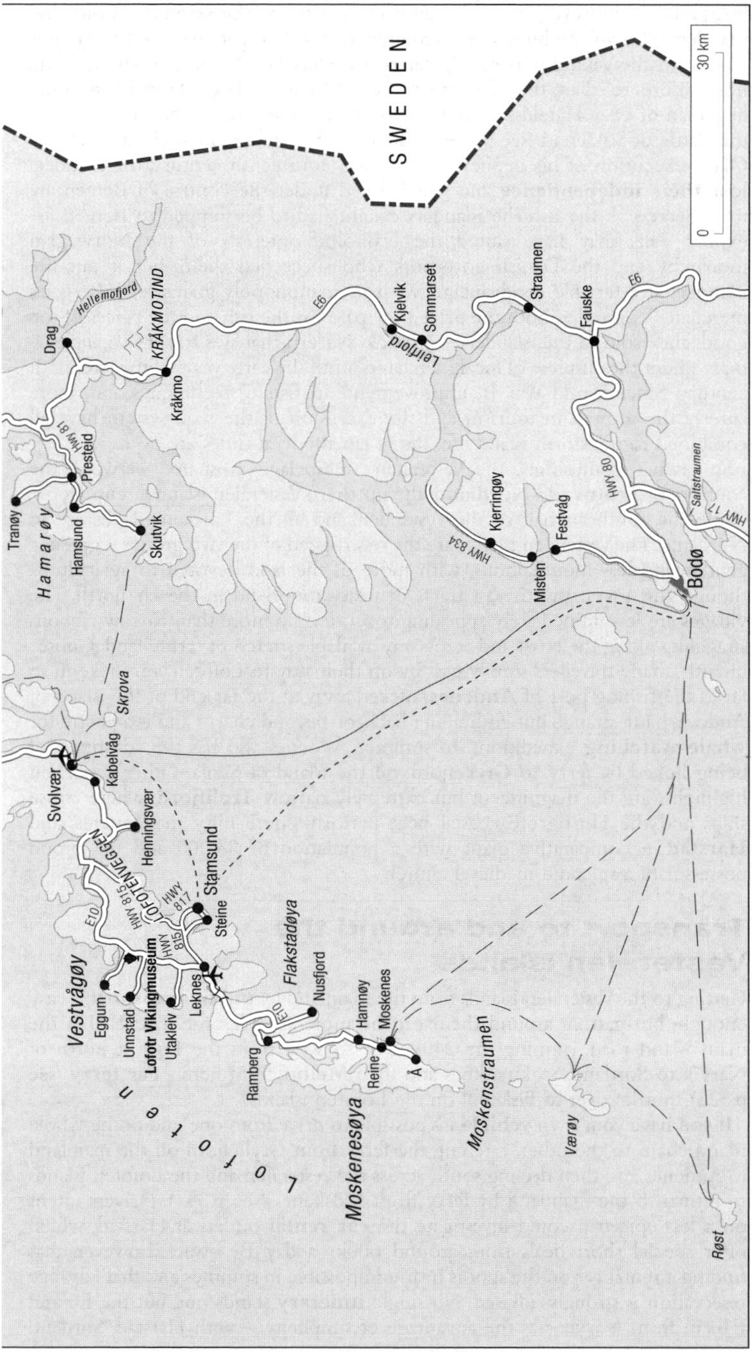

▶ Svartisen Glacier & Kystriksveien

boatbuilding, however, which brought prosperity: by the seventh century, the islanders were able to build ocean-going vessels, a skill that enabled the islanders to join in the Viking bonanza. Local clan leaders became important warlords, none more so than the eleventh-century chieftain **Tore Hund**, one-time liegeman of Olav Haraldsson, and one of the men selected to finish Olav off at the Battle of Stiklestad (see p.300) – the fulfilment of a blood debt incurred by Olav's execution of his nephew. In the early fourteenth century, the islanders **lost their independence** and were placed under the control of Bergen: by royal decree, all the fish the islanders caught had to be shipped to Bergen for export. This may have suited the economic interests of the Norwegian monarchy and the Danish governors who succeeded them, but it put the islanders at a terrible disadvantage. With their monopoly guaranteed, Bergen's merchants controlled both the price they paid for the fish and the prices of the goods they sold to the islanders – a **truck system** that was to survive, increasingly under the auspices of local merchants, until the early years of the twentieth century. Since World War II, improvements in fishing techniques and, more latterly, the growth in tourism and the extension of the road system have all combined to transform island life, and at last the hard times are over.

Somewhat confusingly, the Vesterålen archipelago is shared between the counties of **Troms** and **Nordland**: the northern Vesterålen islands are in Troms, while the southern half of the Vesterålen and all the Lofoten islands are in Nordland. The Vesterålen islands are the less rugged of the two groups – greener, gentler and less mountainous, with more of the land devoted to agriculture, though this gives way to vast tracts of peaty moorland in the far north. The villages are less immediately appealing too, often no more than narrow ribbons straggling along the coast and across any available stretch of fertile land. Consequently, many travellers simply pass by on their way to Lofoten, a mistake in so far as the fishing port of **Andenes**, tucked away at the far end of the island of Andøya, has a strange but enthralling back-of-beyond charm and is a centre for **whale-watching** expeditions. In summer, Andenes also has the advantage of being linked by ferry to Gryllefjord, on the island of Senja. Other Vesterålen highlights are the magnificent but extremely narrow **Trollfjord**, where cruise ships and the Hurtigrute coastal boat perform some nifty manoeuvres, and **Harstad**, a comparative giant with a population of 23,000 and the proud possessor of a splendid medieval church.

Transport to and around the Vesterålen islands

Getting to the Vesterålen islands from the mainland by **public transport** is easy enough, but getting around them can be more troublesome. The **E10** is the main island road, running the 240km or so west from the E6 just north of Narvik to Sortland, Stokmarknes and then **Melbu**; from here a **car ferry** (see p.323) shuttles over to Fiskebøl on the Lofoten islands.

If you have your own **vehicle** it's possible to drive from one end of the whole island chain to the other, catching the ferry from Gryllefjord on the mainland to Andenes and then driving south across the Vesterålen and the Lofoten islands to return to the mainland by ferry from Moskenes (see p.344). Drivers intent on a less epic trip could investigate the **car rental** outlets at Harstad, which offer special short deals from around 600kr a day. Be aware, however, that finding a rental car on the spot is nearly impossible in summer and that advance reservation is strongly advised. No single **itinerary** stands out, but the E6 and E10 in from Narvik has the advantage of simplicity – with Harstad, Sortland

and then Andenes being the obvious route, plus Stokmarknes if you're heading on to Lofoten. On the Vesterålen, **Andenes** has most to offer as a base, thanks to its whale- and bird-watching trips and choice of accommodation.

All Nordland **public transport** timetables – including those for much of Vesterålen – are online at ⓦwww.177nordland.com; you can also call ⓣ177 in Nordland, otherwise ⓣ75 77 24 10.

By car ferry

The principal **car ferry** from the mainland to the Vesterålen islands departs from the jetty at **Bognes**, on the E6 between Fauske and Narvik, and sails to **Lødingen** (late June to mid-Aug 16 daily, mid-Aug to late June 13 daily; 1hr; passengers 51kr, car & driver 163kr; ⓦwww.hurtigruten.no). From Lødingen, it's just 4km to the E10 at a point midway between Harstad and Sortland. A second, but this time seasonal, car ferry runs from remote **Gryllefjord**, 110km west of the E6 well to the north of Narvik, to **Andenes** at the northern tip of the Vesterålen (late May to mid-June & early-to-late Aug 2 daily, mid-June to early Aug 3 daily; 2hr; passengers 145kr; car & driver 375kr). Reservations are strongly advised by email or phone with the ferry company concerned, Senjafergene (ⓣ76 14 12 03, ⓦwww.senjafergene.no). A third car ferry links the Vesterålen islands with Lofoten, running across the Hadselfjord between **Melbu** and **Fiskebøl**, both of which are on the E10 (daily 7am–11pm, every 80min; 30min; passengers 31kr, car & driver 85kr; ⓦwww.177nordland.com).

By boat: the Hurtigrute

Heading north from Bodø (departing daily at 3pm), the **Hurtigrute coastal boat** (ⓦwww.hurtigruten.no) threads a scenic route up through the Lofoten to the Vesterålen islands, where it calls at four places: **Stokmarknes** and **Sortland** in the south, **Risøyhamn** in the north and **Harstad** in the east. The journey time from Bodø to Stokmarknes is 10 hours, 3.5 hours more to Risøyhamn and another 2 hours to Harstad. None of these four destinations is especially appealing, but workaday Risøyhamn is well on the way to Andenes, while Harstad is a regional centre and transport hub with a fine old church (see p.325). Cruising southwards from Tromsø (departing daily at 1.30am), the Hurtigrute follows the same itinerary, but in reverse; the sailing time from Tromsø to Harstad is 6.5 hours. The **passenger fare** from Bodø to Risøyhamn is 792kr in summer, 555kr in winter, 849/594kr to Harstad and 1226/858kr to Tromsø. The all-year fare for transporting a car from Bodø to Harstad is 453kr, 592kr to Tromsø. For vehicles, advance reservations are essential, and can be made either online (ⓦwww.hurtigruten.no) or by phoning the ship – ask down at the harbour or at the port's tourist office for assistance.

Scenically, the highlight of the Hurtigrute cruise through the Lofoten and Vesterålen islands is the **Raftsundet**, a long and narrow sound between Svolvær and Stokmarknes, off which branches the magnificent **Trollfjord**. Unfortunately, the northbound Hurtigrute leaves Svolvær at 10pm and so the Raftsundet is only visible during the period of the midnight sun (late May to mid-July); in the opposite direction, however, boats leave Stokmarknes at a much more convenient 3.15pm. The Svolvær/Stokmarknes trip takes three hours and the passenger fare is 245kr in summer, 172kr in winter; cars cost an extra 353kr throughout the year.

By boat: Hurtigbåt passenger express boats

Hurtigbåt boats provide a speedy alternative to the car ferries and the Hurtigrute. The main **Hurtigbåt** service from the mainland to the **Vesterålen** runs from Tromsø to Harstad (2–4 daily; 2hr 45min; 380kr; ⓦwww.hurtigruten.no).

There's also an especially useful Hurtigbåt boat to the **Lofoten**: Bodø to Svolvær (1 daily; 3hr 30min; 297kr; @www.hurtigruten.no). In both cases, advance reservation – most easily done online – is a good idea.

By bus

Operated by Nor-Way Bussekspress (@www.nor-way.no), the **Fauske Ekspressen** (1–2 daily) runs from Bodø and Fauske to the Bognes-Lødingen car ferry and then continues onto Sortland. This Nor-Way Bussekspress service is supplemented by a number of local buses operated by Veolia (@177 in Nordland, otherwise @75 77 24 10, @www.177nordland.com). Two of Veolia's most useful Vesterålen services link Sortland and Lødingen with Harstad (1 daily; 2hr 30min) and Sortland with Andenes (2–4 daily; 2hr).

By plane – and car rental

Harstad/Narvik, the main **airport** for the Vesterålen, is located in Evenes, in between Harstad and Narvik on the E10. There are regular **flights** to Evenes from Oslo, Trondheim, Bodø and Tromsø, operated by SAS, Norwegian and Widerøe. From the airport, it's a good hour's drive to either city and there's also a good **Flybussen** (@78 40 70 00, @www.flybussen.no) service to Harstad, Narvik and Sortland. **Car rental** is available at the airport – both Avis (@76 98 21 33) and Hertz (@41 58 22 28) have outlets here. If you reserve in advance (which is almost essential in high season), the price can drop to about 600kr a day.

Harstad

Readily reached by car, bus and the Hurtigrute coastal boat, **HARSTAD**, just 130km from Narvik, is easily the largest town on the Vesterålen islands. It's home to much of northern Norway's engineering industry, its sprawling docks a tangle of supply ships, repair yards and cold-storage plants spread out along the gentle slopes of the Vågsfjord. This may not sound too enticing, and it's true that Harstad wins few beauty contests, but the town does have the odd attraction, and if you're tired of sleepy Norwegian villages, it at least provides a bustling interlude.

Arrival and information

Harstad may be easy to reach, but if you're travelling along the E10 it's actually something of a cul-de-sac, involving a thirty-kilometre detour north along Highway 83. Once you've arrived, however, you'll find almost everything you need conveniently clustered together around the harbour. Here, within a few metres of each other, you'll find the **bus station**, jetties for the Hurtigbåt and Hurtigrute **boats** plus the **tourist office**, Torvet 8 (mid-June to mid-Aug daily 10am–6pm; mid-Aug to mid-June Mon–Fri 8am–3.30pm; @77 01 89 89, @www.destinationharstad.no), which has a wide selection of tourist literature on the Vesterålen.

Accommodation

For a town of limited charms, the number of large chain **hotels** in Harstad is relatively high, which is why, especially in summer, walk-in prices can be extremely competitive. The *Arcticus Hotel*, a short walk from the Torvet at Havnegata 3 (@77 04 08 00, @www.choice.no; ❹, sp/r ❷), has the best rates by far, offering recently revamped, retro-chic rooms. A breakfast and dinner buffet is included in the rate, making it very good value. A good alternative, also occupying a modern block near the Torvet, is the neat and trim *Grand Nordic Hotell*, Strandgata 9 (@77 00 30 00, @www.nordic.no; ❹, sp/r ❷), although the

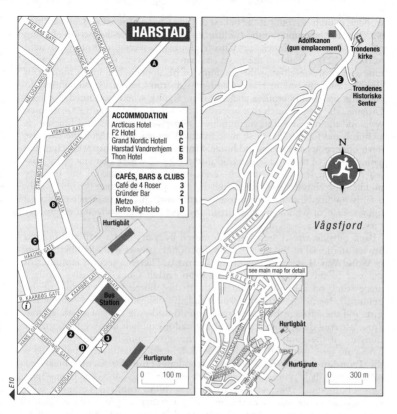

interior could do with a makeover. For something more up to date, try the *F2 Hotel* at Fjordgata 2 (☏77 00 32 00, Ⓦwww.f2hotel.no; ❸) offering 88 smart rooms right in front of the bus station plus a modern indoor spa. Most expensive of the lot is the *Thon Hotel* at Sjøgaten 11 (☏77 00 08 00, Ⓦwww.thonhotels .no; ❻, sp/r ❹), stylishly decorated in a marine theme that complements the harbour view.

Further afield, the HI **hostel** *Harstad Vandrerhjem* (June to mid-Aug; ☏77 04 00 77, Ⓦwww.vandrerhjem.no; dorm beds 295k, doubles ❶; reception closed 4–5pm) has the advantage of a pleasant fjordside location, near the Trondenes kirke. The hostel has self-catering facilities, washing machines and comfortable double rooms, the only problem being that the building is a school for most of the year and so has a rather cold, institutional feel. The hostel is easy to reach on the local "Trondenes" bus from the station (Mon–Sat 1 hourly; 10min).

The sights

Harstad's historical pride and joy is **Trondenes kirke** (opening times vary; free; guided tours mid-June to mid-Aug daily at 5pm; 40kr), which occupies a lovely leafy location beside the fjord 3km north of the town centre at the end of the slender Trondenes peninsula. To get there, take the local "Trondenes" bus (Mon–Sat 1 hourly; 10min), which leaves the bus station beside the tourist office and goes past the church – or take a taxi. By car, follow Highway 83 north from the centre and watch for the signposted turning on the right. The original wooden church was built at the behest of King Øystein (of *rorbuer* fame; see box, p.332) at the beginning of the twelfth century and had the distinction of being the northernmost church in Christendom for several centuries. Øystein (c.1088–1123) was one of the more constructive rulers of the period, spending time and effort developing the economy of his domain, building a number of churches like this one in Harstad and, perhaps most unusual of all, refusing to conspire against his brother and co-ruler, Sigurd, when he joined the First Crusade. The stone church that survives today was erected in the 1300s, its thick walls and the remains of its surrounding ramparts reflecting its dual function as a church and fortress, for these were troubled, violent times. After the exterior, stern of necessity, the warm and homely **interior** comes as a surprise. Here, the dainty arches of the rood screen lead into the choir, where a late medieval, bas-relief wooden triptych surmounts each of the three altars. Of the trio, the middle triptych is the most charming: the main panel, depicting the holy family, is fairly predictable, but down below is a curiously cheerful sequence of biblical figures, each of whom wears a turban and sports a big, bushy and exquisitely carved beard.

Back outside, the churchyard is bordered by a dry-stone wall and holds a Soviet memorial to the eight hundred prisoners of war who died hereabouts in World War II at the hands of the Germans. There's a second reminder of the war in the form of the **Adolfkanon** (Adolf Gun), a massive artillery piece stuck on a hilltop to the north of the church in the middle of the peninsula. It's inside a military zone, and the obligatory guided tour of the **gun** and the adjacent **bunkers** (mid-June to mid-Aug daily at 11am, 1pm & 3pm; late Aug daily at 3pm; 60kr; ⓦwww.adolfkanonen.no), which begins at the gate of the compound, 1km from the gun, stipulates that you have to have your own vehicle to visit. The third sight on the Trondenes peninsula is the **Trondenes Historiske Senter** (Trondenes Historical Centre; mid-June to mid-Aug daily 11am–5pm; mid-Aug to mid-June Mon–Fri 10am–2pm, Sun 11am–4pm; 70kr; ⓦwww.tdm.no), a plush modern complex with exhibitions on the history of the locality – dioramas, mood music, incidental Viking artefacts and the like. It's located along the fjord from the church, back towards the town centre.

As for Harstad itself, the downtown core has little appeal, though the comings and goings of the ferry boats are a diversion and in late June the eight-day **North Norway Arts Festival** (Festspillene i Nord-Norge; ⓦwww.festspillnn.no) provides a spark of interest with its concerts, and drama and dance performances; note, however, that the town's hotels are full to bursting throughout the proceedings.

Eating, drinking and nightlife

Harstad is no gastronomic nirvana, but its saving grace is ⚹ *Café de 4 Roser*, Torvet 7a (☏77 01 27 50; Mon–Sat 10am–10pm), which covers all the culinary bases by having a first-rate French-influenced **restaurant** upstairs and a **café-bar** down below. At the latter, they serve light meals – fish burgers, salads and pasta – during the day before switching to fresh-fruit cocktails after 6pm: it's the best bar in town. A popular hangout both day- and night-time is trendy *Metzo* with many coffee varieties, simple wok dishes for lunch and dinner and DJs at weekends; the heated terrace makes up for the Nordic temperatures. The *Gründer Bar*, at Fjordgata 2, is more traditional with nautical relics on the walls and wraps, tapas and salads on the menu (closed Sun). As for **nightlife**, the *Retro Nightclub* is your best bet, occupying the basement of the *F2 Hotel* right in the centre of town, although they only open on Friday and Saturday nights.

From Harstad, the **Hurtigrute** (ⓦ www.hurtigruten.no) sails north for Tromsø at 8am and south for points in the Vesterålen and Lofoten islands at 8.30am. Alternatively, there's a **Hurtigbåt** service to Tromsø (2–4 daily; 2hr 45min; 480kr; (ⓦ www.hurtigruten.no) and frequent **buses** to Narvik, Sortland (for Andenes) and Lofoten (ⓦ www.177nordland.com). For **car rental**, several firms in Harstad offer short-term deals: try Europcar, Samagata 33 (ⓣ 77 01 86 10), or Hertz, by the harbour (ⓣ 77 06 13 46).

On to Andenes

Back on the **E10** south of Harstad, it's 50km southwest along the fjord to the turning for the Lødingen ferry (see p.323) and 50km more to the bridge that spans the sound over to Sortland (see p.330). On the near side of this Sortland bridge, **Highway 82** begins its 100-kilometre trek north, snaking along the craggy edge of Hinnøya island before crossing a second bridge over to humdrum **Risøyhamn**, the only Hurtigrute stop on **Andøya**, the most northerly of the Vesterålen islands. Beyond Risøyhamn, the scenery is much less dramatic, as the mountains give way to hills in the west and a vast, peaty moor in the east. Highway 82 strips across this moorland and, despite offering panoramic views of the mountains back on the mainland, it's an uneventful journey on to Andenes. If you have time to spare, consider taking the more scenic route along the west coast of Andøya, branching off from Highway 82 just past Risøyhamn to pass through a series of tiny villages like Nordmela, Stave and Bleik (see p.329). There's a palpable sense of desolation here on this wild and isolated coast.

At the old fishing port of **ANDENES**, lines of low-slung buildings lead up to the clutter of wooden warehouses and mini boat-repair yards that edge the harbour and its prominent breakwaters. "It is the fish, and that alone, that draws people to Andenes – the place itself has no other temptations," said the writer Poul Alm when he visited in 1944, and although this is too harsh a judgement today, the main emphasis does indeed remain firmly nautical. Among Scandinavians at least, Andenes is famous for its **Whale Safaris**, four- to five-hour cruises with a marine biologist on board to point out sperm, killer and minke whales as well as dolphin and porpoise; even better, the operators claim – with every justification – a ninety-five percent chance of a whale sighting: the edge of the continental shelf, which is closer to land here than anywhere else in Norway, boasts a large stock of sperm whales, who form the basis of the tours and dawdle in these waters all year. The safari involves tracking and locating the whales with underwater microphones and then waiting for them to surface. Safaris take place at least once daily between late May and mid-September but can be as frequent as five daily in high season, subject to demand. Taking an evening safari during the midnight-sun period can be especially rewarding, as the calmer sea makes it easier to spot the surfacing sperm whales, and the light is simply enchanting. **Tickets** cost 795kr each (children 5–13 years 500kr) and covers the guided tour of the Whale Centre (see p.328) that precedes the boat trip. The safari isn't recommended for children under five as the sea can get rough; warm clothing and sensible shoes are essential. **Reservation** (ⓣ 76 11 56 00, ⓦ www.whalesafari.no) at least a day in advance is strongly advised as the trips are popular, and even with multiple departures in high season, they tend to fill up quickly.

Whaling in Norway

To many foreigners at least, Norway has an unenviable reputation as one of the few countries in the world still **hunting whales** for commercial purposes. In so doing, the Norwegians ignore the worldwide **ban** on commercial whaling adopted by the International Whaling Commission in 1986. While Japan claims to kill whales for scientific reasons, Norway does not disguise its main reason for hunting – human consumption – and its fisheries department works out its own quota (1052 whales in 2008). Whale meat (*hval*) is considered a delicacy by many Norwegians and can still be found on many (north) Norwegian menus, though opinion polls indicate that about one in four Norwegians under thirty oppose the hunt. The method of killing these animals is also subject to bitter debate. Norwegian whalers invented the exploding harpoon and they still use it today. Activists claim there's no humane way to kill a whale, but many abhor this particular method: one in five harpooned whales suffer a long and painful death. Ironically enough, the waters where thousands of tourists venture out on their "Whale-watching Safaris" are the same as those used by the whale hunters. Indeed, in 2006 a whale was shot and dragged aboard a whaler right in front of a whaling safari boat, causing a real brouhaha.

The other recommended boat trip hereabouts is a **Puffin Safari** round the bird island of **Bleiksøya** (June to mid-Aug 1–2 daily; 1hr 30min; 350kr, children 150kr; reservation through the tourist office or direct ☏97 19 52 75, ⓦ www.puffinsafari.no), a pyramid-shaped hunk of rock populated by thousands of puffins, kittiwakes, razorbills and, sometimes, white-tailed eagles. Cruises leave from the jetty at **Bleik** (see p.329), an old and picturesque fishing hamlet around 7km southwest of Andenes that has a clear view of the islet; a local bus often makes the trip from Andenes to coincide with sailings.

Andenes sights

Andenes' **Hvalsenter** (Whale Centre; late May to mid-June & mid-Aug to mid-Sept daily 8am–4pm; mid-June to mid-Aug daily 8am–7.30pm; 60kr; 140kr discount ticket for all of the town's sights on sale at the tourist office), metres from the harbour, may not be the most exciting way to start a safari, but it does give you a good explanation of what you're about to witness on the open ocean. That said, the centre's incidental displays on the life and times of the animal hardly fire the imagination, and neither does the massive – and deliberately dark and gloomy – display of a whale munching its way though a herd of squid, though at least the sperm-whale skeleton, which was washed up on an Andenes beach, gives a clear idea of the sheer size of the animal. More diverting is the **Hisnakul natural history centre** (mid-June to Aug daily 10am–6pm; Sept to mid-June daily 10am–4pm; 50kr), which explores various facets of Andøya life from its premises in a refurbished timber warehouse near the Whale Centre. The centre is short on historical artefacts, plumping instead for imaginative displays such as the two hundred facial casts of local people made in 1994 and an assortment of giant-replica bird-beaks. The adjacent **Nordlyssenteret** (Northern Lights Centre; late June to late Aug daily 10am–6pm; 40kr) provides a comprehensive explanation of the northern lights (see box, p.354) – Andenes is a particularly good spot to see them – illustrated by first-class photographs and a slide show.

Close by, **Andenes fyr** (Andenes lighthouse; mid-June to Aug daily noon–4pm; 35kr) is a 40m-high maroon structure dating from the 1850s and offering wide views over the town from its top. From the lighthouse, it's a brief stroll south to the **Polarmuseet** (Polar Museum; late June to mid-Aug daily 10am–6pm; 30kr), inside a modest little building with a pretty wooden porch. Its main exhibit is the giant stuffed polar bear gazing at you from a frightening height; it was allegedly shot by accident on a recent expedition to Spitsbergen. The rest of the interior is mostly dedicated to the Arctic knick-knacks accumulated by a certain Hilmar Nøis, an Andøy man who wintered on Svalbard no fewer than 38 times. Unfortunately all the labelling is in Norwegian, but the helpful staff are willing to translate.

Practicalities

Bisecting the town, Andenes' long and straight main street, **Storgata**, ends abruptly at the seafront. The **bus station** is just a few metres to the east of Storgata, just back from the seafront, while the **tourist office** is on the harbour, sharing the same premises as the Northern Lights Centre (mid-June to Aug daily 10am–6pm; Sept to mid-June daily 9am–4pm; ☎76 14 12 03, ⓦwww .andoyturist.no). The office has a comprehensive range of local information and can make reservations for bird-island boat trips, whale safaris and the car ferry to Gryllefjord (see p.323). It also has details of local **bicycle rental** and of **hiking trails** in the surrounding district.

Andenes has a fair sprinkling of inexpensive **accommodation** and several households offer **private rooms** (❷–❸) – look out for the signs – but, considering how isolated a spot this is, you'd be well advised to make a reservation before you get here. One of the nicest places to stay is a guesthouse, the ❧*Fargeklatten Veita*, Sjøgata 38 (☎97 76 00 20, ⓦwww.fargeklatten.no; May–Sept; ❷), a cluster of eighteenth- and nineteenth-century buildings that incorporates a small museum showing fishermen's odds and ends, an art gallery and a stylishly decorated guesthouse near the harbour. Nearby, on the seafront, is the green-timbered *Grønnbua* (☎76 14 14 99, ⓦwww.rorbucamping.no), comprising two *sjøhus* (for more about a *sjøhus*, see p.332), each of which has been parcelled up into **apartments**: one set is cosy and modern (from 865kr), the other older and slightly shabbier (from 540kr), though both have good views over the water. As an alternative to Andenes, you might also consider staying in tiny **BLEIK**, a pretty little place where a string of clapboard houses huddles between craggy hills and a long sandy beach. Bleik is just 7km southwest down along the coast from Andenes and it's home to the *Norlandia Bleik Apartments* (☎76 14 12 22, ⓦwww.norlandia .no/bleik), where there are modern double rooms (❹) and apartments (from 700kr) in a handful of *sjøhus*. Pushing on from Bleik, it's a further 8km south to the minuscule village of **STAVE**, which is home to *Stave Camping* (☎76 14 65 62, ⓦwww.stavecamping.no; cabins (from 390kr) with its king-sized hot pools on a hill overlooking the ocean.

Moving on from Andenes – and the coastal route north to Tromsø

Operated by **Veolia** (☎177 in Nordland, otherwise ☎75 77 24 10, ⓦwww.177nordland .com), local **buses** run south from Andenes to Risøyhamn and Sortland for the E10 (2–4 daily; 1hr/2hr). Heading north, it's possible to weave your way up along the coast from Andenes to Tromsø (see p.354), beginning with the seasonal **Senjafergene car ferry** (☎76 14 12 03, ⓦwww.senjafergene.no) linking Andenes with **Gryllefjord** on the mainland, but note that advance reservations are strongly advised (late May to mid-June & early-to-late Aug 2 daily, mid-June to early Aug 3 daily; 2hr; passengers 145kr, car & driver 375kr). From Gryllefjord, it's about 220km to Tromsø via Highway 86 to Finnsnes, then along the scenic Highway 861 to **Botnhamn**, where a second Senjafergene car ferry crosses over to **Brensholmen** (May–Aug 5–7 daily; 45min; passengers 60kr, cars 155kr); from Brensholmen it's 70km or so on to Tromsø.

As regards **food**, nothing really stands out, but the timber terrace of the *Grønnbua II* is very pleasant and prices are reasonable with main courses – like whale steak (conscience permitting) – averaging 175kr. For daytime snacks, head for *Jul. Nilsens Bakeri* (Mon–Fri am–4.30pm, Sat 8.30am–2.30pm), close to the bus station at Kong Hansgate 1.

Sortland and points south to Melbu

Small-town **SORTLAND** is little more than an unappetizing modern sprawl that straggles along the coast beside the bridge linking the islands of Hinnøya and Langøya. By virtue of its location, Sortland is also something of a **transport hub**, and bus passengers sometimes have to change here for the onward journey south to Stokmarknes and Lofoten, and always to catch the local bus north to Andenes (see p.327), which originates here. The **tourist office** at Kjøpmanns-gata 2 (mid-June to late Aug Mon–Fri 9am–6pm, Sat 10am–2pm, Sun 10am–noon; Sept to mid-June Mon–Fri 8am–4pm; ☎76 11 14 80, ⓦwww.visitvesteralen.no) is in the centre of town, a couple of hundred metres from the Hurtigrute quay and a five- to ten-minute walk from the bus station.

Stokmarknes – and the Trollfjord

Travelling southwest from Sortland, the E10 hugs the shoreline for 30km before shooting over the two bridges that span the straits between Langøya and Hadseløya; the longer bridge is equipped with a high-frequency sound device that is supposed to stop Langøya's foxes in their tracks, keeping its smaller neighbour fox-free. On the far side of the straits is **STOKMARKNES**, an unremarkable little town whose mediocrity is partly relieved by its pleasant shoreline setting. Here also you can sample the delights of the **Hurtigrutemuseet** (mid-May to mid-June & mid-Aug to mid-Sept daily noon–4pm; mid-June to mid-Aug daily 10am–6pm; mid-Sept to mid-May Mon–Fri 2–4pm, Sat noon–4pm & Sun 2–4pm; 80kr; ⓦwww.hurtigrutemuseet.no), which is entirely devoted to the history of the Hurtigrute coastal boat, with a genuine 1950s ferry, the M/S *Finnmarken*, parked up outside on the quayside, looking very much its age. Also on the quayside is a statue of Richard With, the skipper responsible for stream-lining the coastal ferry service in the 1890s. Before With, long-distance coastal boats did not stick to a rigorous timetable and anchored up during darkness; With changed all that and became something of a folk hero hereabouts as a result.

The Trollfjord on the Hurtigrute

Museum aside, the main reason to stop off in **Stokmarknes** is to catch the **Hurtigrute coastal boat** south to Svolvær via the Trollfjord. The boat leaves daily at 3.15pm, sailing down the **Raftsundet**, the narrow sound separating the harsh, rocky shanks of Hinnøya and Austvågøya. Towards the southern end of the sound, the ship usually makes a short detour to the **Trollfjord**, a majestic tear in the landscape just 2-kilometre long. Slowing to a gentle chug, the vessels inch up the narrow gorge, smooth stone towering high above and blocking out the light. At the head of the Trollfjord, the boats effect a nautical three-point turn and then crawl back to rejoin the main waterway. It's very atmospheric, and the effect is perhaps even more extraordinary when the weather is up. One caution: the Hurtigrute will not enter the Trollfjord when there's the danger of a rock fall, but pauses at the fjord's mouth instead. Check locally before embarkation, though you're only likely to miss out, if at all, in spring. The Hurtigrute cruise from Sortland to Svolvær takes a little over three hours and costs 207kr per passenger in winter, 295kr in summer; cars cost 377kr all year. It's also possible to visit the Trollfjord on special boat trips from Svolvær – see p.323 & p.336..

Stokmarknes practicalities

Buses to Stokmarknes pull in near the harbourfront tourist office (late May to mid-Aug Mon–Fri 10am–5pm, Sat & Sun 10am–3pm; ☎76 16 46 60), which has details of what little local **accommodation** there is both in and around town. The best choice is the *Turistsenteret* (☎76 15 29 99, ⓦwww .hurtigrutenshus.com; ❺, sp/r ❸), a brassy, modern hotel-cum-conference centre plonked on Børøya islet, about fifteen-minutes' walk from the museum, at the far end of the first of two bridges back towards Sortland. The modern *rorbuer* that constitute the hotel all have magnificent views of the Hurtigrute as it makes its way into Stokmarknes harbour.

From Stokmarknes, it's 15km south along the E10 to **MELBU**, from where there is a **car ferry** over to Fiskebøl on Lofoten (daily 7am–11pm, every 90min; 25min; passengers 31kr, car & driver 85kr; ☎177, ⓦwww.177nordland.com).

The Lofoten islands

A skeletal curve of mountainous rock stretched out across the Norwegian Sea, the **Lofoten islands** have been the focal point of northern Norway's winter fishing from time immemorial. At the turn of the year, cod migrate from the Barents Sea to spawn here, where the coldness of the water is tempered by the Gulf Stream. The season only lasts from February to April, but fishing impinges on all aspects of island life and is impossible to ignore at any time of the year. At almost every harbour stand the massed ranks of wooden racks used for drying the cod, burgeoning and odiferous in winter, empty in summer like so many abandoned climbing frames.

Sharing the same history, but better known and more beautiful than their neighbours the Vesterålen, the Lofoten islands have everything from sea-bird colonies in the south to beaches and fjords in the north. The traditional approach is by boat from Bodø and this brings visitors face to face with the islands' most striking feature, the towering peaks of the **Lofotenveggen** (Lofoten Wall), a 160-kilometre stretch of mountains, whose jagged teeth bite into the skyline, trapping a string of tiny fishing villages tight against the shore. The mountains are set so close together that on first inspection there seems to be no way through, but in fact the islands are riddled with straights, sounds and fjords.

The Lofoten have their own relaxed pace, and are perfect for a simple, uncluttered few days. For somewhere so far north, the weather can be exceptionally mild: summer days can be spent sunbathing on the rocks or hiking and biking around the superb coastline, and when it rains – as it frequently does – life focuses on the *rorbuer* (fishermen's huts), where freshly caught fish are cooked over wood-burning stoves, stories are told and time gently wasted. If that sounds rather contrived, in a sense it is – the way of life here is to some extent preserved like this for tourists – but it's rare to find anyone who isn't less than completely enthralled by it all.

The **E10** weaves a scenic route across Lofoten, running the 170km from **Fiskebøl** in the north to **Å** in the south, hopping from island to island by bridge and causeway and by occasionally tunnelling through the mountains and under the sea. The highway passes through or within a few kilometres of all the islands' main villages, Among which **Henningsvær** and **Å** are breathtakingly beautiful, with **Stamsund** coming in close behind. All three make great bases for further explorations on foot or by boat. Indeed, there's an abundance of marine activity with everything on offer from island cruises, sea-rafting and fishing excursions through to birdwatching trips. Scores of places also rent out

Staying in a rorbu or sjøhus

Right across Lofoten, **rorbuer** (fishermen's shacks) are rented out to tourists for both overnight stays and longer periods. The name *rorbu* is derived from *ror*, "to row" and *bu*, literally "dwelling" – and some older islanders still ask "Will you row this winter?", meaning "Will you go fishing this winter?" *Rorbuer* date back to the twelfth century, when King Øystein ordered the first of them to be built round the Lofoten coastline to provide shelter for visiting fishermen who had previously been obliged to sleep under their upturned boats. Traditionally, *rorbu* were built on the shore, often on poles sticking out of the sea, and usually coloured with a red paint based on cod-liver oil. They consisted of two sections, a sleeping and eating room and a smaller storage area.

At the peak of the fisheries in the 1930s, some 30,000 men were accommodated in *rorbuer*, but during the 1960s fishing boats became more comfortable and since then many fishermen have preferred to sleep aboard. Most of the original *rorbuer* disappeared years ago, and, although a few have survived, visitors today are much more likely to stay in a modern version, mostly prefabricated units churned out by the dozen with the tourist trade in mind. At their best, they are comfortable and cosy seashore cabins, sometimes a well-planned conversion of an original *rorbu* with bunk beds and wood-fired stoves; at their worst, they are little better than prefabricated hutches in the middle of nowhere. Most have space for between four and six guests and the charge for a hut averages around 1000kr per night – though some cost as little as 600kr, while others rise to about 2000kr. Similar rates are charged for the islands' **sjøhus** (literally sea-houses), originally the large quayside halls where the catch was processed and the workers slept. Most of the original *sjøhus* have been cleverly converted into attractive apartments with self-catering facilities, a few into dormitory-style accommodation – and again, as with the *rorbuer*, the quality varies enormously. A full list of *rorbuer* and *sjøhus* is given in the *Lofoten Info-Guide*, a free pamphlet that you can pick up at any local tourist office and on ⓦwww.lofoten.info.

fishing boats and equipment, although, because of the strong currents, you should always seek advice about local conditions. Back on land, the islands may not have a well-developed network of huts and hiking trails, but the byroads, where you'll rarely see a car, provide mile after mile of excellent **walking** as they delve deep into the heart of the landscape. There's plenty of scope for **mountaineering** too: Austvågøya has the finest climbing, with some of the best ascents in Norway, and there's a prestigious climbing school at Henningsvær. There's more walking and yet more solitude on mountainous **Værøy** and flatter, more agricultural Røst, a pair of inhabited islands to the south of Å, reachable by ferry from Moskenes and Bodø.

As regards accommodation, the Lofoten islands have a sprinkling of **hotels**, a few of which are first-rate, though some are blandly modern, as well as three HI **hostels**, numerous **campsites** and the local speciality, the **rorbuer** (see box, above). There's comprehensive tourist information on ⓦwww.lofoten.info, though ⓦwww.lofoten-info.no covers two of the more southerly islands, Moskenesøya and Flakstadøya, in greater detail.

Transport to and around the Lofoten islands

The opening of the **Lofast**, the new stretch of road between Gullesfjordbotn and Fiskebøl, has made it much easier to get to the Lofoten and it's now possible to **drive** from Evenes (Harstad/Narvik) airport to Svolvær in less than three hours. This new route is ferry free, but you can still reach the Lofoten by car **ferry**, Hurtigbåt passenger express boat and the Hurtigrute coastal boat. Once you've got to the Lofoten, you'll find **public transport** thin on the ground. What local bus services there are stick almost exclusively to the E10, the islands' only main road, and elsewhere you'll mostly have to **walk** – hardly an onerous task in such beautiful surroundings. Alternatively, **bike rental** is available at most hostels, hotels and guesthouses, and the detailed *Cycling in Lofoten* booklet, which includes route maps, is sold at all tourist offices.

If you have your own **vehicle**, village-hopping is easy and quick, but it's only when you leave the car and head off into the landscape that the real character of Lofoten begins to reveal itself; allow time for at least one walk or sea trip. Conversely, if you don't have a vehicle and want to reach the islands' remoter spots, it's worth considering renting a car, an inexpensive option if a few people share the cost. There are local **car rental** outlets at Svolvær, Stamsund, and Svolvær and Leknes airports, where special short-term deals can bring costs down to around 600kr a day.

All Nordland **public transport** timetables – including those for Lofoten – are online at Ⓦ www.177nordland.com; you can also call Ⓣ 177 within Nordland, otherwise Ⓣ 75 77 24 10.

By car ferry

From the mainland, the traditional approach to the Lofoten is by **car ferry** from **Bodø**. There are three destinations to choose from, all on the southern peripheries of the archipelago: **Moskenes**, a tiny port just a few kilometres from the end of the E10, and the islets of **Værøy** and **Røst**. The ferry route varies, but there's almost always one ferry a day (and sometimes more) to Moskenes throughout the year, with marginally less frequent services to the two islets; Moskenes is often the first port of call. The trip from Bodø to Moskenes takes about four hours; allow a further two hours to Værøy, and two more for Røst, and be prepared for a rough crossing. The **fare** from Bodø to Moskenes is 155kr for passengers, 561kr for a car and driver; for details of fares to the islets, see p.346. All these ferries are operated by **Hurtigruten** (Ⓦ www.hurtigruten.no) on a first-come, first-served basis, so it's a good idea to turn up a couple of hours before departure. Note, however, that in the summertime (June–Aug) advance reservations are permitted – and are strongly recommended: Bodø tourist office will arrange things for you or you can contact Hurtigruten direct, either online or on the company's reservation line Ⓣ 810 30 000.

The shortest **car ferry** service to the Lofoten links **Skutvik**, 35km west of the E6 midway between Fauske and Narvik, with **Svolvær** (1 daily; 2hr; passengers 76kr, car & driver 262kr). This is also operated by Hurtigruten (Ⓦ www.hurtigruten.no) and, given the infrequency of the service, advance reservations are strongly advised – either with Hurtigruten direct (see above) or at Bodø tourist office.

Heading for the Lofoten from the **Vesterålen**, you can either use the Lofast connection or take the **Melbu-to-Fiskebøl** car ferry (daily 7am–11pm, every 80min; 30min; passengers 31kr, car & driver 85kr; Ⓣ 177 in Nordland, otherwise Ⓣ 75 77 24 10, Ⓦ www.177nordland.com).

By boat: the Hurtigrute

The northbound **Hurtigrute** leaves Bodø daily at 3pm calling at two ports in the Lofoten islands – Stamsund and Svolvær – before nudging through the Raftsundet en route to Stokmarknes, on the Vesterålen. The passenger fare for the four-and-a-half-hour cruise from Bodø to Stamsund is 397kr in summer,

278kr in winter, and cars cost 353kr all year; the six-hour journey to Svolvær costs 425/297kr, cars 377kr. Advance reservations for cars are essential, and can be made online (ⓦwww.hurtigruten.no) or by phoning the ship – ask down at the harbour or at the port's tourist office for assistance.

By boat: Hurtigbåt passenger express boats

A **Hurtigbåt** passenger express boat service runs from **Bodø to Svolvær** (1 daily; 3hr 30min; 297kr; ⓣ177 in Nordland, otherwise ⓣ75 77 24 10, ⓦwww.hurtigruten.no). Advance reservation is advised.

By bus

The long-distance **Lofoten Ekspressen**, operated by Nor-Way Bussekspress (ⓦwww.nor-way.no) in conjunction with a couple of smaller companies provides the main bus service from the mainland to the Lofoten. It leaves Narvik twice daily to run along the E6 and then the E10, calling at Evenes airport and Lødingen before taking the Lofast highway to Fiskebøl in the Lofoten; it then proceeds on to Svolvær, where one bus daily continues on to Kabelvåg and Leknes, or you change for the once-daily bus to Leknes and Å. As an example of **journey times**, Narvik to Leknes takes six hours, just under eight hours to Å.

This long-distance bus service is supported by a number of somewhat intermittent **local buses** operated by **Veolia** (ⓣ177 in Nordland, otherwise ⓣ75 77 24 10, ⓦwww.177nordland.com). Two of Veolia's more useful offerings are Svolvær to Kabelvåg and Henningsvær (Mon–Sat 4–7 daily) and Leknes to Stamsund (Mon–Sat 3–6 daily).

By plane – and car rental

Flights leave Bodø for the Lofoten airports – or rather airstrips – at Svolvær and Leknes four to seven times a day. The operator is **Widerøe** (ⓦwww .wideroe.no), an SAS subsidiary, and tickets can be purchased at any travel agent or SAS agent as well as online; fares from Bodø to the islands vary enormously, but a standard summer return ticket costs in the region of 900kr, half that one-way. Note also that whereas Svolvær airport is merely 5km from town, Leknes airport is miles from anywhere you might want to visit, and the onward taxi will cost an arm and a leg. There is **car rental** at both airports: Svolvær has, for instance, Avis (ⓣ76 07 11 40) and Hertz (ⓣ76 07 07 20) outlets, as does Leknes – Hertz (ⓣ76 08 18 44) and Avis (ⓣ76 08 01 04). Good-value short-term deals abound – from around 600kr per day.

Svolvær

SVOLVÆR strings over and around several headlands and bays on the southeast coast of **Austvågøya**, the largest of the Lofoten islands, but somehow contrives to be a somewhat disappointing introduction to the archipelago. The region's administrative and transport centre, it has all the bustle but little of the charm of the other island towns, though it does have more accommodation and better restaurants than its neighbours and – to be fair – its surroundings are suitably mountainous. The town also possesses three attractions of some interest, beginning with the **Lofoten Krigsminnemuseum**, close to the Hurtigrute quay (War Museum; June–Sept Mon–Fri 10am–4pm, Sat 11am–3pm & Sun noon–3pm; by appointment out of season; 50kr; ⓦwww.lofotenkrigmus.no), which chronicles the British commando raids on Lofoten (see box, p.337) by means of photographs and original artefacts. There's also **Magic Ice** (mid-June to mid-Aug daily noon–11pm; mid-Aug

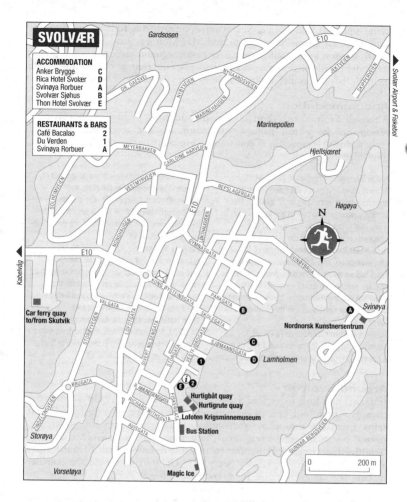

to mid-June daily 6–10pm; 95kr; Ⓦwww.magic-ice.no), a quayside gallery depicting Lofoten life in winter by means of giant ice sculptures. The temperature is permanently below zero, so warm jackets and boots are issued for free. Finally, the **Nordnorsk Kunstnersentrum**, across the bridge from the centre on the islet of Svinøya (mid-June to late Aug daily 10am–6pm; late Aug to mid-June Wed–Sun 11am–3pm; 30kr; Ⓦwww.nnks.no), has some fine paintings by Gunnar Berg (1863–93), including the *Battle of the Trollfjord*, as well as work by contemporary Norwegian artists.

Arrival and information

Ferries to Svolvær dock about 1km west of the town centre, whereas the Hurtigrute docks in the centre, a brief walk from the **bus station** and the busy **tourist office**, just off the main town square near the harbour (late May to mid-June Mon–Fri 9am–4pm & Sat 10am–2pm; mid- to late June Mon–Fri 9am–8pm, Sat 10am–2pm & Sun 4–8pm; late June to early Aug Mon–Fri

9am–10pm, Sat 9am–8pm & Sun 10am–8pm; early Aug to late Aug Mon–Fri 9am–8pm, Sat 10am–2pm; Sept to mid-May Mon–Fri 9am–3.30pm; ☏76 06 98 07, ⊛www.lofoten.info); they have maps, accommodation lists and public transport details. Svolvær is also a good place to **rent a car**: Europcar, for example, have an outlet at Sivert Nilsens Gate 43 (☏76 07 00 00).

Accommodation

Although Svolvær isn't short of **accommodation**, finding a room in high season can be a real pain. Consequently, advance reservation is highly recommended – especially if you want to avoid the town's clutch of mundane, mini-high-rise hotels.

Anker Brygge Lamholmen ☏76 06 64 80, ⊛www.anker-brygge.no. The town's smartest accommodation, consisting of 22 spacious and tastefully decorated *rorbuer* in a prime location on a tiny islet – Lamholmen – at the end of a causeway in the middle of the harbour. ❻
Rica Hotel Svolvær Lamholmen ☏76 07 22 22, ⊛www.rica.no. This well-above-average chain hotel has an attractive modern design, its acres of glass perched on top of timber piles. Has small but comfortable rooms, half with balcony. On the islet of Lamholmen in the middle of the harbour. ❻
Svinøya Rorbuer Svinøya ☏76 06 99 30, ⊛www.svinoya.no. At the northeast end of town, a causeway crosses over to the long and slender

island of Svinøya, which is home to this set of *rorbuer*. They range from the plain and simple (❷) to the deluxe (❺–❻) and there's a low-budget, summertime hostel here too, with large and clean double rooms that are exceptionally good value at ❶.
Svolvær Sjøhus Parkgata ☏76 07 03 36, ⊛www.svolver-sjohuscamp.com. Modest rooms here at this long-established place by the seashore at the foot of Parkgata. To get there from the square, turn right up the hill along Vestfjordgata and it's to the right, past the library. ❶
Thon Hotel Svolvær O. J. Kaalbøes gate 5 ☏76 04 90 00, ⊛www.thonhotels.no. Smart, recently revamped chain hotel right in the centre of town. Thirty neat, efficient bedrooms. ❺

Around Svolvær

It doesn't take long to explore Svolvær, and afterwards you could do no better than to venture out into its dramatic environs on one of several local **boat trips**. Every day throughout the summer boats (return trip 3hr; 400kr; buy tickets on board; ⊛www.lofoten-charterboat.no) leave Svolvær for the **Trollfjord**, an impossibly narrow, two-kilometre-long stretch of water that's also on the Hurtigrute itinerary (see p.323). The intrepid should also consider making the same excursion by **speedboat** – heavy jackets and goggles are included (return trip 2hr; 500kr; ⊛www.lofoten-explorer.com).

Alternatively, take a stroll on the pretty islet of **Skrova**, just offshore from Svolvær. Skrova's only settlement trails along a slender rocky spit, its harbour dominated by the country's largest whaling station. The village is attached by a causeway to the main body of island, which is dominated by the steep Mount Høgskrova (258m). There are two to four ferries daily to Skrova, taking just thirty minutes and costing 32kr each way; ferry times almost always make a day-trip feasible.

Svolvær also boasts one of the archipelago's most famous **climbs**, the haul up to the top of the **Svolværgeita** (the "Svolvær Goat"), a twin-pronged peak that rises high above the E10 to the northeast of town. The lower slopes of the mountain are hard enough, but the last 40m – up the horns of the "Goat" – require considerable expertise. Daring-daft mountaineers complete the thrill by jumping from one pinnacle to the other.

Restaurants and bars

Svolvær has a reasonable selection of bars and restaurants, the best you'll find on Lofoten, though they don't come cheap. The 🍴 *Café Bacalao*, down on the quay, is a spacious café-restaurant with snappy service and a menu that mixes Mediterranean and Norwegian cuisine with flair and imagination: lunches, and main courses in the evening, hover around 175kr. It serves excellent coffee too, and at night turns into the town's liveliest bar, jam-packed at the weekend. If you're considering splashing out on dinner, *Du Verden*, in the centre at J.E. Paulsens gate 12 (T 76 07 70 99), is your best bet. The creative menu features the freshest of local ingredients with main courses averaging around 250kr. At lunchtime the place is a snip – try the mouthwatering fish soup. Alternatively, the restaurant at the *Svinøya Rorbuer* is highly competent, with seafood its forte; mains from around 240kr.

Kabelvåg

With its pretty wooden centre draped around the shore of a narrow and knobbly inlet, **KABELVÅG** is immediately more appealing than Svolvær, its near neighbour, just 6km away. The most important village on Lofoten from Viking times until the early years of the twentieth century, Kabelvåg was once the centre of the fishery and home to the islands' first *rorbuer*, built in 1120, as well as the first inn, which dates from 1792. The late nineteenth-century **Vågan kirke** (May–Aug Mon–Fri 9.30am–6pm, Sun noon–6pm; 20kr), a big and breezy timber church beside the E10 on the eastern edge of the village, is a reminder of those busier times, its hangar-like interior built to accommodate a congregation of over a thousand.

The village holds other attractions too, primarily the **Lofotmuseet**, located 1500m west of the centre by the seashore in the **Storvågan** neighbourhood (Lofoten Museum; May Mon–Fri 9am–3pm, Sat & Sun 11am–3pm; June–Aug daily 9am–6pm; Sept Mon–Fri 9am–3pm & Sun 11am–3pm; Oct–April Mon–Fri 9am–3pm; 60kr, but with a Storvågan multi-ticket including the gallery and aquarium 140kr; W www.lofotmuseet.no). This traces the history of the islands' fisheries and displays the definitive collection of fishing equipment and other cultural paraphernalia. Nearby, also in Storvågan, is the **Galleri Espolin** (May daily 11am–3pm; early June daily 10am–6pm; mid-June to mid-Aug daily 10am–7pm; late Aug daily 10am–6pm; Sept–April Mon–Fri & Sun 11am–3pm; 60kr; W www.galleri-espolin.no), which features paintings and sketches by Kaare Espolin Johnson (1907–94), a renowned Norwegian artist of romantic inclination, who specialized in Arctic images and imagery. Storvågan's third attraction is the **Lofotakvariet** (Aquarium; May daily 11am–3pm; June–Aug daily 10am–7pm; Sept–Nov and Feb–April Mon–Fri & Sun 11am–3pm; 80kr; @www.lofotakvariet.no), displaying a wide variety of Atlantic species.

Kabelvåg does a good line in **outdoor pursuits**. The main operator is Lofoten Aktiv, Rødmyrveien 26 (⊕99 23 11 00, @www.lofoten-aktiv.no), which organizes everything from sea-kayaking and trekking through to skiing, fishing and cycling trips, though the sea-kayaking courses are a speciality. Divers should contact Lofotdykk, in the centre of Kabelvåg at Kaiveien 15 (⊕99 63 91 66, @www.lofotdykk.no), for all manner of marine activities, including sea-rafting, orca-watching safaris (Oct–Dec) and, of course, diving.

Arrival and accommodation

Buses to Kabelvåg, from Svolvær and Henningsvær (3–10 daily), drop passengers right in the centre of the village, from where it's a five-minute stroll up the hill to the pleasant *Kabelvåg Hotel* (⊕76 07 88 00, ❹), which occupies an old timber building just back from the harbour. The village also possesses a spartan HI **hostel**, *Kabelvåg Sommerhotell* (⊕76 06 98 80, @www.vandrerhjem.no; dorm beds 240kr, doubles ❷; June to mid-Aug), in the school building east of the centre, 500m from the E10; the facilities here aren't luxurious, and neither are they always impeccably clean, but they do serve a great big breakfast. Perhaps a better budget bet is the well-equipped house run by diving specialists *Lofotdykk* (⊕99 63 91 66, @www.lofotdykk.no), which comes complete with a sauna and outdoor *badestamp*; basic quads here go for 180kr per person per night. By far the most luxurious choice is the *Nyvågar Rorbuhotell* in Storvågan (⊕76 06 97 00, @www.nyvaagar.no), comprising a scattering of smart four-bedded *rorbuer* (750–1200kr) – the best-positioned are on the water-front. Their secluded terrace overlooking the water is a fine and scenic spot to enjoy a glass of wine. For a taste of old Lofoten, head for the *Lofoten Rorbuferie* at Vikabakken 25 (⊕76 07 84 44, @www.lofoten-rorbuferie.no (from 700kr) near the breakwater. The old *rorbuer* here were built with government money in 1923 and give you a good impression of traditional life on the fishery. Kabelvåg also has two fjordside **campsites**, *Sandvika Camping* (⊕76 07 81 45, @www .lofotferie.no) being the better equipped, with modern cabins from 950kr, a small beach and boats for hire.

Eating and drinking

As regards **food**, the *Krambua Restaurant* (⊕76 07 88 00; mid-June to mid-Aug), in the *Kabelvåg Hotel*, is a quiet, stylish affair with a menu that leans heavily towards quality seafood with main courses averaging 250kr. Much livelier – in fact it's the heart of the Kabelvåg social scene – is the *Prestenbrygga Pub*, right in the centre of the village overlooking the dock. Here they serve enormous, excellent-value pizzas from 80kr, have a popular bottomless-cup-of-coffee deal, and feature a locally famous fish soup in autumn and winter and the best *bacalao* you'll taste in summer. The owner is a whisky connoisseur and with 170 different bottles to choose from, has by far the largest collection on Lofoten.

Henningsvær

Heading west from Kabelvåg, it's 11km on the E10 to the 8km-long turning that leads to **HENNINGSVÆR**, the most beguiling of headland villages, a cobweb of cramped and twisting lanes lined with brightly painted wooden houses. These frame a tiny inlet that literally cuts the place in half, forming a sheltered, picture-postcard harbour. Almost inevitably, coach parties are wheeled in and out, despite the narrowness of the two high-arched bridges into the village, but for all the hustle and bustle Henningsvær richly deserves an **overnight stay**.

Cod fishing from Henningsvær

For hundreds of years fishermen have gathered in the waters off Lofoten to catch the **cod** that have migrated here from the Barents Sea to spawn. The fish arrive in late January or early February and the season lasts until April. There are tremendous fluctuations in the number of cod making the journey; although the reasons for this variation are not fully understood, relative water temperatures and, more recently, over-fishing are two key components. Sometimes the cod arrive packed together, at other times they are thinly spread, their distribution dictated by water temperature. The fish prefer a water temperature of about 5 degrees centigrade, which occurs here off Lofoten between the warm and salty bottom current and the colder surface waters: sometimes this band of water is thick, sometimes thin; sometimes it's close to the shore, sometimes it's way out to sea, all of which affect the fishing. If you fancy joining the fishing fleet, **Lofoten Opplevelser**, in Henningsvær (☎76 07 50 01, ⓦwww.lofoten-opplevelser.no), organize two-hour **cod-fishing trips** from the middle of March to the end of the season at a cost of 750kr per person.

One of the town's main draws is the **Galleri Lofotens Hus**, on Hjellskjæret (late May to mid-Sept daily 9am–7pm; 75kr; ⓦwww.galleri-lofoten.no), which exhibits (and sells) the work of the contemporary Norwegian artist Karl Erik Harr. Also on display is a competent selection of late nineteenth- and twentieth-century Lofoten paintings by artists such as Einar Berge, Adelsteen Normann, Gunnar Berg and Otto Sinding – you can't miss the latter's whopping *Funeral in Lofoten* of 1886 – plus historic and contemporary photographs and slides mostly of the islands. Henningsvær's Arctic light, plus the might of the mountains, have long attracted Norwegian painters, making it something of an arts centre, and, indeed, there's more art for sale – plus ceramics and glassware – at the nearby **Engelskmannsbrygga**, on the main square (late Feb to early June & mid-Aug to Dec Tues–Fri 10am–4pm, Sat & Sun noon–4pm; mid-June to early Aug daily 10am–8pm; free; ⓦwww.engelskmannsbrygga.no).

The intrepid should make a beeline for Lofoten's best mountaineering school, **Nord Norsk Klatreskole** (☎90 57 42 08, ⓦwww.nordnorskklatreskole.no), who operate a range of all-inclusive **climbing holidays** in the mountains near Henningsvær, catering for various degrees of fitness and experience. Prices vary depending on the trip, but a three-day, one-climb-a-day package costs in the region of 4800kr per person, including equipment, food and accommodation. Much less strenuous are **fishing trips** (see box above), a morning's or afternoon's excursion for around 450kr, which can be booked down at the harbour, or **sea-eagle safaris** (370kr; ☎90 58 14 75, ⓦwww.lofoten-opplevelser.no), which depart daily at 2.30pm throughout the summer. Finally, Henningsvær's an especially windy little place – so come (or be) prepared.

Arrival and accommodation

The Lofoten Ekspressen **bus** (see p.334) does not detour off the E10 to get to Henningsvær, but there is a local bus service from Svolvær and Kabelvåg (7 daily). The town has ample **accommodation**, the smartest hotel being the quayside *Henningsvær Bryggehotell* (☎76 07 47 50, ⓦwww.henningsvaer .no; ❺–❻), an attractive modern building in traditional style right on the waterfront. Another stylish option is the *Henningsvær Rorbuer* (☎76 06 60 00, ⓦwww .henningsvar-rorbuer.no), offering 26 well-equipped *rorbuer* (930–2600kr) at the far end of the town. A far more economical choice is the frugal *Den Siste Viking*, Misværveien 10 (☎90 57 42 08, ⓦwww.nordnorskklatreskole.no; ❶), which provides unadorned lodgings also right in the centre; the place doubles as the island's mountaineering school (see p.339). Perhaps the most cheerful hotel is the *Henningsvær Hotell* (☎76 07 07 00, ⓦwww.nordnorskenytelser .no; ❸), where all the rooms are themed up in different colour schemes and there's a spacious restaurant downstairs (see below).

Eating and drinking

Henningsvær has a good supply of **cafés and restaurants**, beginning with the inviting *Klatrekafeen*, at *Den Siste Viking* (see p.339), which serves up a good range of Norwegian stand-bys from 100kr, plus soup and salads and some killer chocolate cupcakes, all washed down with first-rate coffee; climbing relics and candle lightgives the place oodles of atmosphere. A good alternative is the *Bakeriteateret* with its stylish interior and tasty waffles and coffee; at night-time, the place doubles as a bar. For something a little more unusual, consider having lunch in the *Lysstøperi* – the local candle shop at Gammelveien 2 – where they serve *kanelsnurr* and *skolebolle*, both sweet treats designed to test your dental fillings. The classiest restaurant is the waterside *Fiskekrogen*, Dreyersgate 19 (☎76 07 46 52), where the seafood in general, and the fish soup in particular, are simply superb; main courses like cod, monkfish and mussels from 225kr. A smashing second option is the spacious restaurant at the *Henningsvær Hotell*, which specializes in halibut, codfish and *bacalao*.

Vestvågøy: Stamsund

It's the next large island to the southwest of Austvågøya, **Vestvågøy**, that captivates many travellers to Lofoten. This is due in no small part to the laid-back charm of **STAMSUND**, whose older buildings string along the rocky, fretted seashore in an amiable jumble of crusty port buildings, wooden houses and *rorbuer*. There have been some recent additions to the Stamsund stew, but it's all pretty low-key; the modern art gallery, **Galleri 2** (June–Aug Tues–Sun noon– 4pm & 6.30–9.30pm; 20kr; ⓦwww.galleri2.no), about 100m from the Hurtigrute dock, is well worth a gander.

The main **bus** service to Stamsund (Mon–Sat 3–4 daily) is from Leknes, both the dull administrative centre of Vestvågøy and the site of the island's **airport**, just 15km away to the west; Leknes is reachable on the long-distance **Lofoten Ekspressen** (see p.334). Stamsund is also the first port at which the Hurtigrute **coastal boat** docks on its way north from Bodø. By **car**, the quickest way to Stamsund from Svolvær is to turn south off the E10 down Highway 815, a scenic forty-kilometre coastal drive.

Stamsund: eating, drinking, accommodation and fishing

The best place to **stay** in Stamsund is the 🅗 HI **hostel** (☎76 08 93 34, ⓦwww .vandrerhjem.no; March to mid-Oct; dorm beds 120kr, doubles ❶), about a kilometre down the road from the port. The hostel consists of several *rorbuer* and a *sjøhus* perched over a bonny, pin-sized bay, and has a washing machine and tumble drier, and self-catering facilities. You can rent **bikes** here at 100kr a day, and the warden is very knowledgeable on everything about Vestvågøy, from cycling through to hiking and fishing. The **fishing** is, in fact, first-class: you can borrow the hostel's rowing boats and lines to take out on the (usually still) water. Afterwards you can barbecue your catch and eat alfresco on the veranda overlooking the bay – it's this sort of easygoing activity that makes the place incredibly popular. For something a little more conventionally comfortable – or just conventional – head for the stylishly decorated and intelligently revamped old *rorbuer* at *Skjærbrygga* (☎76 05 46 00, ⓦwww.skjaerbrygga.no; ❹), right in the centre of Stamsund by the harbour. The old *Skjærbrygga sjøhus* has been attractively renovated too, and now contains a café and an excellent restaurant, which features the freshest of local ingredients; main courses at the restaurant go for around 250kr, much less at the café. Less pricey *rorbuer* can also be found 3 kilometre west along the coast from Stamsund in the minuscule hamlet of **STEINE**, where the cosy if rather spartan *Steine Rorbuer & Hytter* (☎76 08 92 83; from 650kr) snuggle tight against the seashore.

The northwest coast of Vestvågøy

Fans of wild scenery should consider heading out to Vestvågøy's blustery **northwest coast**, where a few hardy fishing villages struggled on until they were finally abandoned to the birds, the wind and the sea in the 1950s – give or take the occasional summer resident. This coast is accessed by a series of turnings off the **E10** as it slices across Vestvågøy's drab central valley: you'll need your own car, however, as cyclists face stiff gradients and often strong winds and, although the bus service along the E10 itself is reasonable, there are no regular buses off it to the northwest coast.

To Utakleiv

Beginning in Stamsund, the first part of the excursion is the hilly fifteen-kilometre haul up to **Leknes**. Here, you turn north along the **E10** for the three-kilometre journey to the first signposted byroad, which leads the 10km over the hills, along the seashore and through a narrow tunnel to **UTAKLEIV**, on the edge of a wide and windy bay surrounded by austere cliffs. The old village is itself remarkably flat, with grazing sheep and cows dotting the pastureland, and there are two crispy white beaches just before the tunnel where you can **camp** for 100kr per night.

Unstad, Eggum and the Lofotr Vikingmuseum

There's more stern scenery at the end of the next significant turning off the E10, this time at **UNSTAD**, a huddle of houses in a diminutive river valley set beneath the mountains and with wide views out to sea. The main draw here is the ocean: this is by far the best **surfing** spot on the island with a great and stable swell attracting each and every passing surfer. The only accommodation, *Unstad Camping* (☎76 08 64 33, ⓦwww.unstadcamping.no), rents out surf gear and has four-hour surf clinics (600kr). If surfing isn't your cup of tea, you can always consider a hike. From Unstad, a popular nine-kilometre **trail** runs east with mountains and lakes on one side and the surging ocean on the other as far as **EGGUM**. En route, you'll pass the remains of a radar station built by the Germans during World War II. The tiny hamlet of Eggum is an especially pretty spot, its handful of houses clinging on to a precarious headland dwarfed by the mountains behind and with a whopping pebble beach in front.

Eggum can also be reached by road from the **E10** – it's the next turning along from the Unstad road – but before you reach the Eggum turn-off you'll pass the flashy **Lofotr Vikingmuseum**, 14km from Leknes (early to late May & late Aug to mid-Sept daily 11am–5pm; June to late Aug daily 10am–7pm; 100kr; ⓦwww.lofotr.no). Inspired by the accidental discovery of the remains of a Viking chieftain's house by a local farmer in 1981, the museum is housed within a reconstructed 83-metre Viking house, with flickering lights, wood-tar smells and so forth all adding to the atmosphere. There's also a permanent exhibition of Viking artefacts found in the vicinity, and the boathouse contains a full-sized replica of the Gokstad ship displayed in Oslo (see p.100).

South to Nusfjord

By any standard, the next two islands of the archipelago, **Flakstadøya** – known to the Vikings as "Vargfot", or wolf's paw, on account of its shape – and **Moskenesøya**, are extraordinarily beautiful. As the Lofoten taper towards their southerly conclusion, the rearing peaks of the Lofotenveggen crimp the sea-shredded coastline, providing a thunderously scenic backdrop to a necklace of tiny fishing villages. The E10 travels along almost all of this shoreline, leaving Leknes to tunnel west under the sound separating Vestvågøy from Flakstadøya. About 20km from Leknes, an even more improbable byroad somehow wiggles the 6km through the mountains to **NUSFJORD**, an extravagantly picturesque fishing village in a tight and forbidding cove. Unlike many *rorbuer* elsewhere in Lofoten, the ones here are the genuine nineteenth-century article, and the

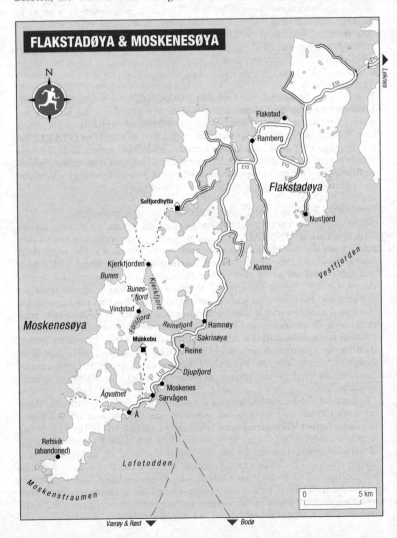

FLAKSTADØYA & MOSKENESØYA

general store, with its wooden floors and antique appearance, fits in nicely too. Perhaps inevitably, it's tourism that keeps the local economy afloat and indeed the place is now so popular with day-trippers that there's a 50kr fee to get in. Don't let that deter you: some of the buildings, like the cod-liver refinery, the smithy and the saw-mill, have been attractively restored and in the evening, when the crowds have disappeared, Nusfjord is truly beguiling.

Nusfjord Rorbu Holidays (⊤76 09 30 20, Ⓦwww.nusfjord.no) offer **accommodation** here in over forty comfortably refurbished *rorbuer*. There are various types of *rorbuer*, ranging from simple, standard versions holding up to four people (1050kr for two people) to luxurious two-bedroom affairs that cost an arm and a leg (2000kr for two people); advance reservations are strongly advised. **Bike rental** is available here too, as is fishing gear and you can go **deep-sea diving** nearby with Aqua Lofoten (⊤99 01 90 42, Ⓦwww .aqualofoten.no; 450kr for one dive).

On to Hamnøy and Sakrisøya

Back on the E10, it's a further 5km to **Flakstad kirke**, a distinctive onion-domed, red timber church built in 1780. The church's ornate pulpit was painted by the itinerant German artist Gottfried Ezechiel (see also the Bodin kirke, p.311), as was the painting above the altar, whose main motif is the Last Supper. The church announces the beginning of **RAMBERG**, the island's administrative centre – if that's what you can call the smattering of services (garage, super-market and suchlike) that strings along the sandy beach. Pressing on over the first of several narrow bridges, you're soon on **Moskenesøya**, where the road squirms across the mouth of the Reinefjord, hopping from islet to islet to link the fishing villages of **HAMNØY**, on the north side of the inlet, with Reine (see below) a little to the south. Both villages boast impossibly picturesque settings and Hamnøy also lays claim to an excellent **restaurant**, *Hamnøy Mat & Vinbu* (⊤76 09 21 45; May–Sept), whose short menu provides traditional Norwegian cuisine at its best, with excellent seafood including cods' tongues – an island delicacy – and the rarely seen, but delicious, sago pudding. Hamnøy also possesses some very plain *rorbuer – Hamnøy Rorbuer* (⊤76 09 23 20, Ⓦwww .lofoten-info.no/hamnoy; 600–900kr), but far more appealing are those on the tiny islet of **Sakrisøya**, midway between Hamnøy and Reine, where the pretty, original 1870 cabins of ⚓ *Sakrisøy Rorbuer* (⊤76 09 21 43, Ⓦwww.lofoten.ws; 500–1100kr) are both well kept and cosy with a wood stove adding to the atmosphere. The owners of the *rorbuer* also run the little fishmongers opposite, where they dish out delicious home-made fish burgers and sell freshly caught fish. A tiny dolls' museum and bric-a-brac store complete the scene.

Reine

On the far side of the inlet, **REINE** has a fabulous location, ambling along a tiny islet, which is connected to the rest of Moskenesøya by a narrow causeway branching off the E10. Right next to the boat dock, the **Eva Harr gallery** (late May to late Aug daily 10.30am–6pm; Ⓦwww.evaharr.no; 60kr) is devoted to Harr – a contemporary artist, whose paintings of Lofoten are displayed alongside a selection of her graphic work. The best place to stay in the village is the *Reine Rorbuer* (⊤76 09 22 22, Ⓦwww.reinerorbuer.no; 1100–2100kr for two persons), consisting of 22 recently renovated *rorbuer* and three apartments in what was once the police station. The restaurant occupies the old general store (May–Aug) and offers top-notch seafood risottos, local lamb and marinated salmon with a terrace overlooking the harbour; mains from 180kr.

Reine is a departure point for a variety of **boat trips**. Apart from the excursion to Vindstad (see below), there are also midnight-sun cruises, coastal voyages, fishing expeditions and excursions to the MoskeNstraumen (see p.345). For further information about these trips, ask around locally or contact the Moskenes tourist office (see below).

From Reine to Bunes by boat and on foot

Throughout the year, passenger **ferries** (2–3 daily; 45kr each way; ☎99 49 18 05) leave Reine for the thirty-minute journey up the **Reinefjord** to minuscule **VINDSTAD**. There's only one permanent inhabitant here in this eerily deserted village – though there are a number of holiday homes – but Vindstad is the starting point for the ninety-minute hike over to Moskenesøya's northwest coast. The first thirty minutes of the hike, along an old dirt trail, are not especially enjoyable, but things improve thereafter as you proceed along the west shore of the narrow and very steep Bunesfjord with jagged mountains rearing up in every direction. Just past the cemetery, the dirt trail ends abruptly and you have to make a sharp left, continuing up a steep grass path that takes you over a ridge between the mountains. Beyond is the sandy cove of **Bunes**, the epitome of isolation and a smashing place to watch the midnight sun. This is not a difficult hike, but given that the last section can get very slippery and the weather can change in minutes, you'll need to be properly equipped.

Moskenes

From Reine, it's about 5km to **MOSKENES**, the main island port to and from Bodø – not that there's much here beyond a handful of houses dotted round a horseshoe-shaped bay. There is, however, a helpful **tourist office** by the jetty (March–April & Sept Mon–Fri 10am–2pm; early to mid-June & mid- to late Aug daily 10am–5pm; late June to early Aug daily 9am–7pm; ☎98 01 75 64, ⓦwww.lofoten-info.no), and a basic **campsite** (☎99 48 94 05; June–Aug), up a gravel track a five-minute walk away.

##

Five kilometres south of Moskenes the road ends abruptly at tersely named **Å**, one of Lofoten's most delightful villages, its huddle of old buildings rambling along a foreshore that's wedged in tight between the grey-green mountains and the surging sea. Unusually, so much of the nineteenth-century village has survived that a good portion of Å has been incorporated into the **Norsk Fiske-vaersmuseum** (Norwegian Fishing Village Museum; late June to late Aug daily 10am–5.30pm; late Aug to late June Mon–Fri 11am–3.30pm; 50kr; ⓦwww .lofoten-info.no/nfmuseum), an engaging attempt to re-create life here at the end of the nineteenth century. There are about fifteen buildings to examine, including a boathouse, forge, cod-liver-oil processing plant, *rorbuer*, and the houses of both the traders who dominated things hereabouts and the fishermen who did their bidding. According to the census of 1900, Å had 91 inhabitants, of whom ten were traders and their relatives, 18 servants, and 63 fishermen and their dependants. It was a rigidly hierarchical society underpinned by terms and conditions akin to serfdom: the fishermen did not own any land and had to pay rent for the ground on which their houses stood. Payment was made in the form of unpaid labour on the merchant's farmland during the summer harvest and, to rub salt into the wound, neither could the fishermen control the price of the fish upon which they were reliant – no wonder Norwegians emigrated in their thousands. The museum has a series of **displays** detailing every aspect

The Vikings

In a country that only became a separate kingdom in 1905, the Vikings remain a potent symbol of independence. It's all rather tongue-in-cheek – plastic Viking helmets are hardly the stuff of fervent nationalism – but it is a strong sentiment all the same, and accounts for the diligence with which the Norwegians preserve their Viking artefacts, most memorably the longships, the stave churches and the ancient burial mounds that attract visitors right across south and central Norway.

From raider to colonizer

Norway's **Vikings** sailed west in their longships, falling upon Scotland and Ireland with ferocious force in the ninth century. At first, the Vikings raided, robbed and then sailed away, but later they conquered and settled, creating a Norse world that at its peak stretched west to Greenland and south to Scotland, England and France. A terror to their enemies, the raiders seemed invincible, but with time they were to prove more of a historical interlude than a major turning point. Within a few generations, the Viking settlers blended in with the local population – William the Conqueror (1027–87), the epitome of the French baron, was the descendant of a Viking chieftain.

The sagas

Bow of a Viking ship ▲

Sigurd with a broken sword at an anvil ▼

Norwegian Vikings colonized Iceland in the ninth century, and it was on this remote island, between the twelfth and the fourteenth centuries, that the **sagas** were first transcribed. Written in prose, they were distilled from Norse oral tradition and mostly feature historical figures and events – albeit embroidered – revealing much about the Viking world of feuds and rivalries, superstition and magic. There are also sagas devoted to the semi-mythical heroes of the "ancient times"; the most important of these is the **Volsunga Saga**, relating the story of Sigurd the Dragonslayer. Poor old Sigurd had a terrible time: as if killing a dragon wasn't difficult enough, his foster father tried to swindle him and then the queen slipped him a magic potion, which induced Sigurd to leave the woman he loved, Brynhild, for the queen's daughter. It got worse: out of pique, Brynhild persuaded a kinsman to murder Sigurd, but immediately regretted it and threw herself on his funeral pyre. Most Norwegians know their sagas well and Sigurd is, for instance, still a common name. For more on sagas and folklore, see p.413.

Viking jewellery

The Vikings were particularly keen on **jewellery**, both as a form of adornment and as a way of showing their wealth. Silver was the primary metal of value, as gold was in desperately short supply and only used by the most privileged. The early Vikings were quite content to wear imported – or indeed looted – jewellery of pretty much any description, but by the tenth century it was the silver- and goldsmiths back home who produced the most valued pieces, decorated with

▲ Woodcut of a Viking raid on the English coast

▼ Heddal stave church

Stave churches

Only 29 stave medieval churches survive of some 750 built in Norway. Though not from the Viking period as such, they were all greatly influenced by Viking design and some, such as Urnes stave church, incorporate carved wooden panels salvaged from earlier Viking churches. Architecturally, their key feature is that the timbers are placed vertically in the ground with upright bracing posts – or staves – at each corner, but more interesting by far is the decoration: dragon finials reminiscent of longship prows protrude from their roofs, and the doorframes sport forceful, intricate carvings of men and beasts entwined in dense foliage. The most enchanting churches are Borgund (see p.187) and Urnes (see p.249), though Hopperstad (see p.237), Lom (see p.252) and Heddal (see p.191) run them close. For more on the construction of stave churches, see p.187.

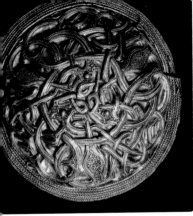

Silver brooch ▲

Gaia, a replica Viking ship ▼

a densely wrought filigree of abstract patterns. Viking gold- and silver work is categorized into several different periods, beginning with the intricate Oseberg and Borre styles of the ninth century and culminating in the more sophisticated Jellinge and Urnes styles of the tenth. However, only the wealthier Vikings could afford gold and silver and most had to make do with bronze jewellery, which was mass-produced in clay moulds. The most common items were bracelets and brooches, armlets and buckles, neck rings and pendants; earrings were unknown and finger rings rare. The two finest collections of surviving Viking silverwork are in Oslo – at the Kulturhistorisk Museum (see p.87), and at the Vikingskipshuset (see p.99); there are also displays at the Midgard Historical Centre (see p.128) and beside Borgund stave church (see p.187).

Burying a Viking

The Vikings were not hot on theology, their paganism being a hotchpotch of competing beliefs and rival gods, and had no particular rules about how to mark a **death**. Some Vikings were cremated, while others were buried in simple holes in the ground or beneath large earthen mounds. Some were buried with their treasure, others weren't; some were interred in their longships, others next to symbolic representations of their ship; and a few had their slaves killed and thrown in the tomb with them. A few graves of Vikings buried in their longships have survived remarkably well – most notably the **Oseberg ship** (see p.99), on display in Oslo and unearthed complete with a fantastic haul of treasure, including swords, daggers, fancily carved animal heads, and ornate sleighs and wagons.

of village life – and very well presented it is too. Afterwards, you can extend your knowledge of all things fishy by visiting the **Tørrfiskmuseum** (Stockfish Museum; early to late June Mon–Fri 11am–4pm; late June to late Aug daily 10am–5.30pm; 40kr) – stockfish being the air-dried fish that was the staple diet of most Norwegians well into the twentieth century.

Hiking and boat trips from Å – the MoskeNstraumen

Å doesn't offer too much in the way of hiking trails, but there is an enjoyable route leading west from the village to the other side of the island. This begins by skirting the south shore of Lake Ågvatnet, before climbing over a steep ridge and then pushing on to the sea cliffs of the exposed west coast. The hike takes a whole day, and shouldn't be attempted in bad weather. Less energetic are the **boat trips** that leave from Å's jetty from May through to September, including day-long fishing expeditions (500kr per person), coastal cruises (3hr; 500kr), and, weather and tides permitting, cruises to the abandoned fishing village of Refsvik and the **MoskeNstraumen** (5hr; 800kr), the dramatic maelstrom at the southern tip of Moskenesøya. There are other places to see similar phenomena in Norway – Bodø's Saltstraumen springs to mind – but this is the most dramatic and was described by **Edgar Allan** Poe in his short story *A Descent into the Maelstrom*:

Even while I gazed, this current acquired a monstrous velocity. Each moment added to its speed – to its headlong impetuosity. In five minutes the whole sea ... was lashed into ungovernable fury... Here the vast bed of the waters seamed and scarred into a thousand conflicting channels, burst suddenly into frenzied convulsion – heaving, boiling, hissing...

Practicalities

Beginning in Narvik – and using the Lofast highway – the **Lofoten Ekspressen bus** (Ⓦ www.177nordland.com) runs the length of the E10 all the way down to Svolvær twice daily; from Svolvær, one bus daily continues on to Leknes and Å. The journey time from Narvik to Å is about eight hours, a little under four hours from Svolvær. Times do not, however, usually coincide with ferry sailings to and from Moskenes. Consequently, if you're heading from the Moskenes ferry port to Å, you'll either have to walk – it's an easy 5km – or take a taxi.

Most of the **accommodation** in Å is run by one family, who own the year-round HI **hostel** (singles 180kr, doubles ❶); an assortment of smart one- to eight-bedded *rorbuer* that surround the dock (850–1550kr per *rorbu*); and the adjacent *sjøhus*, which offers comfortable and equally smart hotel-standard rooms (❷). The same family also runs the cosy bar, with seagull-egg bar snacks, and the only restaurant, where the seafood is excellent. Bookings for all these can be made on ☎ 76 09 11 21, Ⓦ www.lofoten-rorbu.com. While you are here, you should also try the cinnamon buns made at the old bakery, which still uses the original, vintage oven.

Å is, to some extent at least, a victim of its own success and in summertime it can heave with tourists. Don't despair. From the village, it's a short (600m) walk back down the road to **TIND**, much less visited and with fifteen spacious but cosy *rorbuer* (☎ 92 89 36 74, Ⓦ www.tindlofoten.no; ❸); the spa and outdoor hot tubs here are a real treat.

Værøy & Røst

Værøy and **Røst** are the most southerly of the Lofoten islands, and the most time-consuming to reach: indeed, unless you're careful, the irregular ferry schedules can leave you stranded on either for a couple of days. The ferry operator is Hurtigruten (☎177 in Nordland, otherwise ☎75 77 24 10, ⓦwww.hurtigruten.no) and the gist of their timetable is that **car ferries** run from Bodø to Værøy and/or Røst once or twice a day, and all of them call at Moskenes. The fare from Bodø to Værøy is 143kr per person and 514kr for a car and driver; Bodø to Røst is 171kr and 621kr; and between Værøy and Røst it's 76kr and 262kr. In the summer, from June to August, advance ferry reservations are advised, but for the rest of the year the ferries are first-come, first-served, so it's a good idea to turn up at least an hour before departure. Much quicker, though, is **flying** to the islands: Røst has a tiny airstrip with flights from Bodø, which take just twenty minutes (1–2 daily; around 650kr one-way; ⓦwww.katoair.no); and Værøy can be reached from Bodø by the world's most northerly helicopter service (1–3 daily; 20min; ☎75 50 48 94, ⓦwww.wideroe.no).

Both Værøy and Røst are internationally famous for their **bird colonies**, hosting a multitude of puffins, eiders and gulls, as well as cormorants, terns, kittiwakes, guillemots, rare sea eagles and more recent immigrants like the fulmar and gannet. There are lots of **bird trips** to choose from, and for a three-hour excursion you can reckon on paying between 350kr and 450kr. The weather in the islands is uncommonly mild throughout the year, potential hiking routes are ubiquitous, and the occasional beach glorious and deserted.

Værøy

Of the two islands, **Værøy**, just 8km long, is the more visually appealing, comprising a slender, lightly populated, grassy-green coastal strip that ends suddenly in the steep, bare mountains that backbone the island. Værøy's few kilometres of roads primarily connect the farmsteads of the plain, but one squeezes through the mountains to wiggle along a portion of the west coast. The island is, however, best explored on **foot**, either along the steep (and sometimes dangerous) footpaths of the mountains, or on the easier and clearer paths that lead out along the Nupsneset promontory. The most popular walk is, however, the hiking trail that leads along the west coast from the end of the road to the isolated village of **Måstad**, abandoned in the 1950s; it's a tricky walk which takes two to three hours each way. The inhabitants of Måstad varied their fishy diet by catching puffins from the neighbouring sea cliffs, a hard and difficult task in which they were assisted by specially bred dogs known as puffin dogs, or **Lundehund**. These small – 32–38cm high – innocuous-looking dogs have three distinctive features: they have six toes; can close their ears against dust and moisture; and can bend their heads right round on to their backs. Værøy's most important **bird cliffs** occupy the southwest corner of the island, but they are much too steep and slippery to approach on foot, so the best bet is to take a **boat trip**. There are several island operators – just ask around – and expect to pay about 400kr for a three-hour excursion.

Practicalities

Ferries to Værøy dock at the southeast tip of the island, about 800m from the **tourist office** (June–Oct Mon–Fri 9am–3pm; ☎76 05 15 00); they can advise on boat tours and **accommodation** – though you would be foolhardy not to arrange this beforehand. The options are limited to a well-kept guesthouse at the old vicarage, the *Gamle Prestegård*, on the northern side of the island (☎76 09 54 11, ⓦwww.prestegaarden.no; ❷), and a line of *rorbuer* (from 650kr) belonging to the *Kornelius Kro pub* in the centre of the village (☎76 09 52 99, ⓦwww.lofotenportal.com).

Finding a decent **meal** can a problem, but there are pizzas and snacks at *Kunsthavna Pub & Kafe*, the old airport at the end of the northern road. Back in the village, *Kornelius Kro* serves similar fare and they have the added benefit of a hot tub on the back terrace.

Røst

Even smaller than its neighbour, with a population of just 600, **Røst** is immediately different, its smattering of lonely farmsteads dotted over a flat, marshy landscape interrupted by dozens of tiny lakes. It was here in 1431 that the lifeboat of a shipwrecked Italian nobleman, Pietro Querini, was washed up after weeks at sea. Querini, and his fellow Venetians, stayed the winter and his written account is one of the few surviving records of everyday life in Nordland in the Middle Ages.

Ferries to Røst dock at the southwest corner of the island, about 3km from the main village. The tourist office (late June to late Aug Mon–Sat 10am–1.30pm & usually when the boat comes in; ☎76 09 64 11) is close to the jetty. As for **accommodation**, there are plain and inexpensive lodgings at *Kårøy Rorbucamping* (☎76 09 62 38, ⊕ www.karoy.no; ❷), and much more comfortable rooms at the *Røst Bryggehotell* complex (☎76 05 08 00, ⊕ www.rostbryggehotell.no; ❸). The latter organizes **boat trips** to the jagged islets that rise high above the ocean to the southwest of Røst, their steep cliffs sheltering myriad seabird colonies.

Travel details

Principal train services (⊕www.nsb.no)

Trondheim to: Bodø (2 daily; 10hr); Fauske (2 daily; 9hr); Lønsdal (2 daily; 8hr; request stop); Mo-i-Rana (3 daily; 6hr 30min); Mosjøen (3 daily; 5hr); Oslo via Dombås (4 daily via Dombås, Lillehammer and Oslo Gardermoen airport; 5hr, some services 7hr); Oslo via Røros (1 daily; 8hr 30min; change at Hamar); Røros (3 daily; 2hr 30min); Steinkjer (3–4 daily; 2hr); Stockholm (2 daily; 12hr); Verdal (3–4 daily; 1hr 30min).

Ofotbanen trains from Narvik operated by SJ (⊕www.sj.se)

Narvik to: Kiruna, Sweden (2–3 daily; 3hr); Luleå, Sweden (2–3 daily; 6hr 30min); Riksgränsen, Sweden (2–3 daily; 50min).

Principal Nor-Way Bussekspress bus services (⊕www.nor-way.no)

(Note that the Lofoten Ekspressen from Narvik to the Lofotens is operated by Nor-Way Bussekspress in conjunction with two other companies.)
Bodø to: Fauske (2–3 daily; 1hr 10min); Lødingen (2 daily; 6hr); Narvik (2 daily; 6hr 30min); Sortland (2 daily; 7hr).

Fauske to: Bodø (2–3 daily; 1hr 10min); Lødingen (2 daily; 4hr); Narvik (2 daily; 5hr 30min); Sortland (2 daily; 5hr).
Narvik to: Å (1 daily; 7hr 50min); Alta (2 daily except Sat; 9hr 30min); Bodø (2 daily; 6hr 30min); Fauske (2 daily; 5hr 30min); Gullesfjordbotn (2 daily; 3hr); Kabelvåg (1 daily; 4hr 30min); Leknes (2 daily; 6hr); Lødingen (2 daily; 2hr 30min); Svolvær (2 daily; 4hr 20min); Tromsø (2–3 daily; 4hr).
Sortland to: Fauske (2 daily; 5hr).
Svolvær to: Kabelvåg (1 daily; 15min); Leknes (2 daily; 1hr 30min); Narvik (2 daily; 4hr 20min).
Trondheim to: Ålesund (3–4 daily; 7hr); Bergen (1 daily; 14hr 30min); Loen (1 daily; 8hr); Lom (1 daily; 5hr 40min); Oslo (1–3 daily; 8hr); Otta (1 daily; 4hr 30min); Stryn (1 daily; 8hr); .

Nor-Way Bussekspress's Nord-Norgeekspressen and Nordkappekspressen (⊕www.nor-way.no)

The **Nord-Norgeekspressen** (North Norway Express Bus) complements the railway system. It runs north from Bodø and Fauske to Alta in three segments: Bodø to Narvik via Fauske (2 daily; 6hr 30min); Narvik to Tromsø (1–3 daily; 4hr); and Tromsø to Alta (1 daily; 6hr 30min). Alternatively, the **Nordkappekspressen** (North Cape Express Bus) runs direct from Narvik to Alta (2 daily except

Sat; 9hr 30min), where passengers overnight before picking up the second leg of the Nordkappekspressen to Honningsvåg and Nordkapp (see p.388 for details).

The Lofoten Ekspressen

The long-distance **Lofoten Ekspressen**, operated by Nor-Way Bussekspress (⊛www.nor-way.no) in conjunction with a couple of smaller companies, provides the main bus service from the mainland to the Lofoten. It leaves Narvik twice daily to run along the E6 and then the E10, calling at Evenes airport and Lødingen before taking the Lofast highway to Fiskebøl in the Lofoten; it then proceeds on to Svolvær, where one bus daily continues on to Kabelvåg and Leknes, or you change for the once-daily bus to Leknes and Å. As an example of journey times, Narvik to Leknes takes six hours, just under eight hours to Å. Selected local bus services (⊛www.177nordland.com)
Å to: Harstad (1 daily; 7hr 15min); Kabelvåg (2 daily; 3hr); Leknes (2–3 daily; 1hr 40min); Reine (2–3 daily; 20min); Sortland (3 daily; 5hr 45min); Stokmarknes (3 daily; 5hr 15min); Svolvær (1–2 daily; 3hr 15min).
Andenes to: Sortland (2–4 daily; 2hr).
Harstad to: Å (1 daily; 7hr 15min); Lødingen (2 daily; 1hr 30min); Svolvær (2–4 daily; 3hr 45min).
Sortland to: Å (1–3 daily; 5hr 45min); Andenes (2–4 daily; 2hr); Svolvær (1–3 daily; 2hr 15min).
Svolvær to: Å (1–2 daily; 3hr 15min); Harstad (2–4 daily; 3hr 45min); Leknes (3–6 daily; 1hr 30min); Sortland (1–3 daily; 2hr 15min); Stokmarknes (1–4 daily; 1hr 45min).

Principal Hurtigruten car ferries (⊛www.hurtigruten.no)

Bodø to: Moskenes (June–Aug 5–6 daily; Sept–May 1–2 daily except Sat; 3hr 45min); Røst (June–Aug 1–2 daily; Sept–May 4 weekly; 4hr

45min); Værøy (June–Aug 1–2 daily except Sun; Sept–May 4 weekly; 6hr 30min).
Bognes to: Lødingen (every 1hr – 2hr daily; 1hr); Skarberget (every 1hr or 90min; 25min).
Skutvik to: Svolvær (1 daily; 2hr).
Svolvær to: Skutvik (1 daily; 2hr).
Other car ferry services:
Andenes to: Gryllefjord (late May to mid-June & early to late Aug 2 daily, mid-June to early Aug 3 daily; 2hr) with Senjafergene (⊛www.senjafergene.no).
Botnhamn to: Brensholmen (May to Aug 5–7 daily; 45min) with Senjafergene (⊛www.senjafergene.no).
Fiskebøl to: Melbu (daily 7am–11pm, every 90min; 25min) with Veolia (⊛www.177nordland.com).

Hurtigbåt passenger express boats

Bodø to: Svolvær (1 daily; 3hr 30min) with Hurtigruten car ferries (⊛www.hurtigruten.no).
Harstad to: Tromsø (2–3 daily; 2hr 45min) with Hurtigruten car ferries. (⊛www.hurtigruten.no).
Trondheim to: Kristiansund (1–3 daily; 3hr 15min) on the Kystekspressen (⊛www.kystekspressen.no).

Hurtigrute coastal boat (⊛www.hurtigruten.no)

Northbound departures: daily from Trondheim at noon; Bodø at 3pm; Stamsund at 7.30pm; Svolvær at 10pm; Stokmarknes at 1am; Sortland at 3am & Harstad at 8am.
Southbound departures: daily from Harstad at 8.30am; Sortland at 1pm; Stokmarknes at 3.15pm; Svolvær at 7.30pm; Stamsund at 9.30pm; Bodø at 4am & Trondheim at 10am.
Journey times: Trondheim to Harstad 43hr; Trondheim to Tromsø 51hr.

North Norway

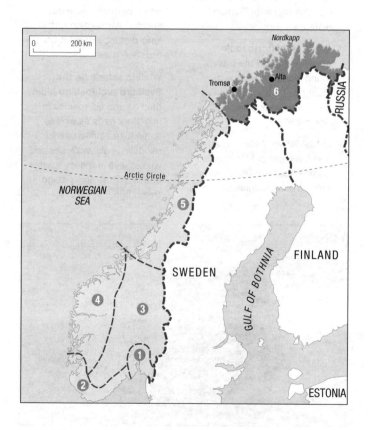

CHAPTER 6

Highlights

✳ **Rica Ishavshotel, Tromsø**
Classy chain hotel slap-bang
on the waterfront in Tromsø
with all sorts of tasty little
touches. **See p.357**

✳ **Emmas Drømmekjøkken**
Try the Arctic specialities –
reindeer and char for instance
– at this exquisite Tromsø
restaurant. **See p.360**

✳ **Alta's prehistoric rock
carvings** Follow the trail
round Northern Europe's
most extensive collection of
prehistoric rock carvings.
See p.363

✳ **Juhls' Silver Gallery** The first
and foremost of Finnmark's
Sámi-influenced jewellery-
makers and designers.
See p.367

✳ **Repvåg** An old fishing station
with traditional red-painted
wooden buildings on stilts,
framed by a picture-postcard
setting. **See p.376**

✳ **The Hurtigrute** Sail around
the northern tip of Norway
and across the Barents
Sea – perhaps the most
spectacular section of this
long-distance coastal boat
trip. **See p.381**

✳ **Wildlife safaris on the
Svalbard archipelago** More
than a hundred species of
migratory birds as well as
arctic foxes, polar bears,
reindeer, seals, walruses and
whales, live in the icy wastes
of this remote archipelago.
See p.385

▲ Bearded seal

6

North Norway

aedeker, writing a hundred years ago about Norway's remote **northern provinces** of Troms and Finnmark, observed that they "possess attractions for the scientific traveller and the sportsman, but can hardly be recommended for the ordinary tourist" – a comment that isn't too wide of the mark even today. These are enticing lands, no question; the natural environment they offer is stunning in its extremes, with the midnight sun and polar night emphasizing the strangeness of the terrain, but the travelling can be hard, the specific sights widely separated and, when you reach them, subtle in their appeal.

Troms's intricate, fretted coastline has shaped its history since the days when powerful Viking lords operated a trading empire from its islands. Indeed, over half the population still lives offshore in dozens of tiny fishing villages, but the place to aim for is **Tromsø**, the so-called "Capital of the North" and a lively university town where King Håkon and his government proclaimed a "Free Norway" in 1940, before fleeing into exile. Beyond Tromsø, the long trek north begins in earnest as you enter **Finnmark**, a vast wilderness covering 48,000 square kilometres, but home to just two percent of the Norwegian population. Much of the land was laid waste during World War II, the combined effect of the Russian advance and the retreating German army's scorched-earth policy, and it's now possible to drive for hours without coming across a building more than sixty or so years old. The first obvious target in Finnmark is **Alta**, a sprawling settlement and important crossroads famous for its prehistoric rock carvings. From here, most visitors head straight for the steely cliffs of **Nordkapp** (the North Cape), supposedly but not actually Europe's northernmost point, with or without a detour to the likeable port of **Hammerfest**, and leave it at that; but some doggedly press on to **Kirkenes**, the last town before the Russian border, where you feel as if you're about to drop off the end of the world. From Alta, the other main alternative is to travel inland across the eerily endless scrubland of the **Finnmarksvidda**, where winter temperatures plummet to -35°C. This high plateau is the last stronghold of the **Sámi**, northern Norway's indigenous people, some of whom still live a semi-nomadic life tied to the movement of their reindeer herds. You'll spot Sámi in their brightly coloured traditional gear all across the region, but especially in the remote towns of **Kautokeino** and **Karasjok**, strange, disconsolate places in the middle of the plain.

Finally, and even more adventurously, there is the **Svalbard** archipelago, whose icy mountains rise out of the Arctic Ocean 640km north of mainland Norway. Once the exclusive haunt of trappers, fishermen and coal miners, Svalbard now makes a tidy income from adventure tourism – everything from guided glacier walks to snowmobile excursions and whale-watching. You can

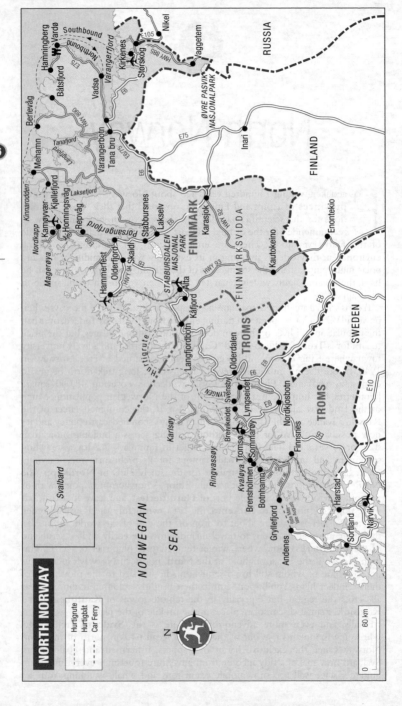

NORTH NORWAY

Hurtigrute
Hurtigbåt
Car Ferry

Svalbard

NORWEGIAN SEA

N

0   60 km

RUSSIA

FINLAND

SWEDEN

FINNMARK

FINNMARKSVIDDA

TROMS

TROMS

Nikel
Vaggetem
E105
HWY 886
Kirkenes
Storskog
Varangerfjord
ØVRE PASVIK NASJONALPARK
Vardø
Hanningberg
Vadsø
Berlevåg
E75
Southbound
Northbound
E6
Varangerbotn
Tana bru
HWY 890
Tanafjord
Mehamn
Laksefjord
Kinnarodden
Inari
E75
E6
Kjøllefjord
Honningsvåg
Kamøyvær
Repvåg
Stabbursnes
Lakselv
Karasjok
HWY 92
Enontekiö
Nordkapp
Magerøya
E69
Porsangerfjord
Skaidi
STABBURSDALEN NASJONAL PARK
HWY 98
Olderfjord
HWY 94
Hammerfest
Alta
HWY 93
Kautokeino
E8
Kåfjord
Langfjordbotn
Hurtigrute
Olderdalen
E6   E8
LYNGEN
Svensby
Lyngseidet
E8
Nordkjosbotn
Karlsøy
Breivikeidet
Tromsø
Skjervøy
E6
Finnsnes
E10
Ringvassøy
Kvaløya
Sommarøy
Brensholmen
Botnhamn
HWY 86
Gryllefjord
Andenes
HWY 83/85
Harstad
Sortland
Narvik

fly there independently from most of Norway's larger towns, including Tromsø, at bearable prices, though most people opt for a package tour.

Transport practicalities

Public transport in the provinces of Troms and Finnmark is by **bus**, the **Hurtigrute** coastal boat and **plane** – there are no trains. For all but the most truncated of tours, the best idea is to pick and mix these different forms of transport – for example by flying from Tromsø to Kirkenes and then taking the Hurtigrute back, or vice versa. What you should try to avoid is endless doubling-back on the **E6**, though this is often difficult as it is the only road to run right across the region. To give an idea of the distances involved, from Tromsø it's 400km to Alta, 640km to Nordkapp and 970km to Kirkenes.

Norway's principal long-distance bus company, Nor-Way Bussekspress (ⓦ www.nor-way.no), provides two services in the region – the **Nord-Norgeekspressen**, which links Tromsø with Narvik and Alta once daily, and the **Nordkappekspressen**, linking Narvik and Alta twice daily except on Saturdays. At Alta, passengers overnight before proceeding on the next leg of the Nordkappekspressen journey north to Honningsvåg, where – from early June to late August – they can change on to the connecting bus to Nordkapp. Alta is also where you can pick up local buses to Hammerfest, Kautokeino, Karasjok and Kirkenes. Bus **timetables** are available at most tourist offices and bus stations; they are also available online – Cominor for Tromsø and its environs (ⓣ 177, ⓦ www.cominor.no) and FFR for the whole of Finnmark (ⓣ 177, ⓦ www.ffr.no). On the longer rides, it's a good idea to buy **tickets** in advance, or turn up early, as buses fill up fast in the summer.

Northern Norway's main **highways** are all well maintained, but **drivers** will find the going a little slow as they have to negotiate some pretty tough terrain. You can cover 250–300km in a day without any problem, but much more and it all becomes rather wearisome. Be warned also that in July and August the E6 north of Alta can get congested with caravans and motorhomes on their way to Nordkapp. You can avoid the crush by starting early or, for that matter, by driving overnight – an eerie experience when it's bright sunlight in the wee hours of the morning. In **winter**, driving conditions can be appalling and, although the Norwegians make a spirited effort to keep the E6 open, they don't always succeed. If you're not used to driving in these sorts of conditions, don't start here – especially during the polar night. If you intend to use the region's minor, **unpaved roads**, be prepared for the worst and take food and drink, warm clothes and a mobile phone. Keep an eye on the fuel indicator too, as **petrol stations** are confined to the larger settlements and they may be 100 to 200km apart. Car repairs can take time since workshops are scarce and parts often have to be ordered from the south.

Much more leisurely is the **Hurtigrute coastal boat**, which takes the best part of two days to cross the huge fjords between Tromsø and Kirkenes. En route, it calls at eleven ports, mostly remote fishing villages but also Hammerfest and Honningsvåg, where northbound ferries pause for four hours so that special buses can cart passengers off to Nordkapp and back. One especially appealing option, though this has more to do with comfort than speed, is to combine **car and boat** travel. Special deals on the Hurtigrute can make this surprisingly affordable and tourist offices at the Hurtigrute's ports of call will make bookings. If you are renting a car, taking your vehicle on to the Hurtigrute may well work out a lot cheaper than leaving it at your port of embarkation: car-hire drop-off charges in Norway are notoriously expensive, reaching anything up to 8000kr. At the other end of the nautical extreme, the region has two **Hurtigbåt passenger express boat** services – Alta to Hammerfest and Tromsø to Harstad.

The region has several **airports**, including those at Alta, Hammerfest, Honningsvåg, Kirkenes, Tromsø and Longyearbyen, on Svalbard. SAS and its subsidiary, Widerøe, have the widest range of flights to northern Norway, but Norwegian Airlines chips in too, flying to Tromsø, Alta and Kirkenes. Standard return fares are usually expensive, but discounts are legion and Norwegian airlines are most economical.

As for **accommodation**, all the major settlements have at least a couple of hotels and the main roads are sprinkled with campsites. If you have a tent and a well-insulated sleeping bag, you can, in theory, bed down more or less where you like, but the hostility of the climate and the ferocity of the mosquitoes, especially in the marshy areas of the Finnmarksvidda, make most people think (at least) twice. There are HI **hostels** at Tromsø, Alta, Honningsvåg, Lakselv and Karasjok.

Tromsø

TROMSØ has been called, rather preposterously, the "Paris of the North", and though even the tourist office doesn't make any pretence to such grandiose titles today, the city is without question the effective capital of northern Norway. Easily the region's most populous town, its credentials go back to the Middle Ages and beyond, when seafarers used its sheltered harbour, and there's been a church here since the thirteenth century. Tromsø received its municipal charter in 1794, when it was primarily a fishing port and trading station, and flourished in the middle of

---

Arctic phenomena

On and above the **Arctic Circle**, an imaginary line drawn round the earth at latitude 66.5 degrees north, there is a period around midsummer during which the sun never makes it below the horizon, even at midnight – hence the **midnight sun**. On the Arctic Circle itself, this only happens on one night of the year – at the summer solstice – but the further north you go, the greater the number of nights affected: in Bodø, it's from the first week of June to early July; in Tromsø from late May to late July; in Alta, from the third week in May to the end of July; in Hammerfest, mid-May to late July; and in Nordkapp, early May to the end of July. Obviously, the midnight sun is best experienced on a clear night, but fog or cloud can turn the sun into a glowing, red ball – a spectacle that can be wonderful but also strangely disconcerting. All the region's tourist offices have the exact dates of the midnight sun, though note that these are calculated at sea level; climb up a hill and you can extend the dates by a day or two. The converse of all this is the **polar night**, a period of constant darkness either side of the winter solstice; again the further north of the Arctic Circle you are, the longer this lasts.

The Arctic Circle also marks the typical southern limit of the **northern lights**, or **Aurora Borealis**, though this extraordinary phenomenon has been seen as far south as latitude 40 degrees north. Caused by the bombardment of the atmosphere by electrons, carried away from the sun by the solar wind, the northern lights take various forms and are highly mobile – either flickering in one spot or travelling across the sky. At relatively low latitudes hereabouts, the aurora is tilted at an angle and is often coloured red – the sagas tell of Vikings being half scared to death by them – but nearer the pole, they hang like gigantic luminous curtains, often tinted greenish blue. Naturally enough, there's no predicting when the northern lights will occur, but in wintertime they are not uncommon – and on a clear night they can be strangely humbling.

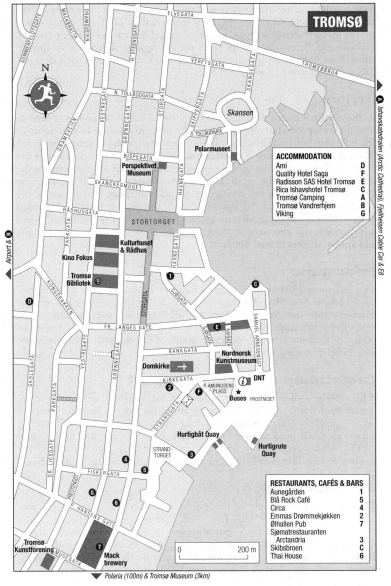

TROMSØ

ELVEGATA
SØMMERFELDTSGATE
MACKRABTA
DRAMSVEIEN
R. STEENSGATE
VERFTSGATA
TROMSØBRUA
SKANSEGATA
N. TOLLBODGATA
VESTREGATA
GRØNNEGATA
STORGATA
SKIPPERGATA
S. TOLLBODGATE
Skansen
DRAMSVEIEN
HAVNEGATA
BISPEGATA
Polarmuseet
Perspektivet
Museum
SKANCKESMUGET
RÅDHUSGATA
PARKGATA
STORTORGET
Kulturhuset
& Rådhus
Kino Fokus
HAVNEGATA
Tromsø
Bibliotek
@
SJØGATA
STORGATA
SJØGATA
KAIGATA
SAMUEL ARNESENGT
FR. LANGES GATE
VESTREGATA
GRØNNEGATA
BANKGATA
Nordnorsk
Kunstmuseum
Domkirke
KIRKEGATA
R. AMUNDSENS
PLASS
DNT
STRANDGATA
Buses
PROSTNESET
Hurtigbåt Quay
STRAND-
TORGET
Hurtigrute
Quay
SKOLEGATA
PARKGATA
DR. LIESGATE
FISKERGATA
PRESTVNGT
P. HANSENS GATE
Tromsø
Kunstforening
MUSÉGATA
Mack
brewery

Airport & B

A. Ishavskatedralen (Arctic Cathedral), Fjellheisen Cable Car & E8

ACCOMMODATION	
Ami	D
Quality Hotel Saga	F
Radisson SAS Hotel Tromsø	E
Rica Ishavshotel Tromsø	C
Tromsø Camping	A
Tromsø Vandrerhjem	B
Viking	G

RESTAURANTS, CAFÉS & BARS	
Aunegården	1
Blå Rock Café	5
Circa	4
Emmas Drømmekjøkken	2
Ølhallen Pub	7
Sjømatrestauranten	
Arctandria	3
Skibsbroen	C
Thai House	6

0   200 m

Polaria (100m) & Tromsø Museum (3km)

the nineteenth century when its seamen ventured north to Svalbard to reap rich rewards hunting arctic fox, polar bears reindeer, walrus and, most profitable of all, seal. Subsequently, Tromsø became famous as the jumping-off point for a string of Arctic expeditions, its celebrity status assured when the explorer Roald Amundsen flew from here to his death somewhere on the Arctic icecap in 1928. Since those heady days, Tromsø has grown into an urbane and likeable small city with a population of 63,000 employed in a wide range of industries and at the university. It's become an important port too, for although the city is some 360km north of the Arctic Circle, its climate is moderated by the Gulf Stream, which sweeps up the Norwegian coast and keeps its harbour ice-free. Give or take the odd museum, Tromsø is perhaps short on top-ranking **sights**, but its amiable atmosphere, fine mountain-and-fjord setting, and clutch of lively restaurants and bars more than compensate.

Arrival

At the northern end of the E8, 73km from the E6 and 260km north of Narvik, Tromsø's compact centre slopes up from the waterfront on the eastern shores of the hilly island of Tromsøya. The island is connected to the mainland by bridge and tunnel. The **Hurtigrute coastal boat** docks in the town centre beside the Prostneset quay at the foot of Kirkegata, while **Hurtigbåt** services arrive at the jetty about 150m to the south. Long-distance **buses** pull in at the stops on Prostneset, metres from the Hurtigrute quay. The **airport** is 5km west of the centre on the other side of Tromsøya; from the airport, frequent Flybussen (Mon–Fri 5am–7pm every 30min–1hr, Sat 5am–3pm hourly, Sun 9am–7.30pm hourly; 55kr) run into the city, stopping at the *Radisson SAS Hotel* on Sjøgata and at several other central hotels.

Information

Tromsø's **tourist office** is a few paces from the Prostneset quay at Kirkegata 2 (mid-May to Aug Mon–Fri 9am–7pm, Sat & Sun 10am–5pm; rest of year Mon–Fri 9am–4pm, Sat 10am–4pm; ☎77 61 00 00, ⊛www.visittromso.no). It issues free town maps, has a small supply of B&Bs (see below), and provides oodles of local information, including details of bus and boat sightseeing trips around neighbouring islands.

Orientation and city transport

A five-minute **walk** from one side to the other, the busiest part of the town centre spreads south from Stortorget, the main square, along Storgata, the main street and north–south axis, as far as Kirkegata and the harbourfront. For Tromsø's outlying attractions you'll need to catch a local **bus**. These are operated by Cominor (☎177, ⊛www.cominor.no) with the standard, flat-rate fare for a local bus journey costing 25kr. Another option is to **rent a bike** from the tourist office.

Accommodation

Tromsø has a good supply of modern, central **hotels**, though the majority occupy chunky concrete high-rises. Less expensive – and sometimes more distinctive – are the town's **guesthouses** (*pensjonater*) and there's also a rudimentary HI **hostel**. In addition, the tourist office has a small list of **B&Bs** (❶–❷), but most are stuck out in the suburbs. Tromsø is a popular destination, so advance reservation is recommended, especially in the summer.

Hotels

Ami Skolegata 24 ☎77 62 10 00, ⊛www.amihotel .no. With seventeen simple rooms, this guesthouse/hotel has wide views over the city from the hillside behind the town centre. Free internet access too. ❷
Quality Hotel Saga Richard Withsplass 2 ☎77 60 70 00, ⊛www.choicehotels.no. Although there has

been some Ikea-ization at this medium-sized, 1960s chain hotel, the public areas remain reassuringly old-fashioned with lots of pine (rather than chipboard). Right in the centre of town opposite the Domkirke. ❻, sp/r ❸
Radisson SAS Hotel Tromsø Sjøgata 7 ☎77 60 00 00, ⊛www.tromso.radissonsas.com. The

biggest hotel in town, occupying two large and clumpy tower blocks down by the harbour. The rooms are kitted out in standard-issue, chain-hotel style – unadventurous but perfectly adequate. Ultra-efficient service. ❼, sp/r ❺

🏃 **Rica Ishavshotel Tromsø** Fr. Langes gate 2 ☎77 66 64 00, ⓦwww.rica.no. Perched on the harbourfront, this imaginatively designed hotel is partly built in the style of a ship, complete with a sort of crow's-nest bar. Lovely rooms and unbeatable views over the harbour with the mountains glinting behind make it the best place in town. ❼, sp/r ❻
Viking Grønnegata 18 ☎77 64 77 30, ⓦwww .viking-hotell.no. Modern, bright and breezy hotel-cum-guesthouse with 24 fully functional guest rooms. Centrally located near the Mack brewery. Very competitive prices. ❸

The City

Completed in 1861, the Lutheran **Domkirke** (Cathedral; June–Aug Tues–Sat noon–4pm, Sun 10am–4pm; Sept–May Tues–Sat noon–4pm, Sun 10am–2pm; free), bang in the centre on Kirkegata, bears witness to the prosperity of the town's nineteenth-century merchants, who became rich on the back of the barter trade with Russia. They part-funded the cathedral's construction, the result being the large and handsome structure of today, whose slender spire and dinky little tower pokes high into the sky above the neo-Gothic pointed windows of the nave.

In a large old building just along from the church is the **Nordnorsk Kunstmuseum** at Sjøgata 1 (Art Museum of Northern Norway; late June to late Aug daily noon–6pm; rest of year Tues–Fri 10am–5pm, Sat & Sun noon–5pm; ⓦwww.museumsnett.no/nordnorsk-kunstmuseum; free). It's not a large ensemble, but the museum's permanent collection, which is enhanced – and sometimes disturbed – by an ambitious programme of temporary exhibitions, covers all of Norway's artistic bases, beginning in the nineteenth century with the ingenious landscapes of Thomas Fearnley and Johan Dahl (for more on whom, see p.88) and several Romantic peasant scenes by Adolph Tidemand (1814–76). There are lots of North Norway landscapes and seascapes here too, including several delightful paintings by Kongsberg-born Otto Sinding (1842–1909) – look out for his *Spring Day in Lofoten* – as well as a whole battery of paintings by the talented and prolific Axel Revold (1887–1962), whose work typically maintains a gentle, heart-warming lyricism. By contrast, Willi Midelfarts (1904–75) was clearly enraged when he painted his bloody *Assault on the House of Karl Liebknecht*, a reference to the murder of one of Germany's leading Marxists in 1919. The museum also owns a handful of minor works by Edvard Munch (see p.106), including a modest portrait entitled *Parisian Model*.

To Stortorget and the Perspektivet

Back in front of the Domkirke, it's a gentle five-minute stroll north past the shops of Storgata to the main square, **Stortorget**, site of a daily open-air **market** selling flowers and knick-knacks. The square nudges down towards the waterfront, where fresh fish and prawns are sold direct from inshore fishing boats throughout the summer. Just beyond the square, at Storgata 95, is the **Perspektivet Museum** (June–Aug Tues–Sun 11am–5pm; Sept–May Tues–Fri 11am–3pm, Thurs till 7pm; free), where the emphasis is on all things local, with a lively programme of temporary exhibitions concerning Tromsø and its inhabitants. The building itself, dating from 1838, is also of interest as the one-time home of the local writer **Cora Sandel** (1880–1974), who was born Sara Fabricius and lived in Tromsø from 1893 to 1905, before shipping out to Paris. Sandel's most important work was the *Alberta Trilogy*, a set of semi-autobiographical novels following the trials and tribulations of a young woman as she attempts to establish her own independent identity. The museum has a small section on Sandel on the first floor, but it is confined to a few of her knick-knacks and several photos of her on walkabout in Tromsø.

Polarmuseet

From the **Perspektivet Museum**, it's a brief walk east to the modest knoll known as **Skansen**, which marks the sight of Tromsø's eighteenth-century fort, and, down by the water, the old wooden warehouse that holds the city's most enjoyable museum, the **Polarmuseet** (Polar Museum; daily: mid-June to mid-Aug 10am–7pm; March to mid-June & mid-Aug to Sept 11am–5pm; Oct–Feb 11am–4pm; ⓦwww.polarmuseum.no; 50kr). The collection begins with a rather unappetizing series of displays on trapping in the Arctic, but beyond is an outstanding section on Svalbard, including archeological finds retrieved in the 1980s from an eighteenth-century **Russian whaling station**. Most of the artefacts come from graves that were preserved intact by the permafrost and, among many items, there are combs, leather boots, parts of a sledge, slippers and even – just to prove illicit smoking is not a recent phenomenon – a clay pipe from a period when the Russian company in charge of affairs did not allow trappers to smoke. Two other sections on the first floor focus on **seal hunting**, an important part of the local economy until the 1950s.

Upstairs, on the second floor, a further section is devoted to the exploits of one **Henry Rudi** (1889–1970), the so-called "Isbjørnkongen" (King of the Polar Bears), who spent 27 winters on Svalbard and Greenland, bludgeoning his way through the local wildlife, killing over seven hundred polar bears in the process. Rather more edifying is the extensive display on the polar explorer **Roald Amundsen** (1872–1928), who spent thirty years searching out the secrets of the polar regions. In 1901, he purchased a sealer, the *Gjøa*, here in Tromsø and then spent three years sailing and charting the **Northwest Passage** between the Atlantic and the Pacific. The *Gjøa* (now on display in Olso; see p.100) was the first vessel to complete this extraordinary voyage, which tested Amundsen and his crew to the very limits. Long searched for, the Passage had for centuries been something of a nautical Holy Grail and the progress of the voyage – and at times the lack of it – was headline news right across the world. In 1910, Amundsen set out in a new ship, the *Fram* (also exhibited in Oslo; see p.100), for the Antarctic, or more specifically the **South Pole**. On December 14, 1911, Amundsen and four of his crew became the first men to reach the South Pole, famously just ahead of his British rival Captain Scott. The museum exhibits all sorts of oddments used by Amundsen and his men – from long johns and pipes through to boots and ice picks – but it's the photos that steal the show, providing a fascinating insight into the way Amundsen's polar expeditions were organized and the hardships endured. Amundsen clearly liked having his picture taken, judging from the heroic poses he struck, his derring-do emphasized by the finest set of eyebrows north of Oslo.

Finally, there's another extensive section on Amundsen's contemporary **Fridtjof Nansen** (1861–1930), a polar explorer of similar renown who, in his later years, became a leading figure in international famine relief. In 1895, Nansen and his colleague Hjalmar Johansen made an abortive effort to reach the North Pole by dog sledge after their ship was trapped by pack ice. It took them fifteen months to get back to safety, a journey of such epic proportions that tales of it captivated all of Scandinavia.

Mack brewery, Tromsø Kunstforening and Polaria

Just to the south of the town centre, at the corner of Storgata and Musegata, the profitable **Mack brewery** proudly claims to be the world's northernmost brewery – and dreams up all sorts of bottle labels with ice and polar bears to hammer home the point. Nearby, just up Musegata, **Tromsø Kunstforening** (Tromsø Art Society; Tues–Sun noon–5pm; 30kr; ⓦwww.tromsokunstforening.no) occupies part of a large and attractive Neoclassical building dating from the 1890s. The art society puts on imaginative temporary exhibitions of Norwegian contemporary art with the emphasis on the work of Nordland artists.

Doubling back down Musegata, it's a couple of hundred metres south along Storgata to **Polaria** (daily: mid-May to mid-Aug 10am–7pm; mid-Aug to mid-May noon–5pm; ⓦwww.polaria.no; 100kr), a lavish waterfront complex which deals with all things Arctic. There's an aquarium filled with Arctic species, a 180-degree cinema showing a film on Svalbard and several exhibitions on polar research. Parked outside in a glass greenhouse is a 1940s sealing ship, **M/S Polstjerna**.

South of the centre: Tromsø Museum

About 3km south of the centre, near the southern tip of Tromsøya, is the university's **Tromsø Museum** (June–Aug daily 9am–6pm; rest of year Mon–Fri 9am–3.30pm, Sat noon–3pm & Sun 11am–4pm; 30kr), whose varied collections feature nature and the sciences downstairs, and culture and history above. Pride of place goes to the **medieval religious carvings**, naïve but evocative pieces retrieved from various Nordland churches. There's also an enjoyable section on the Sámi featuring displays on every aspect of Sámi life – from dwellings, tools and equipment through to traditional costume and hunting techniques.

To get to the museum, take bus #37 from the centre (every 30min; ⓦwww .cominor.no).

East of the centre: Ishavskatedralen and the Fjellheisen cable car

East of the city centre, over the spindly Tromsø bridge, rises the desperately modern **Ishavskatedralen** (Arctic Cathedral; June to mid-Aug Mon–Sat 9am–7pm, Sun 1–7pm; mid-Aug to May daily 4–6pm; 25kr). Completed in 1965, the church has a strikingly white, glacier-like appearance, achieved by means of eleven immense triangular concrete sections, representing the eleven Apostles left after the betrayal. The entire east wall is formed by a huge stained-glass window, one of the largest in Europe, and the organ is unusual too, built to represent a ship when viewed from beneath – recalling the tradition, still seen in many a Norwegian church, of suspending a ship from the roof as a good-luck talisman for seafarers. Among several bus services, #20 (every 20–30min; ⓦwww.cominor.no) comes this way, but it's only a few minutes' walk over the bridge from the centre.

From the Ishavskatedralen, it's a fifteen-minute walk – or a short ride on bus #26 – southeast to the **Fjellheisen cable car** (daily: April to late May 10am–5pm; late May to mid-Aug 10am–1am; mid-Aug to mid-Sept 10am-10pm; late Sept 10am–5pm; 95kr; ⓦwww.fjellheisen.no), which whisks up Mount Storsteinen. From the top, at 421m, the views of the city and its surroundings are extensive and it's a smashing spot to catch the midnight sun; there's a café at the top. Note that cable-car services are suspended during poor weather.

Eating, drinking and nightlife

With a clutch of first-rate **restaurants**, several enjoyable **cafés** and a good supply of late-night **bars**, Tromsø is as well served as any comparable Norwegian city. The best of the cafés and restaurants are concentrated in the vicinity of the Domkirke, and most of the livelier bars – many of which sell Mack, the local brew – are in the centre, too.

The **Kulturhuset**, beside Grønnegata (☎77 66 38 10, ⓦwww.kulturhuset .tr.no), is the principal venue for cultural events of all kinds, while the main **cinema**, Kino Fokus, is next door (☎90 88 99 00, ⓦwww.tromsokino.no).

Cafés and restaurants

Aunegården Sjøgata 29. Cosy and popular café-restaurant within the old – and listed – late nineteenth-century Aunegården building. All the standard Norwegian dishes are served, at moderate prices (mains 80–100kr), but these are as nothing when compared with the cakes – wonderful confections, which are made at their own bakery. Weep with pleasure as you nibble at the cheesecake. Mon–Sat 10.30am–11pm, Sun noon–6pm.

Emmas Drømmekjøkken Kirkegata 8 ☎77 63 77 30. Much praised in the national press as a gourmet treat, "Emma's dream kitchen" lives up to its name, with an imaginative and wide-ranging menu focused on Norwegian produce. The grilled arctic char with chanterelle risotto is a treat and, giving reindeer a wide berth, a delicious venison dish with rowanberries is handled with finesse. Excellent service in smart premises. Main courses are 126kr and up. Mon–Sat from 6pm; closed Sun.

Sjømatrestauranten Arctandria Strand-torget 1 ☎77 60 07 20. Some of the best food in town. The upstairs restaurant serves a superb range of fish, with the emphasis on Arctic species, and there's also reindeer and seal; main courses start at around 260kr. Prices are about twenty percent less at the café-bar *Vertshuset Skarven*, downstairs, where there's a slightly less varied menu. Mon–Sat 4pm–midnight.

Thai House Storgata 22 ☎77 67 05 26. Decent Thai cooking with the welcome inclusion of some excellent fish and vegetable dishes; the Thai spicy salads are especially good, and prices are moderate (mains from around 160kr). Daily 3–11pm.

Bars

Blå Rock Café Strandgata 14 ⓦwww.blarock .no. Definitely the place to go for loud rock music – with and without the roll. Occasional live acts too, plus delicious burgers. Mon–Thurs 11.30am–2am, Fri & Sat 11.30am–3.30am, Sun 1pm–2am.

Circa Storgata 36. With DJs Thurs–Sat and intimate jazz concerts at least once a week, the sense of fun in this laid-back bar makes it one of the best in town. Mon–Thurs 11.30am–1.30am, Fri & Sat 11.30am–3.30am, Sun 1pm–1.30am.

Ølhallen Pub Storgata 4. Solid (some would say staid) basement pub adjoining the Mack brewery, whose various ales are its speciality. It's the first pub in town to start serving, and so pulls in the serious drinkers. Mon–Thurs 9am–5pm, Fri 9am–6pm & Sat 9am–3pm.

Skibsbroen Fr. Langes gate 2. Inside the *Rica Ishavshotel* (see p.357), this smart little bar overlooks the waterfront from on high – it occupies the top of a slender tower with wide windows and sea views. Relaxed atmosphere; lots of tourists. Mon–Thurs 6pm–1.30am, Fri & Sat 3pm–3am; closed Sun.

Listings

Airlines Norwegian ☎815 21 815; SAS ☎05400; Widerøe ☎810 01 200.
Car rental Europcar, Alkeveien 5 and at the airport (☎77 67 56 00); Hertz, Richard Withsplass 4 and at the airport (☎77 62 44 00).
Diving and sea rafting Dykkersenteret AS, Stakkevollveien 72 (☎77 69 66 00, ⓦwww.dykkersenteret.no), organizes guided diving tours to local wrecks in the surrounding fjords. Also runs fishing and midnight-sun excursions and does equipment rental.

DNT Troms Turlag, next door to the tourist office at Kirkegata 2 (Wed noon–4pm, Thurs noon–6pm & Fri noon–2pm; ☎77 68 51 75, ⓦwww .turistforeningen.no/troms). DNT affiliate with bags of information on local hiking trails and DNT huts.
Hiking See DNT (above) and Outdoor Pursuits (p.361).
Internet Free access at Tromsø Bibliotek, on Grønnegata near Stortorget (Mon–Thurs 9am–7pm, Fri 9am–5pm, Sat 11am–3pm & Sun noon–4pm).

Maps and books Bokhuset Libris, Storgata 86 (℡77 68 30 36).

Outdoor pursuits Among several wilderness-tour specialists, Tromsø Villmarkssenter (Tromsø Wilderness Centre; ℡77 69 60 02, ⓦwww .villmarkssenter.no) offers a wide range of activities from guided glacier walks, kayak paddling and mountain climbing in summer, to ski trips and dog-sled rides in winter. Overnight trips staying in a *lavvo* (a Sámi tent) can also be arrranged. The Centre is located about 6km from downtown Tromsø, beyond the airport at Kvaløysletta, on the island of Kvaløya. See also Diving and DNT, p.360.

Pharmacy Vitus Apotek, opposite the *Radisson SAS Hotel* at Fr. Langes gate 9 (Mon–Fri 8.30am–4.30pm & Sat 10am–2pm).

Post office Main office at Strandgata 41 (Mon–Fri 8.30am–5pm, Sat 10am–2pm).

Taxi Tromsø Taxi ℡77 60 30 00 (24hr).

Vinmonopolet Grønnegata 64 (Mon–Fri 10am–6pm & Sat 10am–3pm).

Moving on from Tromsø – and Sommarøy

Running up from Narvik, Nor-Way Bussekspress's (ⓦwww.nor-way.no) **Nord-Norgeekspressen bus** leaves Tromsø to push on north to Alta (1 daily; 6hr 30min); it's a fine journey that begins on the E8, but then detours off along Highway 91 to take in two car-ferry rides – Breivikeidet to Svendsby and Lyngseidet to Olderdalen, which is back on the E6. At Alta, passengers change – and overnight – to catch the same company's **Nordkappekspressen bus** on to Honningsvåg (1–2 daily; 4hr), where they change again to get to Nordkapp (early June to late Aug 2 daily; 45min). There are also FFR buses (ⓦwww.ffr.no) from Alta to Hammerfest (Aug–June 1–3 daily except Sat, July 1–3 daily; 2hr 30min), Karasjok (1–2 daily except Sat; 5hr), Kautokeino (1–2 daily except Sat; 2hr 15min) and Kirkenes (3 weekly; 10–13hr).

Northbound, the **Hurtigrute coastal boat** (ⓦwww.hurtigruten.no) leaves Tromsø daily at 6.30pm, taking twelve hours to reach Hammerfest; southbound it sails at 1.30am, arriving in Harstad six and a half hours later. The main **Hurtigbåt passenger express boat** service links Tromsø with Harstad (2–3 daily; 2hr 45min; ⓦwww .hurtigruten.no); there are no boats between Tromsø and Alta.

For **drivers**, the quickest route from Tromsø to Alta is south along the E8 and then north on the E6, a total distance of about 410km. The shortest route – and also the prettiest – is, however, the one followed by the Nord-Norgeekspressen bus along Highway 91 and taking in a couple of car ferries – Breivikeidet to Svendsby (every 1–2hr; Mon–Fri 6am–10pm, Sat 8am–8pm, Sun 10am–9pm; 25min; ⓦwww.bjorklid .no) and Lyngseidet to Olderdalen, on the E6 (every 1–2hr; Mon–Fri 7am–8pm, Sat 9am–7pm, Sun 10.30am–8pm; 40min; ⓦwww.bjorklid.no).

As you drive west from Tromsø past the airport, Highway 862 crosses the Sandnessundet straits to reach the mountainous island of **Kvaløya**, whose three distinct parts are joined by a couple of narrow isthmuses. On the far side of the straits, Highway 862 meanders south offering lovely fjord and mountain views en route to the **Brensholmen–Botnhamn** car ferry (May–Aug 5–7 daily; 45min; ⓦwww.senjafergene .no), about 60km from Tromsø. From Botnhamn, it's a further 160km to Gryllefjord, where a second car ferry (late May to mid-June & early to late Aug 2 daily; mid-June to early Aug 3 daily; 2hr; ⓦwww.senjafergene.no; reservations advised) takes you across to Andenes on Vesterålen (see p.327).

The best place to break your journey hereabouts is on the tiny islet of **Sommarøy**, which is linked to Kvaløya by a causeway that branches off Highway 862 a few kilometres short of Brensholmen. Sommarøy is home to the relaxing *Sommarøy Kurs og Feriesenter* (℡77 66 40 00, ⓦwww.sommaroy.no), which offers hotel accommodation (❺) in the main building, plus high-quality, well-equipped seashore cabins for up to ten people; the smallest, the six-berth cabins, cost 1590kr per day. The restaurant is excellent too, particularly its Arctic specialities, and there are two traditional *badestamp* – wooden hot-tubs seating up to ten people – one inside and one outdoors, next to the ocean.

Into Finnmark: from Tromsø to Alta

Beyond Tromsø, the vast sweep of the northern landscape slowly unfolds, with silent fjords cutting deep into the coastline beneath ice-tipped peaks which themselves fade into the high plateau of the interior. This forbidding, elemental terrain is interrupted by the occasional valley, where those few souls hardy enough to make a living in these parts struggle on – often by dairy farming. In summer, cut grass dries everywhere, stretched over wooden poles that form long lines on the hillsides. Curiously enough, a particular problem for the farmers here is the abundance of Siberian garlic (*Allium sibiricum*): the cows love the stuff, but if they eat a lot of it, the milk they produce tastes of onions.

Slipping along the valleys and traversing the mountains in between, the **E8** and then the **E6** follow the coast pretty much all the way from Tromsø to Alta, some 410km – and about nine-hours' drive – to the north. Drivers can save around 100km (although not necessarily time and certainly not money) by turning off the E8 25km south of Tromsø on to **Highway 91** – a quieter, even more scenic route, offering extravagant fjord and mountain views. Highway 91 begins by cutting across the rocky peninsula that backs on to Tromsø to reach the **Breivikeidet–Svendsby car ferry** (every 1–2hr; Mon–Fri 6am–10pm, Sat 8am–8pm, Sun 10am–9pm; 25min; 76kr car and driver; ℡177, ⓦwww.bjorklid .no) over to the glaciated Lyngen peninsula. From the Svendsby ferry dock, it's just 24km over the Lyngen to the **Lyngseidet–Olderdalen car ferry** (every 1–2hr; Mon–Fri 7am–8pm, Sat 9am–7pm, Sun 10.30am–8pm; 40min; 107kr car and driver; ℡177, ⓦwww.bjorklid.no), by means of which you can rejoin the E6 at Olderdalen, some 220km south of Alta. This route is at its most spectacular between Svendsby and Lyngseidet, with the road nudging along a narrow channel flanked by the imposing peaks of the Lyngsalpene, or Lyngen Alps.

Beyond Olderdalen, the E6 eventually enters the province of **Finnmark** as it approaches the hamlet of **LANGFJORDBOTN**, at the head of the long and slender Langfjord. Thereafter, the road sticks tight against the coast to reach, after another 60km, the tiny village of **KÅFJORD**, whose sympathetically restored nineteenth-century church was built by the English company who operated the area's copper mines until they were abandoned as uneconomic in the 1870s. The Kåfjord itself is a narrow and sheltered arm of the Altafjord, which was used as an Arctic hideaway by the *Tirpitz* and other German battleships during World War II. From here, it's just 20km further to Alta.

Alta

First impressions of **ALTA** are not encouraging. With a population of just 17,000, the town comprises a string of unenticing, modern settlements that spread along the E6 for several kilometres. The ugliest part is **Alta Sentrum**, now befuddled by a platoon of soulless concrete blocks. Alta was interesting once – for a couple of centuries not Norwegian at all but Finnish and Sámi, and host to an ancient and much-visited Sámi fair. World War II polished off the fair and destroyed all the old wooden buildings that once clustered together in Alta's oldest district, **Bossekop**, where Dutch whalers settled in the seventeenth century.

Alta's prehistoric rock carvings

For all that, Alta does have one remarkable feature, the most extensive area of **prehistoric rock carvings** in northern Europe, the **Helleristningene i Hjemmeluft** (Rock Carvings in Hjemmeluft), which are impressive enough to have been designated a UNESCO World Heritage Site. The carvings are located

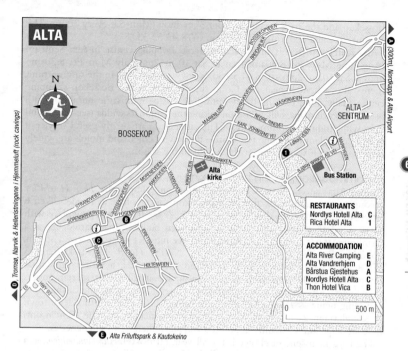

Within the map image:
ALTA

N

BOSSEKOP

ALTA SENTRUM

Alta kirke

Bus Station

RESTAURANTS
Nordlys Hotell Alta   C
Rica Hotel Alta   1

ACCOMMODATION
Alta River Camping   E
Alta Vandrerhjem   D
Bårstua Gjestehus   A
Nordlys Hotell Alta   C
Thon Hotel Vica   B

0   500 m

Tromsø, Narvik & Hellerisitningene i Hjemmeluft (rock cavings)

(300m), Nordkapp & Alta Airport

E, Alta Friluftspark & Kautokeino

beside the E6, some 2.5km before the Bossekop district as you approach Alta from the southwest, and they form part of the **Alta Museum** (May daily 9am–6pm; June to late Aug daily 8am–9pm; late Aug daily 8am–6pm; Sept daily 9am–6pm; Oct–April Mon–Fri 9am–3pm, Sat & Sun 11am–4pm; ⓦwww.alta .museum.no; May–Sept 85kr, Oct–April 45kr). A visit begins in the museum building, where there's a wealth of background information on the carvings in particular and on prehistoric Finnmark in general. It also offers a potted history of the Alta area, with exhibitions on the salmon-fishing industry, copper mining and so forth. The **rock carvings** themselves extend down the hill from the museum to the fjordside. A clear and easy-to-follow footpath and boardwalk circumnavigate the site, taking in all the carvings in about an hour. On the trail, there are a dozen or so **vantage points** offering close-up views of the carvings, recognizable though highly stylized representations of boats, animals and people picked out in red pigment (the colours have been retouched by researchers). They make up an extraordinarily complex tableau, whose minor variations – there are **four identifiable bands** – in subject matter and design indicate successive historical periods. The carvings were executed between 2500 and 6000 years ago, and are indisputably impressive: clear, stylish, and touching in their simplicity. They provide an insight into a prehistoric culture that was essentially settled and largely reliant on the hunting of land animals, who were killed with flint and bone implements; sealing and fishing were of lesser importance. Many experts think it likely the carvings had spiritual significance because of the effort that was expended by the people who created them, but this is the stuff of conjecture.

Practicalities

Long-distance buses pull into the **bus station** just off the E6 at Alta Sentrum. From the bus station, there's a limited local bus service – *bybussen* – south to

Bossekop and the rock carvings, about 5km away (Mon–Sat every 30min–1hr; 10min). To call a taxi, ring Alta Taxi on ☎78 43 53 53.

Alta **tourist office** is in the Parksenteret shopping centre in Alta Sentrum (Aug–June Mon–Fri 8.30am–4pm & Sat 10am–2pm; July Mon–Fri 8.30am–6pm & Sat 10am–2pm; ☎78 44 50 50, ⓦwww.visitalta.no). In the summertime, there's also a branch near the Coop supermarket in the Bossekop shopping centre (daily: June & Aug 10am–6pm; July 10am–8pm; same number). Both issue free town maps, will advise on hiking the Finnmarksvidda (see p.370) and help with finding accommodation. The latter is a particularly useful service if you're dependent on public transport – the town's hotels and motels are widely dispersed – or if you're here at the height of the season.

Accommodation, eating and drinking

Among Alta's several **hotels**, one of the more appealing is the *Thon Hotel Vica*, a couple of minutes' walk from the Bossekop tourist office at Fogdebakken 6 (☎78 48 22 22, ⓦwww.thonhotels.com; ❼, sp/r ❹). It's a small, cosy place with smart, modern rooms, and occupies a wooden building that started out as a farmhouse; it has a suntrap of a terrace and free internet access. A second option, opposite the Bossekop tourist office, is *Nordlys Hotell Alta*, Bekkefaret 3 (☎78 45 72 00, ⓦwww.nordlyshotell.no; ❺, sp/r ❹), a rather uninviting mishmash of styles, but with large, comfortable if somewhat spartan rooms nonetheless. Alta also possesses a handful of guesthouses, with one of the more appealing being ⚔ *Bårstua Gjestehus*, just off the E6 on the north side of town at Kongleveien 2a (☎78 43 33 33, ⓦwww.baarstua.no; ❸). The eight rooms here are large and pleasantly appointed and all of them have kitchenettes.

The bargain-basement choice is the all-year, HI **hostel**, *Alta Vandrerhjem*, in a plain chalet in the countryside off the E6 about 6km southwest of Alta (☎48 24 11 69, ⓦwww.vandrerhjem.no; dorm beds 300–350kr, doubles ❷). The hostel has self-catering facilities, a café and a laundry. There's no public transport, but they will pick you up from Alta by prior arrangement. In the vicinity of Alta are several **campsites**. The best is the well-equipped, four-star *Alta River Camping* (☎78 43 43 53, ⓦwww.alta-river-camping.no), by the river about 5km out of town along Highway 93, which branches off the E6 in between Bossekop and the rock paintings. They have tent spaces here as well as hotel-style rooms (❷) and cabins (from 500kr per night for two).

Two of Alta's restaurants are members of the Arctic Menu scheme (see p.303) – one at *Nordlys Hotell Alta* (see above), the other at the (large and very smart) *Rica Hotel Alta*, in Alta Sentrum at Løkkeveien 61 (☎78 48 27 00). Both specialize in regional delicacies – cloudberries, reindeer and the like – and mains at both cost around 200kr.

Around Alta: Alta Friluftspark

Aside from the rock carvings, the only reason to linger hereabouts is the **Alta Friluftspark** (☎78 43 33 78, ⓦwww.alta-friluftspark.no), 20km to the south of town off Highway 93, beside the river in Storelvdalen. Here, all manner of Finnmark experiences are on offer, from snowmobile tours, dog-sled trips, ice-fishing and reindeer racing in winter, to summer fishing and boat trips along the 400m-deep Sautso canyon, Scandinavia's largest.

The Friluftspark also boasts an **Igloo Hotell** (mid-Jan to mid-April; ❾), a 100-bed, 1100-square-metre hotel built entirely out of ice and snow, including the beds and the glasses in the bar. Staying here is really fun, but the hotel is fantastically popular, so advance reservations are well-nigh essential.

Moving on from Alta

Alta is something of a transport hub. The **Nordkappekspressen** (North Cape Express Bus; ⓦwww.nor-way.no) runs direct from Narvik to Alta (2 daily except Sat; 9hr 30min), where passengers overnight before picking up the second leg of the Nordkappekspressen to Honningsvåg (1–3 daily; 4hr); here they change for Nordkapp (early June to late Aug 2 daily; 45min). The Nordkappekspressen links in with the **Nord-Norgeekspressen** (North Norway Express Bus), which runs north from Bodø and Fauske to Alta in three segments: Bodø to Narvik via Fauske (2 daily; 6hr 30min); Narvik to Tromsø (1–3 daily; 4hr); and Tromsø to Alta (1 daily; 6hr 30min).

Other long-distance routings from Alta are provided by **FFR** (☏177, ⓦwww.ffr.no). They operate buses from Alta to Karasjok (1–2 daily except Sat; 5hr) and Kirkenes (3 weekly; 10–13hr) along the E6; to Hammerfest (Aug–June 1–3 daily except Sat, July 1–3 daily; 2hr 30min); and across the Finnmarksvidda to Kautokeino (1–2 daily except Sat; 2hr 15min). Note, however, that there are no buses between Kautokeino and Karasjok. Finally, there is also an FFR **Hurtigbåt passenger express boat** from Alta to Hammerfest (1 daily; 1hr 30min; 266kr one-way)

The Finnmarksvidda

Venture far inland from Alta and you enter the **Finnmarksvidda**, a vast mountain plateau which spreads southeast up to and beyond the Finnish border. Rivers, lakes and marshes lattice the region, but there's barely a tree, let alone a mountain, to break the contours of a landscape whose wide skies and deep horizons are eerily beautiful. Distances are hard to gauge – a dot of a storm can soon be upon you, breaking with alarming ferocity – and the air is crystal clear, giving a whiteish lustre to the sunshine. A couple of roads cross this expanse, but for the most part it remains the preserve of the few thousand semi-nomadic **Sámi** who make up the majority of the local population. Many still wear traditional dress, a brightly coloured affair of red bonnets and blue jerkins or dresses, all trimmed with red, white and yellow embroidery. You'll see permutations on this traditional costume all over Finnmark, but especially at roadside souvenir stalls and, on Sundays, outside Sámi churches.

Despite the slow encroachments of the tourist industry, lifestyles on the Finnmarksvidda have remained remarkably constant for centuries. The main occupation is **reindeer herding**, supplemented by hunting and fishing, and the pattern of Sámi life is still mostly dictated by these animals. During the winter, the reindeer graze the flat plains and shallow valleys of the interior, migrating towards the coast in early May as the snow begins to melt, and temperatures inland begin to climb, even reaching 30°C on occasion. By October, both people and reindeer are journeying back from their temporary summer quarters. The long, dark winter is spent in preparation for the great **Easter festivals**, when weddings and baptisms are celebrated in the region's two principal settlements, **Karasjok** and – more especially – **Kautokeino**. As neither place is particularly appealing in itself, this is without question the best time to be here, when the inhabitants celebrate the end of the polar night and the arrival of spring. There are folk-music concerts, church services and traditional sports, including the famed reindeer races – not, thank goodness, reindeers racing each other (they would never cooperate), but reindeer pulling passenger-laden sleds. Details of the Easter festivals are available at any Finnmark tourist office. Summer visits, on the other hand, can be disappointing, since many families and their reindeer are at coastal pastures and there is precious little activity.

From Alta, the only direct route into the Finnmarksvidda is south along **Highway 93** to Kautokeino, a distance of 130km. Just short of Kautokeino, about 100km from Alta, Highway 93 connects with **Highway 92**, which travels the 100km or so northeast to Karasjok, where you can rejoin the E6 (but well beyond the turning to Nordkapp). Operated by FFR (℡177, ⓦ www.ffr.no), **bus** services across the Finnmarksvidda are patchy: except on Saturdays, there are one or two buses a day from Alta to Kautokeino, a journey that takes two hours, but nothing between Kautokeino and Karasjok. There's also an FFR bus service from Alta to Karasjok along the E6 and this takes five hours and runs once or twice daily except on Saturdays when it doesn't run at all. A further service links Karasjok with Hammerfest once or twice daily (except on Sat) in just over four hours.

The best time to **hike** the Finnmarksvidda is in August and early September, after the peak mosquito season and before the weather turns cold. For the most part the plateau vegetation is scrub and open birch forest, which makes the going fairly easy, though the many marshes, rivers and lakes often impede progress. There are a handful of clearly demarcated **hiking trails** as well as a

The Sámi

The northernmost reaches of Norway, Sweden and Finland, plus the Kola peninsula of northwest Russia, are collectively known as **Lapland**. Traditionally, the indigenous population were called "Lapps", but in recent years this name has fallen out of favour and been replaced by the term **Sámi**, although the change is by no means universal. The new name comes from the Sámi word *sámpi* meaning both the land and its people, who now number around 70,000 scattered across the whole of the region. Among the oldest peoples in Europe, the Sámi are probably descended from prehistoric clans who migrated here from the east by way of the Baltic. Their **language** is closely related to Finnish and Estonian, though it's somewhat misleading to speak of a "Sámi language" as there are, in fact, three distinct versions, and each of these breaks down into a number of markedly different regional dialects. All three share many common features, however, including a superabundance of words and phrases to express variations in snow and ice conditions.

Originally, the Sámi were a semi-nomadic people, living in small communities (*siidas*), each of which had a degree of control over the surrounding hunting grounds. They mixed hunting, fishing and trapping, preying on all the edible creatures of the north, but it was the wild reindeer that supplied most of their needs. This changed in the sixteenth century when the Sámi switched over to **reindeer herding**, with communities following the seasonal movements of the animals. What little contact the early Sámi had with other Scandinavians was almost always to their disadvantage – as early as the ninth century, a Norse chieftain by the name of Ottar boasted to the English king Alfred the Great of his success in imposing a fur, feather and hide tax on his Sámi neighbours.

These early depredations were, however, nothing compared with the **dislocation of Sámi culture** that followed the efforts of Sweden, Russia and Norway to control and colonize Sámi land from the seventeenth century onwards. It took the best part of two hundred years for the competing nations finally to agree their northern frontiers – the last treaty, between Norway and Russia, was signed in 1826 – and meanwhile hundreds of farmers had settled in "Lapland", to the consternation of its native population. At the same time, in the manner of many colonized peoples, Norway's Sámi had accepted the **religion** of their colonizers, succumbing to the missionary endeavours of Pietist Protestants in the early eighteenth century. Predictably, the missionaries frowned upon the Sámi's traditional shamanism, although the more progressive among them did support the use of Sámi languages and even translated hundreds of books into their language. Things, however, got even worse smattering of appropriately sited but unstaffed huts; for detailed information, ask at Alta tourist office (see p.364).

Kautokeino

It's a two-hour drive or bus ride from Alta across the Finnmarksvidda to **KAUTOKEINO** (Guovdageaidnu in Sámi), the principal winter camp of the Norwegian Sámi and the site of a huge reindeer market in spring and autumn. The Sámi are not, however, easy town dwellers and although Kautokeino is very useful to them as a supply base, it's still a desultory, desolate-looking place straggling along Highway 93 for a couple of kilometres, with the handful of buildings that pass for the town centre gathered at the point where the road crosses the Kautokeinoelva river. Nevertheless, the settlement has become something of a tourist draw on account of the **jewellers**, who set up their stalls here every summer, attracting Finnish day-trippers like flies. The jewellery bigwigs hereabouts are **Frank and Regine Juhls**, who braved all sorts of

for the Norwegian Sámi towards the end of the nineteenth century, when the government, influenced by the Social Darwinism of the day, embarked on an aggressive policy of "**Norwegianization**". New laws banned the use of indigenous languages in schools, and only allowed Sámi to buy land if they could speak Norwegian. It was only in the 1950s that these policies were abandoned and slowly replaced by a more considerate, progressive approach.

More recently, the Sámi were dealt yet another grievous blow by the **Chernobyl nuclear disaster** of 1986. This contaminated not only the lichen that feeds the reindeer in winter, but also the game, fish, berries and fungi that supplement the Sámi diet. Contamination of the reindeer meat meant the collapse of the export market, and promises of compensation by the various national governments only appeared late in the day. Furthermore, the cash failed to address the fact that this wasn't just an economic disaster for the Sámi, but a threat to their traditional way of life, based around reindeer herding. Partly because of the necessarily reduced role of reindeer – reindeer herding is now the main occupation of just one-fifth of the Sámi population – other expressions of Sámi **culture** have expanded. Traditional arts and crafts are now widely available in all of Scandinavia's major cities and the first of several Sámi films, *Veiviseren* (The Pathfinder), was released to critical acclaim in 1987. Sámi music (*joik*) has also been given a hearing by world-music and jazz buffs. Although their provenance is uncertain, the rhythmic song-poems that constitute *joik* were probably devised to soothe anxious reindeer; the words are subordinated to the unaccompanied singing and at times are replaced altogether by meaningless, sung syllables.

Since the international anti-colonial struggles of the 1960s, the Norwegians have been obliged to thoroughly re-evaluate their relationship with the Sámi. In 1988, the country's constitution was amended by the addition of an article that read: "It is the responsibility of the authorities of the state to create conditions enabling the Sámi people to preserve and develop their language, culture and way of life." The following year a Sámi Parliament, the **Sameting**, was opened in Karasjok. Certain deep-seated problems do remain and, in common with other aboriginal peoples marooned in industrialized countries, there have been heated debates about land and mineral rights and the future of the Sámi as a people, above and beyond one country's international borders. Neither is it clear quite how the Norwegian Sámi will adjust to having something akin to dual status – as an indigenous, partly autonomous people and as citizens of a particular country – but at least Oslo is asking the right questions.

difficulties to set up their workshop here in 1959. It was a bold move at a time when the Sámi were very much a neglected minority, but the Juhls had a keen interest in nomadic cultures and, although the Sámi had no tradition of jewellery-making, they did adorn themselves with all sorts of unusual items traded in from the outside world. The Juhls were much influenced by this Sámi style of self-adornment, repeating and developing it in their own work, and

▲ Sámi couple in traditional costumes

their business prospered – perhaps beyond their wildest dreams – and they now have shops in Oslo (see p.120) and Bergen (see p.221). As further testimony to the Juhls' commercial success, the plain and simple workshop they first built has been replaced by **Juhls' Silver Gallery** (daily: June to early Aug 8.30am–9pm; early Aug to May 9am–6pm; ring in winter to confirm hours on ☏78 48 43 30, ⓦwww.juhls.no), an extensive complex of low-lying showrooms and workshops, whose pagoda-like roofs are derived from the Sámi. Exquisitely beautiful, high-quality silver work is made and sold here alongside a much broader range of classy craftwork. The complex's **interior** (regular, free guided tours; 30min) is intriguing in its own right, with some rooms decorated in crisp, modern pan-Scandinavian style, others done out in an elaborate version of Sámi design. The gallery is located on a ridge above the west bank of the Kautokeinoelva, 2.5km south of the town centre – follow the signs.

The rest of Kautokeino

Also south of the centre is the modern **Kautokeino kirke** (June to mid-Aug daily 9am–9pm; free), a delightful wooden building whose interior is decorated in bright, typically Sámi colours; it looks particularly appealing when the Sámi turn up here in their Sunday best. There are two more modest attractions on the north side of the river, beginning with the small **Kautokeino Bygdetun og Museum** (Guovdageaidnu Gilisillju or Kautokeino Parish Museum; mid-June to mid-Aug Mon–Sat 9am–7pm, Sun noon–7pm; mid-Aug to mid-June Mon–Fri 9am–3pm; 30kr), which features a history of the town inside and a number of draughty-looking Sámi dwellings outside. You'll spot the same little turf huts and skin tents (known as *lavvo*) all over Finnmark – often housing souvenir stalls. Not far away, and clearly signposted to the north, is the **Kautokeino Kulturhuset** (Guovdageaidnu Kulturviessu or Cultural Centre; ⓦwww.beaivvas.no). Winner of various architectural awards, the building houses the only state-sponsored Sámi theatre in Norway.

Practicalities

Buses to Kautokeino stop beside Highway 93 in the town centre on the north side of the river – and about 300m to the north of the **tourist office** (daily: late June to early Aug 9am–4pm; July 9am–8pm; ☏78 48 65 00, ⓦwww.kautokeino.nu). The latter provides town maps and has details of local events and activities, from fishing and hiking through to "**Sámi adventures**", which typically include a boat trip and a visit to a *lavvo* ("tent") where you can sample traditional Sámi food and listen to *joik* (rhythmic song-poems) for around 350kr. One leading local tour operator is Cavzo Safari (☏78 48 75 88, ⓦwww.cavzo.no).

Easily the largest **hotel** in Kautokeino is the *Thon Hotel Kautokeino*, in a fortress-like modern structure north of the river just off Highway 93 at Biedjovaggeluodda 2 (☏78 48 70 00, ⓦwww.thonhotels.no; June–Dec; ❼). There are seventy guest rooms here and each is decorated in a bright and breezy style. Alternatives include the modest and modern *Kautokeino Villmarkssenter*, across the highway from the tourist office at Hannoluohka 2 (☏78 48 76 02; ❷), and the *Arctic Motell & Camping*, near the river on the southern edge of town at Suomaluodda 16 (☏78 48 54 00, ⓦwww.kauto.no) with cabins (from 400kr) and a few frugal motel rooms (❷).

Eating establishments are thin on the ground, but there's good coffee, cakes and sandwiches at *Kaffe Galleriet*, behind the tourist office, and a full-scale restaurant at the *Thon Hotel*, which specializes in local dishes; mains here average 250kr.

Karasjok

The only other settlement of any size on the Finnmarksvidda is **KARASJOK** (Kárásjohka in Sámi), Norway's Sámi capital, which straddles the E6 on the main route from Finland to Nordkapp – and consequently sees plenty of tourists. Spread across a wooded river valley, the town has none of the desolation of Kautokeino, yet it still conspires to be fairly mundane despite the presence of the Sámi Parliament and the country's best Sámi museum. The busiest place in town is the **tourist office**, Karasjok Opplevelser (early June to mid-Aug daily 9am–7pm; rest of year Mon–Fri 9am–4pm; ☎78 46 88 00, ⓦwww.karasjokinfo.no), located on the north side of the river beside the E6 and Highway 92 crossroads, which is, to all intents and purposes, the centre of town. Staff here issue free town maps, book overnight accommodation and organize authentic(ish) Sámi expeditions. The office is also incorporated within a miniature Sámi theme park, **Sámpi Park** (same times; 100kr), which offers a fancy multimedia introduction to the Sámi in the Stálubákti ("Magic Theatre"). Here also are examples of traditional Sámi dwellings, Sámi shops and a restaurant plus displays of various ancient Sámi skills with the obligatory reindeer brought along as decoration or to be roped and coralled.

From the tourist office, it's a 200-metre walk north along the Nordkapp road to Museumsgata, where you turn right for **De Samiske Samlinger** (Sámi vourká dávvirat, Sámi Museum; June–Aug Mon–Fri 9am–6pm, Sat & Sun 10am–6pm; Sept–May Tues–Fri 9am–3pm; 75kr; ⓦwww.rdm.no). This attempts an overview of Sámi culture and history, with the outdoor exhibits comprising an assortment of old dwellings that illustrate the frugality of Sámi life. Inside, a large and clearly presented collection of incidental bygones includes a colourful sample of folkloric Sámi costumes.

Gamle kirke and the Samisk Kunstnersenter

On the south side of the river, just off Highway 92, you might also want to take a peek at the **Gamle kirke** (June–Aug daily 8am–9pm; free), the only building left standing in Karasjok at the end of World War II. Of simple design, it dates from 1807, making it easily the oldest-surviving church in Finnmark.

Carry on from the Gamle kirke along Highway 92, and the next major turning on the right leads along to the **Samisk Kunstnersenter** (Sámi daiddaguovddás, Sámi Artists' Centre; Mon–Fri 10am–5pm, Sat & Sun 1–4pm; free; ⓦwww.samiskkunstnersenter.no). This unassuming gallery showcases the work of contemporary Sámi artists, but don't expect folksy paintings – Sámi artists are a diverse bunch and as likely to be influenced by post modernism as reindeer herding.

Hikes and tours into the Finnmarksvidda

However diverting Karasjok's sights may be, you'll only get a real feel for the Finnmarksvidda if you venture out of town. The tourist office has the details of a wide range of local **guided tours**: options include dog-sledging, a visit to a Sámi camp, a boat trip on the Karasjokka river, cross-country skiing and even gold-panning. The region's most popular long-distance **hike** is the five-day haul across the heart of the Finnmarksvidda, from Karasjok to Alta via a string of strategically located huts; ask at Alta's tourist office (see p.364) for details, but note that this is not for the faint-hearted or inexperienced. A more gentle walk is the 3.5-kilometre **Ássebákti nature trail**, which passes more than a hundred Sámi cultural monuments – *lavvo* and so forth – on the way. Clearly signed, the trail head is about 16km west of Karasjok along Highway 92 towards Kautokeino.

Practicalities

There's a limited **bus** service from Alta to Karasjok along the E6 (1–2 daily except Sat; 5hr; ℡177, ⓦwww.ffr.no) and another FFR service from Hammerfest to Karasjok (1–2 daily except on Sat; 4hr), but there are currently no buses from Kautokeino. Schedules mean that it's often possible to spend a couple of hours here before moving on, which is quite enough to see the sights, but not nearly long enough to get the true flavour of the place. Buses pull into Karasjok **bus station**, on Storgata, from where it's a signposted five- to ten-minute walk west to the **tourist office** (see opposite).

The best **hotel** in town is the *Rica Hotel Karasjok* (℡78 46 88 60, ⓦwww .rica.no; ❼, sp/r ❺), a breezy modern establishment in a large chalet-like building a short stroll north of the tourist office along the E6. Much more distinctive, however, is ⚮ *Engholm's Husky Lodge* (℡78 46 71 66, ⓦwww .engholm.no), a fantastic all-year HI **hostel and lodge**, which has a number of home-made **cabins** from the large (23 dorm beds at 300kr per person) through to cosy four- to six-bed versions (800kr per night for 2 in a shared cabin, 600kr singles; full board 1800kr, 1000kr per person respectively). The hostel is open all year and offers self-catering facilities, a sauna and Arctic dinners, sitting on reindeer skins around an open fire. The owner, the illustrious Sven, is an expert dog-sled racer and keeps about forty huskies; he uses them on a variety of winter guided tours – dog-sledding and so forth – and in summer organizes everything from fishing trips and guided wilderness hikes to horseback riding. The hostel is 7km west out of town on the Kautokeino road (Highway 92), but that's no problem as Sven will pick up guests from Karasjok by prior arrangement for 100kr.

Sven hits all the gastronomic buttons, but the *Rica Hotel Karasjok* possesses the unusual *Storgammen* restaurant, a set of turf-covered huts where Sámi-style meals are served. It's all good fun, but the choices are pretty much limited to reindeer or salmon plus (delightful) cloudberries with sweetened cream. Reckon on 220kr for a main course.

From Karasjok, it's 130km west to Kautokeino, 270km north to Nordkapp, 220km northwest to Hammerfest, and 330km east to Kirkenes.

Hammerfest

HAMMERFEST, some 150km north of Alta, is, as its tourist office takes great pains to point out, the world's northernmost town. It was also, they add, the first town in Europe to have electric street-lighting. Hardly fascinating facts perhaps, but both give a glimpse of the pride the locals take in making the most of what is, indisputably, an inhospitable location. Indeed, it's a wonder the town has survived at all: a hurricane flattened the place in 1856; it was burnt to the ground in 1890; and the retreating Germans mauled it at the end of World War II. Yet, instead of being abandoned, Hammerfest was stubbornly rebuilt for a third time. Nor is it the grim industrial town you might expect from the proximity of the offshore oil wells, but a bright, cheerful port that drapes around a **horseshoe-shaped harbour** sheltered from the elements by a steep, rocky hill. Hammerfest also benefits from the occasional dignified wooden building that recalls its nineteenth-century heyday as the centre of the *Pomor* trade in which Norwegian fish were traded for boat-loads of Russian flour. But don't get too carried away: Bill Bryson, in *Neither Here Nor There*, hit the nail on the head with his description of

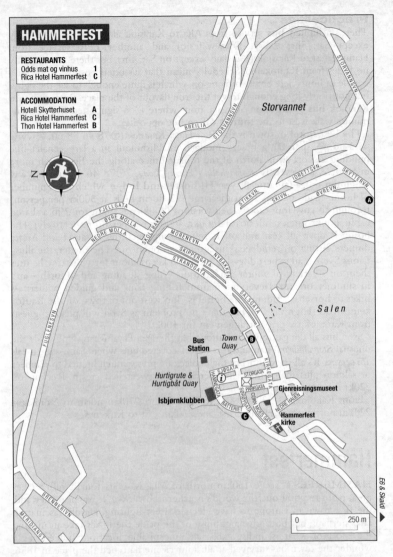

Hammerfest as "an agreeable enough town in a thank-you-God-for-not-making-me-live-here sort of way".

The Town

Running parallel to the waterfront, **Strandgata**, the town's principal street, is a busy, 500-metre-long run of supermarkets, clothes and souvenir shops, partly inspired by the town's role as a stop off for cruise ships on the way to Nordkapp. However, most of the activity takes place on the **old town** quay, off Sjøgata, with tourists emerging from the liners to beetle around the harbourfront, eating shellfish from the stalls along the wharf or buying souvenirs in the small, summertime Sámi market. The Hurtigrute spends a couple of hours at Hammerfest too, arriving at an unsociable 5.15am on its way north, and at a more palatable 11.15am heading south.

Beyond that, it's the general atmosphere of the place that appeals rather than any specific sight, though Hammerfest's tiny town centre does muster a couple of attractions, beginning with the **Isbjørnklubben** (Royal and Ancient Polar Bear Society; mid-June to mid-Aug Mon–Fri 6am–4pm, Sat & Sun 6am–3pm; rest of year Mon–Fri 10am–2pm, Sat & Sun 10.30am–1.30pm; 40kr), in the main quayside building at Hamnegata 3. The society's pint-sized museum – filled with stuffed polar bears and seal-skin-covered furniture – tells the story of Hammerfest as a trapping centre for polar bears, eagles and arctic fox, and gives the background to the creation of the society itself in 1963. Be sure you avoid the ceremony of being "knighted" with a walrus's penis bone – not only will it set you back 225kr, but it will make you cringe with embarrassment for weeks on end.

Gjenreisningsmuseet and Salen

Of more general interest is the purpose-built **Gjenreisningsmuseet** (Museum of Postwar Reconstruction; mid-June to mid-Aug Mon–Fri 9am–4pm, Sat & Sun 10am–2pm; mid-Aug to mid-June daily 11am–2pm; 50kr; ⓦwww.gjenreisningsmuseet.no), a five-minute walk west of the old town quay up Kirkegata. This begins with a fascinating section on the hardships endured by the inhabitants of Finnmark during the German retreat in the face of the advancing Russians in late 1944. The Germans ordered a general evacuation and then applied a scorched-earth policy, which left almost all of the region's towns and villages in ruins. Just in case any of his soldiers got the wrong idea, Hitler's orders stipulated that "Compassion for the population is out of place." Refugees in their own country, the Norwegians found shelter wherever they could and several thousand hid out in caves until May 1945, though many died from cold and malnutrition. Subsequent sections of the museum deal with postwar reconstruction, giving a sharply critical account of the central government bureaucracy initially put in charge. Under the weight of complaints, it was disbanded in 1948 and control was passed back to the municipalities. Interestingly, the left-wing Labour Party, who co-ordinated the reconstruction programme, adopted an almost evangelical stance, crusading against dirtiness, inequality and drunkenness in equal measure. As the labelling is only in Norwegian – though this may change – it's worth investing in the English-language guidebook.

For something a little more energetic, take the **footpath** that zigzags up **Salen**, the hill behind town. It takes about fifteen minutes to reach the plateau at the top, from where there are panoramic views out across the town and over to the nearby islands. The footpath begins a couple of minutes' walk from the old town quay on Salsgata, one block south of Strandgata.

Arrival and information

Some 60km from the E6 along Highway 94, Hammerfest is situated on the western shore of the rugged island of Kvaløya, which is linked to the mainland by bridge. Buses pull into Hammerfest **bus station** at the foot of Sjøgata; the **Hurtigrute coastal boat** docks at the adjacent quay, as does the FFR (ⓉI177 or locally Ⓣ78 41 73 50, Ⓦwww.ffr.no) **Hurtigbåt passenger express boat** from Alta (1–2 daily except Sat; 1hr 30min; 266kr). The **tourist office** (mid-June to mid-Aug daily 9am–5pm; mid-Aug to mid-June daily 10.30am–1.30pm;

⊤78 41 31 00, ⓦwww.hammerfest-turist.no) is just a few metres away at Hamnegata 3, in the same building as the Isbjørnklubben (see p.373). It issues free town maps and has details of local excursions, easily the most popular of which are the fishing trips and the summertime sea cruises to local bird cliffs, which seethe and squawk with guillemot, gannet and kittiwake, Among many other types of sea birds.

Accommodation and eating

Hammerfest is light on places to stay, but there are two good **hotels**. First choice should be the 🛪 *Rica Hotel Hammerfest*, Sørøygata 15 (⊤78 42 57 00, ⓦwww.rica.no; ➐, sp/r ➍), an attractive and well-maintained modern place with sea views that sits on a grassy knoll a couple of minutes' walk west of the main quay. There's also the enjoyable *Thon Hotel Hammerfest*, Strandgata 2–4 (⊤78 42 96 00, ⓦwww.thonhotels.no; ➐, sp/r ➍), which occupies a prime spot just metres from the old town quay; it's housed in a routine modern block, but the cosy interior has a pleasant, slightly old-fashioned air, the bedrooms equipped with chunky wooden fittings that (mostly) predate the chipboard mania of today. The only budget hotel is *Hotell Skytterhuset*, Skytterveien 24 (⊤78 41 15 11, ⓦwww.skytterhuset.no; ➍, sp/r ➋), which, despite appearances – it's in a long, low prefabricated block originally built to house migrant fish-factory workers – has a pleasant, modern interior of pastel furnishings and laminate wooden floors. The only drawback is the location: the hotel is stuck on a windswept hillside, some 3km from and behind the town centre. To get there by car, head northeast from the main harbourfront along Strandgata and, after about 500m, just over the stream, turn right along Skolebakken. This leads into Storvannsveien, which circum-navigates Lake Storvannet, a gloomy pool at the bottom of a steep-sided valley dotted with the houses of Hammerfest's one and only suburb; the

---

Moving on from Hammerfest

From Hammerfest, **FFR buses** (⊤177, ⓦwww.ffr.no) run to Alta (Aug–June 1–3 daily except Sat; July 1–3 daily; 2hr 30min), Karasjok along the E6 (1–2 daily except Sat; 4hr) and Kirkenes (2 weekly; 10hr). All these buses pass through **Skaidi**, on the E6, where you change for the **Nordkappekspressen bus** (ⓦwww.nor-way.no) service on to Honningsvåg (1–3 daily); at Honningsvåg, you change yet again for Nordkapp (early June to early Sept 2 daily; 45min). Note that not all the Hammerfest buses make the Nordkappekspressen connection at Skaidi, so check at the bus station before you set out. FFR also operates **Hurtigbåt passenger express boats** from Hammerfest to Alta (1–2 daily except Sat; 1hr 30min; 266kr).

The **Hurtigrute** coastal boat (ⓦwww.hurtigruten.no) sails north daily from Hammerfest at 6.45am and reaches Honningsvåg at 11.45am. At Honningsvåg, it pauses for three and a half hours, plenty enough time for special connecting buses to make the return trip to Nordkapp. Southbound, the Hurtigrute does not overlay at Honningsvåg and reaches Hammerfest at 11.15am, departing 12.45pm and taking eleven hours to reach its next major port of call, Tromsø. Port-to-port passenger fares are bearable: Hammerfest to Honningsvåg costs just 440kr from mid-April to mid-September, 308kr from mid-September to mid-April.

Finally, Hammerfest has several **car rental** companies and they frequently offer attractive short-term deals from around 700kr a day unlimited mileage. Try Europcar (⊤93 00 44 55) or Hertz (⊤78 41 71 66). If, however, Nordkapp is your goal, comparable rental deals may be available at Honningsvåg (see p.377), 180km north from Hammerfest.

hotel is on the hillside above the far side of the lake – the turning is clearly signed. Unless you're particularly energetic, you'll not want to walk here from the centre – it's too hilly – so take a taxi.

For **food**, the *Rica Hotel Hammerfest* (see opposite*)* possesses the best **restaurant** in town, with ocean views and delicious seafood; main courses start at around 250kr. Slightly more economical is *Odds mat og vinhus*, Strandgata 24 (Mon–Fri 2.30pm–midnight, Sat 6pm–1am; ☎78 41 37 66), where they specialize in local ingredients, from grouse and hare to salmon and char; mains here begin at 220kr.

Magerøya and Nordkapp

At the northern tip of Norway, the treeless and windswept island of **Magerøya** is mainly of interest to travellers as the location of the **Nordkapp** (North Cape), generally regarded as Europe's northernmost point – though in fact it isn't: that distinction belongs to **Kinnarodden**, a remote headland about 80km further to the east on a different island altogether. Somehow, everyone seems to have conspired to ignore this simple latitudinal fact and now, while Nordkapp has become one of the most popular tourist destinations in the country, there isn't even a road to Kinnarodden, which can only be reached on a long and difficult 25-kilometre hike from the Hurtigrute port of **Mehamn**. Neither has the development of the Nordkapp as a tourist spot been without its critics, who argue that the large and lavish visitor centre – **Nordkapphallen** – is crass and grossly overpriced; their opponents simply point to the huge number of people who visit. Whichever side you're on, it's hard to imagine making the long trip to Magerøya without at least dropping by Nordkapp, and the island has other charms too, notably a bleak, rugged beauty that's readily seen from the **E69** as it threads across the mountainous interior from Honningsvåg, on the south coast, to Nordkapp, a distance of 34km.

The obvious base for a visit to Nordkapp is the island's main settlement, **Honningsvåg**, a middling fishing village with a clutch of chain hotels. More appealing, however, is the tiny hamlet of **Kamøyvær**, nestling beside a narrow fjord just off the E69 between Honningsvåg and Nordkapp, and with a couple of family-run guesthouses. Bear in mind also that Nordkapp is within easy striking distance of other places back on the mainland – certainly the picturesque fishing-station-cum-hotel at **Repvåg**, and maybe even Hammerfest (see p.371) and Alta (see p.362), respectively 210km and 240km away.

Getting to Magerøya and Nordkapp

Arriving along the E6 and then the E69 from Alta and Skaidi (for Hammerfest), Nor-Way Bussekspress's **Nordkappekspressen bus** (1–3 daily; ⊛www .nor-way.no) stops at Honningsvåg, where passengers change for the FFR service (☎177, ⊛www.ffr.no) on to Nordkapp (early June to early Sept 2 daily; 45min). The schedule is such that if you take the first bus from Honningsvåg to Nordkapp, you can spend a couple of hours there before catching the first bus back. If you take the second bus, you'll arrive at Nordkapp at 10.15pm with the return bus departing two hours later at 12.15am, which means, of course, that you can view the midnight sun. Note also that, depending on timings, you can wait for as little as fifteen minutes and as much as two and a half hours between arriving at Honningsvåg on the Nordkappekspressen and leaving for Nordkapp with FFR. Finally, the Hurtigrute coastal boat arrives in Honningsvåg twice

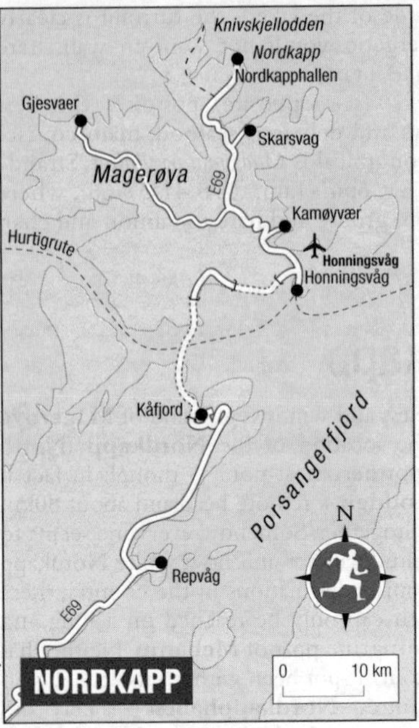
Knivskjellodden
Nordkapp
Nordkapphallen
Gjesvaer
Skarsvag
Magerøya
E69
Kamøyvær
Hurtigrute
Honningsvåg
Honningsvåg
Kåfjord
Porsangerfjord
N
Repvåg
E69
Olderfjord & E6
NORDKAPP
0
10 km

daily (once going north, once south), but on neither occasion does its arrival match FFR bus times; alternative transport to Nordkapp is provided for passengers, however – ask on board.

Buses apart, the best way of proceeding from Honningsvåg to Nordkapp is to rent a car or take a taxi. Honningsvåg tourist office has the details of local **car hire** companies offering special deals – reckon on 800kr for a five-hour rental. The **taxi fare** to Nordkapp, including an hour's waiting time after you get there, is about 900kr return, 500kr one-way; contact Nordkapp Taxisentral (☎78 47 22 34). Arriving **by car**, bear in mind that the last stretch of the Honningsvåg–Nordkapp road is closed by snow in winter, roughly from November to early April. To stand a chance of seeing the northern lights, try to go when the weather is clear.

North from Skaidi to Repvåg and Magerøya island

Beyond the **Skaidi** crossroads, located at the end of Highway 94 from Hammerfest, the **E6** veers east to clip across a bleak plateau that brings it, 23km later, to the turning for Nordkapp. This turning, the **E69**, scuttles north along the shore of the **Porsangerfjord**, a deep and wide inlet flanked by bare, low-lying hills whose stone has been fractured and made flaky by the biting cold of winter. Here and there, massive monoliths interrupt the coast, but for the most part the scenery is unusually tame and the shoreline accommodates a string of fishermen's houses – plus the wooden racks used to air-dry their catch. After 48km, the E69 zips past the byroad to **REPVÅG**, an old timber fishing-station on a promontory just 2km off the main highway. A rare and particularly picturesque survivor from pre war days, the station is painted red in the traditional manner and perches on stilts on the water's edge. The whole complex has been turned into the *Repvåg Fjordhotell og Rorbusenter* (☎78 47 54 40, ⓦwww.repvag-fjordhotell.no; May to late Sept), with simple, unassuming rooms (❷–❸) in the main building, as well as a cluster of old fishermen's shacks – *rorbuer* (650–750kr for 2). It's a charming place to stay – solitary and scenic in equal proportions, the public areas of the hotel decked out with authentic nautical tackle and cosy furniture. Neither is tourism the only concern of the owners, as is evidenced by the split cod nailed to the outside walls to dry. Repvåg is an ideal base from which to reach Nordkapp, though once you're ensconced here, you may settle instead for one of the hotel's boat and fishing trips out on the Porsangerfjord. Almost inevitably, the hotel **restaurant** specializes in seafood – and very good it is too.

Back on the E69, it's about 25km to the ambitious series of tunnels and bridges (145kr toll) that spans the straits between the mainland and Honningsvåg, on the island of **Magerøya**, which you'll spy long before you get there, a hunk of brown rock looking like an inverted blancmange.

Honningsvåg

HONNINGSVÅG, 180km from Hammerfest and just 2km off the E69, is officially classified as a village, which robs it of the title of the world's north-ernmost town – hard luck considering it's barely any smaller nor less hardy in the face of adversity than its neighbour and rival, Hammerfest. The village largely comprises a jumble of well-worn modern buildings that reflect its role as a minor fishing- and sea-port. It straggles along the seashore, sheltered from the blizzards of winter by the surrounding crags – though, given the conditions, sheltered is a comparative term. Honningsvåg has accumulated several chain hotels, which make a steady living from the tourists who stream through bound for the Nordkapp, and is at its prettiest at the **head of the harbour**, where an assortment of timber warehouses, dating back to the days when the village was entirely reliant on fish, makes an attractive ensemble. Draped with fishing nets and tackle, these good-looking buildings perch on crusty timber stilts that jut out into the water. They have wide eaves to protect against the snow, and each has its own jetty where fishing smacks are roped in tight against the wind.

Practicalities

Honningsvåg strings out along its main drag for about 1km. Buses from the mainland, including the long-distance Nord-Norgeekspressen, pull into the **bus station** at its southern end. **Hurtigrute** coastal boats dock at the adjacent jetty, with northbound boats arriving at 11.45am and departing 3.15pm; southbound, the boats don't overlay here, arriving and departing at 6.15am; the northbound service is met by special Nordkapp excursion buses – details on board. The **tourist office** is here too (mid-June to mid-Aug Mon–Fri 8.30am–8pm, Sat & Sun noon–8pm; rest of year Mon–Fri 8.30am–4pm; ☎78 47 70 30, ⓦ www .nordkapp.no).

All of Honningsvåg's **hotels** are along or near the main street. Walking south from the bus station, it's a few metres to the first, the *Rica Hotel Honningsvåg* (☎78 47 72 20, ⓦ www.rica.no; mid-May to Aug; ❹), a routine modern block with nearly two hundred modern rooms. Its sister hotel, the *Rica Bryggen* (☎78 47 72 50, ⓦ www.rica.no; June–Aug; ❺), occupies a similar but slightly smarter concrete high-rise about 500m to the east, down at the head of the harbour. The rooms here are bright, modern and comfortable, but hardly inspiring. More appealing is the adjacent *Honningsvåg Brygge Hotel* (☎78 47 64 64, ⓦ www.hvg-brygge.no; ❺), a tasteful and intel-ligent conversion of a set of wooden warehouses perched on one of the old jetties. The rooms are neat and cosy – and advance reservations are strongly advised. For lighter wallets, there's an HI **hostel**, *Nordkapp Vandrerhjem*, a twenty-minute walk north of Honningsvåg – and just 1km from the end of the tunnel from the mainland (☎91 82 41 56, ⓦ www.vandrerhjem.no; May–Dec; dorm beds 330kr, doubles ❷). There are self-catering facilities here, but no café or restaurant. Also at the bargain end of things is *NAF Nordkapp Camping* (☎78 47 33 77, ⓦ www.nordkappcamping.no; May–Sept), comprising a **campsite** and **cabins** (from 500kr per night) and located 9km from Honningsvåg on the road to Nordkapp.

For **food**, the *Honningsvåg Brygge Hotel* boasts the best **restaurant** by far, the *Sjøhuset* (June to early Aug daily 2–11pm; limited hours the rest of year), where the seafood is delicious and main courses hover around 220kr; reservations are strongly advised, as preference is given to hotel guests.

North from Honningsvåg

The E69 winds its way out of Honningsvåg, staying close to the shore for the first part of its journey north. After 9km, just beyond the conspicuous *Rica Hotel Nordkapp*, you'll spot the turning for **KAMØYVÆR**, a pretty little village tucked in tight between the sea and the hills, just 2km from the main road. Here, metres from the jetty, is the *Hotel Árran Nordkapp* (℡78 47 51 29, ⊛www.arran .as; ❹; May to early Sept), a pleasant, family-run hotel, whose forty-odd guest rooms are distributed among several brightly painted and well-tended houses. They serve dinner here too, though it's best to book it ahead of time.

Beyond the Kamøyvær turning, the E69 twists a solitary course up through the hills to cross a high-tundra plateau, the mountains stretching away on either side. It's a fine run, with snow and ice lingering well into the summer and impressive views over the treeless and elemental Arctic terrain. From June to October this is pastureland for herds of reindeer, who graze right up to the road, paying little heed to the passing vehicles unless they wander too close. The Sámi, who bring them here by boat, combine herding with souvenir selling, setting up camp at the roadside in full costume to peddle clothes, jewellery and sets of antlers, which some motorists are daft enough to attach to the front of their vehicles. About 29km from Honningsvåg, the E69 passes the start of the well-marked **hiking trail** that leads to the headland of **Knivskjellodden**, stretching about 1500m further north than its famous neighbour. The eighteen-kilometre hike – there and back – takes between two and three hours each way, but although the terrain isn't so severe, the climate is too unpredictable for the novice or poorly equipped hiker.

Nordkapp

When they finally reach **Nordkapp** (North Cape), many visitors feel desperately disappointed – it is, after all, only a cliff and, at 307m, it isn't even all that high. But for others there's something about this greyish-black hunk of slate, stuck at the end of a bare, wind-battered promontory, that exhilarates the senses. Some such feeling must have inspired the prehistoric Sámi to establish a sacrificial site here, and the Nordkapp certainly stirred the romantic notions of earlier generations of tourists, often inspiring them to metaphysical ruminations. In 1802, the Italian naturalist Giuseppe Acerbi, author of *Travels through Sweden, Finland and Lapland*, exclaimed, "The northern sun, creeping at midnight along the horizon, and the immeasurable ocean in apparent contact with the skies, form the grand outlines in the sublime picture presented to the astonished spectator." Quite – though the seventeenth-century traveller Francesco Negri wasn't far behind: "Here, where the world comes to an end, my curiosity does as well, and now I can return home content."

Flights of fancy apart, North Cape was named by the English explorer **Richard Chancellor** in 1553, as he drifted along the Norwegian coast in an attempt to find the Northeast Passage from the Atlantic to the Pacific. He failed, but managed to reach the White Sea, from where he and his crew travelled overland to Moscow, thereby opening a new, northern trade route to Russia. Chancellor's account, published in the geographer Richard Hakluyt's *Naviga-tions*, brought his exploits to the attention of seamen across Europe, but it was to be another three hundred years before the Northeast Passage was finally negoti-ated by the Swede, Nils Nordenskjøld, in 1879. In the meantime, just a trickle of visitors ventured to the Nordkapp. Among them, in 1795, was the exiled Louis Philippe of Orleans (subsequently king of France), but it was the visit of the Norwegian king **Oscar II** in 1873 that opened the tourist floodgates.

Nordkapphallen

Nowadays the lavish **Nordkapphallen** (North Cape Hall; daily: early May 11am–3pm; late May to Aug 11am–1am; Sept 11am–3pm; 200kr for 48hr, including parking; ⓦwww.rica.no), cut into the rock of the Cape, entertains hundreds of visitors every day. Fronted by a statue of King Oscar II, the main building contains a restaurant, café, a post office where you get your letters specially stamped, and a cinema showing – you guessed it – films about the Cape. There's a viewing area too, but there's not much to see except the sea – and, weather permitting, the midnight sun from May 12 to July 29. Gluttons for financial punishment can stay here too, from May to September, in *Suite 71° 10' 21"* (ⓣ78 47 68 60, ⓦwww.rica.no) – as in Nordkapp's latitude. At the top of the building's one and only tower, the suite offers a 270-degree view through its enormous windows and is a favourite with honeymooners, though quite why this should be considered a romantic spot is hard to discern. If it's booked in advance, the suite costs around 4000kr per night, but the price tumbles to half that if it's rented on spec.

A **tunnel** runs from the main building to the cliff face. It's flanked by a couple of little side-chambers, in one of which is a chapel where you can get married, and by a series of displays detailing past events and visitors, including the unlikely appearance of the king of Siam in 1907, who was so ill that he had to be carried up here from his boat on a stretcher. At the far end, the cavernous *Grotten Bar* offers caviar and champagne, long views out to sea through the massive glass wall and (of all things) a mock bird-cliff. Alternatively, to escape the hurly-burly, you may decide to walk out on to the surrounding headland, though this is too bleak a spot to be much fun.

East to Kirkenes

East of Nordkapp the landscape is more of the same – a relentless expanse of barren plateaux, mountain and ocean. Occasionally a determined village relieves the monotony with commanding views over the fjords that slice deep into the mainland, but generally there is little for the eyes of a tourist. Nor is there much to do in what are predominantly fishing and industrial settlements, and there are few tangible attractions beyond the sheer impossibility of the chill wilderness.

The **E6** weaves a circuitous course across this vast territory, hugging the Finnish border for much of its length. The only obvious target is the Sámi centre of **Karasjok** (see p.370), 270km from Nordkapp and 220km from Hammerfest and easily the region's most interesting town. Frankly, there's not much reason to push on further east unless you're intent on picking up the **Hurtigrute coastal boat** as it bobs along the remote and spectacular shores of the Barents Sea. Among the Hurtigrute's several ports of call, perhaps the most diverting is **Kirkenes**, 320km to the east of Karasjok at the end of the E6 and near the Russian frontier: if any European town comes close to defining remoteness then this surely must be it. Kirkenes is the northern terminus of the Hurtigrute, from where it begins its long journey south to Bergen. Taking the boat also means that you can avoid the long haul back the way you came – and by the time you reach Kirkenes you'll certainly be heartily sick of the E6. The other shortcut is to **fly**: Kirkenes has its own airport and from here there are regular Widerøe (ⓦ www.wideroe.no) flights to a hatful of north Norwegian towns, including Alta, Hammerfest and Tromsø; as a sample fare, a single ticket from Kirkenes to Alta can go for as little as 600kr, though 800kr is a more usual fare. A subsidiary of SAS airlines, Widerøe flies to no fewer than fourteen airports – and airstrips – in Troms and Finnmark. As regards **buses**, FFR (ⓣ 177, ⓦ www.ffr.no) reaches most corners of Finnmark with reasonable regularity, but its principal long-distance services link Hammerfest with Alta and Alta with Kirkenes along the E6, via Skaidi, Olderfjord, Karasjok and Tana Bru; the whole Alta–Kirkenes journey takes between ten and thirteen hours and there are three buses weekly. Many of FFR's services operate all year, as the E6 and some other main roads are kept open throughout the winter, but this does not imply that **drivers** will find conditions straightforward: ice and snow can make the roads treacherous, if not temporarily impassable, at any time, and driving through the long polar darkness (late Nov to late Jan) is extremely disorientating. Note also that if you are using a **car hire**, one-way, drop-off charges in Norway are almost invariably exorbitant.

Finally, **accommodation** is very thin on the ground, being confined to a handful of the larger communities. Reservations, therefore, are strongly advised. Campsites are more frequent and usually have cabins for rent, but they are mostly stuck in the middle of nowhere.

East from Nordkapp on the E6

Beyond its junction with the E69 Nordkapp road, the **E6** bangs along the western shore of the **Porsangerfjord**, a wide inlet that slowly shelves up into the sticky marshes and mud flats at its head. After about 45km, the road reaches the hamlet of **STABBURSNES**, which is home to the small but enjoyable **Stabbursnes Naturhus og Museum** (Stabbursnes Nature House and Museum; early June daily 11am–6pm; mid-June to mid-Aug daily 9am–8pm; late Aug daily 9am–6pm; Sept–May Tues & Thurs noon–3pm, Wed noon–4pm; 50kr), which provides an overview of the region's flora and fauna. There are diagrams of the elaborate heat-exchanger in the reindeer's nose that helps stop the animal from freezing to death in winter, and blow-ups of the warble fly which torments it in summer. There are also examples of traditional Sámi handicrafts and a good section on Finnmark's topography, examining, for example, how and why some of the region's rivers are slow and sluggish, while others have cut deep gashes in the landscape. The museum is on the eastern periphery of – and acts as an information centre for – the **Stabbursdalen Nasjonalpark**, a large slab of wilderness that contains the world's most northerly pine forest – covering the slopes of the Stabbursdalen river valley, which runs down from the Finnmarksvidda plateau to the Porsangerfjord. The lower end of the valley is broad and marshy, but beyond lie precipitous canyons and chasms – challenging terrain, with a couple of marked hiking trails. If that sounds too much like hard work, opt instead for the easy 2.8-kilometre stroll east from the museum along the clearly marked nature trail that traverses the thick gravel banks of the Stabbursdalen river where it trickles into the Porsangerfjord. It's an eerily chill landscape and there's a good chance of spotting several species of **wetland bird** in spring and summer: ducks, geese and waders like the lapwing, the curlew and the arctic knot are common. Indeed, these salt marshes and mud flats are such an important resting and feeding area for migratory wetland birds that they have been protected as the Stabbursnes **nature reserve**.

Lakselv

From Stabbursnes, it's about 15km south on the E6 to **LAKSELV**, an inconsequential fishing village at the head of the Porsangerfjord, and another 75km to Karasjok (see p.370), the best place hereabouts to spend the night. Pushing on, the **E6** weaves its way northeast along the Finnish border, joining with the **E75** from Finland long before it reaches, 180km from Karasjok, **TANA BRU**, a Sámi settlement clustered around a suspension bridge over the River Tana. Some 300km long, the River Tana, which rattles down to the Tanafjord, an inlet of the Barents Sea, is one of Europe's best salmon rivers, but although the fishing is outstanding, it's hedged with restrictions about what you can catch and when: **Tana Tourist Information** (late June to late Aug Mon–Fri 9am–6pm, Sat & Sun 10am–5pm; rest of year Mon–Fri 8am–3.30pm; ☎78 92 53 00, ⒲www .tana.kommune.no), at the *Hotel Tana*, beside the main road as you near the bridge, will advise. The only **hotel** in Tana is the very same *Hotel Tana* (☎78 92 81 98, ⒲www.hoteltana.no; ❻), a chalet-like affair with competently comfortable rooms and a restaurant; they allow camping here too.

Varangerbotn

On the east side of Tana bridge, Highway 890 branches off north bound for the coast at Berlevåg (see below) 140km away, while the E6/E75 pushes east for another 18km to **VARANGERBOTN**, at the head of the long and deep **Varangerfjord**. This is where the E-roads diverge: the E75 heads off to Vadsø (see p.383) and Vardø (see below), but the E6 continues on to Kirkenes, another 130-kilometre haul to the east. Initially, the E6 tracks along the southern shores of the Varangerfjord, a bleak, weather-beaten run with all colour and vegetation being confined to the northern shore, with its scattered farms and painted fishing boats, but then the road loops inland, clipping across the tundra, before it regains the coast for its final spurt into Kirkenes (see p.383).

East from Nordkapp on the Hurtigrute

Beyond Nordkapp, the Hurtigrute steers a fine route round the top of the country, nudging its way between tiny islets and craggy bluffs, and stopping at a series of solitary fishing villages. Among them the prettiest is **BERLEVÅG**, which sits amid a landscape of eerie greenish-grey rock, splashes of colour in a land otherwise stripped by the elements. It's a tiny village, with a population of just 1200, but its cultural traditions and tight community spirit were deftly explored in Knut Jensen's documentary *Heftig og Begeistret* (Cool & Crazy), released in 2001. The **film** received rave reviews both in Norway and across Europe, a welcome fillip to Berlevåg in general and the subject matter of the film – the local men's choir, the **Berlevåg Mannsangforening** – in particular.

Berlevåg has a couple of places **to stay**, including the *Berlevåg Pensjonat og Camping*, on Havnegata (☎78 98 16 10, ⒲www.berlevag-pensjonat.no), with tent pitches (June–Sept) and four simple, straightforward guest rooms (all year; ❷). If you're after a room, you'd be well advised to reserve ahead of time given Berlevåg's remote location. Northbound, the Hurtigrute calls here at 10.45pm, southbound at 10.30pm; the journey time to and from Honningsvåg is a little under eight hours. Local buses link Berlevåg with Tana Bru, but it's an infrequent service – Tana Tourist Information *(see above)* will have the times.

Vardø

From Berlevåg, it's just over five hours on the Hurtigrute to **VARDØ**, Norway's most easterly town and a busy fishing port of 2700 souls. Like everywhere else in Finnmark, Vardø was savaged in World War II and the modern town that grew up in the 1950s could hardly be described as beautiful, though its geography is at least unusual: Vardø spreads out over two little islets connected by a narrow causeway, which in turn forms the apex of the town's harbour; a tunnel connects Vardø with the mainland, just a couple of kilometres away.

Vardø's main attraction is the **Vardøhus Festning** (Vardø fortress; daily: mid-April to mid-Sept 10am–9pm; mid-Sept to mid-April 10am–6pm; 30kr), a tiny star-shaped fortress, located about 600m southwest of the Hurtigrute quay. The site was first fortified in 1300, but the present structure dates from the 1730s, built at the behest of King Christian VI. When this singularly unprepossessing monarch toured Finnmark he was greeted, according to one of his courtiers, with "expressions of abject flattery in atrocious verse" – and the king loved it. Christian had the fortress built to guard the northeastern approaches to his kingdom, but it has never seen active service – hence its excellent state of preservation. A small **museum** gives further details of the fort's history.

Vardøhus museum

The town's main museum is the **Vardøhus museum**, Pers Larssengate 32 (mid-June to mid-Aug Mon–Fri 9am–6pm, Sat & Sun 11am–6pm; mid-Aug to mid-June Mon–Fri 9am–3pm; 40kr), which occupies a sturdy stone building, Lushaugen, on the northwest edge of Vardø, about fifteen-minutes' walk from the Hurtigrute quay. Spread over three floors, a series of well-presented displays explains Vardø's history, with sections devoted to explorers such as Willem Barents and Fridtjof Nansen, plus others examining local flora and fauna. Most interesting of all is the section on the **witch-hunting** fever that gripped Finnmark in the seventeenth century. Although the Church had long regarded the extremes of Finnmark as the realm of the devil, witch-finding only took a hold in the 1620s – half a century or so later than the rest of Europe – when, it was alleged, a coven set up shop in a cave on the edge of town. Over the next sixty years more than eighty women were burned alive in Vardø, a huge number considering the size of the population.

Around Vardø

Of Vardø's outdoor attractions, top of the list is the **boat trips** (April to mid-Oct daily; 175kr per person), which leave Vardø harbour to cruise round nearby **Hornøya**, a rocky islet and bird reserve where thousands of sea birds nest each summer. Advance bookings are essential (contact the tourist office; see below).

Alternatively, a recently completed byroad threads its way northwest from Vardø along the coast, passing through a lunar-like landscape to reach the (largely) abandoned fishing village of **Hamningberg** after 45km. It's a picturesque spot and scores of locals walk here during Vardø's main festival – Pomordagene (Pomor Days), in early July.

Vardø practicalities

The northbound **Hurtigrute** reaches Vardø at 4am and leaves just fifteen minutes later; southbound it docks at 4pm and leaves an hour later. FFR **buses** (☎177, ⊛www.ffr.no) run the 50km from Varangerbotn on the E6 to Vadsø (1–2 daily except Sat; 50min), where a second bus heads the 75km on to Vardø (1–2 daily; 1hr 30min); sometimes these services connect, sometimes they don't – check before you set out; the Varangerbotn–Vadsø bus starts in Kirkenes. Vardø **tourist office** is metres from the Hurtigrute quay (mid-June to late Aug Mon–Fri 10am–7pm, Sat & Sun noon–7pm; ☎78 98 69 07, ⊛www.varanger .com), and close by is the only **hotel** in town, the workaday *Vardo Hotell*, at Kaigata 8 (☎78 98 77 61, ⊛www.vardohotel.no; ❹).

Vadsø

VADSØ, four hours by **Hurtigrute** from Vardø (northbound only), used to be largely Finnish-speaking, and even now half the population of 6100 claims Finnish descent. Its main claim to fame is as the administrative centre of Finnmark, which − to be blunt − isn't much to get excited about. Russian bombers and German soldiers between them destroyed almost all the old town during World War II, the result being the mundanely modern town-centre of today. There's really no reason to get off the boat here, but there are a couple of minor sights to see if you do, most notably the **Innvandrermonumentet** (the Immigration Monument), bang in the centre of town, which commemorates the many Finns who migrated here in the eighteenth and nineteenth centuries.

FFR **buses** (℡177, ⓦwww.ffr.no) from Kirkenes/Varangerbotn (1−2 daily except Sat; 3hr 30min/50min) as well as Vardø (see p.381) pull into Vadsø **bus station** on Strandgata, which is located on a stumpy promontory − 500m by 300m − in the centre of town. From here, it's about 1km to the Hurtigrute dock, over the bridge on Vadsøya island. The best **hotel** in town is the *Rica Hotel Vadsø*, a large, modern and really rather pleasant affair in the town centre, at Oscars gate 4 (℡78 95 52 50, ⓦwww.rica.no; ❼, sp/r ❹).

After Vadsø, the **Hurtigrute** takes a couple of hours to cross the deep blueblack waters of the **Varangerfjord** on the last stage of its journey to Kirkenes. There's snow on the mainland here even in July, which makes for a picturesque chug across the fjord, the odd fishing boat the only sign of life.

Kirkenes

During World War II, the mining town and ice-free port of **KIRKENES** was bombed more heavily than any other place in Europe apart from Malta. The retreating German army torched what was left as they fled in the face of liberating Soviet soldiers, who found 3500 locals hiding in the nearby iron-ore mines. The mines finally closed in 1996, threatening the future of this 4000-strong community, which is now trying hard to kindle trade with Russia to keep itself afloat.

Kirkenes is almost entirely modern, with long rows of uniform houses spreading out along the Bøkfjord, a narrow arm of the Barents Sea. If that sounds dull, it's not to slight the town, which makes the most of its inhospitable surroundings with some pleasant public gardens, lakes and residential areas − it's just that it seems an awfully long way to come for not very much. That said, once you've finally got here it seems churlish to leave quickly, and it's certainly worth searching out the **Sør-Varanger museum** (early June to mid-Aug daily 10am−6pm; mid-Aug to early June daily 10am−3.30pm; 40kr; ⓦwww .sor-varanger.museum.no), one of whose sections − the **Grenselandmuseet (Frontier Museum)** − focuses on the history of the region and its people, and includes a detailed account of the events of World War II, illustrated by some fascinating old photos. In the same building is a display of the work of **John Savio** (1902−38), a local Sámi artist whose life was brief and tragic. Orphaned at the age of three, Savio was ill from childhood onwards and died in poverty of tuberculosis at the age of 36. This lends poignancy to his woodcuts and paintings, with their lonely evocations of the Sámi way of life and the overbearing power of nature. The museum is about 1.5km south of the main harbourfront at the end of Solheimsveien (the E6), beside one of the town's several little lakes.

The sterling part Kirkenes played in the war is also recalled by a couple of **monuments** − one dedicated to the town's wartime women in the main square, and a second to the Red Army, plonked on Roald Amundsens gate, just to the east.

Practicalities

Kirkenes is the northern terminus of the **Hurtigrute** coastal boat, which arrives here at 10am and departs for points south at 12.45pm. The Hurtigrute uses the quay just over 1km east of the town centre; a local bus shuttles between the two. Kirkenes **airport** is 15km west of town just off the E6; Flybussen (2–5 daily; 20min; 85kr one-way) connect the airport with the centre. The **bus station** is at the west end of the main harbourfront, and from here it's about 400m east along Kirkegata to the **tourist office**, at Presteveien 1 (June–Aug Mon–Fri 10am–6pm, Sat & Sun 10am–4pm; Sept–May Mon–Fri 9am–4pm; ℡78 99 25 44, Ⓦwww.kirkenesinfo.no).

The town's best **hotel** is the *Rica Arctic*, whose eighty well-appointed rooms occupy a smart modern block in the centre near the town square at Kongensgate 1 (℡78 99 59 00, Ⓦwww.rica.no; ❻, sp/r ❹). The similarly modern *Rica Hotel Kirkenes* is in a three-storey block about 800m south of the main square at Pasvikveien 63 (℡78 99 14 91, Ⓦwww.rica.no; ❻, sp/r ❹).

As for **food**, the *Rica Arctic Hotel* has a very competent restaurant, though it's slightly bettered by *Vin og Vilt*, Kirkegata 5 (daily 6–11pm; ℡78 99 38 11), where they serve up an excellent range of Arctic specialities from reindeer to char and beyond. Main courses at both hover at around 260kr.

Around Kirkenes: Øvre Pasvik Nasjonalpark

Hidden away some 120km south of Kirkenes, where the borders of Norway, Finland and Russia intersect, is the ten-by-nine-kilometre parcel of wilderness that comprises the **Øvre Pasvik Nasjonalpark**, a western offshoot of the Siberian taiga. The park's subarctic pine forest covers a series of low-lying hills that make up about half the total area, and below lie swamps, marshes and lakes. Wolverines and bears live in the forest, and there are also traces of the prehistoric Komsa culture, notably the vague remains of pit-traps beside **Lake Ødevatn**. The Kirkenes tourist office has details of guided tours to the park, which are useful as you have to be an expert wilderness-hiker-cum-survivalist to delve into the park under your own steam. The absence of natural landmarks makes it easy to get lost, especially as there

---

Crossing into Russia

From Kirkenes, it's just 16km southeast along the **E105** to **Storskog**, Norway's only official border crossing point with Russia. You can take photographs of the frontier, provided you don't snap any Russian personnel or military installations – which rather limits the options as there's little else to see. The crossing is busy for much of the year, but it's not open for casual day-trippers; in any case, the only convenient settlement nearby is the ugly Russian mining town of **Nikel**, around 40km further to the south, from where you can – extraordinarily enough – travel by train all the way to Vladivostok. Several Kirkenes travel agents organize day-and weekend tours into Russia, the most worthwhile being those to the Arctic port of **Murmansk**. The trips include a visa (500kr for one day, 675kr for three), which the agents can arrange in a few hours once they have your passport, a completed visa application form, an extra passport photo and the money; if you do it on your own, reckon on sixteen days. Among these travel agents, Pasvikturist, in the centre at Dr. Wesselsgate 9 (℡78 99 50 80, Ⓦwww.pasvikturist.no), is as good as any. They have details of trips to Murmansk, both one-night (2090kr per person) and weekend (2390kr) excursions. Incidentally, there is a Russian consulate in Kirkenes, at Arbeidergata 6 (℡78 99 37 37), but they will not short-cut the visa process. If a Russian jaunt proves impossible, you'll have to be content with the reflection that if you have made it to Kirkenes and the border, you are further east than Istanbul and as far north as Alaska.

are no marked footpaths, nor is there any map that can be relied upon. If you're undeterred, and have your own vehicle (there's no public transport), then drive south from Kirkenes for about 100km along Highway 885 through the pine forests of the Pasvik river valley as far as **Vaggatem**. Turn off the main road 1.5km or so further on and then follow the nine-kilometre, rough forest road south to a lake, **Sortbrysttjern (Sortabaetluobbal)**, from where a footpath takes you into the park at another lake, **Ellenvatnet**. If you want to **stay** hereabouts, the only option is Vaggatem's all-year *Øvre Pasvik Café and Camping* (☎78 99 55 30, ⓦwww .pasvik-cafe.no), which rents out ten simple wooden cabins (500–600kr for 2).

Svalbard

The **Svalbard archipelago** is one of the most hostile places on earth. Some 640km north of the Norwegian mainland – and just 1300km from the North Pole – two-thirds of its surface is covered by glaciers, the soil frozen to a depth of up to 500m. The archipelago was probably discovered in the twelfth century by Icelandic seamen, though it lay ignored until 1596 when the Dutch explorer Willem Barents named the main island, **Spitsbergen**, after its needle-like mountains. However, apart from a smattering of determined adventurers – from seventeenth-century whalers to eighteenth-century monks and trappers – few people ever lived here until, in 1899, rich **coal** deposits were discovered, the geological residue of a prehistoric tropical forest. The first coal mine was opened by an American seven years later and passed into Norwegian hands in 1916. Meanwhile, other countries, particularly Russia and Sweden, were getting into the coal-mining act, and when, in 1920, Norway's sovereignty over the archipelago was ratified by international treaty, it was on condition that those other countries who were operating mines could continue to do so. It was also agreed that the islands would be a demilitarized zone, which made them, incidentally, sitting ducks for a German squadron, which arrived here to bombard the Norwegian coal mines during World War II.

Despite the hardships, there are convincing reasons to make a trip to this oddly fertile land, covering around 63,000 square kilometres. Between late April and late August there's continuous daylight and, with temperatures bobbing up into the late teens, the snow has all but disappeared by July, leaving the valleys covered in wild flowers. And then there's the **wildlife**, an abundance of Arctic fauna, including over a hundred species of migratory birds, arctic foxes, polar bears and reindeer on land, and seals, walruses and whales offshore. In winter, it's a different story: the polar night, during which the sun never rises above the horizon, lasts from late October to mid-February, and the record low tempera-ture is a staggering -46°C – and that's not counting the wind-chill factor.

Practicalities

The simplest way to reach Svalbard is to **fly** to the archipelago's airport at Longyearbyen, on the main island, Spitsbergen. SAS operates direct services there from Tromsø and Oslo Gardermoen. The Tromsø–Longyearbyen flight takes an hour and forty minutes and a return ticket without restrictions is a steep 4500kr return, though special deals are commonplace, reducing this to 2500–3500kr. If any of the budget airlines get a toe-hold on the Svalbard routes, as is rumoured, then prices will no doubt dip. Before you book your flight, you'll need to reserve accommodation in Longyearbyen (see p.387) and – unless you're happy to be stuck in your lodgings – you'd be well advised to pre-book the **guided excursions** you fancy too.

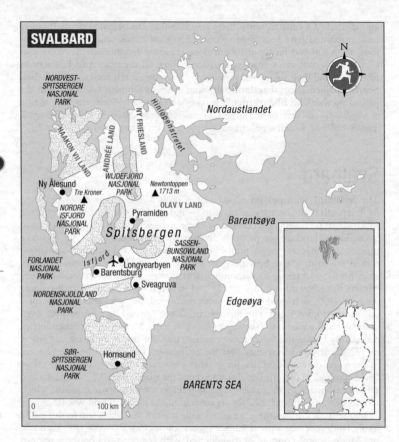

Guided tours are big business on Svalbard and you can choose anything from hiking and climbing through to kayaking, snowmobiling, dog-sledging, glacier walking, helicopter rides, Zodiac boat trips, wildlife safaris and ice-caving, not to mention trips into a former coal mine. In the first instance, further information is available from Longyearbyen's official tourist office, **Svalbard Tourism** (☎79 02 55 50, ⊛www.svalbard.net), or try the excellent **Spitsbergen Travel**, also in Longyearbyen (☎79 02 61 00, ⊛www.spitsbergentravel.no). You can, of course, book a whole holiday with an operator back home (see Basics, p.32) or even take pot luck when you get there, but be warned that wilderness excursions are often fully booked weeks in advance. Finally, if you are determined to strike out into the wilderness independently, you first have to seek permission from, and log your itinerary with, the governor's office, Sysselmannen på Svalbard, Postboks 633, N-9171 Longyearbyen (☎79 02 43 00, ⊛www .sysselmannen.svalbard.no) – and they will certainly expect you to carry a gun and a "shocking device" – a signal pistol or suchlike – to ward off polar bears.

Spitsbergen

The main island of the Svalbard archipelago, **Spitsbergen**, is the only one that is permanently inhabited; it has five settlements in total – three Norwegian, one

Russian and one Polish – with a total population of around 3000. With just over 2000 inhabitants, the only Norwegian settlement of any size is **LONGYEAR-BYEN**, which huddles on the narrow coastal plain below the mountains and beside the Isfjorden, roughly in the middle of the island. It was founded in 1906, when John M. Longyear, an American mine-owner, established the Arctic Coal Company here. Today, Longyearbyen is well equipped with services, including shops, cafés, a post office, bank, swimming pool, several tour companies, a campsite, a couple of guesthouses and three hotels, though advance reservations are essential for all accommodation.

Ny Ålesund, Sveagruva, Barentsburg and Hornsund

Of the other Norwegian settlements, **Ny Ålesund** (40–100 inhabitants, depending on the season) is a polar research centre to the northwest of Longyearbyen, and the **Sveagruva** mining community (200 day-workers) lies to the southeast. The only Russian settlement is the coal-mining township of **Barentsburg** (900) to the west of Longyearbyen. A second Russian mining settlement, Pyramiden, to the north of Longyearbyen, was abandoned in 2001 when the coal seams ran out. Since then, there have been lengthy debates as to what to do with it – the establishment of an international science station seems the most popular option. **Hornsund**, the Polish settlement, is the smallest of the five, comprising a research station with just a dozen or so scientists based there. There are no road connections between any of Svalbard's settlements, though there is about 50km of road around Longyearbyen. Public transport is limited to the airport bus, occasional cargo ships from Longyearbyen to both Barentsburg and Ny Ålesund, and a light-aircraft service from Longyearbyen to Ny Ålesund, though government employees and researchers take priority on these flights.

Longyearbyen: arrival and information

Longyearbyen airport is 5km west of the town centre and the airport **bus** links the two, its schedule coinciding with flight arrivals and departures. The town itself trails back from the Isfjord for a couple of kilometres on either side of the Longyearelva river, altogether a ramshackle sort of place hunkered and bunkered down against the blast of winter. The few buildings that pass for the town centre are located about 500m in from the fjord just to the east of the river, and this is where you'll find the year-round **tourist office** (May–Sept daily 10am–5pm; Oct–April daily noon–5pm; ☏79 02 55 50, Ⓦwww.svalbard .net), which has information on a wide range of trips, from dog-sledging and ice-caving to snowmobile excursions and glacier walks.

Longyearbyen: accommodation and food

Longyearbyen's smartest **hotel** is the *Radisson SAS Polar Hotel* (☏79 02 34 50, Ⓦwww.radissonsas.com; ❼, sp/r ❻), a modern chalet-like affair with nearly a hundred rooms, the pick of which have views over to the Isfjord; the hotel is near the tourist office. More distinctive, if rather more spartan, **lodgings** are to be found in several former miners' quarters, basically low-slung modern blocks parcelled up into small rooms with shared bathrooms. One of the most appealing of these is *Mary Ann's Polarrigg* (☏79 02 37 02, Ⓦwww.polarriggen .com; ❸), where the main block has thirty rooms with shared facilities and the newer annexe has nine en-suite rooms; it's located on the west side of the river, opposite the *SAS Polar Hotel*. For something even more classically "Arctic", there are also fifteen rooms in *Basecamp Spitzbergen* (☏79 02 46 00, Ⓦwww .basecampexplorer.com; ❾), a sort of enlarged mock-up of a trapper's cabin, complete with sealskins and a sauna and mostly made from old, recycled lumber; it's all a bit hoochie, but great fun all the same – and very convivial – and it's handily located about 600m south of the tourist office.

The *Polar Hotel*'s *Brasseri Nansen* is the best place **to eat** in town, serving all manner of Arctic specialities from char to reindeer, seal and (like it or not) whale. A slightly less expensive option is *Huset* (T79 02 25 00), which also specializes in Arctic dishes with main courses at around 250kr, much less if you eat at the attached **bar**. *Huset* is on the west side of the river at the southern end of town in the same building as the cinema.

Travel details

Principal Nor-Way Bussekspress bus services (ⓦwww.nor-way.no)

Alta to: Honningsvåg (1–2 daily; 4hr); Narvik (2 daily except Sat; 9hr 30min); Tromsø (1 daily; 7hr).
Honningsvåg to: Alta (1–2 daily; 4hr); Nordkapp (early June to late Aug 2 daily; 45min).
Tromsø to: Alta (1 daily; 7hr); Narvik (2–3 daily; 4hr).

Principal FFR bus services (ⓦwww.ffr.no)

Alta to: Hammerfest (Aug–June 1–3 daily except Sat, July 1–3 daily; 2hr 30min); Karasjok (1–2 daily except Sat; 5hr); Kautokeino (1–2 daily except Sat; 2hr 15min); Kirkenes (3 weekly; 10–13hr).
Hammerfest to: Alta (Aug–June 1–3 daily except Sat, July 1–3 daily; 2hr 30min); Karasjok (1–2 daily except Sat; 4hr); Kirkenes (2 weekly; 10hr).
Note that all these services are routed through Skaidi, where you change for points north and south along the E6 – but check connecting times before you set out.
Karasjok to: Alta (1–2 daily except Sat; 5hr); Hammerfest (1–2 daily except Sat; 4hr); Kirkenes (2 weekly; 5–7hr).
Kautokeino to: Alta (1–2 daily except Sat; 2hr 15min).
Kirkenes to: Alta (3 weekly; 10–13hr); Hammerfest (2 weekly; 10); Karasjok (2 weekly; 5–7hr).

Nor-Way Bussekspress's Nord-Norgeekspressen and Nord-kappekspressen (ⓦwww.nor-way.no)

The **Nord-Norgeekspressen** (North Norway Express Bus) complements the railway system. It runs north from Bodø and Fauske to Alta in three segments: Bodø to Narvik via Fauske (2 daily; 6hr 30min); Narvik to Tromsø (1–3 daily; 4hr); and Tromsø to Alta (1 daily; 6hr 30min). Alternatively, the **Nordkappekspressen** (North Cape Express

Bus) runs direct from Narvik to Alta (2 daily except Sat; 9hr 30min), where passengers overnight before picking up the second leg of the Nordkappekspressen to Honningsvåg (1–2 daily; 4hr), where they change again to reach Nordkapp (early June to late Aug 2 daily; 45min).

Principal car ferries

Breivikeidet to: Svendsby (every 1–2hr; Mon–Fri 6am–10pm, Sat 8am–8pm, Sun 10am–9pm; 25min) with Bjørklids (ⓦwww.bjorklid.no).
Brensholmen to: Botnhamn (May to Aug 5–7 daily; 45min) with Senjafergene (ⓦwww.senjafergene.no).
Gryllefjord to: Andenes (late May to mid-June & early to late Aug 2 daily, mid-June to early Aug 3 daily; 2hr) with Senjafergene (ⓦwww.senjafergene.no).
Lyngseidet to: Olderdalen (every 1–2hr; Mon–Fri 7am–8pm, Sat 9am–7pm, Sun 10.30am–8pm; 40min) with Bjørklids (ⓦwww.bjorklid.no).

Principal Hurtigbåt passenger express boats

Alta to: Hammerfest (1–2 daily except Sat; 1hr 30min) with FFR (ⓦwww.ffr.no).
Tromsø to: Harstad (2–3 daily; 2hr 45min) with Hurtigruten car ferries (ⓦwww.hurtigruten.no).

Hurtigrute coastal boat (year-round; daily; ⓦwww.hurtigruten.no)

Northbound from: Tromsø at 6.30pm; Hammerfest at 6.45am; Honningsvåg at 3.15pm; Berlevåg at 10.45pm; Vardø at 4.15am; Vadsø at 8.15am; terminates at Kirkenes at 10am.
Southbound from: Kirkenes at 12.45pm; Vardø at 5pm; (no southbound stop at Vadsø); Berlevåg at 10.30pm; Honningsvåg at 6.15am; Hammerfest at 12.45pm; Tromsø at 1.30am.
The Tromsø–Kirkenes journey time is 40hr.

Contexts

Contexts

History

D espite its low contemporary profile, Norway has a fascinating past. As early as the tenth century its people had explored – and conquered – much of northern Europe, and roamed the Atlantic as far as the North American mainland. These heady days came to an end, however, when Norway lost its independence in the fourteenth century, coming under the sway of first Denmark and then Sweden. Independent again from 1905, Norway was propelled into World War II by the German invasion of 1940, an act of aggression that transformed the Norwegians' attitude to the outside world. Gone was the old insular neutrality, replaced by a liberal internationalism exemplified by Norway's leading role in the environmental movement.

Early civilizations

The earliest signs of human habitation in Norway date from the end of the last Ice Age, around 10,000 BC. In the Finnmark region of north Norway, the **Komsa culture** was reliant upon sealing, whereas the peoples of the **Fosna culture**, further south near present-day Kristiansund, hunted both seals and reindeer. Both these societies were essentially static, dependent upon flint and bone implements. At Alta, the Komsa people left behind hundreds of **rock carvings and drawings** (see p.363), naturalistic representations of their way of life dating from the seventh to the third millennium BC.

As the edges of the icecap retreated from the western coastline, so new migrants slowly filtered north. These new peoples, of the **Nøstvet-økser culture**, were also hunters and fishers, but they were able to manufacture stone axes, examples of which were first unearthed at Nøstvet, near Oslo. Beginning around 2700 BC, immigrants from the east, principally the semi-nomadic **Boat Axe** and **Battle-Axe peoples** – so named because of the distinctive shape of their stone weapons/tools – introduced animal husbandry and agriculture. The new arrivals did not, however, overwhelm their predecessors; the two groups coexisted, each picking up hints from the other – a reflection of the harsh infertility of the land.

Into the Bronze Age

These **late Stone Age** cultures flourished at a time when other, more southerly countries were already using metal. Norway was poor and had little to trade, but the Danes and Swedes exchanged amber for copper and tin from the bronze-making countries of central Europe. A fraction of the imported bronze subsequently passed into Norway, mostly to the Battle-Axe people, who appear to have had a comparatively prosperous aristocracy. This was the beginning of the Norwegian **Bronze Age** (1500–500 BC), which also saw a change in burial customs. In the Stone Age, the Battle-Axe peoples had dug shallow earth graves, but these were now supplanted by **burial mounds** enclosing coffins in which supplies were placed in readiness for the after life. Building the mounds involved a substantial amount of effort, suggesting the existence of powerful chieftains who could organize the work, and who may also have been priests. **Rock carvings** became prevalent in southern Norway during this period too – workaday images of men ploughing with oxen, riding horses, carrying arms and using boats to navigate the coastal waters, which were supplemented by drawings of religious or symbolic significance. In general terms, however, the Bronze Age was characterized more by the development of agriculture than by the use of metal, and stone implements remained the norm.

500 BC to 200 AD

Around **500 BC** Norway was affected by two adverse changes: the climate deteriorated, and trade relations with the Mediterranean were disrupted by the westward movement of the Celts across central Europe. The former encouraged the development of settled, communal farming in an attempt to improve winter shelter and storage, with each clan resident in a large stone, turf and timber dwelling; the latter cut the supply of tin and copper and subsequently isolated Norway from the early Iron Age. The country's isolation continued through much of the Classical period. The Greek geographer Pytheas of Marseilles, who went far enough north to note the short summer nights, probably visited southern Norway, but the regions beyond remained the subject of vague speculation. Pliny the Elder mentions "Nerigon" as the great island south of the legendary "**Ultima Thule**", the outermost region of the earth, while Tacitus, in his *Germania*, demonstrated knowledge only of the Danes and Swedes.

The expansion of the Roman Empire in the first and second centuries AD revived Norway's **trading links with the Mediterranean**. Evidence of these renewed contacts is provided across Scandinavia by **runes**, carved inscriptions dating from around 200 AD, whose 24-letter alphabet – the *futhark* – was clearly influenced by Greek and Latin capitals. Initially, runes were seen as having magical powers and it was to gain their knowledge that the god Odin hung for nine nights on *Yggdrasill*, the tree of life, with a spear in his side; they also turn up in the sagas with Egil, in *Egil's Saga* for instance, destroying a whale bone carved with runes because they contained "Ten secret characters, [which] gave the young girl [the daughter of his friend] her grinding pain." But gradually rune usage became more prosaic, and most of the eight hundred or so runic inscriptions extant across southern Norway commemorate events and individuals: mothers and fathers, sons and slain comrades.

The Norwegian Iron Age and early medieval Norway

The renewal of trade with the Mediterranean also spread the use of **iron**. Norway's agriculture was transformed by the use of iron tools, and the pace of change accelerated in the fifth century AD, when the Norwegians learned how to smelt the brown iron ore, limonite, that lay in their bogs and lakes – hence its common name, **bog-iron**. Clearing the forests with iron axes was relatively easy and, with more land available, the pattern of settlement became less concentrated. Family homesteads leapfrogged up the valleys, and a class of wealthy farmers emerged, their prosperity based on fields and flocks. Above them in the pecking order were local chieftains, the nature of whose authority varied considerably. Inland, the chieftains' power was based on landed wealth and constrained by feudal responsibilities, whereas the coastal lords, who had often accumulated influence from trade, piracy and military prowess, were less encumbered. Like the farmers, these seafarers had also benefited from the **iron axe**, which made boat building much easier. An early seventh-century ship found at Kvalsund, near Hammerfest, was 18m long, its skilfully crafted oak hull equipped with a high prow and stern, prefiguring the vessels of the Vikings.

By the **middle of the eighth century**, Norway had become a country of small, independent kingships, its geography impeding the development of any central authority. In the event, it was the Yngling chieftains of southeast Norway who attempted to assert some sort of wider control. Their first leaders are listed in the *Ynglinga Tal*, a paean compiled by the Norwegian *skald* (court poet) Thjodolf in the ninth century. According to Thjodolf, early royal life had its ups and downs: King Domaldi was sacrificed to ensure the fertility of his land; Dag was killed by an accidental blow from a pitchfork; and Fjolnir got up in the night to take a leak, fell into a vat of mead and drowned.

The Vikings

Overpopulation, clan discord, and the lure of plunder and commerce all contributed to the sudden explosion that launched the **Vikings** (from the Norse word *vik*, meaning creek, and *-ing*, frequenter of), upon an unsuspecting Europe in the ninth century. The patterns of attack and eventual settlement were dictated by the geographical position of the various Scandinavian countries. The Swedish Vikings turned eastwards, the Danes headed south and southwest, while the **Norwegians sailed west**, their longships landing on the Hebrides, Shetland, Orkney, the Scottish mainland and western Ireland. The Pictish population was unable to muster much resistance and the islands were quickly overrun, becoming, together with the Isle of Man, the nucleus of a new Norse kingdom that provided a base for further attacks on Scotland and Ireland.

The Norwegians founded Dublin in 836, and from Ireland turned their attention eastward to northern Britain. Elsewhere, Norwegian Vikings settled the Faroe Islands and Iceland, and even raided as far south as Moorish Spain, attacking Seville in 844. The raiders soon became settlers, sometimes colonizing the entire country – as in Iceland and the Faroes – but mostly intermingling with the local population. The speed of their assimilation is, in fact, one of the Vikings' most striking features: **William the Conqueror** (1027–87) was the epitome of the Norman baron, yet he was also the descendant of Rollo, the Viking warrior whose army had overrun Normandy just a century before.

The whole of Norway felt the **stimulating effect**s of the Viking expeditions. The economy was boosted by the spoils of war and the population grew in physical stature as health and nutrition improved. Farmland was no longer in such short supply; cereal and dairy farming were extended into new areas in eastern Norway; new vegetables, such as cabbages and turnips, were introduced from Britain; and farming methods were improved by overseas contact – the Celts, for instance, taught the Norwegians how to thresh grain with flails.

Alfred the Great and Ottar

The Vikings also rigorously exploited the hunting and fishing peoples who roamed the far north of Norway. Detailed information on Finnmark in the late ninth century comes from a surprising source, the court of **Alfred the Great**, which was visited by a Norwegian chieftain named **Ottar** in about 890. Ottar dwelt, so he claimed, "northernmost of all Norsemen", and he regaled Alfred with tales of his native land, which the king promptly incorporated within his translation of a fifth-century Latin text, the *History of the World* by Paulus Orosius. Ottar, who boasted that he owed political allegiance to no one, had a few cows, sheep and pigs and a tiny slice of arable land, which he ploughed with horses, but his real wealth came from other sources. Fishing, whaling and walrus hunting provided both food for his retinue and exportable commodities. He also possessed a herd of six hundred tame reindeer – plus six decoy animals used to snare wild reindeer – and extracted a heavy tribute from the Sámi (see p.366), payable in furs and hides.

Viking religion and art

The Vikings' brand of **paganism** (see p.414), with its wayward, unscrupulous deities, underpinned their inclination to vendettas and clan warfare. Nevertheless, institutions slowly developed which helped regulate the blood-letting. Western Norway adopted the Germanic *wergeld* system of cash-for-injury compensation; every free man was entitled to attend the local *Thing* (*Ting*) or parliament, while a regional *Allthing* made laws and settled disputes. Justice was class-based, however, with society divided into three main categories: the lord, the freeman, and the thrall or slave, who was worth about eight cows. The Vikings were industrious slavers, opening slave markets wherever they went, sending thousands to work on their land back home and supplying the needs of other buyers.

Viking **decorative art** was also pan-Scandinavian, with the most distinguished work being the elaborate and often grotesque animal motifs that adorned their ships, sledges, buildings and furniture. This craftsmanship is seen to good advantage in the **ship burials** of Oseberg and Gokstad, the retrieved artefacts which are on display in Oslo's Viking Ships Museum (p.99). The Oseberg ship is thought to be the burial ship of Åse, wife of the early ninth-century **Yngling** king, Gudrød Storlatnes. She was also the mother of Halfdan the Black, whose body had a very different fate from her own – it was chopped up, and the bits were buried across his kingdom to ensure the fertility of the land.

Norway's first kings

It was from the **Ynglings of Vestfold** that Norway's first widely recognized king, **Harald Hårfagri** (Fair-Hair; c.880–930), claimed descent. Shortly before 900 (the exact date is unclear), Harald won a decisive victory at Hafrsfjord (near modern Stavanger), which gave him control of the coastal region as far north as Trøndelag. It sparked an exodus of minor rulers, most of whom left to settle in Iceland. The thirteenth-century *Laxdaela Saga* records the departure of one such family, the Ketils of Romsdal, who would not be "forced to become Harald's vassals or be denied compensation for fallen kinsmen". Harald's long rule was based on personal pledges of fealty and, with the notable exception of the regional *Allthings*, there were no institutions to sustain it; consequently, when he died, Harald's kingdom broke up into its component parts. Harald did, however, leave a less tangible but extremely important legacy: from now on every ambitious chieftain was not content to be a local lord, but strove to be ruler of a kingdom stretching from the Trøndelag to Vestfold.

Harald's son, **Erik Bloodaxe** (d.954), struggled to hold his father's kingdom together, but was outmanoeuvred by his youngest brother, **Håkon the Good** (920–60), who secured the allegiance of the major chieftains before returning home from England where he had been raised (and Christianized) at the court of King Athelstan of Wessex. Erik fled to Northumbria to become king of Viking York. Initially, Håkon was well-received, and, although his attempts to introduce Christianity failed, he did carry out a number of far-ranging reforms. He established a common legal code for the whole of Vestfold and Trøndelag, and also introduced the system of *Leidangr*, the division of the coastal districts into areas, each of which was responsible for maintaining and manning a warship.

Harald Greycloak Eriksson and Håkon Sigurdsson

Håkon's rule was, however, punctuated by struggles against Erik's heirs. With the backing of the Danish king Harald Bluetooth, they defeated and killed Håkon in battle in 960. Håkon's kingdom then passed to one of Erik's sons, **Harald Greycloak Eriksson** (935–70). This forceful man set about extending his territories with gusto. Indeed, he was, in Bluetooth's opinion, much too successful; keen to keep Norway within his sphere of influence, the Dane slaughtered Greycloak on the battlefield in 970 and replaced him with a Danish appointee, **Håkon Sigurdsson** (d.995), the last genuine heathen to rule Norway. But again Bluetooth seems to have got more than he bargained for. Sigurdsson based himself in Trøndelag, a decent distance from his overlord, and it's believed he soon refused to recognize Danish suzerainty: certainly the Christian Bluetooth would not have sanctioned Sigurdsson's restitution of pagan sacred sites.

Olav Tryggvason

In 995 the redoubtable **Olav Tryggvason** (c.968-1000; see p.293), another Viking chieftain who had been baptized in England, sailed to Norway to challenge Sigurdsson, who was conveniently dispatched by one of his own servants before the fighting started. Olav quickly asserted control over the Trøndelag and parts of southern and western Norway. He founded Nidaros (now Trondheim), from where he launched a sustained and brutal campaign against his pagan compatriots – which incidentally secured him the adulation of later saga-writers. Despite his evangelical zeal, Olav's religious beliefs are something of an enigma: he had pagan magicians in his personal retinue, and was so good at predicting the future from bird bones that he was called *Craccaben* (Crowbone). Olav's real problem remained the enmity of the Danish-controlled southeastern regions of Norway, and of Bluetooth's son **Svein Forkbeard** (d.1014), who regarded Norway as his rightful inheritance. In alliance with the Swedish king, Svein defeated Olav at a sea battle in the Skaggerak in 1000, and Norway was divided up among the victors.

West across the Atlantic

Meanwhile, Norwegian settlers were laying the foundations of independent Norse communities in the Faroes and Iceland, where they established a parliament, the *Allthing*, in 930. The Norwegian Vikings went on to make further discoveries: Erik the Red, exiled from Norway and then banished from Iceland for three years for murder, set out in 985 with 25 ships, fourteen of which arrived in **Greenland**. The new colony prospered, and by the start of the eleventh century there were about three thousand settlers. This created a shortage of good farmland, making another push west inevitable. The two **Vinland sagas** (see p.396) provide the only surviving account of these further explorations, recounting the exploits of Leif Eriksson the Lucky, who founded a colony he called Vinland on the shores of **North America** around 1000 AD.

Norse settlers continued to secure resources from the Vinland region for the next few decades, until the native population drove them out. The Viking site discovered at L'Anse aux Meadows in Newfoundland may have been either Vinland itself or the result of one of these further foragings. The Greenland colonists carried on collecting timber from Labrador up until the fourteenth century, when the climate is known to have cooled and deteriorated, making the sea trip too dangerous. Attacks by the Inuit and the difficulties of maintaining trading links with Norway then took their toll on the main Greenland colonies. All contact with the outside world was lost in around 1410, and the last of the half-starved, disease-ridden survivors died out towards the end of the fifteenth century, just as **Christopher Columbus** was eyeing up his "New World".

The arrival of Christianity

In 1015, **Olav Haraldsson** (995–1030), a prominent Viking chieftain, sailed for Norway from England, intent upon conquering his homeland. Significantly, he arrived by merchant ship with just 100 men, rather than with a fleet of longships and an army, a clear sign of the passing of the Viking heyday. He gained the support of the yeoman farmers of the interior – a new force in Norway that was rapidly supplanting the old warrior aristocracy – and with Svein Forkbeard's son and successor Knut (King Canute of England) otherwise engaged, Haraldsson soon assumed the mantle of king of much of the country.

For twelve years Olav ruled in peace, founding Norway's first national government. His authority was based on the regional *Things* – consultative and broadly democratic bodies which administered local law – and on his willingness to deliver justice without fear or favour. The king's most enduring achievement, however, was to make Norway **Christian**. Olav had been converted during his days as a Viking, and vigorously imposed his new faith on his countrymen. Wherever necessary he executed persistent heathens and destroyed their sacred places. The dominant position of the new religion was ensured by the foundation of the Norwegian Church, whose first priests were consecrated in Bremen in Germany.

Olav's death and Magnus the Good

It was foreign policy rather than pagan enmity that brought about Olav's downfall. By scheming with the Swedish king against **Knut** (d.1035), who had now consolidated his position as king of Denmark and England, Olav provoked a Danish invasion, whose course was smoothed by massive bribes. The Norwegian chieftains, who had suffered at the hands of Olav, could be expected to help Knut, but even the yeomen failed to rally to Olav's cause, possibly alienated by his imperious ways. In 1028, Olav was forced to flee, first to

Sweden and then to Russia, while Knut's young son Svein and his mother, the English queen Aelfgifu, took the Norwegian crown. Two years later, Olav made a sensational return at the head of a scratch army, only to be defeated and killed by an alliance of wealthy landowners and chieftains at **Stiklestad**, the first major Norwegian land battle (see p.300).

The petty chieftains and yeomen-farmers who had opposed Olav soon fell out with their new king: Svein had no intention of relaxing the royal grip and his rule was at least as arbitrary as that of his predecessor. The rebellion that ensued seems also to have had nationalistic undertones – many Norwegians had no wish to be ruled by a Dane. Svein fled the country, and Olav's old enemies popped over to Sweden to bring back Olav's young son, **Magnus the Good** (1024–47), who became king in 1035.

The chastening experience of Svein's short rule transformed the popular memory of Olav. With surprising speed, he came to be regarded as a heroic champion, and there was talk of miracles brought about by the dead king's body. The Norwegian Church, looking for a local saint to enhance its position, fostered the legends and had Olav canonized. The remains of **St Olav** were then re-interred ceremoniously at Nidaros, today's Trondheim, where the miracles increased in scope, hastening the conversion of what remained of heathen Norway.

Harald Hardrada

On Magnus's death in 1047, **Harald Hardrada** (1015–66), Olav Haraldsson's half-brother, became king, and soon consolidated his grip on the whole of Norway from the Trøndelag to the Oslofjord. The last of the Viking heroes, Hardrada was a giant of a man, reputedly almost seven feet tall with a sweeping moustache and eccentric eyebrows, and a warrior who had fought alongside Olav at Stiklestad. After the battle, he and his men had fled east, fighting as mercenaries in Russia and ultimately Byzantium, where Hardrada was appointed the commander of the Varangians, the Norse bodyguard of the Byzantine emperor.

Back in Norway, Harald dominated the country by force of arms for over twenty years, earning the soubriquet "Hardrada" (the Hard) for his ruthless treatment of his enemies, many of whom he made "kiss the thin lips of the axe" as the saga writers put it. Neither was Hardrada satisfied with being king of just Norway. At first he tried to batter Denmark into submission through regular raiding, but the stratagem failed and he finally made peace with the Danish king, Svein, in 1064.

In 1066, the death of Edward the Confessor presented Harald with an opportunity to press his claim to the English throne. The Norwegian promptly sailed on England, landing near York with a massive fleet, but just outside the city, at **Stamford Bridge**, his army was surprised and trounced by Harold Godwinson, the new Saxon king of England. It was a battle of crucial importance, and one that gave rise to all sorts of legends, penned by both Norse and English writers. The two kings are supposed to have eyed each other up like prize fighters, with Hardrada proclaiming his rival "a small king, but one that stood well in his stirrups", and Harold promising the Norwegian "seven feet of English ground, or as much more as he is taller than other men". Hardrada was defeated and killed, and the threat of a Norwegian conquest of England had – though no one realized it at the time – gone forever. Not that the victory did much good for Godwinson, whose weakened army trudged back south to be defeated by William of Normandy at the **Battle of Hastings**.

Medieval consolidation

Harald's son, **Olav Kyrre** (the Peaceful; d.1093) – whose life had been spared after Stamford Bridge on the promise never to attack England again – went on to reign as king of Norway for the next 25 years. Peace engendered economic prosperity, and treaties with Denmark ensured Norwegian independence. Three native bishoprics were established, and cathedrals built at Nidaros, Bergen and Oslo. It's from this period, too, that Norway's surviving **stave churches** date: wooden structures resembling an upturned keel, they were lavishly decorated with dragon heads and scenes from Norse mythology, proof that the traditions of the pagan world were slow to disappear. (For more on stave churches, see p.187.)

The first decades of the twelfth century witnessed the further consolidation of Norway's position as an independent power, despite internal disorder as the descendants of Olav Kyrre competed for influence. Civil war ceased only when **Håkon IV** (1204–63) took the throne in 1240, ushering in what is often called "**The Period of Greatness**". Secure at home, Håkon strengthened the Norwegian hold on the Faroe and Shetland islands, and in 1262 both Iceland and Greenland accepted Norwegian sovereignty. A year later, however, the king died in the Orkneys during a campaign to assert his control over the Hebrides, and three years later the Hebrides and the Isle of Man (always the weakest links in the Norwegian empire) were sold to the Scottish Crown by Håkon's successor, **Magnus the Lawmender** (1238–80).

Under Magnus, Norway prospered. Law and order were maintained, trade flourished and, in striking contrast to the rough-and-ready ways of Hardrada, the king's court even followed a code of etiquette compiled in what became known as the *Konungs skuggsja* or "King's Mirror". Neither was the power of the monarchy threatened by feudal barons as elsewhere in thirteenth-century Europe: Norway's scattered farms were not susceptible to feudal tutelage and, as a consequence, the nobility lacked both local autonomy and resources. Castles remained few and far between and instead the energies of the nobility were drawn into the centralized administration of the state, a process that only happened several centuries later in the rest of western Europe. Norwegian **Gothic art** reached its full maturity in this period, as construction began on the nave at Nidaros Cathedral and on Håkon's Hall in Bergen.

Magnus was succeeded by his sons, first the undistinguished Erik and then **Håkon V** (1270–1319), the last of medieval Norway's talented kings. Håkon continued the policy of his predecessors, making further improvements to central government and asserting royal control of Finnmark through the construction of a fortress at Vardø. His achievements, however, were soon to be swept away along with the independence of Norway itself.

Loss of sovereignty

Norway's independence was threatened from two quarters. With strongholds in Bergen and Oslo, the merchants of the **Hanseatic League** had steadily increased their influence, exerting a virtual monopoly on the region's imports and controlling inland trade. They also came to exercise undue influence on the royal household, which grew dependent on the taxes the merchants paid.

The second threat was **dynastic**. When Håkon died in 1319 he left no male heir and was succeeded by his grandson, the 3-year-old son of a Swedish duke. The boy, **Magnus Eriksson** (1316–74), was elected Swedish king two months later, marking the virtual end of Norway as an independent country until 1905.

Magnus assumed full power over both countries in 1332, but his reign was a difficult one. When the Norwegian nobility rebelled he agreed that the monarchy should again be split: his 3-year-old son, Håkon, would become Norwegian king when he came of age, while the Swedes agreed to elect his eldest son Erik to the Swedish throne. It was then, in 1349, that the **Black Death** struck, spreading quickly along the coast and up the valleys, killing almost two-thirds of the Norwegian population. It was a catastrophe of unimaginable proportions, its effects compounded by the way the country's agriculture was structured. Animal husbandry was easily the most important part of Norwegian farming, and harvesting and drying winter fodder was labour-intensive. Without the labourers, the animals died in their hundreds and famine conditions prevailed for several generations.

Many farms were abandoned and, deprived of their rents, the petty chieftains who had once dominated rural Norway were, as a class, almost entirely swept away. The vacuum was filled by royal officials, the **syslemenn**, each of whom exercised control over a large chunk of territory on behalf of a Royal Council. The collapse of local governance was compounded by dynastic toing and froing at the top of the social ladder. In 1380, Håkon died and Norway passed into Danish control with **Olav**, the son of Håkon and the Danish princess Margaret, becoming ruler of the two kingdoms.

The Kalmar Union

Despite Olav's early death in 1387, the resourceful Margaret persevered with the union. Proclaimed regent by both the Danish and (what remained of the) Norwegian nobility, she engineered a treaty with the Swedish nobles that not only recognized her as regent of Sweden but also agreed to accept any king she should nominate. Her chosen heir, **Erik of Pomerania** (1382–1459), was foisted on the Norwegians in 1389. When he reached the age of majority in 1397, Margaret organized a grand coronation with Erik crowned king of all three countries at Kalmar in Sweden – hence the **Kalmar Union**.

After Margaret's death in 1412, all power was concentrated in Denmark. In Norway, foreigners were preferred in both state and church, and the country became impoverished by the taxes levied to pay for Erik's various wars. Incompetent and brutal in equal measure, Erik managed to get himself deposed in all three countries at the same time, ending his days as a Baltic pirate.

Union with Denmark

In 1439, Sweden left the union, and in 1450 a Danish count, **Christian of Oldenburg**, was crowned king of Norway and Denmark. Thereafter, Norway simply ceased to take any meaningful part in Scandinavian affairs. Successive monarchs continued to appoint foreigners to important positions, appropriating

Norwegian funds for Danish purposes and even mortgaging Orkney and Shetland in 1469 to the Scots. Danish became the official tongue, replacing **Old Norse**, which came to be regarded as the language of the ignorant and inconsequential. Of local institutions, only the Norwegian Church retained any power, though this was soon to be squashed by the Reformation, and only once did it look as if Norway might break the Danish stranglehold. This was in 1501, when a Swedish-Norwegian nobleman, **Knut Alvsson**, crossed the border and overran southern Norway, but the Danes soon fought back and Alvsson was treacherously murdered as he sued for peace.

The Danish victor, King **Christian II** (1481–1559), imposed a crash programme of "Danicization" on the Norwegians and mercilessly hunted down his opponents, but his attempts to dominate the Swedes led to his forced abdication in 1523. The leaders of the Norwegian opposition rallied under the archbishop of Nidaros, Olav Engelbrektsson, but their attempt to gain terms from the new king Frederik I failed. The Danish civil war that followed the death of Frederik resulted in the victory of the Protestant **Christian III** (1503–59) and the loss of Norway's last independent national institution, the Catholic Church. In 1536 Christian III declared that Norway should cease to be a separate country and that the Lutheran faith should be established there. Christian even carted the silver casket that had contained the bones of St Olav back to Copenhagen, where he melted it down into coins.

Thereafter, Norway became, to all intents and purposes, simply a source of raw materials – fish, timber and iron ore – whose proceeds lined the Danish royal purse. Naturally enough, the Swedes coveted these materials too, the upshot being a long and inconclusive war (1563–70), which saw much of Norway ravaged by competing bands of mercenaries. Ironically, the Swedish attempt to capture Norway induced a change of attitude in Copenhagen: keen to keep their subjects happy, a degree of decentralization became the order of the day, and the Danes appointed a **Governor-General** (*Stattholder*) to administer justice in accordance with traditional Norwegian law.

The Reformation

Though slow to take root among the Norwegian peasantry, **Lutheranism** served as a powerful instrument in establishing Danish control. The Bible, catechism and hymnal were all in Danish and the bishops were all Danes too. Thus, the Norwegian **Reformation** was very much an instrument of Danish colonization rather than a reflection of widespread intellectual ferment: the urban apprentices and craftsmen who fired the movement elsewhere in Europe simply didn't exist in significant numbers here in rustic Norway. Neither had the **Renaissance** made much impact here: the first printing press wasn't established in Norway until 1643, and the reading public remained minuscule, though the country did produce a surprising number of humanist writers. Nonetheless, something of the Renaissance spirit did arrive in the form of **Christian IV** (1588–1648). Among the Danish kings of the period, he proved the most sympathetic to Norway. He visited the country often, improving the quality of its administration and founding new towns – including Kongsberg, Kristiansand and Christiania (later Oslo) – whose buildings were laid out on a spacious gridiron plan.

At last, in the **late sixteenth century**, the Norwegian economy began to pick up. The population grew, trade increased and, benefiting from the decline of the Hanseatic League, a native bourgeoisie began to take control of certain parts of the economy, most notably the herring industry. But Norwegian cultural self-esteem remained at a low ebb: the country's merchants spoke Danish, mimicked Danish manners and read Danish literature. What's more, Norway was a constant bone of contention between Sweden and Denmark, the result being a long series of wars in which competing armies regularly overran its more easterly provinces.

The beginnings of Danish absolutism

The year **1660** marked a turning point in the constitutional arrangements governing Norway. For centuries, the Danish Council of State had had the power to elect the monarch and impose limitations on his or her rule. Now, a powerful alliance of merchants and clergy swept these powers away to make **Frederik III** (1609–70) absolute ruler. This was, however, not a reactionary coup, but an attempt to limit the power of the conservative-minded nobility. In addition, the development of a centralized state machine would, many calculated, provide all sorts of job opportunities to the low-born but adept. As a result, Norway was incorporated into the administrative structure of Denmark with royal authority delegated to the beefed-up office of *Stattholder*, who governed through what soon became a veritable army of professional bureaucrats.

In the event, there were indeed positive advantages for Norway: the country acquired better defences, simpler taxes, a separate High Court and further doses of Norwegian law, but once again power was exercised almost exclusively by Danes. The functionaries were allowed to charge for their services, and there was no fixed tariff – a swindler's charter for which the peasantry paid heavily. So much so, in fact, that one of the *Stattholders*, **Ulrik Gyldenløve**, launched a vigorous campaign against corruption, his efforts rewarded by a far-reaching series of reforming edicts promulgated in 1684.

The eighteenth century

The **absolute monarchy** established by Frederik III soon came to concern itself with every aspect of Norwegian life. The ranks and duties of a host of minor officials were carefully delineated, religious observances tightly regulated and restrictions were imposed on everything from begging and dress through to the food and drink that could be consumed at weddings and funerals. This extraordinary superstructure placed a leaden hand on imagination and invention. Neither was it impartial: there were some benefits for the country's farmers and fishermen, but by and large the system worked **in favour of the middle class**. The merchants of every small town were allocated exclusive rights to trade in a particular area and competition between towns was forbidden. These local monopolies placed the peasantry at a dreadful disadvantage, nowhere more iniquitously than in the Lofoten islands, where fishermen not only had to buy supplies and equipment at the price set by the merchant, but had to sell their fish at the price set by him too.

The Dano-Norwegian functionaries who controlled Norway also set the **cultural agenda**, patronizing an insipid and imitative art and literature. The writings of **Petter Dass** stand out from the dross, however – heartfelt verses and descriptions of life in the Nordland where he worked as a pastor. There were liberal, vaguely nationalist stirrings too, in the foundation of the Norwegian Society in Copenhagen twelve years later.

Missionaries into the north

There was also renewed missionary interest in Norway's old colony of **Greenland**. Part of it was down to the eccentric ethnic obsession of the clergyman concerned, one **Hans Egede** (1686–1758), who was looking for Inuit with Viking features, but Bergen's merchants went along with Egede on condition that he build them a fur-trading station there. In the event, it was a poor investment, as the trading monopoly was given to a Dane. There was also missionary work in Finnmark, where a determined effort was made to convert the Sámi (see pp.366–367). This was a very different undertaking from Egede's, and one that reflected the changing temperament of the Lutheran Church of Norway, which had been reinvigorated by **pietist** clergymen. One of their number, **Thomas von Westen**, learned the Sámi language and led an extraordinarily successful mission to the far north. He was certainly a good deal more popular than many of his fellow pietists down south who persuaded **Christian VI** (1730–46) to impose draconian penalties for such crimes as not observing the Sabbath or not going to church regularly.

War, peace and religious revival

In the meantime, there were more wars between Denmark and Sweden. In 1700, **Frederik IV** (1699–1730) made the rash decision to attack the Swedes at the time when their king, Karl XII, was generally reckoned to be one of Europe's most brilliant military strategists. Predictably, the Danes were defeated and only the intervention of the British saved Copenhagen from falling into Swedish hands. Undeterred, Frederik tried again, and this time Karl retaliated by launching a full-scale invasion of Norway. The Swedes rapidly occupied southern Norway, but then, much to everyone's amazement, things began to go wrong. The Norwegians successfully held out in the Akershus fortress in Christiania (Oslo) and added insult to injury by holding on to Halden too. Furthermore, a naval commander, one **Peter Tordenskiold**, became a national hero in Norway when he caught the Swedish fleet napping and ripped it to pieces off Strømstad. Karl was forced to retreat, but returned with a new army two years later. He promptly besieged the fortress at Halden for a second time, but while he was inspecting his troops someone shot him in the head – whether it was one of his own soldiers or a Norwegian has been the subject of heated debate (in Scandinavia) ever since. Whatever the truth, Karl's death enabled the protagonists to agree the **Peace of Frederiksborg** (1720), which ended hostilities for the rest of the eighteenth century.

Peace favoured the growth of trade, but although Norway's economy prospered it was hampered by the increasing **centralization** of the Dano-Norwegian state. Regulations pushed more and more trade through Copenhagen, to the irritation of the majority of Norwegian merchants who were accustomed to trading direct with their customers. Increasingly, they wanted the same privileges as the Danes, and especially, given the chronic shortage of capital and credit, their own national bank. In the 1760s, Copenhagen did a dramatic U-turn, abolishing monopolies, removing trade barriers and even permitting a free press – and the Norwegian economy boomed. Nonetheless, the bulk of the population remained impoverished and prey to famine whenever the harvest was poor. The number of landless agricultural labourers rose dramatically, partly because more prosperous farmers were buying up large slices of land, and for the first time Norway had something akin to a proletariat.

Despite this, Norway was one of the few European countries little affected by the French Revolution. Instead of political action, there was a **religious revival**, with Hans Nielson Hauge emerging as an evangelical leader. The movement's characteristic hostility to officialdom caused concern, and Hauge was imprisoned, but in reality it posed little threat to the status quo. The end result was rather the foundation of a **Christian fundamentalist movement** that is still a force to be reckoned with in parts of west Norway.

The end of union with Denmark – the early nineteenth century

Denmark-Norway had remained neutral throughout the Seven Years' War (1756–63) between England and France, and renewed that neutrality in 1792, during the period leading up to the **Napoleonic Wars**. The prewar years were good for Norway: overseas trade, especially with England, flourished, and demand for Norwegian timber, iron and cargo-space heralded a period of unparalleled prosperity at least for the bourgeoisie. However, when Napoleon implemented a trade blockade – the Continental System – against Britain, he roped in the Danes. As a result, the British fleet bombarded Copenhagen in 1807 and forced the surrender of the entire Dano-Norwegian fleet. Denmark, in retaliation, declared war on England and Sweden. The move was disastrous for the Norwegian economy, which had also suffered bad harvests in 1807 and 1808, and the English blockade of its seaports ruined trade.

By 1811 it was obvious to many Norwegians that the Danes had backed the wrong side in the war, and the idea of a union of equals with Sweden, which had supported Britain, became increasingly attractive. By attaching their coat-tails to the victors, they hoped to restore the commercially vital trade with England. They also thought that the new Swedish king would be able to deal with the Danes if it came to a fight – just as the Swedes had themselves calculated when they appointed him in 1810. The man concerned, **Karl XIV Johan**, was, curiously enough, none other than Jean-Baptiste Bernadotte, formerly one of Napoleon's marshals. With perfect timing, he had helped the British defeat Napoleon at Leipzig in 1813. His reward came in the **Treaty of Kiel** the following year, when the great powers instructed the Danes to cede to Sweden all rights in Norway (although they did keep the dependencies of Iceland, Greenland and the Faroes). Four hundred years of union had ended.

Union with Sweden 1814–1905

The high-handed transfer of Norway from Denmark to Sweden did nothing to assuage the growing demands for greater Norwegian independence. Furthermore, the Danish Crown Prince Christian Frederik roamed Norway stirring up fears of Swedish intentions. The prince and his supporters convened a Constituent Assembly, which met in a country house outside Eidsvoll (see p.166) in April 1814 and produced a **constitution**. Issued on May 17, 1814 (still a national holiday), this declared Norway to be a "free, independent and indivisible realm" with Christian Frederik as its king. Not surprisingly, Karl Johan would have none of this and, with the support of the great powers, he invaded Norway. Completely outgunned, Christian Frederik barely mounted any resistance. In exchange for Swedish promises to recognize the Norwegian constitution and the *Storting* (parliament), he abdicated as soon as he had signed a peace treaty – the so-called **Convention of Moss** – in August 1814.

The ensuing period was marred by struggles between the *Storting* and **Karl XIV Johan** over the nature of the union. Although the constitution emphasized Norway's independence, Johan had a suspensive veto over the *Storting*'s actions, the post of *Stattholder* in Norway could only be held by a Swede, and foreign and diplomatic matters concerning Norway remained entirely in Swedish hands. Despite this, Karl Johan proved popular in Norway, and during his reign the country enjoyed a degree of independence. The Swedes allowed all the highest offices in Norway to be filled by Norwegians and democratic local councils were established, in part due to the rise of the peasant farmers as a political force.

Under both Oscar I (1844–59) and Karl XV (1859–72), however, it was **pan-Scandinavianism** that ruled the intellectual roost. This belief in the natural solidarity of Denmark, Norway and Sweden was espoused by the leading artists of the period, but died a toothless death in 1864 when the Norwegians and the Swedes refused to help Denmark when it was attacked by Austria and Prussia; some of the loudest cries of treachery came from a young writer by the name of Henrik Ibsen, whose poetic drama, *Brand*, was a spirited indictment of Norwegian perfidy.

Domestic politics and the end of the union with Sweden

Domestic politics were changing too, with the rise to power in the 1850s of **Johan Sverdrup** (1816–92), who started a long and ultimately successful campaign to wrest executive power from the king and transfer it to the *Storting*. By the mid-1880s, Sverdrup and his political allies had pretty much won the day, though a further bout of sabre-rattling between the supporters of Norwegian independence and the Swedish king **Oscar II** (1872–1907) was necessary before both sides would accept a plebiscite. This took place in August 1905, when there was an overwhelming vote in favour of the **dissolution of the union**, which was duly confirmed by the Treaty of Karlstad. A second plebiscite determined that independent Norway should be a monarchy rather than a republic, and, in November 1905, Prince Karl of Denmark (Edward VII of England's son-in-law) was elected to the throne as **Håkon VII** (1872–1957).

Norway's National Romantic movement

Meanwhile, the gradual increase in prosperity had been having important **social and cultural implications**. The layout and buildings of modern Oslo – the Royal Palace, Karl Johans gate, the university – date from this period, while Johan Christian Dahl, the most distinguished Scandinavian landscape painter of his day, was instrumental in the foundation of the Nasjonalgalleriet (National Gallery; see p.88) in Oslo in 1836. More importantly, Dahl and other prominent members of the bourgeoisie formed the nucleus of a **National Romantic movement** that championed all things Norwegian. The movement's serious intent was flagged up by Jens Kraft, who produced a massive six-volume topographical survey of the country, and the poet, prose writer and propagandist **Henrik Wergeland**, who decried the civil-servant culture that had dominated Norway for so long in favour of the more sincere qualities of the peasant farmer. Indeed, the movement endowed the Norwegian peasantry with all sorts of previously unidentified qualities, while the **temperance movement** sought to bring them up to these lofty ideals by promoting laws to prohibit the use of small stills, once found on every farm. The government obliged by formally banning these stills in 1844, and by the mid-nineteenth century, consumption of spirits had dropped drastically and coffee rivalled beer as the national drink.

Similarly, the **Norwegian language** and its folklore was rediscovered by a number of academics, further restoring the country's cultural self-respect. Following on were authors like Alexander Kielland, whose key works were published between 1880 and 1891, and Knut Hamsun, whose most characteristic novel, *Hunger*, was published in 1890. In music, **Edvard Grieg** (1843–1907) was inspired by old Norwegian folk melodies, composing some of his most famous music for Ibsen's *Peer Gynt*, while the artist **Edvard Munch** (1863–1944) completed many of his major works in the 1880s and 1890s. Finally, the internationally acclaimed dramatist **Henrik Ibsen** (1828–1906) returned to Oslo in 1891 after a prolonged self-imposed exile.

Early independence: 1905–30

Norway's **independence** came at a time of further economic advance, engendered by the introduction of hydroelectric power and underpinned by a burgeoning merchant navy, the third-largest after the USA and Britain. Social reforms also saw funds being made available for unemployment relief, accident insurance schemes and a Factory Act (1909), governing safety in the workplace. An extension to the franchise gave the vote to all men over 25, and, in 1913, to women too. The education system was reorganized, and substantial sums were spent on new arms and defence. This prewar period also saw the emergence of a strong trade-union movement and of a Labour Party committed to revolutionary change.

Since 1814 Norway had had little to do with European affairs, and at the outbreak of **World War I** it declared itself strictly neutral. Its sympathy, though, lay largely with the Western Allies, and the Norwegian economy boomed as its ships and timber were in great demand. By 1916, however, Norway had begun to feel the pinch as German submarine action hit both enemy and neutral shipping, and by the end of the war Norway had lost half its chartered tonnage and 2000 crew. The Norwegian economy also suffered after the USA entered the war because the Americans imposed strict trade restrictions in their attempt to prevent supplies getting to Germany, and rationing had to be introduced across Norway. Indeed, the price of neutrality turned out to be high: there was a rise in state expenditure, a soaring cost of living and, at the end of the war, no seat at the conference table. In spite of its losses, Norway got no share of confiscated German shipping, although it was partly compensated by gaining sovereignty of Spitsbergen and its coal deposits – the first extension of the Norwegian frontiers for 500 years. In 1920 Norway also entered the new League of Nations.

The late 1920s

In the **late 1920s**, the decline in world trade led to decreased demand for Norway's shipping. Bank failures and currency fluctuation were rife, and, as unemployment and industrial strife increased, a strengthening Norwegian **Labour Party** took advantage. With the franchise extended and the introduction of larger constituencies, it had a chance to win seats outside the large towns for the first time. At the 1927 election the Labour Party, together with the Social Democrats from whom they'd split, were the biggest grouping in the *Storting*. However, they had no overall majority and because many feared their revolutionary rhetoric, they were manoeuvred out of office after only fourteen days. Trade disputes and lockouts continued and troops had to be used to protect scabs.

The early 1930s

During the war, **Prohibition** had been introduced as a temporary measure and a referendum of 1919 showed a clear majority in favour of its continuation. But the ban did little to quell – and even exacerbated – drunkenness, and it was abandoned in 1932, replaced by the government monopoly on the sale of wines and spirits that remains in force today. The **1933 election** gave the Labour Party more seats than ever. Having shed its revolutionary image, a campaigning, reformist Labour Party benefited from the growing popular conviction that state control and a centrally planned economy were the only answer to Norway's economic problems. In 1935 the Labour Party, in alliance with the Agrarian Party, took power – an unlikely combination since the Agrarians were profoundly nationalist in outlook, so much so that one of their defence spokesmen had been the rabid anti-Semite **Vidkun Quisling**. Frustrated by the democratic process, Quisling had left the Agrarians in 1933 to found **Nasjonal Samling** (National Unification), a fascist movement which proposed, among other things, that both Hitler and Mussolini should be nominated for the Nobel Peace Prize. Quisling had good contacts with Nazi Germany but little support in Norway – local elections in 1937 reduced his local representation to a mere seven, and party membership fell to 1500.

The Labour government under **Johan Nygaardsvold** presided over an improving economy. By 1938 industrial production was 75 percent higher than it had been in 1914 and unemployment dropped as expenditure on roads, railways and public works increased. Social-welfare reforms were implemented and trade-union membership increased. When war broke out in 1939, Norway was lacking only one thing – adequate defence. A vigorous member of the League of Nations, the country had pursued disarmament- and peace-oriented policies since the end of World War I and was determined to remain **neutral**.

World War II

In early **1940**, despite the threat posed by Hitler, the Norwegians were preoccupied with Allied mine-laying off the Norwegian coast – part of their attempt to prevent Swedish iron ore being shipped from Narvik to Germany. Indeed, such was Norwegian naivety that they made a formal protest to Britain on the day of the **German invasion**. Caught napping, the Norwegian army offered little initial resistance and the south and central regions of the country were quickly overrun. King Håkon and the *Storting* were forced into a hasty evacuation of Oslo and headed north to Elverum, evading capture by just a couple of hours. Here, at the government's temporary headquarters, the executive was granted full powers to take whatever decisions were necessary in the interests of

Norway – a mandate which later formed the basis of the Norwegian government-in-exile in Britain.

The Germans contacted the king and his government in Elverum, demanding, among other things, that Quisling be accepted as prime minister as a condition of surrender. Though their situation was desperate, the Norwegians rejected this outright and instead chose resistance. The ensuing campaign lasted for two months and, although the Norwegians fought determinedly with the help of a few British regulars, they were no match for the German army. In June both king and government fled to Britain from Tromsø in northern Norway. The country was rapidly brought under Nazi control, Hitler sending **Josef Terboven** to take full charge of Norwegian affairs.

The fascist **Nasjonal Samling** was declared the only legal party and the media, civil servants and teachers were brought under its control. As **civil resistance** grew, a state of emergency was declared: two trade-union leaders were shot, arrests increased and a concentration camp was set up outside Oslo. In February 1942 Quisling was installed as "Minister President" of Norway, but it soon became clear that his government didn't have the support of the Norwegian people. The Church refused to cooperate, schoolteachers protested and trade-union members and officials resigned en masse. In response, deportations increased, death sentences were announced and a compulsory labour scheme was introduced.

The Resistance

Military resistance escalated. A military organization (**MILORG**) was established as a branch of the armed forces under the control of the High Command in London. By May 1941 it had enlisted 20,000 men (32,000 by 1944) in clandestine groups all over the country. Arms and instructors came from Britain, radio stations were set up and a continuous flow of intelligence about Nazi movements sent back. Sabotage operations were legion, the most notable being the destruction of the heavy-water plant at **Rjukan** (see p.193), foiling a German attempt to produce an atomic bomb. Reprisals against the resistance were severe and some were carried out by several thousand Norwegian collaborators, including the 15,000 who enlisted in the German army.

The **government-in-exile** in London continued to represent free Norway to the world, mobilizing support on behalf of the Allies. Most of the Norwegian merchant fleet was abroad when the Nazis invaded, and by 1943 the Norwegian navy had seventy ships helping the Allied convoys. With the German position deteriorating, neutral Sweden adopted a more sympathetic policy to its Norwegian neighbours, allowing the creation of thinly disguised training grounds for resistance fighters. These camps also served to produce the police detachments that were to secure law and order after liberation.

German surrender

When the Allies landed in Normandy in June 1944, overt action against the occupying Germans in Norway was temporarily discouraged as the US and Britain could not guarantee military supplies. Help was at hand, however, in the form of the **Soviets** who crossed into the far north of Norway in late October, driving back the Germans at double speed. Unfortunately, the Germans chose to burn everything in their path as they retreated, a scorched-earth policy that inflicted untold suffering on the local population, many of whom hid in the forests and caves. To prevent the Germans reinforcing their beleaguered

Finnmark battalions, the resistance organized a campaign of mass railway sabotage, stopping three-quarters of the troop movements overnight. With their control of Norway crumbling, the Germans finally **surrendered** on May 7, 1945. King Håkon returned to Norway on June 7, five years to the day since he'd left for exile.

Terboven committed suicide and the NS collaborators were rounded up. A caretaker government took office, staffed by resistance leaders, and was replaced in October 1945 by a majority **Labour government**. The Communists won eleven seats, reflecting the efforts of Communist saboteurs in the war and the prestige that the Soviet Union enjoyed in Norway after the liberation. Quisling was shot, along with 24 other high-ranking traitors, and thousands of collaborators were punished with varying degrees of severity.

Postwar reconstruction

At the end of the war, Norway was on its knees: the far north – Finnmark – had been laid waste, half the mercantile fleet lost, and production was at a standstill. Nevertheless, recovery, fostered by a sense of national unity, was quick and it was only three years before GNP was at its prewar level. In addition, Norway's part in the war had increased her international prestige. The country became one of the founding members of the **United Nations** in 1945, and the first UN Secretary-General, Trygve Lie, was, at the time of his appointment, Norwegian Foreign Minister. With the failure of discussions to promote a Scandinavian defence union, the *Storting* also voted to enter **NATO** in 1949.

Domestically, there was general agreement about the form that **social reconstruction** should take. In 1948, the *Storting* passed the laws that introduced the Welfare State almost unanimously. The 1949 election saw the government returned with a larger majority, and Labour governments continued to be elected throughout the following decade, with the dominant political figure being **Einar Gerhardsen**. As national prosperity increased, society became ever more egalitarian, levelling up rather than down. Subsidies were paid to the agricultural and fishing industries, wages increased, and a comprehensive social security system helped to eradicate poverty. The state ran the important mining industry, was the largest shareholder in the national hydroelectric company and built an enormous steel works at Mo-i-Rana to help develop the economy of the devastated northern counties. Rationing ended in 1952 and, as the demand for higher education grew, so new universities were created in Bergen, Trondheim and Tromsø.

Beyond consensus: the 1960s to the 1970s

The political consensus began to fragment in the early 1960s. Following the restructuring of rural constituencies in the 1950s, there was a realignment in centre politics, the outmoded Agrarian Party becoming the **Centre Party**. There was change on the left too, where defence squabbles within the Labour

Party led to the formation of the **Socialist People's Party (SF)**, which wanted Norway out of NATO and sought a renunciation of nuclear weapons. The Labour Party's 1961 declaration that no nuclear weapons would be stationed in Norway except under an immediate threat of war did not placate the SF, who unexpectedly took two seats at the election that year. Holding the balance of power, the SF voted with the Labour Party until 1963, when it helped bring down the government over mismanagement of state industries. A replacement coalition collapsed after only one month, but the writing was on the wall. Rising prices, dissatisfaction with high taxation and a continuing housing shortage meant that the 1965 election put a **non-socialist coalition** in power for the first time in twenty years.

Under the leadership of **Per Borten** of the Centre Party, the coalition's programme was unambitious. Nonetheless, living standards continued to rise, and although the 1969 election saw a marked increase in Labour Party support, the coalition hung on to power. Also that year, **oil and gas** were discovered beneath the North Sea and, as the vast extent of the reserves became obvious, it became clear that the Norwegians were to enjoy a magnificent bonanza – one which was destined to pay about 25 percent of the government's annual bills.

Elsewhere, Norway's politicians, who had applied twice previously for membership of the **European Economic Community (EEC)** – in 1962 and 1967 – believed that de Gaulle's fall in France presented a good opportunity for a third application, which was made in 1970. There was great concern, though, about the effect of membership on Norwegian agriculture and fisheries, and in 1971 Per Borten was forced to resign following his indiscreet handling of the negotiations. The Labour Party, the majority of its representatives in favour of EEC membership, formed a minority administration, but when the **1972 referendum** narrowly voted "No" to joining the EEC, the government resigned.

With the 1973 election producing another minority Labour government, the uncertain political pattern of the previous ten years continued. Even the postwar consensus on **Norwegian security policy** broke down on various issues – primarily the question of a northern European nuclear-free zone and the stocking of Allied material in Norway – although there remained strong agreement for continued NATO membership.

The 1980s and early 1990s

In 1983, the Christian Democrats and the Centre Party joined together in a non-socialist coalition, which lasted only two years. It was replaced in 1986 by a minority Labour administration, led by **Dr Gro Harlem Brundtland**, Norway's first woman prime minister. She made sweeping changes to the way the country was run, introducing seven women into her eighteen-member cabinet, but her government was beset by problems for the three years of its life: tumbling oil prices led to a recession, unemployment rose (though only to four percent) and there was widespread dissatisfaction with Labour's high taxation policies.

At the **general election** in September 1989, Labour lost eight seats and was forced out of office – the worst result the party had suffered since 1930. More surprising was the success of the extremist parties on both political wings – the anti-NATO, leftist Socialist Party and the right-wing, anti-immigrant Progress Party both scored spectacular results, winning almost a quarter of the votes cast,

▲ Dr Gro Harlem Brundtland

and increasing their representation in the *Storting* many times over. This deprived the Conservative Party (one of whose leaders, bizarrely, was Gro Harlem Brundtland's husband) of the majority it might have expected, the result being yet another shaky minority administration – this time a **centre-right coalition** between the Conservatives, the Centre Party and the Christian Democrats, led by Jan Syse.

The new government immediately faced problems familiar to the last Labour administration. In particular, there was continuing conflict over joining the **European Community** (as the European Union was then known), a policy still supported by many in the Norwegian establishment but flatly rejected by the Centre Party. It was this, in part, that signalled the end of the coalition, for after just over a year in office, the Centre Party withdrew its support and forced the downfall of Syse. In October 1990, Gro Harlem Brundtland was put back in power at the head of a **minority Labour administration**, remaining in office till her re-election for a fourth minority term in 1993. The 1993 elections saw a revival in Labour Party fortunes and, to the relief of the majority, the collapse of the Progress Party vote. However, it was also an untidy, confusing affair where the main issue, membership of the EU, cut across the traditional left-versus-right divide.

The 1990s – political argy-bargy

Following the 1993 election, the country tumbled into a long and fiercely conducted campaign over **membership of the EU**. Brundtland and her main political opponents wanted in, but despite the near-unanimity of the political class, the Norwegians narrowly rejected the EU in a 1994 referendum. It was a close call (52.5 percent versus 47.5 percent), but in the end farmers and fishermen afraid of the economic results of joining, as well as women's groups and environmentalists, who felt that Norway's high standards of social care and "green" controls would suffer, came together to swing opinion against joining. Afterwards, and unlike the Labour government of 1972, the Brundtland administration soldiered on, wisely soothing ruffled feathers by promising to shelve the whole EU membership issue until at least 2000. Nonetheless, the **1997 election** saw a move to the right, the main beneficiaries being the Christian Democratic Party and the ultra-conservative Progress Party. In itself, this was not enough to remove the Labour-led coalition from office – indeed Labour remained comfortably the largest party – but the right was dealt a trump card by the new Labour leader, **Thorbjørn Jagland**. During the campaign Jagland had promised that the Labour Party would step down from office if it failed to elicit more than the 36.9 percent of the vote it had secured in 1993. Much to the chagrin of his colleagues, Jagland's political chickens came home to roost when Labour only received 35 percent of the vote – and they had to go, leaving power in the hands of an unwieldy right-of-centre, minority coalition. Bargaining with its rivals from a position of parliamentary weakness, the new government found it difficult to cut a clear path – or at least one very different from its predecessor – apart from managing to antagonize the women's movement by some reactionary social legislation whose none-too-hidden subtext seemed to read "A woman's place is in the home". In the spring of 2000, the government resigned and the Labour Party resumed command.

Norway today

The Labour Party administration that took over the reins of government in 2000 didn't last long: in elections the following year, they took a drubbing and the right prospered, paving the way for an ungainly centre-right coalition. This coalition battled on until October 2005 when the Labour Party, along with its allies the Socialist Left Party and the Centre Party, won a general election, with the politically experienced **Jens Stoltenberg** becoming Prime Minister – as he remains at time of writing. Stoltenberg has bolted together one of Norway's more secure coalitions and his political agenda was – and remains – standard-issue centre-left: for instance, a flexible retirement from the age of 62 (it's currently 67) will be introduced in 2010; a careful incomes policy is geared to the needs of both employer and employee; there's a commitment to develop and strengthen Sámi culture; and there are detailed promises on tackling climate change and global warming. As Stoltenberg put it himself at the time of his election victory "Our gains are due to a clear political message about jobs, education, and giving people security in their old age. Our aim is to give this country a stable and predictable government."

In the summer of 2008, however, the wheels began to come off the coalition wagon with arguments about the killing of wolves, corruption, and the state of the health-care system. Stoltenberg's popularity sank, but then came the banking crisis and, with Norway's banks hit hard, Stoltenberg started to look more like a prime minister who could take care of business – and the opinion polls gave him and his Labour Party a better rating. Quite whether this revival will save the Labour Party and its allies from defeat in the next general election in September 2009 remains to be seen.

The future

In the long term, quite what Norway will make of its splendid **isolation from the EU** is unclear, though the situation is mitigated by Norway's membership of the European Economic Agreement (EEA), a free-trade deal of January 1994 that covers both Norway and the EU. Whatever happens, and whether or not there is another EU referendum, it's hard to imagine that the Norwegians will suffer any permanent economic harm. They have, after all, a superabundance of natural resources and arguably the most educated workforce in the world. Which isn't to say the country doesn't collectively **fret** – a modest increase in the amount of drug addiction and street crime has produced much heart-searching, the theory being that an advanced and progressive social policy should be able to eliminate such barbarisms. This thoughtful approach, so typical of Norway, is very much to the country's credit, as is the refusal to accept a residual level of unemployment (of about 2–4 percent) that is the envy of many other Western governments. Neither are fretting and a sense of happiness mutually exclusive: Norway's Lutheran roots run deep and, if an old joke is to be believed, the low point of the average Norwegian's year is the summer vacation.

The Norwegians also fret (and argue) about **environmental** issues, with one hot potato being the country's **road building** programme. A curse afflicting prewar Norway had always been rural isolation and the Norwegians of 1945 were determined to connect (almost) all of the country's villages to the road system. Give or take the occasional hamlet, this has now been achieved and a second phase is underway, involving the upgrading of roads and the construction of innumerable tunnels. Wherever this makes conditions safer, the popular consensus for the programme survives, but there is increasing opposition to the prestige projects so beloved by politicians – the enormous tunnel near Flåm (see p.239) being a case in point. There is, however, precious little internal argument when it comes to **whaling and sealing**, with the majority continuing to support the hunting of these animals as has been the custom for centuries – indeed, for some Norwegians whaling and sealing go some way to defining what they consider to be the national identity. This is inexplicable to many Western Europeans, who point to Norway's eminently liberal approach to most other matters, but the Norwegians see things very differently: why, many of them ask, is the culling of seals and mink seen in a different light from the mass slaughter of farmed animals?

Legends and folklore

Norway has an exceptionally rich body of **historical legend and folk tradition**, and it's one that plays an important part in the national consciousness. Most famous are the **sagas**, mainly written in Iceland between the twelfth and fourteenth centuries and constituting a vast collection of part-historical, part-fictionalized stories covering several centuries of Norse history. Thanks to the survival of one of these sagas, the *Poetic Edda* (see p.413), our knowledge of **Norse mythology** is far from conjectural. Furthermore, much that was not recorded there survived in the oral tradition, to be revived from the 1830s onwards by the artists and writers of the National Romantic movement. Some members of this movement also set about collecting the **folk tales** and legends of the rural regions. The difficulties they experienced in rendering the Norwegian dialects into written form – there was no written Norwegian language per se – fuelled the language movement, and sent the academic Ivar Aasen roaming the countryside to assemble the material from which he formulated *Landsmål* (see p.461).

Sagas

The Norwegian Vikings settled in Iceland in the ninth century and throughout the medieval period the Icelanders had a deep attachment to, and interest in, their original homeland. The result was a body of work that remains one of the richest sources of European medieval literature. That so much of it has survived is due to Iceland's isolation – most Norwegian sources disappeared centuries ago.

All the **sagas** feature real people and tell of events which are usually known to have happened, though the plots are embroidered to suit the tales' heroic style. They reveal much about a Norse culture in which arguments between individuals might spring from comparatively trivial disputes over horses or sheep, but where a strict code of honour and revenge meant that every insult, whether real or imagined, had to be avenged. Thus personal disputes soon turned into clan vendettas. Plots are complex, the dialogue laconic, and the pared-down prose omits unnecessary detail. New characters are often introduced by means of tedious genealogies, necessary to explain the motivation behind their later actions (though the more adept translations render these explanations as footnotes). Personality is only revealed through speech, facial expressions and general demeanour, or the comments and gossip of others.

The earliest Icelandic work, the **Elder** or **Poetic Edda** (various English editions are available), comprises 34 lays dating from as early as the eighth century, and they combine to give a detailed insight into early Norse culture and pagan cosmogony and belief. It's not to be confused with the **Younger** or **Prose Edda**, written centuries later by Snorri Sturluson, the most distinguished of the saga writers.

Also noteworthy are *The Vinland Saga*, *Njal's Saga* and the *Laxdaela Saga*, tales of ninth- and tenth-century Icelandic derring-do; and *Harald's Saga*, a rattling good yarn celebrating the life and times of Harald Hardrada. English translations of all the above are published by Penguin.

Norse mythology

The Vikings shared a common **pagan faith**, whose polytheistic tenets were upheld right across Scandinavia. The deities were worshipped at a thousand village shrines, usually by means of sacrifices in which animals, weapons, boats and other artefacts, even humans, were gifted to the gods. There was very little theology to sanctify these rituals; instead the principal gods – Odin, Thor and Frey – were surrounded by mythical tales attributing to them a bewildering variety of strengths, weaknesses and powers.

The god of war, wisdom, poetry and magic, **Odin** was untrustworthy, violent and wise in equal measure. The most powerful of the twelve Viking deities, the Aesir, who lived at Asgard, he was also lord of the **Valkyries**, women warrior-servants who tended his needs while he held court at **Valhalla**, the hall of dead heroes. As with many of the other pagan gods, he had the power to change into any form he desired. Odin's wife, **Frigga**, was the goddess protecting the home and the family.

At the beginning of time, it was Odin who made heaven and earth from the body of the giant Ymir, and created man from an ash tree, woman from an alder. However, **Yggdrasil**, the tree of life that supported the whole universe, was beyond his control; the Vikings believed that eventually the tree would die and both gods and mortals would perish in the **Ragnarok**, the twilight of the gods. Among the Anglo-Saxons, the equivalent of Odin was Woden, hence the origin of the word "Wednesday".

One of Odin's sons, **Thor** appears to have been the most worshipped of the Norse gods. A giant with superhuman strength, he was the short-tempered god of thunder, fire and lightning. He regularly fought with the evil Frost Giants in the Jotunheim mountains (see p.415), his favourite weapon being the hammer, Mjolnir, which the trolls (see p.415) had fashioned for him. His chariot was drawn by two goats – Cracktooth and Gaptooth – who could be killed and eaten at night, but would be fully recovered the next morning, providing none of their bones were broken. It's from Thor that we get "Thursday".

A negative force, **Loki** personified cunning and trickery. His treachery turned the other deities against him, and he was chained up beneath a serpent that dripped venom onto his face. His wife, **Sigyn**, remained loyal and held a bowl over his head to catch the venom, but when the bowl was full she had to turn away to empty it, and in those moments his squirmings would cause earthquakes.

The god of fertility, **Frey**'s pride and joy was Skidbladnir, a ship that was large enough to carry all the gods, but could still be folded up and put into his bag. He often lived with the elves (see p.415) in Elfheim.

Freya was the goddess of love, healing and fertility. "Friday" was named after her.

The goddess of the dead, **Hel** lived on brains and bone marrow. She presided over "Hel", where those who died of illness or old age went, living a miserable existence under the roots of Yggdrasil, the tree of life.

Representing the past, the present and the future, the **Norns** were the three goddesses of fate, casting lots over the cradle of every new born child.

Folk tales and legends

Norway's extensive oral folklore was first written down in the early nineteenth century, most famously by **Peter Christen Asbjørnsen** and **Jørgen Moe**, the first of whose compilations appeared to great popular acclaim in 1842. Despite all the nationalist kerfuffle regarding the Norwegianness of the tales, many of them were in fact far from unique to Norway. But while they shared many characteristics – and had the same roots – as folk tales across the whole of northern Europe, they were populated by stock characters who were recognizably Norwegian – the king, for example, was always pictured as a wealthy Norwegian farmer.

There are three types of Norwegian **folk tale**: comical tales; animal yarns, in which the beasts concerned – most frequently the wolf, fox and bear – talk and behave like human beings; and most common of all, magical stories populated by a host of supernatural creatures. The folk tale is always written matter-of-factly, no matter how fantastic the events it retells. In this respect it has much in common with the **folk legend**, though the latter purports to be factual. Norwegian legends "explain" scores of unusual natural phenomena – the location of boulders, holes in cliffs, etc – and are crammed with supernatural beings, again as is broadly familiar right across northern Europe.

The assorted **supernatural creatures** of folk tale and legend hark back to the pagan myths of the pre-Christian era, but whereas the Vikings held them of secondary importance to their gods, in Norwegian folk tales they take centre stage. In post-pagan Norwegian folk tradition, these creatures were regarded as the descendants of children that Eve hid from God. When they were discovered by him, they were assigned particular realms in which to dwell, but their illicit wanderings were legion. Towards the end of the nineteenth century, book illustrations by **Erik Werenskiold** and **Theodor Kittelsen** effectively defined what the various supernatural creatures looked like in the Norwegian public's imagination.

As mythologized in Norway, the creatures of the folk tales possess a confusing range of virtues and vices. Here's a brief guide to some of the more important.

Enormous in size and strength, the **giants** of Norwegian folklore were reputed to be rather stupid and capable both of kindly actions and great cruelty towards humans. They usually had a human appearance, but some were monsters with many heads. They were fond of carrying parts of the landscape from one place to another, dropping boulders and even islands as they went. According to the Eddic cosmogony, the first giant, Ymir, was killed by Odin and the world made from his body – his blood formed the sea, his bones the mountains and so on. Ymir was the ancestor of the evil **Frost Giants**, who lived in Jotunheim, and who regularly fought with Thor.

Spirits of the underground, **trolls** were ambivalent figures, able both to hinder and help humans – and were arguably a folkloric expression of the id. The first trolls were depicted as giants, but later versions were small, strong, misshapen and of pale countenance from living underground; sunlight would turn them into stone. They worked in metals and wood and were fabulous craftsmen. They made Odin's spear and Thor's hammer, though Thor's inclination to throw the weapon at them made them hate noise; as late as the eighteenth century, Norwegian villagers would ring church bells for hours on end to drive them away. If the trolls were forced to make something for a human, they would put a secret curse on it; this would render it dangerous to the owner. Some trolls had a penchant for stealing children and others carried off women to be their wives.

Akin to fairies, **elves** were usually divided between good-hearted but mischievous white elves, and nasty black elves, who brought injury and sickness. Both lived underground in a world, Elfheim, that echoed that of humans – with farms, animals and the like – but made excursions into the glades and groves of the forests up above. At night, the white elves liked singing and dancing to the accompaniment of the harp. They were normally invisible, though you could spot their dancing places wherever the grass grew more luxuriantly in circular patterns than elsewhere. The black elves were also invisible, a good job considering they were extremely ugly and had long, filthy noses. If struck by a sunbeam, they would turn to stone. Both types of elf were prone to entice humans into their kingdom, usually for a short period – but sometimes forever.

In pre-Christian times, the Vikings believed their lands to be populated with invisible guardian spirits, the **wights** (*vetter*), who needed to be treated with respect. One result was that when a longship was approaching the shore, the fearsome figurehead at its prow was removed so as not to frighten the *vetter* away. Bad luck would follow if a *vetter* left the locality.

Personifying all those who have died at sea, the **draugen** was a ghostly apparition who appeared as a headless fisherman in oilskins. He sailed the seas in half a boat and wailed when someone was about to drown. Other water spirits included the malicious river sprite, the **nixie**, who could assume different forms to lure the unsuspecting to a watery grave. There were also the shy and benign **mermaids** and **mermen**, half-fish and half-human, who dived into the water whenever they spied a human. However, they also liked to dress up as humans to go to market.

As with **witches** across the rest of Europe, the Scandinavian version was an old woman who had made a pact with the Devil, swapping her soul in return for special powers. The witch could inflict injury and illness, especially if she had something the victim had touched or owned – anything from a lock of hair to an item of clothing. She could disguise herself as an animal, and had familiars – usually insects or cats – which assisted her in foul deeds. Most witches travelled through the air on broomsticks, but some rode on wolves bridled with snakes.

Viking customs and rituals

T he **Vikings** have long been the subject of historical myth and legend, but accurate and unbiased contemporary accounts are few and far between. A remarkable exception is the annals of **Ibn Fadlan**, a member of a diplomatic delegation sent from the Baghdad Caliphate to Bulgar on the Volga in 921–922AD. In the following extracts Fadlan details the habits and rituals of a tribe of Swedish Vikings, the **Rus**, who dealt in furs and slaves. The first piece notes with disgust the finer points of Viking personal hygiene, the second provides a sober eyewitness account of the rituals of a Viking ship burial.

Habits and rituals

I saw the Rus when they arrived on their trading mission and anchored at the River Atul (Volga). Never had I seen people of more perfect physique; they are tall as date-palms, and reddish in colour. They wear neither mantle nor coat, but each man carries a cape, which covers one half of his body, leaving one hand free. Their swords are Frankish in pattern, broad, flat and fluted. Each man has (tattooed upon him) trees, figures and the like from the finger-nails to the neck. Each woman carries on her bosom a container made of iron, silver, copper or gold – its size and substance depending on her man's wealth. Attached to the container is a ring carrying her knife, which is also tied to her bosom. Round her neck she wears gold or silver rings; when a man amasses 10,000 *dirhems* he makes his wife one gold ring; when he has 20,000 he makes two; and so the woman gets a new ring for every 10,000 *dirhems* her husband acquires, and often a woman has many of these rings. Their finest ornaments are green beads made from clay. They will go to any length to get hold of these; for one *dirhem* they procure one such bead and they string these into necklaces for their women.

They are the filthiest of god's creatures. They do not wash after discharging their natural functions, neither do they wash their hands after meals. They are as stray donkeys. They arrive from their distant lands and lay their ships alongside the banks of the Atul, which is a great river, and there they build big wooden houses on its shores. Ten or twenty of them may live together in one house, and each of them has a couch of his own where he sits and diverts himself with the pretty slave-girls whom he has brought along to offer for sale. He will make love with one of them in the presence of his comrades, sometimes this develops into a communal orgy and, if a customer should turn up to buy a girl, the Rus will not let her go till he has finished with her.

Every day they wash their faces and heads, all using the same water which is as filthy as can be imagined. This is how it is done. Every morning a girl brings her master a large bowl of water in which he washes his face and hands and hair, combing it also over the bowl, then blows his nose and spits into the water. No dirt is left on him which doesn't go into the water. When he has finished the girl takes the same bowl to his neighbour – who repeats the performance – until the bowl has gone round the entire household. All have blown their noses, spat and washed their faces and hair in the water.

On anchoring their vessels, each man goes ashore carrying bread, meat, onions, milk, and *nabid* [wine], and these he takes to a large wooden stake with a face like that of a human being, surrounded by smaller figures, and behind them tall poles in the ground. Each man prostrates himself before the large post and recites: "O Lord, I have come from distant parts with so many girls, so many furs (and whatever other commodities he is carrying). I now bring you this offering." He then presents his gift and continues "Please send me a merchant who has many dinars and *dirhems*, and who will trade favourably with me without too much bartering." Then he retires. If, after this, business does not pick up quickly and go well, he returns to the statue to present further gifts. If results continue slow, he then presents gifts to the minor figures and begs their intercession, saying, "These are our Lord's wives, daughters and sons." Then he pleads before each figure in turn, begging them to intercede for him and humbling himself before them. Often trade picks up, and he says "My Lord has required my needs, and now it is my duty to repay him." Whereupon he sacrifices goats or cattle, some of which he distributes as alms. The rest he lays before the statues, large and small, and the heads of the beasts he plants upon the poles. After dark, of course, the dogs come and devour the lot – and the successful trader says, "My Lord is pleased with me, and has eaten my offerings."

If one of the Rus falls sick they put him in a tent by himself and leave bread and water for him. They do not visit him, however, or speak to him, especially if he is a serf. Should he recover he rejoins the others; if he dies they burn him. If he happens to be a serf, however, they leave him for the dogs and vultures to devour. If they catch a robber they hang him in a tree until he is torn to shreds by wind and weather …

The burial

… I had been told that when their chieftains died cremation was the least part of their whole funeral procedure, and I was, therefore, very much interested to find out more about this. One day I heard that one of their leaders had died. They laid him forthwith in a grave, which they covered up for ten days till they had finished cutting-out and sewing his costume. If the dead man is poor they make a little ship, put him in it, and burn it. If he is wealthy, however, they divide his property and goods into three parts: one for his family, one to pay for his costume, and one to make *nabid*. This they drink on the day when the slave woman of the dead man is killed and burnt together with her master. They are deeply addicted to *nabid*, drinking it day and night; and often one of them has been found dead with a beaker in his hand. When a chieftain among them has died, his family demands of his slave women and servants: "Which of you wishes to die with him?" Then one of them says "I do" – and having said that the person concerned is forced to do so, and no backing out is possible. Those who are willing are mostly the slave women.

So when this man died they said to his slave women "Which of you wants to die with him?" One of them answered "I do." From that moment she was put in the constant care of two other women servants who took care of her to the extent of washing her feet with their own hands. They began to get things ready for the dead man, to cut his costume and so on, while every day the doomed woman drank and sang as though in anticipation of a joyous event.

When the day arrived on which the chieftain and his slave woman were going to be burnt, I went to the river where his ship was moored. It had been hauled ashore and four posts were made for it of birch and other wood. Further there was arranged around it what looked like a big store of wood. Then the ship was hauled near and placed on the wood. People now began to walk about talking in a language I could not understand, and the corpse still lay in the grave; they had not taken it out. They then produced a wooden bench, placed it on the ship, and covered it with carpets of Byzantine *dibag* (painted silk) and with cushions of Byzantine *dibag*. Then came an old woman whom they called "the Angel of Death", and she spread these cushions out over the bench. She was in charge of the whole affair from dressing the corpse to the killing of the slave woman. I noticed that she was an old giant-woman, a massive and grim figure. When they came to his grave they removed the earth from the wooden frame and they also took the frame away. They then divested the corpse of the clothes in which he had died. The body, I noticed, had turned black because of the intense frost. When they first put him in the grave, they had also given him beer, fruit, and a lute, all of which they now removed. Strangely enough the corpse did not smell, nor had anything about him changed save the colour of his flesh. They now proceeded to dress him in hose, and trousers, boots, coat, and a mantle of *dibag* adorned with gold buttons; put on his head a cap of *dibag* and sable fur; and carried him to the tent on the ship, where they put him on the blanket and supported him with cushions. They then produced *nabid*, fruit, and aromatic plants, and put these round his body; and they also brought bread, meat, and onions which they flung before him. Next they took a dog, cut it in half, and flung the pieces into the ship, and after this they took all his weapons and placed them beside him.

Next they brought two horses and ran them about until they were in a sweat, after which they cut them to pieces with swords and flung their meat into the ship; this also happened to two cows. Then they produced a cock and a hen, killed them, and threw them in. Meanwhile the slave woman who wished to be killed walked up and down, going into one tent after the other, and the owner of each tent had sexual intercourse with her, saying "Tell your master I did this out of love for him."

It was now Friday afternoon and they took the slave woman away to something which they had made resembling a doorframe. Then she placed her legs on the palms of the men and reached high enough to look over the frame, and she said something in a foreign language, after which they took her down. And they lifted her again and she did the same as the first time. Then they took her down and lifted her a third time and she did the same as the first and second times. Then they gave her a chicken and she cut its head off and threw it away; they took the hen and threw it into the ship. Then I asked the interpreter what she had done. He answered: "The first time they lifted her she said: 'Look! I see my mother and father.' The second time she said: 'Look! I see all my dead relatives sitting around.' The third time she said: 'Look! I see my master in Paradise, and Paradise is beautiful and green and together with him are men and young boys. He calls me. Let me join him then.'"

They now led her towards the ship. Then she took off two bracelets she was wearing and gave them to the old woman, "the Angel of Death", the one who was going to kill her. She next took off two anklets she was wearing and gave them to the daughters of that same woman. They then led her to the ship but did not allow her inside the tent. Then a number of men carrying wooden shields and sticks arrived, and gave her a beaker with *nabid*. She sang over it and emptied it. The interpreter then said to me, "Now with that she is bidding farewell to all her women friends." Then she was given another beaker. She took it and sang a lengthy song; but the old woman told her to hurry and drink up and enter the tent where her master was. When I looked at her she seemed completely bewildered. She wanted to enter the tent and she put her head between it and the ship. Then the woman took her head and managed to get it inside the tent, and the woman herself followed. Then the men began to beat the shields with the wooden sticks, to deaden her shouts so that the other girls would not become afraid and shrink from dying with their masters. Six men entered the tent and all of them had intercourse with her. Thereafter they laid her by the side of her dead master. Two held her hands and two her feet, and the woman called "the Angel of Death" put a cord round the girl's neck, doubled with an end at each side, and gave it to two men to pull. Then she advanced holding a small dagger with a broad blade and began to plunge it between the girl's ribs to and fro while the two men choked her with the cord till she died.

The dead man's nearest kinsman now appeared. He took a piece of wood and ignited it. Then he walked backwards, his back towards the ship and his face towards the crowd, holding the piece of wood in one hand and the other hand on his buttock; and he was naked. In this way the wood was ignited which they had placed under the ship after they had laid the slave woman, whom they had killed, beside her master. Then people came with branches and wood; each brought a burning brand and threw it on the pyre, so that the fire took hold of the wood, then the ship, then the tent and the man and the slave woman and all. Thereafter a strong and terrible wind rose so that the flame stirred and the fire blazed still more.

I heard one of the Rus folk, standing by, say something to my interpreter, and when I inquired what he had said, my interpreter answered: "He said: 'You Arabs are foolish'". "Why?" I asked. "Well, because you throw those you love and honour to the ground where the earth and the maggots and fields devour them, whereas we, on the other hand, burn them up quickly and they go to Paradise that very moment." The man burst out laughing, and on being asked why, he said: "His Lord, out of love for him, has sent this wind to take him away within the hour!" And so it proved, for within that time the ship and the pyre, the girl and the corpse had all become ashes and then dust. On the spot where the ship stood after having been hauled ashore, they built something like a round mould. In the middle of it they raised a large post of birch-wood on which they wrote the names of the dead man and the king of the Rus, and then the crowd dispersed.

The above extract, translated by Karre Stov, was taken from *The Vikings* by Johanes Brøndsted, and is reprinted by permission of Penguin Books.

Flora and fauna

There are significant differences in **climate** between the west coast of Norway, which is warmed by the Gulf Stream, and the interior, but these variations are of much less significance for the country's **flora** than altitude and latitude. With regard to its **fauna**, wild animals survive in significant numbers in the more inaccessible regions, but have been hunted extensively elsewhere, and Norway's west coast is home to dozens of extensive sea-bird colonies.

Flora

Much of the Norwegian landscape is dominated by vast **forests of spruce**, though these are, in fact, a relatively recent feature: the original forest cover was mainly of pine, birch and oak, and only in the last two thousand years has spruce spread across the whole of southeast and central Norway. That said, a rich variety of **deciduous trees** – notably oak, ash, lime, hazel, rowan, elm and maple – still flourishes in a wide belt along the south coast, up through the fjord country and as far north as Trondheim, but only at relatively low altitudes. For their part, **conifers** thin out at around 900m above sea level in the south, 450m in Finnmark, to be replaced by a birch zone, where there are also aspen and mountain ash. Norway's deciduous trees contrive to ripen their seeds despite a short, cool summer, and can consequently be found at low altitudes almost as far north as Nordkapp (North Cape) – as can the pine, the most robust of the conifers. At around 1100m/650m, the birch fizzle out to be replaced by willow and dwarf birch, while above the timber line are bare mountain peaks and huge plateaux, the latter usually dotted with hundreds of lakes.

Norway accommodates in the region of two thousand plant species, but few of them are native. The most sought-after are the **berrying** species that grow wild all over Norway, mainly cranberries, blueberries and yellow **cloudberries**. Common in the country's peat bogs, and now also extensively cultivated, the cloudberry is a small herbaceous bramble whose fruits have a tangy flavour that is much prized in Norway. In drier situations and on the mountain plateaux, **lichens** – the favourite food of the reindeer – predominate, while in all but the thickest of spruce forests, the ground is thickly carpeted with **moss** and **heather**.

Everywhere, spring brings **wild flowers**, splashes of brilliant colour at their most intense on the west coast, where a wide range of mountain plants is nourished by the wet conditions and a geology that varies from limestone to acidic granites. Most of these species can also be found in the Alps, but there are several rarities, notably the **alpine clematis** (*Clematis alpina*) found in the Gudbrandsdal valley, hundreds of miles from its normal homes in eastern Finland and the Carpathian mountains. Another, larger group comprises about thirty **Canadian mountain plants**, found in Europe only in the Dovre and Jotunheim mountains; quite how they come to be there has long baffled botanists.

The mildness of the west-coast winter has allowed certain species to prosper beyond their usual northerly latitudes. Among species that can tolerate very little frost or snow are the star hyacinth (*Scilla verna*) and the purple heather (*Erica purpurea*), while a short distance inland come varieties that can withstand only short icy spells, including the foxglove (*Digitalis purpurea*) and the holly (*Ilex aquifolium*). In the southeastern part of the country, where the winters are harder and the summers hotter, the conditions support species that can lie dormant under the snow for several months a year – for example the blue anemone (*Anemone hepatica*) and the aconite (*Aconitum septentrionale*).

In the far north, certain Siberian species have migrated west down the rivers and along the coasts to the fjords of Finnmark and Troms. The most significant is the **Siberian garlic** (*Allium sibiricum*), which grows in such abundance that farmers have to make sure their cows don't eat too much of it or else the milk becomes garlic-flavoured. Other Siberian species to look out for are the fringed pink (*Dianthus superbus*) and a large, lily-like plant, the sneezewort (*Veratrum album*).

Fauna

The larger Arctic **predators** of Norway, principally the lynx, wolf, wolverine and bear, are virtually extinct, and where they have survived they are mainly confined to the more inaccessible regions of the north. To a degree this has been caused by the timber industry, which has logged out great chunks of forest. The smaller predators – the arctic fox, otter, badger and marten – have fared rather better and remain comparatively common.

In the 1930s, the **beaver** had been reduced to just 500 animals in southern Norway. A total ban on hunting has, however, led to a dramatic increase in their numbers, and the beaver has begun to recolonize its old hunting grounds right across Scandinavia. The elk has benefited from the rolling back of the forests, grazing the newly treeless areas and breeding in sufficient numbers to allow an annual cull of around 40,000 animals; the red deer of the west coast are flourishing too. Otherwise, the Norwegians own about two million sheep and around 200,000 domesticated **reindeer**, most of whom are herded by the Sámi. The last wild reindeer in Europe, some 15,000 beasts, wander the Hardangervidda and its adjacent mountain areas.

Lemmings

Among Norway's rodents, the most interesting is the **lemming**, whose numbers vary over a four-year cycle. In the first three to four years there is a gradual increase, which is followed, in the course of a few months, by a sudden fall. The cause of these variations is not known, though theories are plentiful. In addition to this four-year fluctuation, the lemming population goes through a violent explosion every eleven to twelve years. Competition for food is so ferocious that many animals start to range over wide areas. In these so-called lemming years the mountains and surrounding areas teem with countless thousands of lemmings, and hundreds swarm to their deaths by falling off cliff edges and the like in a stampede of migration (though there is no truth in the idea that they commit mass suicide). In lemming years, predators and birds of prey have an abundant source of food and frequently give birth to twice as many young as normal – not surprising considering the lemmings are extremely easy to catch. More inexplicably, the snowy owl leaves its polar habitat in lemming years, flying south to join in the feast: quite how they know when to turn up is a mystery. The Vikings were particularly fascinated by lemmings, believing that they dropped from the sky during thunderstorms.

Birds

With the exception of the raven, the partridge and the grouse, all the **mountain birds** of Norway are **migratory**, reflecting the harshness of winter conditions. Most fly back and forth from the Mediterranean and Africa, but some winter down on the coast. **Woodland** species include the wood grouse, the black grouse, several different sorts of owl, woodpecker and birds of prey, while the country's **lakes and marshes** are inhabited by cranes, swans, grebes, geese, ducks and many types of wader. Most dramatic of all are the coastal nesting cliffs, where millions of **sea-birds**, such as kittiwake, guillemots, puffin, cormorant and gull, congregate. What you won't see is the great auk, a flightless, 50cm-high bird resembling a penguin that once nested in its millions along the Atlantic seaboard but is now extinct: the last Norwegian great auk was killed in the eighteenth century and the last one of all was shot near Iceland a century later.

Fish

The waters off Norway once teemed with **seals** and **whales**, but indiscriminate hunting has drastically reduced their numbers, prompting several late-in-the-day conservation measures. The commonest species of **fish** – cod, haddock, coalfish and halibut – have been overexploited too, and whereas there were once gigantic shoals of them right along the coast up to the Arctic Sea, they are now much less common. The cod, like several other species, live far out in the Barents Sea, only coming to the coast to spawn, a favourite destination being the waters round the Lofoten islands.

The only fish along Norway's coast that can survive in both salt and fresh water is the **salmon**, which grows to maturity in the sea and only swims up-river to spawn and die. In the following spring the young salmon return to the sea on the spring flood. Trout and char populate the rivers and lakes of western Norway, living on a diet of crustacea, which tints their meat pink, like the salmon. Eastern Norway and Finnmark are the domain of **whitefish**, so-called because they feed on plant remains, insects and animals, which keep their flesh white. In prehistoric times, these species migrated here from the east via what was then the freshwater Baltic; the most important of them are the perch, powan, pike and grayling.

Cinema

Often overshadowed by its Nordic neighbours, **Norwegian cinema** has long struggled to make an impact on the international scene. In the last decade or so, however, a group of talented film makers has emerged, who are responsible for a string of stylish, honest and refreshingly lucid films. Norway in general and northern Norway in particular has also developed a niche as a film location, most famously as the ice planet Hoth at the start of George Lucas's *The Empire Strikes Back* (1980).

Early Norwegian cinematic successes were few and far between, an exception being *Kon-Tiki*, a 1951 Oscar-winning documentary recording Thor Heyerdahl's journey across the Pacific on a balsa raft (see p.101), though the producer (and Oscar recipient) was a Swede, Olle Nordemar. In 1957, *Nine Lives* (*Ni Liv*), produced and directed by the Norwegian **Arne Skouen**, was widely acclaimed for its tale of a betrayed Resistance fighter, who managed to drag himself across northern Norway in winter to safety in neutral Sweden. Two years later **Erik Løchen**'s *The Hunt* (*Jakten*) was much influenced by the French New Wave in its mixture of time and space, dream and reality, as was the early work of **Anja Breien**, whose *Growing Up* (*Jostedalsrypa*) relates the story of a young girl who is the sole survivor from the Black Death in a remote fjordland village. Breien followed this up in 1975 with a successful improvised comedy *Wives* (*Hustruer*), in which three former classmates meet at a school reunion and subsequently share their life experiences. Breien developed this into a trilogy with *Wives Ten Years Later* (*Hustruer ti år efter*) in 1985 and *Wives III* in 1996. She also garnered critical success at Cannes with *Next of Kin* (*Arven*; 1979), and won prizes at the Venice Film Festival with *Witch Hunt* (*Forfølgelsen*; 1982), an exploration of the persecution of women in the Middle Ages.

Liv Ullmann (b.1939) is easily the most famous Norwegian actor, but in Scandinavia she has worked mostly with Swedish and Danish producers and directors, most notably Ingmar Bergman (with whom she also had a daughter). In 1995, Ullmann brought the popular Norwegian writer Sigrid Undset's medieval epic *Kristin Lavransdatter* to the screen in a three-hour film that attracted mixed reviews. Another Norwegian writer to have had his work made into films is Knut Hamsun (see p.315 & p.433): in 1966, the Dane, Henning Carlson, filmed Hamsun's *Hunger* (*Sult*), and in the mid-1990s, the Swedish director Jan Troell filmed the superb biographical *Trial against Hamsun* (*Prosessen mot Hamsun*). In 1993, Oslo's **Erik Gustavson** directed *The Telegraphist* (*Telegrafisten*), based on a Hamsun story, and its success landed him the task of bringing Jostein Gaarder's extraordinarily popular novel *Sophie's World* (*Sofies Verden*; 1999) to the screen.

Nils Gaup's debut film *The Pathfinder* (*Veiviseren*; 1987), an epic adventure based on a medieval Sámi legend, was widely acclaimed both in Norway and abroad when it was released, not least because the dialogue was in the Sámi language. Gaup followed it up with a nautical adventure, *Shipwrecked* (*Håkon Håkonsen*; 1990), and then a thriller *Head Above Water* (*Hodet over vannet;* 1993), which had a pretty woeful Hollywood remake starring Cameron Diaz and Harvey Keitel. Among other Norwegian successes in the 1990s was **Pål Sletaune**'s *Junk Mail* (*Budbringeren*; 1997), a darkly humorous tale of an Oslo postman who opens the mail himself, and **Erik Skjoldbjaerg**'s *Insomnia* (1997), a film noir set in the permanent summer daylight of northern Norway. Stylish and compelling, it impressed Hollywood so much that it was remade in 2002 starring Al Pacino, but the newer version was a big glossy film without the grittiness of the original.

▲ Nils Gaup's debut film The Pathfinder

Much praised, too, are **Berit Nesheim**'s *The Other Side of Sunday* (*Søndagsen-gler*; 1996), the story of a vicar's daughter desperate to escape from her father's oppressive control, and **Eva Isaksen**'s *Death at Oslo Central* (*Døden på Oslo S*; 1990), a moving story of drug abuse and family conflict among the capital's young down-and-outs. There was also **Knut Erik Jensen**'s surprise hit, *Cool and Crazy* (*Heftig og Begeistret*; 2001), a gentle, lyrical documentary about the male voice choir of Berlevåg (see p.381), a remote community in the far north of the country. Much to Jensen's surprise, his film was picked up abroad and became a major hit on the art-house cinema circuit. Similarly successful, though in a very different cinematic vein, was **Peter Næss**'s *Elling* (2001), a sort of tragic-comedy that relates the heart-warming/-rending story of Elling, a fastidious and obsessive ex-mental patient who moves into an Oslo flat with one of the other former patients – an odd coupling if ever there was one. Equally idiosyncratic was **Bent Hamer**'s *Kitchen Stories* (*Salmer fra kjøkkenet*; 2003), a comic tale in which a tester for a Swedish kitchen-design company is dispatched to Norway to study the culinary goings-on of Isak, a farmer who lives a solitary life deep in the countryside. The two become friends, but it's a bumpy business with each having to dispense with his prejudices against the other's nationality.

Cinematic highlights of 2005 included **Sara Johnsen**'s *Kissed by Winter* (*Vinterkyss*), a harrowing tale of death, racism and murder in rural Norway, and an ambitious re working of an Ibsen play, *An Enemy of the People* (*En folkefiende*), by Erik Skjoldbjaerg, in which the contamination of the medicinal baths in a small coastal town becomes a moral barometer, about who wants to admit the disaster and who wants to cover it up. The following year saw a cracking Norwegian horror film, Roar Uthaug's *Cold Prey* (*Fritt Vilt*) as well as Joachim Trier's playful *Reprise*, a subtle film about love and sorrow, success and failure, creativity and friendship.

For the latest news on Norwegian cinema, consult the Norwegian Film Institute website (ⓦ www.nfi.no/english).

Books

P recious few travellers have written in English about the joys of journeying around Norway, though you might always dig out a copy of a vintage *Baedeker's Norway and Sweden*, if only for the phrasebook, from which you can learn such gems as the Norwegian for "Do you want to cheat me?" and "We must rope ourselves together to cross this glacier." Neither has Norwegian history been a major preoccupation – with the notable exception of the **Vikings**, who have attracted the attention of a veritable raft of historians and translators, whose works have often focused on the surviving **Sagas**, a rich body of work mostly written in Iceland between the twelfth and fourteenth centuries. Scandinavian fiction is, however, an entirely different matter, with a flood of translations appearing on the market, a literary charge led by the immaculate crime novels of the Swede, Henning Mankell, with the Norwegians following in his slipstream.

Of the **publishers**, the UK's **Norvik Press**, based at University College London (⌾www.norvikpress.com), maintains an excellent back catalogue of classic Scandinavian novels and plays. In the US, **Dufour Editions** (⌾www .dufoureditions.com) is strong on Scandinavia too and also recommendable is the UK's **Peter Owen** (⌾www.peterowen.com), an independent publishing company that produces fine new translations of modern Scandinavian novels.

Most of the books listed below are **in print and in paperback**, and those that are **out of print (o/p)** should be easy to track down either in second hand bookshops or through Amazon's used and second hand book service (⌾www.amazon.co.uk or ⌾www.amazon.com). Note also that while we recommend all the books we've listed below, we do have favourites – and these have been marked with ⚐.

Travel and general

James Baxter *Scandinavian Mountains and Peaks over 2000 Metres in the Hurrungane* (Jotunheim). Published in 2005, this specialist text details a series of walks, scrambles and climbs in the Jotunheim mountains. Detailed text with maps, but you'll still need to invest in a proper hiking map.

Anthony Dyer *Walks and Scrambles in Norway*. English-language books on Norway's hiking trails are thin on the ground. This one describes over fifty hikes and scrambles from one end of the country to the other, though the majority are in the western fjords (as in our Chapter 4). Lots of photographs, and the text is detailed and thoroughly researched, but the maps are only general and

you'll need to buy specialist hiking ones to supplement them. Published in 2006.

Christer Elfving & Petra de Hamer *New Scandinavian Cooking*. A cook's tour through Scandinavia's capital cities mixing history, culinary trends, and tips on the hottest chefs and restaurants with delicious modern recipes. Good fun, but a little out of date now – it was published in 2001.

Ranulph Fiennes *Ice Fall in Norway* (o/p). A jaunt on the Jostedalsbreen glacier with Fiennes and his pals in 1970, long before he got famous. A quick and enjoyable read, though the occasional sexist comment may make you wince.

Thor Heyerdahl *The Kon-Tiki Expedition.* You may want to read this after visiting Oslo's Kon-Tiki Museum (p.101). Heyerdahl's account of the Kon-Tiki expedition aroused huge interest when it was first published, and it remains a ripping yarn – though surprisingly few people care to read it today. Heyerdahl's further exploits are related in *The Ra Expeditions* and *The Tigris Expedition* as is his long research trip to Easter Island in *Aku-Aku: The Secret of Easter Island.*

Tony Howard *Climbs, Scrambles and Walks in Romsdal.* Thorough exploration of the mighty mountains near Åndalsnes (see p.267). Tips, hints and details of 300 routes with some maps and diagrams.

Roland Huntford *Scott and Amundsen: The Last Place on Earth.* There are dozens of books on the polar explorers Scott, Amundsen and Nansen, but this is one of the more recent, describing with flair and panache the race to the South Pole between Scott and Amundsen. Also worth a read is the same author's *Nansen,* a doorstep-sized biography of the noble explorer, academic and statesman Fridtjof Nansen.

Lucy Jago *The Northern Lights: How One Man Sacrificed Love, Happiness and Sanity to Solve the Mystery of the Aurora Borealis* (o/p). Intriguing biography of Kristian Birkeland, who spent years ferreting around northern Norway bent on understanding the northern lights – a quest for which he paid a heavy personal price.

Mark Kurlansky *Cod: A Biography of the Fish that Changed the World.* This wonderful book tracks the life and times of the cod and the generations of fishermen who have lived off it. There are sections on overfishing and the fish's breeding habits, and recipes are provided too. Norwegians figure frequently – after all, cod was the staple diet of much of the country for centuries. Published in 1998.

Sven Lindqvist *Bench Press.* Delightful little book delving into the nature of weight-training – and the Swedish/Scandinavian attitude to it. Wry and perceptive cultural commentary by one of Sweden's wittiest and most impassioned cultural commentators.

Eva Maagerø and Birte Simonsen (ed) *Norway: Society and Culture.* Published in 2008, this ambitious collection of essays attempts to summarize where Norway is sociologically and culturally – and where it has come from. Among much else, there are essays on the Welfare State, Religion, Literature, Art, Music and Language. Some are very good, but others are really rather pedestrian.

Ben Nimmo *In Forkbeard's Wake: Coasting Around Scandinavia.* Light and lively account of the author's sailing trip around Scandinavia, brimming with sailing mishaps and encounters with Nordic types – divers, fishermen, archeologists and a drunk Swedish dentist. An all-too-rare, modern travel book on the region. Published in 2003.

Bernhard Pollmann *Norway – South, A Rother Walking Guide.* Fifty suggested hikes dotted across southern Norway. The descriptions are clear and concise, the photos helpful and the maps useful for preparation. The walks themselves range from the short and easy to the long and very strenuous. Probably the best of its type on the market; published in 2001.

Alison Raju *The Pilgrim Road to Nidaros* (o/p). The old medieval pilgrims' route from Oslo to Trondheim cathedral has recently been waymarked, and this unusual and exactingly researched book explores its every nook and cranny. Lots of helpful practical information as well as brief descriptions of every sight.

Christoph Ransmayr *The Terrors of Ice and Darkness* (o/p). Clever mingling of fact and fiction as the book's main character follows the route of the doomed Austro-Hungarian Arctic expedition in 1873. A story of obsession and, ultimately, insanity.

Roger Took *Running with Reindeer*. A thoughtful account of Took's extended visit to – and explorations of – Russia's Kola peninsula in the 1990s, with much to say about the Sámi and their current predicaments.

Paul Watkins *The Fellowship of Ghosts*. Modern-day musings as

Watkins travels through the mountains and fjords of southern Norway. Easy reading, but sometimes over-written – and if that doesn't get you, the barrage of jokes probably will. There again, to be fair, there are lots of useful bits and pieces about Norway and its people.

Mary Wollstonecraft *Letters written during a Short Residence in Sweden, Norway and Denmark*. For reasons that have never been entirely clear, Wollstonecraft, the author of *A Vindication of the Rights of Women*, and mother of Mary Shelley, travelled Scandinavia for several months in 1795. Her letters home represent a real historical curiosity, though her trenchant comments on Norway often get sidelined by her intense melancholia.

General history

Jack Adams *The Doomed Expedition* (o/p). Thorough and well-researched account of the 1940 Allied campaign in Norway in all its gallant but incompetent detail.

Martin Conway *No Man's Land*. Anecdotal, vastly entertaining account of the history of Spitsbergen (Svalbard) from 1596 to modern times. Full of intriguing detail, such as Admiral Nelson's near-death experience (aged 14), when he set out on the ice at night to kill a polar bear. Written in 1906 and published by Kessinger in its "Rare Reprints" series.

Fredrik Dahl *Quisling: A Study in Treachery*. A comprehensive biography of the world's most famous traitor, Vidkun Quisling, who got his just deserts at the end of World War II. Well-written and incisive exploration of Quisling's complex character – and one that also sheds a grim light on the nature and extent of Norwegian collabora-

tion. Published by Cambridge University Press.

Rolf Danielsen et al *Norway: A History from the Vikings to Our Own Times* (o/p). Thoughtful and well-presented account investigating the social and economic development of Norway – a modern and well-judged book that avoids the "kings and queens" approach to its subject.

Thomas Kingston Derry *A History of Scandinavia* (o/p). This is a scholarly history of Scandinavia, a detailed and thorough account of the region from prehistoric times onwards and including Iceland and Finland. It's rather better as a reference source than as a read, however, and having been originally published in 1980, parts are out of date.

Tony Griffiths *Scandinavia: At War with Trolls – A Modern History from the Napoleonic Era to the Third Millennium*. Engaging title for an engaging, well-written and well-researched book covering its subject in a very manageable 320 pages. First published in 2004.

Knut Helle et al *The Cambridge History of Scandinavia*. Comprehensive history, from the Stone Age onwards, in three whopping (and expensive) volumes. No stone is left unturned, no rune unread. Published in 2003.

David Howarth *Shetland Bus*. Entertaining and fascinating in equal measure, this excellent book, written by one of the British naval officers involved, details the clandestine wartime missions that shuttled between the Shetlands and occupied Norway.

Chris Mann *Hitler's Arctic War*. A recent account (2002) of the war that raged across the Arctic wastes of Norway, Finland and the USSR from 1940–45, both on sea and land.

Alan Palmer *Bernadotte* (o/p). Biography of Napoleon's marshal, later King Karl Johan of Norway and Sweden, a fascinating if enigmatic figure whom this lively and comprehensive book presents to good effect.

Geoffrey Parker *The Thirty Years' War*. First published in the 1980s, this book provides the authoritative account of the pan-European war that so deeply affected Scandinavia in general and Sweden in particular. Superbly written and researched.

Kathleen Stokker *Folklore Fights the Nazis: Humor in Occupied Norway 1940–1945* (o/p). A book that can't help but make you laugh – and one that also provides a real insight into Norwegian society and its subtle mores. The only problem is that Stokker adopts an encyclopedic approach, which means you have to plough through the poor jokes to get to the good ones. Stokker adopted a similar approach to her more recent *Remedies and Rituals: Folk Medicine in Norway and the New Land*.

Raymond Strait *Queen of Ice, Queen of Shadows: The Unsuspected Life of Sonja Henie* (o/p). In-depth biography of the ice-skating gold medallist, film star and conspicuous consumer, whose art collection was bequeathed to the Oslo museum that bears her name (see p.102).

Eilert Sundt *Sexual Customs in Rural Norway: A Nineteenth-Century Study*. First published in 1857, the product of a research trip by a pioneer sociologist, this book doesn't have much sex, but does have lots about rural life – a hard existence if ever there was one. Interesting sections on diet, clothes and associated manners and mores. An Iowa State hardback, and very expensive.

The Vikings, Norse mythology and folk tales

Peter Christen Asbjørnsen and Jørgen Moe *Norwegian Folk Tales*. Of all the many books on Norwegian folk tales, this is the edition you want – the illustrations by Erik Werenskiold and Theodor Kittelsen are superb. A Pantheon book published in 1991.

Johannes Brøndsted *The Vikings* (o/p). Extremely readable account with fascinating sections on social and cultural life, art, religious beliefs and customs: see pp.417–420 for an extract from this book.

H.R. Ellis Davidson *The Gods and Myths of Northern Europe*. Classic text, first published almost forty years ago, that gives a who's who of Norse mythology, including some useful reviews of the more obscure gods. Importantly, it displaced the classical deities and their world as the most relevant mythological framework for northern and western Europeans.

Paddy Griffith *The Viking Art of War*. This detailed text examines its chosen subject well. Excellently researched with considered if sometimes surprising conclusions.

John Haywood *The Penguin Historical Atlas of the Vikings*. Accessible and attractive sequence of maps charting the Vikings' various wanderings as explorers, settlers, raiders, conquerors, traders and mercenaries. Also *The Encyclopaedia of the Viking Age*, an easy-to-use who's who and what's what of the Viking era.

Gwyn Jones *A History of the Vikings*. Superbly crafted, erudite and very detailed account of the Vikings, with excellent sections on every aspect of their history and culture. The same author wrote *Scandinavian Legends and Folk Tales* (see below).

Gwyn Jones *Scandinavian Legends and Folk Tales* (o/p). The Oxford University Press commissioned this anthology, whose stories are drawn from every part of Scandinavia and cover many themes – from the heroic to the tragic – and are populated by a mixed crew of trolls, wolves, bears and princelings.

Donald Logan *The Vikings in History*. Scholarly – and radical – re-examination of the Vikings' impact on medieval Europe, indispensable for the Vikingophile.

Magnus Magnusson and Hermann Palsson (translators) *The Vinland Sagas: The Norse Discovery of America*. These two sagas tell of the Vikings' settlement of Greenland and

of the "discovery" of North America in the tenth century. The introduction is a particularly interesting and acute analysis of these two colonial outposts. This version was published in 1985, but there's a newer edition by **Leifur Ericksson** (Penguin; 2008). See also Snorri Sturluson (p.413).

Heather O'Donoghue *From Asgard to Valhalla: the Remarkable History of the Norse Myths*. Well, the "remarkable" in the title may well have been dreamed up by someone in PR, as what you get here is a well-researched and detailed investigation/exploration of its subject matter. The chapters are arranged by theme – "Creation and Cosmos" and "Heroes and Humans" for example.

Andrew Orchard *Cassell's Dictionary of Norse Myth and Legend*. Thorough guide to the complete cast of Scandinavian gods, trolls, heroes and monsters, complete with the social and historical background. Also covers key topics, such as burial rites, sacrificial practices and runes.

Else Roesdahl *The Vikings*. A clearly presented, 350-page exploration of Viking history and culture, including sections on art, burial customs, class divisions, jewellery, kingship, kinship and poetry. An excellent introduction to its subject.

Alexander Rumble et al *The Reign of Cnut* (o/p). Often overlooked, King Cnut (aka Canute) ruled a vast swathe of northern Europe – including England and Norway – at the beginning of the eleventh century. This academic book has several interesting chapters on aspects of his reign, for example, military developments and his influence on the names of people and places in England.

Peter Sawyer (ed) *The Oxford Illustrated History of the Vikings* (o/p).

Published in 2001, this book brings together the latest historical research on the Vikings in a series of well-considered essays by leading experts. Includes sections on religion, shipbuilding and diet.

🏃 **Jane Smiley et al** *The Sagas of Icelanders*. Easy-to-read translations of all the main sagas – galloping tales of derring-do from medieval Iceland. The index makes it an excellent reference book too.

Snorri Sturluson *Egil's Saga, Laxdaela Saga, Njal's Saga, and King Harald's Saga*. These Icelandic sagas (for more on which, see p.413) were written in the early years of the thirteenth century, but relate tales of ninth- and tenth-century derring-do. There's clan warfare in the Laxdaela and Njal sagas, more bloodthirstiness in Egil's, and a bit more biography in King Harald's, penned to celebrate one of the last and most ferocious Viking chieftains – Harald Hardrada (see p.397). Among those who have worked on these English translations was the former UK TV celebrity Magnus Magnusson, long a leading light in the effort to popularize the sagas, see also the *Vinland Sagas* and *The Sagas of Icelanders*, above.

Architecture, film and the visual arts

Marie Bang *Johan Christian Dahl* (o/p). Authoritative and lavishly illustrated book on Norway's leading nineteenth-century landscape painter. From the Scandinavian University Press.

Ketil Bjørnstad *The Story of Edvard Munch*. Precise and detailed biography of the great artist that makes liberal use of Munch's own letters and diaries as well as contemporary newspapers and periodicals. A vivid tale indeed, just a shame that Munch isn't more likeable.

Einar Haugen and Camilla Cai *Ole Bull: Norway's Romantic Musician and Cosmopolitan Patriot*. A neglected figure, Ole Bull (see p.217), the nineteenth-century virtuoso violinist and utopian socialist, deserves a better historical fate. This biography attempts to rectify matters by delving into every facet of his life, but it's ponderously written and over-detailed. For Bull lovers only.

🏃 **J.P. Hodin** *Edvard Munch*. The best available general introduction to Munch's life and work, with much interesting historical detail. Beautifully illustrated, as you would expect from a Thames & Hudson publication.

🏃 **Neil Kent** *The Soul of the North: A Social, Architectural and Cultural History of the Nordic Countries 1770–1940*. Immaculately illustrated, erudite chronicle of Scandinavian art and architecture during its most influential periods. Highly recommended; another superb book from Thames & Hudson.

Robert Layton *Grieg*. Clear, concise and attractively illustrated book on Norway's greatest composer. Essential reading if you want to get to grips with the man and his times.

Marion Nelson (ed) *Norwegian Folk Art: The Migration of a Tradition*. Lavishly illustrated book discussing the whole range of folk art, from wood carvings through to bedspreads and traditional dress. It's particularly strong on the influence of

Norwegian folk art in the US, but the text sometimes lacks focus. It's earth-shatteringly expensive too.

Sue Prideaux *Edvard Munch: Behind the Scream*. Not a classic biography perhaps, but a thorough and well-researched trawl through the life of a man who fulfilled most of the stereotypes of the alienated and tormented (drunken) artist. Published by Yale University Press.

Tytti Soila et al *Nordic National Cinemas* and *The Cinema of Scandinavia*. These two books are the best there is on Scandinavian cinema in general and Norwegian cinema in particular. Published in 1998, the first of the two has separate chapters on each of the Nordic countries and each chapter provides a chronological overview. The second book, published in 2005, adopts a more cinematic approach with 24 extended essays on key Scandinavian films – and an intriguing bunch they are too.

Literature and literary biography

Kjell Askildsen *A Sudden Liberating Thought* (o/p). Short stories, in the Kafkaesque tradition, from one of Norway's most uncompromisingly modernist writers.

Paul Binding *With Vine-Leaves in His Hair: The Role of the Artist in Ibsen's Plays*. Academic title ideal for Ibsen lovers/students.

Jens Bjørneboe *The Sharks*. Set at the end of the last century, this is a thrilling tale of shipwreck and mutiny by a well-known Norwegian writer, who had an enviable reputation for challenging authoritarianism of any description. Also recommended is his darker trilogy – *Moment of Freedom* (o/p), *The Powderhouse* and *The Silence* (o/p) – exploring the nature of cruelty and injustice.

Johan Bojer *The Emigrants* (o/p). One of the leading Norwegian novelists of his day, Bojer (1872–1959) wrote extensively about the hardships of rural life. *The Emigrants*, perhaps his most finely crafted work, deals with a group of young Norwegians who emigrate to North Dakota in the 1880s – and the difficulties they experience. In Norway, Bojer is better known for *Last of the Vikings* (o/p), a heart-rending tale of fishermen from the tiny village of Rissa in Nordland, who are forced to row out to the Lofoten winter fishery, no matter what the conditions, to keep from starving. It was first published in 1921.

Lars Saabye Christensen *Herman*. Christensen made a real literary splash with *The Half Brother*, an intense tale focused on four generations of an Oslo family in the years following World War II, the narrator being Barnum, a midget, alcoholic screenplay-writer. It is, however, a real doorstopper of a book and before you embark on such a long read you might want to sample Christensen's *Herman*, a lighter (and much shorter) tale of adolescence with an Oslo backdrop.

Camilla Collett *The District Governor's Daughters* (o/p). Published in 1854, this heartfelt demand for the emotional and intellectual emancipation of women is set within a bourgeois Norwegian milieu. The central character, Sophie, struggles against her conditioning and the expectations of those around her. An important, early feminist novel.

Per Olov Enquist *The Visit of the Royal Physician*. Wonderfully entertaining and beautifully written novel, set in the Danish court in Copenhagen at the end of the eighteenth century – a time when Denmark governed Norway.

Knut Faldbakken *Adam's Diary*. Three former lovers describe their relationships with the same woman – an absorbing and spirited novel by one of Norway's more talented writers.

Robert Ferguson *Enigma: the Life of Knut Hamsun*. Detailed and well-considered biography of Norway's most controversial writer (see p.315). The same author also wrote *Ibsen*, an in-depth biography of the playwright.

Karin Fossum *Calling out for You; Don't Look Back; Black Seconds*. Norway's finest crime writer, Fossum has written a string of superb thrillers in the Inspector Sejer series – and each gives the real flavour of contemporary Norway. These three novels are the best place to get started – but avoid *When the Devil Holds the Candle*, which is a bit of a dud. The first chapter of *Don't Look Back* is printed here on -000.

Jostein Gaarder *Sophie's World*. Hugely popular novel that deserves all the critical praise it has received. Beautifully and gently written, with puffs of whimsy all the way through, it bears comparison with Hawking's *A Brief History of Time*, though the subject matter here is philosophy, and there's an engaging mystery story tucked in too. Also try Gaarder's comparable *Through A Glass Darkly*.

Janet Garton (ed) *Contemporary Norwegian Women's Writing*. Wide-ranging anthology, beginning with the directly political works of the 1970s and culminating in the more fantastical tales typical of the 2000s. Fiction, drama and poetry all make an appearance and there are lots of issues too – from prostitution and abuse

through to women's empowerment. Also *New Norwegian Plays*, comprising four plays written between 1979 and 1983, including work by the feminist writer Bjørg Vik and a Brechtian analysis of Europe in the nuclear age by Edvard Hoem. Both are published by Norvik Press (see p.426).

Knut Hamsun *Hunger*. Norway's leading literary light in the 1920s and early 1930s, Knut Hamsun (1859–1952) was a writer of international acclaim until he disgraced himself by supporting Hitler – for which many Norwegians never forgave him. Of Hamsun's many novels, it was *Hunger* (1890) that made his name, a trip into the psyche of an alienated and angst-ridden young writer, which shocked contemporary readers. The book was to have a seminal influence on the development of the modern novel. In the latter part of his career, Hamsun advocated a return to the soil and basic rural values. He won the Nobel Prize for Literature for one of his works from this period, *Growth of the Soil*, but you have to be pretty determined to plough through its metaphysical claptrap. In recent years, Hamsun has been tentatively accepted back into the Norwegian literary fold and there has been some resurgence of interest in his works; there's also been a biographical film, *Hamsun*, starring Max von Sydow.

William Heinesen *The Black Cauldron*. It would be churlish to omit the Faroe-islander William Heinesen (1900–91), whose evocative novels delve into the subtleties of Faroese life – and thereby shed light on the related culture of western Norway. This particular book, arguably his best, is rigorously modernistic in approach and style – an intriguing, challenging read, with the circling forces of Faroese society set against the British occupation of the Faroes in World War II. If this whets your appetite, carry on with the same author's *The Tower at the Edge of the World*.

Sigbjørn Holmebakk *The Carriage Stone*. Evil and innocence, suffering and redemption, with death lurking in the background, make this a serious and powerful novel. These themes are explored through the character of Eilif Grotteland, a Lutheran priest who loses his faith and resigns his ministry. Holmebakk (1922–81), who was a leading light in the Ban the Bomb movement, wrote several other excellent novels, but none has yet appeared in translation. In particular, look out for *Fimbulvinteren* (The Terrible Winter), set in Finnmark as the Germans applied their scorched-earth policy during their retreat of 1944.

Henrik Ibsen *Four Major Plays*. The key figure of Norwegian literature, Ibsen (see p.86) was a social dramatist with a keen eye for hypocrisy, repression and alienation. Ibsen's most popular plays – primarily *A Doll's House* and *Hedda Gabler* – pop up in all sorts of editions, but this particular collection, in the Oxford World Classics series, contains both these favourites as well as *Ghosts* and *The Master Builder*. What's more, it's inexpensive and translated by one of the leading Ibsen experts, James McFarlane. In print also are several editions of Ibsen's whole oeuvre – the Kessinger Publishing Company's version is currently the least expensive.

Jørgen-Frantz Jacobsen *Barbara*. Jacobsen (1900–38) died young from tuberculosis, leaving this lyrical tale of Faroese life, part historical novel – it's set in the middle of the eighteenth century – partly a tale of female emancipation, all to a stern Faroe-islands background. By implication, gives much of the flavour of western Norway and its domination by the same type of Danish official who ran the Faroes.

Jan Kjærstad (ed) *Leopard VI: The Norwegian Feeling for Real*. Promoted by the queen of Norway no less, this first-rate anthology of modern Norwegian writers hits all the literary buttons – from boozy nights out in Oslo to the loneliness of rural Norway and small-town envy. Contains 28 short stories plus potted biographies of all the writers who appear.

Jan Kjærstad *The Seducer*. This remarkable novel weaves and wanders, rambles and roams around the life of its protagonist, Jonas Wergeland, in a series of digressions as our hero/anti-hero sits in his flat with his murdered wife lying dead in an adjoining room. Mysterious and convoluted, pensive and whimsical, it's a truly extraordinary work that won the Nordic Prize for Literature in 2001.

Björn Larsson *Long John Silver*. Larsson, a veteran Swedish sailor with an extensive knowledge of eighteenth-century British sea lore, uses his specialist knowledge to great effect in this chunky but charming novel that provides an extra twist – or two – to Stevenson's original.

Jonas Lie *The Seer & Other Norwegian Stories* (o/p). Part of the Norwegian literary and cultural revival of the late nineteenth century, Jonas Lie is largely forgotten today, but this collection of mystical folk tales makes for intriguing reading. It is printed alongside his first great success, the novella *The Seer*, in which a teacher is saved from insanity, born of ancient (pagan) superstitions, by the power of Christianity. Also *Weird Tales from Northern Seas: Norwegian Legends*, a collection much enjoyed by no less than Roald Dahl.

Henning Mankell *Faceless Killers*, *Sidetracked*. Cracking yarns from Scandinavia's leading crime writer featuring Inspector Kurt Wallander, a shambolic and melancholic middle-aged police officer struggling to make sense of it all in small-town southern Sweden. Hard to beat.

Michael Meyer *Ibsen* (o/p). Lucid, immaculately researched biography of Norway's greatest playwright. Explores every nook and cranny of the man's life and times in just over six hundred pages.

Jo Nesbø *The Devil's Star*. Nesbø has become one of the big names of contemporary Norwegian crime writing and this racy tale is one of his better offerings, though the name of the detective involved, Harry Hole, doesn't work too well in English. Also *The Redbreast* in which Hole shoots a US secret-service agent by mistake – with a variety of unforeseen consequences.

Per Petterson *Out Stealing Horses*. Doom and gloom, guilt and isolation deep in the Norwegian woods. Hardly cheerful fare perhaps, but stirring, unsettling stuff all the same.

Cora Sandel *Alberta and Freedom, Alberta Alone, Alberta and Jacob*. Set in a small town in early twentieth-century Norway, the Alberta trilogy follows the attempts of a young woman to establish an independent life/identity. Characterized by sharp insights and a wealth of contemporary detail. For more on Sandel, who lived in Tromsø as a young woman, see p.358.

Kjersti Scheen *Final Curtain*. Fast-paced detective story from one of the country's most popular crime writers. Refreshingly, the detective isn't a middle-aged man, but an Oslo-based woman.

Amalie Skram *Under Observation* and *Lucie*. Bergen's Amalie Skram (1846–1905) married young and went through the marital mangle before turning her experiences into several novels and a commitment to women's emancipation. For the period, the novels are extraordinarily progressive, and are an enjoyable read too: see p.436 for an extract from *Lucie*.

Dag Solstad *Shyness & Dignity*. One of the big names of Norwegian literature, Solstad's sombre tale of a middle-aged teacher's psychological collapse is set in a dour Oslo. "What shall become of me?" he complains – yes, what indeed.

Sven Somme *Another Man's Shoes*. In World War II, the redoubtable Sven Somme managed to escape the clutches of the Germans and make his escape over the mountains into neutral Sweden. Sixty years later, his two daughters, now resident in England, retraced his steps as described in his memoirs – and this is the result, a combination of the original text and their comments on their own journey. The title comes from the pair of shoes left behind by Sven and kept by one of the families who helped him.

Sigrid Undset *Kristin Lavransdatter: The Cross, The Bridal Wreath, The Garland & The Mistress of Husaby*. The prolific Undset, one of the country's leading literary lights, can certainly churn it out. This historical series – arguably encapsulating her best work – is set in medieval Norway and has all the excitement of a pulp thriller, along with subtle plots and deft(ish) characterizations.

Herbjørg Wassmo *Dina's Book: A Novel*. Set in rural northern Norway in the middle of the nineteenth century, this strange but engaging tale has a plot centred on a powerful but tormented heroine: see p.442 for an extract. Also *Dina's Son*, again with a nineteenth-century setting, but with intriguing sections focused on the protagonist's move from rural Norway to the city.

Literary extracts

I t was **Jostein Gaarder**'s *Sophie's World* that brought Norwegian literature to a worldwide audience in the 1990s, though in fact the Norwegians have been mining a deep, if somewhat idiosyncratic, literary seam since the middle of the nineteenth century. From Ibsen onwards, the country's authors and playwrights have been deeply influenced by Norway's unyielding geography and stern pietism, their preoccupations often focused on anxiety and alienation. **Amalie Skram**, a contemporary of Ibsen, is largely forgotten today, but her *Lucie* is a sharply observed novel and a pioneering feminist work to boot. *Lucie* provides the first of the three extracts we have included; the others are by **Herbjørg Wassmo** and the crime writer **Karin Fossum**, two of Norway's finest contemporary writers.

Amalie Skram

Born in Bergen in 1846, **Amalie Skram** was the daughter of a shopkeeper, who went bankrupt when she was seventeen – a riches-to-rags story reminiscent of Ibsen's early life (see p.86). She married out of poverty, but the marriage – to a sea captain – went wrong and her husband's refusal to grant a divorce brought on a nervous breakdown in 1877. Recovered, Amalie moved to Christiania (Oslo) in 1881 and here she became involved in both the political movement for an independent Norway and a number of progressive social issues, primarily attempts to regulate prostitution. Amalie also became a familiar figure on the Oslo literary scene and was well known for her controversial or, rather, progressive views. Published in 1888, *Lucie* was a coruscating attack on bourgeois morality in general, and male sexual hypocrisy in particular, with the eponymous heroine gradually ground down into submission. Inevitably, the novel created a huge furore. The extract below describes one key episode in the increasingly oppressive relationship between Lucie and her husband, Gerner.

Lucie

At the Mørks'

Dinner was over, and the women were seated around a table in the sitting room drinking coffee.

Mrs. Mørk was talking about the difficulties she was having with her maids. The nursery maid had got up in the middle of the night to go to a dance, and the baby had screamed until he was blue in the face before they heard it in their bedroom.

"Oh these maids, these maids! And of course they break everything. If your purse was as deep as the ocean it still wouldn't be enough." Mrs. Lunde was speaking. The wife of a sea captain, she had eight children and struggled mightily to get along on her monthly allowance.

And then they launched into stories about their housemaids' wastefulness and profligacy. When one flagged, the other started in.

Lucie listened with a stiff smile. None of the women turned to address her, but almost unconsciously left her out of the conversation. To remedy this painful situation, she feigned interest, shook her head frequently, and said at the right times, "No, you don't say. How dreadful!"

The men strolled in from the smoking room; with glowing faces and smiling eyes, they seated themselves among the women.

A young fellow with red hands and flaxen hair combed into a stiff point over his forehead struck up a conversation with Lucie.

"Has madam gone to many balls this winter?" he asked.

"No, I'm afraid not. My husband doesn't care to dance, unfortunately." Lucie smiled invitingly.

"Is that right?" the gentleman said, exposing all of his large, ugly teeth. "He really should be obliged to, when he has such a young wife, don't you think? I suppose you weren't at the carnival either?"

"An outstanding likeness of Mrs. Mørk, don't you think?" Gerner [her husband] came over to Lucie and handed her a photograph, while turning his back on the man with the teeth.

A slight shock went through Lucie. She had not seen Gerner come in with the others and thought he was still in the smoking room.

"Yes, it's a good likeness," she said, eagerly looking at the photograph.

Gerner pulled a chair over to the table and sat down.

"Don't you think so, too?" In her confusion, Lucie reached behind her husband and handed the photograph to the gentleman, who stood there smiling like an idiot.

"Can't you leave that dolt alone?" Gerner whispered. "Next you'll be asking him how many balls *he's* been to."

"What do you say, Mrs. Gerner," said Mrs. Mørk. "Do you want to play cards or sit and talk?"

"My wife likes to play whist," Gerner hurriedly replied.

"Have I done something wrong again?" Lucie muttered, looking anxiously at Theodor. "He's Mrs. Mørk's brother, you know."

"That shopkeeper," Gerner answered savagely. "Mrs. Mørk's brother, is *that* what you consider refined company? Yes, I'm coming now." Mørk had called out that the table for ombre was ready in the smoking room.

"They're dancing at Mrs. Reinertson's," Lucie said as she shuffled the cards, glancing up at the ceiling, which was actually shaking.

"Now, *there's* a widow who loves to entertain," said Mrs. Mørk. "It hasn't been a week since we were at a big party up there."

"But we didn't dance then," Lucie said with a sigh.

"No, but only the young people were invited tonight. There are loads of cousins in the family."

"It seems a bit unusual for a widow to do that kind of thing," opined Mrs. Lunde.

"Her brother, the pastor in Arendal, is very worldly too," lisped a pregnant little assistant pastor's wife with heavy blue rings under her eyes. "He's always scandalising the congregation, Jensen says."

"And she defends *Albertine* [a controversial novel of the period]," Mrs Lund went on. "Well as I always say, if you don't have any children....I'm so pleased with my eight. I'd rather have sixteen than none. Your lead, Mrs. Gerner."

There was much more talking and gossiping than playing. Lucie tried to get into the conversation a couple of times, but wasn't successful. Feeling uncomfortable and out of place, she pretended to be intent on the cards. When it was finally time to eat supper she breathed a sigh of relief.

"I think that was the doorbell," Mørk said. They had finished supper and were just getting up from the table.

"It must have been the street door," his wife answered. "But what in the world is that?"

They all paused, hands on their chairs, as they were moving them back from the table. Drifting in from the next room came an intermittent muffled clamour and the tones of a violin playing a march. Mrs. Mørk went over and opened the door. The others turned around quickly with a buzz of astonishment.

The sitting room was jammed with people wearing carnival costumes and masks on their faces. It was a gaudy mixture of knights and their ladies, peasants and Italian fishermen, gypsies and dancing girls. In front of them stood a fiddler dressed as a peasant and Mrs. Reinertson in a pale grey silk dress, a gold comb in her shiny brown hair.

"Well, what do you think?" Mrs. Reinertson said laughingly to Mrs. Mørk, who had stopped in the doorway. She clapped her hands. "My guests couldn't be restrained, they're simply wild tonight. First they scared the life out of me by coming in carnival costumes, and then they absolutely insisted on coming down here. You mustn't take offence."

"How could you think that – what a fun idea they had. Come in, do come in."

"Oh now you're shy," Mrs. Reinertson laughed at her guests, who were clustered together with their arms linked, giggling in embarrassment and whispering behind their masks. "What did I say?"

"How marvellous of you to come and liven us up." With a bray of laughter Mørk walked around shaking hands with the masked guests, who bowed and curtsied and made somewhat fruitless attempts to be amusing.

"Now make yourselves at home and *act* your parts to your heart's content. By heaven, we'll have champagne! Here Lina." He handed a ring of keys through the dining room door.

"Now really Aksel," said his wife angrily, snatching the keys away from him. "The maids in the wine cellar …."

"Look, Mrs. Lund!" Lucie was so excited that she impulsively took Mrs. Lund's arm and pointed at a harlequin who was walking on his hands among the armchairs. "Oh Lord. Oh Lord, the lamp!" she cried, clinging tightly to her arm. The harlequin's feet were close to a porcelain lamp on a little marble table.

With a strained expression, Mrs. Lund moved away from Lucie. "A bit common, don't you think," she said to the assistant pastor's wife, taking her by the arm.

Champagne corks were going off explosively in the dining room and Mørk poured. "If you please, ladies and gentlemen!" he called. "People who want champagne must come in here!"

"But first take off your masks!" said Mrs. Reinertson with a clap of her hands, after which they all took off their masks and let them dangle from their arms. Then they began to laugh and talk, recognize and introduce themselves, as they all crowded around the table in the dining room to drink champagne.

There were speeches and toasts, and gradually the somewhat forced animation that had covered embarrassment gave way to a rush of good cheer.

Lucie was looking through narrowed eyes at a good-looking young man, tall and broad-shouldered, with a black moustache, red lips, and gleaming healthy teeth. He was wearing sandals on his feet and a monk's cowl over his lieutenant's uniform.

"Your health, madam," he said clinking his glass against Lucie's. "Long live celibacy!"

"Long live what?" Lucie asked, laughing heartily. "I don't know what you mean."

"You are adorable, madam!" The lieutenant threw back his head and gazed at her rapturously with brown, laughing eyes. "Should I explain it to you? Oh no,

I would rather explain what celibacy is *not*. We'll take our glasses with us." He offered her his arm.

"Don't be such a flirt, Knut," Mrs. Reinertson whispered in his ear, as he and Lucie walked by. "Her husband is so jealous."

"Then we'd better cure him," Knut replied. "She's so sweet and amusing, Aunt."

"Let's sit over here." The lieutenant led Lucie to a little sofa in a corner of the sitting room beneath a tall arrangement of leafy plants, and sat down beside her. He began to chat with her in a soft, confiding tone.

Gerner observed them from the dining room, where he was talking to a knight's lady dressed in black velvet with a tall mother of pearl comb in her hair. He watched Lucie laugh and drink champagne. Occasionally she would lean back and lift her feet off the floor. Once she turned away, as if her admirer had been too forward, and the lieutenant gave her a surprised look and became earnest and intense. Gerner's half-shut eyes were narrowed more than usual and his nostrils twitched nervously.

"What are you staring at?" the knight's lady asked, turning around.

"That monk over there is amusing." – Gerner forced his mouth into a smile. – "That fop of a lieutenant in the monk's cowl."

"Oh Knut Reinertson. Knut Lionheart."

"Oh yes? Why do they call him that?" Gerner interrupted.

"I don't know really, but I suppose it's because he's a heartbreaker. – Who is the lady he's talking to?"

"It's my wife," answered Gerner, looking at the knight's lady with his eyes wide open.

"Oh I see – well I'm sure we were introduced but I didn't hear the name. She is really very charming. – If only he doesn't hypnotize her."

"Hypnotize?"

"Yes, didn't you hear about that? It's quite dreadful the things he gets people to do and say. At a party the other night – papa wouldn't give me permission to try it. – What! Go up to Mrs. Reinertson's and dance? – Oh yes, let's do that!" She clapped her hands.

"What do our guests say?" cried Mrs. Mørk looking over at her husband.

"Let's go up, go up," they all answered.

"Let me lead the way," Mrs. Reinertson said, taking the fiddler by the arm.

"That's what I call hospitable," Mørk exclaimed, offering Mrs. Lund his arm.

Gerner wanted to reach Lucie to tell her they should go home, but he couldn't get past all the people and furniture. He stretched sideways over the others' shoulders in order to catch her glance, but she pretended not to notice.

"Devil take it," Gerner mumbled, when he saw her follow the others out of the door, flushed and laughing on the lieutenant's arm.

"Tonight I intend to enjoy myself," Lucie said to her escort, lifting her knees in a little dance. "It's certainly been a long time. – Imagine, I haven't gone dancing one single time since I got married."

I don't care if he kills me, I'm having a good time tonight, she thought. There'll be a scene anyway, might as well get some fun out of it.

"Do you not have a partner, Gerner?" asked Mrs. Mørk. "Then you'll have to be content with me."

He bowed silently and they left the room.

From the entryway he saw Lucie and the lieutenant turning into the bend of the staircase that led to Mrs. Reinertson's apartment. They were close together. His head was bent toward Lucie's and she was looking up at his face as he spoke.

Mrs. Mørk chattered on and on, but Gerner heard nothing; he just stared up the stairs with a white face and clenched lips.

"I wish I had a sixth sense," said the lieutenant.

"Oh, and why is that?" Lucie asked.

"So I could look into your soul and read my fate." His face was mirthful but his voice was solemn.

"Oh you," Lucie laughed, poking him in the side with her elbow.

"Every young woman's heart is an unresolved riddle, a boundless deep – an ocean of – in a word – riches and possibilities – oh, a bottomless ..." he paused for a moment. "It's a sin to keep such a treasure locked away."

Lord, he's sweet, and it's so poetic, the way he talks, Lucie thought, her face alight with rapture. And he's such a gentleman.

"Oh I think you'd soon have your fill of that treasure, I do, Lieutenant Reinertson." Her voice was trembling with delight and agitation.

"Try me, madam," he begged earnestly. "Tell me what you are thinking, feeling, what delights you, makes you suffer" – he softly squeezed her arm – "especially suffer, for is there any human being who doesn't suffer?" – They had now come upstairs into rooms lit by candelabras and lamps, where the musicians struck up a waltz.

And then the dancing couples whirled down the large, rectangular dining room.

Reinertson clasped Lucie firmly to his chest and danced off. She closed her eyes and leaned back against his arm. Never before had dancing felt so delicious. She felt like she was flying through the air and that her body was almost dissolving in a wonderful, tingling sensation. The furniture, the people, and everything else drifted away. She was conscious only of him and herself, and, from far away, the sound of the music. If only it never, never had to end.

"I'd surrender my soul to the pains of Hell for the key to her rooms," the lieutenant whispered after the dance, when they were sitting in an alcove off the dining room.

Blood pounded in Lucie's ears. She leaned back, fanning herself with her handkerchief. A soft smile trembled at the corners of her mouth, and her breast rose and fell. "Oh, if only I had met you before, Reinertson," she whispered back, and squeezed his hand.

This is getting amusing. She thinks I'm in love with her, thought the lieutenant.

"We can still get to know each other, of course," he said softly, squeezing her hand in return. Rubbish, I can't be bothered with this, he thought a second later, just as Lucie was about to answer. He released her hand and said. "Come, let's dance the gallop together."

They stood up and Lucie took his arm.

In the doorway, they met Gerner.

"Well here you are, finally," he said. "It's time to go home."

Lucie could tell from his voice how much it was costing him to control himself. But she didn't feel the slightest trace of fear, only a boundless joy that she was going to dance with him again.

"Just a couple of times around, counsellor," said Reinertson, "then I'll return her to you."

He danced off with her. Gerner watched them.

"Now I'll take my leave and surrender your wife to the hands of her natural guardian, as they say." The lieutenant had brought Lucie back to Gerner. "Goodnight, madam. Thank you for this evening. Goodnight, counsellor." He bowed and left.

Lucie's eyes followed him through the room with a longing expression. She seemed to have completely forgotten that Gerner was standing beside her.

"Do you hear, we're leaving." He grabbed her firmly by the wrist and walked her towards the door.

"I should say goodbye first, don't you think?" Lucie tried to free her hand.

He tightened his grip and actually pulled her past the dancing couples. "You're coming now!"

"Leave without thanking them?" Lucie said sharply, out in the front hall.

"Don't try to prolong the scandal." Gerner opened the door and pushed Lucie out through it. He could barely get his words out and his hands were shaking.

I don't care if he's in a good mood or a rotten mood, Lucie thought, as they were walking down the stairs. As long as I can see that darling Reinertson again soon.

But when they were putting on their coats in the Mørks' well-lit front hall, the sight of Theodor's pallid cheeks and clenched lips sent a chill through Lucie.

Striding down the street, Theodor took such long steps that Lucie had to trot to keep up with him. Finally she slowed and trailed along behind.

"Is it your intention to play the part of a streetwalker tonight?" Gerner had stopped by the university to wait for Lucie.

"How can anybody keep up when you run like that," Lucie answered angrily and walked past him.

"You are to conduct yourself properly." In a couple of steps Gerner was beside her. "Reminding everybody of what a trollop I married." His voice was distorted with rage.

"You're really so crude," Lucie said indifferently, walking hurriedly, almost running.

"If a man so much as looks at you, your whole body starts to tremble," Gerner went on, getting more and more agitated. "You make me look ridiculous."

"Well, that's not difficult, is it," she said with a scornful breath.

Gerner could have hit her.

"You be careful," he snarled. "You're a tart, and you'll never get that out of your blood."

"A tart! I really have to laugh. You should hear what Mrs. Reinertson has to say. I suppose you were lily-white when you married me."

"Now you start with impertinences – you've wisely refrained from that until now."

"But I won't stand for you treating me this way any more." She spoke breathlessly because of their quick pace on the slippery snow. "I won't stand for it any longer, just so you know. I suppose you think being married to you is so glorious!"

"Be quiet!" He grabbed her shoulders and shook her so violently that her little fur hat flew off her head. They had turned onto Drammensveien, and he gave her a shove that propelled her a few steps along the street.

Without uttering a sound, Lucie bent over to retrieve her hat, then took off down Drammensveien with her hat in her hand, as if she were running for her life.

Translated by Katherine Hanson & Judith Messick; reprinted by permission of Norvik Press.

Herbjørg Wassmo

Two volumes of poetry marked **Herbjørg Wassmo**'s writing debut in 1976, at the age of 34. Shortly afterwards she switched to prose, subsequently writing two series of popular novels about contrasting women. **Dina**, the female protagonist of *Dina's bok* (Dina's Book, 1989) and *Lykkens sønn* (The Son of Fortune, 1992), is wilful to the point of ruthlessness: she eliminates her husband and takes a new lover, while the funeral is in progress elsewhere. Yet beneath her toughness is a deep sense of betrayal: rejected as a child by her father after she accidentally caused her mother's death, Dina has grown up expecting betrayal. Set in the mid-nineteenth century, the Dina stories have as their backdrop a rural community in Wassmo's native northern Norway. The extract below comes from the beginning of *Dina's Book*.

Dina's Book

The eyes of the Lord preserve knowledge, and he overthroweth the words of the transgressor.
Proverbs 22:12

Dina had to take her husband, Jacob, who had gangrene in one foot, to the doctor on the other side of the mountain. November. She was the only one who could handle the wild yearling, which was the fastest horse. And they needed to drive fast. On a rough, icy road.

Jacob's foot already stank. The smell had filled the house for a long time. The cook smelled it even in the pantry. An uneasy atmosphere pervaded every room. A feeling of anxiety.

No one at Reinsnes said anything about the smell of Jacob's foot before he left. Nor did they mention it after Blackie returned to the estate with empty shafts.

But aside from that, people talked. With disbelief and horror. On the neighbouring farms. In the parlours at Strandsted and along the sound. At the pastor's home. Quietly and confidentially.

About Dina, the young wife at Reinsnes, the only daughter of Sheriff Holm. She was like a horse-crazy boy. Even after she got married. Now she had suffered such a sad fate.

They told the story again and again. She had driven so fast that the snow crackled and spurted under the runners. Like a witch. Nevertheless, Jacob Grønelv did not get to the doctor's. Now he no longer existed. Friendly, generous Jacob, who never refused a request for help. Mother Karen's son, who came to Reinsnes when he was quite young.

Dead! No one could understand how such a terrible thing could have happened. That boats capsized, or people disappeared at sea, had to be accepted. But this was the devil's work. First getting gangrene in a fractured leg. Then dying on a sleigh that plunged into the rapids!

Dina had lost the power of speech, and old Mother Karen wept. Jacob's son from his first marriage wandered, fatherless, around Copenhagen, and Blackie could not stand the sight of sleighs.

The authorities came to the estate to conduct an inquiry into the events that had occurred up to the moment of death. Everything must be stated specifically and nothing hidden, they said.

Dina's father, the sheriff, brought two witnesses and a book for recording the proceedings. He said emphatically that he was there as one of the authorities, not as a father.

Mother Karen found it difficult to see a difference. But she did not say so.

No one brought Dina down from the second floor. Since she was so big and strong, they took no chance that she might resist and make a painful scene. They did not try to force her to come downstairs. Instead it was decided the authorities would go up to her large bedroom.

Extra chairs had been placed in the room. And the curtains on the canopy bed were thoroughly dusted. Heavy gold fabric patterned with rows of rich red flowers. Bought in Hamburg. Sewn for Dina and Jacob's wedding.

Oline and Mother Karen had tried to take the young wife in hand so she would not look completely unpresentable. Oline gave her herb tea with thick cream and plenty of sugar. It was her cure for all ills, from the scurvy to childlessness. Mother Karen assisted with praise, hair brushing, and cautious concern.

The servant girls did as they were told, while looking around with frightened glances.

The words stuck. Dina opened her mouth and formed them. But their sound was in another world. The authorities tried many different approaches.

The sheriff tried using a deep, dispassionate voice, peering into Dina's light-grey eyes. He could just as well have looked through a glass of water.

The witnesses also tried. Seated and standing. With both compassionate and commanding voices.

Finally, Dina laid her head of black, unruly hair on her arms. And she let out sounds that could have come from a half-strangled dog.

Feeling ashamed, the authorities withdrew to the downstairs rooms. In order to reach agreement about what had happened. How things had looked at the place in question. How the young woman had acted.

They decided that the whole matter was a tragedy for the community and the entire district. That Dina Grønelv was beside herself with grief. That she was not culpable and had lost her speech from the shock.

They decided that she had been racing to take her husband to the doctor. That she had taken the curve near the bridge too fast, or that the wild horse had bolted at the edge of the cliff and the shaft fastenings had pulled loose. Both of them.

This was neatly recorded in the official documents.

They did not find the body, at first. People said it had washed out to sea. But did not understand how. For the sea was nearly seven miles away through a rough, shallow riverbed. The rocks there would stop a dead body, which could do nothing itself to reach the sea.

To Mother Karen's despair, they gradually gave up the search.

A month later, an old pauper came to the estate and insisted that the body lay in Veslekulpen, a small backwater some distance below the rapids. Jacob lay crooked around a rock. Stiff as a rod. Battered and bloated, the old fellow said.

He proved to be right.

The water level had evidently subsided when the autumn rains ended. And one clear day in early December, the unfortunate body of Jacob Grønelv appeared. Right before the eyes of the old pauper, who was on his way across the mountain.

Afterward, people said the pauper was clairvoyant. And, in fact, always had been. This is why he had a quiet old age. Nobody wanted to quarrel with a clairvoyant. Even if he was a pauper.

Dina sat in her bedroom, the largest room on the second floor. With the curtains drawn. At first she did not even go to the stable to see her horse.

They left her in peace.

Mother Karen stopped crying, simply because she no longer had time for that. She had assumed the duties that the master and his wife had neglected. Both were dead, each in his or her own way.

Dina sat at the walnut table, staring. No one knew what else she did. Because she confided in no one. The sheets of music that had been piled around the bed were now stuffed away in the clothes closet. Her long dresses swept over them in the draught when she opened the door.

The shadows were deep in the bedroom. A cello stood in one corner, gathering dust. It had remained untouched since the day Jacob was carried from the house and laid on the sleigh.

The solid canopy bed with sumptuous bed curtains occupied much of the room. It was so high that one could lie on the pillows and look out through the windows at the sound. Or one could look at oneself in the large mirror with a black lacquered frame that could be tilted to different angles.

The big round stove roared all day. Behind a triple-panelled folding screen with an embroidered motif of beautiful Leda and the swan in an erotic embrace. Wings and arms. And Leda's long, blond hair spread virtuously over her lap.

A servant girl, Thea, brought wood four times a day. Even so, the supply barely lasted through the night.

No one knew when Dina slept, or if she slept. She paced back and forth in heavy shoes with metal-tipped heels, day and night. From wall to wall. Keeping the whole house awake.

Thea could report that the large family Bible, which Dina had inherited from her mother, always lay open.

Now and then the young wife laughed softly. It was an unpleasant sound. Thea did not know whether her mistress was laughing about the holy text or if she was thinking about something else.

Sometimes she angrily slammed together the thin-as-silk pages and threw the book away like the entrails from a dead fish.

Jacob was not buried until seven days after he was found. In the middle of December. There were so many arrangements to be made. So many people had to be notified. Relatives, friends, and prominent people had to be invited to the funeral. The weather stayed cold, so the battered and swollen corpse could easily remain in the barn during that time. Digging the grave, however, required the use of sledge-hammers and pickaxes.

The moon peered through the barn's tiny windows and observed Jacob's fate with its golden eye. Made no distinction between living and dead. Decorated the barn floor in silver and white. And nearby lay the hay, offering warmth and nourishment, smelling fragrantly of summer and splendour.

One morning before dawn, they dressed for the funeral. The boats were ready. Silence lay over the house like a strange piety. The moon was shining. No one waited for daylight at that time of year.

Dina leaned against the windowsill, as if steeling herself, when they entered her room to help her dress in the black clothes that had been sewn for the funeral. She had refused to try them on.

She seemed to be standing there sensing each muscle and each thought. The sombre, teary-eyed women did not see a single movement in her body.

Still, they did not give up at once. She had to change her clothes. She had to be part of the funeral procession. Anything else was unthinkable. But finally, they did think that thought. For with her guttural, animal-like sounds, she convinced everyone that she was not ready to be the widow at a funeral. At least not this particular day.

Terrified, the women fled the room. One after another. Mother Karen was the last to leave. She gave excuses and soothing explanations. To the aunts, the wives, the other women, and, not least of all, to Dina's father, the sheriff.

He was the hardest to convince. Bellowing loudly, he burst into Dina's room without knocking. Shook her and commanded her, slapped her cheeks with fatherly firmness while his words swarmed around her like angry bees.

Mother Karen had to intervene. The few who stood by kept their eyes lowered.

Then Dina let out the bestial sounds again. While she flailed her arms and tore her hair. The room was charged with something they did not understand. There was an aura of madness and power surrounding the young, half-dressed woman with dishevelled hair and crazed eyes.

Her screams reminded the sheriff of an event he carried with him always. Day and night. In his dreams and in his daily tasks. An event that still, after thirteen years, could make him wander restlessly around the estate. Looking for someone, or something, that could unburden him of his thoughts and feelings.

The people in the room thought Dina Grønelv had a harsh father. But on the other hand, it was not right that such a young woman refused to do what was expected of her.

She tired them out. People decided she was too sick to attend her husband's funeral. Mother Karen explained, loudly and clearly, to everyone she met:

"Dina is so distraught and ill she can't stand on her feet. She does nothing but weep. And the terrible thing is, she's not able to speak."

First came the muffled shouts from the people who were going in the boats. Then came the scraping of wood against iron as the coffin was loaded onto the longboat with its juniper decorations and its weeping, black-clad women. Then the sounds and voices stiffened over the water like a thin crusting of beach ice. And disappeared between the sea and the mountains. Afterward, silence settled over the estate as though this were the true funeral procession. The house held its breath. Merely let out a small sigh among the rafters now and then. A sad, pitiful final honour to Jacob.

The pink waxed-paper carnations fluttered amid the pine and juniper boughs across the sound in a light breeze. There was no point in travelling quickly with such a burden. Death and its detached supporting cast took their time. It was not Blackie who pulled them. And it was not Dina who set the pace. The coffin was heavy. Those who bore it felt the weight. This was the only way to the church with such a burden.

Now five pairs of oars creaked in the oarlocks. The sail flapped idly against the mast, refusing to unfurl. There was no sun. Grey clouds drifted across the sky. The raw air gradually became still.

The boats followed one another. A triumphal procession for Jacob Grønelv. Masts and oars pointed toward ocean and heaven. The ribbons on the wreaths fluttered restlessly. They had only a short time to be seen.

Mother Karen was a yellowed rag. Edged with lace, it is true.

The servant girls were wet balls of wool in the wind.

The men rowed, sweating behind their beards and moustaches. Rowing in rhythm.

At Reinsnes everything was prepared. The sandwiches were arranged on large platters. On the cellar floor and on shelves in the large entry were pewter plates filled with cakes and covered by cloths.

Under Oline's exacting supervision, the glasses had been rubbed to a glistening shine. Now the cups and glasses were arranged neatly in rows on the tables and in the pantry, protected by white linen towels bearing the monograms of

Ingeborg Grønelv and Dina Grønelv. They had to use the linen belonging to both of Jacob's wives today.

Many guests were expected after the burial.

Dina stoked the fire like a madwoman, although there was not even frost on the windows. Her face, which had been grey that morning, began slowly to regain its colour.

She paced restlessly back and forth across the floor with a little smile on her lips. When the clock struck, she raised her head like an animal listening for enemies.

Translated by Nadia Christensen; reprinted by permission of Norvik Press.

Karin Fossum

Born in Sandefjord, on the south coast of Norway, in 1954, **Karin Fossum** began her literary career in the early 1970s with the publication of a collection of poetry. Yet it was not poetry that made her name, but the sharp brilliance of her crime writing in the **Detective Inspector Konrad Sejer** series. In the last decade, Norway has produced an abundance of crime writers, but Fossum is generally regarded as the most talented, her taut and tight tales gripping and unpredictable in equal measure. To the non-Norwegian, they are also appealing in so far as they give the real flavour of that country and an insight into the collective mind of its people (in so far as this exists). The extract below comes from the beginning of a novel, which first appeared in English translation in 2002.

Don't Look Back

Ragnhild opened the door cautiously and peered out. Up on the road everything was quiet, and a breeze that had been playing amongst the buildings during the night had finally died down. She turned and pulled the doll's pram over the threshold.

"We haven't even eaten yet," Marthe complained.

She helped push the pram.

"I have to go home. We're going out shopping," Ragnhild said.

"Shall I come over later?"

"You can if you like. After we've done the shopping."

She was on the gravel now and began to push the pram towards the front gate. It was heavy going, so she turned it around and pulled it instead.

"See you later, Ragnhild."

The door closed behind her – a sharp slam of wood and metal.

Ragnhild struggled with the gate, but she mustn't be careless. Marthe's dog might get out. He was watching her intently from beneath the garden table. When she was sure that the gate was properly closed, she started off across the street in the direction of the garages. She could have taken the short-cut between the buildings, but she had discovered that it was too difficult with the pram. Just then a neighbour closed his garage door. He smiled to her and buttoned up his coat, a little awkwardly, with one hand. A big black Volvo stood in the driveway, rumbling pleasantly.

"Well, Ragnhild, you're out early, aren't you? Hasn't Marthe got up yet?"

"I slept over last night," she said. "On a mattress on the floor."

"I see."

He locked the garage door and glanced at his watch; it was 8.06 am. A moment later he turned the car into the street and drove off.

Ragnhild pushed the pram with both hands. She had reached the downhill stretch, which was rather steep, and she had to hold on tight so as not to lose her grip. Her doll, who was named Elise – after herself, because her name was Ragnhild Elise – slid down to the front of the pram. That didn't look good, so she let go with one hand and put the doll back in place, patted down the blanket, and continued on her way. She was wearing sneakers: one was red with green laces, the other was green with red laces, and that's how it had to be. She had on a red tracksuit with Simba the Lion across the chest and a green anorak over it. Her hair was extraordinarily thin and blond, and not very long, but she had managed to pull it into a topknot with an elastic band. Bright plastic fruit dangled from the band, with her sprout of hair sticking up in the middle like a tiny, neglected palm tree. She was six and a half, but small for her age. Not until she spoke would one guess that she was already at school.

She met no one on the hill, but as she approached the intersection she heard a car. So she stopped, squeezed over to the side, and waited as a van with its paint peeling off wobbled over a speed bump. It slowed even more when the girl in the red outfit came into view. Ragnhild wanted to cross the street. There was a pavement on the other side, and her mother had told her always to walk on the pavement. She waited for the van to pass, but it stopped instead, and the driver rolled down his window.

"You go first, I'll wait," he said.

She hesitated a moment, then crossed the street, turning around again to tug the pram up onto the pavement. The van slid forward a bit, then stopped again. The window on the opposite side was rolled down. His eyes are funny, she thought, really big and round as a ball. They were set wide apart and were pale blue, like thin ice. His mouth was small with full lips, and it pointed down like the mouth of a fish. He stared at her.

"Are you going up Skiferbakken with that pram?"

She nodded. "I live in Granittveien."

"It'll be awfully heavy. What have you got in it, then?"

"Elise," she replied, lifting up the doll.

"Excellent," he said with a broad smile. His mouth looked nicer now.

He scratched his head. His hair was dishevelled, and grew in thick clumps straight from his head like the leaves of a pineapple.

Now it looked even worse.

"I can drive you up there," he said. There's room for your pram in the back."

Ragnhild thought for a moment. She stared up Skiferbakken, which was long and steep. The man pulled on the handbrake and glanced in the back of the van.

"Mama's waiting for me," Ragnhild said.

A bell seemed to ring in the back of her mind, but she couldn't remember what it was for.

"You'll get home sooner if I drive you," he said.

That decided it. Ragnhild was a practical little girl. She wheeled the pram behind the van and the man hopped out. He opened the back door and lifted the pram in with one hand.

"You'll have to sit in the back and hold on to the pram. Otherwise it'll roll about," he said, and lifted in Ragnhild too.

He shut the back doors, climbed into the driver's seat, and released the brake.

"Do you go up this hill every day?" He looked at her in the mirror.

"Only when I've been at Marthe's. I stayed over."

She opened a flowered overnight bag from under the doll's blanket and opened it, checking that everything was in place: her nightgown with the picture of Nala on it, her toothbrush and hairbrush. The van lumbered over another speed bump. The man was still looking at her in the mirror.

"Have you ever seen a toothbrush like this?" Ragnhild said, holding it up for him. It had feet.

"No!" he said. "Where did you get it?"

"Papa bought it for me. You don't have one like it?"

"No, but I'll ask for one for Christmas."

He was finally over the last bump, and he shifted to second gear.

It made an awful grinding noise. The little girl sat on the floor of the van steadying the pram. A very sweet little girl, he thought, red and cute in her tracksuit, like a ripe little berry. He whistled a tune and felt on top of the world, enthroned behind the wheel in the big van with the little girl in the back. Really on top of the world.

The village lay in the bottom of the valley, at the end of the fjord, at the foot of a mountain. Like a pool in a river, where the water was much too still. And everyone knows that only running water is fresh. The village was a stepchild of the municipality, and the roads that led there were indescribably bad. Once in a while a bus deigned to stop by the abandoned dairy and pick up people to take them to town. There were no night buses back to the village.

Kollen, the mountain, was a grey, rounded peak, virtually neglected by those who lived there, but eagerly visited by people from far-off places. This was because of the mountain's unusual minerals and its flora, which was exceptionally rare. On calm days a faint tinkling could be heard from the mountaintop; one might almost believe it was haunted. In fact, the sound was from sheep grazing up there. The ridges around the mountain looked blue and airy through the haze, like soft felt with scattered woollen veils of fog.

Konrad Sejer traced the main highway in the road atlas with a fingertip. They were approaching a roundabout. Police Officer Karlsen was at the wheel, keeping an attentive eye on the fields while following the directions.

"Now you have to turn right on to Gneisveien, then up Skiferbakken, then left at Feltspatveien. Granittveien goes off to the right. A cul-de-sac," Sejer said pensively. "Number 5 should be the third house on the left."

He was tense. His voice was even more brusque than usual.

Karlsen manoeuvred the car into the housing estate and over the speed bumps. As in so many places, the new arrivals had taken up residence in clusters, some distance from the rest of the local community. Apart from giving directions, the two policemen didn't talk much. They approached the house, trying to steel themselves, thinking that perhaps the child might even be back home by now. Perhaps she was sitting on her mother's lap, surprised and embarrassed by all the fuss. It was 1pm, so the girl had been missing for five hours. Two would have been within a reasonable margin, five was definitely too long. Their unease was growing steadily, like a dead spot in the chest where the blood refused to flow. Both of them had children of their own; Karlsen's daughter was eight, Sejer had a grandson of four. The silence was filled with images, which might turn out to be correct – this is what struck Sejer as they drew up in front of the house.

Number 5 was a low, white house with dark blue trim. A typical prefab house with no personality, but embellished like a playroom with decorative shutters and scalloped edges on the gables. The yard was well kept. A large veranda with a prettily turned railing ran around the entire building. The house sat almost at the top of the ridge, with a view over the whole village, a small village, quite lovely, surrounded by farms and fields. A patrol car that had come on ahead of them was parked next to the letterbox.

Sejer went first, wiping his shoes carefully on the mat, and ducking his head as he entered the living room. It only took them a second to see what was happening. She was still missing, and the panic was palpable. On the sofa sat the mother, a stocky woman in a gingham dress. Next to her, with a hand on the mother's arm, sat a woman officer. Sejer could almost smell the terror in the room. The mother was using what little strength she had to hold back her tears, or perhaps even a piercing shriek of terror. The slightest effort made her breathe hard, as was evident when she stood up to shake hands with Sejer.

"Mrs Album," he said. "Someone is out searching, is that correct?"

"Some of the neighbours. They have a dog with them."

She sank back on the sofa.

"We have to help each other."

He sat down in the armchair facing her and leaned forward, keeping his eyes fixed on hers.

"We'll send out a dog patrol. Now, you have to tell me all about Ragnhild. Who she is, what she looks like, what she's wearing."

No reply, just persistent nodding. Her mouth looked stiff and frozen.

"Have you called every possible place where she could be?"

"There aren't many," she murmured. "I've called them all."

"Do you have relatives anywhere else in the village?"

"No, none. We're not from round here."

"Does Ragnhild go to kindergarten or nursery school?"

"There weren't any openings."

"Does she have any brothers or sisters?"

"She's our only child."

He tried to breathe without making a sound.

"First of all," he said, "what was she wearing? Be as precise as you can."

"A red tracksuit," she stammered, "with a lion on the front. Green anorak with a hood. One red shoe and one green shoe."

She spoke in fits and starts. Her voice threatening to break.

"And Ragnhild herself? Describe her for me."

"About four foot tall. Two and a half stone. Very fair hair. We just took her for her sixth-year check-up."

She went over to the wall by the TV, where a number of photos were hanging. Most of them were of Ragnhild, one was of Mrs Album in national costume, and one of a man in a field uniform of the Home Guard, presumably the father. She chose one in which the girl was smiling and handed it to him. Her hair was almost white. The mother's was jet-black, but the father was blond. Some of his hair was visible under his service cap.

"What sort of girl is she?"

"Trusting," she gasped. "Talks to everybody." This admission made her shiver.

"That's just the kind of child that gets along best in this world," he said firmly. "We'll have to take the picture with us."

"I realize that."

"Tell me," he said, sitting back down, "where do the children in the village go walking?"

"Down to the fjord. To Prestegårds Strand or to Horgen. Or to the top of Kollen. Some go up to the reservoir, or they go walking in the woods."

He looked out the window and saw the black firs.

"Has anyone at all seen Ragnhild since she left?"

"Marthe's neighbour met her by his garage when he was leaving for work. I know because I rang his wife."

"Where does Marthe live?"

"In Krystallen, just a few minutes from here."

"She had her doll's pram with her?"

"Yes. A pink Brio."

"What's the neighbour's name?"

"Walther," she said, surprised. "Walther Isaksen."

"Where can I find him?"

"He works at Dyno Industries, in the personnel department."

Sejer stood up, went over to the telephone and called information, then punched in the number, and waited.

"I need to speak to one of your employees immediately. The name is Walther Isaksen."

Mrs Album gave him a worried look from the sofa. Karlsen was studying the view from the window, the blue ridges, the fields, and a white steeple church in the distance.

"Konrad Sejer of the police," Sejer said curtly. "I'm calling from 5 Granittveien and you probably know why."

"Is Ragnhild still missing?"

"Yes. But I understood that you saw her when she left Marthe's house this morning."

"I was shutting my garage door."

"Did you notice the time?"

"It was 8.06am. I was running a little late."

"Are you sure of the time?"

"I have a digital watch."

Sejer was silent, trying to recall the way they had driven.

"So you left at 8.06am by the garage and drove straight to work?"

"Yes."

"Down Gneisveien and out to the main highway?"

"That's correct."

"I would think," Sejer said, "that at that time of day most people are driving towards town and there's probably little traffic going the other way."

"Yes, that's right. There are no main roads going through the village, and no jobs, either."

"Did you pass any cars on the way that were driving towards the village?"

The man was silent for a moment. Sejer waited. The room was as quiet as a tomb.

"Yes, actually, I did pass one, down by the flats, just before the roundabout. A van, I think, ugly and with peeling paint. Driving quite slowly."

"Who was driving it?"

"A man," he said hesitantly. "One man."

"My name is Raymond." He smiled.

Ragnhild looked up, saw the smiling face in the mirror, and Kollen Mountain bathed in the morning light.

"Would you like to go for a drive?"

"Mama's waiting for me."

She said it in a sort of stuck-up voice.

"Have you ever been to the top of Kollen?"

"One time, with Papa. We had a picnic."

"It's possible to drive up there," he explained. "From the back side, that is. Shall we drive up to the top?"

"I want to go home," she said, a bit uncertain now.

He shifted down and stopped.

"Just a short ride?" he asked.

His voice was thin. Ragnhild thought he sounded so sad. And she wasn't used to disappointing the wishes of grown-ups. She got up, walked forward to the front seat and leaned over.

"Just a short ride," she repeated. "Up to the top and then back home right away."

He backed into Feldspatveien and drove back downhill.

"What's your name?" he asked.

"Ragnhild Elise."

He rocked a little from side to side and cleared his throat, as if to admonish her.

"Ragnhild Elise. You can't go shopping so early in the morning. It's only 8.15am. The shops are closed."

She didn't answer. Instead she lifted Elise out of the pram, put her on her lap and straightened her dress. Then she pulled the dummy out of the doll's mouth. Instantly the doll began to scream, a thin, metallic baby cry.

"What's that?" he braked hard and looked in the mirror.

"That's just Elise. She cries when I take her dummy out."

"I don't like that noise! Put it back in!"

He was restless at the wheel now, and the van weaved back and forth.

"Papa is a better driver than you are," she said.

"I had to teach myself," he said sulkily. "Nobody wanted to teach me."

"Why not?"

He didn't reply, just tossed his head. The van was out on the main highway now; he drove in second gear down to the roundabout and passed through the intersection with a hoarse roar.

"Now we're coming to Horgen," she said, delighted.

He didn't reply. Ten minutes later he turned left, up into the wooded mountainside. On the way they passed a couple of farms with red barns and tractors parked here and there. They saw no-one. The road grew narrower and peppered with holes. Ragnhild's arms were starting to grow tired from holding onto the pram, so she laid the doll on the floor and put her foot between the wheels as a brake.

"This is where I live," he said suddenly and stopped.

"With your wife?"

"No, with my father. But he's in bed."

"Hasn't he got up?"

"He's always in bed."

She peered cautiously out of the window and saw a peculiar house. It had been a hut once, and someone had added onto it, first once, then again. The separate parts were all different colours. Next to it stood a garage of corrugated iron. The courtyard was overgrown. A rusty old trowel was being slowly strangled by stinging nettles and dandelions. But Ragnhild wasn't interested in the house; she had her eye on something else.

"Bunnies!" she said faintly.

"Yes," he said "Do you want to look at them?"

He hopped out, opened the back, and lifted her down. He had a peculiar way of walking; his legs were almost unnaturally short and he was severely bowlegged. His feet were small. His wide nose nearly touched his lower lip, which stuck out a bit. Under his nose hung a big, clear drop. Ragnhild thought he wasn't that old, although when he walked he swayed like an old man. But it was funny too. A boy's face on an old body. He wobbled over to the rabbit hutches and opened them. Ragnhild stood spellbound.

"Can I hold one?"

"Yes. Take your pick."

"The little brown one," she said, entranced.

"That's Påsan. He's the nicest."

He opened the hutch and lifted out the rabbit. A chubby, lop-eared rabbit, the colour of coffee with a lot of cream. It kicked its legs vigorously but calmed down as soon as Ragnhild took it in her arms. For a moment she was utterly still. She could feel its heart pounding against her hand, as she stroked one of its ears cautiously. It was like a piece of velvet between her fingers. Its nose shone black and moist like a liquorice drop. Raymond stood next to her and watched. He had a little girl all to himself, and no-one had seen them.

"The picture," Sejer said, "Along with the description, will be sent to the newspapers. Unless they hear otherwise, they'll print it tonight."

Irene Album fell across the table sobbing. The others stared wordlessly at their hands, and at her shaking back. The woman officer sat ready with a handkerchief. Karlsen scraped his chair a bit and glanced at his watch.

"Is Ragnhild afraid of dogs?" Sejer said.

"Why do you ask?" she said with surprise.

'Sometimes when we're searching for children with the dog patrol, they hide when they hear our German shepherds."

"No, she's not afraid of dogs."

The words reverberated in his head. *She's not afraid of dogs.*

"Have you had any luck getting hold of your husband?"

"He's in Narvik on manoeuvres," she whispered. "On the plateau somewhere.

"Don't they use mobile phones?"

"They're out of range."

"The people who are looking for her now, who are they?"

"Boys from the neighbourhood who are home in the daytime. One of them has a phone with him."

"How long have they been gone?"

She looked up at the clock on the wall. "More than two hours."

Her voice was no longer quavering. Now she sounded doped, almost lethargic, as if she were half asleep. Sejer leaned forward and spoke to her as softly and as clearly as he could.

"What you fear most has probably *not* happened. Do you realize that? Usually, children disappear for all sorts of trivial reasons. And it's a fact that children get lost all the time, just because they're children. They have no sense of time or responsibility, and they're so maddeningly curious that they follow any impulse that comes into their head. That's what it's like to be a child, and that's why they get lost. But as a rule they turn up just as suddenly as they disappeared. Often they don't have a good explanation for where they've been or what they were doing. But generally" – he took a breath – "they're quite all right."

"I know!" she said, staring at him. "But she's never gone off like this before!"

"She's growing up and getting bigger," he said persuasively.

"She's becoming more adventurous."

God help me, he thought, I've got an answer for everything. He got up and dialled another number, repressing an urge to look at his watch again – it would be a reminder that time was passing, and they didn't need that. He reached the Duty Officer, gave him a brief summary of the situation and asked him to contact a volunteer rescue group. He gave him the address in Granittveien and gave a quick description of the girl: dressed in red, almost white hair, pink doll's pram. Asked whether any messages had come in, and was told none had been received. He sat down again.

"Has Ragnhild mentioned or named anyone lately whom you didn't know yourself?"

"No."

"Did she have any money? Could she have been looking for a shop?"

"She had no money."

"This is a small village," he went on. "Has she ever been out walking and been given a ride by one of the neighbours?"

"Yes, that happens sometimes. There are about a hundred houses on this ridge, and she knows almost everyone, and she knows their cars. Sometimes she and Marthe have walked down to the church with their prams, and they've been given a ride home with one of the neighbours."

"Is there any special reason why they go to the church?"

"There's a little boy they know buried there. They pick flowers for his grave, and then they come back up here. I think it seems exciting to them."

"You've searched the church?"

"I rang for Ragnhild at ten o'clock. When they told me she had left at eight, I jumped in the car. I left the front door unlocked in case she came back while I was out searching. I drove to the church and down to the Fina petrol station, I looked in the auto workshop and behind the dairy, and then I drove over to the school to look in the schoolyard, because they have jungle gyms and things there. And then I checked the kindergarten. She was so keen on starting school, she …"

Another bout of sobbing took hold. As she wept, the others sat still and waited. Her eyes were puffy now, and she was crumpling her skirt in her fingers in despair. After a while her sobs died away and the lethargy returned – a shield to keep the terrible possibilities at bay.

The phone rang. A sudden ominous jangle. She gave a start and got up to answer it, but caught sight of Sejer's hand held up to stop her. He lifted the receiver.

"Hello, is Irene there?"

It sounded like a boy. "Who's calling?"

"Thorbjørn Haugen. We're looking for Ragnhild."

"You're speaking with the police. Do you have any news?"

"We've been to all the houses on the whole ridge. Every single one. A lot of people weren't home, though we did meet a lady in Feltspatveien. A lorry had backed into her farmyard and turned around, she lives in number 1. A kind of van, she thought. And inside the van she saw a girl with a green jacket and white hair pulled into a topknot on her head. Ragnhild often wears her hair in a topknot."

"Go on."

"It turned halfway up the hill and drove back down. Disappeared around the curve."

"Do you know what time it was?"

"It was 8.15 am."

"Can you come over to Granittveien?"

"We'll be right there, we're at the roundabout now."

He hung up. Irene Album was still standing.

"What was it?" she whispered. "What did they say?"

"Someone saw her," he said slowly. "She got into a van."

Irene Album's scream finally came. It was as if the sound penetrated through the tight forest and created a faint movement in Ragnhild's mind.

"I'm hungry," she said suddenly. "I have to go home."

Raymond looked up. Påsan was shuffling about on the kitchen table and licking up the seeds they had scattered over it. They had forgotten both time and place. They had fed all the rabbits, Raymond had shown her his pictures, cut out of magazines and carefully pasted into a big album. Ragnhild kept roaring with laughter at his funny face. Now she realised it was getting late.

"You can have a slice of bread."

"I have to go home. We're going shopping."

"We'll go up to Kollen first, then I'll drive you home afterwards."

"Now!" she said firmly. "I want to go home now."

Raymond thought desperately for a way to stall her.

"All right. But first I have to go out and buy some milk for Papa, down at Horgen's shop. You can wait here, then it won't take as long."

He stood up and looked at her. Her bright face, with the little heart-shaped mouth that made him think of heart-shaped cinnamon sweets. Her eyes were clear and blue and her eyebrows dark, surprising beneath her white fringe. He sighed heavily, walked over to the back door and opened it.

Ragnhild really wanted to leave but she didn't know the way home so she would have to wait. She padded into the little living room with the rabbit in her arms and curled up in a corner of the sofa. They hadn't slept much last night, she and Marthe, and with the warm animal in the hollow of her throat she quickly grew sleepy. Soon her eyes closed.

It was a while before he came back. For a long time he sat and looked at her, amazed at how quietly she slept. Not a movement, not a single little sigh. He thought she had expanded a bit, become larger and warmer, like a loaf in the oven. After a while he grew uneasy and didn't know what to do with his hands, so he put them in his pockets and rocked a little in his chair. Started kneading the fabric of his trousers between his hands as he rocked and rocked, faster and faster. He looked anxiously out the windows and down the hall to his father's bedroom. His hands worked and worked. The whole time he stared at her hair, which was shiny as silk, almost like rabbit fur. Then he gave a low moan and stopped himself. Stood up and poked her lightly on the shoulder.

"We can go now. Give me Påsan."

For a moment Ragnhild was completely bewildered. She got up slowly and stared at Raymond, then followed him out to the kitchen and pulled on her anorak, and padded out of the house as the little brown ball of fur vanished back into its cage. The pram was still in the back of the van. Raymond looked sad, but he helped her climb in, then got into the driver's seat and turned the key. Nothing happened.

"It won't start." He said, annoyed. "I don't understand. It was running a minute ago. This piece of junk!"

"I have to go home!" Ragnhild said loudly, as if it would help the situation. He kept trying the ignition and stepping on the accelerator; he could hear the starter motor turning, but it kept up a complaining whine and refused to catch.

"We'll have to walk."

"It's much too far!" she whined.

"No, not from here. We're on the side of Kollen now, we're almost at the top, and from there you can look straight down on your house. I'll pull your pram for you."

He put on a jacket that lay on the front seat, got out and opened the door for her. Ragnhild carried her doll and he pulled the pram behind him. It bumped a little on the pot-holed road. Ragnhild could see Kollen looming farther ahead, ringed by dark woods. For a moment they had to pull off to the side of the road as a car passed them noisily at high speed. The dust hung like a thick fog behind it. Raymond knew the way, and he wasn't very fit, so it was no problem for Ragnhild to keep up. After a while the road grew steeper, ending in a turning space, and the path, which went round to the right of Kollen, was soft and dusty. The sheep had widened the path, and their droppings lay as thick as hail. Ragnhild amused herself by treading on them, they were dry and powdery. After a few minutes there was a lovely glistening visible through the trees.

"Serpent Tarn," Raymond said.

She stopped next to him, stared out across the lake and saw the water-lilies, and a little boat that lay upside down on the shore.

"Don't go down to the water," said Raymond. "It's dangerous. You can't swim here, you"d just sink into the sand and disappear. Quicksand," he added, with a serious expression. Ragnhild shuddered. She followed the bank of the tarn with her eyes, a wavy yellow line of rushes, except for one place where what might be called a beach broke the line like a dark indentation. That's what they were staring at. Raymond let go of the pram, and Ragnhild stuck a finger in her mouth.

Thorbjørn stood fiddling with the mobile phone. He was about 16, and had dark shoulder-length hair with a hint of dandruff, held in place with a patterned bandana. The ends stuck out at the knots at his temples like two red feathers, making him look like a pale Indian. He avoided looking at Ragnhild's mother, staring hard at Sejer instead, licking his lips constantly.

"What you have discovered is important," Sejer said. "Please write down her address. Do you remember the name?"

"Helga Moen, in number 1. A grey house with a kennel outside."

He almost spoke in a whisper as he printed the words in big letters on the pad that Sejer gave him.

"Your boys have been over most of the area?" Sejer asked.

"We were up on the Kollen first, then we went down to Serpent Tarn and went over the paths there. We went to the high tarn, Horgens Store and Prestegårds Strand. And the church. Last, we looked at a couple of farms, at Bjerkerud and at the Equestrian Sports Centre. Ragnhild was, uh, I mean *is* very interested in animals."

The slip of the tongue made him blush. Sejer patted him lightly on the shoulder.

"Sit down, Thorbjørn."

He nodded to the sofa where there was room next to Mrs Album. She had graduated to another phase, and was now contemplating the dizzying possibility that Ragnhild might never come home again, and she might have to live the rest of her life without her little girl and her big blue eyes. This realisation came in small stabs of pain. Her whole body was rigid, as if she had a steel rod running up her spine. The woman officer, who had hardly said a word the whole time they had been there, stood up slowly. For the first time she ventured to make a suggestion.

"Mrs Album," she asked quietly, "why don't we make everyone some coffee?"

The woman nodded weakly, got up and followed the officer out to the kitchen. A tap was turned on and there was the sound of cups clattering. Sejer motioned Karlsen over towards the hallway. They stood there muttering to one another. Thorbjørn could just see Sejer's head and the tip of Karlsen's shoe, which was shiny and black. In the dim light they could check their watches without being observed. They did so and nodded in agreement. Ragnhild's disappearance had become a serious matter, all the department's resources would have to be utilised. Sejer scratched his elbow through his shirt.

"I can't face the thought of finding her in a ditch."

He opened the door to get some fresh air. And there she stood. In her red jogging suit, on the bottom step, with a tiny white hand on the railing.

"Ragnhild?" he said in astonishment.

A happy half-hour later, as the car sped down Skiferbakken, Sejer ran his fingers through his hair with satisfaction. Karlsen thought his hair looked like a steel brush now that it was cut shorter than ever. The kind of brush used to clean off old paint. Sejer's lined face looked peaceful, not closed and serious as it usually did. Halfway down the hill they passed the grey house. They saw the kennel and a face at the window. If Helga Moen was hoping for a visit from the police, she would be disappointed. Ragnhild was sitting safely on her mother's lap with two thick slices of bread in her hand.

The moment when the little girl stepped into the living room was etched into the minds of both officers. The mother, hearing her thin little voice, rushed in from the kitchen and threw herself at Ragnhild, lightning fast, like a beast of prey grasping its victim and never wanting to let it go. Ragnhild's thin limbs and the white sprout of hair stuck out through her mother's powerful arms. And there they stood. Not a sound was heard, not a single cry from either of them. Thorbjørn was practically crushing the phone in his hand, the woman officer was making a clatter with the cups, and Karlsen kept twisting his moustache with a blissful grin on his face. The room brightened up as though the sun had suddenly shot a beam through the window. And then finally, with a sobbing laugh:

"YOU TERRIBLE CHILD!"

"I've been thinking," Sejer cleared his throat, "about taking a week's holiday. I have some time off due to me."

Karlsen crossed a speed bump.

"What will you do with it? Go skydiving in Florida?"

"I thought I'd air out my cabin."

"Near Brevik, isn't that where it is?"

"Sand Island."

They turned onto the main road and picked up speed.

"I have to go to Legoland this year," Karlsen muttered. "Can't avoid it any longer. My daughter is pestering me."

"You make it sound like a punishment," Sejer said. "Legoland is beautiful. When you leave I guarantee you'll be weighed down with boxes of Lego and you'll be bitten by the bug. Do go, you won't regret it."

"So, you've been there, have you?"

"I went there with Matteus. Do you know that they've built a statue of Sitting Bull out of nothing but pieces of Lego? One point four million pieces with special colouring. It's unbelievable."

He fell silent as he caught sight of the church off to the left, a little white wooden church a bit off the road between green and yellow fields, surrounded by lush trees. A beautiful little church, he thought; he should have buried his wife in a spot like that, even though it would have been a long way to come. Of course, it was too late now. She had been dead more than eight years and her grave was in the cemetery in the middle of town, right by the busy high street surrounded by exhaust fumes and traffic noise.

"Do you think the girl was all right?"

"She seemed to be. I've asked the mother to ring us when things calm down a bit. She"ll probably want to talk about it eventually. Six hours," he said thoughtfully, "that's quite a while. Must have been a charming lone wolf."

"He evidently had a driver's licence, at least. So he isn't a total hermit."

"We don't know that, do we? That he has a driver's licence?"

"No, damn it, you're right," Karlsen said. He braked abruptly and turned into the petrol station in what they called "downtown", with a post office, bank, hairdresser, and the Fina station. A poster bearing the words "sale on medicine" was displayed in the window of the low-price Kiwi grocery, and the hairdresser had a tempting offer for a new tanning bed.

"I need something to eat. Are you coming?"

They went in and Sejer bought a newspaper and some chocolate.

He peered out the window and down to the fjord.

"Excuse me," said the girl behind the counter, staring nervously at Karlsen's uniform. "Nothing has happened to Ragnhild, has it?"

"Do you know her?" Sejer put some coins on the counter.

"No, I don't know her, but I know who they are. Her mother was here this morning looking for her."

"Ragnhild is all right. She's back at home."

She smiled with relief and gave him his change.

"Are you from round here?" Sejer asked. "Do you know most people?"

"I certainly do. There aren't many of us."

"If I ask you whether you know a man, maybe a little odd, who drives a van, an old, ugly van with its paint peeling off, does that ring a bell?"

"That sounds like Raymond," she said, nodding. "Raymond Lake."

"What do you know about him?"

"He works at the employment centre. Lives in a cabin on the far side of Kollen with his father. Raymond has Down's syndrome. About 30, and very nice. His father used to run this station, by the way, before he retired."

"Does Raymond have a driver's licence?"

"No, but he drives anyway. It's his father's van. He's an invalid so he probably doesn't have much control over what Raymond does. The sheriff knows about it and pulls him over now and then, but it doesn't do much good. He never drives above second gear. Did he pick up Ragnhild?"

"Yes."

"Then she couldn't have been safer," she smiled. "Raymond would stop to let a ladybird cross the road."

They both grinned and went back outside. Karlsen bit into his chocolate and looked around.

"Nice town," he said, chewing.

Sejer, who had bought an old-fashioned marzipan loaf, followed his gaze. "That fjord is deep, more than 300 metres. Never gets above 17 degrees Celsius."

"Do you know anyone here?"

"I don't, but my daughter Ingrid does. She's been here on a folklore walk, the kind of thing they organize in the autumn. "Know your district." She loves stuff like that."

He rolled the candy wrapper into a thin strip and stuck it into his shirt pocket. "Do you think someone with Down's syndrome can be a good driver?"

"No idea," Karlsen said. "But there's nothing wrong with them except for having one chromosome too many. I think their biggest problem is that they take longer to learn something than other people do. They also have bad hearts. They don't live to be very old. And there's something about their hands."

"What's that?"

"They're missing a line on their palm or something."

Sejer gave him a surprised look. "Anyway, Ragnhild certainly let herself be charmed."

"I think the rabbits helped."

Karlsen found a handkerchief in his inside pocket and wiped the chocolate from the corners of his mouth. "I grew up with a Down's syndrome child. We called him "Crazy Gunnar". Now that I think of it, we actually seemed to believe that he came from another planet. He's dead now – only lived to be 35."

They got into the car and drove on. Sejer prepared a simple little speech that he would serve up to the department chief when they were back at headquarters. A few days off to go up to his cabin seemed tremendously important all of a sudden. The timing was right, the long-term prospects were promising, and the girl showing up safe and sound at home had put him in a good mood. He stared over fields and meadows, registered that they had slowed down, and saw the tractor in front of them. A green John Deere with butter-yellow wheel rims was crawling at a snail's pace. They had no chance to overtake it; each time they came to a straight stretch, it proved to be too short. The farmer, who was wearing a gardener's cap and earmuffs, sat like a tree stump, as though he was growing straight up out of the seat. Karlsen changed gears and sighed.

"He's carrying Brussels sprouts. Can't you reach out and grab a box? We could cook them in the kitchen at the canteen."

"Now we're going as fast as Raymond does," muttered Sejer.

"Life in second gear. That really would be something, don't you think?"

He settled his grey head against the head-rest and closed his eyes.

Published by Harvill Press. Reprinted by permission of The Random House Group Ltd.

Language

Language

Norwegian

There are two official Norwegian languages: **Riksmål** or **Bokmål** (book language), a modification of the old Dano-Norwegian tongue left over from the days of Danish dominance; and **Landsmål** or **Nynorsk**, which was codified during the nineteenth-century upsurge of Norwegian nationalism and is based on rural dialects of Old Norse provenance. Roughly ninety percent of schoolchildren have *Bokmål* as their primary language, and the remaining ten percent are *Nynorsk* speakers, concentrated in the fjord country of the west coast and the mountain districts of central Norway. Despite the best efforts of the government, *Nynorsk* is in decline – in 1944 fully one-third of the population used it. As the more common of the two languages, *Bokmål* is what we use here in this Guide.

You don't really need to know any Norwegian to get by in Norway. Almost everyone speaks some English, and in any case many words are not too far removed from their English equivalents; there's also plenty of English (or American) on billboards, the TV and at the cinema. Mastering "hello" or "thank you" will, however, be greatly appreciated, while if you speak either Danish or Swedish you should have few problems being understood. Incidentally, Norwegians find Danish easier to read than Swedish, but orally it's the other way round.

Phrasebooks are fairly thin on the ground, but Berlitz's *Norwegian Phrasebook with Dictionary* has – as you would expect from the title – a mini-dictionary, not to mention a useful grammar section and a menu reader; Dorling Kindersley's *Norwegian Phrasebook* is comparable. There are several **dictionaries** to choose from, all of which include pronunciation tips and so forth. The best is generally considered to be the Collins *English-Norwegian Dictionary*, though this is currently out of print and you might decide to opt for the Berlitz *Norwegian Pocket Dictionary* instead.

Pronunciation

Pronunciation can be tricky. A **vowel** is usually long when it's the final syllable or followed by only one consonant; followed by two it's generally short. Unfamiliar ones are:

æ before an r, as in b**a**d; otherwise as in s**ay**

ø as in f**ur** but without pronouncing the r

å usually as in s**aw**

øy between the ø sound and b**oy**

ei as in s**ay**

Consonants

are pronounced as in English except:

c, q, w, z found only in foreign words and pronounced as in the original language

g before i, y or ei, as in **y**et; otherwise hard

hv as in **v**iew

j, gj, hj, lj as in **y**et

rs almost always as in **sh**ut

k before i, y or j, like the Scottish lo**ch**; otherwise hard

sj, sk before i, y, ø or øy, as in **sh**ut

Words and phrases

Basic phrases

do you speak English?	snakker du engelsk?	you're welcome	vær så god
yes	ja	excuse me	unnskyld
no	nei	good morning	god morgen
do you understand?	forstår du?	good afternoon	god dag
I don't understand	jeg forstår ikke	good night	god natt
I understand	jeg forstår	goodbye	adjø
please (is near enough, though there's no direct equivalent)	vær så god	today	i dag
		tomorrow	i morgen
		day after tomorrow	i overmorgen
		in the morning	om morgenen
		in the afternoon	om ettermiddagen
thank you (very much)	takk (tusen takk)	in the evening	om kvelden

Some signs

entrance	inngang	cycle path	sykkelsti
exit	utgang	no smoking	røyking forbudt
gentlemen	herrer/menn	no camping	camping forbudt
ladies	damer/kvinner	no trespassing	uvedkommende forbudt
open	åpen		
closed	stengt	no entry	ingen adgang
arrival	ankomst	pull/push	trekk/trykk
police	politi	departure	avgang
hospital	sykehus	parking fees	avgift

Questions and directions

where? (where is/are?)	hvor? (hvor er?)	hot/cold	varm/kald
when?	når?	near/far	i nærheten/ langt borte
what?	hva?	good/bad	god/dårlig
how much/many?	hvor mye/hvor mange?	vacant/occupied	ledig/opptatt
why?	hvorfor?	a little/a lot	litt/mye
which?	hvilket?	more/less	mer/mindre
what's that called in Norwegian?	hva kaller man det på norsk?	can we camp here?	kan vi campe her?
can you direct me to ...?	kan de vise meg veien til ...?	is there a youth hostel near here?	er det et vandrerhjem i nærheten?
it is/there is (is it/is there)	det er (er det?)	how do I get to ...?	hvordan kommer jeg til ...?
what time is it?	hvor mange er klokken?	how far is it to ...?	hvor langt er det til ...?
		ticket	billett
big/small	stor/liten	single/return	en vei/tur-retur
cheap/expensive	billig/dyrt	can you give me a lift to ...?	kan jeg få sitte på til ...?
early/late	tidlig/sent	left/right	venstre/høyre
		go straight ahead	kjør rett frem

Numbers

0	null	17	sytten
1	en	18	atten
2	to	19	nitten
3	tre	20	tjue
4	fire	21	tjueen
5	fem	22	tjueto
6	seks	30	tretti
7	sju	40	førti
8	åtte	50	femti
9	ni	60	seksti
10	ti	70	sytti
11	elleve	80	åtti
12	tolv	90	nitti
13	tretten	100	hundre
14	fjorten	101	hundreogen
15	femten	200	to hundre
16	seksten	1000	tusen

Days

Sunday	søndag	Thursday	torsdag
Monday	mandag	Friday	fredag
Tuesday	tirsdag	Saturday	lørdag
Wednesday	onsdag		

Months

January	januar	August	august
February	februar	September	september
March	mars	October	oktober
April	april	November	november
May	mai	December	desember
June	juni	(Note: days and months are never capitalized)	
July	juli		

Menu reader

Basics and snacks

appelsin, marmelade	marmalade	fløte	cream
brød	bread	grønsaker	vegetables
eddik	vinegar	grøt	porridge
egg	egg	iskrem	ice cream
eggerøre	scrambled eggs	kaffefløte	single cream for coffee
flatbrød	crispbread	kake	cake

kaviar	caviar	ris	rice
kjeks	biscuits	rundstykker	bread roll
krem	whipped cream	salat	salad
melk	milk	salt	salt
mineralvann	mineral water	sennep	mustard
nøtter	nuts	smør	butter
olje	oil	smørbrød	open sandwich
omelett	omelette	sukker	sugar
ost	cheese	suppe	soup
pannekake	pancakes	syltetøy	jam
pepper	pepper	varm pølse	hot dog
potetchips	crisps (potato chips)	yoghurt	yoghurt
pommes-frites	chips (French fries)		

Norwegian specialities

brun saus gravy served with most meats, rissoles, fishcakes and sausages.

fenalår marinated mutton that is smoked, sliced, salted, dried and served with crispbread, scrambled egg and beer.

fiskeboller fish balls, served under a white sauce or on open sandwiches.

fiskekabaret shrimps, fish and vegetables in aspic.

fiskesuppe fish soup.

flatbrød a flat unleavened cracker, half barley, half wheat.

gammelost a hard, strong smelling, yellow-brown cheese with veins.

geitost/gjetost goat's cheese, slightly sweet and fudge-coloured. Similar cheeses have different ratios of goat's milk to cow's milk.

gravetlaks salmon marinated in salt, sugar, dill and brandy.

juleskinke marinated boiled ham, served at Christmas.

kjøttkaker med homemade burgers with **surkål** cabbage and a sweet and sour sauce.

koldtbord – a midday buffet with cold meats, herrings, salads, bread and perhaps soup, eggs or hot meats.

lapskaus pork, venison (or other meats) and vegetable stew, common in the south and east, using salted or fresh meat, or leftovers, in a thick brown gravy.

lutefisk fish (usually cod) preserved in an alkali solution and seasoned; an acquired taste.

multer cloudberries – wild berries mostly found north of the Arctic Circle and served with cream (med krem).

mysost brown whey cheese, made from cow's milk.

nedlagtsild marinated herring.

pinnekjøtt western Norwegian Christmas dish of smoked mutton steamed over shredded birch bark, served with cabbage; or accompanied by boiled potatoes and mashed swedes (kålrabistappe).

reinsdyrstek reindeer steak, usually served with boiled potatoes and cranberry sauce.

rekesalat shrimp salad in mayonnaise.

ribbe, julepølse eastern Norwegian Christmas medisterkake dish of pork ribs, sausage and dumplings.

spekemat various types of smoked, dried meat.

Trondhjemsuppea kind of milk broth with raisins, rice, cinnamon and sugar.

Meat (kjøtt) and game (vilt)

dyrestek	venison	postei	pâté
elg	elk	pølser	sausages
kalkun	turkey	reinsdyr	reindeer
kjøttboller	meatballs	ribbe	pork rib
kjøttkaker	rissoles	skinke	ham
kylling	chicken	spekemat	dried meat
lammekjøtt	lamb	stek	steak
lever	liver	svinekjøtt	pork
oksekjøtt	beef	varm pølse	frankfurter/hot dog

Fish (fisk) and shellfish (skalldyr)

ål	eel	piggvar	turbot
ansjos	anchovies (brisling)	reker	shrimps
blåskjell	mussels	rødspette	plaice
brisling	sprats	røkelaks	smoked salmon
hummer	lobster	sardiner	sardines (brisling)
hvitting	whiting	sei	coalfish
kaviar	caviar	sild	herring
krabbe	crab	sjøtunge	sole
kreps	crayfish	småfisk	whitebait
laks	salmon	steinbit	catfish
makrell	mackerel	torsk	cod
ørret	trout	tunfisk	tuna

Vegetables (grønsaker)

agurk	cucumber/gherkin/ pickle	løk	onion
		mais	sweetcorn
blomkål	cauliflower	nepe	turnip
bønner	beans	paprika	peppers
erter	peas	poteter	potatoes
gulrøtter	carrots	rosenkål	Brussels sprouts
hodesalat	lettuce	selleri	celery
hvitløk	garlic	sopp	mushrooms
kål	cabbage	spinat	spinach
linser	lentils	tomater	tomatoes

Fruit (frukt)

ananas	pineapple	grapefrukt	grapefruit
appelsin	orange	jordbær	strawberries
aprikos	apricot	multer	cloudberries
banan	banana	plommer	plums
blåbær	blueberries	pærer	pears
druer	grapes	sitron	lemon
eple	apple	solbær	blackcurrants
fersken	peach	tyttbær	cranberries
fruktsalat	fruit salad		

Cooking terms

blodig	rare, underdone	røkt	smoked
godt stekt	well done	stekt	fried
grillet	grilled	stuet	stewed
grytestekt	braised	sur	sour, pickled
kokt	boiled	syltet	pickled
marinert	marinated	saltet	cured
ovnstekt	baked/roasted		

Bread, cake and desserts

bløtkake cream cake with fruit

fløtelapper pancakes made with cream, served with sugar and jam

havrekjeks oatmeal biscuits, eaten with goat's cheese

knekkebrød crispbread

kransekake cake made from almonds, sugar and eggs, served at celebrations

lomper potato scones-cum-tortillas

riskrem rice pudding with whipped cream and sugar, usually served with **frukt saus**, a slighly thickened fruit sauce

tilslørtbondepiker stewed apples and breadcrumbs, served with cream

trollkrem beaten egg whites (or whipped cream) and sugar mixed with cloudberries (or cranberries)

vafle waffles

Drinks

akevitt	aquavit	te med melk/sitron	tea with milk/lemon
appelsin	orange squash	vann	water
saft/juice	juice	varm sjokolade	hot chocolate
brus	fizzy soft drink	vin	wine
eplesider	cider	søt	sweet
fruktsaft	sweetened fruit juice	tørr	dry
kaffe	coffee	rød	red
melk	milk	hvit	white
mineralvann	mineral water	rosé	rosé
øl	beer	skål	cheers
sitronbrus	lemonade		

Glossary of Norwegian terms

apotek chemist

bakke hill

bokhandel bookshop

bre glacier

bro/bru bridge

brygge quay or wharf

dal valley/dale

DNT (Den Norske Turistforening) nationwide hiking organization whose local affiliates maintain hiking paths across almost all the country.

Domkirke Cathedral

drosje taxi

E.kr AD

elv/bekk river/stream

ferje/ferge ferry

fjell/berg mountain

Flybussen Airport bus (literally "plane bus")

F.kr BC

foss waterfall

gågate urban pedestrianized area

gate (gt.) street

Gamle byen literally "Old Town"; used wherever the old part of town has remained distinct from the rest (eg Fredrikstad, p.123). Also spelt as one word.

hav ocean

havn harbour

Hurtigbåt passenger express boat; usually a catamaran

Hurtigrute literally "quick route", but familiar as the name of the boat service along the west coast from Bergen to Kirkenes.

hytte cottage, cabin

innsjø lake

jernbanestasjon railway station

kirke/kjerke church

Kfum/kfuk Norwegian YMCA/YWCA

klokken/kl. o'clock

klippfisk salted whitefish, usually cod

moderasjon discount or price reduction

Moms or mva sales tax – applied to almost all consumables

museet museum

NAF nationwide Norwegian automobile association. Membership covers rescue and repair.

øy/øya islet

rabatt discount or price reduction

rådhus town hall

rorbu originally a simple wooden cabin built near the fishing grounds for incoming (ie non-local) fishermen. Many cabins are now used as tourist accommodation, especially in the Lofoten (see p.332).

Sámi formerly called Lapps, the Sámi inhabit the northern reaches of Norway, Finland and Sweden – Lapland.

sentrum city or town centre

sjø sea

sjøhus harbourside building where the catch was sorted, salted, filleted and iced. Many are now redundant and some have been turned into tourist accommodation.

skog forest

slott castle, palace

Stavkirke Stave church

Storting Parliament

tilbud special offer

torget main town square, often home to an outdoor market; sometimes spelt Torvet

Vandrerhjem Youth hostel

vann/vatn water or lake

vei/veg/vn. road

Glossary of English art and architectural terms

Ambulatory Covered passage around the outer edge of the choir in the chancel of a church.

Art Deco Geometrical style of art and architecture popular in the 1930s.

Art Nouveau Style of art, architecture and design based on highly stylized vegetal forms. Particularly popular in the early part of the twentieth century.

Baroque The art and architecture of the Counter-Reformation, dating from around 1600 onwards, and distinguished by extreme ornateness, exuberance and the complex but harmonious spatial arrangement of interiors.

Classical Architectural style incorporating Greek and Roman elements – pillars, domes, colonnades, etc – at its height in the seventeenth century and revived, as Neoclassical, in the nineteenth century.

Fresco Wall painting – made durable through applying paint to wet plaster.

Gothic Architectural style of the thirteenth to sixteenth centuries, characterized by pointed arches, rib vaulting, flying buttresses and a general emphasis on verticality.

Misericord Ledge on a choir stall on which the occupant can be supported while standing; often carved with secular subjects (bottoms were not thought worthy of religious ones).

Nave Main body of a church.

Neoclassical Architectural style derived from Greek and Roman elements – pillars, domes, colonnades, etc – popular in Norway throughout the nineteenth century.

Renaissance Movement in art and architecture developed in fifteenth-century Italy.

Rococo Highly florid, light and graceful eighteenth-century style of architecture, painting and interior design, forming the last phase of Baroque.

Rood screen Decorative screen separating the nave from the chancel.

Romanesque Early medieval architecture distinguished by squat forms, rounded arches and naive sculpture.

Stucco Marble-based plaster used to embellish ceilings, etc.

Transept Arms of a cross-shaped church, placed at ninety degrees to nave and chancel.

Triptych Carved or painted work on three panels. Often used as an altarpiece.

Vault An arched ceiling or roof.

Travel store

ROUGH GUIDES

For more information go to www.roughguides.com

Hotel discounts in Norway!

With a Fjord Pass® you get a significant discount on the hotel's rate for standard rooms. With 170 hotels in Norway to choose from, the Fjord Pass® offers you a much greater choice than any other hotel pass. Fjord Pass® only costs NOK 120.

FOR BOOKING AND INFORMATION:
www.fjordpass.no

FJORD PASS®
FJORDTOURS.COM

Small print and

Index

A Rough Guide to Rough Guides

Published in 1982, the first Rough Guide – to Greece – was a student scheme that became a publishing phenomenon. Mark Ellingham, a recent graduate in English from Bristol University, had been travelling in Greece the previous summer and couldn't find the right guidebook. With a small group of friends he wrote his own guide, combining a highly contemporary, journalistic style with a thoroughly practical approach to travellers' needs.

The immediate success of the book spawned a series that rapidly covered dozens of destinations. And, in addition to impecunious backpackers, Rough Guides soon acquired a much broader and older readership that relished the guides' wit and inquisitiveness as much as their enthusiastic, critical approach and value-for-money ethos.

These days, Rough Guides include recommendations from shoestring to luxury and cover more than 200 destinations around the globe, including almost every country in the Americas and Europe, more than half of Africa and most of Asia and Australasia. Our ever-growing team of authors and photographers is spread all over the world, particularly in Europe, the USA and Australia.

In the early 1990s, Rough Guides branched out of travel, with the publication of Rough Guides to World Music, Classical Music and the Internet. All three have become benchmark titles in their fields, spearheading the publication of a wide range of books under the Rough Guide name.

Including the travel series, Rough Guides now number more than 350 titles, covering: phrasebooks, waterproof maps, music guides from Opera to Heavy Metal, reference works as diverse as Conspiracy Theories and Shakespeare, and popular culture books from iPods to Poker. Rough Guides also produce a series of more than 120 World Music CDs in partnership with World Music Network.

Visit www.roughguides.com to see our latest publications.

Rough Guide travel images are available for commercial licensing at www.roughguidespictures.com

SMALL PRINT

Rough Guide credits

Text editor: Tim Locke
Layout: Anita Singh
Cartography: Swati Handoo, Katie Lloyd-Jones
Picture editor: Sarah Cummins
Production: Rebecca Short
Proofreader: Diane Margolis
Cover design: Chloë Roberts
Editorial: Ruth Blackmore, Andy Turner, Keith Drew, Edward Aves, Alice Park, Lucy White, Jo Kirby, James Smart, Natasha Foges, Róisín Cameron, Emma Traynor, Emma Gibbs, Kathryn Lane, Christina Valhouli, Monica Woods, Mani Ramaswamy, Harry Wilson, Lucy Cowie, Helen Ochyra, Alison Roberts, Joe Staines, Peter Buckley, Matthew Milton, Tracy Hopkins, Ruth Tidball; **Delhi** Madhavi Singh, Karen D'Souza, Lubna Shaheen
Design & Pictures: **London** Scott Stickland, Dan May, Diana Jarvis, Mark Thomas, Chloë Roberts, Nicole Newman, Emily Taylor; **Delhi** Umesh Aggarwal, Ajay Verma, Jessica Subramanian, Ankur Guha, Pradeep Thapliyal, Sachin Tanwar, Nikhil Agarwal
Production: Vicky Baldwin

Cartography: **London** Maxine Repath, Ed Wright; **Delhi** Rajesh Chhibber, Ashutosh Bharti, Rajesh Mishra, Animesh Pathak, Jasbir Sandhu, Karobi Gogoi, Alakananda Bhattacharya, Deshpal Dabas
Online: **London** George Atwell, Faye Hellon, Jeanette Angell, Fergus Day, Justine Bright, Clare Bryson, Aine Fearon, Adrian Low, Ezgi Celebi, Amber Bloomfield; **Delhi** Amit Verma, Rahul Kumar, Narender Kumar, Ravi Yadav, Debojit Borah, Rakesh Kumar, Ganesh Sharma, Shisir Basumatari
Marketing & Publicity: **London** Liz Statham, Niki Hanmer, Louise Maher, Jess Carter, Vanessa Godden, Vivienne Watton, Anna Paynton, Rachel Sprackett, Libby Jellie, Laura Vipond, Vanessa McDonald; **New York** Katy Ball, Judi Powers, Nancy Lambert; **Delhi** Ragini Govind
Manager India: Punita Singh
Reference Director: Andrew Lockett
Operations Manager: Helen Phillips
PA to Publishing Director: Nicola Henderson
Publishing Director: Martin Dunford
Commercial Manager: Gino Magnotta
Managing Director: John Duhigg

ROUGH GUIDES

SMALL PRINT

Publishing information

This fifth edition published June 2009 by
Rough Guides Ltd,
80 Strand, London WC2R 0RL
14 Local Shopping Centre, Panchsheel Park,
New Delhi 110017, India
Distributed by the Penguin Group
Penguin Books Ltd,
80 Strand, London WC2R 0RL
Penguin Group (USA)
375 Hudson Street, NY 10014, USA
Penguin Group (Australia)
250 Camberwell Road, Camberwell,
Victoria 3124, Australia
Penguin Group (Canada)
195 Harry Walker Parkway N, Newmarket, ON,
L3Y 7B3 Canada
Penguin Group (NZ)
67 Apollo Drive, Mairangi Bay, Auckland 1310,
New Zealand
Cover concept by Peter Dyer.

Typeset in Bembo and Helvetica to an original design by Henry Iles.
Printed in China
© Phil Lee 2009

488pp includes index
A catalogue record for this book is available from the British Library
ISBN: 978-1-84836-027-3

1 3 5 7 9 8 6 4 2

Help us update

We've gone to a lot of effort to ensure that the fifth edition of **The Rough Guide to Norway** is accurate and up to date. However, things change – places get "discovered", opening hours are notoriously fickle, restaurants and rooms raise prices or lower standards. If you feel we've got it wrong or left something out, we'd like to know, and if you can remember the address, the price, the hours, the phone number, so much the better.

Please send your comments with the subject line "Rough Guide Norway Update" to ℮mail @roughguides.com. We'll credit all contributions and send a copy of the next edition (or any other Rough Guide if you prefer) for the very best emails.

Have your questions answered and tell others about your trip at
ⓦcommunity.roughguides.com

Acknowledgements

Phil Lee would like to thank his editor, Tim Locke, for his good humour and attention to detail during the preparation of this new edition of the Rough Guide to Norway. Special thanks also to Katie Lloyd-Jones and Maxine Repath for working so hard on the maps.

Thanks also to Trine Winther of Scandic Hotels; Linda Kragseth and Anne Gjerstad of Fjord Tours AS; Paul Richards of Ulvik Fjord Hotel; Wenche Berger of NSB railways; Linn Falkenberg of the Bergen Tourist Board; and Annett Brohmann of Visit Oslo.

Readers' letters

Thanks to all the readers who have taken the time to write in with comments and suggestions (and apologies if we've inadvertently omitted or misspelt anyone's name):

Tommy Andreasen; Nigel Barnack; Mike Beasley; Ard Beld; Gavin Bell; Natalie Birk; Stacy Braverman; Ross Brown; Mary Cable; Cathy Crofts; Torben Diklev; Christian Donatzky; Peter Eberth; Gary Elflett; E.K. Edwards; Margaret Fotheringham; Esther Geerling; Hilary & Malcolm Gledhill; Linda Gray; Tanya Gregson; Arlene Hansell; Sheila Hessey; Birgit Hintermann; William Ho; Jane Hollowday; Katja Kraskovic; Alan Kraus; Frances Landeryou; Saila Lehtomaa; Yuri van der Linden; Jonas Ludvigsson; Raymond Maxwell; Greg Minshall; Ghislaine Morris; John Morrison; Leo Nieminen; Zoe Norgate; Vicki Ong; David Paul; Daniel Payne; Benjamin Perl; Dawn Robinson; Peter Rollason; Stacey Ross; Maryam Sherman; Ian Simpson; Katja Siberg; Lyn Smolenska; Alan Tait; Dr F.D. Trevarthen; Stephen Whittaker; Meredith Younghein.

Photo credits

All photos © Rough Guides except the following:

Title page
Puffin, Hornoya © NHPA/Photoshot

Full page
Sognefjord, Vik © Chris Coe/Axiom

Introduction
Dog sled sign, Karasjok © Dan Gair Photographic/Photolibrary
Winter sunset in the forest near Oslo © David Lomax/Robert Harding
Labels on display at the Canning Museum, Stavanger © Anna Watson/Axiom
Captain Roald Amundsen © Bettmann/Corbis
Seven Sisters Falls, Geirangerfjord © Tony Waltham/Robert Harding
Rows of fish hanging out to dry © Loken Bard/Photolibrary
Lofoten islands © Hemis/Axiom
Stavanger, harbourside pub © Anna Watson/Axiom
Midnight sun © Ken Gillham/Photolibrary

Things not to miss
01 Mountain lake and snowy peaks, Jotunheimen National Park © Charles Bowman/Robert Harding
02 Norsk Fiskevaersmuseum © Glyn Thomas/Alamy
03 The Flåmsbana Railway © David Robertson/Alamy
04 Vigelandsparken © Innovation Norway
05 White-tailed eagle © WILDLIFE GmbH/Alamy
06 Prehistoric rock carvings of moose and caribou at Alta © Joel W. Rogers/Corbis
07 Edvard Grieg's home at Troldhaugen © G Richardson/Robert Harding
08 Killer whale © Jonathon Ball/Alamy
09 Briksdalsbreen Glacier ice-climbing, Jostedalsbreen © tbkmedia.de/Alamy
10 Kjerringoy fishing village © Mezzanotte Susy/SIME-4Corners
11 Diving into Olsofjord © Paul A Souders/Corbis
12 Cathedral in Trondheim © superclic/Alamy
13 View over Geirangerfjord © David Robertson/Alamy

14 Detail at Urnes stave church © Innovation Norway

15 Oil painting of girls on the Jetty by Edvard Munch © Burstein Collection/Corbis

16 The Bryggen, Bergen © David Robertson/Alamy

17 Art Nouveau building, Ålesund © David Robertson/Alamy

18 Union Hotel © Phil Lee

19 Hjorundfjord © Phil Lee

20 Evening harbour, Henningsvaer © Arctic-Images/Corbis

21 Polar bears, Svalbard © Thorsten Milse/Robert Harding

22 Northern lights © Innovation Norway

23 Exhibition in the Viking Ship Museum © Caro/Alamy

24 Mandal Beach © Phil Lee

25 Bruennich's guillemot on iceberg, Spitsbergen, Svalbard © Thorsten Milse/Robert Harding

Hiking colour section

Walker standing on a cliff edge overlooking Eikesdalen © David Robertson/Alamy

Tourists walking to Briksdalbreen glacier © David Robertson/Alamy

Hiker reading map in Jotunheimen © Gerhard Zwerger-Schoner/Photolibrary

Helgelandskysten © Terje Rakke/Nordic life/Innovation Norway

Mountain hut and Glacier © imagebroker/Alamy

Ringsdalen © Johan Wildhagen/Innovation Norway

Hardangervidda National Park © Bildagentur Rm/Photolibrary

Dovrefjell National Park © Anders Gjengedal/Innovation Norway View over mountain scenery, Jotunheimen National Park © Gerhard Zwerger-Schoner/Photolibrary

The Vikings colour section

Close-up of Viking ship used as a charter boat, Aker Brygge, Oslo © Robert Harding/Alamy

Bow of Viking ship, Oslo © Doug Scott/Photolibrary

Sigurd on anvil with broken sword, detail, portal Hylestad Kirke Setesdal, second half 12th century © INTERFOTO Pressebildagentur/Alamy

Viking raid on an English Channel coast under Olaf Tryggvason 900s AD © North Wind Picture Archive/Alamy

Heddal stave church © Holger Burmeister/Alamy

Brooch with decoration, Jellinge, silver, c.900 AD © INTERFOTO Pressebildagentur/Alamy

Gaia, replica Viking ship © David Lomax/Photolibrary

Black and whites

p.66 Vigelandsparken © Kim Hart/Robert Harding/Drr.net

p.85 Karl Johans gate © DK

p.97 Akershus Fortress © Perret/Andia.fr/Drr.net

p.112 Clodion Art Café © FAN Travelstock/Alamy

p.130 Tourists at Preikestolen © Pep Roig/Alamy

p.151 Traditional houses at Stavanger © Anna Watson/Alamy

p.162 Kayaking at Rondane National Park © Chris Fredriksson/Alamy

p.178 Hiking at Rondane National Park © Kim Hart/Robert Harding/Drr.net

p.191 Telemark © Vidar Askeland/Innovation Norway

p.198 Houses and Canal of Ålesund © Hideo Kurihara/Alamy

p.225 Hardeangerfjord © F1online digitale Bildagentur GmbH /Alamy

p.245 Bookstall in Fjærland © David Robertson/Drr.net

p.267 Trollstigen road © Nick Gregory/Alamy

p.280 Children watching killer whales from cruise ship © Staffan Widstrand/Corbis

p.294 Old District, Bakklandet, Trondheim © LOOK Die Bildagentur der Fotografen GmbH/Alamy

p.313 View over a ski hut on the Fagernes © Rainer Raffalski/Alamy

p.350 Seal at Svalbard © Louise Murray/Robert Harding/Drr.net

p.368 Sámi couple © Arco Images GmbH/Alamy

p.410 Dr Gro Harlem Brundtland © Reuters/Corbis

p.425 Film still from Pathfinder © The Kobal Collection/Filmkammerterne/Norsk Film

Index

Note that the Norwegian alphabet has three more letters than its English counterpart. These are Æ, Ø and Å. In Norwegian dictionaries, words beginning with these two letters appear at the end after 'Z'. However in this index we follow conventional English alphabetical order, so Æ is listed with 'AE', Ø with 'O' and Å with 'A'.
Map entries are in colour.

INDEX

Map symbols

maps are listed in the full index using coloured text

▬ ▬ ▪ International boundary	∴ Ruin
▬ ▪ ▪ County boundary	⚲ Church (regional maps)
▬ ▬ ▬ Chapter division boundary	🏛 Stately home
═══ Major highways	♜ Castle
═══ Main road	⊙ Statue
═══ Minor road	ⓘ Tourist office
)┈┈(Tunnel	⊠ Post office
═══ Pedestrianized road	☎ Telephone
▭▭▭ Steps	@ Internet access
┈┈┈ Footpath	⊞ Hospital
▬▬▬ Railway	ⵟ Lighthouse
—Ⓜ— T- Bane (underground)	◉ Accommodation
●┈┈● Cable car	■ Restaurant
─ ─ Ferry route	🅿 Parking
═══ Waterway	★ Bus stop
▲ Mountain peak	▪ Building
⚘ Mountain range	⊞ Church (town maps)
⚑ Waterfall	⊞ Cemetery
⬆ Lodge	▨ Park/forest
✈ Airport (International)	░ Sand/beach
✗ Airport (Domestic)	▨ Glacier
♦ General point of interest	

We're covered. Are you?

ROUGH GUIDES Travel Insurance

Visit our website at www.roughguides.com/website/shop or call:

COLUMBUS
Travel Insurance

ROUGH GUIDES

- ⊤ UK: 0800 083 9507
- ⊤ Spain: 900 997 149
- ⊤ Australia: 1300 669 999
- ⊤ New Zealand: 0800 55 99 11
- ⊤ Worldwide: +44 870 890 2843
- ⊤ USA, call toll free on: 1 800 749 4922

Please quote our ref: *Rough Guides books*

Cover for over 46 different nationalities and available in 4 different languages.